MW00450917

STRATEGIC MANAGEMENT

CONCEPTS

SEVENTH EDITION

STRATEGIC MANAGEMENT

CONCEPTS

FRED R. DAVID

Francis Marion University

Prentice Hall
Upper Saddle River, New Jersey 07458

Acquisitions Editor: David Shafer
Associate Editor: Shane Gemza
Editorial Assistant: Shannon Sims
Editor-in-Chief: Natalie Anderson
Marketing Manager: Tami Wederbrand
Production Editor: Lynne Breitfeller
Production Coordinator: Tara Ruggerio
Managing Editor: Dee Josephson
Manufacturing Supervisor: Arnold Vila
Senior Designer: Jill Little
Design Director: Pat Smythe
Cover Design: Michael Fruhbeis
Composition/Project Management: TSI Graphics, Inc.
Photo: Mehau Kulyk, Photo Researchers, Inc.

Copyright © 1999, 1997, 1995, 1993, 1991 by Prentice-Hall, Inc.
A Simon & Schuster Company
Upper Saddle River, New Jersey 07458

All rights reserved. No part of this book may be
reproduced, in any form or by any means,
without permission in writing from the Publisher.

Library of Congress Cataloging-in-Publication Data
David, Fred R.
  Concepts of strategic management / Fred R. David. — 7th ed.
      p.   cm.
  Includes bibliographical references and index.
  ISBN 0-13-080784-2
    1. Strategic planning   2. Strategic planning—Case studies.
  I. Title.
  HD30.28.D3785   1998   98-47067
  658.4′012—dc21   CIP

Printed in the United States of America

10 9 8 7 6 5 4 3 2 1

ISBN 0-13-080784-2

Prentice-Hall International (UK) Limited, London
Prentice-Hall of Australia Pty. Limited, Sydney
Prentice-Hall Canada Inc., Toronto
Prentice-Hall Hispanoamericana, S.A., Mexico
Prentice-Hall of India Private Limited, New Delhi
Prentice-Hall of Japan, Inc., Tokyo
Simon & Schuster Asia Pte. Ltd., Singapore
Editora Prentice-Hall do Brasil, Ltda., Rio de Janeiro

To:
Joy, Forest, Byron, and Meredith—my wife and children—
for their encouragement and love.

Brief Contents

Contents

Preface

The business world today is much different than it was just two years ago when the previous edition of this text was introduced. Internet use has skyrocketed, China peacefully annexed Hong Kong, Europe agreed on a common currency, Southeast Asian stock markets crashed, thousands of firms globalized, and thousands more merged. Downsizing, rightsizing, reengineering and countless divestitures, acquisitions, and liquidations permanently altered the corporate landscape. Hundreds of new strategic management articles appeared in journals, magazines, and newspapers and altered strategic thinking. Changes made in this edition are aimed squarely at illustrating the effect that our rapidly changing world has on strategic management theory and practice.

Our mission in preparing the seventh edition of *Strategic Management* was "to create the most current, well written business policy textbook on the market—a book that is exciting and valuable to both students and professors." To achieve this mission, significant improvements have been on every page and to every piece of the teaching package. The time basis for all cases included in this edition is 1997–1998, representing the most up-to-date compilation of cases ever assembled in a business policy text. New strategic management research and practice from this era are incorporated throughout the chapters. Hundreds of new examples appear throughout the text. The Cohesion Case on Hershey Foods and the Experiential Exercises are fully updated.

Scores of reviewers and I believe you will find this edition to be the best ever, and now the best business policy textbook available, for communicating both the excitement and value of strategic management. Now published in four different languages—English, Chinese, Spanish, and German—this text is perhaps the most widely used strategic planning book in the world.

SPECIAL NOTE TO PROFESSORS

This textbook meets all AACSB guidelines for the business policy and strategic management course at both the graduate and undergraduate level. Previous editions of this text have been used at more than 500 colleges and universities. Prentice Hall maintains a separate Web site for this text at www.prenhall.com/davidsm. The author maintains the Strategic Management Club Online at www.strategyclub.com. Membership is free to professors and $29 for students.

Although structure of this edition parallels the last, great improvements have been made in readability, currentness, and coverage. In keeping with the mission "to become the most current, well written business policy textbook on the market," every page has undergone rethinking and rewriting to streamline, update, and improve the caliber of presentation.

A net result of this activity is that every chapter is shorter in length. The most current concepts and practices in strategic management are presented in a style that is clear, focused, and relevant. Changes in this edition add up to the biggest revision ever made on this popular text.

CHAPTER THEMES

The following three themes permeate all chapters in this edition, and contribute significantly to making this text timely, informative, exciting, and valuable.

1. *Global Factors Affect Virtually All Strategic Decisions*

   The Global theme is enhanced in this edition because doing business globally has become a necessity rather than a luxury in most industries. Growing interdependence among countries and companies worldwide is evidenced by stock markets around the world dramatically affecting volatility of each other. But doing business globally is more risky and complex than ever. The dynamics of political, economic, and cultural differences across countries directly affect strategic management decisions.

2. *Information Technology Is a Vital Strategic Management Tool*

   The Information Technology theme is more deeply integrated in response to accelerating strategic use of computer technology to gather, analyze, send, and receive information. Unlike several years ago, most college students now surf the Web, send e-mail, and use the Internet. Since the last edition, literally thousands of companies have established world wide web home pages and are conducting commerce internationally on the Internet. Important U.S. government documents are now available over the Internet and updated monthly. Using monthly rather than annually updated information makes a tremendous difference in strategic decision making.

3. *Preserving the Natural Environment Is a Vital Strategic Issue*

Unique to strategic management texts, the Natural Environment theme is strengthened in this edition in order to promote the need for firms to conduct operations in an environmentally sound manner, or face increasingly stiff penalties and criticism. Smog in Southeast Asia has killed thousands of people and El Niño devastates coastal areas worldwide. Numerous countries globally have enacted laws to curtail firms from polluting streams, rivers, the air, land, and sea. The strategic efforts of both companies and countries to preserve the natural environment are described. Respect for the natural environment has become an important concern for consumers, companies, society, and the AACSB.

TIME-TESTED FEATURES

This edition continues many of the special *time-tested features* and content that have made this text so successful over the last decade. Trademarks of this text strengthened in this edition are as follows:

Chapters: Time-Tested Features

◆ The text meets AACSB guidelines that support a practitioner orientation rather than a theory/research approach. This text aims to support that effort by taking a skills-oriented approach to developing a mission statement, performing an external audit, conducting an internal assessment, and formulating, implementing, and evaluating strategies.

◆ The author's writing style is concise, conversational, interesting, logical, lively, and supported by numerous current examples throughout.

◆ A simple, integrative strategic-management model appears in all chapters and on the inside front cover of the text.

◆ A fully updated Hershey Foods Cohesion Case appears after chapter 1 and is revisited at the end of each chapter. The Hershey case allows students to apply strategic-management concepts and techniques to a real organization as chapter material is covered. This integrative (cohesive) approach readies students for case analysis. Hershey encourages professors and students to call 1-800-468-1714 for additional information or visit their home page at www.hersheys.com.

◆ End-of-chapter Experiential Exercises effectively apply concepts and techniques in a challenging, meaningful, and enjoyable manner. Eighteen exercises apply text material to the Cohesion Case; ten apply textual material to a college or university; another ten send students into the business world to explore important strategy topics. The exercises are relevant, interesting, and contemporary.

◆ Pedagogy, including Notable Quotes and Objectives to open each chapter, and Key Terms, Current Readings, Discussion Questions, and Experiential Exercises close each chapter.

◆ Excellent coverage of business ethics aimed at more than meeting AACSB standards.

◆ Excellent coverage of strategy implementation issues such as corporate culture, organizational structure, marketing concepts, and financial tools and techniques.

◆ A systematic, analytical approach presented in chapter 6, including matrices such as the TOWS, BCG, IE, GRAND, SPACE, and QSPM.

◆ The chapter material is again published in four color.

◆ "Take It to the Net" Internet exercises available online at www.prenhall.com/davidsm.

◆ The Web site www.prenhall.com/davidsm provides chapter and case updates and support materials.

◆ A paperback version of only the Concepts is available.

◆ An outstanding ancillary package, including:

    ◆ A comprehensive *Instructor's Manual*.

    ◆ An elaborate *Case Solutions Manual* with a complete set of matrices.

    ◆ An extensive transparency package available in PowerPoint format.

    ◆ Seventeen corporate case videos.

    ◆ A computerized test bank.

    ◆ A companion Web site for students and professors at www.prenhall.com/davidsm.

NEW TO THIS EDITION

In addition to the special time-tested trademarks described above, this edition includes some exciting new features designed to position this text as the clear leader and best choice for teaching business policy and strategic management include:

Chapters: New Features

◆ A new Global Perspective boxed insert is integrated into each chapter to support the expanded global nature of the text.

◆ A new Information Technology boxed insert is appropriately integrated into each chapter to portray the increasing reliance upon information technology by both large and small firms.

◆ A new Natural Environment boxed insert appears in each chapter to show increasing strategic relevance of this issue to business.

◆ New topics covered more extensively in the chapters include reengineering, downsizing, rightsizing, restructuring, culture, and use of the Internet for strategic purposes.

◆ New company examples are provided in every chapter.

◆ New research is integrated into every chapter with new current readings at the end of each chapter.

◆ New Web site addresses (over 100) are provided throughout the chapters.

◆ Chapter 10 on International Strategic Management Issues has been completely overhauled and greatly improved.

◆ Chapter 4 on Conducting an External Strategic Management Audit has been shortened and strengthened with new Internet sources of information replacing lists of library sources.

ANCILLARY MATERIALS

◆ *Case Solutions Manual.* Provides a comprehensive teacher's note for all 35 cases. The teacher's notes feature detailed analyses, classroom discussion questions with answers, an external and internal assessment, specific recommendations, strategy-implementation material, analytical matracies and an epilogue for each case.

◆ *Instructor's Manual.* Provides lecture notes, teaching tips, answers to all end-of-chapter Experiential Exercises and Review Questions, additional Experiential Exercises not in the text, a glossary with definitions of all end-of-chapter key terms and concepts, sample course syllabi, and a test bank of 1,364 questions with answers.

◆ *Seventeen Corporate Case Video Segments.* To accompany the Cohesion Case, a 21-minute color video prepared by Hershey Foods Corporation is available to adopters free of charge. Shown near the beginning of the course, the Hershey Foods video can arouse students' interest in studying the Cohesion Case and completing Experiential Exercises that apply chapter material to this case. In addition, a collection of sixteen other case video segments are available free of charge. The segments average 15 minutes each and were professionally prepared by firms used in cases in this text. Videos are provided to accompany the following cases: The Limited, Winnebago Industries, Playboy Enterprises, Banc One, Audubon Zoo, Nike, and Pilgrim's Pride.

◆ *Transparency Masters.* A total of 50 color transparency acetates are available with this text. Half of the transparencies are from exhibits and figures in the text, while the other half are from sources outside the text.

◆ *Printed and Computerized Test Bank.* The test bank for this text includes 737 True/False questions, 425 multiple choice questions, and 202 essay questions for the text chapters. Sample comprehensive tests for chapters 1–5 and chapters 6–10 are also given, and answers to all objective questions are provided. The test questions given in the instructor's manual are also available on computerized test software to facilitate preparing and grading tests.

◆ *PowerPoint Case Solutions Manual Diskette.* Each case is accompanied by a set of PowerPoint slides to assist in class discussion and analysis.

◆ *Companion Web site on PHLIP (Prentice Hall learning on the Internet Partnership):*

—*Interactive Study Guide:* Includes multiple choice and true/false questions for every chapter of the text. Graded by our server, the immediate feedback includes additional help and page references to the text.

—*Current Events Articles and Exercises:* are added bi-monthly, to illustrate how management concepts impact the real world.

—*Management Internet Resources:* include helpful sites linked to the relevant sections of the text.

—*Study Hall and Writing Center:* feature student-orientated links to virtual libraries, dictionaries, on-line tutors and more.

—*Faculty Resource Center:* includes sample syllabi, PowerPoint presentations, using the Internet, and faculty chat rooms.

—*On-Line Course Syllabus Building:* allows the instructor to create a custom on-line syllabus.

SPECIAL NOTE TO STUDENTS

Welcome to business policy. This is a challenging and exciting course that will allow you to function as the owner or chief executive officer of different organizations. Your major task in this course will be to make strategic decisions and to justify those decisions through oral and written communication. Strategic decisions determine the future direction and competitive position of an enterprise for a long time. Decisions to expand geographically or to diversify are examples of strategic decisions.

Strategic decision making occurs in all types and sizes of organizations, from General Motors to a small hardware store. Many people's lives and jobs are affected by strategic decisions, so the stakes are very high. An organization's very survival is often at stake. The overall importance of strategic decisions makes this course especially exciting and challenging. You will be called upon in business policy to demonstrate how your strategic decisions could be successfully implemented.

In this course you can look forward to making strategic decisions both as an individual and as a member of a team. No matter how hard employees work, an organization is in real trouble if strategic decisions are not made effectively. Doing the right things (effectiveness) is more important than doing things right (efficiency). For example, Kodak was prosperous in the early 1990s, but ineffective strategies led to billion dollar losses in the late 1990s.

You will have the opportunity in this course to make actual strategic decisions, perhaps for the first time in your academic career. Do not hesitate to take a stand and defend specific strategies that you determine to be the best. The rationale for your strategic decisions will be more important than the actual decision, because no one knows for sure what the best strategy is for a particular organization at a given point in time. This fact accents the subjective, contingency nature of the strategic-management process. Use the concepts and tools presented in this text, coupled with your own intuition, to recommend strategies that you can defend as being most appropriate for the organizations that you study. You will also need to integrate knowledge acquired in previous business courses. For this reason, business policy is often called a capstone course; you may want to keep this book for your personal library.

This text is practitioner-oriented and applications-oriented. It presents strategic-management concepts that will enable you to formulate, implement, and evaluate strategies in all kinds of profit and nonprofit organizations. The end-of-chapter Experiential Exercises allow you to apply what you've read in each chapter to the Hershey Foods Cohesion Case and to your own university.

Consider joining the Strategic Management Club Online at www.strategyclub.com. The templates and links there will save you time in performing analyses and will make your work look professional. Work hard in policy this term and have fun. Good luck!

ACKNOWLEDGMENTS

Many persons have contributed time, energy, ideas, and suggestions for improving this text over four editions. The strength of this text is largely attributed to the collective wisdom, work, and experiences of business policy professors, strategic-management researchers, students, and practitioners. Names of particular individuals whose published research is referenced in the fourth edition of this text are listed alphabetically in the Name Index. To all individuals involved in making this text so popular and successful, I am indebted and thankful.

Many special persons and reviewers contributed valuable material and suggestions for this edition. I would like to thank my colleagues and friends at Auburn University, Mississippi State University, East Carolina University, and Francis Marion University. These are universities where I have served on the management

faculty. Scores of students and professors at these schools shaped development of this text.

Scores of Prentice Hall employees and salespersons have worked diligently behind the scenes to make this text a leader in the business policy market. I appreciate the continued hard work of all those persons.

I also want to thank you, the reader, for investing time and effort reading and studying this text. As we approach the twenty-first century together, this book will help you formulate, implement, and evaluate strategies for organizations with which you become associated. I hope you come to share my enthusiasm for the rich subject area of strategic management and for the systematic learning approach taken in this text.

Finally, I want to welcome and invite your suggestions, ideas, thoughts, and comments and questions regarding any part of this test or the ancillary materials. Please call me at 843-661-1431/1419, fax me at 843-661-1432, e-mail me at Fdavid@Fmarion.edu, or write me at the School of Business, Francis Marion University, Florence, South Carolina 29501. I appreciate and need your input to continually improve this text in future editions. Drawing my attention to specific errors or deficiencies in coverage or exposition will especially be appreciated.

Thank you for using this text.

Cases to accompany this text can be ordered on an individual basis by visiting the Prentice Hall Custom Case Web site at: http://www.emissary.com.

Seventh Edition Cases

1. The Limited, Inc.—1998
2. Wal-Mart Stores, Inc.—1998
3. Dayton Hudson Corporation—1998
4. Circus Circus Enterprises, Inc.—1998
5. Harrah's Entertainment, Inc.—1998
6. Banc One Corporation—1998
7. Citicorp—1998
8. Audubon Zoo—1997
9. Riverbanks Zoological Park and Botanical Garden—1997
10. Dakota, Minnesota & Eastern Railroad Corporation—1997
11. RailTex, Inc.—1998
12. Greyhound Lines, Inc.—1998
13. Carnival Corporation—1998
14. Southwest Airlines Co.—1998
15. Central United Methodist Church—1998
16. Elkins Lake Baptist Church—1997
17. Grace Lutheran Church—1997
18. Classic Car Club of America, Inc.—1997

How to Analyze a Business Policy Case

OBJECTIVES

After studying this chapter, you should be able to do the following:

1. Describe the case method for learning strategic-management concepts.

2. Identify the steps in preparing a comprehensive written case analysis.

3. Describe how to give an effective oral case analysis presentation.

4. Discuss fifty tips for doing case analysis.

NOTABLE QUOTES

The essential fact that makes the case method an educational experience of the greatest power is that it makes the student an active rather than a passive participant.——WALLACE B. DONHAM

The great aim of education is not knowledge, but action.——HERBERT SPENCER

Two heads are better than one.——UNKNOWN AUTHOR

Good writers do not turn in their first draft. Ask someone else to read your written case analysis, and read it out loud to yourself. That way, you can find rough areas to clear up.——LAWRENCE JAUCH

One reaction frequently heard is, "I don't have enough information." In reality, strategists never have enough information because some information is not available and some is too costly.——WILLIAM GLUECK

I keep six honest serving men. They taught me all I know. Their names are What, Why, When, How, Where, and Who.——RUDYARD KIPLING

Don't recommend anything you would not be prepared to do yourself if you were in the decision maker's shoes.——A.J. STRICKLAND III

A picture is worth a thousand words.——UNKNOWN AUTHOR

The purpose of this section is to help you analyze business policy cases. Guidelines for preparing written and oral case analyses are given, and suggestions for preparing cases for class discussion are presented. Steps to follow in preparing case analyses are provided. Guidelines for making an oral presentation are described.

WHAT IS A BUSINESS POLICY CASE?

A *business policy case* describes an organization's external and internal condition and raises issues concerning the firm's mission, strategies, objectives, and policies. Most of the information in a business policy case is established fact, but some information may be opinions, judgments, and beliefs. Business policy cases are more comprehensive than those you may have studied in other courses. They generally include a description of related management, marketing, finance/accounting, production/operations, R&D, computer information systems, and natural environment issues. A business policy case puts the reader on the scene of the action by describing a firm's situation at some point in time. business policy cases are written to give you practice applying strategic-management concepts. The case method for studying strategic management is often called *learning by doing*.

GUIDELINES FOR PREPARING CASE ANALYSES

THE NEED FOR PRACTICALITY   There is no such thing as a complete case, and no case ever gives you all the information you need to conduct analyses and make recommendations. Likewise, in the business world, strategists never have all the information they need to make decisions: information may be unavailable, too costly to obtain, or may take too much time to obtain. So, in preparing business policy cases, do what strategists do every day—make reasonable assumptions about unknowns, state assumptions clearly, perform appropriate analyses, and make decisions. *Be practical.* For example, in performing a pro forma financial analysis, make reasonable assumptions, state them appropriately, and proceed to show what impact your recommendations are expected to have on the organization's financial position. Avoid saying, "I don't have enough information." You can always supplement the information provided in a case with research in your college library. Library research is required in case analyses.

THE NEED FOR JUSTIFICATION   The most important part of analyzing cases is not what strategies you recommend, but rather how you support your decisions and how you propose that they be implemented. There is no single best solution or one right answer to a case, so give ample justification for your recommendations. This is important. In the business world, strategists usually do not know if their decisions are right until resources have been allocated and consumed. Then it is often too late to reverse the decisions. This cold fact accents the need for careful integration of intuition and analysis in preparing business policy case analyses.

THE NEED FOR REALISM   Avoid recommending a course of action beyond an organization's means. *Be realistic.* No organization can possibly pursue all the strategies that could potentially benefit the firm. Estimate how much capital will be required to implement what you recommended. Determine whether debt, stock, or a combination of debt and stock could be used to obtain the capital. Make sure your recommendations are feasible. Do not prepare a case analysis that omits all arguments and information not supportive of your recommendations. Rather, present the major advantages and disadvantages of several feasible alternatives. Try not to exaggerate, stereotype, prejudge, or overdramatize. Strive to demonstrate that your interpretation of the evidence is reasonable and objective.

THE NEED FOR SPECIFICITY   Do not make broad generalizations such as "The company should pursue a market penetration strategy." *Be specific* by telling what, why, when, how, where, and who. Failure to use specifics is the single major shortcoming of most oral and written case analyses. For example, in an internal audit say, "The firm's current ratio fell from 2.2 in 1998 to 1.3 in 1999, and this is considered to be a major weakness," instead of, "The firm's financial condition is bad." Rather than concluding from a SPACE Matrix that a firm should be defensive, be more specific, saying, "The firm should consider closing three plants, laying off 280 employees, and divesting itself of its chemical division, for a net savings of $20.2 million in 1998." Use ratios, percentages, numbers, and dollar estimates. Businesspeople dislike generalities and vagueness.

THE NEED FOR ORIGINALITY   Do not necessarily recommend the course of action that the firm plans to take or actually undertook, even if those actions resulted in improved revenues and earnings. The aim of case analysis is for you to consider all the facts and information relevant to the organization at the time, generate feasible alternative strategies, choose among those alternatives, and defend your recommendations. Put yourself back in time to the point when strategic decisions were being made by the firm's strategists. Based on information available then, what would you have done? Support your position with charts, graphs, ratios, analyses, and the like—not a revelation from the library. You can become a good strategist by thinking through situations, making management assessments, and proposing plans yourself. *Be original.* Compare and contrast what you recommend versus what the company plans to do or did.

THE NEED TO CONTRIBUTE   Strategy formulation, implementation, and evaluation decisions are commonly made by a group of individuals rather than by a single person. Therefore, your professor may divide the class into three- or four-person teams to prepare written or oral case analyses. Members of a strategic-management team, in class or in the business world, differ on their aversion to risk, their concern for short-run versus long-run benefits, their attitudes toward social responsibility, and their views concerning globalization. There are no perfect people, so there are no perfect strategists. Be open-minded to others' views. *Be a good listener and a good contributor.*

PREPARING A CASE FOR CLASS DISCUSSION

Your professor may ask you to prepare a case for class discussion. Preparing a case for class discussion means that you need to read the case before class, make notes regarding the organization's external opportunities/threats and internal strengths/weaknesses, perform appropriate analyses, and come to class prepared to offer and defend some specific recommendations.

THE CASE METHOD VERSUS LECTURE APPROACH   The case method of teaching is radically different from the traditional lecture approach, in which little or no preparation is needed by students before class. The *case method* involves a classroom situation in which students do most of the talking; your professor facilitates discussion by asking questions and encouraging student interaction regarding ideas, analyses, and recommendations. Be prepared for a discussion along the lines of, "What would you do, why would you do it, when would you do it, and how would you do it?" Prepare answers to the following types of questions:

◆ What are the firm's most important external opportunities and threats?

◆ What are the organization's major strengths and weaknesses?

◆ How would you describe the organization's financial condition?

◆ What are the firm's existing strategies and objectives?

◆ Who are the firm's competitors and what are their strategies?

◆ What objectives and strategies do you recommend for this organization? Explain your reasoning. How does what you recommend compare to what the company plans?

◆ How could the organization best implement what you recommend? What implementation problems do you envision? How could the firm avoid or solve those problems?

THE CROSS-EXAMINATION   Do not hesitate to take a stand on the issues and to support your position with objective analyses and outside research. Strive to apply strategic-management concepts and tools in preparing your case for class discussion. Seek defensible arguments and positions. Support opinions and judgments with facts, reasons, and evidence. Crunch the numbers before class! Be willing to describe your recommendations to the class without fear of disapproval. Respect the ideas of others, but be willing to go against the majority opinion when you can justify a better position.

Business policy case analysis gives you the opportunity to learn more about yourself, your colleagues, strategic management, and the decision-making process in organizations. The rewards of this experience will depend upon the effort you put forth, so do a good job. Discussing business policy cases in class is exciting and challenging. Expect views counter to those you present. Different students will place emphasis on different aspects of an organization's situation and submit different recommendations for scrutiny and rebuttal. Cross-examination discussions commonly arise, just as they occur in a real business organization. Avoid being a silent observer.

PREPARING A WRITTEN CASE ANALYSIS

In addition to asking you to prepare a case for class discussion, your professor may ask you to prepare a written case analysis. Preparing a written case analysis is similar to preparing a case for class discussion, except written reports are generally more structured and more detailed. There is no ironclad procedure for preparing a written case analysis because cases differ in focus; the type, size, and complexity of the organizations being analyzed also vary.

When writing a strategic-management report or case analysis, avoid using jargon, vague or redundant words, acronyms, abbreviations, sexist language, and ethnic or racial slurs, and watch your spelling. Use short sentences and paragraphs and simple words and phrases. Use quite a few subheadings. Arrange issues and ideas from the most important to the least important. Arrange recommendations from the least controversial to the most controversial. Use the active voice rather than the passive voice for all verbs; for example, say, "Our team recommends that the company diversify," rather than, "It is recommended by our team to diversify." Use many examples to add specificity and clarity. Tables, figures, pie charts, bar charts, time lines, and other kinds of exhibits help communicate important points and ideas. Sometimes a picture *is* worth a thousand words.

THE EXECUTIVE SUMMARY   Your professor may ask you to focus the written case analysis on a particular aspect of the strategic-management process, such as (1) to identify and evaluate the organization's existing mission, objectives, and strategies; or (2) to propose and defend specific recommendations for the company; or (3) to develop an industry analysis by describing the competitors, products, selling techniques, and market conditions in a given industry. These types of written reports are sometimes called *executive summaries*. An executive summary usually ranges from three to five pages of text in length, plus exhibits.

THE COMPREHENSIVE WRITTEN ANALYSIS   Your professor may ask you to prepare a *comprehensive written analysis*. This assignment requires you to apply the entire strategic-management process to the particular organization. When preparing a comprehensive written analysis, picture yourself as a consultant who has been asked by a company to conduct a study of its external and internal environment and make specific recommendations for its future. Prepare exhibits to support your recommendations. Highlight exhibits with some discussion in the paper. Comprehensive written analyses are usually about ten pages in length, plus exhibits.

STEPS IN PREPARING A COMPREHENSIVE WRITTEN ANALYSIS   In preparing a comprehensive written analysis, you could follow the steps outlined here, which correlate to the stages in the strategic-management process and the chapters in this text.

Step 1 Identify the firm's existing mission, objectives, and strategies.

Step 2 Develop a mission statement for the organization.

Step 3 Identify the organization's external opportunities and threats.

Step 4 Construct a Competitive Profile Matrix.

Step 5 Construct an EFE Matrix.

Step 6 Identify the organization's internal strengths and weaknesses.

Step 7 Construct an IFE Matrix.

Step 8 Prepare a TOWS Matrix, SPACE Matrix, BCG Matrix, IE Matrix, Grand Strategy Matrix, and QSPM as appropriate. Give advantages and disadvantages of alternative strategies.

Step 9 Recommend specific strategies and long-term objectives. Show how much your recommendations will cost. Itemize these costs clearly for each projected year. Compare your recommendations to actual strategies planned by the company.

Step 10 Specify how your recommendations can be implemented and what results you can expect. Prepare forecasted ratios and pro forma financial statements. Present a timetable or agenda for action.

Step 11 Recommend specific annual objectives and policies.

Step 12 Recommend procedures for strategy review and evaluation.

MAKING AN ORAL PRESENTATION

Your professor may ask you to prepare a business policy case analysis, individually or as a group, and present your analysis to the class. Oral presentations are usually graded on two parts: content and delivery. *Content* refers to the quality, quantity, correctness, and appropriateness of analyses presented, including such dimensions as logical flow through the presentation, coverage of major issues, use of specifics, avoidance of generalities, absence of mistakes, and feasibility of recommendations. *Delivery* includes such dimensions as audience attentiveness, clarity of visual aids, appropriate dress, persuasiveness of arguments, tone of voice, eye contact, and posture. Great ideas are of no value unless others can be convinced of their merit through clear communication. The guidelines presented here can help you make an effective oral presentation.

ORGANIZING THE PRESENTATION   Begin your presentation by introducing yourself and giving a clear outline of topics to be covered. If a team is presenting, specify the sequence of speakers and the areas each person will address. At the beginning of an oral presentation, try to capture your audience's interest and attention. You could do this by displaying some products made by the company, telling an interesting short story about the company, or sharing an experience that you had related to the company, its products, or its services. You could develop or obtain a video to show at the beginning of class; you could visit a local distributor of the firm's products and tape a personal interview with the business owner or manager. A light or humorous introduction can be effective at the beginning of a presentation.

Be sure the setting of your presentation is well organized, with chairs, flip charts, a transparency projector, and whatever else you plan to use. Arrive at least 15 minutes early at the classroom to organize the setting, and be sure your materials are ready to go. Make sure everyone can see your visual aids well.

CONTROLLING YOUR VOICE   An effective rate of speaking ranges from 100 to 125 words per minute. Practice your presentation out loud to determine if you are going too fast. Individuals commonly speak too fast when nervous. Breathe deeply before and during the presentation to help yourself slow down. Have a cup of water available; pausing to take a drink will wet your throat, give you time to collect your thoughts, control your nervousness, slow you down, and signal to the audience a change in topic.

Avoid a monotone by placing emphasis on different words or sentences. Speak loudly and clearly, but don't shout. Silence can be used effectively to break a monotone voice. Stop at the end of each sentence, rather than running sentences together with *and* or *uh*.

MANAGING BODY LANGUAGE   Be sure not to fold your arms, lean on the podium, put your hands in your pockets, or put your hands behind you. Keep a straight posture, with one foot slightly in front of the other. Do not turn your back to the audience, which is not only rude but which also prevents your voice from projecting well. Avoid using too many hand gestures. On occasion leave the podium or table and walk toward your audience, but do not walk around too much. Never block the audience's view of your visual aids.

Maintain good eye contact throughout the presentation. This is the best way to persuade your audience. There is nothing more reassuring to a speaker than to see members of the audience nod in agreement or smile. Try to look everyone in the eye at least once during your presentation, but focus more on individuals who look interested than on persons who seem bored. Use humor and smiles as appropriate throughout your presentation to stay in touch with your audience. A presentation should never be dull!

SPEAKING FROM NOTES   Be sure not to read to your audience, because reading puts people to sleep. Perhaps worse than reading is memorizing. Do not try to memorize anything. Rather, practice using notes unobtrusively. Make sure your notes are written clearly so you will not flounder trying to read your own writing. Include only main ideas on your note cards. Keep note cards on a podium or table if possible so that you won't drop them or get them out of order; walking with note cards tends to be distracting.

CONSTRUCTING VISUAL AIDS   Make sure your visual aids are legible to individuals in the back of the room. Use color to highlight special items. Avoid putting complete sentences on visual aids; rather, use short phrases and then elaborate on issues orally as you make your presentation. Generally, there should be no more than four to six lines of text on each visual aid. Use clear headings and subheadings. Be careful about spelling and grammar; use a consistent style of lettering. Use masking tape or an easel for posters—do not hold posters in your hand. Transparencies and handouts are excellent aids; however, be careful not to use too many handouts or your audience may concentrate on them instead of you during the presentation.

ANSWERING QUESTIONS   It is best to field questions at the end of your presentation, rather than during the presentation itself. Encourage questions and take your time to respond to each one. Answering questions can be persuasive because it involves you with the audience. If a team is giving the presentation, the audience should direct questions to a specific person. During the question and answer period, be polite, confident, and courteous. Avoid verbose responses. Do not get defensive with your answers, even if a hostile or confrontational question is asked. Staying calm during potentially disruptive situations such as a cross-examination reflects self-confidence, maturity, poise, and command of the particular company and its industry. Stand up throughout the question and answer period.

FIFTY TIPS FOR SUCCESS IN CASE ANALYSIS

Business policy students who have used this text over six editions offer you the following fifty tips for success in doing case analysis:

1. View your case analysis and presentation as a product that must have some competitive factor to differentiate it favorably from the case analyses of other students.

2. Prepare your case analysis far enough in advance of the due date to allow time for reflection and practice. Do not procrastinate.

3. Develop a mind-set of "why," continually questioning your own and others' assumptions and assertions.

4. The best ideas are lost if not communicated to the reader, so as ideas develop, think of their most appropriate presentation.

5. Maintain a positive attitude about the class, working *with* problems rather than against them.

6. Keep in tune with your professor and understand his or her values and expectations.

7. Since business policy is a capstone course, seek the help of professors in other specialty areas as needed.

8. Other students will have strengths in functional areas that will complement your weaknesses, so develop a cooperative spirit that moderates competitiveness in group work.

9. Read your case frequently as work progresses so you don't overlook details.

10. When preparing a case analysis as a group, divide into separate teams to work on the external analysis and internal analysis. Each team should write its section as if it were to go into the paper; then give each group member a copy.

11. At the end of each group session, assign each member of the group a task to be completed for the next meeting.

12. Have a good sense of humor.

13. Capitalize on the strengths of each member of the group; volunteer your services in your areas of strength.

14. Set goals for yourself and your team; budget your time to attain them.

15. Become friends with the library.

16. Foster attitudes that encourage group participation and interaction. Do not be hasty to judge group members.

17. Be creative and innovative throughout the case analysis process.

18. Be prepared to work. There will be times when you will have to do more than your share. Accept it, and do what you have to do to move the team forward.

19. Think of your case analysis as if it were really happening; do not reduce case analysis to a mechanical process.

20. To uncover flaws in your analysis and to prepare the group for questions during an oral presentation, assign one person in the group to actively play the devil's advocate.

21. Do not schedule excessively long group meetings; two-hour sessions are about right.

22. A goal of case analysis is to improve your ability to think clearly in ambiguous and confusing situations; do not get frustrated that there is no single best answer.

23. Push your ideas hard enough to get them listened to, but then let up; listen to others and try to follow their lines of thinking; follow the flow of group discussion, recognizing when you need to get back on track; do not repeat yourself or others unless clarity or progress demands repetition.

24. Do not confuse symptoms with causes; do not develop conclusions and solutions prematurely; recognize that information may be misleading, conflicting, or wrong.

25. Work hard to develop the ability to formulate reasonable, consistent, and creative plans; put yourself in the strategist's position.

26. Develop confidence in using quantitative tools for analysis. They are not inherently difficult; it is just practice and familiarity you need.

27. Develop a case-writing style that is direct, assertive, and convincing; be concise, precise, fluent, and correct.

28. Have fun when at all possible. It is frustrating at times, but enjoy it while you can; it may be several years before you are playing CEO again.

29. Acquire a professional typist and proofreader. Do not perform either task alone.

30. Strive for excellence in writing and technical preparation of your case. Prepare nice charts, tables, diagrams, and graphs. Use color and unique pictures. No messy exhibits!

31. In group cases do not allow personality differences to interfere. When they occur, they must be understood for what they are and put aside.

32. Do not forget that the objective is to learn; explore areas with which you are not familiar.

33. Pay attention to detail.

34. Think through alternative implications fully and realistically. The consequences of decisions are not always apparent. They often affect many different aspects of a firm's operations.

35. Get things written down (drafts) as soon as possible.

36. Read everything that other group members write, and comment on it in writing. This allows group input into all aspects of case preparation.

37. Provide answers to such fundamental questions as what, when, where, why, and how.

38. Adaptation and flexibility are keys to success; be creative and innovative.

39. Do not merely recite ratios or present figures. Rather, develop ideas and conclusions concerning the possible trends. Show the importance of these figures to the corporation.

40. Support reasoning and judgment with factual data whenever possible.

41. Neatness is a real plus; your case analysis should look professional.

42. Your analysis should be as detailed and specific as possible.

43. A picture speaks a thousand words, and a creative picture gets you an A in many classes.

44. Let someone else read and critique your paper several days before you turn it in.

45. Emphasize the Strategy Selection and Strategy Implementation sections. A common mistake is to spend too much time on the external or internal analysis parts of your paper. Always remember that the meat of the paper or presentation is the strategy selection and implementation sections.

46. Make special efforts to get to know your group members. This leads to more openness in the group and allows for more interchange of ideas. Put in the time and effort necessary to develop these relationships.

47. Be constructively critical of your group members' work. Do not dominate group discussions. Be a good listener and contributor.

48. Learn from past mistakes and deficiencies. Improve upon weak aspects of other case presentations.

49. Learn from the positive approaches and accomplishments of classmates.

50. Be considerate, dependable, reliable, and trustworthy.

CURRENT READINGS

Fielen, John. "Clear Writing Is Not Enough." *Management Review* (April 1989): 49–53.

Holcombe, M., and J. Stein. *Presentation for Decision Makers* (Belmont, Calif.: Lifetime Learning Publications, 1983).

_____ *Writing for Decision Makers* (Belmont, Calif.: Lifetime Learning Publications, 1981).

Jeffries, J., and J. Bates. *The Executive's Guide to Meetings, Conferences, and Audiovisual Presentations* (New York: McGraw-Hill, 1983).

Shurter, R., J. P. Williamson, and W. Broehl. *Business Research and Report Writing* (New York: McGraw-Hill, 1965).

Strunk, W., and E. B. White. *The Elements of Style* (New York: Macmillan, 1978).

Zall, P., and L. Franc. *Practical Writing in Business and Industry* (North Scituate, Mass.: Duxbury Press, 1978).

Instructions for Using the Strategy Formulator Software

The *Strategy Formulator* software that accompanies this text is user-friendly programs that run on any IBM or IBM-compatible machine with at least one floppy disk drive and 512K (or greater) memory. A copy can be found in the back of your instructors Case Solution Manual or downloaded from the Web site that accompanies this text: www.prenhall.com/davidsm. Step-by-step instructions for using this software are provided in this section. *Strategy Formulator* will greatly reduce the time it takes you to prepare quantitative, professional exhibits to support your oral case presentations and written case assignments.

The *Strategy Formulator* program generates strategy-formulation matrices that are widely used among organizations. The matrices are described in chapters 4, 5, and 6 of the text. You will want to use *Strategy Formulator* in analyzing all business policy cases. No prior experience with computers is needed to use this software, which is DOS-based.

MAKING A BACKUP COPY OF THE DISKETTES   It is a good idea to make a working copy of the *Strategy Formulator* diskettes. Keep the original copies in a safe place as a backup. The operating system manual that came with your computer contains instructions on how to make backup copies. Follow instructions in your computer manual for creating a subdirectory, (or folder) and copy the original diskette to that subdirectory (or folder).

THE *STRATEGY FORMULATOR* SOFTWARE

Strategy Formulator is an innovative program that enables managers and students to formulate strategies for organizations. This personal computer software program incorporates the most modern strategic planning techniques in a simple way. The simplicity of *Strategy Formulator* enables this software to facilitate the process of strategic planning by promoting communication, understanding, creativity, and forward thinking among users.

Strategy Formulator is not a spreadsheet or database program; it is a structured brainstorming tool that enhances participation in strategy formulation. The software begins with development of an organizational mission statement as described in chapter 3. Then, the software guides you through an internal strategic planning audit of the company, followed by an external audit of the firm as described in chapters 4 and 5. Next, the software generates alternative strategies for the firm, using analytical tools discussed in chapter 6.

Strategy Formulator enables students or managers to create an organizational mission statement, identify key internal strengths and weaknesses as well as key external opportunities and threats, and then generate, evaluate, and prioritize alternative strategies that the firm could pursue. Individuals can work through the software independently and then meet to discuss particular strategies.

Strategy Formulator runs on any IBM-compatible personal computer system that has a high density (HD) disk drive. It includes numerous help screens and examples and offers clear printouts. No documentation manual is needed with *Strategy Formulator.* Simply boot DOS, type SF, and follow directions.

Strategy Formulator gives you hands-on experience using actual strategic planning software and facilitates business policy case analysis. This new software is similar to the CheckMATE strategic planning software that is widely used among organizations worldwide. (For additional information about CheckMATE, contact the author at Strategic Planning Systems, P.O. Box 13065, Florence, SC 29504; Phone 843-669-6960; Fax 843-673-9460, e-mail strategy29@aol.com) CheckMATE is Windows-based and costs $195.

THE STRUCTURE AND FUNCTION OF *STRATEGY FORMULATOR* The first and second screens that appear in the *Strategy Formulator* software are given in Figures 1 and 2. Note from the first screen that the F1, F2, and F3 keys are the Save key, Load key, and Print key, respectively. Note that the second screen gives an outline or flowchart of the *Strategy Formulator* program. This second screen is a main menu that returns throughout the program; you simply highlight the particular area you wish to work on and hit Enter to begin that part of the program.

FIGURE 1
THE FIRST SCREEN

***Strategy Formulator* Software**

The *Strategy Formulator* program provides a systematic approach for managers to devise strategies their organizations could pursue. *Strategy Formulator* incorporates the most modern strategic planning techniques in a simple way.

The recommended approach for using *Strategy Formulator* is for managers to work through the software independently and then meet together to discuss the results and develop a single set of joint recommendations. This approach to strategic planning facilitates communication, forward thinking, understanding, commitment, and performance. The help key (F1) is available at all times throughout the *Formulator* program to give you more information. Press the F1 key now to obtain information about the Save key (F2), Load key (F3), Print key (F4), and Escape key.

Press the Return key on the highlighted topic on the menu to activate the various parts of the program.

FIGURE 2
THE SECOND SCREEN

The Structure and Function of *Strategy Formulator*

   I. Create a Mission Statement
  II. Identify Key Internal Strengths and Weaknesses
 III. Identify Key External Opportunities and Threats
 IV. Generate Alternative Strategies Using:
      IE Analysis
      TOWS Analysis
      SPACE Analysis
      GRAND Analysis
  V. Refine Alternative Strategies
 VI. Select Strategies to Pursue
     Other functions:
      Load Data from Disk
      Save Data to Disk
      Print
      Quit Program

GETTING STARTED Run the *Strategy Formulator* software by typing SF at the DOS prompt or double click on the SF.EXE program from Windows Explorer.

Read the first screen. Hit the F1 key just to get familiar with the Help routine. Hit the Escape key to return to the main menu. Hit Enter to go to the second screen. Note from the second screen that you may simply highlight the Create a Mission Statement line and hit Enter to begin work on developing a mission statement—which is the first activity in formulating strategies. Hit Enter again when you are ready to return to the main menu. You may hit the F1 key anytime in the program for help. The Program Mechanics Help, as shown in Figure 3, will appear on the screen if you hit the F1 key twice.

After completing the mission statement, highlight the next line, Identify Key Internal Strengths and Weaknesses. Hit Enter and begin development of a list of the company's key strengths and weaknesses. When you have completed this work, return to the main menu. Continue working sequentially in this manner through the program.

THE SAVE AND LOAD ROUTINES It is easy to save and load your work in the *Strategy Formulator* program. The Help Screens (F1 key) associated with the Save and Load routines are given in Figures 4 and 5.

THE PRINT ROUTINE The *Strategy Formulator* software generates nine planning reports that can be printed separately or together, (as indicated on a print screen as shown in Figure 6) that appears near the end of the program.

Simply highlight the reports you desire to be printed, and hit Enter to begin printing your work. You could highlight Print All Reports to print all of your work. If you press the F1 key, the screen shown in Figure 7 appears.

FIGURE 3
THE PROGRAM MECHANICS HELP SCREEN

- Movement between screens within a module is accomplished by pressing the UP and DOWN arrows. This is true both within the Help facility and within the main program.
- If you wish to delete to the left of the cursor, you should press the BACKSPACE key. If you wish to delete to the right of the cursor, you should press the DELETE key.
- If you wish to insert text, place the cursor where you wish to begin the insertion and press the INSERT key. When the insert mode is in operation, the cursor changes its size and the word "Insert" appears in the bottom right corner of the screen. Insert is turned off again either by pressing the INSERT key or by moving to another answer.
- You can access the HELP facility at any time by pressing the F1 key. From the Help facility, you can return to the screen you were working on by pressing the ESCAPE key.
- You can SAVE all of your work at any time by pressing the F2 key.
- You can LOAD all of your work at any time by pressing the F3 key.
- You can PRINT all or part of your work at any time by pressing the F4 key.
- You can return to the menu at any time by pressing the ESCAPE key.

FIGURE 4
THE SAVE ROUTINE HELP SCREEN

The Save routine is where the information that has been entered into the system is saved for later use.

The Drive is the disk drive where the data is saved.

The Path is the logical place on the drive where the information is saved. You should either read up on this in the DOS manual or go with the default. The default is the drive and path where the program is located.

The File Name is the name that is given to the information that is saved. This name is used later to retrieve the information. It is eight characters long.

The Directory List will give you a list of files that already exist. If you save over a file (use the same name), the contents of that file are lost. It is a good idea to save your files in two places so that there will be a backup if the primary file is lost. To do this, put a floppy disk in the drive and change the disk drive letter to the letter corresponding to the drive you are using. Usually the letter is A; sometimes it is B.

FIGURE 5
THE LOAD ROUTINE HELP SCREEN

The Load routine is where the information that has been saved on the disk is brought back into the system.

The Drive is the disk drive where the data is saved.

The Path is the logical place on the drive where the information is saved. For more information on this, you should read the DOS manual.

The File Name is the name that is given to the information that is saved. This name is used to retrieve the information. It is eight characters long.

The Directory List will give you a list of files that exist on the disk and path that are listed on the screen. The name must show up on the directory in order for the information to be read.

FIGURE 6
***STRATEGY FORMULATOR* PRINT REPORTS**

Print ALL Reports	TOWS Analysis Report
Mission Statement Report	SPACE Analysis Report
Internal Analysis Report	GRAND Analysis Report
External Analysis Report	Alternative Strategies Report
E Analysis Report	Selected Strategies Report

FIGURE 7
THE PRINT ROUTINE HELP SCREEN

The Print routine is accessed by hitting the F4 key or the print option on the main menu.

Within the print menu, select the report you wish by pressing the up and down arrow keys. You can print all reports or individual ones.

If there is a "printer off line" error, you should locate the on-line button on your printer and press it. This should put your printer on-line.

If there is a "printer paper out" error, you should load paper into your printer. This should correct this problem.

If you wish to bypass the program's printer error detection features for any reason, press the "D" (for disable) key. This is usually not needed, but if the user has nonstandard software or hardware, it may be necessary.

PART 1

OVERVIEW OF STRATEGIC MANAGEMENT

CHAPTER 1

The Nature of Strategic Management

CHAPTER OUTLINE

- ◆ WHAT IS STRATEGIC MANAGEMENT?
- ◆ KEY TERMS IN STRATEGIC MANAGEMENT
- ◆ THE STRATEGIC-MANAGEMENT MODEL
- ◆ BENEFITS OF STRATEGIC MANAGEMENT
- ◆ BUSINESS ETHICS AND STRATEGIC MANAGEMENT
- ◆ COMPARING BUSINESS AND MILITARY STRATEGY
- ◆ THE COHESION CASE AND EXPERIENTIAL EXERCISES

- ◆ THE COHESION CASE: HERSHEY FOODS CORPORATION—1998

- ■ EXPERIENTIAL EXERCISE 1A
  Strategy Analysis for Hershey Foods
- ■ EXPERIENTIAL EXERCISE 1B
  Developing a Code of Business Ethics for Hershey Foods
- ■ EXPERIENTIAL EXERCISE 1C
  The Ethics of Spying on Competitors
- ■ EXPERIENTIAL EXERCISE 1D
  Strategic Planning for My University
- ■ EXPERIENTIAL EXERCISE 1E
  Strategic Planning at a Local Company

CHAPTER OBJECTIVES

After studying this chapter, you should be able to do the following:

1. Describe the strategic-management process.
2. Explain the need for integrating analysis and intuition in strategic management.
3. Define and give examples of key terms in strategic management.
4. Discuss the nature of strategy formulation, implementation, and evaluation activities.
5. Describe the benefits of good strategic management.
6. Explain why good ethics is good business in strategic management.

*I*f we know where we are and something about how we got there, we might see where we are trending—and if the outcomes which lie naturally in our course are unacceptable, to make timely change.
—ABRAHAM LINCOLN

*W*ithout a strategy, an organization is like a ship without a rudder, going around in circles. It's like a tramp; it has no place to go.—JOEL ROSS AND MICHAEL KAMI

*P*lans are less important than planning.—DALE MCCONKEY

*T*he formulation of strategy can develop competitive advantage only to the extent that the process can give meaning to workers in the trenches.—DAVID HURST

*M*ost of us fear change. Even when our minds say change is normal, our stomachs quiver at the prospect. But for strategists and managers today, there is no choice but to change.—ROBERT WATERMAN, JR.

*I*f business is not based on ethical grounds, it is of no benefit to society, and will, like all other unethical combinations, pass into oblivion.—C. MAX KILLAN

*I*f a man take no thought about what is distant, he will find sorrow near at hand. He who will not worry about what is far off will soon find something worse than worry.—CONFUCIUS

*I*t is human nature to make decisions based on emotion, rather than fact. But nothing could be more illogical.—TOSHIBA CORPORATION

*N*o business can do everything. Even if it has the money, it will never have enough good people. It has to set priorities. The worst thing to do is a little bit of everything. This makes sure that nothing is being accomplished. It is better to pick the wrong priority than none at all.—PETER DRUCKER

*E*xecutives, consultants, and B-school professors all agree that strategic planning is now the single most important management issue and will remain so for the next five years. Strategy has become a part of the main agenda at lots of organizations today. Strategic planning is back with a vengeance.
—JOHN BYRNE

This chapter provides an overview of strategic management. It introduces a practical, integrative model of the strategic-management process and defines basic activities and terms in strategic management and discusses the importance of business ethics.

This chapter initiates several themes that permeate all chapters of this text. First, *global considerations impact virtually all strategic decisions!* The boundaries of countries no longer can define the limits of our imaginations. To see and appreciate the world from the perspective of others has become a matter of survival for businesses. The underpinnings of strategic management hinge upon managers' gaining an understanding of competitors, markets, prices, suppliers, distributors, governments, creditors, shareholders, and customers worldwide. The price and quality of a firm's products and services must be competitive on a worldwide basis, not just a local basis. A Global Perspective is provided in all chapters of this text to emphasize the importance of global factors in strategic management.

A second theme is that *information technology has become a vital strategic-management tool.* An increasing number of companies are gaining competitive advantage by using the Internet for communication with suppliers, customers, creditors, partners, shareholders, clients, and competitors who may be dispersed globally. On-line services allow firms to sell products, advertise, purchase supplies, bypass intermediaries, track inventory, eliminate paperwork, and share information. In total, *electronic commerce* is minimizing the expense and cumbersomeness of time, distance, and space in doing business, which yields better customer service, greater efficiency, improved products, and higher profitability. Acquiring up-to-date information as a basis for decisions is a key benefit offered a firm operating on-line.

The Internet and personal computers are changing the way we organize our lives; inhabit our homes; and relate to and interact with family, friends, neighbors, and even ourselves. Personal-computer penetration of U.S. households topped 52 percent in 1998. More than 72 percent of U.S. households with an annual income above $40,000 have personal computers. Less than half of these households use the Internet, but the percentage is increasing rapidly. Estimates are that more than $100 billion of goods will be bought annually over the Internet in the United States by the year 2000. An Information Technology Perspective is included in each chapter to illustrate how electronic commerce impacts the strategic-management process.

A third theme is that *the natural environment has become an important strategic issue.* With the demise of communism and the end of the cold war, perhaps there is now no greater threat to business and society than the continuous exploitation and decimation of our natural environment. Mark Starik at George Washington University says, "Halting and reversing worldwide ecological destruction and deterioration . . . is a strategic issue that needs immediate and substantive attention by all businesses and managers." A Natural Environment Perspective is provided in all chapters to illustrate how firms are addressing environmental concerns.

WHAT IS STRATEGIC MANAGEMENT?

Once there were two company presidents who competed in the same industry. These two presidents decided to go on a camping trip to discuss a possible merger. They hiked deep into the woods. Suddenly, they came upon a grizzly bear that rose up on its hind legs and snarled. Instantly, the first president took off his knapsack and got out a pair of jogging shoes. The second president said, "Hey, you can't outrun that bear." The first president responded, "Maybe I can't outrun that bear, but I surely can outrun you!" This story captures the notion of strategic management.

DEFINING STRATEGIC MANAGEMENT *Strategic management* can be defined as the art and science of formulating, implementing, and evaluating cross-functional decisions that enable an organization to achieve its objectives. As this definition implies, strategic management focuses on integrating management, marketing, finance/accounting, production/operations, research and development, and computer information systems to achieve organizational success. The term *strategic management* is used at many colleges and universities as the subtitle for the capstone course in business administration, Business Policy, which integrates material from all business courses. Consider joining the Strategic Management Club Online at www.strategyclub.com that offers many benefits for business policy students.

STAGES OF STRATEGIC MANAGEMENT The *strategic-management process* consists of three stages: strategy formulation, strategy implementation, and strategy evaluation. *Strategy formulation* includes developing a business mission, identifying an organization's external opportunities and threats, determining internal strengths and weaknesses, establishing long-term objectives, generating alternative strategies, and choosing particular strategies to pursue. Strategy-formulation issues include deciding what new businesses to enter, what businesses to abandon, how to allocate resources, whether to expand operations or diversify, whether to enter international markets, whether to merge or form a joint venture, and how to avoid a hostile takeover.

Because no organization has unlimited resources, strategists must decide which alternative strategies will benefit the firm most. Strategy-formulation decisions commit an organization to specific products, markets, resources, and technologies over an extended period of time. Strategies determine long-term competitive advantages. For better or worse, strategic decisions have major multifunctional consequences and enduring effects on an organization. Top managers have the best perspective to understand fully the ramifications of formulation decisions; they have the authority to commit the resources necessary for implementation.

Strategy implementation requires a firm to establish annual objectives, devise policies, motivate employees, and allocate resources so that formulated strategies can be executed; strategy implementation includes developing a strategy-supportive culture, creating an effective organizational structure, redirecting marketing efforts, preparing budgets, developing and utilizing information systems, and linking employee compensation to organizational performance.

Strategy implementation often is called the action stage of strategic management. Implementing strategy means mobilizing employees and managers to put formulated strategies into action. Often considered to be the most difficult stage in strategic management, strategy implementation requires personal discipline, commitment, and sacrifice. Successful strategy implementation hinges upon managers' ability to motivate employees, which is more an art than a science. Strategies formulated but not implemented serve no useful purpose.

Interpersonal skills are especially critical for successful strategy implementation. Strategy-implementation activities affect all employees and managers in an organization. Every division and department must decide on answers to questions such as "What must we do to implement our part of the organization's strategy?" and "How best can we get the job done?" The challenge of implementation is to stimulate managers and employees throughout an organization to work with pride and enthusiasm toward achieving stated objectives.

Strategy evaluation is the final stage in strategic management. Managers desperately need to know when particular strategies are not working well; strategy evaluation is the primary means for obtaining this information. All strategies are subject to future modification because external and internal factors are constantly changing. Three fundamental strategy-evaluation activities are (1) reviewing external and internal factors that are the bases for current strategies, (2) measuring performance, and (3) taking corrective actions. Strategy evaluation is needed because success today is no guarantee of success tomorrow! Success always creates new and different problems; complacent organizations experience demise.

Strategy formulation, implementation, and evaluation activities occur at three hierarchical levels in a large organization: corporate, divisional or strategic business unit, and functional. By fostering communication and interaction among managers and employees across hierarchical levels, strategic management helps a firm function as a competitive team. Most small businesses and some large businesses do not have divisions or strategic business units; they have only the corporate and functional levels. Nevertheless, managers and employees at these two levels should be actively involved in strategic-management activities.

Peter Drucker says the prime task of strategic management is thinking through the overall mission of a business:

> . . . that is, of asking the question, "What is our Business?" This leads to the setting of objectives, the development of strategies, and the making of today's decisions for tomorrow's results. This clearly must be done by a part of the organization that can see the entire business; that can balance objectives and the needs of today against the needs of tomorrow; and that can allocate resources of men and money to key results.[1]

INTEGRATING INTUITION AND ANALYSIS The strategic-management process can be described as an objective, logical, systematic approach for making major decisions in an organization. It attempts to organize qualitative and quantitative information in a way that allows effective decisions to be made under conditions of uncertainty. Yet, strategic management is not a pure science that lends itself to a nice, neat, one-two-three approach.

Based on past experiences, judgment, and feelings, *intuition* is essential to making good strategic decisions. Intuition is particularly useful for making decisions in situations of great uncertainty or little precedent. It is also helpful when highly interrelated variables exist, when there is immense pressure to be right, or when it is necessary to choose from several plausible alternatives.[2] These situations describe the very nature and heart of strategic management.

Some managers and owners of businesses profess to have extraordinary abilities for using intuition alone in devising brilliant strategies. For example, Will Durant, who organized General Motors Corporation, was described by Alfred Sloan as "a man who would proceed on a course of action guided solely, as far as I could tell, by some intuitive flash of brilliance. He never felt obliged to make an engineering hunt for the facts. Yet at times, he was astoundingly correct in his judgment."[3] Albert Einstein acknowledged the importance of intuition when he said, "I believe in intuition and inspiration. At times I feel certain that I am right while not knowing the reason. Imagination is more important than knowledge, because knowledge is limited, whereas imagination embraces the entire world."[4]

Although some organizations today may survive and prosper because they have intuitive geniuses managing them, most are not so fortunate. Most organizations can benefit from strategic management, which is based upon integrating intuition and analysis in decision making. Choosing an intuitive or analytic approach to decision making is not an either-or proposition. Managers at all levels in an organization should inject their intuition and judgment into strategic-management analyses. Analytical thinking and intuitive thinking complement each other.

Operating from the I've-already-made-up-my-mind-don't-bother-me-with-the-facts mode is not management by intuition; it is management by ignorance.[5] Drucker says, "I believe in intuition only if you discipline it. 'Hunch' artists, who make a diagnosis but don't check it out with the facts, are the ones in medicine who kill people, and in management kill businesses."[6] As Henderson notes:

> The accelerating rate of change today is producing a business world in which customary managerial habits in organizations are increasingly inadequate. Experience alone was an adequate guide when changes could be made in small increments. But intuitive and experience-based management philosophies are grossly inadequate when decisions are strategic and have major, irreversible consequences.[7]

In a sense, the strategic-management process is an attempt to duplicate what goes on in the mind of a brilliant, intuitive person who knows the business and hinge it with analysis.

ADAPTING TO CHANGE   The strategic-management process is based on the belief that organizations should continually monitor internal and external events and trends so that timely changes can be made as needed. The rate and magnitude of changes that affect organizations are increasing dramatically. Consider, for example, Windows 98, Internet commerce, laser medicine, laser weapons, the aging population, and merger mania. To survive, all organizations must be capable of astutely identifying and adapting to change. The strategic-management process is aimed at allowing organizations to adapt effectively to change over the long run.

> In today's business environment, more than any preceding era, the only constant is change. Successful organizations effectively manage change, continuously adapting their bureaucracies, strategies, systems, products, and cultures to survive the shocks and prosper from the forces that decimate the competition.[8]

Information technology and globalization are external changes that are transforming business and society today. On a political map, the boundaries between countries may be clear, but on a competitive map showing the real flow of financial and industrial activity, the boundaries have largely disappeared.[9] Speedy flow of information has eaten away at national boundaries so that people worldwide readily see for themselves how other people live. People are traveling abroad more; 10 million Japanese travel abroad annually. People are emigrating more; Germans to England and Mexicans to the United States are examples. As the Global Perspective indicates, U.S. firms are challenged by competitors in many industries. We are becoming a borderless world with global citizens, global competitors, global customers, global suppliers, and global distributors!

The need to adapt to change leads organizations to key strategic-management questions, such as, What kind of business should we become? Are we in the right fields? Should we reshape our business? What new competitors are entering our industry? What strategies should we pursue? How are our customers changing? Are new technologies being developed that could put us out of business?

KEY TERMS IN STRATEGIC MANAGEMENT

Before we go any further in discussing strategic management, we should define eight key terms: strategists, mission statements, external opportunities and threats, internal strengths and weaknesses, long-term objectives, strategies, annual objectives, and policies.

GLOBAL PERSPECTIVE
Do U.S. Firms Dominate All Industries?

The Wall Street Journal's annual ranking of the world's largest companies reveals that U.S. firm's are being challenged in many industries. The world's 10 largest insurance companies, banks, and electronics firms, for example, are listed below in rank order. Note that Japanese firms dominate these three industries.

INSURANCE FIRMS

Nippon Life, Japan
Zenkyoren, Japan
Dai-Ichi Mutual Life, Japan
Axa, France
Allianz Holding, Germany
Sumitomo Life, Japan
Metropolitan Life, U.S.
Compagnie UAP, France
Internationale Nederlanden
  Group, Netherlands
Prudential Insurance, U.S.

BANKS

Bank of Tokyo-Mitsubishi, Japan
Deutsche Bank, Germany
Sumitomo Bank, Japan
Dai-Ichi Kangyo Bank, Japan
Fuji Bank, Japan
Sanwa Bank, Japan
ABN Amro Holdings,
  Netherlands
Sakura Bank, Japan
Industrial & Commercial Bank,
  China
HSBC Holdings, U.K.

ELECTRONICS FIRMS

General Electric U.S.
Hitachi, Japan
Matsushita Electronic, Japan
Siemens, Germany
Sony, Japan
Toshiba, Japan
NEC, Japan
Philips Electronics,
  Netherlands
ABB Asea Brown Boveri,
  Switzerland
Mitsubishi Electric, Japan

Source: Adapted from Urban Lehner, "The Global Giants," The Wall Street Journal (September 18, 1997): R. 25.

STRATEGISTS   *Strategists* are individuals who are most responsible for the success or failure of an organization. Strategists have various job titles, such as chief executive officer, president, owner, chair of the board, executive director, chancellor, dean, or entrepreneur. Jonas, Fry, and Srivastva contend that strategists' three principal responsibilities in organizations are creating a context for change, building commitment and ownership, and balancing stability and innovation.[10]

Strategists are expected to change in ways outlined in Table 1–1. For example, strategists in the 2000s will provide more visionary leadership, better link compensation to performance, communicate more frequently with employees, and emphasize business ethics more.

Strategists differ as much as organizations themselves, and these differences must be considered in the formulation, implementation, and evaluation of strategies. Some strategists will not consider some types of strategies due to their personal philosophies. Strategists differ in their attitudes, values, ethics, willingness to take risks, concern for social responsibility, concern for profitability, concern for short-run versus long-run aims, and management style. The founder of Hershey Foods, Milton Hershey, built the company to manage an orphanage. From corporate profits Hershey Foods today cares for over 1,000 boys and girls in its School for Orphans.

Some strategists agree with Ralph Nader, who proclaims that organizations have tremendous social obligations. Others agree with Milton Friedman, an economist, who maintains that organizations have no obligation to do any more for society than is legally required. Most strategists agree that the first social responsibility of any business must be to make enough profit to cover the costs of the future, because if this is not achieved, no other social responsibility can be met. Strategists should examine social problems in terms of potential costs and benefits to the firm, and address social issues that could benefit the firm most.

TABLE 1–1
What Traits CEOs Have—and Will Need: Percent Describing Traits or Talents Dominant in the CEO in 1989 and Important for the CEO in 2000

PERSONAL BEHAVIOR	1989	2000	KNOWLEDGE AND SKILLS	1989	2000
Conveys Strong Sense of Vision	75	98	Strategy Formulation	68	78
Links Compensation to Performance	66	91	Human Resource Management	41	53
Communicates Frequently with Employees	59	89	International Economics and Politics	10	19
Emphasizes Ethics	74	85	Science and Technology	11	15
Plans for Management Succession	56	85	Computer Literacy	3	7
Communicates Frequently with Customers	41	78	Marketing and Sales	50	48
Reassigns or Terminates Unsatisfactory Employees	34	71	Negotiation	34	24
Rewards Loyalty	48	44	Accounting and Finance	33	24
Makes All Major Decisions	39	21	Handling Media and Public Speaking	16	13
Behaves Conservatively	32	13	Production	21	9

Note: This information is based on a Columbia University survey of 1,500 senior executives, 870 of them CEOs, in 20 countries.
Source: Lester Korn, "How the Next CEO Will Be Different." *Fortune* (May 22, 1989): 157.

MISSION STATEMENTS *Mission statements* are "enduring statements of purpose that distinguish one business from other similar firms. A mission statement identifies the scope of a firm's operations in product and market terms."[11] It addresses the basic question that faces all strategists: "What is our business?" A clear mission statement describes the values and priorities of an organization. Developing a business mission compels strategists to think about the nature and scope of present operations and to assess the potential attractiveness of future markets and activities. A mission statement broadly charts the future direction of an organization.

Research suggests that about 60 percent of all organizations have developed a formal mission statement and that high-performing firms have more well-developed mission statements than low-performing firms.[12] Note that the mission statement of Adolph Coors Company below should, but does not, reveal that Coors is in the brewery business:

We are a highly successful, innovative company of stand alone and self-sustaining businesses. We are leaders in technology, quality products and services that provide recognizably superior customer satisfaction. We are growth and profit oriented, developing new businesses from internally generated technology and synergistic acquisitions. Our business is known for quality relationships which are honest, ethical, and caring. Our employees grow personally as the company grows. Our work life is exciting, challenging and rewarding in a friendly atmosphere of teamwork and mutual respect. We are socially responsible and strive for the betterment of society.[13]

EXTERNAL OPPORTUNITIES AND THREATS *External opportunities* and *external threats* refer to economic, social, cultural, demographic, environmental, political, legal, governmental, technological, and competitive trends and events that could significantly benefit or harm an organization in the future. Opportunities and threats are largely beyond the control of a single organization, thus the term *external*. The computer revolution, biotechnology, population shifts, changing work values and attitudes, space exploration, recyclable packages, and increased competition from foreign companies are examples of opportunities or threats for companies. These types of changes are creating a different type of consumer and consequently a need for different types of products, services, and strategies. As indicated in the Information Technology Perspective, adding phone lines in underdeveloped countries is an opportunity for many companies.

Other opportunities and threats may include the passage of a law, the introduction of a new product by a competitor, a national catastrophe, or the declining value of the dollar.

A competitor's strength could be a threat. Unrest in Eastern Europe, rising interest rates, or the war against drugs could represent an opportunity or a threat.

A basic tenet of strategic management is that firms need to formulate strategies to take advantage of external opportunities and to avoid or reduce the impact of external threats. For this reason, identifying, monitoring, and evaluating external opportunities and threats is essential for success. This process of conducting research and gathering and assimilating external information is sometimes called *environmental scanning* or industry analysis.

INTERNAL STRENGTHS AND WEAKNESSES   *Internal strengths* and *internal weaknesses* are an organization's controllable activities that are performed especially well or poorly. They arise in the management, marketing, finance/accounting, production/operations, research and development, and computer information systems activities of a business. Identifying and evaluating organizational strengths and weaknesses in the functional areas of a business is an essential strategic-management activity. Organizations strive to pursue strategies that capitalize on internal strengths and improve on internal weaknesses.

Strengths and weaknesses are determined relative to competitors. *Relative* deficiency or superiority is important information. Also, strengths and weaknesses can be determined by elements of being rather than performance. For example, a strength may involve ownership of natural resources or an historic reputation for quality. Strengths and weaknesses may be determined relative to a firm's own objectives. For example, high levels of inventory turnover may not be a strength to a firm that seeks never to stock-out.

Internal factors can be determined in a number of ways that include computing ratios, measuring performance, and comparing to past periods and industry averages. Various types of surveys also can be developed and administered to examine internal factors such as employee morale, production efficiency, advertising effectiveness, and customer loyalty. Robert H. Short, chief executive officer of Portland General Corporation, described his firm's strategy in terms of strengths and weaknesses:

> First and foremost we are an energy company for the people of Oregon. Indeed, energy is our fundamental strength, and we intend to pursue growth aggressively in this business. To build on our strengths, however, we must mitigate or eliminate our weaknesses. I am proud of the way Portland General is drawing on its strengths to build for another century of success.[14]

LONG-TERM OBJECTIVES   *Objectives* can be defined as specific results that an organization seeks to achieve in pursuing its basic mission. *Long-term* means more than one year. Objectives are essential for organizational success because they state direction; aid in evaluation; create synergy; reveal priorities; focus coordination; and provide a basis for effective planning, organizing, motivating, and controlling activities. Objectives should be challenging, measurable, consistent, reasonable, and clear. In a multidimensional firm, objectives should be established for the overall company and for each division. Minnesota Power's long-term objectives are to achieve a 13 percent return on equity (ROE) in their core electric utility, 14 percent ROE on water resource operations, and 15 percent ROE on support businesses. Minnesota Power also strives to stay in the top 25 percent of electric utilities in the United States in terms of common stock's market-to-book ratio and to maintain an annual growth in earnings per share of 5 percent.

STRATEGIES   *Strategies* are the means by which long-term objectives will be achieved. Business strategies may include geographic expansion, diversification, acquisition, product development, market penetration, retrenchment, divestiture, liquidation, and joint venture. Strategies currently being pursued by E*Trade and Promus Hotels are described in Table 1–2.

INFORMATION TECHNOLOGY

Developing Countries Want to Call Home

In 1996 only 15 percent of the world's population has 71 percent of the world's phones. More than 50 percent of the world's people have never even used a phone. Over two-thirds of households around the world have no telephone. Cambodia has about the fewest phones of any country, only 0.06 phone lines per 100 inhabitants. The United States has close to 60 phone lines per 100 inhabitants. There are 47 countries with less than 1 phone line per 100 people.

Developing countries now realize they cannot develop their own economies or compete in world markets without phones. They must be able to communicate to survive. So, third-world countries are quickly adding phone lines. Underdeveloped countries are increasing their number of phone lines by an average 11.7 percent a year for the next 5 years (compared to 3.7 percent for the world's 24 highest-income countries). For example, China will install 100 million phones between 1996 and 1999.

An integral component of any computer system is the telephone. A phone is essential for using a modem and a fax machine. As indicated in the following table, there is explosive telephone growth in many developing countries. Analysts expect computer growth in these countries to follow on the heels of the phone growth. Implications of these two trends for all kinds of companies is immense.

Recognize that when countries add phones, their people become potential consumers of many new products and services. The addition of phones thus opens whole new markets. For example, Brazil has the ninth-largest econ-omy in the world and 150 million people, but a phone-line density of only 6.8 per 100 inhabitants. (About 721,000 Brazilians have cellular phones in 1996, but that number is expected to reach 6 million by 1998.) The situation in Indonesia, a nation of 190 million, is similar. In Africa there are only 0.8 phone lines per 100 people.

MCI, Sprint, AT&T, Motorola, Nynex, BellSouth, U.S. West, Northern Telecom, and Bell Atlantic are competing aggressively with foreign phone companies to service developing countries. Note that the dollar infrastructure investment required to install phone lines in a country is huge.

Source: Adapted from Catherine Arnst, "The Last Frontier," Business Week (September 18, 1995): 98–114.

Country	1992 Phone Lines per 100 People	2000 Phone Lines per 100 People	1992–2000 Investment for Phones (as expressed in million $U.S.)
China	0.98	3.50	$53.3
Thailand	3.10	9.35	6.6
India	0.77	1.52	13.7
Hungary	12.54	23.80	1.6
Poland	10.28	16.62	4.0
Russia	15.28	24.50	23.3
Chile	8.92	19.71	2.8
Brazil	6.83	9.49	10.2
Mexico	7.54	12.49	9.4
USA	56.49	65.92	55.8

Source: Adapted from Catherine Arnst, "The Last Frontier," Business Week (September 18, 1995): 106.

ANNUAL OBJECTIVES   *Annual objectives* are short-term milestones that organizations must achieve to reach long-term objectives. Like long-term objectives, annual objectives should be measurable, quantitative, challenging, realistic, consistent, and prioritized. They should be established at the corporate, divisional, and functional levels in a large organization. Annual objectives should be stated in terms of management, marketing, finance/accounting, production/operations, research and development, and information systems accomplishments. A set of annual objectives is needed for each long-term objective. Annual objectives are especially important in strategy implementation, whereas long-term objectives are particularly important in strategy formulation. Annual objectives represent the basis for allocating resources.

TABLE 1–2
Two Organizations'
Strategies in 1998

E*TRADE (www.etrade.com)

Headquartered in Palo Alto, California, tiny E*Trade now accounts for 13 percent of all on-line stock trades, tied with Fidelity and behind only Schwab's 35 percent market share. E*Trade's strategy is to become a "great financial company for the twenty-first century." E*Trade has about 230,000 accounts and is opening more than 600 new ones daily—and with only 475 employees total. The average age of an E*Trader is 38 versus 45 for Schwab's average customer. E*Trade's primary strategies are market penetration; spending heavily on advertising; and product development by offering stocks first, mutual funds next, then bonds, then IRAs, and then credit cards. E*Trade's business of on-line stock trading is growing by the hour.

PROMUS HOTELS (www.promus-inc.com)

Headquartered in Memphis, Tennessee, Promus Hotels aggressively is pursuing horizontal integration. With the acquisition of Doubletree and Red Lion hotels in 1997, Promus became the third-largest hotel chain in the United States behind Holiday Inn and Marriott. Promus already owns Embassy Suites, Hampton Inns, and Homewood Suites hotels. (Consolidation in the hotel industry is gaining momentum. Marriott recently acquired Renaissance Hotels, Cendant acquired both Ramada and Best Western, and in the largest lodging merger of 1997, Starwood Motels acquired ITT Corporation for $10.2 billion.) Promus now has over $5 billion in annual revenues.

Source: Lister, Harry, "Patriat Gains," *Lodging* (January 1998): 9.

Campbell Soup Corporation has an annual objective to achieve 20 percent growth in earnings, a 20 percent ROE, and a 20 percent return on invested cash. The company calls this ERC, for earnings, returns, and cash.

The Tribune Company (the nation's fifth-largest publisher of newspapers and owner of the Chicago Cubs baseball team) is another firm that has clear annual objectives. Stanton Cook, president and chief executive officer of Tribune, emphasizes annual objectives. Tribune strives to have an 18 percent annual ROE (net income divided by average stockholders' investment) and a 30 percent debt to total capital ratio.

POLICIES *Policies* are the means by which annual objectives will be achieved. Policies include guidelines, rules, and procedures established to support efforts to achieve stated objectives. Policies are guides to decision making and address repetitive or recurring situations.

Policies are most often stated in terms of management, marketing, finance/accounting, production/operations, research and development, and computer information systems activities. Policies can be established at the corporate level and apply to an entire organization, at the divisional level and apply to a single division, or at the functional level and apply to particular operational activities or departments. Policies, like annual objectives, are especially important in strategy implementation because they outline an organization's expectations of its employees and managers. Policies allow consistency and coordination within and between organizational departments.

Substantial research suggests that a healthier workforce can more effectively and efficiently implement strategies. The National Center for Health Promotion estimates that more than 80 percent of all American corporations have No Smoking policies. No Smoking policies are usually derived from annual objectives that seek to reduce corporate medical costs associated with absenteeism and to provide a healthy workplace. Pullman Company in Garden Grove, California, charges smokers $10 more each month for health insurance than it charges nonsmokers.

THE STRATEGIC-MANAGEMENT MODEL

The strategic-management process best can be studied and applied using a model. Every model represents some kind of process. The framework illustrated in Figure 1–1 is a widely accepted, comprehensive model of the strategic-management process.[15] This model does not guarantee success, but it does represent a clear and practical approach for formulating, implementing, and evaluating strategies. Relationships among major components of the strategic-management process are shown in the model, which appears in all subsequent chapters with appropriate areas shaped to show the particular focus of each chapter.

Identifying an organization's existing mission, objectives, and strategies is the logical starting point for strategic management because a firm's present situation and condition may preclude certain strategies and may even dictate a particular course of action. Every organization has a mission, objectives, and strategy, even if these elements are not consciously designed, written, or communicated. The answer to where an organization is going can be determined largely by where the organization has been!

The strategic-management process is dynamic and continuous. A change in any one of the major components in the model can necessitate a change in any or all of the other components. For instance, a shift in the economy could represent a major opportunity and require a change in long-term objectives and strategies; a failure to accomplish annual objectives could require a change in policy; or a major competitor's change in strategy could require a change in the firm's mission. Therefore, strategy formulation, implementation, and evaluation activities should be performed on a continual basis, not just at the end of the year or semiannually. The strategic-management process never really ends.

The strategic-management process is not as cleanly divided and neatly performed in practice as the strategic-management model suggests. Strategists do not go through the process in lockstep fashion. Generally, there is give-and-take among hierarchical levels of an organization. Many organizations conduct formal meetings semiannually to discuss and update the firm's mission, opportunities/threats, strengths/weaknesses, strategies, objectives, policies, and performance. These meetings are commonly held off-premises and called *retreats*. The rationale for periodically conducting strategic-management meetings away from the work site is to encourage more creativity and candor among participants. Good communication and feedback are needed throughout the strategic-management process.

As shown in Figure 1–2, a number of different forces affect the formality of strategic management in organizations. Size of organization is a key factor; smaller firms are less formal in performing strategic-management tasks. Other variables that affect formality are management styles, complexity of environment, complexity of the production process, nature of problems, and purpose of the planning system.

BENEFITS OF STRATEGIC MANAGEMENT

Strategic management allows an organization to be more proactive than reactive in shaping its own future; it allows an organization to initiate and influence (rather than just respond to) activities, and thus to exert control over its own destiny. Small business owners, chief executive officers, presidents, and managers of many for-profit and nonprofit organizations have recognized and realized the benefits of strategic management.

FIGURE 1-1
A Comprehensive Strategic-Management Model

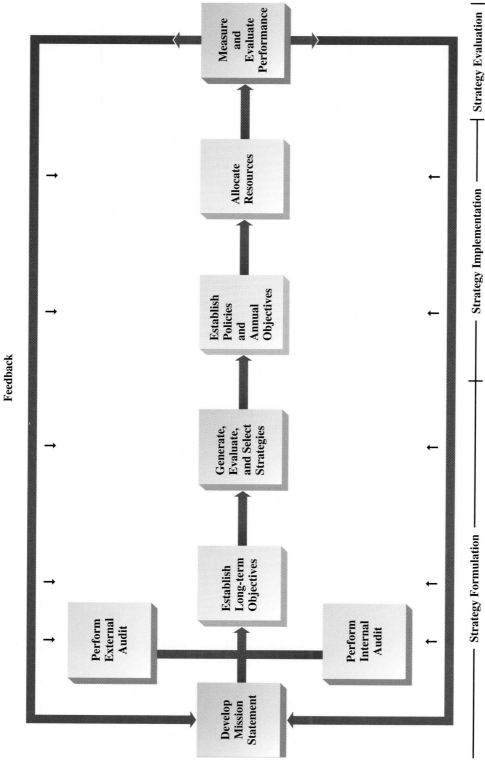

Source: Fred R. David, "How Companies Define Their Mission," *Long Range Planning* 22, no. 3 (June 1988): 40.

FIGURE 1–2
Forces Influencing Design of Strategic-Management Systems

Toward more formality and more details

Toward less formality and fewer details

Organization

Small one-plant companies ——————————→

←—————————— Large companies

Management styles

←—————————— Policy maker

Democratic-permissive ——————————→

←—————————— Authoritarian

Day-to-day operational thinker ——————————→

Intuitive thinker ——————————→

←—————————— Experienced in planning

Inexperienced in planning ——————————→

Complexity of environment

←—————————— Stable environment

Turbulent environment ——————————→

←—————————— Little competition

←—————————— Many markets and customers

Single market and customer ——————————→

Competition severe ——————————→

Complexity of production processes

←—————————— Long production lead times

Short production lead times ——————————→

←—————————— Capital-intensive

←—————————— Labor-intensive

←—————————— Integrated manufacturing processes

Simple manufacturing processes ——————————→

←—————————— High technology

Low technology ——————————→

Market reaction time for new production is short ——————————→

←—————————— Market reaction time is long

Nature of problems

←—————————— Facing new, complex, tough problems having long-range aspects

Facing tough short-range problems ——————————→

Purpose of planning system

←—————————— Coordinate division activities

Train managers ——————————→

Source: Reprinted with permission of the Free Press, a Division of Macmillan, Inc., from *Strategic Planning: What Every Manager Must Know* by George A. Steiner (New York: Free Press, 1979): 54. Copyright 1979 by the Free Press.

Historically, the principal benefit of strategic management has been to help organizations make better strategies through the use of a more systematic, logical, and rational approach to strategic choice. This certainly continues to be a major benefit of strategic management, but research studies now indicate that the process, rather than the decision or document, is the more important contribution of strategic management.[16] *Communication is a key to successful strategic management.* Through involvement in the process, managers and employees become committed to supporting the organization. Dialogue and participation are essential ingredients. The chief executive officer of Rockwell International explains, "We believe that fundamental to effective strategic management is fully informed employees at all organizational levels. We expect every business segment to inform every employee about the business objectives, the direction of the business, the progress towards achieving objectives, and our customers, competitors and product plans."

The manner in which strategic management is carried out is thus exceptionally important. A major aim of the process is to achieve understanding and commitment from all managers and employees. Understanding may be the most important benefit of strategic management, followed by commitment. When managers and employees understand what the organization is doing and why, they often feel a part of the firm and become committed to assisting it. This is especially true when employees also understand linkages between their own compensation and organizational performance. Managers and employees become surprisingly creative and innovative when they understand and support the firm's mission, objectives, and strategies. A great benefit of strategic management, then, is the opportunity that the process provides to empower individuals. *Empowerment* is the act of strengthening employees' sense of effectiveness by encouraging and rewarding them to participate in decision making and exercise initiative and imagination. *The Wall Street Journal* reports that 40 percent of U.S. manufacturers have adopted empowerment, usually through creation of self-directed work teams.[17]

More and more organizations are decentralizing the strategic-management process, recognizing that planning must involve lower-level managers and employees. The notion of centralized staff planning is being replaced in organizations by decentralized line-manager planning. The process is a learning, helping, educating, and supporting activity, not merely a paper-shuffling activity among top executives. Strategic-management dialogue is more important than a nicely bound strategic-management document.[18] The worst thing strategists can do is develop strategic plans themselves and then present them to operating managers to execute. Through involvement in the process, line managers become "owners" of the strategy. Ownership of strategies by the people who have to execute them is a key to success!

Although making good strategic decisions is the major responsibility of an organization's owner or chief executive officer, managers and employees both must also be involved in strategy formulation, implementation, and evaluation activities. Participation is a key to gaining commitment for needed changes.

An increasing number of corporations and institutions are using strategic management to make effective decisions. Over 75 percent of all companies now use strategic-management techniques, compared to less than 25 percent in 1979.[19] But strategic management is not a guarantee for success; it can be dysfunctional if conducted haphazardly. The benefits of strategic management to Rockwell International Corporation, Columbia Gas System Service Corporation, and Ogden Corporation are evidenced in Table 1–3.

William Dearden of Hershey Foods Corporation attributes his company's success to strategic management: "Planning for the long-term future has been entrenched as a way of life at Hershey, and we certainly plan to strengthen and rely on the process going forward."[20]

FINANCIAL BENEFITS   Research indicates that organizations using strategic-management concepts are more profitable and successful than those that do not. For example, a longitudinal study of 101 retail, service, and manufacturing firms over a 3-year period concluded that businesses using strategic-management concepts showed significant improvement in sales, profitability, and productivity compared to firms without systematic planning activities; another study reported that up to 80 percent of the improvement possible in a firm's profitability is achieved through changes in a company's strategic direction: Cook and Ferris reported that the practices of high-performing firms reflect a more strategic orientation and longer-term focus.[21] High-performing firms tend to do systematic planning to prepare

TABLE 1–3
Top Managers Discuss Strategic Management in Their Firms

ROCKWELL INTERNATIONAL CORPORATION (www.rockwell.com)

We expect every business segment head to be responsible for the strategic direction of the business and the business team to be very knowledgeable about their business in the worldwide marketplace, to know where they are taking the business long term; and how they are going to position the business vis-à-vis worldwide competition, as well as the marketplace as a whole. We also expect every business to make full use of the corporation's resources in developing functionally integrated implementation strategies that will beat the best of the competition. We will distinguish ourselves as a strategically managed worldwide company through the care and thoroughness with which our strategic management is linked to operational decision making. (Donald Beall, chief executive officer of Rockwell International, *Internal Report*, 1990.)

COLUMBIA GAS SYSTEM SERVICE CORPORATION (www.columbiaenergy.com)

Headquartered in Wilmington, Delaware, Columbia Gas System's Strategic Plan forms the basis of all other planning activities—marketing plans, capital programs, financial plans, and so forth. Strategic management goes far beyond operational planning that has been traditional throughout Columbia. We are not just looking at projections of how much gas we'll need and where it will come from. The first part of our Strategic Plan is the Mission Statement, which sets the direction for the company. All operating units have their own mission statements, defining their business and their corporate reason for existing. These in turn are followed by long-term objectives which are broad statements of what the company intends to do, followed by annual objectives which for the most part are quantified. (James D. Little, executive vice president of Columbia Gas System, *Columbia Today,* Winter 1985–86, p. 2.)

OGDEN CORPORATION (www.ogdencorp.com)

The best long-run results come from good strategic decisions, which ensure doing the right things (effectiveness), and the combination of design, technology, and automation, which ensure doing things right (efficiency). To predict . . . without the ability to adapt is simply to foresee one's own end! The strategic objectives Ogden has achieved have enabled the adaptation necessary to cope with the changing economic environment for the balance of this century. We are describing a classic example of evolution; in this case, corporate evolution. To survive, both organisms and corporations must adapt to new circumstances. (Ralph Ablon, chair of the board, Ogden Corporation.)

for future fluctuations in their external and internal environments. Firms with planning systems more closely resembling strategic-management theory generally exhibit superior long-term financial performance relative to their industry.

High-performing firms seem to make more informed decisions with good anticipation of both short- and long-term consequences. On the other hand, firms that perform poorly often engage in activities that are shortsighted and do not reflect good forecasting of future conditions. Michael Allen found that strategic management demonstrated impressive power by dramatically improving the performance of a number of major companies that had implemented it, including General Electric, American Express, Allied Corporation, Dun & Bradstreet, and Pitney Bowes.[22] Strategists of low-performing organizations are often preoccupied with solving internal problems and meeting paperwork deadlines. They typically underestimate their competitors' strengths and overestimate their own firm's strengths. They often attribute weak performance to uncontrollable factors such as poor economy, technological change, or foreign competition.

Dun & Bradstreet reports that more than 100,000 businesses in the United States fail annually. Business failures include bankruptcies, foreclosures, liquidations, and court-mandated receiverships. Although many factors besides a lack of effective strategic management can lead to business failure, the planning concepts and tools described in this text can yield substantial financial benefits for any organization. An excellent Web site for businesses engaged in strategic planning is www.checkmateplan.com.

NONFINANCIAL BENEFITS Besides helping firms avoid financial demise, strategic management offers other tangible benefits, such as an enhanced awareness of external threats, an improved understanding of competitors' strategies, increased employee productivity, reduced resistance to change, and a clearer understanding of performance-reward relationships. Strategic management enhances the problem-prevention capabilities of organizations because it promotes interaction among managers at all divisional and functional levels. Interaction can enable firms to turn on their managers and employees by nurturing them, sharing organizational objectives with them, empowering them to help improve the product or service, and recognizing their contributions. According to Tom Peters, the difference between a turned-on and a turned-off worker is not 5 percent or 10 percent, but 100 percent to 200 percent.[23]

In addition to empowering managers and employees, strategic management often brings order and discipline to an otherwise floundering firm. It can be the beginning of an efficient and effective managerial system. Strategic management may renew confidence in the current business strategy or point to the need for corrective actions. The strategic-management process provides a basis for identifying and rationalizing the need for change to all managers and employees of a firm; it helps them view change as an opportunity rather than a threat.

Greenley stated that strategic management offers the following benefits:

1. It allows for identification, prioritization, and exploitation of opportunities.
2. It provides an objective view of management problems.
3. It represents a framework for improved coordination and control of activities.
4. It minimizes the effects of adverse conditions and changes.
5. It allows major decisions to better support established objectives.
6. It allows more effective allocation of time and resources to identified opportunities.
7. It allows fewer resources and less time to be devoted to correcting erroneous or ad hoc decisions.
8. It creates a framework for internal communication among personnel.
9. It helps to integrate the behavior of individuals into a total effort.
10. It provides a basis for the clarification of individual responsibilities.
11. It gives encouragement to forward thinking.
12. It provides a cooperative, integrated, and enthusiastic approach to tackling problems and opportunities.
13. It encourages a favorable attitude toward change.
14. It gives a degree of discipline and formality to the management of a business.[24]

BUSINESS ETHICS AND STRATEGIC MANAGEMENT

Business ethics can be defined as principles of conduct within organizations that guide decision making and behavior. Good business ethics is a prerequisite for good strategic management; good ethics is just good business!

A rising tide of consciousness about the importance of business ethics is sweeping America and the world. Strategists are the individuals primarily responsible for ensuring that high ethical principles are espoused and practiced in an organization. All strategy formulation, implementation, and evaluation decisions have ethical ramifications.

Newspapers and business magazines daily report legal and moral breaches of ethical conduct by both public and private organizations. As the Natural Environment Perspective indicates, firms increasingly view cooperation with environmental groups as more effective than confrontation. Harming the natural environment is unethical, illegal, and costly; as more countries and companies realize this fact, export opportunities for pollution control equipment abound.

A new wave of ethics issues related to product safety, employee health, sexual harassment, AIDS in the workplace, smoking, acid rain, affirmative action, waste disposal, foreign business practices, cover-ups, takeover tactics, conflicts of interest, employee privacy, inappropriate gifts, security of company records, and layoffs has accented the need for strategists to develop a clear code of business ethics. United Technologies Corporation has issued a 21-page Code of Ethics and named a new vice president of business ethics. Baxter Travenol Laboratories, IBM, Caterpillar Tractor, Chemical Bank, Exxon, Dow Corning, and Celanese are firms that have a formal code of business ethics. Note how clearly BellSouth's *code of business ethics* in Table 1–4 outlines the standards of behavior expected of all managers and employees. A code of business ethics can provide a basis on which policies can be devised to guide daily behavior and decisions at the work site.

Merely having a code of ethics, however, is not sufficient to ensure ethical business behavior. A code of ethics can be viewed as a public relations gimmick, a set of platitudes, or window dressing. To ensure that the code is read, understood, believed, and remembered, organizations need to conduct periodic ethics workshops to sensitize people to workplace circumstances in which ethics issues may arise.[25]

Internet privacy is an emerging ethical issue of immense proportions. There is a national push for industry assurances that children have parental permission before giving out their names, ages, and other private details to companies that run Web sites. Privacy advocates increasingly argue for new government regulations to enforce protection of young users.

Netscape recently revealed a flaw in its browsing software that allows some Web site operators to access the personal computers of users. This flaw was corrected quickly but is indicative of privacy problems that plague the Internet.

Millions of computer users are worried about privacy on the Internet and want the U.S. government to pass laws about how data can be collected and used. Advertisers, marketers, companies, and people with various reasons to snoop on other people now can discover easily on the Internet others' buying preferences, hobbies, incomes, medical data, social security numbers, addresses, previous addresses, sexual preferences, credit card purchases, traffic tickets, divorce settlements, and much more. Many Internet users are ready for what they call "some law and order" in cyberspace.

Consumers using the Internet sacrifice privacy and anonymity. People today are being laid off and rejected for jobs without ever knowing the reason, sometimes due to something someone discovered on the Internet. America Online sold its subscriber list of over 11 million people and even cross-referenced that information with data from Donnelley Marketing and other companies. Privacy is important, but some people contend that access to reliable information is at least as important.

The U.S. Supreme Court's 1997 decision to strike down the Communications Decency Act paved the way for even less regulation and even less privacy on the Internet. Justice John Paul Stevens stated that "the interest in encouraging freedom of expression in a democratic society outweighs any theoretical but unproved benefit of censorship. Government regulation of the content of speech is more likely to interfere with the free exchange of ideas than to encourage it. The Internet is not as invasive as radio or television. Users seldom encounter content by accident." With the ruling, telecommunications executives and free-speech advocates were elated, but many consumers, parents, and privacy advocates were disappointed.

TABLE 1–4
BellSouth's Code of Conduct

COUNT ON US!

We are committed to the highest ethical standards because we want people to know they can count on us. This commitment flows naturally from our responsibilities to our customers, our owners, our vendors and suppliers, our families, the communities where we live and work, and to each other. Trust is at the heart of these connections, and trust can only be built on honest and dependability—on ethical conduct.

OUR CUSTOMERS CAN COUNT ON US

We believe our first responsibility is to the people who count on us for their telecommunications needs—in the office, on the road, at home, wherever they might be. All else hinges on this. We will deal with customers straightforwardly and honestly. They will know they can depend not only on our products and services, but on our word and our character. We will promise only what we can deliver. When we err, we will make things right.

OUR OWNERS CAN COUNT ON US

We will provide the highest quality at a reasonable price. As we do so, we will earn a fair return on our owners' investment. Our aim is to increase the value of their investment over the years.

OUR VENDORS AND SUPPLIERS CAN COUNT ON US

Vendors and suppliers must know we will be fair. BellSouth's interests will dictate our decisions about what products and services to buy; our decisions will be based on factors such as quality, price, service, and reliability.

OUR FAMILIES CAN COUNT ON US

We want our families to be proud of our character as individuals in the jobs we do and proud that we work for a company known for its integrity. We seek a healthy balance between our work and our family life.

OUR COMMUNITIES CAN COUNT ON US

Beyond the quality, day-to-day service they expect from us in telecommunications, the cities and towns where we operate can also count on us for help in civic, charitable, and other community activities.

WE CAN COUNT ON EACH OTHER

We take pride in the quality of our collective efforts as BellSouth; we take pride in the integrity of our company. A company's reputation is built on what its people do every day. BellSouth's reputation was built on the honesty of hundreds of thousands of people over the years, and we recognize that we can diminish that reputation in one single instant. We also know, however, that we can reinforce it every day. And since you and I inherited a company with a reputation for honesty and integrity, we are obligated to pass the heritage on to the women and men who follow us.

Ｗe will be even-handed with everyone around us—in scheduling work, in assigning jobs, in awarding incentives and promotions, and in the way we treat one another generally.

Each of us expects to be heard and we in turn pledge to listen. We want honesty and openness—about mistakes as well as successes.

We will speak out when we see ethical lapses. We expect that no one will ask us to do anything wrong. Likewise, we will not ask anyone else to do anything wrong.

Satisfying the letter of the law is not enough. Ours is a higher standard. BellSouth's obligations are for the long term—not just for this quarter or this year. These obligations demand this pledge of us on professional, industry and personal ethics: We will build on BellSouth's heritage of integrity so that people will have an abiding trust in the company and our employees; they will know they can count on us. This is our pledge.

Source: BellSouth Corporation, *Internal Report,* 1993.

NATURAL ENVIRONMENT

Is Cooperation Better Than Confrontation?

More U.S. firms today actively seek out environmental groups and the Environmental Protection Agency (EPA) to engage proactively in dialogue aimed at setting environmental standards for the firm and industry. The old, reactive, command-and-control approach to environmental affairs no longer is considered the most effective. Ciba-Geigy, Monsanto, Exxon, Amoco, and General Motors are just a few among thousands of firms that today actively engage trade associations; regulatory bodies; and state, national, and foreign legislatures in setting industry natural environment standards. Companies find that many environmentalists are highly competent technologically and operationally. Dialogue thus often results in new processes that significantly improve corporate efficiency as well as environmental effectiveness.

Benefits of this activity far exceed public relations.

Before a firm engages an environmental group in discussions, the following seven recommendations can pave the way for success:

- Be sincere in wanting their input.
- Be willing to accept some advice.
- Be part of the issue, so you have credibility.
- Look at the larger interests, see the big picture.
- Staff the meeting with decision makers.
- Have a good corporate reputation.
- Reach out on other issues, also.

When organizations today face criminal charges for polluting the environment, firms increasingly are turning on their managers and employees to win leniency for themselves. Employee firings and demotions are becoming common in pollution-related legal suits. Managers being recently fired at Darling International, Inc., and Niagara Mohawk Power Corporation for being indirectly responsible for their firms' polluting water exemplifies this corporate trend. Therefore, managers and employees today must be careful not to ignore, conceal, or disregard a pollution problem or they may find themselves personally liable.

Source: Adapted from Gail Dutton, "Green Partnerships," Management Review (January 1996): 24–28. Also, Dean Starkman, "Pollution Case Highlights Trend to Let Employees Take the Rap," The Wall Street Journal, (October 9, 1997): B10.

Given the global nature of the Internet, any U.S. government regulations to inhibit free flow of information will not carry much weight anyway in places such as Moldova, home of a phone-porn scam. But perhaps the United States at least should set a standard for Internet rules and regulations that other countries could consider adopting.

An ethics "culture" needs to permeate organizations! To help create an ethics culture, Citicorp developed a business ethics board game that is played by 40,000 employees in 45 countries. Called *The Work Ethic*, this game asks players business ethics questions, such as how to deal with a customer who offers you football tickets in exchange for a new, backdated IRA. Diana Robertson at the Wharton School believes the game is effective because it is interactive. Many organizations, such as Prime Computer and Kmart, have developed a code-of-conduct manual outlining ethical expectations and giving examples of situations that commonly arise in their businesses. Harris Corporation's managers and employees are warned that failing to report an ethical violation by others could bring discharge.

One reason strategists' salaries are high compared to those of other individuals in an organization is that strategists must take the moral risks of the firm. Strategists are responsible for developing, communicating, and enforcing the code of business ethics for their organizations. Although primary responsibility for ensuring ethical behavior rests with a firm's strategists, an integral part of the responsibility of all managers is to provide ethics leadership by constant example and demonstration. Managers hold positions that enable them to influence and educate many people. This makes managers responsible for the development and implementation of ethical decision making. Gellerman and Drucker respectively offer some good advice for managers:

All managers risk giving too much because of what their companies demand from them. But the same superiors who keep pressing you to do more, or to do it better, or faster, or less expensively, will turn on you should you cross that fuzzy line between right and wrong. They will blame you for exceeding instructions or for ignoring their warnings. The smartest managers already know that the best answer to the question "How far is too far?" is don't try to find out.[26]

A man (or woman) might know too little, perform poorly, lack judgment and ability, and yet not do too much damage as a manager. But if that person lacks character and integrity—no matter how knowledgeable, how brilliant, how successful—he destroys. He destroys people, the most valuable resource of the enterprise. He destroys spirit. And he destroys performance. This is particularly true of the people at the head of an enterprise. For the spirit of an organization is created from the top. If an organization is great in spirit, it is because the spirit of its top people is great. If it decays, it does so because the top rots. As the proverb has it, "Trees die from the top." No one should ever become a strategist unless he or she is willing to have his or her character serve as the model for subordinates.[27]

According to John Akers, ethics and competitiveness are inseparable.[28] No society anywhere in the world can compete very long or successfully with people stealing from one another or not trusting one another, with every bit of information requiring notarized confirmation, with every disagreement ending up in litigation, or with government having to regulate businesses to keep them honest. Akers stated that being unethical is a recipe for headaches, inefficiency, and waste. History has proven that the greater the trust and confidence of people in the ethics of an institution or society, the greater its economic strength. Business relationships are built mostly on mutual trust and reputation. Short-term decisions based on greed and questionable ethics will preclude the necessary self-respect to gain the trust of others. More and more firms believe that ethics training and an ethics culture create strategic advantage.

Some business actions *always* considered to be unethical include misleading advertising or labeling, causing environmental harm, poor product or service safety, padding expense accounts, insider trading, dumping banned or flawed products in foreign markets, lack of equal opportunities for women and minorities, overpricing, hostile takeovers, moving jobs overseas, and using nonunion labor in a union shop.[29] Recent research also suggests that Japanese firms are perceived by consumers to be more ethical than American firms.[30]

Ethics training programs should include messages from the CEO emphasizing ethical business practices, development and discussion of codes of ethics, and procedures for discussing and reporting unethical behavior. Firms can align ethical and strategic decision making by incorporating ethical considerations into long-term planning, integrating ethical decision making into the performance appraisal process, encouraging whistle-blowing or the reporting of unethical practices, and monitoring departmental and corporate performance regarding ethical issues.

In a final analysis, ethical standards come out of history and heritage. Our fathers and mothers and brothers and sisters of the past left to us an ethical foundation to build upon. Even the legendary football coach Vince Lombardi knew that some things were worth more than winning, and he required his players to have three kinds of loyalty: to God, to their families, and to the Green Bay Packers, "in that order."

COMPARING BUSINESS AND MILITARY STRATEGY

A strong military heritage underlies the study of strategic management. Terms such as *objectives, mission, strengths,* and *weaknesses* first were formulated to address problems on the battlefield. In many respects, business strategy is like military strategy, and military strategists have learned much over the centuries that can benefit business strategists today. Both business and military organizations try to use their own strengths to exploit competitors' weaknesses. If an organization's overall strategy is wrong (ineffective), then all the efficiency in the world may not be enough to allow success. Business or military success is generally not the happy result of accidental strategies. Rather, success is the product of continuous attention to changing external and internal conditions and the formulation and implementation of insightful adaptations to those conditions. The element of surprise provides great competitive advantages in both military and business strategy; information systems that provide data on opponents' or competitors' strategies and resources are also vitally important.

Of course, a fundamental difference between military and business strategy is that business strategy is formulated, implemented, and evaluated with an assumption of *competition,* whereas military strategy is based on an assumption of *conflict.* Nonetheless, military conflict and business competition are so similar that many strategic-management techniques apply equally to both. Business strategists have access to valuable insights that military thinkers have refined over time. Superior strategy formulation and implementation can overcome an opponent's superiority in numbers and resources.

Both business and military organizations must adapt to change and constantly improve to be successful. Too often, firms do not change their strategies when their environment and competitive conditions dictate the need to change. Gluck offered a classic military example of this:

> When Napoleon won it was because his opponents were committed to the strategy, tactics, and organization of earlier wars. When he lost—against Wellington, the Russians, and the Spaniards—it was because he, in turn, used tried-and-true strategies against enemies who thought afresh, who were developing the strategies not of the last war, but of the next.[31]

CONCLUSION

All firms have a strategy, even if it is informal, unstructured, and sporadic. All organizations are heading somewhere, but unfortunately some organizations do not know where. The old saying "If you do not know where you are going, then any road will lead you there!" accents the need for organizations to use strategic-management concepts and techniques. The strategic-management process is becoming more widely used by small firms, large companies, nonprofit institutions, governmental organizations, and multinational conglomerates alike. The process of empowering managers and employees has almost limitless benefits.

Organizations should take a proactive rather than a reactive approach in their industry, and should strive to influence, anticipate, and initiate rather than just respond to events. The strategic-management process embodies this approach to decision making. It represents a logical, systematic, and objective approach for determining an enterprise's future direction. The stakes are generally too high for strategists to use intuition alone in choosing among alternative courses of action. Successful strategists take the time to think about their businesses, where they are with the businesses, and what they want to be as organizations, and then implement programs and policies to get from where they are to where they want to be in a reasonable period of time.

It is a known and accepted fact that people and organizations that plan ahead are much more likely to become what they want to become than those who do not plan at all. A good strategist plans and controls his or her plans, while a bad strategist never plans and then tries to control people! This textbook is devoted to providing you with the tools necessary to be a good strategist.

We invite you to visit the DAVID page on the Prentice Hall Web site at
www.prenhall.com/davidsm
for this chapter's World Wide Web exercises.

KEY TERMS AND CONCEPTS

Annual Objectives	(p. 11)	Internal Strengths	(p. 9)	Strategic-Management Model	(p. 13)
Business Ethics	(p. 18)	Internal Weaknesses	(p. 9)	Strategic-Management Process	(p. 5)
Code of Business Ethics	(p. 19)	Intuition	(p. 6)	Strategies	(p. 11)
Electronic Commerce	(p. 4)	Long-Term Objectives	(p. 10)	Strategists	(p. 8)
Empowerment	(p. 16)	Mission Statements	(p. 9)	Strategy Evaluation	(p. 5)
Environmental Scanning	(p. 10)	Policies	(p. 12)	Strategy Formulation	(p. 5)
External Opportunities	(p. 9)	Strategic Management	(p. 4)	Strategy Implementation	(p. 5)
External Threats	(p. 9)				

ISSUES FOR REVIEW AND DISCUSSION

1. Explain why Business Policy often is called a "capstone course."

2. Read one of the suggested readings at the end of this chapter. Prepare a 1-page written summary that includes your personal thoughts on the subject.

3. What aspect of strategy formulation do you think requires the most time? Why?

4. Why is strategy implementation often considered the most difficult stage in the strategic-management process?

5. Why is it so important to integrate intuition and analysis in strategic management?

6. Explain the importance of a formal mission statement.

7. Discuss relationships among objectives, strategies, and policies.

8. Why do you think some chief executive officers fail to use a strategic-management approach to decision making?

9. Discuss the importance of feedback in the strategic-management model.

10. How can strategists best ensure that strategies will be effectively implemented?

11. Give an example of a recent political development that changed the overall strategy of an organization.

12. Who are the major competitors of your college or university? What are their strengths and weaknesses? What are their strategies? How successful are these institutions compared to your college?

13. If you owned a small business, would you develop a code of business conduct? If yes, what variables would you include? If no, how would you ensure that ethical business standards were being followed by your employees?

14. Would strategic-management concepts and techniques benefit foreign businesses as much as domestic firms? Justify your answer.

15. What do you believe are some potential pitfalls or risks in using a strategic-management approach to decision making?

16. In your opinion, what is the single major benefit of using a strategic-management approach to decision making? Justify your answer.

17. Compare business strategy and military strategy.

18. What do you feel is the relationship between personal ethics and business ethics? Are they, or should they be, the same?

NOTES

1. Peter Drucker, *Management: Tasks, Responsibilities, and Practices* (New York: Harper & Row, 1974): 611.

2. Weston Agor, "How Top Executives Use Their Intuition to Make Important Decisions," *Business Horizons* 29, no. 1 (January–February 1986): 6. Also, see Andrew Campbell, "Brief Case: Strategy and Intuition—A Conversation with Henry Mintzberg," *Long Range Planning* 24, no. 2. (April 1991): 108–10.

3. Alfred Sloan, Jr., *Adventures of the White Collar Man* (New York: Doubleday, 1941): 104.

4. Quoted in Eugene Raudsepp, "Can You Trust Your Hunches?" *Management Review* 49, no. 4 (April 1960): 7.

5. Stephen Harper, "Intuition: What Separates Executives from Managers," *Business Horizons* 31, no. 5 (September–October 1988): 16.

6. Ron Nelson, "How to Be a Manager," *Success* (July–August 1985): 69.

7. Bruce Henderson, *Henderson on Corporate Strategy* (Boston: Abt Books, 1979): 6.

8. Robert Waterman, Jr., *The Renewal Factor: How the Best Get and Keep the Competitive Edge* (New York: Bantam, 1987). See also *Business Week* (September 14, 1987): 100. Also, see *Academy of Management Executive* 3, no. 2 (May 1989): 115.

9. Kenichi Ohmae, "Managing in a Borderless World," *Harvard Business Review* 67, no. 3 (May–June 1989): 153.

10. Harry Jonas III, Ronald Fry, and Suresh Srivasta. "The Office of the CEO: Understanding the Executive Experience." *Academy of Management Executive* 4, no. 3 (August 1990): 36.

11. John Pearce II and Fred David, "The Bottom Line on Corporate Mission Statements," *Academy of Management Executive* 1, no. 2 (May 1987): 109.

12. Ibid., 112. See also John A. Pearce and Fred R. David, "Corporate Mission Statements: The Bottom Line," *Academy of Management Executive* 1, no. 2 (May 1987): 109; and Fred R. David. "How Companies Define Their Mission." *Long Range Planning* 22, no. 1 (February 1989): 90.

13. Adolph Coors Company, *Annual Report* (1988): 1.

14. Portland General Corporation, *Annual Report* (1986): 2, 3.

15. Fred R. David, "How Companies Define Their Mission." *Long Range Planning* 22, no. 1 (February 1989): 91.

16. Ann Langley, "The Roles of Formal Strategic Planning," *Long Range Planning* 21, no. 3 (June 1988): 40.

17. Timothy Aepel, "Not All Workers Find Idea of Empowerment as Neat as It Sounds," *The Wall Street Journal* (September 8, 1997): A1.

18. Bernard Reimann, "Getting Value from Strategic Planning," *Planning Review* 16, no. 3 (May–June 1988): 42.

19. Michael Allen, "Strategic Management Hits Its Stride," *Planning Review* 13, no. 5 (September–October 1985): 6.

20. Hershey Foods Corporation, *Annual Report* (1983): 3.

21. Richard Robinson, Jr., "The Importance of Outsiders in Small Firm Strategic Planning," *Academy of Management Journal* 25, no. 1 (March 1982): 80. Also, S. Schoeffler, Robert Buzzell, and Donald Heany. "Impact of Strategic Planning on Profit Performance," *Harvard Business Review* (March 1974): 137; Lawrence Rhyne, "The Relationship of Strategic Planning to Financial Performance," *Strategic Management Journal* 7 (1986): 432; and Deborah Cook and Gerald Ferris, "Strategic Human Resource Management and Firm Effectiveness in Industries Experiencing Decline," *Human Resource Management* 25, no. 3 (Fall 1986): 454.

22. Allen, 6.

23. Tom Peters, "Passion for Excellence," Public Broadcasting System videotape, 1987.

24. Gordon Greenley, "Does Strategic Planning Improve Company Performance?" *Long Range Planning* 19, no. 2 (April 1986): 106.

25. Saul Gellerman, "Managing Ethics from the Top Down," *Sloan Management Review* (Winter 1989): 77.

26. Saul Gellerman, "Why 'Good' Managers Make Bad Ethical Choices," *Harvard Business Review* 64, no. 4 (July–August 1986): 88.

27. Drucker, 462, 463.

28. John Akers, "Ethics and Competitiveness—Putting First Things First," *Sloan Management Review* (Winter 1989): 69–71.

29. Gene Laczniak, Marvin Berkowitz, Russell Brooker, and James Hale, "The Ethics of Business: Improving or Deteriorating?" *Business Horizons* 38, no. 1 (January–February 1995): 43.

30. Ibid, p. 42.

31. Frederick Gluck, "Taking the Mystique Out of Planning," *Across the Board* (July–August 1985): 59.

CURRENT READINGS

Arnesen, David W., C. Patrick Fleenor, and Rex S. Toh. "The Ethical Dimensions of Airline Frequent Flier Programs." *Business Horizons* 40, no. 1 (January–February): 47–56.

Azzone, Giovanni, Umberto Bertelé, and Giuliano Noci. "At Last We Are Creating Environmental Strategies Which Work." *Long Range Planning* 30, no. 4 (August 1997): 562–571.

Barnett, W. P. and R. A. Burgelman. "Evolutionary Perspectives on Strategy." *Strategic Management Journal* 17, Special Issue (Summer 1996): 5–20.

Barry, David and Michael Elmes. "Strategy Retold: Toward a Narrative View of Strategic Discourse." *Academy of Management Review* 22, no. 2 (April 1997): 429–452.

Bauerschmidt, A. "Speaking of Strategy." *Strategic Management Journal* 17, no. 8 (October 1996): 665–668.

Boeker, Warren. "Strategic Change: The Influence of Managerial Characteristics and Organizational Growth." *Academy of Management Journal* 40, no. 1 (February 1997): 152–170.

Bonn, Ingrid and Chris Christodoulou. "From Strategic Planning to Strategic Management." *Long Range Planning* 29, no. 4 (August 1996): 543–551.

Bowman, Cliff and Andrew Kakabadse. "Top Management Ownership of the Strategy Problem." *Long Range Planning* 30, no. 2 (April 1997): 197–208.

Burgelman, R. A. "A Process Model of Strategic Business Exit: Implications for an Evolutionary Perspective on Strategy." *Strategic Management Journal* 17, Special Issue (Summer 1996): 193–214.

Cannella, Albert A., Jr. "Contrasting Perspectives on Strategic Leaders: Toward a More Realistic View of Top Managers." *Journal of Management* 23, no. 3 (1997): 213–238.

Chakravarthy, Bala. "A New Strategy Framework for Coping with Turbulence." *Sloan Management Review* 38, no. 2 (Winter 1997): 69–82.

Cravens, David W., Gordon Greenley, Nigel F. Piercy, and Stanley Slater. "Integrating Contemporary Strategic Management Perspectives." *Long Range Planning* 30, no. 4 (August 1997): 493–503.

Daily, Catherine M. and Jonathan L. Johnson. "Sources of CEO Power and Firm Financial Performance: A Longitudinal Assessment." *Journal of Management* 23, no. 2 (1997): 97–118.

Dean, James W., Jr., and Mark P. Sharfman. "Does Decision Process Matter? A Study of Strategic Decision-Making Effectiveness." *Academy of Management Journal* 39, no. 2 (April 1996): 368–396.

Donaldson, Thomas. "Values in Tension: Ethics Away From Home." *Harvard Business Review* (September–October 1996): 48–139.

Duening, Tom. "Our Turbulent Times? The Case for Evolutionary Organizational Change." *Business Horizons* 40, no. 1 (January–February 1997): 2–8.

Epstein, Marc J. "You've Got a Great Environmental Strategy—Now What?" *Business Horizons* 39, no. 5 (September–October 1996): 53–59.

Farjoun, M. and L. Lai. "Similarity Judgments in Strategy Formulation: Role, Process and Implications." *Strategic Management Journal* 18, no. 4 (April 1997): 255–274.

Farkas, Charles M. and Suzy Wetlaufer. "The Ways Chief Executive Officers Lead." *Harvard Business Review* (May–June 1996): 110–124.

Gaddis, Paul O. "Strategy Under Attack." *Long Range Planning* 30, no. 1 (February 1997): 38–45.

Gellerman, Saul W. and Robert J. Potter. "The Ultimate Strategic Question." *Business Horizons* 39, no. 2 (March–April 1996): 5–10.

Ginsberg, Ari. "Strategy at the Leading Edge—'New Age' Strategic Planning: Bridging Theory and Practice." *Long Range Planning* 30, no. 1 (February 1997): 125–128.

Hamel, Gary. "Strategy As Revolution." *Harvard Business Review* (July–August 1996): 69–83.

Hart, Stuart L. "Beyond Greening: Strategies for a Sustainable World." *Harvard Business Review* (January–February 1997): 66–77.

Hartman, Cathy L. and Edwin R. Stafford. "Green Alliances: Building New Business with Environmental Groups." *Long Range Planning* 30, no. 2 (April 1997): 184–196.

Hosmer, L. T. "Response to 'Do Good Ethics Always Make for Good Business?'" *Strategic Management Journal* 17, no. 6 (June 1996): 501–511.

Iaquinto, A. L. and J. W. Fredrickson. "Top Management Team Agreement About the Strategic Decision Process: A Test of Some of Its Determinants and Consequences." *Strategic Management Journal* 18, no. 1 (January 1997): 63–76.

Inkpen, A. C. "The Seeking of Strategy Where It Is Not: Towards a Theory of Strategy Absence: A Reply to Bauerschmidt." *Strategic Management Journal* 17, no. 8 (October 1996): 669–679.

Liebeskind, J. P. "Knowledge, Strategy, and the Theory of the Firm." *Strategic Management Journal* 17, Special Issue (Winter 1996): 93–108.

Markides, Constantinos. "Strategic Innovation." *Sloan Management Review* 38, no. 3 (Spring 1997): 9–24.

Miller, Danny, Theresa K. Lant, Frances J. Milliken, and Helaine J. Korn. "The Evolution of Strategic Simplicity: Exploring Two Models of Organizational Adaptation." *Journal of Management* 22, no. 6 (1996): 863–888.

Near, Janet P. and Marcia P. Miceli. "Whistle-Blowing: Myth and Reality." *Journal of Management* 22, no. 3 (1996): 507–517.

Nehrt, C. "Timing and Intensity Effects of Environmental Investments." *Strategic Management Journal* 17, no. 7 (July 1996): 535–548.

Porter, Michael E. "What is Strategy?" *Harvard Business Review* (November–December 1996): 61–80.

Rajagopalan, Nandini and Deepak K. Datta. "CEO Characteristics: Does Industry Matter?" *Academy of Management Journal* 39, no. 1 (February 1996): 197–207.

Ross, Jeanne W., Cynthia M. Beath, and Dale L. Goodhue. "Develop Long-Term Competitiveness Through IT Assets." *Sloan Management Review* 38, no. 1 (Fall 1996): 31–42.

Russo, Michael V. and Paul A. Fouts. "A Resource-Based Perspective on Corporate Environmental Performance and Profitability." *Academy of Management Journal* 40, no. 3 (June 1997): 534–559.

Schwab, B. "A Note on Ethics and Strategy: Do Good Ethics Always Make for Good Business?" *Strategic Management Journal* 17, no. 6 (June 1996): 499–500.

Sahlman, William A. "How to Write a Great Business Plan." *Harvard Business Review* (July–August 1997): 98–109.

Stafford, Edwin R. and Cathy L. Hartman. "Green Alliances: Strategic Relations between Businesses and Environmental Groups." *Business Horizons* 39, no. 2 (March–April 1996): 50–59.

Teece, D. J., Pisano, G., and A. Shuen. "Dynamic Capabilities and Strategic Management." *Strategic Management Journal* 18, no. 7 (August 1997): 509–534.

Tushman, Michael L. and Charles A. O'Reilly III. "The Ambidextrous Organization: Managing Evolutionary and Revolutionary Change." *California Management Review* 38, no. 4 (Summer 1996): 8–30.

Whittington, Richard. "Strategy at the Leading Edge—Strategy as Practice." *Long Range Planning* 29, no. 5 (October 1996): 733–735.

THE COHESION CASE AND EXPERIENTIAL EXERCISES

Two special features of this text are introduced here: (1) the Cohesion Case and (2) the Experiential Exercises. As strategic-management concepts and techniques are introduced in this text, they are applied to the Cohesion Case through Experiential Exercises. The Cohesion Case enters on Hershey Foods Corporation in 1998. As the term *cohesion* implies, the Hershey Foods case and related exercises integrate material presented throughout the text. At least one exercise at the end of each chapter applies textual material to the Hershey Foods case. The Cohesion Case and Experiential Exercises thus work together to give students practice applying strategic-management concepts and tools as they are presented in the text. In this way, students become prepared to perform case analyses as the policy course progresses.

Based in Hershey, Pennsylvania, and a leading manufacturer of candy and pasta, Hershey Foods was selected as the Cohesion Case for several important reasons. First, Hershey is a multinational corporation, so global issues can be discussed in class. Second, Hershey is a multidivisional organization, thus allowing strategic-management concepts to be applied at the corporate, divisional, and functional levels. Third, Hershey is undergoing extensive strategic changes. Fourth, you probably have eaten Hershey candy and pasta; this familiarity will help you learn this business. Fifth, Hershey is an exemplary organization in terms of business ethics and social responsibility; a significant part of Hershey's profits go toward operating the Milton Hershey School for Orphaned Children. Finally, Hershey is very cooperative with students and professors who call to obtain additional information about the company.

Some Experiential Exercises in the text do not relate specifically to the Cohesion Case. At least one exercise at the end of each chapter applies strategic-management concepts to your university. As a student nearing graduation, you are quite knowledgeable about your university. Apply concepts learned in this course to assist your institution. More colleges and universities are instituting strategic management.

After reading the text and applying concepts and tools to the Cohesion Case through Experiential Exercises, you should be well prepared to analyze business policy cases. The objectives of the case method are as follows:

1. to give you experience applying strategic-management concepts and techniques to different organizations
2. to give you experience applying and integrating the knowledge you have gained in prior courses and work experience
3. to give you decision-making experience in real organizations
4. to improve your understanding of relationships among the functional areas of business and the strategic-management process
5. to improve your self-confidence; because there is no one right answer to a case, you will gain experience justifying and defending your own ideas, analyses, and recommendations
6. to improve your oral and written communication skills
7. to sharpen your analytical and intuitive skills

THE COHESION CASE
Fred R. David
Francis Marion University

HERSHEY FOODS CORPORATION—1998
www.hersheys.com

What is your favorite candy bar? Mr. Goodbar, Reese's, Kit Kat, Big Block, Whatcha-macallit, Allsorts, Rolo, Krackel, BarNone, Mounds, Almond Joy, 5th Avenue, Snickers, or Baby Ruth? Did you know that all of these are made by Hershey Foods (except Snickers made by M&M Mars and Baby Ruth made by Nestlé)? Mars and Nestlé are Hershey's two major competitors. Hershey can be phoned toll-free at 1-800-HERSHEY or phoned at 717-534-4900.

Have you ever been to Hershey, Pennsylvania, the home of Hershey Foods Corporation? It is known as "Chocolate Town, USA." The air in the city actually smells like chocolate. There you can walk down Chocolate Avenue, see sidewalks lit with lights in the shape of Hershey Kisses, visit the Hershey Zoo, and see the Chocolate Kiss Tower in Hershey Park. Hershey's Chocolate World is America's most popular corporate visitors' center with more than 2 million guests annually.[1] Admission is free. Even the White House in Washington, D.C., only attracts about 1.5 million visitors annually. Calendar 1998 was the twenty-fifth birthday of the Hershey's Chocolate World and celebrations went on there daily.

Hershey grew from a one-product, one-plant operation in 1894 to a nearly $4 billion company producing an array of quality chocolate, nonchocolate, pasta, and grocery products in 1998. Hershey entered 1998 as the largest candy maker in the United States with about a 34.1 percent market share, just ahead of M&M Mars. Hershey is also the largest pasta manufacturer in the United States with a 27.0 percent market share, just ahead of Borden.

But Hershey does have problems. Hershey's international sales have declined drastically and at year-end 1997 made up only 4.46 percent of total revenues. Hershey remains inexperienced, ineffective, and uncommitted in markets outside the United States, Mexico, and Canada, even though the candy and pasta industries are globalized. Mars, Borden, Nestlé, and other competitors have a growing and effective presence in international markets. In contrast, Hershey recently divested its two main European businesses, Gubor in Germany and Sperlari in Italy, and divested its Canadian Planter's business. Hershey also recently divested its OZF Jamin confectionery and grocery operations in the Netherlands and Belgium and divested Petybon S.A., its pasta and biscuit manufacturer in Brazil.

Hershey's candy and pasta market shares declined slightly in 1997 and long-term debt nearly increased 57 percent to $1.029 billion. Analysts question whether Hershey can continue to survive as a domestic producer of candy and pasta, while its competitors gain economies of scale and experience in world markets. Shareholders are becoming concerned, too. Hershey needs a clear strategic plan to guide future operations and decisions.

HISTORY

Milton Hershey's love for candy making began with a childhood apprenticeship under candy maker Joe Royer of Lancaster, Pennsylvania. Mr. Hershey was eager to own a candy-making business. After numerous attempts and even bankruptcy, he finally gained success in the caramel business. Upon seeing the first chocolate-making equipment at the Chicago Exhibition in 1893, Mr. Hershey envisioned endless opportunities for the chocolate industry.

By 1901, the chocolate industry in America was growing rapidly. Hershey's sales reached $662,000 that year, creating the need for a new factory. Mr. Hershey moved his company to Derry Church, Pennsylvania, a town that was renamed Hershey in 1906. The new Hershey factory provided a means of mass producing a single chocolate product. In 1909, the Milton Hershey School for Orphans was founded. Mr. and Mrs. Hershey could not have children, so for years the Hershey Chocolate Company operated mainly to provide funds for the orphanage. Hershey's sales reached $5 million in 1911.

In 1927, the Hershey Chocolate Company was incorporated under the laws of the state of Delaware and listed on the New York Stock Exchange. That same year, 20 percent of Hershey's stock was sold to the public. Between 1930 and 1960, Hershey went through rapid growth; the name "Hershey" became a household word. The legendary Milton Hershey died in 1945.

In the 1960s, Hershey acquired the H. B. Reese Candy Company, which makes Reese's Peanut Butter Cups, Reese's Pieces, and Reese's Peanut Butter Chips. Hershey also acquired San Giorgio Macaroni and Delmonico Foods, both pasta manufacturers. In 1968, Hershey Chocolate Corporation changed its name to Hershey Foods Corporation. Between 1976 and 1984, William Dearden served as Hershey's chief executive officer. An orphan who grew up in the Milton Hershey School for Orphans, Dearden diversified the company to reduce its dependence on fluctuating cocoa and sugar prices.

In the 1970s, Hershey acquired Y&S Candy Corporation, a manufacturer of licorice-type products, such as Y&S Twizzlers, Nibs, and Bassett's Allsorts. Hershey purchased a pasta company named Procino-Rossi and the Skinner Macaroni Company. During the 1980s, Hershey acquired both A. B. Marabou of Sweden and the Dietrich Corporation, maker of Luden's Throat Drops, Luden's Mellomints, Queen Anne Chocolate-Covered Cherries, and 5th Avenue candy bars. Hershey also acquired the Canadian confectionery (chocolate and nonchocolate candy), as well as the snack nut operations of Nabisco Brands Ltd., which gave them candies such as Oh Henry!, Eatmore, Cherry Blossom, Glosettes, Lowney, Life Savers, Breath Savers, Planter's nuts, Beaver nuts, Chipits chocolate chips, Moirs boxed chocolates, Care*Free gum, and Bubble Yum gum. Hershey acquired Peter Paul/Cadbury's U.S. candy operations, which gave them Mounds, Almond Joy, York Peppermint Pattie, Cadbury Dairy Milk, Cadbury Fruit & Nut, Cadbury Caramello, and Cadbury Creme Eggs. Hershey received rights to market the Peter Paul products worldwide.

In the 1990s, Hershey acquired Ronzoni Foods Corporation from Kraft General Foods Corporation for $80 million. The purchase included the dry pasta, pasta sauce, and cheese businesses of Ronzoni Foods and strengthened Hershey's position as a branded pasta supplier in the United States. Hershey purchased Nacional de Dulces (NDD) and renamed it Hershey Mexico; today, it produces, imports, and markets chocolate products for the Mexican market under the Hershey brand name. In 1996, Hershey acquired Leaf North America to gain market share leadership in North America in nonchocolate confectionery candies.

MISSION STATEMENT

Hershey Foods's mission statement as of the mid-1990s is given below:

> Hershey Foods Corporation's mission is to become a major diversified food company and a leading company in every aspect of our business as:
>
>> The number-one confectionery company in North America, moving toward worldwide confectionery market share leadership.
>>
>> A respected and valued supplier of high-quality, branded consumer food products in North America and selected international markets.[2]

Hershey's mission statement later was modified and reads as follows:

> to be a focused food company in North America and selected international markets and a leader in every aspect of our business. Our goal is to enhance our number one position in the North American confectionery market, be the leader in U.S. pasta and chocolate-related grocery products, and to build leadership positions in selected international markets.[3]

Note that the current statement is shorter and backs off from aspiring to be a world leader in the confectionery industry. It also lacks a number of components generally included in a good mission statement.

HERSHEY CHOCOLATE NORTH AMERICA

This division combines Hershey's Mexican, Canadian, and U.S. confectionery operations and generated 77.6 percent of total company 1997 sales. Sales and profits of this division increased 15 percent and 11 percent respectively in 1997. Most of the volume gains came from the Leaf acquisition and new products as the base business revenues were flat. U.S. market share decreased from 34.2 percent in 1996 to 34.1 percent in 1997. U.S. confectionery market share information for the six leading competitors is given in Case Figure 1–1.

Hershey's U.S. confectionery manufacturing operations are located in:

Hershey, PA
Oakdale, CA
Stuarts Draft, VA
Reading, PA
Hazelton, PA
Lancaster, PA
Naugatuck, CT
Memphis, TN
Denver, CO
Robinson, IL
New Brunswick, NJ

The Leaf facilities and Henry Heide's confectionery operations are located in the last four cities cited above. Canadian operations are located in Smith Falls, Ontario; Montreal, Quebec; and Dartmouth, Nova Scotia. Mexican operations are located in Guadalajara, Mexico.

Hershey Chocolate North America produces an extensive line of chocolate and non-chocolate products sold in the form of single bars, bagged goods, and boxed items. Hershey introduced its first full-line boxed chocolate named Pot of Gold in late 1996. Its products are marketed under more than 60 brand names, and sold in over 2 million retail outlets in the United States, including grocery wholesalers, chain stores, mass merchandisers, drug stores, vending companies, wholesale clubs, convenience stores, and food distributors. Sales to Wal-Mart Stores account for 12 percent of Hershey's total revenues.

The U.S. confectionery market is growing only 2 percent annually in sales volume. The nonchocolate segment, which accounts for about one-third of the overall sweets market, is growing at 5 percent annually, while the chocolate segment is growing at 1 percent. Hershey has only 4 percent of the nonchocolate confectionery market, and the leader is RJR Nabisco with 18 percent. RJR's Life Savers and Gummy Life Savers compete with Hershey's Amazin' Fruit Gummy Bears. The "other" category for 1997 includes Tootsie Roll/Charms (2.9%), Favorite Brands (3.7%), and Russell Stover (7.0%).

HERSHEY INTERNATIONAL

This division is a big trouble spot for Hershey. Hershey exports confectionery and grocery products to over 60 countries outside of North America although these sales represent less than 5 percent of Hershey's sales. All company business outside of North America, including confectionery, grocery, and pasta, is handled under this division. Hershey's International sales declined from $330 million in 1996 to only $192 million in 1997.

Europeans have the highest per capita chocolate consumption rates in the world, but Hershey has no plans to overtake or even threaten Nestlé or Mars in Europe. In the Far East, Hershey has signed licensing agreements with Selecta Dairy Products to manufacture Hershey's ice cream products in the Philippines and with Kuang Chuan Dairy in Taiwan to manufacture Hershey's beverages. Hershey introduced its products into Russia, the Philippines, and Taiwan in 1994. Overall, however, Hershey is not planning sustained efforts anywhere outside the United States.

HERSHEY PASTA AND GROCERY

Hershey consolidated its pasta and grocery divisions in late 1996, a move widely criticized by analysts. Hershey's pasta sales declined nearly 3 percent in 1997 while grocery sales increased 7.9 percent. For 1997, Hershey's pasta sales declined to $400 million from $412 million the prior year, while grocery sales increased to $370 million from $343 million.

CASE FIGURE 1–1
U.S. Confectionery Market Share Percentages

COMPANY	1997	1996	1995
Hershey	34.1	34.2	34.0
Mars	22.3	26.3	26.1
Nestlé	7.9	9.1	8.9
Brach & Brock	4.6	7.4	8.6
Leaf	NA	3.8	3.8
RJR Nabisco	3.5	3.4	3.3
Other	27.6	15.8	15.3

Source: Credit Suisse First Boston Corporation, *Investment Report* (March 2, 1998): 10.

In terms of pasta market share, Hershey had a 27.0 percent share at year-end 1997, versus 27.2 percent for 1996. This compares to Borden (20.1 percent versus 24.5 percent), Private Label (17.1 percent versus 15.2 percent), and CPC (9.8 percent versus 11.0 percent). The Italian pasta maker Barrilla and other foreign firms continue to take market share away from Hershey through heavy promotional and merchandising activity.

The pasta and grocery divisions contributed 17.9 percent of Hershey's 1997 total company sales as indicated in Case Figure 1–2. Pasta imports in the United States are increasing much more rapidly than pasta consumption. The flood of low-priced imported pasta into the United States is coming primarily from Italy and Turkey. This is a major external threat for Hershey. United States pasta market share data is given in Case Figure 1–3.

Hershey first expanded its business into pasta with its 1996 acquisition of San Giorgio Macaroni in Lebanon, Pennsylvania. Hershey owns pasta facilities in Louisville, Kentucky; Auburn, New York; Omaha, Nebraska; Philadelphia, Pennsylvania; and Excelsior Springs, Missouri. Hershey's pasta brands include San Giorgio, Skinner, Delmonico, P&R, Light 'n Fluffy, American Beauty, Perfection, Pastamania, and Ronzoni. Sales of these brands surpass Borden's Creamette brand. Hershey's main pasta manufacturing facility is in Winchester, Virginia. Hershey manufactures and distributes pasta throughout the United States, but does no exporting of pasta and has no plans to build pasta facilities anywhere outside the United States.

CASE FIGURE 1–2
Hershey Foods Sales and Profit (EBIT) Data By Segment (in millions of dollars)

DIVISION SALES	1997		1996		1995	
Hershey Chocolate North America	$3,340	77.64%	$2,904	72.80%	$2,595	70.31%
International	192	4.46%	330	8.27%	335	9.08%
Grocery	370	8.60%	343	8.60%	341	9.24%
Pasta	400	9.30%	412	10.66%	420	11.37%
Total	$4,302	100.00%	$3,989	100.00%	$3,691	100.00%

DIVISION PROFITS (EBIT)						
Hershey Chocolate North America	$548	87.13%	$494	87.59%	$440	86.27%
International	6	.95%	7	1.24%	3	.58%
Grocery	37	5.88%	31	5.50%	33	6.47%
Pasta	38	6.04%	32	5.67%	34	6.67%
Total	$629	100.00%	$564	100.00%	$510	100.00%

Source: www.freeedgar.com.

CASE FIGURE 1–3
U.S. Pasta Market Share Percentages

COMPANY	1997	1996	1995
Hershey	27.0	27.2	27.0
Borden	20.1	24.5	26.0
Private labels	17.1	15.2	15.2
CPC International	9.8	11.0	11.4
Imports	NA	10.7	9.9
Quaker Oats	NA	2.9	2.9
Archer Daniels	NA	1.0	1.1
Other	NA	6.5	6.5

Source: Merrill Lynch Capital, *Investment Report* (January 29, 1998): 8.

HERSHEY'S OPERATIONS

SOCIAL RESPONSIBILITY

Hershey Foods Corporation is committed to the values of its founder, Milton S. Hershey—that is, the highest standards of quality, honesty, fairness, integrity, and respect. The firm makes annual contributions of cash, products, and services to a variety of national and local charitable organizations. Hershey is the sole sponsor of the Hershey National Track and Field Youth Program. Hershey also makes contributions to the Children's Miracle Network, a national program benefiting children's hospitals across the United States.

The corporation operates the Milton Hershey School, whose mission is to provide all costs and full-time care and education for disadvantaged children, primarily orphans. The school currently cares for over 1,000 boys and girls in grades kindergarten through 12. The Hershey School Trust owns over 75 percent of all Hershey Corporation's common stock.

CORPORATE STRUCTURE

Hershey in 1997 reorganized its corporate structure, changing from a four-division structure (Hershey Chocolate North America, Hershey Grocery, Hershey International, and Hershey Pasta Group) to a three-division structure (Hershey Chocolate North America, Hershey Pasta and Grocery, and Hershey International). Hershey's current organizational chart is shown in Case Figure 1–4.

FINANCE

Hershey annually spends about $26 million on research and development. Hershey's recent financial statements are given in Case Figures 1–5 and 1–6.

CASE FIGURE 1–4
Hershey's Chain of Command

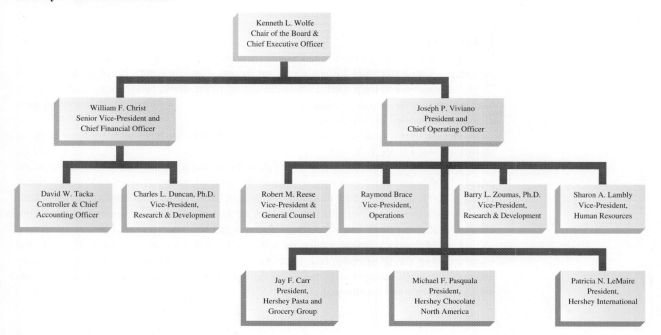

Source: Hershey Foods, *Annual Report* (1997): 40.

CASE FIGURE 1–5
Hershey Foods Corporation
CONSOLIDATED STATEMENTS OF INCOME
In thousands of dollars except per share amounts

FOR THE YEARS ENDED DECEMBER 31,	1997	1996	1995	1994
NET SALES	$4,302,236	$3,989,308	$3,690,667	$3,606,271
COSTS AND EXPENSES:				
Cost of sales	2,488,896	2,302,089	2,126,274	2,097,556
Selling, marketing and administrative	1,183,130	1,124,087	1,053,758	1,034,115
Total costs and expenses	3,672,026	3,426,178	3,180,032	3,131,671
RESTRUCTURING CREDIT (CHARGE)	—	—	151	(106,105)
LOSS ON DISPOSAL OF BUSINESSES	—	(35,352)	—	—
INCOME BEFORE INTEREST AND INCOME TAXES	630,210	527,780	510,786	368,495
Interest expense, net	76,255	48,043	44,833	35,357
INCOME BEFORE INCOME TAXES	553,955	479,737	465,953	333,138
Provision for income taxes	217,704	206,551	184,034	148,919
NET INCOME	$ 336,251	$ 273,186	$ 281,919	$ 184,219
NET INCOME PER SHARE	$ 2.25	$ 1.77	$ 1.70	$ 1.06
CASH DIVIDENDS PAID PER SHARE:				
Common Stock	$ .8400	$ .7600	$ .6850	$ .6250
Class B Common Stock	.7600	.6850	.6200	.5675

Source: Hershey Foods, *Annual Report* (1997): 34.

MARKETING

Per capita candy sales in the United States increased by 7.1 percent over the last 5 years. Americans spend over $21 billion a year on sweets. Upscale candy items such as Mars's Dove Promises are selling well. People are eating more ethnic foods today than 10 years ago, which means they are eating more garlic and flavorings; breath freshener–type candies are selling well in response to this trend.

Hershey's expenditures on advertising and promotion have increased annually as shown in Case Figure 1–7.

Conventional wisdom in the candy industry is that a person rarely selects the same brand of candy bar twice in a row; consequently, product variety is crucial to success. Marketing issues relative to health, nutrition, and weight consciousness are important. The media Hershey uses most for advertising are network television, followed by syndicated television, spot television, magazines, network radio, and spot radio.

Confectionery sales generally are lowest during the second quarter of the year and highest during the third and fourth quarters, due mainly to the holiday seasons. Hershey generates about 20 percent of annual sales during the second quarter and 30 percent of annual sales during the fourth quarter.

CASE FIGURE 1–6
Hershey Foods Corporation
CONSOLIDATED BALANCE SHEETS
In thousands of dollars

DECEMBER 31,	1997	1996	1995
ASSETS			
CURRENT ASSETS:			
Cash and cash equivalents	54,237	61,422	32,346
Accounts receivable—trade	360,831	294,606	326,024
Inventories	505,525	474,978	397,570
Deferred income taxes	84,024	94,464	84,785
Prepaid expenses and other	30,197	60,759	81,598
Total current assets	1,034,814	986,229	922,323
PROPERTY, PLANT AND EQUIPMENT, NET	1,648,237	1,601,895	1,436,009
INTANGIBLES RESULTING FROM BUSINESS ACQUISITIONS	551,849	565,962	428,714
OTHER ASSETS	56,336	30,710	43,577
Total assets	3,291,236	3,184,796	2,830,623
LIABILITIES AND STOCKHOLDERS' EQUITY			
CURRENT LIABILITIES:			
Accounts payable	146,932	134,213	127,067
Accrued liabilities	371,545	357,828	308,123
Accrued income taxes	19,692	10,254	15,514
Short-term debt	232,451	299,469	413,268
Current portion of long-term debt	25,095	15,510	383
Total current liabilities	795,715	817,274	864,355
LONG-TERM DEBT	$1,029,136	655,289	357,034
OTHER LONG-TERM LIABILITIES	346,500	327,209	333,814
DEFERRED INCOME TAXES	267,079	224,003	192,461
Total liabilities	2,438,430	2,023,775	1,747,664
STOCKHOLDERS' EQUITY:			
Preferred Stock, shares issued: none in 1997, 1996, and 1995	—	—	—
Common Stock, shares issued: 149,484,964 in 1997;			
149,471,964 in 1996; and 74,733,982 on a pre-split basis in 1995	149,485	149,472	74,734
Class B Common Stock, shares issued: 30,465,908 in 1997;			
30,478,908 in 1996; and 15,241,454 on a pre-split basis in 1995	30,465	30,478	15,241
Additional paid-in capital	33,852	42,432	47,732
Cumulative foreign currency translation adjustments	(42,243)	(32,875)	(29,240)
Unearned ESOP compensation	(28,741)	(31,935)	(35,128)
Retained earnings	1,977,849	1,763,144	1,694,696
Treasury—Common Stock shares, at cost: 37,018,566 in 1997;			
27,009,316 in 1996; and 12,709,553 on a pre-split basis in 1995	(1,267,861)	(759,695)	(685,076)
Total stockholders' equity	852,806	1,161,021	1,082,959
Total liabilities and stockholders' equity	3,291,236	3,184,796	2,830,623

Source: www.freeedgar.com.

CASE FIGURE 1–7
Hershey's Expenditures on Advertising and Promotion (in millions of dollars)

YEAR	$ ADVERTISING	$ PROMOTION	$ TOTAL
1992	137	398	535
1993	130	444	574
1994	120	419	539
1995	159	403	562
1996	174	429	603
1997	—	—	650

Source: www.freeedgar.com.

GLOBAL ISSUES

The chocolate/cocoa products industry is SIC 2066 and candy/confectionery is SIC 2064. The main distribution channels for chocolate are grocery, drug, and department stores as well as vending machines. Almost all of these distributors are local, regional, or national; only a few are multinational. Although chocolate producers have not yet developed globally uniform marketing programs, the situation is changing. European unification extended grocery and department store channels of distribution. For example, Safeway, a U.S. grocery chain, now operates stores in Canada, Britain, Germany, and Saudi Arabia. As global channels of distribution become more available for chocolate manufacturers, global marketing uniformity will become more prevalent in the industry. Global cultural convergence is accelerating the need for global marketing uniformity in the confectionery industry. Hershey's competitors are taking advantage of this globalization trend.

The confectionery industry is characterized by high manufacturing economies of scale. Hershey's main chocolate factory, for example, occupies more than 2 million square feet, is highly automated, and contains a great deal of heavy equipment, vats, and containers. It is the largest chocolate plant in the world. High manufacturing costs in any industry encourages global market expansion, globally standardized products, and globally centralized production.

The confectionery industry also is characterized by high transportation costs for moving milk and sugar, the primary raw materials. This fact motivates companies such as Hershey to locate near their sources of supply. Because milk can be obtained in large volumes in many countries, chocolate producers have many options in locating plants. Also, producing chocolate is not labor-intensive, nor does it require highly skilled labor.

Product development costs in the confectionery industry are relatively low because the process mostly involves mixing different combinations of the same ingredients. Whenever product development costs are low in an industry, firms are spurred to globalize existing brands rather than develop new ones for different countries.

Industry analysts expect the candy industry to continue to grow. Consumption of chocolate, according to industry analysts, is closely related to national income, although the Far East is an exception to this rule. Candy consumption varies in the major markets of the developed nations. Americans consume about 22 pounds of candy annually per person and Europeans consume about 27 pounds of candy per person annually.

Chocolate accounts for about 54 percent of all candy consumed. Northern Europeans consume almost twice as much chocolate per capita as Americans. Among European countries, Switzerland, Norway, and the United Kingdom citizens consume the most chocolate, whereas Finland, Yugoslavia, and Italy citizens consume the least. The Japanese consume very little chocolate—about 1.4 kilos per capita. Throughout Asia and Southern Europe, there is a preference for types of sweets other than chocolate, partly because of the high incidence of lactose intolerance (difficulty in digesting dairy products) in those populations.

Many consumers worldwide are becoming weight-conscious and health-oriented. Numerous organizations and individuals discourage candy consumption and promote the need for exercise and nutrition. The teenage customer base that historically has consumed so much chocolate is shrinking in the United States and most other countries. These persons are being replaced by older, wealthier consumers who prefer more sophisticated chocolates. In countries where birth rates and numbers of youth are still growing, disposable income tends to be low, which is a barrier to market entry for candy makers.

The most important raw material used in production of Hershey's products is cocoa beans. This commodity is imported from West Africa, South America, and Far Eastern equatorial regions. West Africa grows approximately 60 percent of the world's crop. Cocoa beans exhibit wide fluctuations in price, flavor, and quality, due to (a) weather and other conditions affecting crop size; (b) consuming countries' demand requirements; (c) producing countries' sales policies; (d) speculative influences; and (e) international economics and currency movements.

Hershey purchases roughly 180,000 tons of cocoa per year, representing about 15 percent of the company's total cost of goods sold. Hershey purchases and sells cocoa futures contracts. Hershey maintains West African and Brazilian crop-forecasting operations and continually monitors economic and political factors affecting market conditions. Cocoa prices rose moderately in both 1996 and 1997.

Hershey's second most important raw material is sugar. Sugar is subject to price supports under domestic farm legislation. Due to import quotas and duties, sugar prices paid by U.S. users are substantially higher than prices on the world market. The average wholesale list price for refined sugar has remained stable at $0.30 per pound over recent years.

Other raw materials that Hershey Corporation purchases in substantial quantities include semolina milled from durum wheat, milk, peanuts, almonds, and coconut. The prices of milk and peanuts are affected by federal marketing orders and subsidy programs of the U.S. Department of Agriculture. Raising and lowering price supports on milk and peanuts greatly affect the cost of Hershey's raw materials. Market prices of peanuts and almonds generally are determined in the latter months of each year, after harvest.

Tariffs imposed by different countries can greatly impede or promote globalization within an industry. For example, U.S. tariffs on chocolate are very low, ranging from 35 cents per pound for mass-produced chocolate to about $2.50 for some premium brands. Even a 10-cent difference in price among competing brands makes a big difference to consumers.

Nationalistic tariffs as they impact candy are falling but still are high enough to be a concern. Japan, Korea, and Taiwan, for example, have reduced their tariffs on imported chocolate from 20 percent to 10 percent. Europe is retaining its 12 percent tariff on chocolate imports from outside Europe. The United States has a 5 percent tariff on solid chocolate products and a 7 percent tariff on all other chocolate confectionery products. Technology standards across countries are similar to tariffs in that they vary and can impact global strategy plans. Japan, for example, prohibits the sale of chocolates that contain the additives BHT and TBHQ, which are approved by the U.S. Food & Drug Administration.

COMPETITORS

Some of Hershey's competitors do much of their business outside North America. For example, Cadbury-Schweppes obtains 50 percent from international sales and Mars obtains

50 percent, while Hershey obtains the least (10 percent). Hershey's two major candy competitors are Mars and Nestlé.

MARS

Mars is present in Europe, Asia, Mexico, Russia, and Japan. Mars gained 12 percent of the market in Mexico only 1 year after entering that market. Analysts estimate Mars's worldwide sales and profits to be over $7 billion and $1 billion respectively. Mars was successful introducing its Bounty chocolate candy from Europe into the United States without test marketing. Mars uses uniform marketing globally. The company's M&M candies slogan, "It melts in your mouth, not in your hands," is used worldwide. In contrast, Hershey's successful BarNone candy is named Temptation in Canada.

Mars is controlled by the Mars family through two brothers, John and Forrest, Jr. A marketing executive at Mars recently said, "Being Number 2 doesn't sit well with the brothers, and that's the biggest motivator." Mars is one of the world's largest private, closely held companies. It is a secretive company, unwilling to divulge financial information or corporate strategies. Recently, Mars has not been performing well and there are reports of high turnover in their executive and sales staff.

Unlike Hershey, Mars historically has relied on extensive marketing and advertising expenditures rather than on product innovation to gain market share. Mars has been repackaging, restyling, and reformulating its leading brands, including Snickers, M&M's, Milky Way, and 3 Musketeers, and is supplementing that strategy with extensive product development. New Mars products include Bounty, Balisto, and PB Max. It also successfully developed and marketed frozen Snickers ice cream bars. The product was so successful that it dislodged Eskimo Pie and Original Klondike from the number-one ice cream snack slot without any assistance from promotional advertising. Mars has world-class production facilities in Hackettstown, New Jersey; from that plant it ships products worldwide. Mars also has manufacturing plants in Mexico and several European locations.

NESTLÉ

With annual sales of $7.3 billion in the United States and the recent acquisition of Carnation, Nestlé is the largest food company in the world (see Case Figure 1–7). Nestlé's U.S. operations are headquartered in Glendale, California (818-549-6000). With corporate headquarters in Vevey, Switzerland (021-924-2111), Nestlé is a major competitor in Europe, the Far East, and South America. Nestlé sells products in over 360 countries on five continents, including many in the Third World. It is the world's largest instant-coffee manufacturer, with Nescafé as the dominant product. Nestlé also produces and markets chocolate and malt drinks, and is the world's largest producer of milk powder and condensed milk.

Nestlé's chocolate and confectionery products carry some popular brand names including Callier, Crunch, and Yes. With the acquisition of Rowntree, additional notable brands were added to the product line, including Smarties, After Eight, and Quality Street. Nestlé's Perugina division produces Baci. Through the RJR Nabisco acquisition, Nestlé acquired Curtiss Brand, a U.S. confectionery producer with such products as Baby Ruth and Butterfinger. Based in Switzerland, Nestlé is the world leader in many food categories, including candy. Almost 98 percent of Nestlé's revenues come from international sales. Nestlé manufactures chocolate in 23 countries, particularly in Switzerland and Latin America. Each factory is highly automated and employs an average of 250 people.

Another major product concentration for Nestlé is frozen foods and other refrigerated products. Findus in Europe and Stouffer in the United States represent the bulk of Nestlé's frozen food sales with well-known brands such as Lean Cuisine. Nestlé also manufactures a fast-developing range of fresh pasta and sauces in Europe and the United States under the name Contadina.

CONCLUSION

A major strategic issue facing Hershey today is where, when, and how to best expand internationally. Perhaps Hershey should expand into the Far East because currencies of those countries are depressed. China and India are huge untapped markets. Malaysia, Indonesia, Vietnam, and Thailand also are untapped. Should Hershey wait for Mars and Nestlé to gain a foothold in those countries?

Some analysts contend that Hershey International as a separate division producing and selling diverse products is an ineffective structural design. Critics also contend that Hershey's merging its pasta and grocery operations was a mistake. Can you recommend an improved organizational design for Hershey?

Should Hershey acquire firms in other foreign countries? Analysis is needed to identify and value specific acquisition candidates. In developing an overall strategic plan, what recommendations would you present to Hershey CEO Kenneth Wolfe? What relative emphasis should Hershey place on chocolate versus pasta in 1999 through 2001? Should Hershey diversify more into nonchocolate candies because that segment is growing most rapidly? Should Hershey build a new manufacturing plant in Asia or in Europe?

Design a global marketing strategy that could enable Hershey to boost exports of both chocolate and pasta. Should Hershey increase its debt further or dilute ownership of its stock further to raise the capital needed to implement your recommended strategies? Develop pro forma financial statements to fully assess and evaluate the impact of your proposed strategies.

NOTES

1. www.hersheys.com.
2. Hershey Foods, *Annual Report* (1994): 1.
3. Hershey Foods, *Annual Report* (1997): 1.

EXPERIENTIAL EXERCISES

Experiential Exercise 1A

STRATEGY ANALYSIS FOR HERSHEY FOODS

PURPOSE

The purpose of this exercise is to give you experience identifying an organization's opportunities, threats, strengths, and weaknesses. This information is vital to generating and selecting among alternative strategies.

INSTRUCTIONS

Step 1 Identify what you consider to be Hershey's major opportunities, threats, strengths, and weaknesses. On a separate sheet of paper, list these key factors under separate headings. State each factor in specific terms.

Step 2 Through class discussion, compare your lists of external and internal factors to those developed by other students. From the discussion, add to your lists of factors. Keep this information for use in later exercises.

Experiential Exercise 1B

DEVELOPING A CODE OF BUSINESS ETHICS FOR HERSHEY FOODS

PURPOSE

This exercise can give you practice developing a code of business ethics. In 1989, research was conducted to examine codes of business ethics from large manufacturing and service firms in the United States. The 28 variables listed below were found to be included in a sample of more than 80 codes of business ethics. The variables are presented in order of how frequently they occurred. Thus the first variable, "Conduct business in compliance with all laws," was most often included in the sample documents; "Firearms at work are prohibited" was least often included.

1. Conduct business in compliance with all laws.
2. Payments for unlawful purposes are prohibited.
3. Avoid outside activities that impair duties.
4. Comply with all antitrust and trade regulations.
5. Comply with accounting rules and controls.
6. Bribes are prohibited.
7. Maintain confidentiality of records.
8. Participate in community and political activities.
9. Provide products and services of the highest quality.
10. Exhibit standards of personal integrity and conduct.
11. Do not propagate false or misleading information.

12. Perform assigned duties to the best of your ability.
13. Conserve resources and protect the environment.
14. Comply with safety, health, and security regulations.
15. Racial, ethnic, religious, and sexual harassment at work is prohibited.
16. Report unethical and illegal activities to your manager.
17. Convey true claims in product advertisements.
18. Make decisions without regard for personal gain.
19. Do not use company property for personal benefit.
20. Demonstrate courtesy, respect, honesty, and fairness.
21. Illegal drugs and alcohol at work are prohibited.
22. Manage personal finances well.
23. Employees are personally accountable for company funds.
24. Exhibit good attendance and punctuality.
25. Follow directives of supervisors.
26. Do not use abusive language.
27. Dress in businesslike attire.
28. Firearms at work are prohibited.[1]

INSTRUCTIONS

Step 1 On a separate sheet of paper, write a code of business ethics for Hershey. Include as many variables listed above as you believe appropriate to Hershey's business. Limit your document to 100 words or less.

Step 2 Read your code of ethics to the class. Comment on why you did or did not include certain variables.

Step 3 Explain why having a code of ethics is not sufficient for ensuring ethical behavior in an organization. What else does it take?

NOTES

1. Donald Robin, Michael Giallourakis, Fred R. David, and Thomas E. Moritz. "A Different Look at Codes of Ethics," *Business Horizons* 32, no. 1 (January–February 1989): 66–73.

Experiential Exercise 1C

THE ETHICS OF SPYING ON COMPETITORS

PURPOSE

This exercise gives you an opportunity to discuss ethical and legal issues in class as related to methods being used by many companies to spy on competing firms. Gathering and using information about competitors is an area of strategic management that Japanese firms do more proficiently than American firms.

INSTRUCTIONS

On a separate sheet of paper, number from 1 to 18. For the 18 spying activities listed below, indicate whether or not you believe the activity is Ethical or Unethical and Legal or Illegal. Place either an *E* for ethical or *U* for unethical, and either an *L* for legal or an *I* for illegal for each activity. Compare your answers to your classmates' and discuss any differences.

1. Buying competitors' garbage.
2. Dissecting competitors' products.
3. Taking competitors' plant tours anonymously.
4. Counting tractor-trailer trucks leaving competitors' loading bays.
5. Studying aerial photographs of competitors' facilities.
6. Analyzing competitors' labor contracts.
7. Analyzing competitors' help wanted ads.
8. Quizzing customers and buyers about the sales of competitors' products.
9. Infiltrating customers' and competitors' business operations.
10. Quizzing suppliers about competitors' level of manufacturing.
11. Using customers to buy out phony bids.
12. Encouraging key customers to reveal competitive information.
13. Quizzing competitors' former employees.
14. Interviewing consultants who may have worked with competitors.
15. Hiring key managers away from competitors.
16. Conducting phony job interviews to get competitors' employees to reveal information.
17. Sending engineers to trade meetings to quiz competitors' technical employees.
18. Quizzing potential employees who worked for or with competitors.

Experiential Exercise 1D

STRATEGIC PLANNING FOR MY UNIVERSITY

PURPOSE

External and internal factors are the underlying bases of strategies formulated and implemented by organizations. Your college or university faces numerous external opportunities/threats and has many internal strengths/weaknesses. The purpose of this exercise is to illustrate the process of identifying critical external and internal factors.

External influences include trends in the following areas: economic, social, cultural, demographic, environmental, technological, political, legal, governmental, and competitive. External factors could include declining numbers of high school graduates; population shifts; community relations; increased competitiveness among colleges and universities; rising number of adults returning to college; decreased support from local, state, and federal agencies; and increasing number of foreign students attending American colleges.

Internal factors of a college or university include faculty, students, staff, alumni, athletic programs, physical plant, grounds and maintenance, student housing, administration, fund raising, academic programs, food services, parking, placement, clubs, fraternities, sororities, and public relations.

INSTRUCTIONS

Step 1 On a separate sheet of paper, make four headings: External Opportunities, External Threats, Internal Strengths, and Internal Weaknesses.

Step 2 As related to your college or university, list five factors under each of the four headings.

Step 3 Discuss the factors as a class. Write the factors on the board.

Step 4 What new things did you learn about your university from the class discussion? How could this type of discussion benefit an organization?

Experiential Exercise 1E

STRATEGIC PLANNING AT A LOCAL COMPANY

PURPOSE

This activity is aimed at giving you practical knowledge about how organizations in your city or town are doing strategic planning. This exercise also will give you experience interacting on a professional basis with local business leaders.

INSTRUCTIONS

Step 1 Use the telephone to contact several business owners or top managers. Find an organization that does strategic planning. Make an appointment to visit with the strategist (president, chief executive officer, or owner) of that business.

Step 2 Seek answers to the following questions during the interview:
   a. How does your firm formally conduct strategic planning? Who is involved in the process?
   b. Does your firm have a written mission statement? How was the statement developed? When was the statement last changed?
   c. What are the benefits of engaging in strategic planning?
   d. What are the major costs or problems in doing strategic planning in your business?
   e. Do you anticipate making any changes in the strategic planning process at your company? If yes, please explain.

Step 3 Report your findings to the class.

CHAPTER 2

Strategies in Action

CHAPTER OUTLINE

- ◆ TYPES OF STRATEGIES
- ◆ INTEGRATION STRATEGIES
- ◆ INTENSIVE STRATEGIES
- ◆ DIVERSIFICATION STRATEGIES
- ◆ DEFENSIVE STRATEGIES
- ◆ GUIDELINES FOR PURSUING STRATEGIES
- ◆ MERGERS AND LEVERAGED BUYOUTS
- ◆ MICHAEL PORTER'S GENERIC STRATEGIES
- ◆ STRATEGIC MANAGEMENT IN NONPROFIT AND GOVERNMENTAL ORGANIZATIONS
- ◆ STRATEGIC MANAGEMENT IN SMALL FIRMS

- ■ EXPERIENTIAL EXERCISE 2A
  What Happened at Hershey Foods in 1998?
- ■ EXPERIENTIAL EXERCISE 2B
  Examining Strategy Articles
- ■ EXPERIENTIAL EXERCISE 2C
  Classifying 1998 Strategies
- ■ EXPERIENTIAL EXERCISE 2D
  Strategic Management at the Dynamic Computer Company
- ■ EXPERIENTIAL EXERCISE 2E
  How Risky Are Various Alternative Strategies?
- ■ EXPERIENTIAL EXERCISE 2F
  Developing Alternative Strategies for My University

CHAPTER OBJECTIVES

After studying this chapter, you should be able to do the following:

1. Identify 16 types of business strategies.
2. Identify numerous examples of organizations pursuing different types of strategies.
3. Discuss guidelines when generic strategies are most appropriate to pursue.
4. Discuss Porter's generic strategies.
5. Describe strategic management in nonprofit, governmental, and small organizations.

NOTABLE QUOTES

Alice said, "Would you please tell me which way to go from here?" The cat said, "That depends on where you want to get to."—LEWIS CARROLL

Tomorrow always arrives. It is always different. And even the mightiest company is in trouble if it has not worked on the future. Being surprised by what happens is a risk that even the largest and richest company cannot afford, and even the smallest business need not run.—PETER DRUCKER

Planning. Doing things today to make us better tomorrow. Because the future belongs to those who make the hard decisions today.—EATON CORPORATION

By taking over companies and breaking them up, corporate raiders thrive on failed corporate strategies. Fueled by junk bond financing and growing acceptability, raiders can expose any company to takeover, no matter how large or blue chip.—MICHAEL PORTER

When organizations reach a fork in the road, forces are in motion that will, if not halted, drive a planning process towards the end-state of a self-perpetuating bureaucracy.—R. T. LENZ

One big problem with American business is that when it gets into trouble, it redoubles its effort. It's like digging for gold. If you dig down twenty feet and haven't found it, one of the strategies you could use is to dig twice as deep. But if the gold is twenty feet to the side, you could dig a long time and not find it.—EDWARD DE BONO

If you don't invest for the long term, there is no short term.—GEORGE DAVID

Innovate or evaporate. Particularly in technology-driven businesses, nothing quite recedes like success.—BILL SAPORITO

The demise of strategic planning has been exaggerated. The process has simply moved from corporate staff down to operating managers.—BERNARD REIMANN

Hundreds of companies today, including Sears, IBM, Searle, and Hewlett-Packard, have embraced strategic planning fully in their quest for higher revenues and profits. Kent Nelson, chair of UPS, explains why his company has created a new strategic planning department: "Because we're making bigger bets on investments in technology, we can't afford to spend a whole lot of money in one direction and then find out 5 years later it was the wrong direction."[1]

This chapter brings strategic management to life with many contemporary examples. Sixteen types of strategies are defined and exemplified, including Michael Porter's generic strategies: cost leadership, differentiation, and focus. Guidelines are presented for determining when different types of strategies are most appropriate to pursue. An overview of strategic management in nonprofit organizations, governmental agencies, and small firms is provided.

TYPES OF STRATEGIES

The model illustrated in Figure 2–1 provides a conceptual basis for applying strategic management. Defined and exemplified in Table 2–1, alternative strategies that an enterprise could pursue can be categorized into 13 actions—forward integration, backward integration, horizontal integration, market penetration, market development, product development, concentric diversification, conglomerate diversification, horizontal diversification, joint venture, retrenchment, divestiture, and liquidation—and a combination strategy. Each alternative strategy has countless variations. For example, market penetration can include adding salespersons, increasing advertising expenditures, couponing, and using similar actions to increase market share in a given geographic area.

INTEGRATION STRATEGIES

Forward integration, backward integration, and horizontal integration are sometimes collectively referred to as *vertical integration* strategies. Vertical integration strategies allow a firm to gain control over distributors, suppliers, and/or competitors.

FORWARD INTEGRATION *Forward integration* involves gaining ownership or increased control over distributors or retailers. One company that is betting a large part of its future on forward integration is Boeing. It recently engaged in negotiations with American, Delta, and Continental Airlines whereby those airlines purchase Boeing jets exclusively. The airlines like Boeing's forward integration strategy because it gets them a better price on new jets and saves maintenance and training costs. Boeing's major competitor, Europe's Airbus, vehemently opposes exclusivity pacts.

Another example of forward integration strategy underway today is in the computer industry where Packard Bell has begun to sell personal computers directly to business customers, hoping to emulate the success of Dell Computer Corp. Packard Bell's new strategy aimed at cutting inventory while attracting new customers is, however, angering many current retailers. Dell's build-to-order approach eliminates reseller markups, hastens inventory turnover, and allows the firm to quickly take advantage of falling component prices. Compaq, too, is instituting a new forward integration, build-to-order strategy.

FIGURE 2–1
A Comprehensive Strategic-Management Model

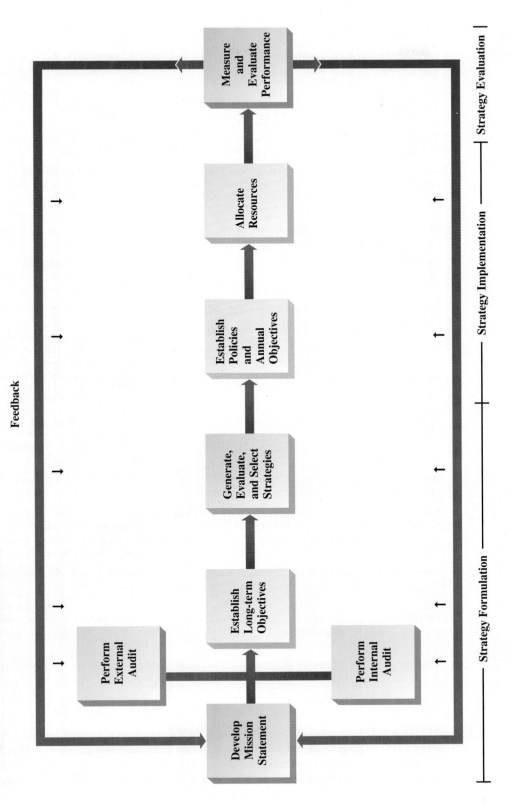

TABLE 2–1
Alternative Strategies Defined and Exemplified

STRATEGY	DEFINITION	EXAMPLE
Forward Integration	Gaining ownership or increased control over distributors or retailers	AT&T opened 45 retail stores, named AT&T Wireless Services, in 1997
Backward Integration	Seeking ownership or increased control of a firm's suppliers	Motel-8 acquired a furniture manufacturer.
Horizontal Integration	Seeking ownership or increased control over competitors	First Union Bank acquired First Fidelity Bancorp.
Market Penetration	Seeking increased market share for present products or services in present markets through greater marketing efforts	Johnson Insurance doubled its number of agents in Mexico.
Market Development	Introducing present products or services into new geographic area	Anheuser-Busch acquired Mexico's largest brewer, Grupo Modelo SA.
Product Development	Seeking increased sales by improving present products or services or developing new ones	Ford developed stand-alone service centers away from dealer locations.
Concentric Diversification	Adding new, but related, products or services	Walt Disney Co. built high-tech arcades for families and teens that feature interactive games and motion-simulator rides, some based on Disney characters. Disney's first arcade, occupying 100,000 square feet in Orlando, Florida, opened in 1998.
Conglomerate Diversification	Adding new, unrelated products or services	Britain's Misys, a banking and insurance firm, acquired Medic Computer Systems, a health care software firm.
Horizontal Diversification	Adding new, unrelated products or services for present customers	First Union acquired Wheat First Butcher Singer.
Joint Venture	Two or more sponsoring firms forming a separate organization for cooperative purposes	Lucent Technologies and Philips Electronics NV formed Philips Consumer Communications to make and sell telephones.
Retrenchment	Regrouping through cost and asset reduction to reverse declining sales and profit	Wells Fargo Bank cut 12,600 jobs during 1996 and 1997.
Divestiture	Selling a division or part of an organization	Raytheon sold its Amana appliance unit for $750 million to Goodman Holding.
Liquidation	Selling all of a company's assets, in parts, for their tangible worth	Ribol sold all its assets and ceases business.

An effective means of implementing forward integration is *franchising*. Approximately 2,000 companies in about 50 different industries in the United States use franchising to distribute their products or services. Businesses can expand rapidly by franchising because costs and opportunities are spread among many individuals. Total sales by franchises in the United States are about $1 trillion annually.

BACKWARD INTEGRATION   Both manufacturers and retailers purchase need materials from suppliers. *Backward integration* is a strategy of seeking ownership or increased control of a firm's suppliers. This strategy can be especially appropriate when a firm's current suppliers are unreliable, too costly, or cannot meet the firm's needs.

When you buy a box of Pampers diapers at Wal-Mart, a scanner at the store's checkout counter instantly zaps an order to Procter & Gamble Company. In contrast, in most hospitals, reordering supplies is a logistics nightmare. Inefficiency due to lack of control of suppliers in the health care industry is, however, rapidly changing as many giant health care purchasers, such as the Defense Department and Columbia/HCA Healthcare Corporation, move to require electronic bar codes on every supply item purchased. This allows instant tracking and reordering without invoices and paperwork. Of the estimated $83 billion spent annually on hospital supplies, industry reports indicate that $11 billion can be eliminated through more effective backward integration.

Some industries in the United States (such as the automotive and aluminum industries) are reducing their historical pursuit of backward integration. Instead of owning their suppliers, companies negotiate with several outside suppliers. Ford and Chrysler buy over half of their components parts from outside suppliers such as TRW, Eaton, General Electric, and Johnson Controls. Deintegration makes sense in industries that have global sources of supply. *Outsourcing*, whereby companies use outside suppliers, shop around, play one seller against another, and go with the best deal, is becoming widely practiced. US Airways recently outsourced its internal reservations system, being performed by 875 of its own workers, to Sabre Group Holdings. Sabre agreed to offer jobs to all displaced US Airways workers, but this business deal still surprised analysts because 82 percent of Sabre is owned by American Airlines.

Global competition also is spurring firms to reduce their number of suppliers and to demand higher levels of service and quality from those they keep. Although traditionally relying on many suppliers to ensure uninterrupted supplies and low prices, American firms now are following the lead of Japanese firms, which have far fewer suppliers and closer, long-term relationships with those few. "Keeping track of so many suppliers is onerous," says Mark Shimelonis of Xerox.

HORIZONTAL INTEGRATION   *Horizontal integration* refers to a strategy of seeking ownership of or increased control over a firm's competitors. One of the most significant trends in strategic management today is the increased use of horizontal integration as a growth strategy. Mergers, acquisitions, and takeovers among competitors allow for increased economies of scale and enhanced transfer of resources and competencies. Kenneth Davidson makes the following observation about horizontal integration:

> The trend towards horizontal integration seems to reflect strategists' misgivings about their ability to operate many unrelated businesses. Mergers between direct competitors are more likely to create efficiencies than mergers between unrelated businesses, both because there is a greater potential for eliminating duplicate facilities and because the management of the acquiring firm is more likely to understand the business of the target.[2]

Horizontal integration has become the most favored growth strategy in many industries. For example, Compaq Computer recently acquired Tandem Computers for $3 billion. Already the world's largest maker of PCs, Compaq received from Tandem advanced computers used by telephone companies and stock exchanges as well as a new 4,000-member sales force with access to hundreds of big companies. Prior to the acquisition, Compaq computers were sold mainly by retailers. Another recent example of horizontal integration occurred when North Carolina–based Wachovia Bank acquired Central Fidelity Banks in Virginia for $2.3 billion, moving Wachovia ahead of NationsBank as the largest bank in Virginia.

INTENSIVE STRATEGIES

Market penetration, market development, and product development are sometimes referred to as *intensive strategies* because they require intensive efforts to improve a firm's competitive position with existing products.

MARKET PENETRATION   A *market-penetration* strategy seeks to increase market share for present products or services in present markets through greater marketing efforts. This strategy is widely used alone and in combination with other strategies. Market penetration includes increasing the number of salespersons, increasing advertising expenditures, offering extensive sales promotion items, or increasing publicity efforts. Procter & Gamble is an example of this, spending heavily on advertising to increase market share of Venezia, its upscale perfume. Its advertising campaign includes full-page ads with scent strips in glossy magazines. Microsoft's multimillion-dollar advertising campaign to promote the new Windows 98 software is another example, as is the increasing use of e-mail for advertising by all kinds of companies. Note in the Information Technology Perspective that more than 100 million users of e-mail are projected within the United States by the year 2000.

MARKET DEVELOPMENT   *Market development* involves introducing present products or services into new geographic areas. The climate for international market development is becoming more favorable. In many industries, such as airlines, it is going to be hard to maintain a competitive edge by staying close to home. U.S. exports reached a

INFORMATION TECHNOLOGY

How Pervasive Is Technology in U.S. Households?

PERCENTAGE PENETRATION OF TECHNOLOGY INTO U.S. HOUSEHOLDS (1997)

Color TV	98	Home CD player	49	Computer with CD-ROM	21
Radio	98	Personal computer	40	Modem or fax/modem	19
Corded phone	96	Computer printer	38	Direct-view satellite dish	10
VCR	89	Cellular phone	34	Fax machine	9
Cordless phone	66	Pager	28		
Telephone answering device	65	Camcorder	26		

Source: Consumer Electronics Manufacturers Association

PAST AND PROJECTED CONSUMER USE OF E-MAIL IN THE UNITED STATES

YEAR	USERS (MILLIONS)	MESSAGES/DAY (MILLIONS)	MESSAGES/DAY/PERSON
1996	40	100	2.5
1997	55	150	2.7
1998	75	225	3.0
1999	95	313	3.3
2000	115	402	3.5
2001	135	500	3.7
2005	170	5,000	29.4

Source: Forrestor Research, Inc.

record $78.4 billion in June 1997, which was 10.6 percent more than in June 1996, and increases continue. Foreigners are increasingly eager to buy U.S. products and services, even though the value of the U.S. dollar rose 9.4 percent in 1997 compared to currencies of 19 other major countries. The rising value of the dollar makes U.S. products and services more expensive in overseas markets.

Wal-Mart is an example firm that aggressively is pursuing a market development strategy. Wal-Mart recently purchased Cifra SA in Mexico for $1.2 billion, marking the company's first major entry into international markets. Less than 5 percent of Wal-Mart's more than 2,500 stores are located outside the United States, but the giant retailer plans to increase its foreign operations and stores significantly in the near future.

PRODUCT DEVELOPMENT   *Product development* is a strategy that seeks increased sales by improving or modifying present products or services. Product development usually entails large research and development expenditures. An example firm betting its future on a product development strategy is NetMedia, which launched a new feature on its Web site called Net Saver Alert that provides airline and hotel discount deals continuously. Just go to www.ltravel.com, click on last-minute deals, fill out the form, and give your e-mail address. In another bold product development strategy, Canadian cigarette maker Imperial Tobacco introduced Mercer, a "natural cigarette without additives." R. J. Reynolds recently introduced Salem Preferred, a low-smoke cigarette, into Japan. As indicated in the Natural Environment Perspective, a decreasing number of firms appear to be actively developing green products—in response to an alarming decline in consumer interest in such efforts.

NATURAL ENVIRONMENT

Is Consumer Concern for Environmental Matters Declining?

Americans are not as vigilant about environmentally driven purchases as they used to be, partly because they feel businesses are making changes. There is a declining willingness among consumers to spend extra money on green products. The only natural environment activity that has gained support in recent years has been recycling, but even this activity may be waning as supply/demand/price relationships hinder company and community efforts.

The national recycling rate for all products in the United States reached 27 percent in 1995, up from only 7 percent in 1970. Many states such as Indiana, California, Colorado, and New York have a goal to recycle 50 percent of their trash by the year 2000. But prices for recycled materials have dropped dramatically since 1996, so the costs of recycling in the eyes of many consumers and businesses now exceed the benefits. For example, old cardboard boxes fetched about $200/ton in 1995, but only $65/ton in 1997. Washington, D.C., recently scrapped its recycling program due to high costs that included more trucks and more workers to pick up separated trash. Many communities find that it costs four times as much to collect and process recyclables as it does to dump trash in landfills. More trucks and more sorting plants also add to pollution. Professors at Carnegie Mellon University recently concluded that recycling benefits the environment, but at too high a cost.

Other environmental activities such as avoiding restaurants using Styrofoam, avoiding ecologically irresponsible companies, buying refillable packages, buying products made of recycled materials, using biodegradable soaps, avoiding aerosols, and reading labels for environmental impacts have less support today than in 1990. The percentage of American adults who care nothing at all about the natural environment has risen from 28 percent in 1990 to 37 percent today. Research suggests that consumers' buying habits are increasingly determined by past experience, price, brand recognition, others' recommendations, and convenience rather than environmental impact. Although Americans do not shop with environmental purpose as they once did, they have internalized deep concerns for the welfare of earth's living plants and animals. Indirect, displaced, and often hidden costs, such as pain and suffering associated with pollution, far exceed direct costs such as cleanup and equipment.

Source: Adapted from Tibbett Speer, "Growing the Green Market," American Demographics, (August 1997): 45–50; and Laura Litvan, "Has Recycling Reached Its Limit?" Investors Business Daily (August 6, 1997): 1.

Large expenditures in product development are a major reason why automotive and computer firms, such as General Motors, Ford, IBM, and Apple, do not own their distributors or dealers. Tandy is the only computer company that owns its distributors, which are Radio Shack stores. By the year 2000, GM plans to launch new car models monthly. The end of the fall new-car season is almost here.

DIVERSIFICATION STRATEGIES

There are three general types of *diversification strategies*: concentric, horizontal, and conglomerate. Overall, diversification strategies are becoming less popular as organizations are finding it more difficult to manage diverse business activities. In the 1960s and 1970s, the trend was to diversify so as not to be dependent on any single industry, but the 1980s saw a general reversal of that thinking. Diversification is now on the retreat. Michael Porter of the Harvard Business School says, "Management found they couldn't manage the beast." Hence, businesses are selling, or closing, less profitable divisions in order to focus on core businesses.

There are, however, a few companies today that pride themselves on being a conglomerate, from small firms such as Pentair Inc. and Blount International to huge companies such as Textron, Allied Signal, Emerson Electric and, of course, the reigning monarch of the conglomerate world, General Electric. Conglomerates prove that focus and diversity are not always mutually exclusive. Even Walt Disney Company competes in hotels, merchandising, television, and theme parks, but makes a case that all its businesses are entertainment-related.

Peters and Waterman's advice to firms is to "stick to the knitting" and not to stray too far from the firm's basic areas of competence. However, diversification is still an appropriate and successful strategy sometimes. For example, Philip Morris derives 60 percent of its profits from sales of Marlboro cigarettes. Hamish Maxwell, Philip Morris's CEO, says, "We want to become a consumer-products company." Diversification makes sense for Philip Morris because cigarette consumption is declining, product liability suits are a risk, and some investors reject tobacco stocks on principle. In a diversification move, Philip Morris spent $12.9 billion in a hostile takeover of Kraft General Foods, the world's second-largest food producer behind Nestlé.

CONCENTRIC DIVERSIFICATION Adding new, but related, products or services is widely called *concentric diversification*. An example of this strategy is the recent acquisition of Baltimore-based brokerage Alexander Brown by Bankers Trust New York for $1.6 billion, representing the largest purchase ever of a brokerage firm by a commercial bank. This is part of a growing merger trend between banks, brokerage companies, and insurance firms in response to deregulation of the financial services industry. Banks can now derive up to 25 percent of securities-related revenue from underwriting, versus 10 percent in the mid-1990s. Less than halfway through calendar 1997, more than $75 billion in financial services mergers and acquisitions were consummated in the United States—a record pace.

HORIZONTAL DIVERSIFICATION Adding new, unrelated products or services for present customers is called *horizontal diversification*. This strategy is not as risky as conglomerate diversification because a firm already should be familiar with its present customers. For example, beverage behemoths Pepsi and Coca-Cola recently entered the $3.6 billion bottled water market controlled mainly by Perrier, which makes Arrowhead, Poland Spring, and Great Bear brands of water. Pepsi introduced Aquafina, its first domestic bottled water. Bottled water is the nation's fastest-growing beverage category, growing 8 percent per year, more than twice that of carbonated drinks. Small, 16-ounce bottles of water are growing 30 percent per year. A few years ago, Pepsi and Coca-Cola entered the bottled tea market and quickly emerged as the top two firms with their Lipton and Nestea brands respectively, overtaking Snapple.

CONGLOMERATE DIVERSIFICATION   Adding new, unrelated products or services is called *conglomerate diversification*. Some firms pursue conglomerate diversification based in part on an expectation of profits from breaking up acquired firms and selling divisions piecemeal. Richard West, dean of New York University's School of Business, says, "The stock market is rewarding deconglomerations, saying company assets are worth more separately than together. There is a kind of antisynergy, the whole being worth less than the parts."

Supermarkets beginning to sell gasoline is a recent conglomerate diversification strategy. Albertson's had 12 stores selling gas in late 1997, Food Lion had 10 stores selling gas, and Kroger had 2 stores selling gas. U.S. West pursued a diversification strategy. U.S. West, a telecommunications firm, now owns operations in industries such as cable TV, equipment financing, advertising services, real estate development, cellular telephones, and publishing. Based in Denver, U.S. West recently purchased Financial Security Assurance for $345 million, further diversifying into financial services.

General Electric is an example of a firm that is highly diversified. GE makes locomotives, lightbulbs, power plants, and refrigerators; GE manages more credit cards than American Express; GE owns more commercial aircraft than American Airlines.

DEFENSIVE STRATEGIES

In addition to integrative, intensive, and diversification strategies, organizations also could pursue joint venture, retrenchment, divestiture, or liquidation.

JOINT VENTURE   *Joint venture* is a popular strategy that occurs when two or more companies form a temporary partnership or consortium for the purpose of capitalizing on some opportunity. This strategy can be considered defensive only because the firm is not undertaking the project alone. Often, the two or more sponsoring firms form a separate organization and have shared equity ownership in the new entity. Other types of *cooperative arrangements* include research and development partnerships, cross-distribution agreements, cross-licensing agreements, cross-manufacturing agreements, and joint-bidding consortia.

Joint ventures and cooperative arrangements are being used increasingly because they allow companies to improve communications and networking, to globalize operations, and to minimize risk. Lucent Technologies and the Dutch consumer electronics giant Philips Electronics recently created a joint venture firm named Philips Consumer Communications, which today is the largest telephone maker in the world with annual revenue over $2.5 billion. The new venture combined Lucent's research and manufacturing skills with Phillips's experience in consumer marketing overseas. Kathryn Rudie Harrigan, professor of strategic management at Columbia University, summarizes the trend toward increased joint venturing:

> In today's global business environment of scarce resources, rapid rates of technological change, and rising capital requirements, the important question is no longer "Shall we form a joint venture?" Now the question is "Which joint ventures and cooperative arrangements are most appropriate for our needs and expectations?" followed by "How do we manage these ventures most effectively?"[3]

Cooperative agreements even between competitors are becoming popular. For example, Canon supplies photocopies to Kodak, France's Thomson and Japan's FVC manufacture videocassette recorders, Siemens and Fujitsu work together, and General Motors and Toyota assemble automobiles. Italian automaker Piat SpA and Russia's Gorky Automobile Factory recently formed a joint venture to produce 150,000 cars annually for the Russian market. Gorky is Russia's largest and most successful automaker. For collaboration between competitors to succeed, both firms must contribute something distinctive, such as technology, distribution, basic research, or manufacturing capacity. But a major risk is that unintended transfers of important skills or technology may occur at organizational levels below where the deal was signed.[4] Information not covered in the formal agreement often gets traded in day-to-day interactions and dealings of engineers, marketers, and product developers. American firms often give away too much information to foreign firms when operating under cooperative agreements! Tighter formal agreements are needed, and Western companies must become better learners since leadership in many industries has shifted to the Far East and Europe.

RETRENCHMENT   *Retrenchment* occurs when an organization regroups through cost and asset reduction to reverse declining sales and profits. Sometimes called a turnaround or reorganizational strategy, retrenchment is designed to fortify an organization's basic distinctive competence. During retrenchment, strategists work with limited resources and face pressure from shareholders, employees, and the media. Retrenchment can entail selling off land and buildings to raise needed cash, pruning product lines, closing marginal businesses, closing obsolete factories, automating processes, reducing the number of employees, and instituting expense control systems.

Wal-Mart implemented a retrenchment strategy in 1998 when the retailer closed 48 of its 61 Bud's Discount City Outlets with plans to close the other 13 soon. Most Bud's Outlets were losing money. International Paper also announced a retrenchment strategy cutting 9,000 jobs, more than 10 percent of its workforce, and eliminating certain production operations. Kodak recently laid off 200 senior and middle managers and trimmed 10 percent of its administrative staff.

In some cases, *bankruptcy* can be an effective type of retrenchment strategy. Bankruptcy can allow a firm to avoid major debt obligations and to void union contracts. Levitz Furniture, the home-furniture retailer in the United States behind Helig-Myers, filed for bankruptcy in late 1997. Levitz is closing 21 of its 129 stores as part of the restructuring.

Corporate America appears to be gearing for continued large layoffs of managers and employees. Corporate downsizing in the United States is evidenced in Table 2–2.

There are five major types of bankruptcy: Chapter 7, Chapter 9, Chapter 11, Chapter 12, and Chapter 13.

Chapter 7 bankruptcy is a liquidation procedure used only when a corporation sees no hope of being able to operate successfully or to obtain the necessary creditor agreement. All the organization's assets are sold in parts for their tangible worth.

Chapter 9 bankruptcy applies to municipalities. The most recent municipality successfully declaring bankruptcy is Bridgeport, the largest city in Connecticut. Some states do not allow municipalities to declare bankruptcy.

Chapter 11 bankruptcy allows organizations to reorganize and come back after filing a petition for protection. Declaring Chapter 11 bankruptcy allowed the Manville Corporation and Continental Products to gain protection from liability suits filed over their manufacturing of asbestos products. Million-dollar judgments against these companies would have required liquidation, so bankruptcy was a good strategy for these two firms. Similarly, Wang Laboratories recently emerged from Chapter 11 with one of the strongest balance sheets in the computer industry.

TABLE 2–2
Corporate Downsizing in the United States

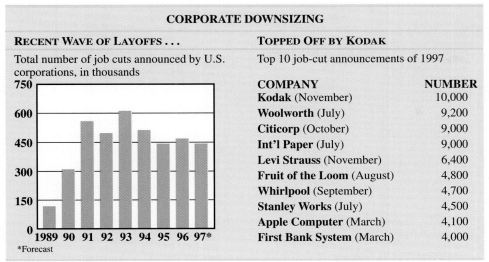

CORPORATE DOWNSIZING	
RECENT WAVE OF LAYOFFS . . .	**TOPPED OFF BY KODAK**

Total number of job cuts announced by U.S. corporations, in thousands

Top 10 job-cut announcements of 1997

COMPANY	NUMBER
Kodak (November)	10,000
Woolworth (July)	9,200
Citicorp (October)	9,000
Int'l Paper (July)	9,000
Levi Strauss (November)	6,400
Fruit of the Loom (August)	4,800
Whirlpool (September)	4,700
Stanley Works (July)	4,500
Apple Computer (March)	4,100
First Bank System (March)	4,000

*Forecast

Source: Adapted from Fred Bleakley, "New Round of Layoffs May Be Beginning," *The Wall Street Journal* (November 13, 1997): A2.

Chapter 12 bankruptcy was created by the Family Farmer Bankruptcy Act of 1986. This law became effective in 1987 and provides special relief to family farmers with debt equal to or less than $1.5 million.

Chapter 13 bankruptcy is a reorganization plan similar to Chapter 11 but available only to small businesses owned by individuals with unsecured debts of less than $100,000 and secured debts of less than $350,000. The Chapter 13 debtor is allowed to operate the business while a plan is being developed to provide for the successful operation of the business in the future.

Personal bankruptcies in the United States exceeded 1.1 million in 1996, a 29 percent increase over 1995. Tennessee, Georgia, and Alabama had the highest personal bankruptcies in the nation with 9.0, 7.3, and 7.2 bankruptcies per 1,000 people respectively, while Maine, Vermont, and Alaska had the fewest personal bankruptcies with 2.3, 2.1, and 1.7 bankruptcies per 1,000 people respectively. The national average is 4.2 personal bankruptcies per 1,000 people.

DIVESTITURE   Selling a division or part of an organization is called *divestiture*. Divestiture often is used to raise capital for further strategic acquisitions or investments. Divestiture can be part of an overall retrenchment strategy to rid an organization of businesses that are unprofitable, that require too much capital, or that do not fit well with the firm's other activities. For example, Columbia/HCA Healthcare Corporation continues to divest all of its operations that are not related to hospitals, including ValueRX and Value Health. Headquartered in Nashville, Tennessee, Columbia is the subject of a massive federal investigation into possible Medicare fraud.

Divestiture has become a very popular strategy as firms try to focus on their core strengths, lessening their level of diversification. A few divestitures consummated in 1998 are given in Table 2–3.

LIQUIDATION   Selling all of a company's assets, in parts, for their tangible worth is called *liquidation*. Liquidation is a recognition of defeat and consequently can be an emotionally difficult strategy. However, it may be better to cease operating than to continue losing large sums of money.

Thousands of small businesses in the United States liquidate annually without ever making the news. It is tough to start and successfully operate a small business. In China

TABLE 2–3
Some Divestitures in 1998

PARENT COMPANY	DIVESTED BUSINESS	ACQUIRING COMPANY
Simon & Schuster	Education divisions	Pearson (British firm)
Merck	A pharmaceutical division	Dupont
Dow Jones & Co.	Telerate	Bridge Information Systems
Black & Decker	Sports equipment division	(to be announced)
General Motors	Seating business	Lear
Xerox	Crum & Forster	Fairfax Financial
Limited	Henri Bendel	(to be announced)
Philips Electronics	PolyGram	(to be announced)
TRW	Odyssey satellite system	ICO Global Communications
Softbank (Japanese firm)	Ziff-Davis (*PC Magazine* and *PC Week*)	(to be announced)
Pennzoil	Jiffy Lube	(to be announced)

and Russia, thousands of government-owned businesses liquidate annually as those countries try to privatize and consolidate industries.

COMBINATION   Many, if not most, organizations pursue a combination of two or more strategies simultaneously, but a *combination strategy* can be exceptionally risky if carried too far. No organization can afford to pursue all the strategies that might benefit the firm. Difficult decisions must be made. Priorities must be established. Organizations, like individuals, have limited resources. Both organizations and individuals must choose among alternative strategies and avoid excessive indebtedness.

Organizations cannot do too many things well because resources and talents get spread thin and competitors gain advantage. In large diversified companies, a combination strategy is commonly employed when different divisions pursue different strategies. Also, organizations struggling to survive may employ a combination of several defensive strategies, such as divestiture, liquidation, and retrenchment, simultaneously.

GUIDELINES FOR PURSUING STRATEGIES

Table 2–4 reveals situations, conditions, and guidelines for when various alternative strategies are most appropriate to pursue. For example, note that a market development strategy is generally most appropriate when new channels of distribution are available that are reliable, inexpensive, and of good quality; when an organization is very successful at what it does; when new untapped or unsaturated markets exist; when an organization has the needed capital and human resources to manage expanded operations; when an organization has excess production capacity; and when an organization's basic industry is rapidly becoming global in scope.

TABLE 2–4
Guidelines for Situations When Particular Strategies Are Most Effective

FORWARD INTEGRATION

- When an organization's present distributors are especially expensive, or unreliable, or incapable of meeting the firm's distribution needs
- When the availability of quality distributors is so limited as to offer a competitive advantage to those firms that integrate forward
- When an organization competes in an industry that is growing and is expected to continue to grow markedly; this is a factor because forward integration reduces an organization's ability to diversify if its basic industry falters

continued

TABLE 2–4   *continued*

- When an organization has both the capital and human resources needed to manage the new business of distributing its own products
- When the advantages of stable production are particularly high; this is a consideration because an organization can increase the predictability of the demand for its output through forward integration
- When present distributors or retailers have high profit margins; this situation suggests that a company profitably could distribute its own products and price them more competitively by integrating forward

BACKWARD INTEGRATION

- When an organization's present suppliers are especially expensive, or unreliable, or incapable of meeting the firm's needs for parts, components, assemblies, or raw materials
- When the number of suppliers is small and the number of competitors is large
- When an organization competes in an industry that is growing rapidly; this is a factor because integrative-type strategies (forward, backward, and horizontal) reduce an organization's ability to diversify in a declining industry
- When an organization has both capital and human resources to manage the new business of supplying its own raw materials
- When the advantages of stable prices are particularly important; this is a factor because an organization can stabilize the cost of its raw materials and the associated price of its product through backward integration
- When present supplies have high profit margins, which suggests that the business of supplying products or services in the given industry is a worthwhile venture
- When an organization needs to acquire a needed resource quickly

HORIZONTAL INTEGRATION

- When an organization can gain monopolistic characteristics in a particular area or region without being challenged by the federal government for "tending substantially" to reduce competition
- When an organization competes in a growing industry
- When increased economies of scale provide major competitive advantages
- When an organization has both the capital and human talent needed to successfully manage an expanded organization
- When competitors are faltering due to a lack of managerial expertise or a need for particular resources that an organization possesses; note that horizontal integration would not be appropriate if competitors are doing poorly because overall industry sales are declining

MARKET PENETRATION

- When current markets are not saturated with a particular product or service
- When the usage rate of present customers could be increased significantly
- When the market shares of major competitors have been declining while total industry sales have been increasing
- When the correlation between dollar sales and dollar marketing expenditures historically has been high
- When increased economies of scale provide major competitive advantages

MARKET DEVELOPMENT

- When new channels of distribution are available that are reliable, inexpensive, and of good quality
- When an organization is very successful at what it does
- When new untapped or unsaturated markets exist
- When an organization has the needed capital and human resources to manage expanded operations
- When an organization has excess production capacity
- When an organization's basic industry rapidly is becoming global in scope

PRODUCT DEVELOPMENT

- When an organization has successful products that are in the maturity stage of the product life cycle; the idea here is to attract satisfied customers to try new (improved) products as a result of their positive experience with the organization's present products or services
- When an organization competes in an industry that is characterized by rapid technological developments
- When major competitors offer better-quality products at comparable prices

continued

TABLE 2–4   *continued*

- When an organization competes in a high-growth industry
- When an organization has especially strong research and development capabilities

CONCENTRIC DIVERSIFICATION

- When an organization competes in a no-growth or a slow-growth industry
- When adding new, but related, products significantly would enhance the sales of current products
- When new, but related, products could be offered at highly competitive prices
- When new, but related, products have seasonal sales levels that counterbalance an organization's existing peaks and valleys
- When an organization's products are currently in the decline stage of the product life cycle
- When an organization has a strong management team

CONGLOMERATE DIVERSIFICATION

- When an organization's basic industry is experiencing declining annual sales and profits
- When an organization has the capital and managerial talent needed to compete successfully in a new industry
- When an organization has the opportunity to purchase an unrelated business that is an attractive investment opportunity
- When there exists financial synergy between the acquired and acquiring firm; note that a key difference between concentric and conglomerate diversification is that the former should be based on some commonality in markets, products, or technology, whereas the latter should be based more on profit considerations
- When existing markets for an organization's present products are saturated
- When antitrust action could be charged against an organization that historically has concentrated on a single industry

HORIZONTAL DIVERSIFICATION

- When revenues derived from an organization's current products or services would increase significantly by adding the new, unrelated products
- When an organization competes in a highly competitive and/or a no-growth industry, as indicated by low industry profit margins and returns
- When an organization's present channels of distribution can be used to market the new products to current customers
- When the new products have countercyclical sales patterns compared to an organization's present products

JOINT VENTURE

- When a privately owned organization is forming a joint venture with a publicly owned organization; there are some advantages of being privately held, such as close ownership; there are some advantages of being publicly held, such as access to stock issuances as a source of capital. Sometimes, the unique advantages of being privately and publicly held can be synergistically combined in a joint venture
- When a domestic organization is forming a joint venture with a foreign company; a joint venture can provide a domestic company with the opportunity for obtaining local management in a foreign country, thereby reducing risks such as expropriation and harassment by host country officials
- When the distinctive competencies of two or more firms complement each other especially well
- When some project is potentially very profitable, but requires overwhelming resources and risks; the Alaskan pipeline is an example
- When two or more smaller firms have trouble competing with a large firm
- When there exists a need to introduce a new technology quickly

RETRENCHMENT

- When an organization has a clearly distinctive competence, but has failed to meet its objectives and goals consistently over time
- When an organization is one of the weaker competitors in a given industry
- When an organization is plagued by inefficiency, low profitability, poor employee morale, and pressure from stockholders to improve performance
- When an organization has failed to capitalize on external opportunities, minimize external threats, take advantage of internal strengths, and overcome internal weaknesses over time; that is, when the organization's strategic managers have failed (and possibly will be replaced by more competent individuals)
- When an organization has grown so large so quickly that major internal reorganization is needed

continued

TABLE 2–4 *continued*

DIVESTITURE
● When an organization has pursued a retrenchment strategy and it failed to accomplish needed improvements
● When a division needs more resources to be competitive than the company can provide
● When a division is responsible for an organization's overall poor performance
● When a division is a misfit with the rest of an organization; this can result from radically different markets, customers, managers, employees, values, or needs
● When a large amount of cash is needed quickly and cannot be obtained reasonably from other sources
● When government antitrust action threatens an organization
LIQUIDATION
● When an organization has pursued both a retrenchment strategy and a divestiture strategy, and neither has been successful
● When an organization's only alternative is bankruptcy; liquidation represents an orderly and planned means of obtaining the greatest possible cash for an organization's assets. A company can legally declare bankruptcy first and then liquidate various divisions to raise needed capital
● When the stockholders of a firm can minimize their losses by selling the organization's assets

Source: Adapted from F. R. David, "How Do We Choose Among Alternative Growth Strategies?" *Managerial Planning* 33, no. 4 (January–February 1985): 14–17, 22.

MERGERS AND LEVERAGED BUYOUTS

Acquisition and merger are two commonly used ways to pursue strategies. An *acquisition* occurs when a large organization purchases (acquires) a smaller firm, or vice versa. A *merger* occurs when two organizations of about equal size unite to form one enterprise. When an acquisition or merger is not desired by both parties, it can be called a *takeover* or *hostile takeover*. Regarding merger-mania restructuring in the United States, *Business Week* offered the following conclusion:

> It is clear now that restructurings are driven by a lot more than tax considerations, low stock prices, raiders' desire for a quick buck, and aggressive merger merchants on Wall Street. . . . Restructuring continues because U.S. industry needs it. Deregulation in industries from financial services to energy, from communications to transportation, has exposed managerial complacency and inefficient practices caused by years of shelter from market forces. . . . Plenty of companies have simply recognized that if they want to compete globally, they must slim down, toughen up, and focus on a narrower range of businesses.[5]

Among mergers, acquisitions, and takeovers in recent years, same-industry combinations have predominated. A general market consolidation is occurring in many industries, especially banking, insurance, defense, and health care, but also pharmaceuticals, food, airlines, accounting, publishing, computers, retailing, financial services, and biotechnology.

Even labor unions are trying to merge. The United Automobile Workers, the International Association of Machinists and Aerospace Workers, and the United Steelworkers of America are engaged in merger talks. Due to mergers, the AFL-CIO today is composed of only 78 unions, and that number is expected to drop to fewer than 50 by 1999. Unions represent only about 14.5 percent of the U.S. workforce today, down from 35 percent in the 1960s.

In 1997, Travelers brokerage subsidiary Smith Barney acquired Saloman Inc. for $9 billion to create the third-largest investment house behind industry leader Merrill Lynch and recently formed Morgan Stanley Dean Witter.

Table 2–5 shows some mergers and acquisitions completed in 1997. There are many reasons for mergers and acquisitions, including the following:

TABLE 2–5
Some Examples of Mergers and Acquisitions Completed in 1997

ACQUIRING FIRM	ACQUIRED FIRM
Dean Witter Discover	Morgan Stanley
First Bank Systems	U.S. Bancorp
Banc One	First USA
Washington Mutual Savings	Great Western Financial
Household International	Transamerica Con. Fin.
American General	USLIFE
Bankers Trust New York	Alexander Brown
Marsh & McLennan	Johnson & Higgins
First Maryland	Dauphin Deposit
Associated Bank	First Financial
Safeco	American States

◆ To provide improved capacity utilization

◆ To make better use of existing sales force

◆ To reduce managerial staff

◆ To gain economies of scale

◆ To smooth out seasonal trends in sales

◆ To gain access to new suppliers, distributors, customers, products, and creditors

◆ To gain new technology

◆ To reduce tax obligations

The volume of mergers completed annually worldwide is growing dramatically and exceeds $1 trillion annually. There are more than 10,000 mergers annually in the United States that total more than $700 billion. Six U.S. mergers in 1996 topped $10 billion each, while over 100 topped $1 billion. For the first 6 months of 1997, nearly 5,000 deals valued at $366 billion were announced versus $314 billion in the year-ago period, a 16 percent increase. The largest merger ever was the 1998 WorldCom acquisition of MCI for $30 billion, exceeding the Bell Atlantic acquisition of Nynex for $25.6 billion.

Globally, merger activity rose to $692 billion in the first half of 1997, up 18 percent from $588 billion in that period for 1996. The three most active industries for mergers are hotels/casinos, brokerages/banks, and oil/gas firms.

The proliferation of mergers is fueled by companies' drive for market share, efficiency, and pricing power as well as by globalization, the need for greater economies of scale, reduced regulation and antitrust concerns, and the stock market rewarding merger activity with higher stock prices.

Mergers do not always give quick results. Of sixty $500 million-plus deals between 1992 and 1995, fifty-five percent of buyers saw their stock underperform their industry average. Many mergers fail because the acquired company is not integrated effectively into the parent firm. For example, when PacifiCare Health Systems acquired rival FHP International Corporation, the former's stock plunged 27 percent. PacifiCare had trouble integrating FHP's computer system, culture, and operations. Similarly, shares of United HealthCare dropped 30 percent after the giant Minnesota HMO acquired MetraHealth Companies recently.

LEVERAGED BUYOUTS (LBOs) A *leveraged buyout* (LBO) occurs when a corporation's shareholders are bought out (hence *buyout*) by the company's management and other private investors using borrowed funds (hence *leveraged*).[6] Besides trying to avoid a hostile takeover, other reasons for initiating an LBO are senior management decisions that particular divisions do not fit into an overall corporate strategy or must be sold to raise cash, or receipt of an attractive offering price. An LBO takes a corporation private.

Borg-Warner, Owen-Illinois, and Jim Walter are companies that experienced leveraged buyouts. Under this arrangement, the debt is paid back later through funds from operations and the sale of assets. Many banks, insurance companies, and other financial institutions are in the buyout business, sometimes called *merchant banking.*

Merchant bankers usually sell companies acquired in leveraged buyouts in pieces and at high profits. In the most profitable leveraged buyout ever recorded, Kohlberg, Kravis, Roberts and Company acquired RJR Nabisco for $25 billion and then began selling divisions separately at premiums. RJR's divestitures included selling its fresh-fruit business for $875 million to Polly Peck, a London-based food company, and its Del Monte canned food business for about $1.48 billion to another leveraged buyout group led by Citicorp Venture Capital.

MICHAEL PORTER'S GENERIC STRATEGIES

Probably the three most widely read books on competitive analysis in the 1980s were Michael Porter's (www.hbs.edu/bios/mporter.) *Competitive Strategy* (Free Press, 1980), *Competitive Advantage* (Free Press, 1985), and *Competitive Advantage of Nations* (Free Press, 1989). According to Porter, strategies allow organizations to gain competitive advantage from three different bases: cost leadership, differentiation, and focus. Porter calls these bases *generic strategies. Cost leadership* emphasizes producing standardized products at very low per-unit cost for consumers who are price-sensitive. *Differentiation* is a strategy aimed at producing products and services considered unique industrywide and directed at consumers who are relatively price-insensitive. *Focus* means producing products and services that fulfill the needs of small groups of consumers.

Porter's strategies imply different organizational arrangements, control procedures, and incentive systems. Larger firms with greater access to resources typically compete on a cost leadership and/or differentiation basis, whereas smaller firms often compete on a focus basis.

Porter stresses the need for strategists to perform cost-benefit analyses to evaluate "sharing opportunities" among a firm's existing and potential business units. Sharing activities and resources enhances competitive advantage by lowering costs or raising differentiation. In addition to prompting sharing, Porter stresses the need for firms to "transfer" skills and expertise among autonomous business units effectively in order to gain competitive advantage. Depending upon factors such as type of industry, size of firm, and nature of competition, various strategies could yield advantages in cost leadership, differentiation, and focus.

COST LEADERSHIP STRATEGIES A primary reason for pursuing forward, backward, and horizontal integration strategies is to gain cost leadership benefits. But cost leadership generally must be pursued in conjunction with differentiation. A number of cost elements affect the relative attractiveness of generic strategies, including economies or diseconomies of scale achieved, learning and experience curve effects, the percentage of capacity utilization achieved, and linkages with suppliers and distributors. Other cost elements to consider in choosing among alternative strategies include the potential for sharing costs and knowledge within the organization, R&D costs associated with new product development or modification of existing products, labor costs, tax rates, energy costs, and shipping costs.

Striving to be the low-cost producer in an industry can be especially effective when the market is composed of many price-sensitive buyers, when there are few ways to achieve product differentiation, when buyers do not care much about differences from brand to brand, or when there are a large number of buyers with significant bargaining power. The basic idea is to underprice competitors and thereby gain market share and sales, driving some competitors out of the market entirely.

A successful cost leadership strategy usually permeates the entire firm, as evidenced by high efficiency, low overhead, limited perks, intolerance of waste, intensive screening of budget requests, wide spans of control, rewards linked to cost containment, and broad employee participation in cost control efforts. Some risks of pursuing cost leadership are that competitors may imitate the strategy, thus driving overall industry profits down; technological breakthroughs in the industry may make the strategy ineffective; or buyer interest may swing to other differentiating features besides price. Several example firms that are well known for their low-cost leadership strategies are Wal-Mart, BIC, McDonald's, Black and Decker, Lincoln Electric, and Briggs and Stratton.

DIFFERENTIATION STRATEGIES   Different strategies offer different degrees of differentiation. Differentiation does not guarantee competitive advantage, especially if standard products sufficiently meet customer needs or if rapid imitation by competitors is possible. Durable products protected by barriers to quick copying by competitors are best. Successful differentiation can mean greater product flexibility, greater compatibility, lower costs, improved service, less maintenance, greater convenience, or more features. Product development is an example of a strategy that offers the advantages of differentiation.

A differentiation strategy should be pursued only after careful study of buyers' needs and preferences to determine the feasibility of incorporating one or more differentiating features into a unique product that features the desired attributes. A successful differentiation strategy allows a firm to charge a higher price for its product and to gain customer loyalty because consumers may become strongly attached to the differentiation features. Special features to differentiate one's product can include superior service, spare parts availability, engineering design, product performance, useful life, gas mileage, or ease of use.

A risk of pursuing a differentiation strategy is that the unique product may not be valued highly enough by customers to justify the higher price. When this happens, a cost leadership strategy easily will defeat a differentiation strategy. Another risk of pursuing a differentiation strategy is that competitors may develop ways to copy the differentiating features quickly. Firms thus must find durable sources of uniqueness that cannot be imitated quickly or cheaply by rival firms.

Common organizational requirements for a successful differentiation strategy include strong coordination among the R&D and marketing functions and substantial amenities to attract scientists and creative people. Firms pursuing a differentiation strategy include Dr. Pepper, Jenn-Air, The Limited, BMW, Grady-White, Ralph Lauren, Maytag, and Cross.

FOCUS STRATEGIES   A successful focus strategy depends upon an industry segment that is of sufficient size, has good growth potential, and is not crucial to the success of other major competitors. Strategies such as market penetration and market development offer substantial focusing advantages. Midsize and large firms effectively can pursue focus-based strategies only in conjunction with differentiation or cost leadership–based strategies. All firms in essence follow a differentiated strategy. Because only one firm can differentiate itself with the lowest cost, the remaining firms in the industry must find other ways to differentiate their products.

Focus strategies are most effective when consumers have distinctive preferences or requirements and when rival firms are not attempting to specialize in the same target segment. Firms pursuing a focus strategy include Midas, Red Lobster, Federal Express, Sprint, MCI, Coors, and Schwinn.

Risks of pursuing a focus strategy include the possibility that numerous competitors recognize the successful focus strategy and copy the strategy, or that consumer preferences drift toward the product attributes desired by the market as a whole. An organization using a focus strategy may concentrate on a particular group of customers, geographic markets, or product line segments in order to serve a well-defined but narrow market better than competitors who serve a broader market.

THE VALUE CHAIN   According to Porter, the business of a firm can best be described as a *value chain* in which total revenues minus total costs of all activities undertaken to develop and market a product or service yields value. All firms in a given industry have a similar value chain, which includes activities such as obtaining raw materials, designing products, building manufacturing facilities, developing cooperative agreements, and providing customer service. A firm will be profitable as long as total revenues exceed the total costs incurred in creating and delivering the product or service. Firms should strive to understand not only their own value chain operations, but also their competitors', suppliers', and distributors' value chains.

THE COMPETITIVE ADVANTAGE OF NATIONS   Some countries around the world, such as Brazil, offer abundant natural resources, while others, such as Mexico, offer cheap labor. Others, such as Japan, offer a high commitment to education, while still others, such as the United States, offer innovativeness and entrepreneurship. Countries differ in what they have to offer businesses, and firms increasingly are relocating various parts of their value chain operations to take advantage of what different countries have to offer.

Porter reveals in his most recent book that some countries seem to have a disproportionate share of successful firms in particular industries. Examples are the United States in entertainment, Italy in ceramic tile, Sweden in trucks, Japan in banking, Switzerland in candy, and Germany in cars. Porter attributes these differences to four decisive elements: (1) availability of strengths in certain narrow, technical fields; (2) high demand in the home country; (3) related and supporting industries in the home country; and (4) strong domestic rivals.[7] Local rivalry, for example, often stimulates growth in local distributors and suppliers. Organizations should strive to pursue strategies that effectively enable the firm to capitalize

GLOBAL PERSPECTIVE
How Extensively Is the Internet Used in Europe?

A lack of personal computers in most households, high connection costs, and currency obstacles have caused the Internet to be used only sparingly in Europe for sales and marketing applications. In France, for example, 20-year-old Minitels are small videotext consoles that link one-quarter of all households and businesses but do not offer access to the Internet. European businesses that do use the Internet for commerce only provide information about their products and services, with no mechanism for actually purchasing goods.

In 1997 in all of Europe, only about 9 million businesses and households logged onto the Internet and consummated only about $500 million in commerce. This number is expected to climb to more than 35 million users by the year 2000 and total over $3 billion in commerce, for two big reasons:

1. Deregulation of Europe's telecommunications industry in scheduled for 1998. Currently, Europeans who log onto the Internet pay 50 percent more than Americans to sign on and, in addition, have to pay 30 cents per minute of connection. These costs should fall in 1998, thus spurring growth of the Internet.

2. Introduction of a single European currency in scheduled for January 1, 1999.

The euro or common coinage for all of Europe will make it much easier to engage in commerce using the Internet because so many different currencies in Europe now make electronic commerce unwieldly and cumbersome. A single currency would spur growth of the Internet.

Source: Adapted from Jack Gee, "Parlez-Vous Internet," Industry Week (April 21, 1997): 78–82.

on the relative strengths of various nations. According to Porter, comparative differences among nations result in the following generalizations for strategic management: devaluation is bad for competitiveness; relaxing antitrust is bad; relaxing product safety and environmental regulations is bad; deregulation is good; promoting interfirm cooperation is bad; orderly marketing agreements are bad; and increasing defense contracts is bad.

The United States is far ahead of rest of the world in use of the Internet for commerce. As indicated in the Global Perspective, Europe lags considerably behind the United States in this regard.

STRATEGIC MANAGEMENT IN NONPROFIT AND GOVERNMENT ORGANIZATIONS

The strategic-management process is being used effectively by countless nonprofit and governmental organizations, such as the Girl Scouts and Boy Scouts, the Red Cross, chambers of commerce, educational institutions, medical institutions, public utilities, libraries, government agencies, and churches. The nonprofit sector, surprisingly, is by far America's largest employer, with 80 million Americans giving on average nearly 5 hours each week to one or more nonprofit organizations. Many nonprofit and governmental organizations outperform private firms and corporations on innovativeness, motivation, productivity, and strategic management. For example, the Salvation Army in Florida is able to rehabilitate 80 percent of persons convicted of their first offense. The Daisy Scouts, a Girl Scout program for 5-year-olds, has grown rapidly to more than 100,000 strong after being initiated only a few years ago.

Compared to for-profit firms, nonprofit and governmental organizations often function as a monopoly, produce a product or service that offers little or no measurability of performance, and are totally dependent on outside financing. Especially for these organizations, strategic management provides an excellent vehicle for developing and justifying requests for needed financial support.

EDUCATIONAL INSTITUTIONS   Educational institutions are using strategic-management techniques and concepts more frequently. Richard Cyert, president of Carnegie-Mellon University, says, "I believe we do a far better job of strategic management than any company I know." Population shifts nationally from the Northeast and Midwest to the Southeast and West are but one factor causing trauma for educational institutions that have not planned for changing enrollments. Ivy League schools in the Northeast are recruiting more heavily in the Southeast and West. This trend represents a significant change in the competitive climate for attracting the best high school graduates each year.

Schools of business in colleges and universities increasingly are developing and offering custom courses for individual companies. At Northwestern University's Kellogg School, for example, custom courses for companies such as Ernst & Young and Johnson & Johnson now make up 40 percent of all executive education offerings. Custom courses account for 59 percent of executive education offerings at the University of Pennsylvania's Wharton School. "In the past, schools felt they were teaching the truth, and everyone would come kneel at their feet," says Nancy Hartigan at Kellogg. "Now companies are much more selective. Schools have to become more responsive to what organizations want." To become accredited by the American Association of Collegiate Schools of Business (AACSB), an elaborate strategic plan must be prepared by the applying school.

MEDICAL ORGANIZATIONS   The $200 billion American hospital industry is experiencing declining margins, excess capacity, bureaucratic overburdening, poorly planned and executed diversification strategies, soaring health care costs, reduced federal support, and high administrator turnover. The seriousness of this problem is accented by a 20 percent annual decline in inpatient use nationwide. Declining occupancy rates, deregulation, and accelerating growth of health maintenance organizations, preferred provider organizations, urgent care centers, outpatient surgery centers, diagnostic centers, specialized clinics, and group practices are other major threats facing hospitals today. Many private and state-supported medical institutions are in financial trouble as a result of traditionally taking a reactive rather than a proactive approach in dealing with their industry.

Hospitals—originally intended to be warehouses for people dying of tuberculosis, smallpox, cancer, pneumonia, and infectious diseases—are creating new strategies today as advances in the diagnosis and treatment of chronic diseases are undercutting that earlier mission. Hospitals are beginning to bring services to the patient as much as bringing the patient to the hospital; in 20 years, health care will be concentrated in the home and in the residential community, not on the hospital campus. Chronic care will require day treatment facilities, electronic monitoring at home, user-friendly ambulatory services, decentralized service networks, and laboratory testing. A successful hospital strategy for the future will require renewed and deepened collaboration with physicians, who are central to hospitals' well-being, and a reallocation of resources from acute to chronic care in home and community settings.

Current strategies being pursued by many hospitals include creating home health services, establishing nursing homes, and forming rehabilitation centers. Backward integration strategies that some hospitals are pursuing include acquiring ambulance services, waste disposal services, and diagnostic services. The Stuart Circle Hospital in Richmond, Virginia, is using newspaper, radio, and outdoor advertising as part of a market penetration strategy. Archbold Memorial Hospital in Thomasville, Georgia, is pursuing a product development strategy by creating an outpatient mental health service, a nurse midwife service, and a substance abuse center. The Children's Memorial Hospital in Chicago has developed a new program called Pediatric Excellence that provides nursing care at home for medically fragile children. This strategy could be considered concentric diversification, as could the strategies of building fitness centers and diet centers. Desert Hospital in Palm Springs, California, has moved its noninvasive cardiac catheterization services out of the hospital and into a joint venture arrangement with physicians.

The 10 most successful hospital strategies today are providing freestanding outpatient surgery centers, freestanding outpatient diagnostic centers, physical rehabilitation centers, home health services, cardiac rehabilitation centers, preferred provider services, industrial medicine services, women's medicine services, skilled nursing units, and psychiatric services.[8]

Due largely to costs, hospitals increasingly are contracting with outside companies to perform services such as providing 24-hour emergency room and life-support systems. Psicor in San Diego, for example, leases equipment and provides technicians for open-heart surgery in 80 hospitals across the country. At least 1,000 hospitals nationwide have contracted with firms such as Coastal Emergency Services in Durham, North Carolina, to provide emergency room services.

GOVERNMENTAL AGENCIES AND DEPARTMENTS Federal, state, county, and municipal agencies and departments, such as police departments, chambers of commerce, forestry associations, and health departments, are responsible for formulating, implementing, and evaluating strategies that use taxpayers' dollars in the most cost-effective way to provide services and programs. Strategic-management concepts increasingly are being used to enable governmental organizations to be more effective and efficient.

But strategists in governmental organizations operate with less strategic autonomy than their counterparts in private firms. Public enterprises generally cannot diversify into unrelated businesses or merge with other firms. Governmental strategists usually enjoy little freedom in altering the organizations' missions or redirecting objectives. Legislators and politicians often have direct or indirect control over major decisions and resources. Strategic issues get discussed and debated in the media and legislatures. Issues become politicized, resulting in fewer strategic choice alternatives. There is more predictability in the management of public sector enterprises.

On the surface, it may seem that strategic management is not applicable to government organizations, but the opposite is true. Government agencies and departments are finding that their employees get excited about the opportunity to participate in the strategic-management process and thereby have an effect on the organization's mission, objectives, strategies, and policies. In addition, government agencies are using a strategic-management approach to develop and substantiate formal requests for additional funding.

STRATEGIC MANAGEMENT IN SMALL FIRMS

Strategic management is vital for large firms' success, but what about small firms? The strategic-management process is just as vital for small companies. From their inception, all organizations have a strategy, even if the strategy just evolves from day-to-day operations. Even if conducted informally or by a single owner/entrepreneur, the strategic-management process significantly can enhance small firms' growth and prosperity. Recent data clearly show that an ever-increasing number of men and women in the United States are starting their own businesses. This means more individuals are becoming strategists. Widespread corporate layoffs have contributed to an explosion in small businesses and new ideas. For example, although less than 1 percent of the 900,000 auto mechanics in the United States are women, Janet Brown of Newport News, Virginia, recently opened and is successfully operating the Women's Auto Clinic, which features women mechanics.

Numerous magazine and journal articles have focused on applying strategic-management concepts to small businesses.[9] A major conclusion of these articles is that a lack of strategic-management knowledge is a serious obstacle for many small business owners. Other problems often encountered in applying strategic-management concepts to small businesses are a lack of both sufficient capital to exploit external opportunities and a day-to-day cognitive frame of reference. Recent research also indicates that strategic management in small firms is more informal than in large firms, but small firms that engage in strategic management outperform those that do not. The CheckMATE strategic planning software at www.checkmateplan.com offers a version especially for small businesses.

CONCLUSION

The main appeal of any managerial approach is the expectation that it will enhance organizational performance. This is especially true of strategic management. Through involvement in strategic-management activities, managers and employees achieve a better understanding of an organization's priorities and operations. Strategic management allows organizations to be efficient, but more importantly, it allows them to be effective. Although strategic management does not guarantee organizational success, the process allows proactive rather than reactive decision making. Strategic management may represent a radical change in philosophy for some organizations, so strategists must be trained to anticipate and constructively respond to questions and issues as they arise. The 16 strategies discussed in this chapter can represent a new beginning for many firms, especially if managers and employees in the organization understand and support the plan for action.

We invite you to visit the DAVID page on the Prentice Hall Web site at
www.prenhall.com/davidsm
for this chapter's World Wide Web exercise.

TAKE IT TO THE NET

KEY TERMS AND CONCEPTS

Acquisition	(p. 59)	Focus	(p. 62)	Market Development	(p. 50)
Backward Integration	(p. 49)	Forward Integration	(p. 46)	Market Penetration	(p. 50)
Bankruptcy	(p. 54)	Franchising	(p. 48)	Merchant Banking	(p. 61)
Combination Strategy	(p. 56)	Generic Strategies	(p. 61)	Merger	(p. 59)
Concentric Diversification	(p. 52)	Horizontal Diversification	(p. 52)	Outsourcing	(p. 49)
Conglomerate Diversification	(p. 53)	Horizontal Integration	(p. 49)	Product Development	(p. 51)
Cooperative Arrangements	(p. 53)	Integration Strategies	(p. 46)	Retrenchment	(p. 54)
Cost Leadership	(p. 61)	Intensive Strategies	(p. 50)	Takeover	(p. 59)
Differentiation	(p. 62)	Joint Venture	(p. 53)	Value Chain	(p. 63)
Diversification Strategies	(p. 52)	Leveraged Buyout	(p. 60)	Vertical Integration	(p. 46)
Divestiture	(p. 55)	Liquidation	(p. 55)		

ISSUES FOR REVIEW AND DISCUSSION

1. How does strategy formulation differ for a small versus a large organization? for a for-profit versus a nonprofit organization?

2. Give recent examples of market penetration, market development, and product development.

3. Give recent examples of forward integration, backward integration, and horizontal integration.

4. Give recent examples of concentric diversification, horizontal diversification, and conglomerate diversification.

5. Give recent examples of joint venture, retrenchment, divestiture, and liquidation.

6. Read one of the suggested readings at the end of this chapter. Prepare a 5-minute oral report on the topic.

7. Do you think hostile takeovers are unethical? Why or why not?

8. What are the major advantages and disadvantages of diversification?

9. What are the major advantages and disadvantages of an integrative strategy?

10. How does strategic management differ in profit and nonprofit organizations?

11. Why is it not advisable to pursue too many strategies at once?

12. Explain Porter's value chain concept.

13. Describe the mechanics of a leveraged buyout.

14. What are the implications of Porter's "competitive advantage of nations" research?

15. Visit the CheckMATE Strategic Planning software Web site at www.checkmateplan.com and discuss the benefits offered.

NOTES

1. John Byrne, "Strategic Planning—It's Back," *Business Week* (August 26, 1996): 46.

2. Kenneth Davidson, "Do Megamergers Make Sense?" *Journal of Business Strategy* 7, no. 3 (Winter 1987): 45.

3. Kathryn Rudie Harrigan, "Joint Ventures: Linking for a Leap Forward," *Planning Review* 14, no. 4 (July–August 1986):10.

4. Gary Hamel, Yves Doz, and C. K. Prahalad, "Collaborate with Your Competitors—and Win," *Harvard Business Review* 67, no. 1 (January–February 1989): 133.

5. "Why Nothing Seems to Make a Dent in Dealmaking," *Business Week* (July 20, 1987): 75.

6. Dan Dalton, "The Ubiquitous Leveraged Buyout (LBO): Management Buyout or Management Sellout?" *Business Horizons* 32, no. 4 (July–August 1989): 36.

7. Bernard Reimann, "Selected Highlights of the 1988 Strategic Management Society Conference," *Planning Review* (January–February 1989): 26–7. See also Michael Porter, *Competitive Advantage of Nations* (New York: Free Press, 1989).

8. *Hospital*, May 5, 1991: 16.

9. Some of these articles are P. H. Thurston, "Should Smaller Companies Make Formal Plans?" *Harvard Business Review* 61, no. 5 (September–October 1983): 162–88; R. Robinson, J. Pearce, G. Vozikis, and T. Mescon, "The Relationship Between Stage of Development and Small Firm Planning and Performance," *Journal of Small Business Management* 22, no. 2 (April 1984): 45–52; L. Nagel, "Strategy Formulation for the Smaller Firm: A Practical Approach," *Long Range Planning* 14, no. 4 (August 1981): 115–20; P. G. Holland and W. Boulton, "Balancing the 'Family' and the 'Business' in Family Business," *Business Horizons* 27, no. 2 (March–April 1984): 16–21; F. R. David, "Computer-Assisted Strategic Planning for Small Businesses," *Journal of Systems Management* 36, no. 7 (July 1985): 24–33.

CURRENT READINGS

Anand, J. and H. Singh. "Asset Redeployment, Acquisitions and Corporate Strategy in Declining Industries." *Strategic Management Journal* 18, Special Issue (Summer 1997): 99–118.

Argyres, N. "Evidence on the Role of Firm Capabilities in Vertical Integration Decisions." *Strategic Management Journal* 17, no. 2 (February 1996): 129–150.

Barkdoll, Gerald and Morris R. Bosin. "Targeted Planning: A Paradigm for the Public Service." *Long Range Planning* 30, no. 4 (August 1997): 529–539.

Bergh, D. D. and G. F. Holbein. "Assessment and Redirection of Longitudinal Analysis: Demonstration with a Study of the Diversification and Divestiture Relationship." *Strategic Management Journal* 18, no. 7 (August 1997): 557–572.

Busija, E. C., H. M. O'Neill, and C. P. Zeithaml. "Diversification Strategy, Entry Mode, and Performance: Evidence of Choice and Constraints." *Strategic Management Journal* 18, no. 4 (April 1997): 321–328.

Byrd, John, Kent Hickman, and Hugh Hunter. "Diversification: A Broader Perspective." *Business Horizons* 40, no. 2 (March–April 1997): 40–44.

Castrogiovanni, Gary J. "Pre-Start-up Planning and the Survival of New Small Businesses: Theoretical Linkages." *Journal of Management* 22, no. 6 (1996): 801–822.

Chang, S. J. "An Evolutionary Perspective on Diversification and Corporate Restructuring Entry, Exit, and Economic Performance During 1981–89." *Strategic Management Journal* 17, no. 8 (October 1996): 587–612.

Dailey, C. M. "Governance Patterns in Bankruptcy Reorganizations." *Strategic Management Journal* 17, no. 5 (May 1996): 355–376.

Dooley, R. S., D. M. Fowler, and A. Miller. "The Benefits of Strategic Homogeneity and Strategic Heterogeneity: Theoretical and Empirical Evidence Resolving Past Differences." *Strategic Management Journal* 17, no. 4 (April 1996): 293–306.

Fiegenbaum, A., J. M. Shaver, and B. Yeung. "Which Firms Expand to the Middle East: The Experience of American Multinationals." *Strategic Management Journal* 18, no. 2 (February 1997): 141–148.

Flanagan, David J. "Announcements of Purely Related and Purely Unrelated Mergers and Shareholder Returns: Reconciling the Relatedness Paradox." *Journal of Management* 22, no. 6 (1996): 823–836.

Goldsmith, Stephen. "Can Business Really Do Business With Government?" *Harvard Business Review* (May–June 1997): 110–122.

Gunz, Hugh P. and R. Michael Jalland. "Managerial Careers and Business Strategies." *Academy of Management Review* 21, no. 3 (July 1996): 718–756.

Hennart, J. F. and S. Reddy. "The Choice between Mergers/Acquisitions and Joint Ventures: The Case of Japanese Investors in the United States." *Strategic Management Journal* 18, no. 1 (January 1997): 1–12.

Hopkins, W. E. and S. A. Hopkins. "Strategic Planning–Financial Performance Relationships in Banks: A Causal Examination." *Strategic Management Journal* 18, no. 8 (September 1997): 635–652.

Inkpen, Andrew C. and Paul W. Beamish. "Knowledge, Bargaining Power, and the Instability of International Joint Ventures." *Academy of Management Review* 22, no. 1 (January 1997): 177–202.

Jennings, David. "Outsourcing Opportunities for Financial Services." *Long Range Planning* 29, no. 3 (June 1996): 393–404.

Kabir, R., D. Cantrijn, and A. Jeunink. "Takeover Defenses, Ownership Structure and Stock Returns in the Netherlands: An

Empirical Analysis." *Strategic Management Journal* 18, no. 2 (February 1997): 97–110.

Khanna, Tarun and Krishna Palepu. "Why Focused Strategies May Be Wrong for Emerging Markets." *Harvard Business Review* (July–August 1997): 41–54.

Krishnan, H. A., A. Miller, and W. Q. Judge. "Diversification and Top Management Team Complementarity: Is Performance Improved by Merging Similar or Dissimilar Teams?" *Strategic Management Journal* 18, no. 5 (May 1997): 361–374.

Khurana, Anil and Stephen R. Rosenthal. "Integrating the Fuzzy Front End of New Product Development." *Sloan Management Review* 38, no. 2 (Winter 1997): 103–113.

Liedtka, Jeanne M. "Collaboration Across Lines of Business for Competitive Advantage." *Academy of Management Executive* 10, no. 2 (May 1996): 20–37.

Lubatkin, Hemant Merchant and Narasimhan Srinivasan. "Merger Strategies and Shareholder Value During Times of Relaxed Antitrust Enforcement: The Case of Large Mergers During the 1980s." *Journal of Management* 23, no. 1 (1997): 61–84.

Milofsky, Carl. "Review of 'Strategic Management for Nonprofit Organizations: Theory and Cases.'" *Academy of Management Review* 22, no. 2 (April 1997): 568–570.

Moulton, Wilbur N., Howard Thomas, and Mark Pruett. "Business Failure Pathways: Environmental Stress and Organizational Response." *Journal of Management* 22, no. 4 (1996): 571–596.

Pearce, Robert J. "Toward Understanding Joint Venture Performance and Survival: A Bargaining and Influence Approach to Transaction Cost Theory." *Academy of Management Review* 22, no. 1 (January 1997): 203–225.

Ramaswamy, Kannah. "The Performance Impact of Strategic Similarity in Horizontal Mergers: Evidence from the U.S. Banking Industry." *Academy of Management Journal* 40, no. 3 (June 1997): 697–715.

Rowe, W. G. and P. M. Wright. "Related and Unrelated Diversification and Their Effect on Human Resource Management Controls." *Strategic Management Journal* 18, no. 4 (April 1997): 329–339.

Saunders, Carol, Mary Gebelt, and Quing Hu. "Achieving Success in Information Systems Outsourcing." *California Management Review* 39, no. 2 (Winter 1997): 63–79.

EXPERIENTIAL EXERCISES

Experiential Exercise 2A

WHAT HAPPENED AT HERSHEY FOODS IN 1998?

PURPOSE

In performing business policy case analysis, you will need to find epilogue information about the respective companies to determine what strategies actually were employed since the time of the case. Comparing *what actually happened* with *what you would have recommended and expected to happen* is an important part of business policy case analysis. Do not recommend what the firm actually did, unless in-depth analysis of the situation at the time reveals those strategies to have been best among all feasible alternatives. This exercise gives you experience conducting library research to determine what strategies Hershey, Mars, and Nestlé pursued in 1998.

INSTRUCTIONS

Step 1 Look up Hershey Foods Corporation, Mars, and Nestlé Corporation on the Internet. Find some recent articles about firms in the confectionery industry. Scan Moody's, Dun & Bradstreet, and Standard & Poor's publications for information. Check the Edgar files at www.sec.gov and Hoover's on-line at www.hoovers.com.

Step 2 Summarize your findings in a three-page report titled "Strategies of Hershey Foods in 1998." Include information about Mars and Nestlé. Also include your personal reaction to Hershey's strategies in terms of their attractiveness.

Experiential Exercise 2B

EXAMINING STRATEGY ARTICLES

PURPOSE

Strategy articles can be found weekly in journals, magazines, and newspapers. By reading and studying strategy articles, you can gain a better understanding of the strategic-management process. Several of the best journals in which to find corporate strategy articles are *Planning Review, Long Range Planning, Journal of Business Strategy,* and *Strategic Management Journal*. These journals are devoted to reporting the results of empirical research in strategic management. They apply strategic-management concepts to specific organizations and industries. They introduce new strategic-management techniques and provide short case studies on selected firms.

Other good journals in which to find strategic-management articles are *Harvard Business Review, Sloan Management Review, Business Horizons, California Management Review, Academy of Management Review, Academy of Management Journal, Academy of Management Executive, Journal of Management,* and *Journal of Small Business Management*.

In addition to journals, many magazines regularly publish articles that focus on business strategies. Several of the best magazines in which to find applied strategy articles are *Dun's Business Month, Fortune, Forbes, Business Week, Inc. Magazine,* and *Industry Week.* Newspapers such as *USA Today, The Wall Street Journal, The New York Times,* and *Barrons* cover strategy events when they occur—for example, a joint venture announcement, a bankruptcy declaration, a new advertising campaign start, acquisition of a company, divestiture of a division, a chief executive officer's hiring or firing, or a hostile takeover attempt.

In combination, journal, magazine, and newspaper articles can make the business policy course more exciting. They allow current strategies of profit and nonprofit organizations to be identified and studied.

INSTRUCTIONS

Step 1 Go to your college library and find a recent journal article that focuses on a strategic-management topic. Select your article from one of the journals listed above, not from a magazine. Copy the article and bring it to class.

Step 2 Give a three-minute oral report summarizing the most important information in your article. Include comments giving your personal reaction to the article. Pass your article around in class.

Experiential Exercise 2c

CLASSIFYING 1998 STRATEGIES

PURPOSE

This exercise can improve your understanding of various strategies by giving you experience classifying strategies. This skill will help you use the strategy-formulation tools presented later. Consider the following strategies announced in 1998 by various firms:

1. Aetna Inc., a huge insurance firm, bought New York Life Insurance Company's health insurance division (NYL Care).
2. Toyota developed a tree that absorbs smog.
3. Merrill Lynch purchased a large European private bank.
4. Pfizer developed and marketed Viagra.
5. Enron withdrew from doing business in California.
6. National Semiconductor laid off 10 percent of its employees.
7. Microsoft developed and marketed Windows 98.
8. CVS, formally Revco, purchased Arbor Drugs.
9. Bethlehem Steel purchased Lukens Steel.
10. Pacific Gas & Electric began selling services outside California.
11. Procter & Gamble began selling Pringles made with Olestra .
12. American Online completed its acquisition of CompuServe.
13. Boeing cut production of 747s from 5 planes to 3.5 a month.
14. General Motors expanded production in Mexico from 300,000 to 600,000 vehicles annually.
15. Digital Equipment merged with Compaq Computer.

16. Japan's NEC acquired 49 percent of Packard Bell.
17. Crescent Real Estate Equities acquired Station Casinos.
18. Apple Computer closed its Claris software unit.
19. J.C. Penney closed 75 stores and cut 4,900 jobs.
20. Dutch retailer Royal Ahold acquired Giant Food.

INSTRUCTIONS

Step 1 On a separate sheet of paper, number from 1 to 20. These numbers correspond to the strategies described above.

Step 2 What type of strategy best describes the 20 actions cited above? Indicate your answers.

Step 3 Exchange papers with a classmate and grade each other's paper as your instructor gives the right answers.

Experiential Exercise 2D

STRATEGIC MANAGEMENT AT THE DYNAMIC COMPUTER COMPANY

PURPOSE

This exercise can give you experience choosing among alternative growth strategies for a specific company. Remember that organizations cannot pursue all the strategies that potentially may benefit the firm. Difficult decisions have to be made to eliminate some options. Use the guidelines given in Table 2–4 to complete this exercise.

BACKGROUND

Dynamic Computer, Inc. (DCI) is a highly regarded personal computer manufacturer based in central California. DCI designs, develops, produces, markets, and services personal computer systems for individuals' needs in business, education, science, engineering, and the home. The company's main product is the Dynamic II personal computer system, complete with optional accessories and software. The company recently announced a new system, the Dynamic III, that is aimed at large business firms. It is much more expensive than the Dynamic II. Dynamic's computer systems are distributed in the United States and Canada by 1,000 independent retail stores and internationally through 21 independent distributors, who resell to 850 foreign retail outlets. Approximately 700 of the retail outlets in the United States and Canada are authorized service centers for Dynamic products, but none of the outlets sell Dynamic products exclusively. Many of these outlets are not marketing Dynamic's products effectively.

TABLE 2D–1
Selected Financial Information for DCI

	1997	1998	1999
Sales	$ 13,000,000	$ 12,000,000	$ 10,000,000
New Income	3,000,000	1,000,000	500,000
Total Assets	180,000,000	200,000,000	250,000,000
Market Share	15%	12%	10%

The American computer industry grew at an inflation-adjusted, compound annual rate of about 20 percent from 1958 through the late 1980s. For the 1990s, real annual growth in the computer industry is expected to have averaged about 18 percent a year. The outlook for personal computers continues to be positive. However, this market is highly competitive and is characterized by rapid technological advances in both hardware and software. Margins on software are nearly double operating margins on hardware. New firms are entering the industry at an increasing rate, and this has resulted in a decline in Dynamic's sales, earnings, and market share in recent years. Many computer companies expect software sales and services to represent 50 percent of their total revenues by 2000. Dynamic is concerned about its future direction and competitiveness. Selected financial information for Dynamic is given in Table 2D–1.

INSTRUCTIONS

The owners of DCI have indicated a willingness to explore a number of alternative growth strategies for the future. They have hired you as a consultant to assist them in making strategic decisions regarding the future allocation of resources. The feeling is that to sustain growth, the company must make some critical decisions. Dynamic is financially capable of investing in several projects. The owners wish to use their resources wisely to produce the highest possible return on investment in the future. They are considering five alternative strategies:

1. Market penetration—establish a nationwide sales force to market Dynamic products to large firms that do not buy through independent retailers.
2. Product development—develop an easier-to-use computer for small business firms.
3. Forward integration—offer major new incentives to distributors who sell and service Dynamic products.
4. Backward integration—purchase a major outside supplier of software.
5. Conglomerate diversification—acquire Toys Unlimited, a large and successful toy manufacturer.

Based on the strategy guidelines given in Chapter 2, your task is to offer specific recommendations to the strategists of DCI. Follow these steps:

Step 1 Across the top of a separate sheet of paper, set up five columns, with the following headings:

Individual Percentage Allocations	Group Percentage Allocations	Expert Percentage Allocations	The Absolute Difference Between Columns 1 and 3	The Absolute Difference Between Columns 2 and 3

Down the left side of your paper, number from 1 to 5. These numbers correspond to the five strategies listed above.

Step 2 Take 10 minutes to determine how you would allocate DCI's resources among the five alternative strategies. Record your answers by placing individual percentage values for strategies 1 through 5 under column 1. Your only constraint is that the total resources allocated must equal 100 percent. Distribute resources in the manner you think will offer the greatest future return on investment and profitability.

Step 3 Join with two other students in class. Develop a set of group percentage allocations and record these values for strategies 1 through 5 under column 2. Do not change your individual percentage allocations once discussion begins in your group.

Step 4 As your teacher reveals the right answer and supporting rationale, record these values for strategies 1 through 5 under column 3.

Step 5 For each row, subtract column 3 values from column 1 values and record the absolute difference (ignore negatives) in column 4. Then, sum the column 4 values.

Step 6 For each row, subtract column 3 values from column 2 values and record the absolute difference (ignore negatives) in column 5. Then, sum the column 5 values.

Step 7 If the sum of column 4 values exceeds the sum of column 5 values, then your group allocation of DCI's resources was better than your individual allocation. However, if the sum of column 4 values is less than the sum of column 5 values, you were a better strategist than your group on this exercise.

Strategic-management research indicates that group strategic decisions are almost always better than individual strategic decisions. Did you do better than your group?

Experiential Exercise 2E

HOW RISKY ARE VARIOUS ALTERNATIVE STRATEGIES?

PURPOSE

This exercise focuses on how risky various alternative strategies are for organizations to pursue. Different degrees of risk are based largely on varying degrees of *externality*, defined as movement away from present business into new markets and products. In general, the greater the degree of externality, the greater the probability of loss resulting from unexpected events. High-risk strategies generally are less attractive than low-risk strategies.

INSTRUCTIONS

Step 1 On a separate sheet of paper, number vertically from 1 to 10. Think of 1 as "most risky," 2 as "next most risky," and so forth to 10, "least risky."

Step 2 Write the following strategies beside the appropriate number to indicate how risky you believe the strategy is to pursue: horizontal integration, horizontal diversification, liquidation, forward integration, backward integration, product development, market development, market penetration, joint venture, and conglomerate diversification.

Step 3 Grade your paper as your teacher gives you the right answers and supporting rationale. Each correct answer is worth 10 points.

This exercise is based on a commonly accepted and published classification of strategies given in James Belohlav and Karen Giddens-Emig, "Selecting a Master Strategy," *Journal of Business Strategy* 7, no. 3 (Winter 1987): 77.

Experiential Exercise 2F

DEVELOPING ALTERNATIVE STRATEGIES FOR MY UNIVERSITY

PURPOSE

It is important for representatives from all areas of a college or university to identify and discuss alternative strategies that could benefit faculty, students, alumni, staff, and other constituencies. As you complete this exercise, notice the learning and understanding that occurs as people express differences of opinions. Recall that *the process of planning is more important than the document.*

INSTRUCTIONS

Step 1 Recall or locate the external opportunity/threat and internal strength/weakness factors that you identified as part of Experiential Exercise 1D. If you did not do that exercise, discuss now as a class important external and internal factors facing your college or university.

Step 2 Identify and put on the chalkboard alternative strategies that you feel could benefit your college or university. Your proposed actions should allow the institution to capitalize on particular strengths, improve upon certain weaknesses, avoid external threats, and/or take advantage of particular external opportunities. List at least 20 possible strategies on the board. Number the strategies as they are written on the board.

Step 3 On a separate sheet of paper, number from 1 to the total number of strategies listed on the board. Everyone in class individually should rate the strategies identified, using a 1 to 3 scale, where 1 = *I do not support implementation*, 2 = *I am neutral about implementation*, and 3 = *I strongly support implementation*. In rating the strategies, recognize that your institution cannot do everything desired or potentially beneficial.

Step 4 Go to the board and record your ratings in a row beside the respective strategies. Everyone in class should do this, going to the board perhaps by rows in the class.

Step 5 Sum the ratings for each strategy so that a prioritized list of recommended strategies is obtained. This prioritized list reflects the collective wisdom of your class. Strategies with the highest score are deemed best.

Step 6 Discuss how this process could enable organizations to achieve understanding and commitment from individuals.

Step 7 Share your class results with a university administrator and ask for comments regarding the process and top strategies recommended.

PART 2

STRATEGY FORMULATION

CHAPTER 3

The Business Mission

CHAPTER OUTLINE

- ◆ **WHAT IS OUR BUSINESS?**
- ◆ **THE IMPORTANCE OF A CLEAR MISSION**
- ◆ **THE NATURE OF A BUSINESS MISSION**
- ◆ **COMPONENTS OF A MISSION STATEMENT**
- ◆ **WRITING AND EVALUATING MISSION STATEMENTS**

- ■ EXPERIENTIAL EXERCISE 3A
  Evaluating Mission Statements

- ■ EXPERIENTIAL EXERCISE 3B
  Writing a Mission Statement for Hershey Foods

- ■ EXPERIENTIAL EXERCISE 3C
  Writing a Mission Statement for My University

- ■ EXPERIENTIAL EXERCISE 3D
  Conducting Mission Statement Research

- ■ EXPERIENTIAL EXERCISE 3E
  Are Mission Statements Esoteric?

CHAPTER OBJECTIVES

After studying this chapter, you should be able to do the following:

1. Describe the nature and role of mission statements in strategic management.
2. Discuss why the process of developing a mission statement is as important as the resulting document.
3. Identify the components of mission statements.
4. Discuss how a clear mission statement can benefit other strategic-management activities.
5. Evaluate mission statements of different organizations.
6. Write good mission statements.

A business is not defined by its name, statutes, or articles of incorporation. It is defined by the business mission. Only a clear definition of the mission and purpose of the organization makes possible clear and realistic business objectives.—PETER DRUCKER

A corporate vision can focus, direct, motivate, unify, and even excite a business into superior performance. The job of a strategist is to identify and project a clear vision.—JOHN KEANE

Where there is no vision, the people perish.—PROVERBS 29:18

Customers are first, employees second, shareholders third, and the community fourth. That's the credo at H. B. Fuller, the century-old adhesives maker in St. Paul.—PATRICIA SELLERS

What is especially difficult is getting different departments working together in the best interest of customers. Yet managers at all levels are the critical link to aligning the entire organization toward the customer.—RICHARD WHITELEY

For strategists, there's a trade-off between the breadth and detail of information needed. It's a bit like an eagle hunting for a rabbit. The eagle has to be high enough to scan a wide area in order to enlarge his chances of seeing prey, but he has to be low enough to see the detail—the movement and features that will allow him to recognize his target. Continually making this trade-off is the job of a strategist—it simply can't be delegated.—FREDERICK GLUCK

The best laid schemes of mice and men often go awry.—ROBERT BURNS (paraphrased)

A strategist's job is to see the company not as it is . . . but as it can become.—JOHN W. TEETS, CHAIRMAN OF GREYHOUND, INC.

That business mission is so rarely given adequate thought is perhaps the most important single cause of business frustration.—PETER DRUCKER

This chapter focuses on the concepts and tools needed to evaluate and write business mission statements. A practical framework for developing mission statements is provided. Actual mission statements from large and small organizations and for-profit and nonprofit enterprises are presented and critically examined. The process of creating a mission statement is discussed.

WHAT IS OUR BUSINESS?

Current thought on mission statements is based largely on guidelines set forth in the mid-1970s by Peter Drucker (www.cgs.edu/faculty/druckerp.html), often called "the father of modern management" for his pioneering studies at General Motors Corporation and for his 22 books and hundreds of articles. *Harvard Business Review* calls Drucker, now in his 80s, "the preeminent management thinker of our time."

Drucker says asking the question "What is our business?" is synonymous with asking the question "What is our mission?" An enduring statement of purpose that distinguishes one organization from other similar enterprises, the *mission statement* is a declaration of an organization's "reason for being." It answers the pivotal question, "What is our business?" A clear mission statement is essential for effectively establishing objectives and formulating strategies.

Sometimes called a *creed statement*, a statement of purpose, a statement of philosophy, a statement of beliefs, a statement of business principles, a vision statement, or a statement "defining our business," a mission statement reveals the long-term vision of an organization in terms of what it wants to be and whom it wants to serve. All organizations have a reason for being, even if strategists have not consciously transformed this into writing. As illustrated in Figure 3–1, a carefully prepared statement of mission is widely recognized by both practitioners and academicians as the first step in strategic management.

A business mission is the foundation for priorities, strategies, plans, and work assignments. It is the starting point for the design of managerial jobs and, above all, for the design of managerial structures. Nothing may seem simpler or more obvious than to know what a company's business is. A steel mill makes steel, a railroad runs trains to carry freight and passengers, an insurance company underwrites fire risks, and a bank lends money. Actually, "What is our business?" is almost always a difficult question and the right answer is usually anything but obvious. The answer to this question is the first responsibility of strategists. Only strategists can make sure that this question receives the attention it deserves and that the answer makes sense and enables the business to plot its course and set its objectives.[1]

We can perhaps best understand a business mission by focusing on a business when it is first started. In the beginning, a new business is simply a collection of ideas. Starting a new business rests on a set of beliefs that the new organization can offer some product or service, to some customers, in some geographic area, using some type of technology, at a profitable price. A new business owner typically believes that the management philosophy of the new enterprise will result in a favorable public image and that this concept of the business can be communicated to, and will be adopted by, important constituencies. When the set of beliefs about a business at its inception is put into writing, the resulting document mirrors the same basic ideas that underlie the mission statement. As a business grows, owners or managers find it necessary to revise the founding set of beliefs, but those original ideas usually are reflected in the revised statement of mission.

Business mission statements often can be found in the front of annual reports. Mission statements often are displayed throughout a firm's premises, and they are distributed

FIGURE 3–1
A Comprehensive Strategic-Management Model

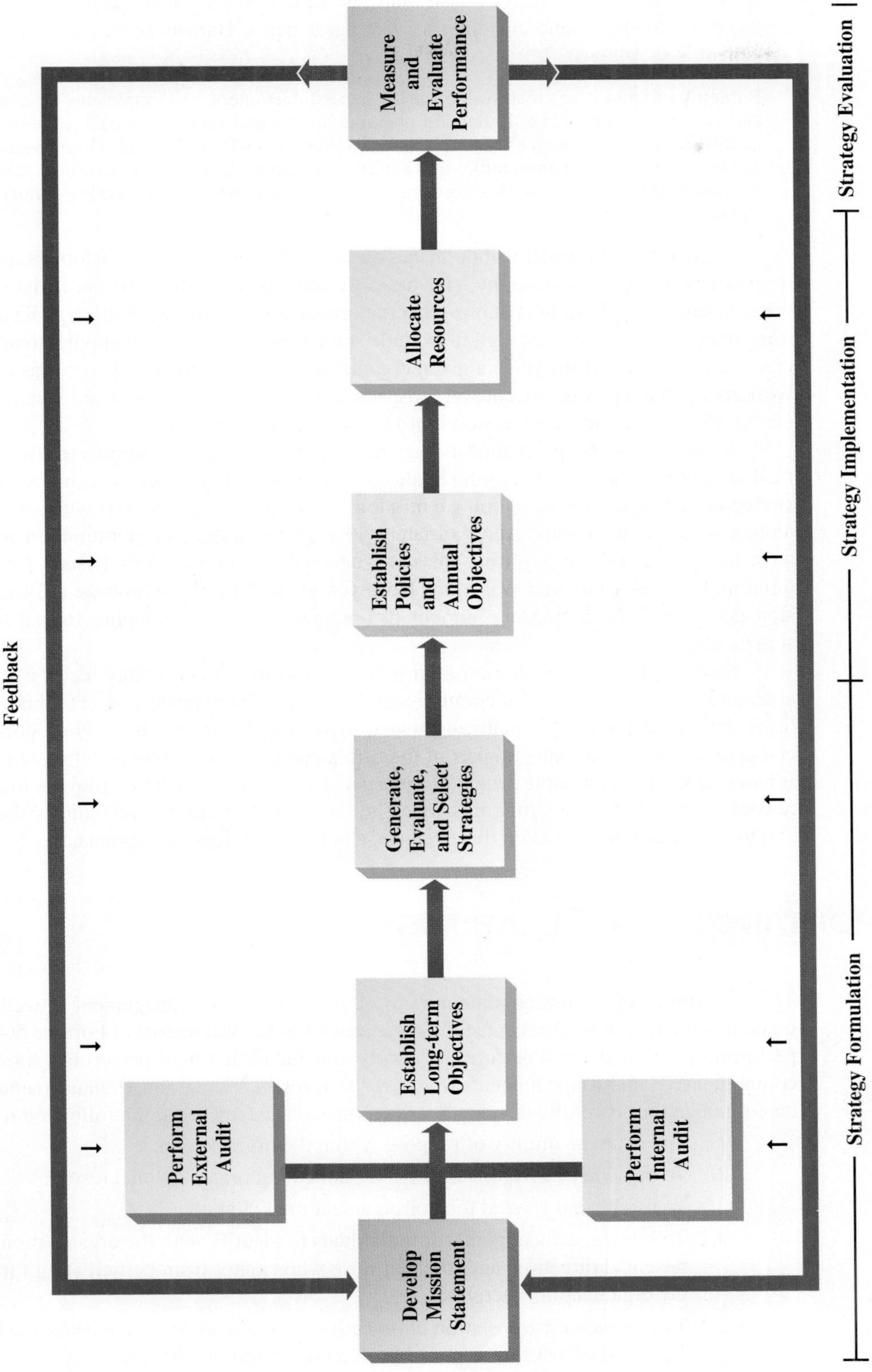

with company information sent to constituencies. The mission statement is a part of numerous internal reports, such as loan requests, supplier agreements, labor relations contracts, business plans, and customer service agreements. Barnett Bank's current mission statement is as follows:

> Barnett's mission is to create value for its owners, customers, and employees by creating and capitalizing on market leadership positions to sell and service a broad range of high quality, profitable financial services. Our sales emphasis will be full service to consumers and businesses in our communities and advisory and processing services to others. We will operate at the lowest possible cost consistent with maintaining high service quality and market leadership.[2]

A good mission statement describes an organization's purpose, customers, products or services, markets, philosophy, and basic technology. According to Vern McGinnis, a mission statement should (1) define what the organization is and what the organization aspires to be, (2) be limited enough to exclude some ventures and broad enough to allow for creative growth, (3) distinguish a given organization from all others, (4) serve as a framework for evaluating both current and prospective activities, and (5) be stated in terms sufficiently clear to be widely understood throughout the organization.[3]

Some strategists spend almost every moment of every day on administrative and tactical concerns, and strategists who rush quickly to establish objectives and implement strategies often overlook developing a mission statement. This problem is widespread even among large organizations. Approximately 40 percent of large corporations in America have not yet developed a formal mission statement, including Walt Disney Company, Grumman Corporation, and Wal-Mart. However, about 60 percent do have a formal mission document.[4] An increasing number of organizations are developing formal mission statements.

Some companies develop mission statements simply because they feel it is fashionable, rather than out of any real commitment. However, as will be described in this chapter, firms that develop and systematically revisit their mission, treat it as a living document, and consider it to be an integral part of the firm's culture realize great benefits. Johnson & Johnson (J&J) is an example firm. J&J managers meet regularly with employees to review, reword, and reaffirm the firm's mission. The entire J&J workforce recognizes the value that top management places on this exercise, and these employees respond accordingly.

THE IMPORTANCE OF A CLEAR MISSION

The importance of a mission statement to effective strategic management is well documented in the literature. A recent study comparing mission statements of Fortune 500 firms performing well and firms performing poorly concluded that high performers have more comprehensive mission statements than low performers.[5] King and Cleland recommend that organizations carefully develop a written mission statement for the following reasons:

1. To ensure unanimity of purpose within the organization.
2. To provide a basis, or standard, for allocating organizational resources.
3. To establish a general tone or organizational climate.
4. To serve as a focal point for individuals to identify with the organization's purpose and direction, and to deter those who cannot from participating further in the organization's activities.
5. To facilitate the translation of objectives into a work structure involving the assignment of tasks to responsible elements within the organization.

6. To specify organizational purposes and the translation of these purposes into objectives in such a way that cost, time, and performance parameters can be assessed and controlled.[6]

Reuben Mark, CEO of Colgate, maintains that a clear mission increasingly must make sense internationally. Colgate's mission can be summarized in five words: "We can be the best." Mark's thoughts on a mission statement are as follows:

> When it comes to rallying everyone to the corporate banner, it's essential to push one vision globally rather than trying to drive home different messages in different cultures. The trick is to keep the vision simple but elevated: "We make the world's fastest computers" or "Telephone service for everyone." You're never going to get anyone to charge the machine guns only for financial objectives. It's got to be something that makes them feel better, feel a part of something.[7]

VISION VERSUS MISSION   Some organizations develop both a mission statement and a vision statement. Whereas the mission statement answers the question "What is our business?" the *vision statement* answers the question "What do we want to become?" Two example companies that have both a mission and vision statement are Amoco Corporation and Harley-Davidson Corporation, as given in Table 3–1.

It can be argued that profit, not mission or vision, is the primary corporate motivator. But profit alone is not enough to motivate people.[8] Profit is perceived negatively by some employees in companies. Employees may see profit as something that they earn and management then uses and even gives away—to shareholders. Although this perception is undesired and disturbing to management, it clearly indicates that both profit and vision are needed to effectively motivate a workforce.

When employees and managers together shape or fashion the vision or mission for a firm, the resultant document can reflect the personal visions that managers and employees have in their hearts and minds about their own futures. Shared vision creates a commonality of interests that can lift workers out of the monotony of daily work and put them into a new world of opportunity and challenge.

THE PROCESS OF DEVELOPING A MISSION STATEMENT   As indicated in the strategic-management model, a clear mission statement is needed before alternative strategies can be formulated and implemented. It is important to involve as many managers as possible in the process of developing a mission statement, because through involvement, people become committed to an organization. Mark's comment about machine guns accents the need for a good mission statement.

A widely used approach to developing a mission statement is first to select several articles about mission statements and ask all managers to read these as background information. Then ask managers themselves to prepare a mission statement for the organization. A facilitator, or committee of top managers, then should merge these statements into a single document and distribute this draft mission statement to all managers. A request for modifications, additions, and deletions is needed next, along with a meeting to revise the document. To the extent that all managers have input into and support the final mission statement document, organizations can more easily obtain managers' support for other strategy formulation, implementation, and evaluation activities. Thus the process of developing a mission statement represents a great opportunity for strategists to obtain needed support from all managers in the firm.

During the process of developing a mission statement, some organizations use discussion groups of managers to develop and modify the mission statement. Some organizations hire an outside consultant or facilitator to manage the process and help draft the language. Sometimes an outside person with expertise in developing mission statements and unbiased views can manage the process more effectively than an internal group or

TABLE 3–1
Two Companies' Mission and Vision Statements

AMOCO CORPORATION (www.amoco.com)

MISSION STATEMENT

Amoco is a worldwide integrated petroleum and chemical company. We find and develop petroleum resources and provide quality products and services for our customers. We conduct our business responsibly to achieve a superior financial return balanced with our long-term growth, benefiting shareholders and fulfilling our commitment to the community and the environment.

VISION STATEMENT

Amoco will be a global business enterprise, recognized throughout the world as preeminent by employees, customers, competitors, investors and the public. We will be the standard by which other businesses measure their performance. Our hallmarks will be the innovation, initiative and teamwork of our people and our ability to anticipate and effectively respond to change and to create opportunity.

HARLEY-DAVIDSON (www.harley-davidson.com)

MISSION STATEMENT

Stay true to the things that make a Harley-Davidson a Harley-Davidson. Keep the heritage alive. From the people in the front office to the craftsmen on our factory floor, that is what we do. And it's why each new generation of Harley-Davidson motorcycles, well refined, contains the best of the ones before it. We have a passion for our product few companies understand. But when you see the result, it all becomes clear. We're not just building motorcycles. We're carrying on a legend. Ask anyone who's ever owned a Harley-Davidson. It gets in your blood. Becomes a part of your life. And once it does, it never leaves. It's something you can't compare with anything else. We know because we've been there. That's why, for 90 years, we've remained firm in our commitment to building the kind of motorcycles that deserve the intense loyalty that Harley-Davidson enjoys. The styling is still pure. The engines still rumble. It's also why you'll see us at major rallies and rides throughout the year, listening and talking to our customers. Staying close to riders and to the sport is how we've kept alive the things that make a Harley-Davidson a Harley-Davidson. Our approach has always been different. But again, so has owning a Harley-Davidson. We wouldn't have it any other way.

VISION STATEMENT

Harley-Davidson, Inc. is an action oriented, international company—a leader in its commitment to continuously improve the quality of profitable relationships with stakeholders (customers, employees, suppliers, shareholders, governments, and society). Harley-Davidson believes the key to success is to balance stakeholders' interests through the empowerment of all employees to focus on value-added activities.

Our Vision is our corporate conscience and helps us to eliminate short-term thinking, such as cashing in on demand for our motorcycles by giving quantity precedence over quality or cutting corners in recreational or commercial vehicles to save a few dollars per unit. It also encourages every employee in our organization to be acutely aware of his or her role in satisfying our stakeholders.

Equally important to our Vision, we live by a Code of Business Conduct that is driven by a value system which promotes honesty, integrity, and personal growth in all our dealings with stakeholders. Our values are the rules by which we operate: Tell the truth; be fair; keep your promises; respect the individual; and encourage intellectual curiosity.

In addition, we never lose sight of the issues we feel must be addressed in order to be successful in the 1990s: Quality, participation, productivity, and cash flow. As a shareholder, you should expect no less from us.

---

committee of managers. Decisions on how best to communicate the mission to all managers, employees, and external constituencies of an organization are needed when the document is in final form. Some organizations even develop a videotape to explain the mission statement and how it was developed.

A recent article by Campbell and Yeung emphasizes that the process of developing a mission statement should create an "emotional bond" and "sense of mission" between the organization and its employees.[9] Commitment to a company's strategy and intellectual agreement on the strategies to be pursued do not necessarily translate into an emotional bond; hence strategies that have been formulated may not be implemented. These researchers stress that an emotional bond comes when an individual personally identifies with the underlying values and behavior of a firm, thus turning intellectual agreement and commitment to strategy into a sense of mission. Campbell and Yeung also differentiate between the terms vision and mission, saying vision is "a possible and desirable future state of an organization" that includes specific goals, whereas mission is more associated with behavior and with the present.

THE NATURE OF A BUSINESS MISSION

A DECLARATION OF ATTITUDE   A mission statement is a declaration of attitude and outlook more than a statement of specific details. It usually is broad in scope for at least two major reasons. First, a good mission statement allows for the generation and consideration of a range of feasible alternative objectives and strategies without unduly stifling management creativity. Excess specificity would limit the potential of creative growth for the organization. On the other hand, an overly general statement that does not exclude any strategy alternatives could be dysfunctional. Apple Computer's mission statement, for example, should not open the possibility for diversification into pesticides, or Ford Motor Company's into food processing. As indicated in the Global Perspective, French mission statements are more general than British mission statements.

Second, a mission statement needs to be broad to effectively reconcile differences among and appeal to an organization's diverse *stakeholders*, the individuals and groups of persons who have a special stake or claim on the company. Stakeholders include employees; managers; stockholders; boards of directors; customers; suppliers; distributors; creditors; governments (local, state, federal, and foreign); unions; competitors; environmental groups; and the general public. Stakeholders affect and are affected by an organization's strategies, yet the claims and concerns of diverse constituencies vary and often conflict. For example, the general public is especially interested in social responsibility, whereas stockholders are more interested in profitability. Claims on any business literally may

GLOBAL PERSPECTIVE
British versus French Mission Statements

Researchers recently studied the mission statements of British and French firms. Results are summarized here.

Researchers found that a highly participative (French) approach to developing a mission statement is more effective in gaining employee commitment than a less participative (British) approach. Differences between British and French statements are rooted in or attributed to different cultural, social, and economic factors in the two countries. For example, in Britain the predominance of equity financing has led to companies frequently being bought and sold like commodities. In contrast, the traditions of family ownership are stronger in France, providing a sense of community and a better basis for development of shared mission statements.

Source: Adapted from "Sharing the Vision: Company Mission Statements in Britain and France," Long Range Planning (February 1994): 84–94.

CHARACTERISTICS OF DOCUMENT	BRITAIN	FRANCE
Length	Short	Long
Specificity	Specific	General
Emphasis	Financial goals	Value to society
Architects	Top managers	All managers and employees
Durability	A year or less	Several years
Focus	Internal	Internal and external

NATURAL ENVIRONMENT

Is Your Firm Environmentally Proactive?

Conducting business in a way that preserves the natural environment is more than just good public relations; it is good business. Preserving the environment is a permanent part of doing business, for the following reasons:

1. Consumer demand for environmentally safe products and packages is high.

2. Public opinion demanding that firms conduct business in ways that preserve the natural environment is strong.

3. Environmental advocacy groups now have over 20 million Americans as members.

4. Federal and state environmental regulations are changing rapidly and becoming more complex.

5. More lenders are examining the environmental liabilities of businesses seeking loans.

6. Many consumers, suppliers, distributors, and investors shun doing business with environmentally weak firms.

7. Liability suits and fines against firms having environment problems are on the rise.

More firms are becoming environmentally proactive, which means they are taking the initiative to develop and implement strategies that preserve the environment while enhancing their efficiency and effectiveness. The old undesirable alternative is to be environmentally reactive—waiting until environmental pressures are thrust upon a firm by law or consumer pressure. A reactive environmental policy often leads to high cleanup costs, numerous liability suits, loss in market share, reduced customer loyalty, and higher medical costs. In contrast, a proactive policy views environmental pressures as opportunities, and includes such actions as developing green products and packages, conserving energy, reducing waste, recycling, and creating a corporate culture that is environmentally sensitive.

A proactive policy forces a company to innovate and upgrade processes; this leads to reduced waste, improved efficiency, better quality, and greater profits. Successful firms today assess "the profit in preserving the environment" in decisions ranging from developing a mission statement to determining plant location, manufacturing technology, product design, packaging, and consumer relations. A proactive environmental policy is simply good business.

Source: Adapted from "The Profit in Preserving America," Forbes (November 11, 1991): 181–189.

number in the thousands, and often include clean air, jobs, taxes, investment opportunities, career opportunities, equal employment opportunities, employee benefits, salaries, wages, clean water, and community services. All stakeholders' claims on an organization cannot be pursued with equal emphasis. A good mission statement indicates the relative attention that an organization will devote to meeting the claims of various stakeholders. More firms are becoming environmentally proactive in response to the concerns of stakeholders.

Reaching the fine balance between specificity and generality is difficult to achieve, but is well worth the effort. George Steiner offers the following insight on the need for a mission statement to be broad in scope:

> Most business statements of mission are expressed at high levels of abstraction. Vagueness nevertheless has its virtues. Mission statements are not designed to express concrete ends, but rather to provide motivation, general direction, an image, a tone, and a philosophy to guide the enterprise. An excess of detail could prove counterproductive since concrete specification could be the base for rallying opposition. Precision might stifle creativity in the formulation of an acceptable mission or purpose. Once an aim is cast in concrete, it creates a rigidity in an organization and resists change. Vagueness leaves room for other managers to fill in the details, perhaps even to modify general patterns. Vagueness permits more flexibility in adapting to changing environments and internal operations. It facilitates flexibility in implementation.[10]

An effective mission statement arouses positive feelings and emotions about an organization; it is inspiring in the sense that it motivates readers to action. An effective mission statement generates the impression that a firm is successful, has direction, and is worthy of time, support, and investment.

It reflects judgments about future growth directions and strategies based upon forward-looking external and internal analyses. A business mission should provide useful criteria for selecting among alternative strategies. A clear mission statement provides a basis for generating and screening strategic options. The statement of mission should be dynamic in orientation, allowing judgments about the most promising growth directions and those considered less promising.

A RESOLUTION OF DIVERGENT VIEWS   What are the reasons some strategists are reluctant to develop a statement of their business mission? First, the question "What is our business?" can create controversy. Raising the question often reveals differences among strategists in the organization. Individuals who have worked together for a long time and who think they know each other suddenly may realize that they are in fundamental disagreement. For example, in a college or university, divergent views regarding the relative importance of teaching, research, and service often are expressed during the mission statement development process. Negotiation, compromise, and eventual agreement on important issues are needed before focusing on more specific strategy formulation activities.

> "What is our mission?" is a genuine decision; and a genuine decision must be based on divergent views to have a chance to be a right and effective decision. Developing a business mission is always a choice between alternatives, each of which rests on different assumptions regarding the reality of the business and its environment. It is always a high-risk decision. A change in mission always leads to changes in objectives, strategies, organization, and behavior. The mission decision is far too important to be made by acclamation. Developing a business mission is a big step toward management effectiveness. Hidden or half-understood disagreements on the definition of a business mission underlie many of the personality problems, communication problems, and irritations that tend to divide a top-management group. Establishing a mission should never be made on plausibility alone, should never be made fast, and should never be made painlessly.[11]

Considerable disagreement among an organization's strategists over basic purpose and mission can cause trouble if not resolved. For example, unresolved disagreement over the business mission was one of the reasons for W. T. Grant's bankruptcy and eventual liquidation. As one executive reported,

> There was a lot of dissension within the company whether we should go the Kmart route or go after the Montgomery Ward and J. C. Penney position. Ed Staley and Lou Lustenberger (two top executives) were at loggerheads over the issue, with the upshot being we took a position between the two and that consequently stood for nothing.[12]

Too often, strategists develop a statement of business mission only when their organization is in trouble. Of course, it is needed then. Developing and communicating a clear mission during troubled times indeed may have spectacular results and even may reverse decline. However, to wait until an organization is in trouble to develop a mission statement is a gamble that characterizes irresponsible management! According to Drucker, the most important time to ask seriously, "What is our business?" is when a company has been successful:

> Success always obsoletes the very behavior that achieved it, always creates new realities, and always creates new and different problems. Only the fairy story ends, "They lived happily ever after." It is never popular to argue with success or to rock the boat. The ancient Greeks knew that the penalty of success can be severe. The management that does not ask, "What is our mission?" when the company is successful is, in effect, smug, lazy, and arrogant. It will not be long before success will turn into failure. Sooner or later, even the most successful answer to the question, "What is our business?" becomes obsolete.[13]

A CUSTOMER ORIENTATION   A good mission statement reflects the anticipations of customers. Rather than developing a product and then trying to find a market, the operating philosophy of organizations should be to identify customers' needs and then provide a product or service to fulfill those needs. Good mission statements identify the utility of a firm's products to its customers. This is why AT&T's mission statement focuses on communication rather than telephones, Exxon's mission statement focuses on energy rather than oil and gas, Union Pacific's mission statement focuses on transportation rather than railroads, and Universal Studios's mission statement focuses on entertainment instead of movies. The following utility statements are relevant in developing a mission statement:

> Do not offer me things.
> Do not offer me clothes. Offer me attractive looks.
> Do not offer me shoes. Offer me comfort for my feet and the pleasure of walking.
> Do not offer me a house. Offer me security, comfort, and a place that is clean and happy.
> Do not offer me books. Offer me hours of pleasure and the benefit of knowledge.
> Do not offer me records. Offer me leisure and the sound of music.
> Do not offer me tools. Offer me the benefit and the pleasure of making beautiful things.
> Do not offer me furniture. Offer me comfort and the quietness of a cozy place.
> Do not offer me things. Offer me ideas, emotions, ambience, feelings, and benefits.
> Please, do not offer me things.

A major reason for developing a business mission is to attract customers who give meaning to an organization. The Information Technology Perspective reveals the top reasons why customers do not purchase products and services over the Internet. A classic description of the purpose of a business reveals the relative importance of customers in a statement of mission:

> It is the customer who determines what a business is. It is the customer alone whose willingness to pay for a good or service converts economic resources into wealth and things into goods. What a business thinks it produces is not of first importance, especially not to the future of the business and to its success. What the customer thinks he/she is buying, what he/she considers value, is decisive—it determines what a business is, what it produces, and whether it

---

INFORMATION TECHNOLOGY

Why People Don't Make Purchases Over the Internet

1. Don't trust payment
   method/security   19.5%
2. No need   14.4%
3. Don't know how   9.3%
4. Prefer store shopping   9.1%
5. Don't have credit card   6.9%
6. Privacy issues   6.7%
7. Nothing worth buying   5.1%

As with automated teller machines (ATMs) of the 1980s and electricity of the 1880s, people are wary of new, complex technology. This is true with the Internet today. Although computer hackers can steal your credit card number if given to purchase goods over the Internet, the fact is that giving your credit card number over the telephone or to a waitress is more risky in terms of it being stolen, used illegally, or intercepted than typing a credit card number into a secure, established Internet site. Although 10 percent of Americans use the Internet regularly today, this percentage is growing dramatically. Sophisticated encryption methods to shield transactions and software to safeguard security are getting better daily, which is spurring more purchases.

Internet businesses actually will have a much harder time calming fears of consumers regarding privacy than about credit card security. Internet sites can regularly monitor your mouse and thus determine what Web pages you call up. Through cross-referencing, they then can determine what type of consumer you are in terms of buying habits. Web site owners can sell this information to advertisers and marketers just as America Online attempted to do recently until its customers threatened boycotts. Internet privacy and security are two key concerns for businesses and individuals today.

Source: Adapted from "Privacy, Security Fears Hinder Acceptance of Internet," USA Today (August 13, 1997): 2B.

will prosper. And what the customer buys and considers value is never a product. It is always utility, meaning what a product or service does for him or her. The customer is the foundation of a business and keeps it in existence.[14]

A DECLARATION OF SOCIAL POLICY The words *social policy* embrace managerial philosophy and thinking at the highest levels of an organization. For this reason, social policy affects the development of a business mission statement. Social issues mandate that strategists consider not only what the organization owes its various stakeholders but also what responsibilities the firm has to consumers, environmentalists, minorities, communities, and other groups. After decades of debate on the topic of social responsibility, many firms still struggle to determine appropriate social policies.

The issue of social responsibility arises when a company establishes its business mission. The impact of society on business and vice versa is becoming more pronounced each year. Social policies directly affect a firm's customers, products and services, markets, technology, profitability, self-concept, and public image. An organization's social policy should be integrated into all strategic-management activities, including the development of a mission statement. Corporate social policy should be designed and articulated during strategy formulation, set and administered during strategy implementation, and reaffirmed or changed during strategy evaluation.[15] The emerging view of social responsibility holds that social issues should be attended to both directly and indirectly in determining strategies.

Firms should strive to engage in social activities that have economic benefits. For example, Merck & Company recently developed the drug ivermectin for treating river blindness, a disease caused by a fly-borne parasitic worm endemic in poor, tropical areas of Africa, the Middle East, and Latin America. In an unprecedented gesture that reflected its corporate commitment to social responsibility, Merck then made ivermectin available at no cost to medical personnel throughout the world. Merck's action highlights the dilemma of orphan drugs, which offer pharmaceutical companies no economic incentive for development and distribution.

Despite differences in approaches, most American companies try to assure outsiders that they conduct business in a socially responsible way. The mission statement is an effective instrument for conveying this message. The Norton Company, for example, concludes its mission statement by saying:

> In order to fulfill this mission, Norton will continue to demonstrate a sense of responsibility to the public interest and to earn the respect and loyalty of its customers, employees, shareholders, and suppliers, and the communities in which it does business.[16]

COMPONENTS OF A MISSION STATEMENT

Mission statements can and do vary in length, content, format, and specificity. Most practitioners and academicians of strategic management consider an effective statement to exhibit nine characteristics or components. Because a mission statement is often the most visible and public part of the strategic-management process, it is important that it includes all of these essential components. Components and corresponding questions that a mission statement should answer are given here.

1. *Customers*: Who are the firm's customers?
2. *Products or services*: What are the firm's major products or services?
3. *Markets*: Geographically, where does the firm compete?
4. *Technology*: Is the firm technologically current?

5. *Concern for survival, growth, and profitability*: Is the firm committed to growth and financial soundness?

6. *Philosophy*: What are the basic beliefs, values, aspirations, and ethical priorities of the firm?

7. *Self-concept*: What is the firm's distinctive competence or major competitive advantage?

8. *Concern for public image*: Is the firm responsive to social, community, and environmental concerns?

9. *Concern for employees*: Are employees a valuable asset of the firm?

Excerpts from the mission statements of different organizations are provided in Table 3–2 to exemplify the nine essential components.

WRITING AND EVALUATING MISSION STATEMENTS

Perhaps the best way to develop a skill for writing and evaluating mission statements is to study actual company missions. Therefore, 11 mission statements are presented in Table 3–3. These statements are then evaluated in Table 3–4 based on the nine criteria presented in the previous section.

There is no one best mission statement for a particular organization, so good judgment is required in evaluating mission statements. In Table 3–4, a *Yes* indicates that the given mission statement answers satisfactorily the question posed in Table 3–3 for the respective evaluative criteria. For example, the *Yes* under customers for the Chase Manhattan mission statement means this statement answers "Who are our customers?" Notice that Chase Manhattan's customers are "individuals, industries, communities, and countries." A *No* would mean a particular mission statement does not answer or answers unsatisfactorily the key question associated with one of the nine evaluative criteria. For example, note that the Apple Computer, AT&T, BellSouth, and Corning mission statements do not identify the organizations' customers. To determine whether a particular statement satisfactorily includes a given component, ask yourself the following question: "If I were responsible for writing a mission statement for this organization, would I have communicated this component better?" If your answer is yes, then record a *No* in the evaluation matrix. Generally, simple inclusion of the word *customers* or *employees* or *technology* is not adequately informative or inspiring in a statement.

Table 3–4 indicates that the Bancorp Hawaii and Chase Manhattan mission statements are the "best" and the Corning mission statement is the "worst" of the examples. Overall, the example mission statements are weakest in the areas of technology; philosophy; and concern for survival, growth, and profitability. The statements are strongest in the areas of products or services, markets, and self-concept.

Let's focus specifically for a moment on the Apple Computer mission statement. Note that the statement does not include coverage of the customer component, which could be individuals, businesses, educational institutions, and governmental agencies. Apple's statement does include the products/services component in saying that Apple provides "exceptional personal computing products and innovative customer services." The statement includes coverage of the market component in saying that Apple helps "people around the world" and includes the technology component in saying that the company finds "innovative ways to use computing technology." No mention of concern for survival, growth, and profitability is given in the statement. Nor is coverage of the philosophy, concern for public image, or concern for employees components. The Apple mission statement includes

TABLE 3–2
Examples of the Nine Essential Components of a Mission Statement

---

1. CUSTOMERS

We believe our first responsibility is to the doctors, nurses, and patients, to mothers and all others who use our products and services. (Johnson & Johnson)

2. PRODUCTS OR SERVICES

AMAX's principal products are molybdenum, coal, iron ore, copper, lead, zinc, petroleum and natural gas, potash, phosphates, nickel, tungsten, silver, gold, and magnesium. (AMAX)
Standard Oil Company (Indiana) is in business to find and produce crude oil, natural gas, and natural gas liquids; to manufacture high-quality products useful to society from these raw materials; and to distribute and market those products and to provide dependable related services to the consuming public at reasonable prices. (Standard Oil Company)

3. MARKETS

We are dedicated to the total success of Corning Glass Works as a worldwide competitor. (Corning Glass Works)
Our emphasis is on North American markets, although global opportunities will be explored. (Blockway)

4. TECHNOLOGY

Control Data is in the business of applying micro-electronics and computer technology in two general areas: computer-related hardware; and computing-enhancing services, which include computation, information, education, and finance. (Control Data)
The common technology in these areas is discrete particle coatings. (Nashua)

5. CONCERN FOR SURVIVAL, GROWTH, AND PROFITABILITY

In this respect, the company will conduct its operations prudently, and will provide the profits and growth which will assure Hoover's ultimate success. (Hoover Universal)
To serve the worldwide need for knowledge at a fair profit by gathering, evaluating, producing, and distributing valuable information in a way that benefits our customers, employees, authors, investors, and our society. (McGraw-Hill)

6. PHILOSOPHY

We believe human development to be the worthiest of the goals of civilization and independence to be the superior condition for nurturing growth in the capabilities of people. (Sun Company)
It's all part of the Mary Kay philosophy—a philosophy based on the golden rule. A spirit of sharing and caring where people give cheerfully of their time, knowledge, and experience. (Mary Kay Cosmetics)

7. SELF-CONCEPT

Crown Zellerbach is committed to leapfrogging competition within 1,000 days by unleashing the constructive and creative abilities and energies of each of its employees. (Crown Zellerbach)

8. CONCERN FOR PUBLIC IMAGE

To share the world's obligation for the protection of the environment. (Dow Chemical)
To contribute to the economic strength of society and function as a good corporate citizen on a local, state, and national basis in all countries in which we do business. (Pfizer)

9. CONCERN FOR EMPLOYEES

To recruit, develop, motivate, reward, and retain personnel of exceptional ability, character, and dedication by providing good working conditions, superior leadership, compensation on the basis of performance, an attractive benefit program, opportunity for growth, and a high degree of employment security. (The Wachovia Corporation)
To compensate its employees with remuneration and fringe benefits competitive with other employment opportunities in its geographical area and commensurate with their contributions toward efficient corporate operations. (Public Service Electric and Gas Company)

---

coverage of self-concept by mentioning education, which is a segment of the industry that Apple does especially well. Overall, the Apple statement includes only three of the nine essential mission statement components.

In multidivisional organizations, strategists should ensure that divisional units perform strategic-management tasks, including the development of a statement of mission.

TABLE 3–3
Mission Statements of Eleven Organizations

AMERICAN HOME PRODUCTS (www.ahp.com)

American Home Products Corporation makes a significant contribution to health care worldwide as a leader in researching, developing, manufacturing and marketing products that meet important health needs.

Our prescription drugs, nutritionals, over-the-counter medications, and medical devices, supplies and instrumentation benefit millions of people. We also produce and market well-known quality food brands in the United States and Canada.

We are focused on improving health care by finding and commercializing innovative, cost-effective therapies and technologies. Key to our efforts are efficient manufacturing, global distribution and marketing, and strict financial controls.

In 1992, American Home Products Corporation achieved record sales and earnings, and the company increased its dividend for the 41st consecutive year.

PFIZER, INC. (www.pfizer.com/main.html)

Pfizer, Inc. is a research-based, global health care company. Our principal mission is to apply scientific knowledge to help people around the world enjoy longer, healthier and more productive lives. The company has four business segments: health care, consumer health care, food science and animal health. We manufacture in 39 countries, and our products are available worldwide.

CHASE MANHATTAN CORPORATION (www.chase.com)

We provide financial services that enhance the well-being and success of individuals, industries, communities and countries around the world.

Through our shared commitment to those we serve, we will be the best financial services company in the world.

Customers will choose us first because we deliver the highest quality service and performance.

People will be proud and eager to work here.

Investors will buy our stock as a superior long-term investment.

To be the best for our customers, we are team players who show respect for our colleagues and commit to the highest standards of quality and professionalism.

Customer focus
Respect for each other
Teamwork
Quality
Professionalism

FOOD LION, INC. (www.foodlion.com)

The Food Lion team will work hard to use our *talents* and *resourcefulness* to satisfy every customer by providing Extra Low Prices on a wide variety of quality products in a *clean*, *convenient*, and *friendly* environment.

APPLE COMPUTER (www.apple.com)

It is Apple's mission to help transform the way customers work, learn and communicate by providing exceptional personal computing products and innovative customer services.

We will pioneer new directions and approaches, finding innovative ways to use computing technology to extend the bounds of human potential.

Apple will make a difference: our products, services and insights will help people around the world shape the ways business and education will be done in the 21st century.

AT&T (www.att.com)

We are dedicated to being the world's best at bringing people together—giving them easy access to each other and to the information and services they want—anytime, anywhere.

BANCORP HAWAII, INC. (www.boh.com/news/970220.html)

The mission of Bancorp Hawaii is to be the finest, most effective financial services organization in the state of Hawaii and the Pacific markets we serve.

As a family of companies built around an outstanding regional bank, we will sell and deliver a broad range of services that meet the needs of our customers at prices which are competitive and consistent with our profit goals.

Our basic business strategy is to identify, understand and then satisfy the financial needs and wants of consumers, businesses, and governments. We will be alert to changes which impact our businesses and exercise initiative to capitalize on new opportunities.

The geographic scope of our business will be expanded only to areas where our unique background, experience and capabilities will give us a competitive advantage and a reasonable opportunity for an adequate financial return. We will introduce only those new financial services which we can perform well.

continued

TABLE 3–3 *continued*

Two primary goals are to achieve significant reductions in noninterest expense through enhanced productivity and automation and to increase noninterest income by marketing fee-based services.

We want to conduct our business under conditions largely determined by ourselves and will, therefore, always maintain a strong financial position. Our goal is to consistently rank among the top 10 percent of our peer group in terms of financial performance. This will ensure that we will fulfill our responsibility to increase the value of our shareholders' investment.

We will maintain a stimulating work environment—one that encourages, recognizes, and rewards high achievers, at all levels of the organization.

We will always conduct ourselves with integrity and endeavor to be a good neighbor and a responsible corporate citizen.

BELLSOUTH CORPORATION (www.bellsouth.com)

BellSouth Corporation provides information services in local exchange and exchange access markets in its nine-state franchised territory. It also provides communications services and products such as advertising and publishing, mobile cellular telephone service, paging, and telecommunications and computer systems through its entities, in both the nine-state region and other major U.S. and international markets.

CORNING, INC. (www.corning.com)

Our purpose is to deliver superior, long-range economic benefits to our customers, our employees, our shareholders, and to the communities in which we operate. We accomplish this by living our corporate values.

NICHOLLS STATE UNIVERSITY (COLLEGE OF BUSINESS) (www.server.nich.edu/~nsu)

The principal mission of the College of Business is to prepare students to participate in society and the work force as educated individuals able to compete in a dynamic global economy. In order to enrich the learning process, the College also contributes to scholarship through applied research and instructional development. In addition to providing support to the employer community through the development of marketable skills in potential employees, the College also enhances the competitive capabilities of regional businesses by providing continuing education courses and consulting services through the Small Business Development Center (SBDC) and the individual efforts of faculty. The faculty advances the welfare of the University, the community, and academic and professional organizations through professional interactions.

SAM HOUSTON STATE UNIVERSITY (COLLEGE OF BUSINESS ADMINISTRATION) (www.shsu.edu)

The mission of the College of Business Administration is to support Sam Houston State University's mission by providing students with the educational experience in the field of business necessary to become productive citizens, to develop successful business-related careers and to provide interested students with the background necessary to pursue advanced studies in the field of business and related fields. The educational experience at the undergraduate and master's levels is designed to provide students with the intellectual flexibility to be successful in a dynamic business environment.

The highest priority of the College of Business Administration is teaching, primarily at the undergraduate level. In addition, the College encourages faculty professional development, scholarly productivity, and service to benefit all stakeholders: students, alumni, donors, regional businesses, and the State of Texas.

Each division should involve its own managers and employees in developing a mission statement consistent with and supportive of the corporative mission. Anchor Hocking is an example of a multinational organization that has developed an overall corporate mission statement and a statement for each of its eight divisions. Notice that the Nicholls State and Sam Houston State mission statements that are given in Table 3–3 are for those in situations at the College of Business rather than in the university at large.

An organization that fails to develop a comprehensive and inspiring mission statement loses the opportunity to present itself favorably to existing and potential stakeholders. All organizations need customers, employees, and managers, and most firms need creditors, suppliers, and distributors. The business mission statement is an effective vehicle for communicating with important internal and external stakeholders. The principal value of a mission statement as a tool of strategic management is derived from its specification of the ultimate aims of a firm:

It provides managers with a unity of direction that transcends individual, parochial, and transitory needs. It promotes a sense of shared expectations among all levels and generations of

TABLE 3–4
An Evaluation Matrix of Mission Statements

	EVALUATIVE CRITERIA				
COMPANY	CUSTOMERS	PRODUCTS/ SERVICES	MARKETS	CONCERN FOR SURVIVAL, GROWTH, AND PROFITABILITY	TECHNOLOGY
American Home Products	Yes	Yes	Yes	Yes	Yes
Pfizer, Inc.	Yes	Yes	Yes	No	No
Chase Manhattan Corporation	Yes	Yes	Yes	No	Yes
Food Lion, Inc.	Yes	No	No	No	No
Apple Computer	No	No	Yes	Yes	No
AT&T	No	No	Yes	No	No
Bancorp Hawaii, Inc.	Yes	Yes	Yes	No	Yes
BellSouth Corporation	No	Yes	Yes	No	No
Corning, Inc.	No	No	No	No	No
Nicholls State University	Yes	Yes	No	No	No
Sam Houston State University	Yes	Yes	Yes	No	No

COMPANY	PHILOSOPHY	SELF-CONCEPT	CONCERN FOR PUBLIC IMAGE	CONCERN FOR EMPLOYEES
American Home Products	No	Yes	No	No
Pfizer, Inc.	No	No	No	No
Chase Manhattan Corporation	Yes	Yes	Yes	Yes
Food Lion, Inc.	No	Yes	No	No
Apple Computer	No	Yes	No	No
AT&T	No	Yes	No	No
Bancorp Hawaii, Inc.	Yes	Yes	Yes	Yes
BellSouth Corporation	No	No	No	No
Corning, Inc.	Yes	No	Yes	Yes
Nicholls State University	No	Yes	Yes	Yes
Sam Houston State University	No	Yes	Yes	Yes

employees. It consolidates values over time and across individuals and interest groups. It projects a sense of worth and intent that can be identified and assimilated by company outsiders. Finally, it affirms the company's commitment to responsible action, which is symbiotic with its need to preserve and protect the essential claims of insiders for sustained survival, growth, and profitability of the firm.[17]

CONCLUSION

Every organization has a unique purpose and reason for being. This uniqueness should be reflected in a statement of mission. The nature of a business mission can represent either a competitive advantage or disadvantage for the firm. An organization achieves a heightened sense of purpose when strategists, managers, and employees develop and communicate a clear business mission. Drucker says developing a clear business mission is the "first responsibility of strategists." A good mission statement reveals an organization's customers, products or services, markets, technology, concern for survival, philosophy, self-concept, concern for public image, and concern for employees. These nine basic components serve as a practical framework for evaluating and writing mission statements. As the first step in strategic management, the mission statement provides direction for all planning activities.

A well-designed mission statement is essential for formulating, implementing, and evaluating strategy. Developing and communicating a clear business mission is one of the most commonly overlooked tasks in strategic management. Without a clear statement of mission, a firm's short-term actions can be counterproductive to long-term interests. A mission statement always should be subject to revision but, if carefully prepared, it will require major changes only infrequently. Organizations usually reexamine their mission statement annually. Effective mission statements stand the test of time.

A mission statement is an essential tool for strategists, a fact illustrated in a short story told by Porsche CEO Peter Schultz:

> Three people were at work on a construction site. All were doing the same job, but when each was asked what his job was, the answers varied. "Breaking rocks," the first replied, "Earning a living," responded the second. "Helping to build a cathedral," said the third. Few of us can build cathedrals. But to the extent we can see the cathedral in whatever cause we are following, the job seems more worthwhile. Good strategists and a clear mission help us find those cathedrals in what otherwise could be dismal issues and empty causes.[18]

We invite you to visit the DAVID page on the Prentice Hall Web site at
www.prenhall.com/davidsm
for this chapter's World Wide Web exercise.

TAKE IT TO THE NET

KEY TERMS AND CONCEPTS

Concern for Employees	(p. 90)	Markets	(p. 89)	Self-Concept	(p. 90)
Concern for Public Image	(p. 90)	Mission Statement	(p. 80)	Social Policy	(p. 89)
Concern for Survival, Growth,		Mission Statement Components	(p. 89)	Stakeholders	(p. 85)
and Profitability	(p. 90)	Philosophy	(p. 90)	Technology	(p. 89)
Creed Statement	(p. 80)	Products or Services	(p. 89)	Vision Statement	(p. 83)
Customers	(p. 89)				

ISSUES FOR REVIEW AND DISCUSSION

1. Do local service stations need to have written mission statements? Why or why not?

2. Why do you think organizations that have a comprehensive mission tend to be high performers? Does having a comprehensive mission cause high performance?

3. Explain why a mission statement should not include strategies and objectives.

4. What is your college or university's self-concept? How would you state that in a mission statement?

5. Explain the principal value of a mission statement.

6. Why is it important for a mission statement to be reconciliatory?

7. In your opinion, what are the three most important components to include in writing a mission statement? Why?

8. How would the mission statements of a for-profit and a nonprofit organization differ?

9. Write a business mission statement for an organization of your choice.

10. Go to your nearest library and look in the annual reports of corporations. Find a mission statement, make a photocopy of the document, bring the copy to class, and evaluate the document.

11. Who are the major stakeholders of the bank that you do business with locally? What are the major claims of those stakeholders?

12. Select one of the current readings at the end of this chapter. Look up that article in your college library and give a 5-minute oral report to the class summarizing the article.

NOTES

1. Peter Drucker, *Management: Tasks, Responsibilities, and Practices* (New York: Harper & Row, 1974): 61.

2. Barnett Bank, Internal document (1993).

3. Vern McGinnis, "The Mission Statement: A Key Step in Strategic Planning," *Business* 31, no. 6 (November–December 1981): 41.

4. Fred David, "How Companies Define Their Mission," *Long Range Planning* 22, no. 1 (February 1989): 90–92. Also, see John Pearce II and Fred David, "Corporate Mission Statements: The Bottom Line," *Academy of Management Executive* 1, no. 2 (May 1987): 110.

5. Pearce and David, 110.

6. W. R. King and D. I. Cleland, *Strategic Planning and Policy* (New York: Van Nostrand Reinhold, 1979): 124.

7. Brian Dumaine, "What the Leaders of Tomorrow See," *Fortune* (July 3, 1989): 50.

8. Joseph Quigley, "Vision: How Leaders Develop It, Share It and Sustain It," *Business Horizons* (September–October 1994): 39.

9. Andrew Campbell and Sally Yeung, "Creating a Sense of Mission," *Long Range Planning* 24, no. 4 (August 1991): 17.

10. George Steiner, *Strategic Planning: What Every Manager Must Know* (New York: The Free Press, 1979): 160.

11. Drucker, 78, 79.

12. "How W. T. Grant Lost $175 Million Last Year," *Business Week* (February 25, 1975): 75.

13. Drucker, 88.

14. Drucker, 61.

15. Archie Carroll and Frank Hoy, "Integrating Corporate Social Policy into Strategic Management," *Journal of Business Strategy* 4, no. 3 (Winter 1984): 57.

16. The Norton Company, *Annual Report* (1981).

17. John Pearce II, "The Company Mission as a Strategic Tool," *Sloan Management Review* 23, no. 3 (Spring 1982): 74.

18. Robert Waterman, Jr., *The Renewal Factor: How the Best Get and Keep the Competitive Edge* (New York: Bantam, 1987). Also, *Business Week* (September 14, 1987): 120.

CURRENT READINGS

Baetz, Mark C. and Christopher K. Bart. "Developing Mission Statements Which Work." *Long Range Planning* 29, no. 4 (August 1996): 526–533.

Bartlett, Christopher A. and Sumantra Ghoshal. "Changing the Role of Top Management: Beyond Strategy to Purpose." *Harvard Business Review* (November–December 1994): 79–90.

Brabet, Julienne and Mary Klemm. "Sharing the Vision: Company Mission Statements in Britain and France." *Long Range Planning* (February 1994): 84–94.

Collins, James C. and Jerry I. Porras. "Building a Visionary Company." *California Management Review* 37, no. 2 (Winter 1995): 80–100.

Collins, James C. and Jerry I. Porras. "Building Your Company's Vision." *Harvard Business Review* (September–October 1996): 65–78.

Cummings, Stephen and John Davies. "Brief Case—Mission, Vision, Fusion." *Long Range Planning* 27, no. 6 (December 1994): 147–150.

Davies, Stuart W. and Keith W. Glaister. "Business School Mission Statements—The Bland Leading the Bland?" *Long Range Planning* 30, no. 4 (August 1997): 594–604.

Gratton, Lynda. "Implementing a Strategic Vision—Key Factors for Success." *Long Range Planning* 29, no. 3 (June 1996): 290–303.

Graves, Samuel B. and Sandra A. Waddock. "Institutional Owners and Corporate Social Performance." *Academy of Management Journal* 37, no. 4 (August 1994): 1034–1046.

Hemphill, Thomas A. "Legislating Corporate Social Responsibility." *Business Horizons* 40, no. 2 (March–April 1997): 53–63.

Larwood, Laurie, Cecilia M. Falbe, Mark P. Kriger, and Paul Miesing. "Structure and Meaning of Organizational Vision." *Academy of Management Journal* 38, no. 3 (June 1995): 740–769.

McTavish, Ron. "One More Time: What Business Are You In?" *Long Range Planning* 28, no. 2 (April 1995): 49–60.

Osborne, Richard L. "Strategic Values: The Corporate Performance Engine." *Business Horizons* 39, no. 5 (September–October 1996): 41–47.

Oswald, S. L., K. W. Mossholder, and S. G. Harris. "Vision Salience and Strategic Involvement: Implications for Psychological Attachment to Organization and Job." *Strategic Management Journal* 15, no. 6 (July 1994): 477–490.

Snyder, Neil H. and Michelle Graves. "The Editor's Chair/Leadership and Vision." *Business Horizons* 37, no. 1 (January–February 1994): 1–7.

Swanson, Diane L. "Addressing a Theoretical Problem by Reorienting the Corporate Social Performance Model." *Academy of Management Review* 20, no. 1 (January 1995): 43–64.

EVALUATING MISSION STATEMENTS

PURPOSE

A business mission statement is an integral part of strategic management. It provides direction for formulating, implementing, and evaluating strategic activities. This exercise will give you practice evaluating mission statements, a skill that is prerequisite to writing a good mission statement.

INSTRUCTIONS

Step 1 Your instructor will select some or all of the following mission statements to evaluate. On a separate sheet of paper, construct an evaluation matrix like the one presented in Table 3–4. Evaluate the mission statements based on the nine criteria presented in the chapter.

Step 2 Record a *yes* in appropriate cells of the evaluation matrix when the respective mission statement satisfactorily meets the desired criteria. Record a *no* in appropriate cells when the respective mission statement does not meet the stated criteria.

MISSION STATEMENTS

Carolina Power & Light Company (www.cplc.com)   It is the mission of the Carolina Power & Light Company to provide the best service to present and future customers at the lowest rates consistent with fair compensation to employees, a fair return to those who have invested in the Company, safety for employees and the public, reasonable protection of the environment, and the development of technology to provide future service. Through the development and contribution of all employees, to the maximum of their potential, the Company will assure total quality performance that results in the highest achievable levels of customer satisfaction and recognition for excellence.

Stetson University (www.stetson.edu)   The mission at Stetson University is to provide an excellent education in an intellectually challenging and collaborative learning community. We pursue excellence through superior teaching, close student-faculty interaction, creative and scholarly activity, and programs solidly grounded in liberal learning. We seek academically talented students with leadership potential and records of personal growth and community service. We prepare them for rewarding careers, selective graduate and professional programs, and a lifetime of learning. Building on Stetson's Christian tradition, we pursue truth in an open and caring environment that is socially and religiously diverse. The University encourages all members of its community to be morally sensitive and effective citizens committed to active forms of social responsibility.

CSX Corporation (www.csx.com)   CSX is a transportation company committed to being a leader in railroad, inland water, and containerized distribution markets.

To attract the human and financial resources necessary to achieve this leadership position, CSX will support our three major constituencies:

For our customers, we will work as a partner to provide excellent service and meet all agreed-upon commitments. For our employees, we will create a work environment that motivates and allows them to grow and develop and perform their jobs to the maximum of their capacity.

For our shareholders, we will meet our goals to provide them with sustainable superior returns.

University of North Carolina at Chapel Hill (www.unc.edu) The University of North Carolina at Chapel Hill has been built by the people of the state and has existed for two centuries as the nation's first state university. Through its excellent undergraduate programs, it has provided higher education to ten generations of students, many of whom have become leaders of the State and the nation. Since the nineteenth century it has offered distinguished graduate and professional programs.

The university is a research university. Fundamental to this designation is a faculty actively involved in research, scholarship, and creative work, whose teaching is transformed by discovery and whose service is informed by current knowledge.

The mission of the university is to serve all the people of the state, and indeed the nation, as a center for scholarship and creative endeavor. The university exists to expand the body of knowledge; to teach students at all levels in an environment of research, free inquiry, and personal responsibility; to improve the condition of human life through service and publication; and to enrich our culture.

To fulfill this mission, the university must

Acquire, discover, preserve, synthesize, and transmit knowledge.

Provide high quality undergraduate instruction to students within a community engaged in original inquiry and creative expression, while committed to intellectual freedom, to personal integrity and justice, and to those values that foster enlightened leadership for the state and the nation.

Provide graduate and professional programs of national distinction at the doctoral and other advanced levels to future generations of research scholars, educators, professionals, and informed citizens.

Extend knowledge-based services and other resources of the university to the citizens of North Carolina and their institutions to enhance the quality of life for all people in the State.

Address, as appropriate, regional, national, and international needs.

This mission imposes special responsibilities upon the faculty, students, staff, administration, trustees, and other governance structures and constituencies of the university in their service and decision-making on behalf of the university.

Federal Express (www.fedex.com) Federal Express is committed to our people-service-profit philosophy. We will produce outstanding financial returns by providing totally reliable, competitively superior global air-ground transportation of high-priority goods and documents that require rapid, time-certain delivery. Equally important, positive control of each package will be maintained utilizing real-time electronic tracking and tracing systems. A complete record of each shipment and delivery will be presented with our request for payment. We will be helpful, courteous, and professional to each other and the public. We will strive to have a satisfied customer at the end of each transaction.

Experiential Exercise 3B

WRITING A MISSION STATEMENT FOR HERSHEY FOODS

PURPOSE

There is no one best mission statement for a given organization. Analysts feel that the Hershey mission statement provided in the Cohesion Case can be improved. Writing a mission statement that includes desired components—and at the same time is inspiring and reconciliatory—requires careful thought. Mission statements should not be too lengthy; statements under 200 words are desirable.

INSTRUCTIONS

Step 1 Take 15 minutes to write a mission statement for Hershey Foods that does not exceed 200 words. Scan the case for needed details as you prepare your mission statement.

Step 2 Join with three other classmates to form a group of four people. Read each other's mission statements silently. As a group, select the best of your group's mission statements.

Step 3 Read that best mission statement to the class.

Experiential Exercise 3C

WRITING A MISSION STATEMENT FOR MY UNIVERSITY

PURPOSE

Most universities have a mission statement, as indicated by the examples provided in this chapter. The purpose of this exercise is to give you practice writing a mission statement for a nonprofit organization such as your own university.

INSTRUCTIONS

Step 1 Take 15 minutes to write a mission statement for your university. Your statement should not exceed 200 words.

Step 2 Read your mission statement to the class.

Step 3 Determine whether your institution has a mission statement. Look in the front of the college handbook. If your institution has a written statement, contact an appropriate administrator of the institution to inquire as to how and when the statement was prepared. Share this information with the class. Analyze your college's mission statement in light of concepts presented in this chapter.

Experiential Exercise 3D

CONDUCTING MISSION STATEMENT RESEARCH

PURPOSE

This exercise gives you the opportunity to study the nature and role of mission statements in strategic management.

INSTRUCTIONS

Step 1 Call various organizations in your city or county to identify firms that have developed a formal mission statement. Contact nonprofit organizations and government agencies in addition to small and large businesses. Ask to speak with the director, owner, or chief executive officer of one organization. Explain that you are studying mission statements in class and are conducting research as part of a class activity.

Step 2 Ask several executives the following four questions and record their answers.
   1. When did your organization first develop a formal mission statement? Who was primarily responsible for its development?

2. How long has your current mission statement existed? When was it last modi-fied? Why was it modified at that point in time?
3. By what process is your firm's mission statement altered?
4. How is your mission statement used in the firm? How does it affect the firm's strategic-planning process?

Step 3 Provide an overview of your findings to the class.

Experiential Exercise 3E

ARE MISSION STATEMENTS ESOTERIC?

PURPOSE

Some large American corporations have publicly denounced the importance of having a clear mission. Louis Gerstner, CEO of IBM, recently said, "The last thing IBM needs now is a vision." Robert Eaton, CEO of Chrysler, recently said, "Internally we don't use the word vision (mission). I believe in quantifiable short-term results—things we can all relate to—as opposed to some esoteric thing no one can quantify." Bill Gates, CEO of Microsoft Corporation, recently said, "Being a visionary (concerned with mission) is trivial." Douglas Lavin of *The Wall Street Journal* recently said, "Vision (mission) may not exactly be dead in corporate America, but a surprising number of CEOs are casting aside their crystal balls to concentrate on the nuts-and-bolts of running their businesses in these leaner times; CEOs whose notion of vision (mission) is a sharp eye on the bottom line include Ronald Compton at Aetna Life & Casualty and John Smith, Jr., at General Motors."

This exercise is adapted from "Robert Eaton Thinks 'Vision' Is Overrated and He's Not Alone," *The Wall Street Journal* (Oct. 4, 1993): A1, A8.

INSTRUCTIONS

Step 1 Decide whether you agree or disagree with the CEO comments cited above. Do you agree with these persons that mission statements are esoteric or a matter for crystal balls? Discuss this issue with several local business executives.

Step 2 Write a 2-page essay explaining your personal views regarding the importance of mission statements.

Step 3 Summarize your views in a 1-minute presentation to the class.

The External Assessment

CHAPTER OUTLINE

CHAPTER OBJECTIVES

After studying this chapter, you should be able to do the following:

1. Describe how to conduct an external strategic-management audit.

2. Discuss 10 major external forces that affect organizations: economic, social, cultural, demo-graphic, environmental, political, governmental, legal, technological, and competitive.

3. Identify key sources of external information, including the Internet.

4. Discuss important forecasting tools used in strategic management.

5. Discuss the importance of monitoring external trends and events.

6. Explain how to develop an EFE Matrix.

7. Explain how to develop a Competitive Profile Matrix.

8. Discuss the importance of gathering competitive intelligence.

9. Describe the trend toward cooperation among competitors.

NOTABLE
QUOTES

*I*f you're not faster than your competitor, you're in a tenuous position, and if you're only half as fast, you're terminal.—GEORGE SALK

*P*ositive trends in the environment breed complacency. That underscores a basic point: In change there is both opportunity and challenge.—CLIFTON GARVIN

*T*he opportunities and threats existing in any situation always exceed the resources needed to exploit the opportunities or avoid the threats. Thus, strategy is essentially a problem of allocating resources. If strategy is to be successful, it must allocate superior resources against a decisive opportunity.—WILLIAM COHEN

*O*rganizations pursue strategies that will disrupt the normal course of industry events and forge new industry conditions to the disadvantage of competitors.—IAN C. MACMILLAN

*T*he idea is to concentrate our strength against our competitor's relative weakness.—BRUCE HENDERSON

*T*here was a time in America when business was easier. We set the pace for the rest of the world. We were immune to serious foreign competition. Many of us were regulated therefore protected. No longer. Today's leaders must recreate themselves and their ways of doing business in order to stay on top and stay competitive.—ROBERT H. WATERMAN, JR.

*C*ompetitive strategy must grow out of a sophisticated understanding of the rules of competition that determine an industry's attractiveness.—MICHAEL PORTER

*T*he main reason for Japan's industrial might is that Japan leads the world in devising ways of creating products derived from basic technologies. America is by no means lacking in technology. But it does lack the creativity to apply new technologies commercially. This is America's biggest problem. On the other hand, it is Japan's strongest point.—AKIO MORITA

*"W*ith the rise of the Internet, a broad shift is underway to a culture that values collaboration and community—attributes more hospitable to women. Ted Leonsis, president of AOL's content division, says the numbers prove this trend: AOL's female membership has grown from 18 percent to 45 percent in the past 2 years."[1]

This chapter examines the tools and concepts needed to conduct an external strategic-management audit (sometimes called *environmental scanning* or *industry analysis*). An *external audit* focuses on identifying and evaluating trends and events beyond the control of a single firm, such as increased foreign competition, population shifts to the Sunbelt, an aging society, information technology, and the computer revolution. An external audit reveals key opportunities and threats confronting an organization so that managers can formulate strategies to take advantage of the opportunities and avoid or reduce the impact of threats. This chapter presents a practical framework for gathering, assimilating, and analyzing external information.

THE NATURE OF AN EXTERNAL AUDIT

The purpose of an external audit is to develop a finite list of opportunities that could benefit a firm and threats that should be avoided. As the term *finite* suggests, the external audit is not aimed at developing an exhaustive list of every possible factor that could influence the business; rather, it is aimed at identifying key variables that offer actionable responses. Firms should be able to respond either offensively or defensively to the factors by formulating strategies that take advantage of external opportunities or that minimize the impact of potential threats. Figure 4–1 illustrates how the external audit fits into the strategic-management process.

KEY EXTERNAL FORCES   *External forces* can be divided into five broad categories: (1) economic forces; (2) social, cultural, demographic, and environmental forces; (3) political, governmental, and legal forces; (4) technological forces; and (5) competitive forces. Relationships among these forces and an organization are depicted in Figure 4–2. External trends and events significantly affect all products, services, markets, and organizations in the world.

Changes in external forces translate into changes in consumer demand for both industrial and consumer products and services. External forces affect the types of products developed, the nature of positioning and market segmentation strategies, the types of services offered, and the choice of businesses to acquire or sell. External forces directly affect both suppliers and distributors. Identifying and evaluating external opportunities and threats enables organizations to develop a clear mission, to design strategies to achieve long-term objectives, and to develop policies to achieve annual objectives.

Some organizations survive solely because they recognize and take advantage of external opportunities. For example, Larson Company in Tucson, Arizona, has capitalized upon the growing concern for our natural environment by creating naturalistic environments for zoos, aquariums, shopping centers, amusement parks, and resort hotels. Larson's sales have grown dramatically to over $20 million annually. Larson contends that large, flashy nature exhibits are a big tourist draw. The new Mirage hotel and casino in Las Vegas, for example, attributes its success to the extensive use of artificial environments, ranging from a giant aquarium behind the registration desk to a 60-foot-high volcano outside the hotel.

The increasing complexity of business today is evidenced by more countries' developing the capacity and will to compete aggressively in world markets. Foreign businesses and countries are willing to learn, adapt, innovate, and invent to compete successfully in

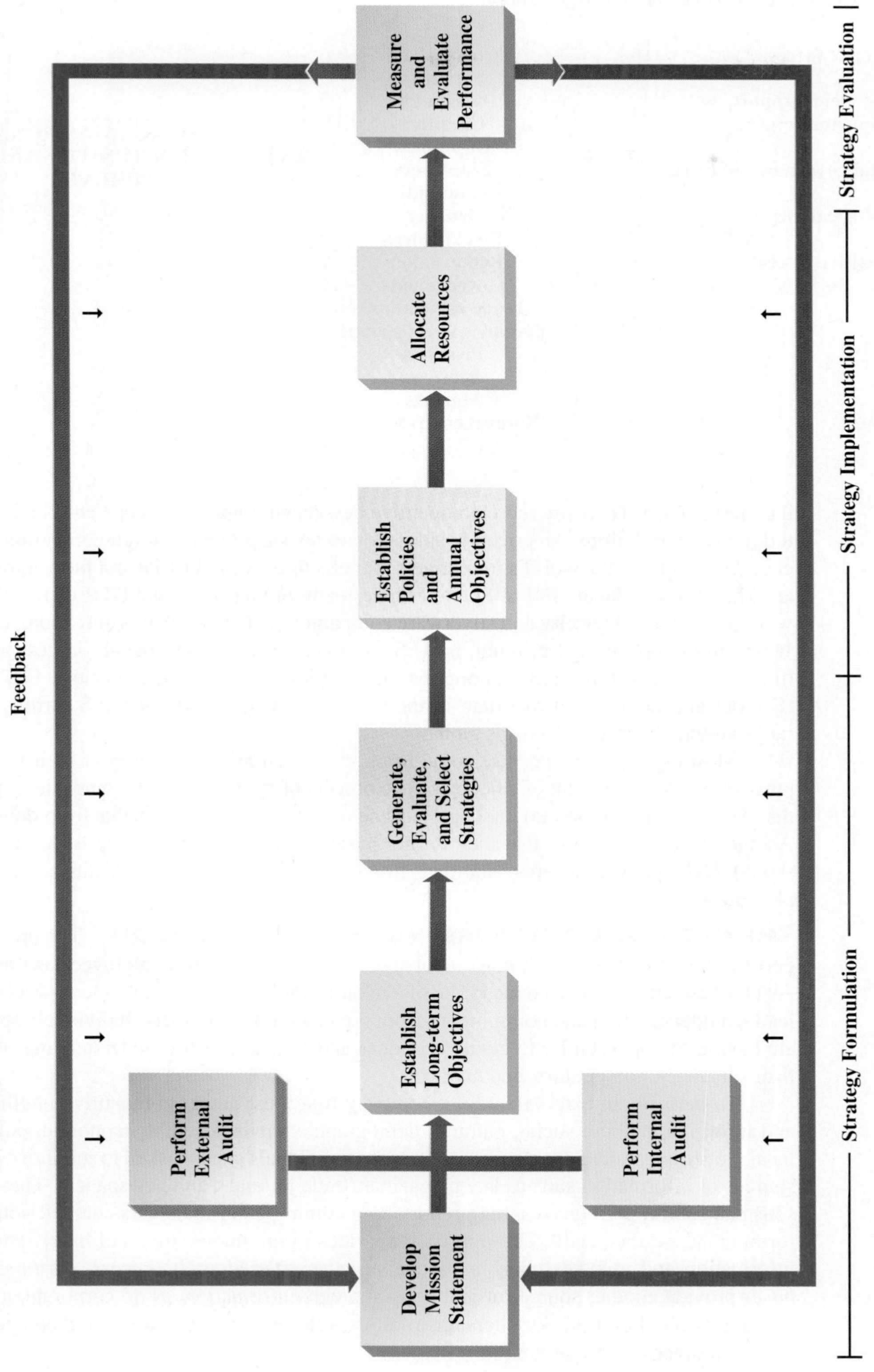

FIGURE 4–1
A Comprehensive Strategic-Management Model

FIGURE 4–2
Relationships Between Key External Forces and an Organization

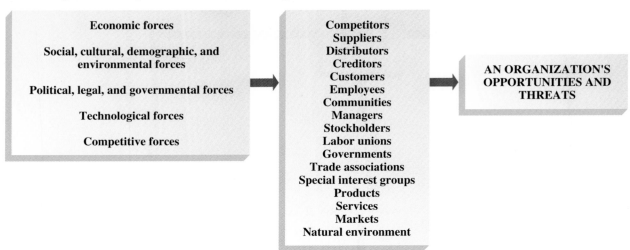

the marketplace. There are more competitive new technologies in Europe and the Far East today than ever before. American businesses can no longer beat foreign competitors with ease. For example, the world's four largest manufacturers of industrial and farm equipment are Mitsubishi of Japan, INI of Spain, Mannesmann of Germany, and BTR of Britain; the world's two largest jewelry and silverware companies are Citizen Watch and Seiko, both of Japan. In publishing and printing, no U.S. company ranks among the six largest; in textiles, no U.S. company ranks among the eight largest; in chemicals, only two U.S. firms (DuPont and Dow Chemical) rank in the top 12; in metals, only one U.S. firm (Alcoa) ranks among the largest 16 firms globally.

Most organizations practice some form of external analysis as part of their planning process. Nearly 75 percent of chief executive officers of the Fortune 500 companies reported that their firms performed external analysis and achieved numerous benefits from doing so.[2] Another 16 percent report that they do not have organized external analysis but probably should. Only 11 percent report that their firms do not conduct external audits and have no plans to begin.

THE PROCESS OF PERFORMING AN EXTERNAL AUDIT   The process of performing an external audit must involve as many managers and employees as possible. As emphasized in earlier chapters, involvement in the strategic-management process can lead to understanding and commitment from organizational members. Individuals appreciate having the opportunity to contribute ideas and to gain a better understanding of their firm's industry, competitors, and markets.

To perform an external audit, a company first must gather competitive intelligence and information about social, cultural, demographic, environmental, economic, political, legal, governmental, and technological trends. Individuals can be asked to monitor various sources of information such as key magazines, trade journals, and newspapers. These persons can submit periodic scanning reports to a committee of managers charged with performing the external audit. This approach provides a continuous stream of timely strategic information and involves many individuals in the external-audit process. *On-line databases* provide another source for gathering strategic information, as do corporate, university, and public libraries. Suppliers, distributors, salespersons, customers, and competitors represent other sources of vital information.

Once information is gathered, it should be assimilated and evaluated. A meeting or series of meetings of up to 20 managers is needed to collectively identify the most important opportunities and threats facing the firm. Critical success factors should be listed on flip charts or a blackboard. A prioritized list of these factors could be obtained by requesting all managers to rank the factors identified, from 1 for the most important opportunity/threat to 20 for the least important opportunity/threat. *Critical success factors* can vary over time and by industry. Relationships with suppliers or distributors are often a critical success factor. Other variables commonly used include market share, breadth of competing products, world economies, foreign affiliates, proprietary and key account advantages, price competitiveness, technological advancements, population shifts, interest rates, and pollution abatement.

Freund emphasized that critical success factors should be (1) important to achieving long-term and annual objectives, (2) measurable, (3) relatively few in number, (4) applicable to all competing firms, and (5) hierarchical in the sense that some will pertain to the overall company and others will be more narrowly focused on functional or divisional areas.[3] A final list of the most important critical success factors should be communicated and distributed widely in the organization. Both opportunities and threats can be critical success factors.

INFORMATION TECHNOLOGY   *Information technology (IT)* has become a powerful tool for conducting an external audit. The quantity and quality of industry and competitive information available to organizations has increased dramatically in recent years. Advanced computer technology, telecommunications, data access and storage devices, fax machines, on-line databases, graphics, and software represent efficient and effective vehicles for identifying and evaluating opportunities and threats. Effective use of the *Internet* as the information superhighway is becoming essential for business success.

The *World Wide Web* is a global network available via the Internet whereby an individual or firm can place information or advertisements for consumption by others around the world—or just within a corporation. Unlike other cyberspace services, Web pages can contain both text and nontext items, including sound clips, graphics, and even movies. Having a Web site in *cyberspace* can allow large savings in paper, copying, phone, and postage. The savings in advertising can be even higher. A Web browser such as Netscape Communications Navigator or America Online on a personal computer can allow anyone to look at what is stored on any Web server in the world.

Using the Internet can be the difference between formulation strategies based on up-to-date rather than out-of-date information. Consultants are readily available to provide assistance.

By the year 2000, millions of people and businesses will each own a small part of cyberspace; they will own their own Web site. Shouldn't your company have its own Web site and peruse the sites of competing companies, suppliers, distributors, and customers? The answer, increasingly, is *yes*. The proliferation of people and companies worldwide using the Web, however, is raising questions about invasion of privacy and breaches of security.

With both private and corporate connections to the Web proliferating, firms must take for granted that every computer on the planet can reach and interact with almost any other. Security and privacy are becoming more of a concern. Linking a firm's computer to cyberspace opens it to potentially millions of largely unidentified visitors, some of whom may have malicious, criminal, or otherwise unethical intent. Verification that senders or receivers on the Internet are who they say they are can be a challenge. A competitor could bombard your system with false messages and information.

The range of products and measures designed to enhance computer security is increasing daily. Software is now available that can generate a new password every few minutes, encrypt all outgoing messages with secret codes or keystrokes, or even block unwanted traffic arriving to your computer from the Internet. Yet, electronic commerce creates vast opportunities for tax evasion, money laundering, and other financial crimes. "There is potential for a serious challenge to the whole political and social order," says Nathaniel Borenstein. "I'm not that sanguine that the government has the control they think they do."

Information technology itself is changing the very nature of opportunities and threats by altering the life cycles of products, increasing the speed of distribution, creating new products and services, erasing limitations of traditional geographic markets, and changing the historical trade-off between production standardization and flexibility. IT is altering economies of scale, changing entry barriers, and redefining the relationship between industries and various suppliers, creditors, customers, and competitors. As an example, consider the airline industry's business travel market:

> Given the current rate of development in telecommunications and office technology, video conferences may become a major substitute for some business air travel soon. This would significantly affect the airline industry's business travel market. Strategists today must address a crucial question: What impact will IT have on our industry over the next five to ten years in terms of products and services, markets, and production economies?[4]

The era of the mainframe computer has given way to a proliferation of affordable microcomputers that are almost as powerful. This trend has created a new basis for competition in virtually all industries and generated new buyers, suppliers, products, and services. The microcomputer revolution especially represents an opportunity for innovative young companies. Entrenched industrial leaders face more competition than ever from small firms using advanced microcomputer technology.

To effectively capitalize on information technology, a number of organizations are establishing two new positions in their firms: *chief information officer (CIO)* and *chief technology officer (CTO)*. This trend reflects the growing importance of information technology in strategic management. A CIO and CTO work together to ensure that information needed to formulate, implement, and evaluate strategies is available where and when it is needed. These persons are responsible for developing, maintaining, and updating a company's information database. The CIO is more a manager, managing the overall external-audit process; the CTO is more a technician, focusing on technical issues such as data acquisition, data processing, decision support systems, and software and hardware acquisition.

ECONOMIC FORCES

In the late 1990s, the United States is benefiting from the best economic conditions in 50 years (U.S. Department of Commerce, www.doc.gov). A balanced federal government budget coupled with low inflation, low interest rates, and low unemployment benefit companies and consumers. Nine states now have no state income tax: Alaska, Florida, Nevada, New Hampshire, South Dakota, Tennessee, Texas, Washington, and Wyoming.

Increasing numbers of two-income households is an economic trend in America. As affluence increases, individuals place a premium on time. Improved customer service, immediate availability, trouble-free operation of products, and dependable maintenance and repair services are becoming more important. Americans today are more willing than ever to pay for good service if it limits inconvenience.

Economic factors have a direct impact on the potential attractiveness of various strategies. For example, if interest rates rise, then funds needed for capital expansion become more costly or unavailable. Also, as interest rates rise, discretionary income declines, and the demand for discretionary goods falls. As stock prices increase, the desirability of equity as a source of capital for market development increases. Also, as the market rises, consumer and business wealth expands. A summary of economic variables that often represent opportunities and threats for organizations is provided in Table 4–1.

Trends in the dollar's value have significant and unequal effects on companies in different industries and in different locations. For example, the pharmaceutical, tourism, entertainment, motor vehicle, aerospace, and forest products industries benefit greatly when the dollar falls against the yen, franc, and mark. Agricultural and petroleum industries are hurt by the dollar's rise against the currencies of Mexico, Brazil, Venezuela, and Australia. Generally, a strong or high dollar makes American goods more expensive on overseas markets. This worsens America's trade deficit. When the value of the dollar falls, tourism-oriented firms benefit because Americans do not travel abroad as much when the value of the dollar is low; rather, foreigners visit and vacation more in the United States. As indicated in the Global Perspective, more foreigners are visiting the United States to receive medical care. U.S. hospitals actively are marketing services to foreigners to capitalize on the rising economic level of many people in foreign countries.

A low value of the dollar means lower imports and higher exports; it helps U.S. companies' competitiveness in world markets. The years 1997 and 1998 have seen the U.S. dollar gaining against virtually every other currency. One benefit of this trend is that consumers pay less for imported goods such as cars and computer memory chips. Domestic firms that manufacture extensively outside the United States also benefit from the rising value of the dollar. If the U.S. budget deficit is cut further, the value of the dollar almost surely will continue to rise, to 150 yen perhaps.

Every business day, thousands of American workers learn that they will lose their jobs. More than 500,000 annual employee layoffs by U.S. firms in the 1990s has led to terms such as *downsizing*, *rightsizing*, and *decruiting* becoming common. European firms, too, are beginning to downsize. The U.S. and world economies face a sustained period of slow, low-inflationary expansion, global overcapacity, high unemployment, price wars, and increased competitiveness. Thousands of laid-off workers are being forced to become entrepreneurs to make a living. The United States is becoming more entrepreneurial every day.

Shift to a service economy in the United States	Import/export factors
Availability of credit	Demand shifts for different categories of goods and services
Level of disposable income	Income differences by region and consumer groups
Propensity of people to spend	Price fluctuations
Interest rates	Exportation of labor and capital from the United States
Inflation rates	
Economies of scale	Monetary policies
Money market rates	Fiscal policies
Federal government budget deficits	Tax rates
Gross domestic product trend	European Economic Community (ECC) policies
Consumption patterns	Organization of Petroleum Exporting Countries (OPEC) policies
Unemployment trends	
Worker productivity levels	Coalitions of Lesser Developed Countries (LDC) policies
Value of the dollar in world markets	
Stock market trends	
Foreign countries' economic conditions	

TABLE 4–1
Key Economic Variables to Be Monitored

GLOBAL PERSPECTIVE
Do U.S. Hospitals Market to Foreigners?

On average, foreign patients pay 20 percent more than American patients with HMOs or Medicare, and for this reason U.S. hospitals actively are marketing themselves to foreigners. The annual rate of increase in foreign patients exceeds 20 percent in many U.S. hospitals. Johns Hopkins and the Mayo Clinic, for example, each treated over 8,000 foreigners in 1997. The rapid influx of foreigners into U.S. hospitals is being spurred by a rising middle class in many foreign countries and rising popularity of employer-based insurance in foreign countries. Insurance companies abroad generally do not discourage treatment in the United States although they don't reimburse travel expenses.

U.S. hospitals actively are pursuing deals with foreign governments, businesses, travel agents, and airlines to get patients. Miami and Houston plan to become medical centers for all of Latin America, South America, and Mexico. U.S. hospitals in the Northeast are targeting Europeans while hospitals in the West are targeting Asians. A common strategy for hospitals is to attract foreign doctors as part of the overall goal of getting foreign patients.

Source: Adapted from Steven Findlay, "U.S. Hospitals Attracting Patients From Abroad," USA Today (July 22, 1997): 2A.

SOCIAL, CULTURAL, DEMOGRAPHIC, AND ENVIRONMENTAL FORCES

Social, cultural, demographic, and environmental changes have a major impact upon virtually all products, services, markets, and customers. Small, large, for-profit and non-profit organizations in all industries are being staggered and challenged by the opportunities and threats arising from changes in social, cultural, demographic, and environmental variables. In every way, the United States is much different in 1999 than it was in 1989, and the year 2009 promises even greater changes.

The United States is getting older and less Caucasian, feeding generational and racial competition for jobs and government money. The gap between rich and poor is growing while the federal bureaucracy gets smaller. America's 76 million baby boomers plan to retire in 2011, and this has lawmakers and younger taxpayers deeply worried and concerned about who will pay their social security, medicare, and medicaid. Persons aged 65 and older in the United States will rise from 12.7 percent of the population to 18.5 percent between 1997 and 2025.

By the year 2075, the United States will have no racial or ethnic majority. This forecast is aggravating tensions over issues such as immigration and affirmative action. Hawaii and New Mexico already have no majority race or ethnic group and by the year 2000, neither will California.

In the year 2050, India is projected to have 1.53 billion people and to overtake China as the world's most populous nation. That year, the United States will have 394 million people. A list of the world's most populous countries is given on page 111.

Social, cultural, demographic, and environmental trends are shaping the way Americans live, work, produce, and consume. New trends are creating a different type of consumer and, consequently, a need for different products, different services, and different strategies. There are now more American households with people living alone or with unrelated people than there are households consisting of married couples with children. Census data suggest that Americans are not returning to traditional life-styles. Church membership fell substantially during the 1980s for nearly all religious denominations, except Southern Baptists and Mormons. It is interesting to note that Protestant churches in

RANK	COUNTRY	1996 POPULATION	RANK	COUNTRY	2025 POPULATION
1.	China	1,217.6	1.	China	1,492.0
2.	India	949.6	2.	India	1,384.6
3.	United States	265.2	3.	United States	335.1
4.	Indonesia	201.4	4.	Indonesia	276.5
5.	Brazil	160.5	5.	Nigeria	246.0
6.	Russia	147.7	6.	Pakistan	232.9
7.	Pakistan	133.5	7.	Brazil	202.3
8.	Japan	125.8	8.	Bangladesh	175.8
9.	Bangladesh	119.8	9.	Russia	153.1
10.	Nigeria	103.9	10.	Mexico	142.1

World's Most Populous Countries (*Estimated, in millions*)

the United States take in over $7 billion in donations annually. The eight largest U.S. church denominations are (in millions of members) Roman Catholic (60.3), Southern Baptist (15.7), National Baptist (11.7), United Methodist (8.5), Lutheran (5.2), Morman (4.7), Presbyterian (3.7), and Episcopalian (3.5).

Significant trends for the 1990s include consumers becoming more educated, the population aging, narcissism replacing the work ethic, minorities becoming more influential, people looking for local rather than federal solutions to problems, fixation on youth decreasing, more emphasis being placed on preserving the natural environment, and more women entering the workforce. The United States Census Bureau projects that the number of Hispanics will increase to 15 percent of the population by 2021, when they will become a larger minority group than African Americans in America. The percentage of African Americans in the U.S. population is expected to increase from 12 percent to 14 percent between 1996 and 2021. Many states currently have more than 500,000 Hispanics as registered voters, including California, New Mexico, Arizona, Texas, Florida, New York, Illinois, and New Jersey. The fastest-growing businesses in the United States are owned by women of color. From 1987 to 1996, the number of firms owned by African American, Asian, Latina, and Native American women increased by 153 percent to 1 million enterprises. Firms owned by women of color employ 1.7 million people and generate $184 billion in sales annually.

During the 1990s, the number of individuals aged 50 and over will increase 18.5 percent, to 76 million. In contrast, the number of Americans under age 50 will grow by just 3.5 percent. The number of babies born in the United States has declined annually since 1990 to a low of 3.7 million in 1998. The trend toward an older America is good news for restaurants, hotels, airlines, cruise lines, tours, resorts, theme parks, luxury products and services, recreational vehicles, home builders, furniture producers, computer manufacturers, travel services, pharmaceutical firms, automakers, and funeral homes. Older Americans are especially interested in health care, financial services, travel, crime prevention, and leisure. The world's longest-living people are the Japanese, with Japanese women living to 86.3 years and men living to 80.1 years on average.

The aging American population affects the strategic orientation of nearly all organizations. Apartment complexes for the elderly, with one meal a day, transportation, and utilities included in the rent, have increased to more than 200,000 units nationwide. Called *lifecare facilities*, these complexes are expected to increase in number to exceed 2 million by 2000. Some well-known companies building these facilities include Avon, Marriott, and Hyatt. By the year 2005, individuals aged 65 and older in the United States will rise to 13 percent of the total population; Japan's elderly population ratio will rise to 17 percent, and Germany's to 19 percent.

Americans are on the move in a population shift to the South and West (Sun Belt) and away from the Northeast and Midwest (Frost Belt). The Internal Revenue Service provides the Census Bureau with massive computer files of demographic data. By comparing individual address changes from year to year, the Census Bureau publishes extensive information about population shifts across the country. For example, Arizona will be the fastest-growing state during the 1990s as its population increases 23 percent. Nevada, New Mexico, and Florida are close behind with projected growth rates above 20 percent. Wyoming will remain the nation's least populated state and California the most populated state. Texas will replace New York as the most populous state. States incurring the greatest loss of people for the 1990s are North Dakota, Wyoming, Pennsylvania, Iowa, and West Virginia. This type of information can be essential for successful strategy formulation, including where to locate new plants and distribution centers and where to focus marketing efforts.

Americans are becoming less interested in fitness and exercise. Fitness participants declined in the United States by 3.5 percent annually in the 1990s. Makers of fitness products, such as Nike, Reebok International, and CML Group—which makes NordicTrack—are experiencing declines in sales growth. American Sports Data in Hartsdale, New York, reports that "the one American in five who exercises regularly is now outnumbered by three couch potatoes."

Mark Starik at George Washington University argues that with the thawing of the Cold War, no greater threat to business and society exists than the voracious, continuous decimation and degradation of our natural environment. The U.S. Clean Air Act went into effect in 1994. The U.S. Clean Water Act went into effect in 1984. As indicated in the Natural Environment Perspective, air and water pollution causes great anguish worldwide. A summary of important social, cultural, demographic, and environmental variables that represent opportunities or threats for virtually all organizations is given in Table 4–2.

TABLE 4–2
Key Social, Cultural, Demographic, and Environmental Variables

Childbearing rates	Attitudes toward retirement
Number of special interest groups	Attitudes toward leisure time
Number of marriages	Attitudes toward product quality
Number of divorces	Attitudes toward customer service
Number of births	Pollution control
Number of deaths	Attitudes toward foreign peoples
Immigration and emigration rates	Energy conservation
Social security programs	Social programs
Life expectancy rates	Number of churches
Per capita income	Number of church members
Location of retailing, manufacturing, and service businesses	Social responsibility
Attitudes toward business	Attitudes toward careers
Life-styles	Population changes by race, age, sex, and level of affluence
Traffic congestion	Attitudes toward authority
Inner-city environments	Population changes by city, county, state, region, and country
Average disposable income	Value placed on leisure time
Trust in government	Regional changes in tastes and preferences
Attitudes toward government	Number of women and minority workers
Attitudes toward work	Number of high school and college graduates by geographic area
Buying habits	Recycling
Ethical concerns	Waste management
Attitudes toward saving	Air pollution
Sex roles	Water pollution
Attitudes toward investing	Ozone depletion
Racial equality	Endangered species
Use of birth control	
Average level of education	
Government regulation	

NATURAL ENVIRONMENT

Is Your Business Polluting the Air or Water?

AIR

More than 1.5 billion people around the world live in urban areas with dangerous levels of air pollution. Alarmingly, cities are growing more rapidly than progress is being made to reverse this trend. Seven of the 10 worst cities for sulfur dioxide and carbon monoxide are in developing countries. These and other pollutants cause acute and chronic lung disease, heart disease, lung cancer, and lead-induced neurological damage in children. Lung cancer alone killed 989,000 people in 1996, and 1.32 million new cases of lung cancer were diagnosed that year. In the European Union countries, a 33 percent increase in female lung cancer cases is predicted by 2005. There is no effective treatment for lung cancer—only 10 percent of patients are alive 5 years after diagnosis. Polluted air knows no city, state, country, or continent boundaries.

The Environmental Protection Agency (EPA) wants to expand air pollution regulation in the United States to cover microscopic particles as tiny as 2.5 micons, down from the current standard of 10 microns. The EPA also wants to expand the allowable level of ozone from 0.12 parts per million cubic feet of air to 0.08 parts per million. The EPA says this will cut premature deaths in the United States by 20,000; cases of aggravated asthma by 250,000; cases of acute childhood respiratory problems by 250,000; bronchitis cases

by 60,000; hospital admissions by 9,000; and cases of major breathing problems by 1.5 million. The total savings of these benefits would exceed $115 billion. Critics say the proposed new regulation will cost too much to U.S. companies and cities.

Source: Adapted from William Miller, "Clean-Air Contention," Industry Week *(May 5, 1997): 14. Also,* World Health Organization Report, *1997.*

WATER

Is your business polluting the water? Contaminated water is blamed for as much as 80 percent of all disease in developing countries. Well over 1 billion people in the world still are without safe water to drink, bathe, cook, and clean. Less than 2 percent of the domestic and industrial wastewater generated in developing countries receives any kind of treatment. It just runs into rivers and groundwater resources, thus poisoning populations, the environment, and the planet. Unsafe drinking water is a prime cause of diarrhea, malaria, cancer, infant deformities, and infant mortality. A few statistics reveal the severity, harshness, and effect of water pollution.

- More than 5 million babies born in developing countries die annually in the first month of life, mainly due to polluted water.

- About 4 million babies are born with deformities annually.

- Diarrhea and dysentery kill 2.5 million people annually.

- Malaria kills 2.1 million people annually.

Industrial discharge, a major water problem even in the United States, contributes significantly to the dramatic rise in cancer both here and abroad. More than 10 million new cases of cancer are diagnosed annually and about 6.5 million people die of cancer annually. More than 1.2 billion of these deaths are due to stomach and colon cancer, two types often associated with poor water and eating habits. Besides deaths, the anguish, sickness, suffering, and expense inflicted upon people directly or indirectly due to contaminated water is immeasurably high even in the United States. Dangerous industrial chemicals are used here as fertilizers, pesticides, solvents, food additives, fuels, medicines, cosmetics, and in a wide range of manufacturing processes.

Source: Adapted from World Health Organization Report, *1997.*

POLITICAL, GOVERNMENTAL, AND LEGAL FORCES

Federal, state, local, and foreign governments are major regulators, deregulators, subsidizers, employers, and customers of organizations. Political, governmental, and legal factors therefore can represent key opportunities or threats for both small and large organizations. For industries and firms that depend heavily on government contracts or subsidies, political forecasts can be the most important part of an external audit. Changes in patent laws, antitrust legislation, tax rates, and lobbying activities can affect firms significantly. The United States Justice Department offers excellent information at its Web site (www.justice2.usdoj.gov) on such topics.

In the world of biopolitics, Americans are still deeply divided over issues such as assisted suicide, genetic testing, genetic engineering, cloning, brain imaging technology, and even abortion. Such political issues have great ramifications for companies in many industries ranging from pharmaceuticals to computers.

The increasing global interdependence among economies, markets, governments, and organizations makes it imperative that firms consider the possible impact of political variables on the formulation and implementation of competitive strategies. A number of nationally known firms forecast political, governmental, and legal variables, including Frost & Sullivan, Probe International, and Arthur D. Little (ADL). ADL forecasts the political climate in foreign countries by examining five criteria: (1) social development, (2) technological advancement, (3) abundance of natural resources, (4) level of domestic tranquility, and (5) type of political system. ADL has found that political unrest follows whenever a country's development in any one of these areas gets too far ahead of the others. Ford, DuPont, Singer, and PepsiCo are among the many companies that use forecasts developed by outside firms to identify key political and governmental opportunities and threats.

Political forecasting can be especially critical and complex for multinational firms that depend on foreign countries for natural resources, facilities, distribution of products, special assistance, or customers. Strategists today must possess skills to deal more legalistically and politically than previous strategists, whose attention was directed more to economic and technical affairs of the firm. Strategists today are spending more time anticipating and influencing public policy actions. They spend more time meeting with government officials, attending hearings and government-sponsored conferences, giving public speeches, and meeting with trade groups, industry associations, and government agency directors. Before entering or expanding international operations, strategists need a good understanding of the political and decision-making processes in countries where their firm may conduct business. For example, republics that made up the former Soviet Union differ greatly in wealth, resources, language, and life-style.

To be considered legally intoxicated even varies considerably among countries. The maximum legal blood alcohol level (.01 percent equals one part alcohol to 10,000 parts blood) for driving in selected countries, with drinks per hour needed to reach it, are as follows:

	LIMIT	DRINKS
Sweden	.02%	2
Japan, France	.05%	3
United States (16 states), United Kingdom	.08%	4
Germany, Italy	.08%	4
United States (34 states, D.C.)	.10%	5

Note: A drink equals 1 oz. whiskey, 5 oz. wine, or 12 oz. beer.

Increasing global competition toward the year 2000 accents the need for accurate political, governmental, and legal forecasts. Many strategists will have to become familiar with political systems in Europe and Asia and with trading currency futures. East Asian countries already have become world leaders in labor-intensive industries. A world market has emerged from what previously was a multitude of distinct national markets, and the climate for international business today would be much more favorable than yesterday. Mass communication and high technology are creating similar patterns of consumption in diverse cultures worldwide! This means that many companies may find it difficult to survive by relying solely on domestic markets.

TABLE 4-3
Some Political, Governmental, and Legal Variables

Government regulations or deregulations	Sino-American relationships
Changes in tax laws	Russian-American relationships
Special tariffs	European-American relationships
Political action committees	African-American relationships
Voter participation rates	Import-export regulations
Number, severity, and location of government protests	Government fiscal and monetary policy changes
Number of patents	Political conditions in foreign countries
Changes in patent laws	Special local, state, and federal laws
Environmental protection laws	Lobbying activities
Level of defense expenditures	Size of government budgets
Legislation on equal employment	World oil, currency, and labor markets
Level of government subsidies	Location and severity of terrorist activities
Antitrust legislation	Local, state, and national elections

It is no exaggeration that in an industry that is, or is rapidly becoming, global, the riskiest possible posture is to remain a domestic competitor. The domestic competitor will watch as more aggressive companies use this growth to capture economies of scale and learning. The domestic competitor will then be faced with an attack on domestic markets using different (and possibly superior) technology, product design, manufacturing, marketing approaches, and economies of scale. A few examples suggest how extensive the phenomenon of world markets has already become. Hewlett-Packard's manufacturing chain reaches halfway around the globe, from well-paid, skilled engineers in California to low-wage assembly workers in Malaysia. General Electric has survived as a manufacturer of inexpensive audio products by centralizing its world production in Singapore.[5]

Local, state, and federal laws, regulatory agencies, and special interest groups can have a major impact on the strategies of small, large, for-profit, and nonprofit organizations. Many companies have altered or abandoned strategies in the past because of political or governmental actions. For example, many nuclear power projects have been halted and many steel plants shut down because of pressure from the Environmental Protection Agency (EPA). Other federal regulatory agencies include the Food and Drug Administration (FDA), the National Highway Traffic and Safety Administration (NHTSA), the Occupational Safety and Health Administration (OSHA), the Consumer Product Safety Commission (CPSC), the Federal Trade Commission (FTC), the Securities Exchange Commission (SEC), the Equal Employment Opportunity Commission (EEOC), the Federal Communications Commission (FCC), the Federal Maritime Commission (FMC), the Interstate Commerce Commission (ICC), the Federal Energy Regulatory Commission (FERC), the National Labor Relations Board (NLRB), and the Civil Aeronautics Board (CAB). A summary of political, governmental, and legal variables that can represent key opportunities or threats to organizations is provided in Table 4–3.

TECHNOLOGICAL FORCES

Revolutionary technological changes and discoveries such as superconductivity, computer engineering, thinking computers, robotics, unstaffed factories, miracle drugs, space communications, space manufacturing, lasers, cloning, satellite networks, fiber optics, biometrics, and electronic funds transfer are having a dramatic impact on organizations. Superconductivity advancements alone, which increase the power of electrical products by lowering resistance to current, are revolutionizing business operations, especially in the transportation, utility, health care, electrical, and computer industries.

Microprocesser-based equipment and process technologies, such as computer-aided design and manufacturing (CAD/CAM), direct numerical control (DNC), computer-centralized numerical control (CNC), flexible production centers (FPC), equipment and process technology (EPT), and computer-integrated manufacturing (CIM), are burgeoning.

Technological forces represent major opportunities and threats that must be considered in formulating strategies. Technological advancements dramatically can affect organizations' products, services, markets, suppliers, distributors, competitors, customers, manufacturing processes, marketing practices, and competitive position. Technological advancements can create new markets, result in a proliferation of new and improved products, change the relative competitive cost positions in an industry, and render existing products and services obsolete. Technological changes can reduce or eliminate cost barriers between businesses, create shorter production runs, create shortages in technical skills, and result in changing values and expectations of employees, managers, and customers. Technological advancements can create new *competitive advantages* that are more powerful than existing advantages. No company or industry today is insulated against emerging technological developments. In high-tech industries identification and evaluation of key technological opportunities and threats can be the most important part of the external strategic-management audit.

Organizations that traditionally have limited technology expenditures to what they can fund after meeting marketing and financial requirements urgently need a reversal in thinking. The pace of technological change is increasing and literally wiping out businesses every day. An emerging consensus holds that technology management is one of the key responsibilities of strategists. Firms should pursue strategies that take advantage of technological opportunities to achieve sustainable, competitive advantages in the marketplace.

> Technology-based issues will underlie nearly every important decision that strategists make. Crucial to those decisions will be the ability to approach technology planning analytically and strategically. . . . technology can be planned and managed using formal techniques similar to those used in business and capital investment planning. An effective technology strategy is built on a penetrating analysis of technology opportunities and threats, and an assessment of the relative importance of these factors to overall corporate strategy.[6]

In practice, critical decisions about technology too often are delegated to lower organizational levels or are made without an understanding of their strategic implications. Many strategists spend countless hours determining market share, positioning products in terms of features and price, forecasting sales and market size, and monitoring distributors; yet too often technology does not receive the same respect:

> The impact of this oversight is devastating. Firms not managing technology to ensure their futures may eventually find their futures managed by technology. Technology's impact reaches far beyond the "high-tech" companies. Although some industries may appear to be relatively technology-insensitive in terms of products and market requirements, they are not immune from the impact of technology; companies in smokestack as well as service industries must carefully monitor emerging technological opportunities and threats.[7]

Not all sectors of the economy are affected equally by technological developments. The communications, electronics, aeronautics, and pharmaceutical industries are much more volatile than the textile, forestry, and metals industries. For strategists in industries affected by rapid technological change, identifying and evaluating technological opportunities and threats can represent the most important part of an external audit.

Some technological advancements expected before the year 2000 in the computer and medical industry are computers that recognize handwriting; voice-controlled computers; gesture-controlled computers; color faxes; picture phones; and defeat of heart disease, AIDS, rheumatoid arthritis, multiple sclerosis, leukemia, and lung cancer. New technological advancements in the computer industry alone are revolutionizing the way businesses operate today.

COMPETITIVE FORCES

The top five U.S. competitors in four different industries are identified in Table 4–4. An important part of an external audit is identifying rival firms and determining their strengths, weaknesses, capabilities, opportunities, threats, objectives, and strategies.

Collecting and evaluating information on competitors is essential for successful strategy formulation. Identifying major competitors is not always easy because many firms have divisions that compete in different industries. Most multidivisional firms generally do not provide sales and profit information on a divisional basis for competitive reasons. Also, privately held firms do not publish any financial or marketing information.

Despite the problems mentioned above, information on leading competitors in particular industries can be found in publications such as *Moody's Manuals, Standard Corporation Descriptions, Value Line Investment Surveys, Ward's Business Directory, Dun's Business Rankings, Standard & Poor's Industry Surveys, Industry Week, Forbes, Fortune,*

TABLE 4–4

The Top Five U.S. Competitors in Four Different Industries in 1997

	1997 SALES IN $ MILLIONS	PERCENTAGE CHANGE FROM 1996	1997 PROFITS IN $ MILLIONS	PERCENTAGE CHANGE FROM 1996
AEROSPACE				
Boeing	45,800.0	+29	−178.0	NM
Lockheed Martin	28,069.0	+4	+1,300.0	−3
United Technologies	24,713.0	+5	+1,072.0	+18
Northrop Grumman	9,153.0	+6	+407.0	+54
General Dynamics	4,062.0	+13	+316.0	+17
FOREST PRODUCTS				
International Paper	20,115.0	0	−151.0	NM
Georgia-Pacific	12,968.0	+1	−86.0	NM
Kimberly-Clark	12,546.6	−5	+884.0	−37
Fort James	7,259.0	−6	+104.5	−68
Champion International	5,735.5	−2	−548.5	NM
COMPUTERS				
IBM	78,508.0	+3	+6,093.0	+12
Hewlett-Packard	42,895.0	+12	+3,119.0	+21
Compaq Computer	24,584.0	+23	+1,855.0	+41
Xerox	18,166.0	+5	+1,452.0	+20
Digital Equipment	13,062.2	−4	+274.8	NM
PUBLISHING				
Time Warner	13,294.0	+32	+301.0	NM
CBS	5,363.0	+29	−131.0	NM
Gannett	4,729.5	+7	+712.7	+14
McGraw-Hill	3,534.1	+15	+290.7	−41
Times Mirror	3,318.5	−2	+250.3	−21

Source: Adapted from Corporate Scoreboard, *Business Week* (March 2, 1998): 113–136.
NM: Not Measurable

Business Week, and *Inc.* In addition, the *Million Dollar Directory* lists key personnel, products, divisions, and SIC codes for over 160,000 U.S. public and private companies whose revenues exceed $500,000. *Standard & Poor's Register of Corporate Directors and Executives* and the *Directory of Corporate Affiliations* are other excellent sources of competitive information. However, many businesses use the Internet to obtain most of their information on competitors. The Internet is fast, thorough, accurate, and increasingly indispensable in this regard. Questions about competitors such as those presented in Table 4–5 are important to address in performing an external audit.

Competition in virtually all industries can be described as intense, and sometimes cutthroat. For example, when United Parcel Service (UPS) employees were on strike in 1997, competitors such as Federal Express, Greyhound, Roadway, and United Airlines lowered prices, doubled advertising efforts, and locked new customers into annual contracts in efforts to leave UPS customer-less when the strike ended. UPS still is struggling to regain its former market share. If a firm detects weakness in a competitor, no mercy at all is shown in capitalizing on its problems.

Seven characteristics describe the most competitive companies in America: (1) Market share matters; the 90th share point isn't as important as the 91st, and nothing is more dangerous than falling to 89; (2) Understand and remember precisely what business you are in; (3) Whether it's broke or not, fix it—make it better; not just products, but the whole company if necessary; (4) Innovate or evaporate; particularly in technology-driven businesses, nothing quite recedes like success; (5) Acquisition is essential to growth; the most successful purchases are in niches that add a technology or a related market; (6) People make a difference; tired of hearing it? Too bad; (7) There is no substitute for quality and no greater threat than failing to be cost-competitive on a global basis; these are complementary concepts, not mutually exclusive ones.[8]

COMPETITIVE INTELLIGENCE PROGRAMS   Senator William Cohen (R-Maine) says, "When France, Germany, Japan, and South Korea are included in a list of nations, we automatically assume that this must be a list of America allies—our military and political partners since the end of the World War II. Unfortunately, this is not only a list of America's trustworthy friends, it is a list of governments that have systematically practiced economic espionage against American companies in the past—and continue to do so to this day. France openly admits that it operates a special department devoted to obtaining confidential information about U.S. companies." Good competitive intelligence in business, as in the military, is one of the keys to success. The more information and knowledge a firm

TABLE 4–5
Key Questions About Competitors

1. What are the major competitors' strengths?
2. What are the major competitors' weaknesses?
3. What are the major competitors' objectives and strategies?
4. How will the major competitors most likely respond to current economic, social, cultural, demographic, environmental, political, governmental, legal, technological, and competitive trends affecting our industry?
5. How vulnerable are the major competitors to our alternative company strategies?
6. How vulnerable are our alternative strategies to successful counterattack by our major competitors?
7. How are our products or services positioned relative to major competitors?
8. To what extent are new firms entering and old firms leaving this industry?
9. What key factors have resulted in our present competitive position in this industry?
10. How have the sales and profit rankings of major competitors in the industry changed over recent years? Why have these rankings changed that way?
11. What is the nature of supplier and distributor relationships in this industry?
12. To what extent could substitute products or services be a threat to competitors in this industry?

can obtain about its competitors, the more likely it can formulate and implement effective strategies. Major competitors' weaknesses can represent external opportunities; major competitors' strengths may represent key threats.

Unfortunately, the majority of U.S. executives grew up in times when American firms dominated foreign competitors so much that gathering competitive intelligence seemed not worth the effort. Too many of these executives still cling to these attitudes, to the detriment of their organizations today. Even most MBA programs do not offer a course in competitive and business intelligence, thus reinforcing this attitude. As a consequence, three strong misperceptions about business intelligence prevail among American executives today:

1. Running an intelligence program requires lots of people, computers, and other resources.

2. Collecting intelligence about competitors violates antitrust laws; business intelligence equals espionage.

3. Intelligence gathering is an unethical business practice.[9]

All three of these perceptions are totally misguided. Any discussions with a competitor about price, market, or geography intentions could violate antitrust statutes, but this fact must not lure a firm into underestimating the need for and benefits of systematically collecting information about competitors for the purpose of enhancing a firm's effectiveness. The Internet has become an excellent medium for gathering competitive intelligence, as indicated in the Information Technology Perspective. Information gathering from employees, managers, suppliers, distributors, customers, creditors, and consultants also can make the difference between having superior or just average intelligence and overall competitiveness.

Firms need an effective *competitive intelligence (CI)* program. The three basic missions of a CI program are (1) to provide a general understanding of an industry and its

INFORMATION TECHNOLOGY

How Can the Internet Be Used to Gain Competitive Intelligence?

The Wall Street Journal recently asked corporate executives and consultants which Web sites are best for gaining competitive intelligence. The results are summarized here. At any given time on the Internet, thousands of people are talking about your company's products and competing products in newsgroups. You can eavesdrop on these discussions most easily using Deja News at www.dejanews.com; this site lets you search these discussions by keyword.

The best all-around starting point for conducting research on the Web is Yahoo! at www.yahoo.com. Unlike AltaVista and other search engines that use computers to automatically index every word at a Web site, Yahoo! is a true directory. So if you type Ford Motor Company into Yahoo!, you get a list of all Ford's

Web sites, whereas typing that name into any other search engine gets you a 12-page list of Web sites that have the name Ford in the title or on the first page. Yahoo! is speedy but not always completely up-to-date.

If you are desperately seeking something that a Yahoo! search does not find, the *WSJ* panelists prefer AltaVista at altavista.digital.com; Excite at www.excite.com; Hotbot at www.hotbot.com; Infoseek at www.infoseek.com; or Lycos at www.lycos.com. These engines are unbelievably thorough. To find a person, Four11 at www.four11.com and Switchboard at www.switchboard.com offer far greater power than a telephone call to directory assistance.

For information on competitors, the *WSJ* panelists prefer to use Hoover's Online at www.hoovers.com; Infospace

at www.infospace.com; and the Securities Exchange Commission's Edgar database at www.sec.gov. To make travel plans, schedule flights, purchase airline tickets, book hotel rooms, and reserve rental cars, the *WSJ* panelists prefer Expedia at www.expedia.com; Mapquest at www.mapquest.com; and Travelocity at www.travelocity.com. Accessing these sites is much easier and quicker than calling a travel agent.

Source: Adapted from Thomas Weber, "Watching the Web: Experts Pick Their Most Useful Sites," The Wall Street Journal, (August 28, 1997): B6.

competitors, (2) to identify areas in which competitors are vulnerable and to asseses the impact strategic actions would have on competitors, and (3) to identify potential moves that a competitor might make that would endanger a firm's position in the market.[10] Competitive information is equally applicable for strategy formulation, implementation, and evaluation decisions. An effective CI program allows all areas of a firm to access consistent and verifiable information in making decisions. All members of an organization, from the chief executive officer to custodians, are valuable intelligence agents and should feel a part of the CI process. Special characteristics of a successful CI program include flexibility, usefulness, timeliness, and cross-functional cooperation.

The increasing emphasis on *competitive analysis* in the United States is evidenced by corporations putting this function on their organizational charts under job titles such as Director of Competitive Analysis, Competitive Strategy Manager, Director of Information Services, or Associate Director of Competitive Assessment. The responsibilities of a *director of competitive analysis* include planning, collecting data, analyzing data, facilitating the process of gathering and analyzing data, disseminating intelligence on a timely basis, researching special issues, and recognizing what information is important and who needs to know. Competitive intelligence is not corporate espionage because 95 percent of the information a company needs to make strategic decisions is available and accessible to the public. Sources of competitive information include trade journals, want ads, newspaper articles, and government filings, as well as customers, suppliers, distributors, and competitors themselves.

Unethical tactics such as bribery, wire tapping, and computer break-ins should never be used to obtain information. Marriott and Motorola—two American companies that do a particularly good job of gathering competitive intelligence—agree that all the information you could wish for can be collected without resorting to unethical tactics. They keep their intelligence staffs small, usually under five people, and spend less than $200,000 per year on gathering competitive intelligence.

COOPERATION AMONG COMPETITORS Strategies that stress cooperation among competitors are being used more. For example, Lockheed recently teamed up with British Aerospace PLC to compete against Boeing Company to develop the next-generation U.S. fighter jet. Lockheed's cooperative strategy with a profitable partner in the Airbus Industrie consortium encourages broader Lockheed-European collaboration as Europe's defense industry consolidates. The British firm offers Lockheed special expertise in the areas of short takeoff and vertical landing technologies, systems integration, and low-cost design and manufacturing.

In the oil industry, Shell Oil and Texaco recently combined their West Coast and Midwestern refining and marketing operations into a new company with $9 billion in assets. Mobil and Amoco are engaged in similar discussions about combining their entire U.S. refining and marketing operations. Marathon Oil and Ashland also are engaged in merger discussions.

The idea of joining forces with a competitor is not easily accepted by Americans, who often view cooperation and partnerships with skepticism and suspicion. Indeed, joint ventures and cooperative arrangements among competitors demand a certain amount of trust to combat paranoia about whether one firm will injure the other. However, multinational firms are becoming more globally cooperative, and increasing numbers of domestic firms are joining forces with competitive foreign firms to reap mutual benefits. Kathryn Harrigan at Columbia University says, "Within a decade, most companies will be members of teams that compete against each other."

American companies often enter alliances primarily to avoid investments, being more interested in reducing the costs and risks of entering new businesses or markets than in acquiring new skills. In contrast, *learning from the partner* is a major reason why Asian and European firms enter into cooperative agreements. American firms, too, should place learning high on the list of reasons to cooperate with competitors. American companies often form alliances with Asian firms to gain an understanding of their manufacturing excellence, but Asian competence in this area is not easily transferable. Manufacturing excellence is a complex system that includes employee training and involvement, integration with suppliers, statistical process controls, value engineering, and design. In contrast, American know-how in technology and related areas more easily can be imitated. American firms thus need to be careful not to give away more intelligence than they receive in cooperative agreements with rival Asian firms.

SOURCES OF EXTERNAL INFORMATION

A wealth of strategic information is available to organizations from both published and unpublished sources. Unpublished sources include customer surveys, market research, speeches at professional and shareholders' meetings, television programs, interviews, and conversations with stakeholders. Published sources of strategic information include periodicals, journals, reports, government documents, abstracts, books, directories, newspapers, and manuals. Computerization and the Internet have made it easier today for firms to gather, assimilate, and evaluate information.

INDEXES   A number of excellent indexes reveal the location of strategic information by subject, topic, source, author, company, and industry. Indexes can save managers considerable time and effort in identifying and evaluating opportunities and threats. A description of major indexes available for locating information is provided in Table 4–6.

TABLE 4–6
Major Indexes That Reference Economic, Social, Political, Technological, and Competitive Information

NAME OF INDEX	TYPE OF INFORMATION	DESCRIPTION
Applied Science & Technology Index	Technological	A subject index that covers more than 200 selected journals in the fields of aeronautics and space science, automation, chemistry, construction, earth sciences, electricity and electronics, engineering, industrial and mechanical arts, materials, mathematics, metallurgy, physics, telecommunication, transportation, and related subjects. *ASTI* is published monthly.
Business Periodicals Index	Economic Social Political Technological Competitive	This is probably the best known index for its overall subject coverage of selected periodicals in the following fields of business: accounting, advertising and public relations, automation, banking, communications, economics, finance and investments, insurance, labor, management, marketing, taxation, and also specific businesses, industries, and trades. This index also includes a review of books appearing in the journals it indexes, listed together under the heading "Book Reviews." *BPI* is published monthly.
Funk & Scott Index of Corporations & Industries	Competitive	This is the best index for current information on companies and industries. It covers a wide selection of business, industrial, and financial periodicals and also a few brokerage house reports. The yellow pages in the weeklies and the green pages in cumulated issues list articles (or data in articles) on all SIC (Standard Industrial Classification) industries; the white pages list articles on companies. Because many of the entries refer to very brief citations, it is important to note that major articles are designated by a black dot that precedes the abbreviated title of the journal. *F&S* is published weekly.
F&S Index International	Competitive Political	A companion of the index above, covering articles on foreign companies and industries that have appeared in some 1,000 foreign and domestic periodicals and other documents. It is arranged in three parts: (1) by SIC number or product; (2) by region and country; (3) by company. *F&SI* is published monthly.

continued

TABLE 4–6 *continued*

Public Affairs Information Service Bulletin	Social Political[a]	This is a selective listing in the areas of economic and social conditions, public adminis-tration, and international relations, published in English throughout the world. The im-portant differences in this index are (1) it only selectively indexes journals to cover those articles pertinent to its subject coverage; (2) it covers not only periodical articles but also selected books, pamphlets, government publications, and reports of public and private agencies. There is a companion index called *Public Affairs Information Service: Foreign Language Index*. The *PAIS* is published weekly.
Readers' Guide to Periodical Literature	Economic Social Political Technological Competitive	A very popular author and subject index to periodicals published in the United States. The *RGPL* is published bimonthly.
Social Sciences Index	Social Economic Political	A subject and author index to articles in over 260 journals that cover the fields of anthro-pology, area studies, economics, environmental science, geography, law and criminology, medical sciences, political science, psychology, public administration, sociology, and re-lated subjects. At the back of each issue is a listing by author of book reviews that appear in the indexed journals. The *SSI* is published quarterly.
New York Times Index	Economic Social Political Technological Competitive	This is an excellent and very detailed index of articles published by the *New York Times* newspaper. The index is arranged alphabetically and includes many helpful cross-references. The *NYTI* is published bimonthly.
Wall Street Journal/ Barron's Index	Economic Social Political Technological Competitive	A valuable index of *Wall Street Journal* and *Barron's* articles. Each issue is in two parts; corporate news and general news. The index includes a list of book reviews. The *WSJ/BI* is published monthly.

[a]"Social" includes cultural, demographic, and environmental information; "Political" includes governmental and legal information.
Source: Adapted from Lorna M. Daniells, *Business Information Sources* (Los Angeles: University of California Press, 1976), 14–17.

INTERNET Millions of people today use on-line services for both business and per-sonal purposes. *America Online* and *Netscape* are leading commercial on-line services. These companies are expanding their menu of available services to include everything from on-line access to most major television networks, newspapers, and magazines to on-line interviewing of celebrities, and they offer access to the furthermost boundaries of the Internet. These companies harness the power of multimedia, combining sound, video, and graphics with text. Excellent sources of strategic management and case re-search information on the World Wide Web are provided in Table 4–7. Table 4–8 pro-vides selected academic and consulting strategic planning Web sites.

The Internet offers consumers and businesses a widening range of services and information resources from all over the world. Interactive services offer users not only access to information worldwide but also the ability to communicate with the person or company that created the information. Historical barriers to personal and business success—time zones and diverse cultures—are being eliminated. The Internet is poised to become as important to our society by the end of this decade as television and newspapers.

TABLE 4–7
Excellent Internet Sources of Information

I. INVESTMENT RESEARCH

American Stock Exchange ⟶ www.amex.com
DBC Online ⟶ www.dbc.com
Hoover's Online ⟶ www.hoovers.com
InvestorGuide ⟶ www.investorguide.com
Wall Street Research Net ⟶ www.wsrn.com
Market Guide ⟶ www.marketguide.com
Money Search - Find It! ⟶ www.moneysearch.com
NASDAQ ⟶ www.nasdaq.com
New York Stock Exchange ⟶ www.nyse.com/public/home.html
PC Financial Network ⟶ www.dljdirect.com
Quote.Com ⟶ www.quote.com
Stock Smart ⟶ www.stocksmart.com
Wright Investors' Service on the World Wide Web ⟶ www.wisi.com
Zacks Investment Research ⟶ www.zacks.com/docs/Bob/hotlinks.htm

II. SEARCH ENGINES

Alta Vista ⟶ www.altavista.digital.com
Deja News ⟶ www.dejanews.com
DogPile ⟶ www.dogpile.com
Excite ⟶ www.excite.com
HotBot ⟶ www.hotbot.com
InfoSeek ⟶ www.infoseek.com
Lycos ⟶ www.lycos.com
Magellan Internet Guide ⟶ www.mckinley.com
Metacrawler ⟶ www.metacrawler.com
Starting Point ⟶ www.stpt.com
WebCrawler ⟶ webcrawler.com
Yahoo! ⟶ www.yahoo.com

III. DIRECTORIES

Argus Clearinghouse ⟶ www.clearinghouse.net
BigBook ⟶ www.bigbook.com
ComFind ⟶ www.comfind.com
U.S. Business Advisor ⟶ www.business.gov/business.html
Thomas Publishing Co. ⟶ www.thomaspublishing.com
Competitive Intelligence Guide ⟶ www.fuld.com

IV. NEWS, MAGAZINES, AND NEWSPAPERS

PR Newswire ⟶ www.prnewswire.com
American Demographics ⟶ www.marketingtools.com
Barron's Magazine ⟶ www.barrons.com
Business Week ⟶ www.businessweek.com
CNNfn ⟶ www.cnnfn.com/search
Financial Times ⟶ www.usa.ft.com
Forbes Magazine On-line ⟶ www.forbes.com
Fortune Magazine ⟶ www.fortune.com
USA Today ⟶ www.usatoday.com
Wall Street Journal ⟶ www.wsj.com
Washington Post Online ⟶ www.washingtonpost.com

V. U.S. GOVERNMENT

Better Business Bureau ⟶ www.bbb.org
Census Bureau ⟶ www.census.gov
Federal Trade Commission ⟶ www.ftc.gov
FreeEDGAR ⟶ www.freeedgar.com
Edgar-Online ⟶ www.edgar-online.com

continued

TABLE 4–7 *continued*

> General Printing Office ⟶ www.gpo.gov
> Internal Revenue Service ⟶ www.irs.ustreas.gov
> Library of Congress ⟶ www.loc.gov
> SEC's Edgar Database ⟶ www.sec.gov/edgarhp.htm
> Small Business Administration ⟶ www.sba.gov
> U.S. Department of Commerce ⟶ www.doc.gov
> U.S. Department of the Treasury ⟶ www.ustreas.gov
> Environmental Protection Agency ⟶ www.epa.gov
> National Aeronautics and Space Administration ⟶ www.hq.nasa.gov

TABLE 4–8
Important Strategic Planning Web Sites

I. ACADEMIC

1. NEW MEXICO STATE UNIVERSITY—www.nmsu.edu/strategic/
This site provides a full description of the strategic planning process at New Mexico State University, including a chart, reading material on strategic planning, and guidelines about how to do strategic planning. A great site for seeing strategic planning in action.

2. STRATEGIC MANAGEMENT SOCIETY—www.virtual-indiana.com/sms/
This is a not-for-profit professional society composed of nearly 2,000 academic, business, and consulting members from 45 countries. This group publishes the *Strategic Management Journal* and offers annual meetings and conferences. The Web site is well designed and outlines the society's services and resources.

3. AMERICAN MANAGEMENT ASSOCIATION—www.amanet.org
AMA provides educational forums worldwide for businesses to learn practical business skills. This Web site is comprehensive in providing access to all AMA seminars, videos, and courses worldwide, including strategic planning products. AMA publishes *Management Review.*

4. ACADEMY OF MANAGEMENT ONLINE—www.aom.pace.edu
This not-for-profit organization is the leading professional association for management research and education in the United States. Almost 10,000 members from businesses and universities around the world participate. About 2,500 of these members specify Business Policy and Strategy as their primary interest. This site provides a search engine to locate and contact all these members. Many links and personal Web pages are provided. This organization publishes *Academy of Management Executive*, *Academy of Management Review*, and *Academy of Management Journal.*

5. STRATEGIC LEADERSHIP FORUM—www.slfnet.org
This is an international organization of executives focusing on strategic management and planning. The Web site is outstanding. Many excellent strategic planning links are provided. The Forum publishes *Strategy and Leadership* (formerly *Planning Review*).

II. CONSULTANTS

1. STRATEGIC PLANNING SYSTEMS—www.checkmateplan.com
This site provides CheckMATE, the industry leader in strategic planning software worldwide. This software is Windows-based and easy to use. Twenty-three different industry versions are available. Also provided on this site is a strategic planning video and workbook, as well as free links to scores for other good sites for gathering strategic planning information.

2. MIND TOOLS—www.mindtools.com/planpage.html
This is an excellent Web site for providing strategic planning information. More than 30 pages of narrative about how and why to do strategic planning are provided. Planning templates are provided.

3. PERFORMANCE STRATEGIES, INC.—www.perfstrat.com/articles/ptp.htm
This Web site offers about 20 pages of excellent narrative about how and why to do strategic planning. A model of the planning process is provided, as well as excellent discussion of mission, benefits of planning, objectives, priorities, and timing.

continued

TABLE 4–8   *continued*

4.   *PALO ALTO SOFTWARE—www.bizplans.com*
This Web site offers a model of the business planning process with excellent narrative as well as seven example business plans from real firms. This is one of the two best sites available for business planning information. (The other is the Small Business Administration Web site.)

5.   *CENTER FOR STRATEGIC MANAGEMENT—www.csmweb.com*
This Web site describes strategic management training, seminars, and facilitation services. The site also provides excellent links to other strategic planning academic and government sites.

6.   *BOSTON CONSULTING GROUP—www.bcg.com*
This perhaps is the best-known strategic planning consulting firm. The Web site offers some nice discussion of strategic planning but focuses mostly on getting a job with BCG rather than on strategic planning information.

7.   *FULD & COMPANY—www.fuld.cum*
This Web site specializes in competitive intelligence. Nice links are provided regarding the importance of gathering information about competitors. This site offers audio answers to key questions about intelligence systems.

FORECASTING TOOLS AND TECHNIQUES

Forecasts are educated assumptions about future trends and events. Forecasting is a complex activity due to factors such as technological innovation, cultural changes, new products, improved services, stronger competitors, shifts in government priorities, changing social values, unstable economic conditions, and unforeseen events. Managers often must rely upon published forecasts to identify key external opportunities and threats effectively.

Many publications and sources on the Internet forecast external variables. Several published examples include *Industry Week*'s "Trends and Forecasts," *Business Week*'s "Investment Outlook," and Standard & Poor's *Industry Survey*. The reputation and continued success of these publications depend partly on accurate forecasts, so published sources of information can offer excellent projections.

Sometimes organizations must develop their own projections. Most organizations forecast (project) their own revenues and profits annually. Organizations sometimes forecast market share or customer loyalty in local areas. Because forecasting is so important in strategic management and because the ability to forecast (in contrast to the ability to use a forecast) is essential, selected forecasting tools are examined further here.

Forecasting tools can be broadly categorized into two groups: quantitative techniques and qualitative techniques. Quantitative forecasts are most appropriate when historical data are available and when the relationships among key variables are expected to remain the same in the future. The three basic types of quantitative forecasting techniques are econometric models, regression, and *trend extrapolation. Econometric models* are based on simultaneous systems of regression equations that forecast variables such as interest rates and money supply. With the advent of sophisticated computer software, econometric models have become the most widely used approach for forecasting economic variables.

All quantitative forecasts, regardless of statistical sophistication and complexity, are based on historical relationships among key variables. *Linear regression*, for example, is based on the assumption that the future will be just like the past—which, of course, it never is. As historical relationships become less stable, quantitative forecasts becomes less accurate.

The six basic qualitative approaches to forecasting are (1) sales force estimates, (2) juries of executive opinion, (3) anticipatory surveys or market research, (4) scenario forecasts, (5) delphi forecasts, and (6) brainstorming. Qualitative or judgmental forecasts are particularly useful when historical data are not available or when constituent variables are expected to change significantly in the future.

Due to advancements in computer technology, quantitative forecasting techniques are usually cheaper and faster than qualitative methods. Quantitative techniques such as multiple regression can generate measures of error that allow a manager to estimate the degree of confidence associated with a given forecast. Forecasting tools must be used carefully or the results can be more misleading than helpful, but qualitative techniques require more intuitive judgment than do quantitative ones. Managers sometimes erroneously forecast what they would like to occur.

No forecast is perfect, and some forecasts are even wildly inaccurate. This fact accents the need for strategists to devote sufficient time and effort to study the underlying bases for published forecasts and to develop internal forecasts of their own. Key external opportunities and threats can be effectively identified only through good forecasts. Accurate forecasts can provide major competitive advantages for organizations. Forecasts are vital to the strategic-management process and to the success of organizations.

MAKING ASSUMPTIONS Planning would be impossible without assumptions. McConkey defines assumptions as "best present estimates of the impact of major external factors, over which the manager has little if any control, but which may exert a significant impact on performance or the ability to achieve desired results.[11] Strategists are faced with countless variables and imponderables that can be neither controlled nor predicted with 100 percent accuracy.

By identifying future occurrences that could have a major effect on the firm and making reasonable assumptions about those factors, strategists can carry the strategic-management process forward. Assumptions are needed only for future trends and events that are most likely to have a significant effect on the company's business. Based on the best information at the time, assumptions serve as checkpoints on the validity of strategies. If future occurrences deviate significantly from assumptions, strategists know that corrective actions may be needed. Without reasonable assumptions, the strategy-formulation process could not proceed effectively. Firms that have the best information generally make the most accurate assumptions, which can lead to major competitive advantages.

COMPETITIVE ANALYSIS: PORTER'S FIVE-FORCES MODEL

As illustrated in Figure 4–3, *Porter's Five-Forces Model* of competitive analysis is a widely used approach for developing strategies in many industries. The intensity of competition among firms varies widely across industries. Table 4–9 reveals the average return on equity for firms in 24 different industries in 1996. Intensity of competition is highest in lower-return industries. According to Porter, the nature of competitiveness in a given industry can be viewed as a composite of five forces:

1. Rivalry among competitive firms
2. Potential entry of new competitors
3. Potential development of substitute products
4. Bargaining power of suppliers
5. Bargaining power of consumers

FIGURE 4-3
The Five-Forces Model of Competition

RIVALRY AMONG COMPETING FIRMS Rivalry among competing firms is usually the most powerful of the five competitive forces. The strategies pursued by one firm can be successful only to the extent that they provide competitive advantage over the strategies pursued by rival firms. Changes in strategy by one firm may be met with retaliatory countermoves, such as lowering prices, enhancing quality, adding features, providing services, extending warranties, and increasing advertising.

TABLE 4-9
Intensity of Competition Among Firms in Different Industries–1996 and 1997 Results Provided

INDUSTRY	1996/1997 AVERAGE RETURN ON EQUITY	1996/1997 AVERAGE EARNINGS PER SHARE
Consumer Products	26.5/27.7	2.25/1.90
Health Care	24.8/21.9	2.39/1.78
Telecommunications	23.1/18.1	2.59/2.25
Chemicals	22.3/18.8	2.96/2.31
Manufacturing	20.4/18.2	2.56/2.18
Conglomerates	20.4/20.6	3.07/2.05
Food	19.4/17.3	1.54/1.07
Automotive	19.3/23.6	3.96/5.16
Fuel	17.1/17.6	4.13/3.17
Office Equipment and Computers	16.8/19.7	1.59/1.55
Aerospace and Defense	16.8/11.7	2.44/1.77
Banks	15.7/16.3	4.16/3.59
Transportation	15.3/16.7	3.45/2.95
Nonbank Financial	15.1/16.0	3.19/3.35
Housing and Real Estate	14.9/20.1	1.64/2.03
Electrical and Electronics	14.3/15.8	2.11/2.21
Leisure Time Industries	13.7/11.4	1.82/1.48
Publishing and Broadcasting	12.0/4.9	1.35/0.54
Utilities and Power	11.4/10.1	2.10/1.87
Discount and Fashion Retailing	11.3/13.5	1.10/1.34
Paper and Forest Products	9.4/3.2	2.06/0.52
Containers and Packaging	9.0/6.5	1.25/0.70
Metals and Mining	8.5/12.2	1.26/1.82
Service Industries	8.3/10.9	0.79/0.98

Source: Adapted from "Corporate Scoreboard," *Business Week* (March 3, 1997): 95–115. Also, "Corporate Scoreboard," *Business Week* (March 2, 1998): 113–136.

The intensity of rivalry among competing firms tends to increase as the number of competitors increases, as competitors become more equal in size and capability, as demand for the industry's products declines, and as price cutting becomes common. Rivalry also increases when consumers can switch brands easily; when barriers to leaving the market are high; when fixed costs are high; when the product is perishable; when rival firms are diverse in strategies, origins, and culture; and when mergers and acquisitions are common in the industry. As rivalry among competing firms intensifies, industry profits decline, in some cases to the point where an industry becomes inherently unattractive.

POTENTIAL ENTRY OF NEW COMPETITORS   Whenever new firms can easily enter a particular industry, the intensity of competitiveness among firms increases. Barriers to entry, however, can include the need to gain economies of scale quickly, the need to gain technology and specialized know-how, the lack of experience, strong customer loyalty, strong brand preferences, large capital requirements, lack of adequate distribution channels, government regulatory policies, tariffs, lack of access to raw materials, possession of patents, undesirable locations, counterattack by entrenched firms, and potential saturation of the market.

Despite numerous barriers to entry, new firms sometimes enter industries with higher-quality products, lower prices, and substantial marketing resources. Compaq's entering the personal computer market and Wal-Mart's entering the discount market are examples. The strategist's job, therefore, is to identify potential new firms entering the market, to monitor the new rival firms' strategies, to counterattack as needed, and to capitalize on existing strengths and opportunities.

POTENTIAL DEVELOPMENT OF SUBSTITUTE PRODUCTS   In many industries, firms are in close competition with producers of substitute products in other industries. Examples are plastic container producers competing with glass, paperboard, and aluminum can producers, and acetaminophen manufacturers competing with other manufacturers of pain and headache remedies. The presence of substitute products puts a ceiling on the price that can be charged before the consumers will switch to the substitute product.

Competitive pressures arising from substitute products increase as the relative price of substitute products declines and as consumers' switching costs decrease. The competitive strength of substitute products is best measured by the inroads into market share those products obtain, as well as those firms' plans for increased capacity and market penetration.

BARGAINING POWER OF SUPPLIERS   The bargaining power of suppliers affects the intensity of competition in an industry, especially when there is a large number of suppliers, when there are only a few good substitute raw materials, or when the cost of switching raw materials is especially costly. It often is in the best interest of both suppliers and producers to assist each other with reasonable prices, improved quality, development of new services, just-in-time deliveries, and reduced inventory costs, thus enhancing long-term profitability for all concerned.

Firms may pursue a backward integration strategy to gain control or ownership of suppliers. This strategy is especially effective when suppliers are unreliable, too costly, or not capable of meeting a firm's needs on a consistent basis. Firms generally can negotiate more favorable terms with suppliers when backward integration is a commonly used strategy among rival firms in an industry.

BARGAINING POWER OF CONSUMERS   When customers are concentrated or large, or buy in volume, their bargaining power represents a major force affecting intensity of competition in an industry. Rival firms may offer extended warranties or special services to gain customer loyalty whenever the bargaining power of consumers is substantial. Bargaining power of consumers also is higher when the products being purchased are standard or undifferentiated. When this is the case, consumers often can negotiate selling price, warranty coverage, and accessory packages to a greater extent.

INDUSTRY ANALYSIS: THE EXTERNAL FACTOR EVALUATION (EFE) MATRIX

An *External Factor Evaluation (EFE) Matrix* allows strategists to summarize and evaluate economic, social, cultural, demographic, environmental, political, governmental, legal, technological, and competitive information. There are five steps in developing an EFE Matrix:

1. List key external factors as identified in the external-audit process. Include a total of from 10 to 20 factors, including both opportunities and threats affecting the firm and its industry. List the opportunities first and then the threats. Be as specific as possible, using percentages, ratios, and comparative numbers whenever possible.

2. Assign to each factor a weight that ranges from 0.0 (not important) to 1.0 (very important). The weight indicates the relative importance of that factor to being successful in the firm's industry. Opportunities often receive higher weights than threats, but threats too can receive high weights if they are especially severe or threatening. Appropriate weights can be determined by comparing successful with unsuccessful competitors or by discussing the factor and reaching a group consensus. The sum of all weights assigned to the factors must equal 1.0.

3. Assign a 1-to-4 rating to each critical success factor to indicate how effectively the firm's current strategies respond to the factor, where 4 = *the response is superior*, 3 = *the response is above average*, 2 = *the response is average*, and 1 = *the response is poor*. Ratings are based on effectiveness of the firm's strategies. Ratings are thus company-based, whereas the weights in Step 2 are industry-based.

4. Multiply each factor's weight by its rating to determine a weighted score.

5. Sum the weighted scores for each variable to determine the total weighted score for the organization.

Regardless of the number of key opportunities and threats included in an EFE Matrix, the highest possible total weighted score for an organization is 4.0 and the lowest possible total weighted score is 1.0. The average total weighted score is 2.5. A total weighted score of 4.0 indicates that an organization is responding in an outstanding way to existing opportunities and threats in its industry. In other words, the firm's strategies effectively take advantage of existing opportunities and minimize the potential adverse effect of external threats. A total score of 1.0 indicates that the firm's strategies are not capitalizing on opportunities or avoiding external threats.

An example of an EFE Matrix is provided in Table 4–10 for UST, Inc., the manufacturer of Skoal and Copenhagen smokeless tobacco. Note that the Clinton Administration was considered to be the most important factor affecting this industry, as indicated by the weight of 0.20. UST was not pursuing strategies that effectively capitalize on this opportunity, as indicated by the rating of 1.01. The total weighted score of 2.10 indicates that UST is below average in its effort to pursue strategies that capitalize on external opportunities and avoid threats. It is important to note here that a thorough understanding of the factors being used in the EFE Matrix is more important than the actual weights and ratings assigned.

TABLE 4–10
An Example External
Factor Evaluation Matrix
for UST, Inc.

KEY EXTERNAL FACTORS	WEIGHT	RATING	WEIGHTED SCORE
OPPORTUNITIES			
1. Global markets are practically untapped by smokeless tobacco market	.15	1	.15
2. Increased demand due to public banning of smoking	.05	3	.15
3. Astronomical Internet advertising growth	.05	1	.05
4. Pinkerton is leader in discount tobacco market	.15	4	.60
5. More social pressure to quit smoking, thus leading users to switch to alternatives	.10	3	.30
THREATS			
1. Legislation against the tobacco industry	.10	2	.20
2. Production limits on tobacco increases competition for production	.05	3	.15
3. Smokeless tobacco market is concentrated in southeast region of United States	.05	2	.10
4. Bad media exposure from the FDA	.10	2	.20
5. Clinton Administration	.20	1	.20
TOTAL	1.00		2.10

THE COMPETITIVE PROFILE MATRIX (CPM)

The *Competitive Profile Matrix (CPM)* identifies a firm's major competitors and their particular strengths and weaknesses in relation to a sample firm's strategic position. The weights and total weighted scores in both a CPM and EFE have the same meaning. However, the factors in a CPM include both internal and external issues; the ratings refer to strengths and weaknesses. There are some important differences between the EFE and CPM. First of all, the critical success factors in a CPM are broader; they do not include specific or factual data and even may focus on internal issues. The critical success factors in a CPM also are not grouped into opportunities and threats as they are in an EFE. In a CPM the ratings and total weighted scores for rival firms can be compared to the sample firm. This comparative analysis provides important internal strategic information.

A sample Competitive Profile Matrix is provided in Table 4–11. In this example, advertising and global expansion are the most important critical success factors, as indicated by a weight of 0.20. Avon's and L'Oreal's product quality are superior, as evidenced by a rating of 4; L'Oreal's "financial position" is good, as indicated by a rating of 3; Procter & Gamble is the weakest firm overall, as indicated by a total weighted score of 2.80.

TABLE 4–11
A Competitive Profile Matrix

CRITICAL SUCCESS FACTORS	WEIGHT	AVON		L'OREAL		PROCTER & GAMBLE	
		RATING	SCORE	RATING	SCORE	RATING	SCORE
Advertising	0.20	1	0.20	4	0.80	3	0.60
Product Quality	0.10	4	0.40	4	0.40	3	0.30
Price Competitiveness	0.10	3	0.30	3	0.30	4	0.40
Management	0.10	4	0.40	3	0.30	3	0.30
Financial Position	0.15	4	0.60	3	0.45	3	0.45
Customer Loyalty	0.10	4	0.40	4	0.40	2	0.20
Global Expansion	0.20	4	0.80	2	0.40	2	0.40
Market Share	0.05	1	0.05	4	0.20	3	0.15
TOTAL	1.00		3.15		3.25		2.80

Note: (1) The ratings values are as follows: 1 = major weakness, 2 = minor weakness, 3 = minor strength, 4 = major strength. (2) As indicated by the total weighted score of 2.8, Competitor 3 is weakest. (3) Only eight critical success factors are included for simplicity; this is too few in actuality.

A word on interpretation: Just because one firm receives a 3.2 rating and another receives a 2.8 rating in a Competitive Profile Matrix, it does not follow that the first firm is 20 percent better than the second. Numbers reveal the relative strength of firms, but their implied precision is an illusion. Numbers are not magic. The aim is not to arrive at a single number, but rather to assimilate and evaluate information in a meaningful way that aids in decision making.

CONCLUSION

Due to increasing turbulence in markets and industries around the world, the external audit has become an explicit and vital part of the strategic-management process. This chapter provides a framework for collecting and evaluating economic, social, cultural, demographic, environmental, political, governmental, legal, technological, and competitive information. Firms that do not mobilize and empower their managers and employees to identify, monitor, forecast, and evaluate key external forces may fail to anticipate emerging opportunities and threats and, consequently, may pursue ineffective strategies, miss opportunities, and invite organizational demise. Firms not taking advantage of the Internet are falling behind technologically.

A major responsibility of strategists is to ensure development of an effective external-audit system. This includes using information technology to devise a competitive intelligence system that works. The external-audit approach described in this chapter can be used effectively by any size or type of organization. Typically, the external-audit process is more informal in small firms, but the need to understand key trends and events is no less important for these firms. The EFE Matrix and five-forces model can help strategists evaluate the market and industry, but these tools must be accompanied by good intuitive judgment. Multinational firms especially need a systematic and effective external-audit system because external forces among foreign countries vary so greatly.

We invite you to visit the DAVID page on the Prentice Hall Web site at
www.prenhall.com/davidsm
for this chapter's World Wide Web exercises.

 TAKE IT TO THE NET

KEY TERMS AND CONCEPTS

America Online	(p. 122)	Director of Competitive Analysis	(p. 120)	Internet	(p. 107)
Chief Information Officer (CIO)	(p. 108)			Learning from the Partner	(p. 120)
Chief Technology Officer (CTO)	(p. 108)	Downsizing	(p. 109)	Linear Regression	(p. 125)
Competitive Advantages	(p. 116)	Econometric Models	(p. 125)	Lifecare Facilities	(p. 111)
Competitive Analysis	(p. 120)	Environmental Scanning	(p. 104)	Porter's Five-Forces Model	(p. 126)
Competitive Intelligence (CI)	(p. 119)	External Audit	(p. 104)	Netscape	(p. 122)
Competitive Profile Matrix (CPM)	(p. 130)	External Factor Evaluation (EFE) Matrix	(p. 129)	On-Line Databases	(p. 107)
				Rightsizing	(p. 109)
Critical Success Factors	(p. 107)	External Forces	(p. 104)	Trend Extrapolation	(p. 125)
Cyberspace	(p. 107)	Industry Analysis	(p. 104)	World Wide Web	(p. 107)
Decruiting	(p. 109)	Information Technology (IT)	(p. 107)		

ISSUES FOR REVIEW AND DISCUSSION

1. Explain how to conduct an external strategic-management audit.

2. Identify a recent economic, social, political, or technological trend that significantly affects financial institutions.

3. Discuss the following statement: Major opportunities and threats usually result from an interaction among key environmental trends rather than from a single external event or factor.

4. Identify two industries experiencing rapid technological changes and three industries that are experiencing little technological change. How does the need for technological forecasting differ in these industries? Why?

5. Use Porter's five-forces model to evaluate competitiveness within the U.S. banking industry.

6. What major forecasting techniques would you use to identify (1) economic opportunities and threats and (2) demographic opportunities and threats? Why are these techniques most appropriate?

7. How does the external audit affect other components of the strategic-management process?

8. As the owner of a small business, explain how you would organize a strategic-information scanning system. How would you organize such a system in a large organization?

9. Construct an EFE Matrix for an organization of your choice.

10. Make an appointment with a librarian at your university to learn how to use on-line databases. Report your findings in class.

11. Give some advantages and disadvantages of cooperative versus competitive strategies.

12. As strategist for a local bank, explain when you would use qualitative versus quantitative forecasts.

13. What is your forecast for interest rates and the stock market in the next several months? As the stock market moves up, do interest rates always move down? Why? What are the strategic implications of these trends?

14. Explain how information technology affects strategies of the organization where you worked most recently.

15. Let's say your boss develops an EFE Matrix that includes 62 factors. How would you suggest reducing the number of factors to 20?

16. Select one of the current readings at the end of this chapter. Prepare a 1-page written summary that includes your personal opinion of the article.

17. Discuss the ethics of gathering competitive intelligence.

18. Discuss the ethics of cooperating with rival firms.

19. Visit the SEC Web site at www.sec.gov and discuss the benefits of using information provided there.

NOTES

1. Paul Judge, "Is the Net Redefining Our Identity?" *Business Week*, (May 12, 1997): 102.

2. John Diffenbach, "Corporate Environmental Analysis in Large U.S. Corporations," *Long Range Planning* 16, no. 3 (June 1983): 109.

3. York Freund, "Critical Success Factors," *Planning Review* 16, no. 4 (July–August 1988): 20.

4. Gregory Parsons, "Information Technology: A New Competitive Weapon," *Sloan Management Review* 25, no. 1 (Fall 1983): 5.

5. Frederick Gluck, "Global Competition in the 1990s," *Journal of Business Strategy* (Spring 1983): 22, 24.

6. John Harris, Robert Shaw, Jr., and William Sommers, "The Strategic Management of Technology," *Planning Review* 11, no. 1 (January–February 1983): 28, 35.

7. Susan Levine and Michael Yalowitz, "Managing Technology: The Key to Successful Business Growth," *Management Review* 72, no. 9 (September 1983): 44.

8. Bill Saporito, "Companies That Compete Best," *Fortune* (May 22, 1989): 36.

9. Kenneth Sawka, "Demystifying Business Intelligence," *Management Review*, (October 1996): 49.

10. John Prescott and Daniel Smith, "The Largest Survey of 'Leading-Edge' Competitor Intelligence Managers," *Planning Review* 17, no. 3 (May–June 1989): 6–13.

11. Dale McConkey, "Planning in a Changing Environment," *Business Horizons* 31, no. 5 (September–October 1988): 67.

CURRENT READINGS

Baum, Joel A. C. and Helaine J. Korn. "Competitive Dynamics of Interfirm Rivalry." *Academy of Management Journal* 39, no. 2 (April 1996): 255–291.

Belohlav, James A. "The Evolving Competitive Paradigm." *Business Horizons* 39, no. 2 (March–April 1996): 11–19.

Brooks, Ian and Jon Reast. "Redesigning the Value Chain at Scania Trucks." *Long Range Planning* 29, no. 4 (August 1996): 514–525.

Cheng, Joseph and Idalene F. Kesner. "Organizational Slack and Response to Environmental Shifts: The Impact of Resource Allocation Patterns." *Journal of Management* 23, no. 1 (Spring 1997): 1–18.

Cheng, Ming-Jer. "Competitor Analysis and Interfirm Rivalry: Toward a Theoretical Integration." *Academy of Management Review* 21, no. 1 (January 1996): 100–134.

Doz, Y. L. "The Evolution of Cooperation in Strategic Alliances: Initial Conditions or Learning Processes?" *Strategic Management Journal* 17, Special Issue (Summer 1996): 55–84.

Elenkov, D. S. "Strategic Uncertainty and Environmental Scanning: The Case for Institutional Influences on Scanning Behavior." *Strategic Management Journal* 18, no. 4 (April 1997): 287–302.

Evans, Philip B. and Thomas S. Wurster. "Strategy and the New Economics of Information." *Harvard Business Review* (September–October 1997): 70–83.

Gleb, Betsy D. and Linda Hayes. "When Your Competitor Turns Obstructionist . . ." *Business Horizons* 40, no. 2 (March–April 1997): 33–39.

Goll, I. and A.M.A. Rasheed. "Rational Decision-Making and Firm Performance: The Moderating Role of Environment." *Strategic Management Journal* 18, no. 7 (August 1997): 583–593.

Gruca, Thomas S., Deepika Nath, and Ajay Mehra. "Exploiting Synergy for Competitive Advantage." *Long Range Planning* 30, no. 4 (August 1997): 605–611.

Harrison, Jeffrey S. and Caron H. St. John. "Managing and Partnering with External Stakeholders." *Academy of Management Executive* 10, no. 2 (May 1996): 46–60.

Jose, P. D. "Corporate Strategy and the Environment: A Portfolio Approach." *Long Range Planning* 29, no. 4 (August 1996): 462–472.

Lado, Augustine A., Nancy G. Boyd, and Susan C. Hanlon. "Competition, Cooperation, and the Search for Economic Rents: A Syncretic Model." *Academy of Management Review* 22, no. 1 (January 1997): 110–141.

McGahan, A. M. and M. E. Porter. "How Much Does Industry Matter, Really?" *Strategic Management Journal* 18, Special Issue (Summer 1997): 15–30.

Mowery, D. C., J. E. Oxley, and B. S. Silverman. "Strategic Alliances and Interfirm Knowledge Transfer." *Strategic Management Journal* 17, Special Issue (Winter 1996): 77–92.

Newman, Victor and Kazem Chaharbaghi. "Strategic Alliances in Fast-Moving Markets." *Long Range Planning* 29, no. 6 (December 1996): 850–856.

Pawar, Badrinarayan Shankar and Ramesh Sharda. "Obtaining Business Intelligence on the Internet." *Long Range Planning* 30, no. 1 (February 1997): 110–121.

Powell, T. C. and A. Kent-Micallef. "Information Technology as Competitive Advantage: The Role of Human, Business, and Technology Resources." *Strategic Management Journal* 18, no. 5 (May 1997): 375–406.

Price, Robert M. "Executive Forum: Technology and Strategic Advantage." *California Management Review* 38, no. 3 (Spring 1996): 38–56.

Randall, Doug. "Consumer Strategies for the Internet: Four Scenarios." *Long Range Planning* 30, no. 2 (April 1997): 157–168.

Spekman, Robert E., Lynn A. Isabella, Thomas C. MacAvoy, and Theodore Forbes III. "Creating Strategic Alliances Which Endure." *Long Range Planning* 29, no. 3 (June 1996): 346–357.

Stimpert, J. L. and Irene M. Duhaime. "Seeing the Big Picture: The Influence of Industry, Diversification, and Business Strategy on Performance." *Academy of Management Journal* 40, no. 3 (June 1997): 560–583.

Zahra, Shaker A. "Governance, Ownership, and Corporate Entrepreneurship: The Moderating Impact of Industry Technological Opportunities." *Academy of Management Journal* 39, no. 6 (December 1996): 1713–1735.

EXPERIENTIAL EXERCISES

DEVELOPING AN EFE MATRIX FOR HERSHEY FOODS

PURPOSE

This exercise will give you practice developing an EFE Matrix. An EFE Matrix summarizes the results of an external audit. This is an important tool widely used by strategists.

INSTRUCTIONS

Step 1 Join with two other students in class and jointly prepare an EFE Matrix for Hershey Foods. Refer back to the Cohesion Case and to Experiential Exercise 1A if needed to identify external opportunities and threats.

Step 2 All three-person teams participating in this exercise should record their EFE total weighted scores on the board. Put your initials after your score to identify it as your team's.

Step 3 Compare the total weighted scores. Which team's score came closest to the instructor's answer? Discuss reasons for variation in the scores reported on the board.

THE LIBRARY SEARCH

PURPOSE

This exercise will help you become familiar with important sources of external information available in your college library. A key part of preparing an external audit is examining published sources of information for relevant economic, social, cultural, demographic, environmental, political, governmental, legal, technological, and competitive trends and events. External opportunities and threats must be identified and evaluated before strategies can be formulated effectively.

INSTRUCTIONS

Step 1 Select a company or business located in your county. Go to your college library and conduct an external audit for this company. Find opportunities and threats in recent issues of the local newspaper. Also check magazines. Search for information using the Internet.

Step 2 On a separate sheet of paper, list 10 opportunities and 10 threats that face this company. Be specific in stating each factor by including percentages and numbers wherever possible.

Step 3 Include a bibliography to reveal where you found the information.

Step 4 Share your information with a manager of that company. Ask for his or her comments and additions.

Step 5 Write a three-page summary of your findings and submit it to your teacher.

Experiential Exercise 4C

DEVELOPING AN EFE MATRIX FOR MY UNIVERSITY

PURPOSE

More colleges and universities are embarking upon the strategic-management process. Institutions are consciously and systematically identifying and evaluating external opportunities and threats facing higher education in your state, the nation, and the world.

INSTRUCTIONS

Step 1 Join with two other individuals in class and jointly prepare an EFE Matrix for your institution.

Step 2 Go to the board and record your total weighted score in a column that includes the scores by all three-person teams participating. Put your initials after your score to identify it as your team's.

Step 3 Which team viewed your college's strategies most positively; which team viewed your college's strategies most negatively? Discuss the nature of the differences.

Experiential Exercise 4D

DEVELOPING A COMPETITIVE PROFILE MATRIX FOR HERSHEY FOODS

PURPOSE

Monitoring competitors' performance and strategies is a key aspect of an external audit. This exercise is designed to give you practice evaluating the competitive position of organizations in a given industry and assimilating that information in the form of a Competitive Profile Matrix.

INSTRUCTIONS

Step 1 Turn back to the Cohesion Case and review the section on competitors.

Step 2 On a separate sheet of paper, prepare a Competitive Profile Matrix that includes Hershey Foods, Nestlé, and Mars.

Step 3 Turn in your Competitive Profile Matrix for a classwork grade.

DEVELOPING A COMPETITIVE PROFILE MATRIX FOR MY UNIVERSITY

PURPOSE

Your college or university competes with all other educational institutions in the world, especially those in your own state. State funds, students, faculty, staff, endowments, gifts, and federal funds are areas of competitiveness. The purpose of this exercise is to give you practice thinking competitively about the business of education in your state.

INSTRUCTIONS

Step 1 Identify two colleges or universities in your state that compete directly with your institution for students. Interview several persons who are aware of particular strengths and weaknesses of those universities. Record information about the two competing universities.

Step 2 Prepare a Competitive Profile Matrix that includes your institution and the two competing institutions. Include the following factors in your analysis:
1. Tuition costs
2. Quality of faculty
3. Academic reputation
4. Average class size
5. Campus landscaping
6. Athletic programs
7. Quality of students
8. Graduate programs
9. Location of campus
10. Campus culture

Step 3 Submit your Competitive Profile Matrix to your instructor for evaluation.

CHAPTER 5

The Internal Assessment

CHAPTER OUTLINE

- ◆ THE NATURE OF AN INTERNAL AUDIT
- ◆ RELATIONSHIPS AMONG THE FUNCTIONAL AREAS OF BUSINESS
- ◆ MANAGEMENT
- ◆ MARKETING
- ◆ FINANCE/ACCOUNTING
- ◆ PRODUCTION/OPERATIONS
- ◆ RESEARCH AND DEVELOPMENT
- ◆ COMPUTER INFORMATION SYSTEMS

- ◆ INTERNAL AUDIT CHECKLISTS
- ◆ THE INTERNAL FACTOR EVALUATION (IFE) MATRIX

- ■ EXPERIENTIAL EXERCISE 5A
  Performing a Financial Ratio Analysis for Hershey Foods

- ■ EXPERIENTIAL EXERCISE 5B
  Constructing an IFE Matrix for Hershey Foods

- ■ EXPERIENTIAL EXERCISE 5C
  Constructing an IFE Matrix for My University

CHAPTER OBJECTIVES

After studying this chapter, you should be able to do the following:

1. Describe how to perform an internal strategic-management audit.

2. Discuss key interrelationships among the functional areas of business.

3. Identify the basic functions or activities that make up management, marketing, finance/accounting, production/operations, research and development, and computer information systems.

4. Explain how to determine and prioritize a firm's internal strengths and weaknesses.

5. Explain the importance of financial ratio analysis.

6. Discuss the nature and role of computer information systems in strategic management.

7. Develop an Internal Factor Evaluation (IFE) Matrix.

NOTABLE QUOTES

*L*ike a product or service, the planning process itself must be managed and shaped, if it is to serve executives as a vehicle for strategic decision-making.—ROBERT LENZ

*T*he difference between now and five years ago is that information systems had limited function. You weren't betting your company on it. Now you are.—WILLIAM GRUBER

*W*eak leadership can wreck the soundest strategy.—SUN ZI

A firm that continues to employ a previously successful strategy eventually and inevitably falls victim to a competitor.—WILLIAM COHEN

*I*t is the ability of an organization to move information and ideas from the bottom to the top and back again in continuous dialogue that the Japanese value above all things. As this dialogue is pursued, strategy evolves.—L. J. ROSENBERG AND C. D. SCHEWE

*A*n organization should approach all tasks with the idea that they can be accomplished in a superior fashion.—THOMAS WATSON, JR.

*W*orld-class information technologies are proving to be a significant strategic advantage, helping North American companies maintain and expand their position in the global marketplace.—Y. NAKAMURA

*B*y 2010, managers will have to handle greater cultural diversity. Managers will have to understand that employees don't think alike about such basics as "handling confrontation" or even what it means "to do a good day's work."—JEFFREY SONNENFELD

*T*here is no substitute for quality and no greater threat than failing to be cost-competitive on a global basis. These are complementary concepts, not mutually exclusive ones.—BILL SAPORITO

This chapter focuses on identifying and evaluating a firm's strengths and weaknesses in the functional areas of business, including management, marketing, finance/accounting, production/operations, research and development, and computer information systems. Relationships among these areas of business are examined. Strategic implications of important functional area concepts are examined. The process of performing an internal audit is described.

THE NATURE OF AN INTERNAL AUDIT

All organizations have strengths and weaknesses in the functional areas of business. No enterprise is equally strong or weak in all areas. Maytag, for example, is known for excellent production and product design, whereas Procter & Gamble is known for superb marketing. Internal strengths/weaknesses, coupled with external opportunities/threats and a clear statement of mission, provide the basis for establishing objectives and strategies. Objectives and strategies are established with the intention of capitalizing upon internal strengths and overcoming weaknesses! The internal-audit part of the strategic-management process is emphasized in Figure 5–1.

KEY INTERNAL FORCES   It is not possible in a business policy text to review in depth all the material presented in courses such as marketing, finance, accounting, management, computer information systems, and production/operations; there are many subareas within these functions, such as customer service, warranties, advertising, packaging, and pricing under marketing.

For different types of organizations, such as hospitals, universities, and government agencies, the functional business areas, of course, differ. In a hospital, for example, functional areas may include cardiology, hematology, nursing, maintenance, physician support, and receivables. Functional areas of a university can include athletic programs, placement services, housing, fund raising, academic research, counseling, and intramural programs. Within large organizations, each division has certain strengths and weaknesses. For example, AT&T is strong in communications and weak in computers.

A firm's strengths that cannot be easily matched or imitated by competitors are called *distinctive competencies*. Building competitive advantages involves taking advantage of distinctive competencies. For example, 3M exploits its distinctive competence in research and development by producing a wide range of innovative products. Strategies are designed in part to improve on a firm's weaknesses, turning them into strengths, and maybe even into distinctive competencies.

Some researchers emphasize the importance of the internal audit part of the strategic-management process by comparing it to the external audit. Robert Grant concluded that the internal audit is more important, saying:

> In a world where customer preferences are volatile, the identity of customers is changing, and the technologies for serving customer requirements are continually evolving, an externally focused orientation does not provide a secure foundation for formulating long-term strategy. When the external environment is in a state of flux, the firm's own resources and capabilities may be a much more stable basis on which to define its identity. Hence, a definition of a business in terms of what it is capable of doing may offer a more durable basis for strategy than a definition based upon the needs which the business seeks to satisfy.[1]

THE PROCESS OF PERFORMING AN INTERNAL AUDIT   The process of performing an *internal audit* closely parallels the process of performing an external audit. Representative managers and employees from throughout the firm need to be involved in

FIGURE 5–1
A Comprehensive Strategic-Management Model

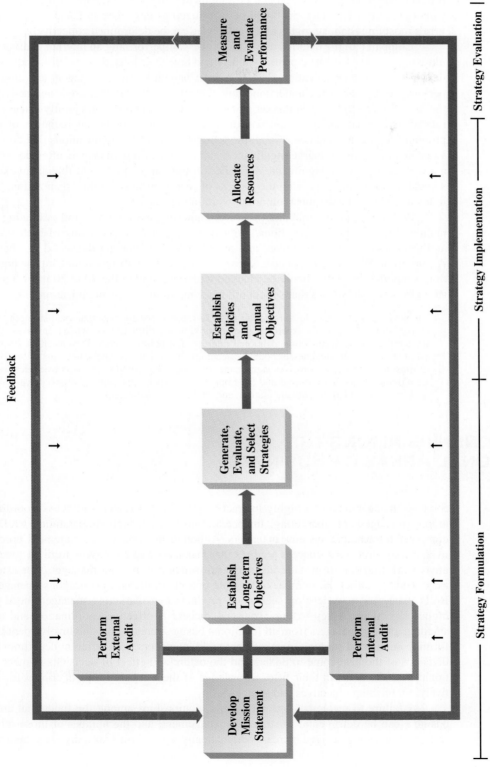

determining a firm's strengths and weaknesses. The internal audit requires gathering and assimilating information about the firm's management, marketing, finance/accounting, production/operations, research and development (R&D), and computer information systems operations. Key factors should be prioritized as described in Chapter 4 so that the firm's most important strengths and weaknesses can be determined collectively.

Compared to the external audit, the process of performing an internal audit provides more opportunity for participants to understand how their jobs, departments, and divisions fit into the whole organization. This is a great benefit because managers and employees perform better when they understand how their work affects other areas and activities of the firm. For example, when marketing and manufacturing managers jointly discuss issues related to internal strengths and weaknesses, they gain a better appreciation of issues, problems, concerns, and needs in all the functional areas. In organizations that do not use strategic management, marketing, finance, and manufacturing managers often do not interact with each other in significant ways. Performing an internal audit thus is an excellent vehicle or forum for improving the process of communication in the organization. "Communication" may be the most important word in management.

Performing an internal audit requires gathering, assimilating, and evaluating information about the firm's operations. Critical success factors, consisting of both strengths and weaknesses, can be identified and prioritized in the manner discussed in Chapter 4. According to William King, a task force of managers from different units of the organization, supported by staff, should be charged with determining the 10 to 20 most important strengths and weaknesses that should influence the future of the organization:

> The development of conclusions on the 10 to 20 most important organizational strengths and weaknesses can be, as any experienced manager knows, a difficult task, when it involves managers representing various organizational interests and points of view. Developing a 20-page list of strengths and weaknesses could be accomplished relatively easily, but a list of the 10 to 15 most important ones involves significant analysis and negotiation. This is true because of the judgments that are required and the impact which such a list will inevitably have as it is used in the formulation, implementation, and evaluation of strategies.[2]

RELATIONSHIPS AMONG THE FUNCTIONAL AREAS OF BUSINESS

Strategic management is a highly interactive process that requires effective coordination among management, marketing, finance/accounting, production/operations, R&D, and computer information systems managers. Although the strategic-management process is overseen by strategists, success requires that managers and employees from all functional areas work together to provide ideas and information. Financial managers, for example, may need to restrict the number of feasible options available to operations managers, or R&D managers may develop such good products that marketing managers need to set higher objectives. A key to organizational success is effective coordination and understanding among managers from all functional business areas! Through involvement in performing an internal strategic-management audit, managers from different departments and divisions of the firm come to understand the nature and effect of decisions in other functional business areas in their firm. Knowledge of these relationships is critical for effectively establishing objectives and strategies.

A failure to recognize and understand relationships among the functional areas of business can be detrimental to strategic management, and the number of those relationships that must be managed increases dramatically with a firm's size, diversity, geographic dispersion, and the number of products or services offered. Governmental and nonprofit enterprises traditionally have not placed sufficient emphasis on relationships among the business functions. For example, some state governments, utilities, universities, and hospitals only recently have begun to establish marketing objectives and policies that are consistent with their financial capabilities and limitations. Some firms place too great an emphasis on one function at the expense of others. Ansoff explained:

> During the first fifty years, successful firms focused their energies on optimizing the performance of one of the principal functions: production/operations, R&D, or marketing. Today, due to the growing complexity and dynamism of the environment, success increasingly depends on a judicious combination of several functional influences. This transition from a single function focus to a multifunction focus is essential for successful strategic management.[3]

Financial ratio analysis exemplifies the complexity of relationships among the functional areas of business. A declining return on investment or profit margin ratio could be the result of ineffective marketing, poor management policies, research and development errors, or a weak computer information system. The effectiveness of strategy formulation, implementation, and evaluation activities hinges upon a clear understanding of how major business functions affect one another. For strategies to succeed, a coordinated effort among all the functional areas of business is needed. In the case of planning, George wrote:

> We may conceptually separate planning for the purpose of theoretical discussion and analysis, but in practice, neither is it a distinct entity nor is it capable of being separated. The planning function is mixed with all other business functions and, like ink once mixed with water, it cannot be set apart. It is spread throughout and is a part of the whole of managing an organization.[4]

INTEGRATING STRATEGY AND CULTURE Relationships among a firm's functional business activities perhaps can be exemplified best by focusing on organizational culture, an internal phenomenon that permeates all departments and divisions of an organization. *Organizational culture* can be defined as "a pattern of behavior developed by an organization as it learns to cope with its problem of external adaptation and internal integration, that has worked well enough to be considered valid and to be taught to new members as the correct way to perceive, think, and feel."[5] This definition emphasizes the importance of matching external with internal factors in making strategic decisions.

Organizational culture captures the subtle, elusive, and largely unconscious forces that shape a workplace. Remarkably resistant to change, culture can represent a major strength or weakness for the firm. It can be an underlying reason for strengths or weaknesses in any of the major business functions.

Defined in Table 5–1, *cultural products* include values, beliefs, rites, rituals, ceremonies, myths, stories, legends, sagas, language, metaphors, symbols, heroes, and heroines. These products or dimensions are levers that strategists can use to influence and direct strategy formulation, implementation, and evaluation activities. An organization's culture compares to an individual's personality in the sense that no organization has the same culture and no individual has the same personality. Both culture and personality are fairly enduring and can be warm, aggressive, friendly, open, innovative, conservative, liberal, harsh, or likable.

Dimensions of organizational culture permeate all the functional areas of business. It is something of an art to uncover the basic values and beliefs that are buried deeply in an organization's rich collection of stories, language, heroes, and rituals, but cultural products can represent important strengths and weaknesses. Culture is an aspect of organizations that no longer can be taken for granted in performing an internal strategic-management audit because culture and strategy must work together.

The strategic-management process takes place largely within a particular organization's culture. Lorsch found that executives in successful companies are emotionally

TABLE 5–1
Cultural Products and Associated Definitions

Rites	Relatively elaborate, dramatic, planned sets of activities that consolidate various forms of cultural expressions into one event, carried out through social interactions, usually for the benefit of an audience
Ceremonial	A system of several rites connected with a single occasion or event
Ritual	A standardized, detailed set of techniques and behaviors that manage anxieties, but seldom produce intended, technical consequences of practical importance
Myth	A dramatic narrative of imagined events, usually used to explain origins or transformations of something. Also, an unquestioned belief about the practical benefits of certain techniques and behaviors that is not supported by facts
Saga	An historical narrative describing the unique accomplishments of a group and its leaders, usually in heroic terms
Legend	A handed-down narrative of some wonderful event that is based on history but has been embellished with fictional details
Story	A narrative based on true events, sometimes a combination of truth and fiction
Folktale	A completely fictional narrative
Symbol	Any object, act, event, quality, or relation that serves as a vehicle for conveying meaning, usually by representing another thing
Language	A particular form or manner in which members of a group use sounds and written signs to convey meanings to each other
Metaphors	Shorthand words used to capture a vision or to reinforce old or new values
Values	Life-directing attitudes that serve as behavioral guidelines
Belief	An understanding of a particular phenomenon
Heroes/Heroines	Individuals whom the organization has legitimized to model behavior for others

Source: Adapted from H.M. Trice and J.M. Beyer, "Studying Organizational Cultures Through Rites and Ceremonials," *Academy of Management Review* 9, no. 4 (October 1984): 655.

committed to the firm's culture, but he concluded that culture can inhibit strategic management in two basic ways. First, managers frequently miss the significance of changing external conditions because they are blinded by strongly held beliefs. Second, when a particular culture has been effective in the past, the natural response is to stick with it in the future, even during times of major strategic change.[6] An organization's culture must support the collective commitment of its people to a common purpose. It must foster competence and enthusiasm among managers and employees.

Organizational culture significantly affects business decisions and thus must be evaluated during an internal strategic-management audit. If strategies can capitalize on cultural strengths, such as a strong work ethic or highly ethical beliefs, then management often can implement changes swiftly and easily. However, if the firm's culture is not supportive, strategic changes may be ineffective or even counterproductive. A firm's culture can become antagonistic to new strategies, with the result being confusion and disorientation. An organization's culture should infuse individuals with enthusiasm for implementing strategies. Allarie and Firsirotu emphasized the need to understand culture:

> Culture provides an explanation for the insuperable difficulties a firm encounters when it attempts to shift its strategic direction. Not only has the "right" culture become the essence and foundation of corporate excellence, it is also claimed that success or failure of reforms hinges on management's sagacity and ability to change the firm's driving culture in time and in tune with required changes in strategies.[7]

The potential value of organizational culture has not been realized fully in the study of strategic management. Ignoring the effect that culture can have on relationships among the functional areas of business can result in barriers to communication, lack of coordination, and an inability to adapt to changing conditions. Some tension between culture and a firm's strategy is inevitable, but the tension should be monitored so that it does not reach a point at which relationships are severed and the culture becomes antagonistic. The resulting disarray among members of the organization would disrupt strategy formulation, implementation, and evaluation. On the other hand, a supportive organizational culture can make managing much easier.

Internal strengths and weaknesses associated with a firm's culture sometimes are overlooked due to the interfunctional nature of this phenomenon. It is important, therefore, for strategists to understand their firm as a sociocultural system. Success is often determined by linkages between a firm's culture and strategies. The challenge of strategic management today is to bring about the changes in organizational culture and individual mind-sets necessary to support the formulation, implementation, and evaluation of strategies. As indicated in the Global Perspective, this challenge becomes greater as a firm initiates or expands multinational operations. Note how managers in the Far East differ from U.S. and European managers in style and behavior.

OPERATING AS IF THE NATURAL ENVIRONMENT MATTERS Both employees and consumers are becoming especially resentful of firms that take from more than they give to the natural environment; likewise, people today are especially appreciative of firms that conduct operations in a way that mends rather than harms the environment.

The U.S. Justice Department recently issued new guidelines for companies to uncover environmental wrongdoing among their managers and employees without exposing

GLOBAL PERSPECTIVE
How Cultures of Countries Vary

There are two basic types of cultures in the world—high-context and low-context. High-context cultures are oral cultures in which what a person says in writing is *less important* than who a person is and what the social context is surrounding a business agreement. In low-context cultures, what a person says in writing is *more important* than who a person is and what the social context is surrounding a business agreement. The following diagram gives an arrangement of high-context and low-context cultures worldwide:

Chinese — High-Context Culture
Korean
Japanese
Vietnamese
Arab
Greek
Spanish
Italian
English
North American
Scandinavian
Swiss
German — Low-Context Culture

There are numerous implications of the high-context/low-context culture analysis that should be considered in doing business globally. For example:

1. In high-context countries, casual conversations have a level of business significance far beyond the content being discussed. High-context foreign nationals want to know a lot about people personally and about their companies before making business commitments.

2. Businesspeople in high-context cultures expect a presentation to be in short, separate segments to allow time for questions and digestion of what has been presented. Frequent deviations from the major business topic are expected. High-context persons are not time- or efficiency-oriented and thus like to relax some during business meetings.

3. In high-context cultures, age, seniority, and experience are very important, so sending a young expert to conduct a meeting or close a sale would often be interpreted negatively.

4. A passive, impersonal style of communication is best with low-context cultures. Avoid exaggeration, hyperbole, superlatives, and egocentrism.

Source: Adapted from Ronald Dulek, John Fielden, and John Hill, "International Communication: An Executive Primer," Business Horizons (January–February 1991): 19–25. Also, Edward Hall, "How Cultures Collide," Psychology Today (July 1976): 67–74.

themselves to potential criminal liability. The new guidelines give nine hypothetical examples to illustrate the new legal requirements. The examples include Company A, which regularly conducts a comprehensive environmental audit, goes straight to the government as soon as something wrong is turned up, disciplines the responsible people in the company, and gives their names as well as all relevant documentation to the government. The Justice Department will prosecute but be lenient in this case. The extreme example is Company K, which tries to cover up an environmental violation and does not cooperate with the government or provide names. Its audit is narrow, and its compliance program is "no more than a collection of paper." No leniency is likely for this firm. United Technologies Corporation, for example, recently was a Company K and incurred a $5.3 million fine for abuses in handling and discharging hazardous wastes.

MANAGEMENT

The *functions of management* consist of five basic activities: planning, organizing, motivating, staffing, and controlling. An overview of these activities is provided in Table 5–2.

PLANNING The only thing certain about the future of any organization is change, and *planning* is the essential bridge between the present and the future that increases the likelihood of achieving desired results. Planning is the cornerstone of effective strategy formulation. But even though it is considered the foundation of management, it is commonly the task that managers neglect most. Planning is essential for successful strategy implementation and

TABLE 5–2
The Basic Functions of Management

FUNCTION	DESCRIPTION	STAGE OF STRATEGIC-MANAGEMENT PROCESS WHEN MOST IMPORTANT
Planning	Planning consists of all those managerial activities related to preparing for the future. Specific tasks include forecasting, establishing objectives, devising strategies, developing policies, and setting goals.	Strategy Formulation
Organizing	Organizing includes all those managerial activities that result in a structure of task and authority relationships. Specific areas include organizational design, job specialization, job descriptions, job specifications, span of the control, unity of command, coordination, job design, and job analysis.	Strategy Implementation
Motivating	Motivating involves efforts directed toward shaping human behavior. Specific topics include leadership, communication, work groups, behavior modification, delegation of authority, job enrichment, job satisfaction, needs fulfillment, organizational change, employee morale, and managerial morale.	Strategy Implementation
Staffing	Staffing activities are centered on personnel or human resource management. Included are wage and salary administration, employee benefits, interviewing, hiring, firing, training, management development, employee safety, affirmative action, equal employment opportunity, union relations, career development, personnel research, discipline policies, grievance procedures, and public relations.	Strategy Implementation
Controlling	Controlling refers to all those managerial activities directed toward ensuring that actual results are consistent with planned results. Key areas of concern include quality control, financial control, sales control, inventory control, expense control, analysis of variances, rewards, and sanctions.	Strategy Evaluation

strategy evaluation, largely because organizing, motivating, staffing, and controlling activities are dependent upon good planning.

The process of planning must include involvement of managers and employees throughout an organization. As noted in Figure 5–2, the time horizon for planning decreases from two to five years for top-level to less than six months for lower-level managers. The important point is that all managers do planning and should involve subordinates in the process to facilitate employee understanding and commitment.

Planning can have a positive impact on organizational and individual performance. Planning allows an organization to identify and take advantage of external opportunities and minimize the impact of external threats. Planning is more than extrapolating from the past and present into the future. It also includes developing a mission, forecasting future events and trends, establishing objectives, and choosing strategies to pursue.

An organization can develop synergy through planning. *Synergy* exists when everyone pulls together as a team that knows what it wants to achieve; synergy is the $2 + 2 = 5$ effect. By establishing and communicating clear objectives, employees and managers can work together toward desired results. Synergy can result in powerful competitive advantages. The strategic-management process itself is aimed at creating synergy in an organization.

FIGURE 5–2
The Three Levels of Planning

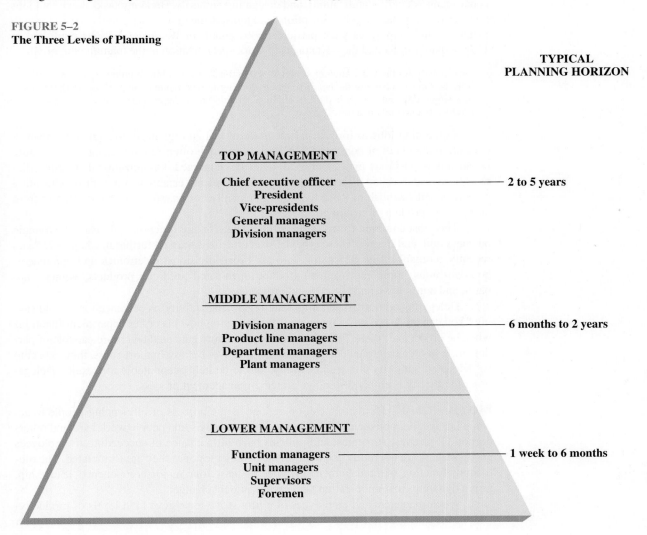

TYPICAL
PLANNING HORIZON

TOP MANAGEMENT

Chief executive officer ———————— 2 to 5 years
President
Vice-presidents
General managers
Division managers

MIDDLE MANAGEMENT

Division managers ———————— 6 months to 2 years
Product line managers
Department managers
Plant managers

LOWER MANAGEMENT

Function managers ———————— 1 week to 6 months
Unit managers
Supervisors
Foremen

Planning allows a firm to adapt to changing markets and thus shape its own destiny. Strategic management can be viewed as a formal planning process that allows an organization to pursue proactive rather than reactive strategies. Successful organizations strive to control their own futures rather than merely react to external forces and events as they occur. Historically, organisms and organizations that have not adapted to changing conditions have become extinct. Swift adaptation is needed today more than ever before because changes in markets, economies, and competitors worldwide are accelerating.

ORGANIZING   The purpose of *organizing* is to achieve coordinated effort by defining task and authority relationships. Organizing means determining who does what and who reports to whom. There are countless examples in history of well-organized enterprises successfully competing against, and in some cases defeating, much stronger but less-organized firms. A well-organized firm generally has motivated managers and employees who are committed to seeing the organization succeed. Resources are allocated more effectively and used more efficiently in a well-organized firm than in a disorganized firm.

The organizing function of management can be viewed as consisting of three sequential activities: breaking tasks down into jobs (work specialization), combining jobs to form departments (departmentalization), and delegating authority. Breaking tasks down into jobs requires development of job descriptions and job specifications. These tools clarify for both managers and employees what particular jobs entail. In *Wealth of Nations* published in 1776, Adam Smith cited the advantages of work specialization in the manufacture of pins:

> One man draws the wire, another straightens it, a third cuts it, a fourth points it, a fifth grinds it at the top for receiving the head. Ten men working in this manner can produce 48,000 pins in a single day, but if they had all wrought separately and independently, each might at best produce twenty pins in a day.[8]

Combining jobs to form departments results in an organizational structure, span of control, and a chain of command. Changes in strategy often require changes in structure because new positions may be created, deleted, or merged. Organizational structure dictates how resources are allocated and how objectives are established in a firm. Allocating resources and establishing objectives geographically, for example, is much different from doing so by product or customer.

The most common forms of departmentalization are functional, divisional, strategic business unit, and matrix. These types of structure are discussed further in Chapter 7. Sears recently reorganized its 825 stores into six broad divisions: electronics and appliances, home fashions, home improvement products, men's and children's products, women's apparel, and automotive and recreational products.

Delegating authority is an important organizing activity, as evidenced in the old saying "You can tell how good a manager is by observing how his or her department functions when he or she isn't there." Employees today are more educated and more capable of participating in organizational decision making than ever before. In most cases, they expect to be delegated authority and responsibility, and to be held accountable for results. Delegation of authority is embedded in the strategic-management process.

MOTIVATING   *Motivating* can be defined as the process of influencing people to accomplish specific objectives.[9] Motivation explains why some people work hard and others do not. Objectives, strategies, and policies have little chance of succeeding if employees and managers are not motivated to implement strategies once they are formulated. The motivating function of management includes at least four major components: leadership, group dynamics, communication, and organizational change.

When managers and employees of a firm strive to achieve high levels of productivity, this indicates that the firm's strategists are good leaders. Good leaders establish rapport with subordinates, empathize with their needs and concerns, set a good example, and are trustworthy and fair. Leadership includes developing a vision of the firm's future and inspiring people to work hard to achieve that vision. Kirkpatrick and Locke reported that certain traits also characterize effective leaders: knowledge of the business, cognitive ability, self-confidence, honesty, integrity, and drive.[10]

Research suggests that democratic behavior on the part of leaders results in more positive attitudes toward change and higher productivity than does autocratic behavior. Drucker said:

> Leadership is not a magnetic personality. That can just as well be demagoguery. It is not "making friends and influencing people." That is flattery. Leadership is the lifting of a person's vision to higher sights, the raising of a person's performance to a higher standard, the building of a person's personality beyond its normal limitations.[11]

Group dynamics play a major role in employee morale and satisfaction. Informal groups or coalitions form in every organization. The norms of coalitions can range from being very positive to very negative toward management. It is important, therefore, that strategists identify the composition and nature of informal groups in an organization to facilitate strategy formulation, implementation, and evaluation. Leaders of informal groups are especially important in formulating and implementing strategy changes.

Communication, perhaps the most important word in management, is a major component in motivation. An organization's system of communication determines whether strategies can be implemented successfully. Good two-way communication is vital for gaining support for departmental and divisional objectives and policies. Top-down communication can encourage bottom-up communication. The strategic-management process becomes a lot easier when subordinates are encouraged to discuss their concerns, reveal their problems, provide recommendations, and give suggestions. A primary reason for instituting strategic management is to build and support effective communication networks throughout the firm.

> The manager of tomorrow must be able to get his people to commit themselves to the business, whether they are machine operators or junior vice-presidents. Ah, you say, participative management. Have a cigar. But just because most managers tug a forelock at the P word doesn't mean they know how to make it work. In the 1990s, throwing together a few quality circles won't suffice. The key issue will be empowerment, a term whose strength suggests the need to get beyond merely sharing a little information and a bit of decision making.[12]

STAFFING The management function of *staffing*, also called *personnel management* or *human resource management*, includes activities such as recruiting, interviewing, testing, selecting, orienting, training, developing, caring for, evaluating, rewarding, disciplining, promoting, transferring, demoting, and dismissing employees, and managing union relations. After the Teamsters strike at United Parcel Service, the rhetoric of labor activists implied a strong union revival in the United States. Facts, however, do not support the rhetoric. Unions in the Southeast United States held 32 percent fewer elections in 1996 than in 1990. Union membership as a percentage of the workforce in the Southeast continues to plummet, to 5.3 percent in 1996 from 8.1 percent in 1986. In the entire United States, there were 3,623 union elections in 1990 but only 2,792 in 1996. North and South Carolina still rank 49th and 50th among states in percentage of union members among all workers.

Staffing activities play a major role in strategy-implementation efforts, and for this reason human resource managers are becoming more actively involved in the strategic-management process. Strengths and weaknesses in the staffing area are important to identify.

The complexity and importance of human resource activities have increased to such a degree that all but the smallest organizations now need a full-time human resource manager.

Numerous court cases that directly affect staffing activities are decided each day. Organizations and individuals can be penalized severely for not following federal, state, and local laws and guidelines related to staffing.[13] Line managers simply cannot stay abreast of all the legal developments and requirements regarding staffing. The human resources department coordinates staffing decisions in the firm so that an organization as a whole meets legal requirements. This department also provides needed consistency in administering company rules, wages, and policies.

Human resources management is particularly challenging for international companies. For example, the inability of spouses and children to adapt to new surroundings has become a major staffing problem in overseas transfers. The problems include premature returns, job performance slumps, resignations, discharges, low morale, marital discord, and general discontent. Firms such as Ford Motor and Exxon have begun screening and interviewing spouses and children before assigning persons to overseas positions. 3M Corporation introduces children to peers in the target country and offers spouses educational benefits.

Strategists are becoming increasingly aware of how important human resources are to effective strategic management. Human resource managers are becoming more involved and more proactive in formulating and implementing strategies. They provide leadership for organizations that are restructuring or allowing employees to work at home as suggested in the Information Technology Perspective.

Waterman described staffing activities among successful companies:

> Successful (renewing) companies are busy taking out layers of management, cutting staff, and pushing decisions down. Nucor Corporation runs a successful, near billion-dollar steel enterprise from a headquarters office and complement of seven people in a Charlotte, N.C., shopping mall. At Dana Corporation, President Woody Morcott and others take extraordinary pride in the fact that today there are only five layers between the chief executive's office and the person on the factory floor. In the mid-1970s there were 14. . . . Leaner organizations set the stage for success (renewal). They make each one of us more important. They empower the individual.[14]

INFORMATION TECHNOLOGY

The Officeless Office

In many firms information technology is doing away with the workplace and allowing employees to work at home or anywhere, anytime. The number of work-at-home employees and managers is expected to exceed 13 million by 1998 in the United States. "There is nothing I can do in an office that I can't do at home," says William Holtz, vice-president for global enterprise services with Northern Telecom. From his home in Philadelphia, Holtz supervises a staff of 1,000 in Nashville, Tennessee. Managers are moving away from the mindset of having to see their employees and watch them work.

The mobile concept of work allows employees to work the traditional 9-to-5 workday across any of the 24 time zones around the globe. Affordable desktop videoconferencing software developed by AT&T, Intel, Lotus, or Vivo Software allows employees to beam in whenever needed. Any manager or employee who travels a lot away from the office may be a good candidate for working at home rather than in an office provided by the firm. Salespersons and consultants are good examples, but any person whose job largely involves talking to others or handling information could easily operate at home with the proper computer system and software. The accounting firm Ernst & Young has reduced its office space requirements by 2 million square feet over the past three years by allowing employees to work at home.

Many people see the officeless office trend as leading to a resurgence of family togetherness in American society. Even the design of homes may change from having large open areas to having more private small areas conducive to getting work done.

Source: Adapted from Edward Baig, "Welcome to the Officeless Office," Business Week (June 26, 1995): 104.

CONTROLLING The *controlling* function of management includes all those activities undertaken to ensure that actual operations conform to planned operations. All managers in an organization have controlling responsibilities, such as conducting performance evaluations and taking necessary action to minimize inefficiencies. The controlling function of management is particularly important for effective strategy evaluation. Controlling consists of four basic steps:

1. Establishing performance standards
2. Measuring individual and organizational performance
3. Comparing actual performance to planned performance standards
4. Taking corrective actions

Measuring individual performance is often conducted ineffectively or not at all in organizations. Some reasons for this shortcoming are that evaluation can create confrontations that most managers prefer to avoid, can take more time than most managers are willing to give, and can require skills that many managers lack. No single approach to measuring individual performance is without limitations. For this reason, an organization should examine various methods, such as the graphic rating scale, the behaviorally anchored rating scale, and the critical incident method, and then develop or select a performance appraisal approach that best suits the firm's needs. Increasingly, firms are striving to link organizational performance with managers' and employees' pay. This topic is discussed further in Chapter 7.

MARKETING

Marketing can be described as the process of defining, anticipating, creating, and fulfilling customers' needs and wants for products and services. Joel Evans and Barry Bergman suggested that there are nine basic *functions of marketing*: (1) customer analysis, (2) buying supplies, (3) selling products/services, (4) product and service planning, (5) pricing, (6) distribution, (7) marketing research, (8) opportunity analysis, and (9) social responsibility.[15] Understanding these functions helps strategists identify and evaluate marketing strengths and weaknesses.

CUSTOMER ANALYSIS *Customer analysis*—the examination and evaluation of consumer needs, desires, and wants—involves administering customer surveys, analyzing consumer information, evaluating market positioning strategies, developing customer profiles, and determining optimal market segmentation strategies. The information generated by customer analysis can be essential in developing an effective mission statement. Customer profiles can reveal the demographic characteristics of an organization's customers. Buyers, sellers, distributors, salespeople, managers, wholesalers, retailers, suppliers, and creditors can all participate in gathering information to identify customers' needs and wants successfully. Successful organizations continually monitor present and potential customers' buying patterns.

BUYING SUPPLIES The second function of marketing is buying supplies needed to produce and sell a product or service. *Buying* consists of evaluating alternative suppliers or vendors, selecting the best suppliers, arranging acceptable terms with suppliers, and procuring the supplies. The buying process can be complicated by such factors as price controls, recession, foreign trade restrictions, strikes, walkouts, and machine breakdowns. Even the weather can significantly disrupt procurement of needed supplies. Quite often, the question arises whether to make or buy needed supplies and services. Recall that backward integration, gaining control over suppliers, is a particularly attractive strategy when suppliers are unreliable, costly, or incapable of meeting company needs.

SELLING PRODUCTS/SERVICES   Successful strategy implementation generally rests upon the ability of an organization to sell some product or service. *Selling* includes many marketing activities such as advertising, sales promotion, publicity, personal selling, sales force management, customer relations, and dealer relations. These activities are especially critical when a firm pursues a market penetration strategy. The effectiveness of various selling tools for consumer and industrial products varies. Personal selling is most important for industrial goods companies, and advertising is most important for consumer goods companies. Determining organizational strengths and weaknesses in the selling function of marketing is an important part of performing an internal strategic-management audit.

With regard to advertising products and services on the Internet, a new trend is to base advertising rates exclusively on sale rates. This new accountability contrasts sharply with traditional broadcast and print advertising that bases rates on the number of persons expected to see a given advertisement. The new cost-per-sale on-line advertising rates are possible because any Web site can monitor which user clicks on which advertisement and then can record whether that consumer actually buys the product. If there are no sales, then the advertisement is free.

Some mass retailers such as Amazon Books and CUC International are paying millions of dollars in sales commissions and advertising fees in exchange for prominent placement on high-traffic Web sites, search engines, and home pages of on-line service providers such as America Online.

Anheuser-Busch currently is being investigated by the U.S. Justice Department to determine whether the company's sales practices are a violation of antitrust laws. Anheuser has 45 percent of the U.S. beer market, followed by Miller's 22 percent, Coors's 10 percent, Stroh's' 8.3 percent, Import's 6.5 percent, and Pabst's 2.5 percent.[16]

PRODUCT AND SERVICE PLANNING   *Product and service planning* includes activities such as test marketing; product and brand positioning; devising warranties; packaging; determining product options, product features, product style, and product quality; deleting old products; and providing for customer service. Product and service planning is particularly important when a company is pursuing product development or diversification.

One of the most effective product and service planning techniques is *test marketing*. Test markets allow an organization to test alternative marketing plans and to forecast future sales of new products. In conducting a test market project, an organization must decide how many cities to include, which cities to include, how long to run the test, what information to collect during the test, and what action to take after the test has been completed. Test marketing is used more frequently by consumer goods companies than by industrial goods companies. Test marketing can allow an organization to avoid substantial losses by revealing weak products and ineffective marketing approaches before large-scale production begins.

PRICING   Five major stakeholders affect *pricing* decisions: consumers, governments, suppliers, distributors, and competitors. Sometimes an organization will pursue a forward integration strategy primarily to gain better control over prices charged to consumers. Governments can impose constraints on price fixing, price discrimination, minimum prices, unit pricing, price advertising, and price controls. For example, the Robinson-Patman Act prohibits manufacturers and wholesalers from discriminating in price among channel member purchasers (suppliers and distributors) if competition is injured.

Competing organizations must be careful not to coordinate discounts, credit terms, or condition of sale; not to discuss prices, markups, and costs at trade association meetings; and not to arrange to issue new price lists on the same date, to rotate low bids on contracts, or to uniformly restrict production to maintain high prices. Strategists should view price from both a short-run and a long-run perspective, because competitors can copy price changes with relative ease. Often a dominant firm will aggressively match all price cuts by competitors.

With regard to pricing, as the value of the dollar increases, which it has been doing steadily, U.S. multinational companies have a choice. They can raise prices in the local currency of a foreign country or risk losing sales and market share. Alternatively, multinational firms can keep prices steady and face reduced profit when their export revenue is reported in the United States in dollars.

DISTRIBUTION   *Distribution* includes warehousing, distribution channels, distribution coverage, retail site locations, sales territories, inventory levels and location, transportation carriers, wholesaling, and retailing. Most producers today do not sell their goods directly to consumers. Various marketing entities act as intermediaries; they bear a variety of names such as wholesalers, retailers, brokers, facilitators, agents, middlemen, vendors, or simply distributors.

Major cargo carriers in the United States, including trains, trucks, ships, and planes, are being swamped with business in the late 1990s. Union Pacific, the nation's largest railroad, has such a monumental backlog that the firm now ships goods by sea, through the Panama Canal. Freight in the United States has piled up at rail terminals, ship docks, and trucking centers. Trucks move 80 percent of consumer goods in the United States. There is a widespread shortage of both truck drivers and trucks in this country.

Distribution becomes especially important when a firm is striving to implement a market development or forward integration strategy. Some of the most complex and challenging decisions facing a firm concern product distribution. Intermediaries flourish in our economy because many producers lack the financial resources and expertise to carry out direct marketing. Manufacturers who could afford to sell directly to the public often can gain greater returns by expanding and improving their manufacturing operations. Even General Motors would find it very difficult to buy out its more than 18,000 independent dealers.

Successful organizations identify and evaluate alternative ways to reach their ultimate market. Possible approaches vary from direct selling to using just one or many wholesalers and retailers. Strengths and weaknesses of each channel alternative should be determined according to economic, control, and adaptive criteria. Organizations should consider the costs and benefits of various wholesaling and retailing options. They must consider the need to motivate and control channel members and the need to adapt to changes in the future. Once a marketing channel is chosen, an organization usually must adhere to it for an extended period of time.

MARKETING RESEARCH   *Marketing research* is the systematic gathering, recording, and analyzing of data about problems relating to the marketing of goods and services. Marketing research can uncover critical strengths and weaknesses, and marketing researchers employ numerous scales, instruments, procedures, concepts, and techniques to gather information. Recent market research regarding the top 10 selling brands of liquor and wine are provided in Table 5–3. Marketing research activities support all of the major business functions of an organization. Organizations that possess excellent marketing research skills have a definite strength in pursuing generic strategies.

> The President of PepsiCo says, "Looking at the competition is the company's best form of market research. The majority of our strategic successes are ideas that we borrow from the marketplace, usually from a small regional or local competitor. In each case, we spot a promising new idea, improve on it, and then out-execute our competitor."[17]

About 20,000 new products are introduced by U.S. companies annually, but 85 percent of these fail within three years. Many CEOs continue to trust their own best judgment

TABLE 5–3
Leading Liquor and Wind Brands

LEADING LIQUOR BRANDS *(IN THOUSANDS OF 9-LITER CASE SALES)*				
			CASE SALES	
BRAND	**MARKETER**	**TYPE**	**1995**	**1996**
Bacardi	Bacardi	Rum	6,120	6,050
Smirnoff	Heublein	Vodka	5,785	5,950
Seagram's	Seagram	Gin	3,840	3,625
Absolut	Carillon	Vodka	3,165	3,330
Jim Beam	Beam	Bourbon	3,260	3,080
Seagram's 7 Crown	Seagram	Whiskey	3,050	3,015
Jack Daniel's Black	Brown-Forman	Whiskey	3,000	3,010
Canadian Mist	Brown-Forman	Whiskey	2,960	2,885
Popov	Heublein	Vodka	3,000	2,805
E & J	E & J Gallo	Brandy	2,525	2,775

TOP 10 WINE BRANDS *(IN THOUSANDS OF 9-LITER CASE SALES)*				
			CASE SALES	
	BRAND	**COMPANY**	**1995**	**1996**
1.	Franzia	The Wine Group	13,000	15,800
2.	Carlo Rossi	E&J Gallo Winery	11,695	11,800
3.	Gallo Livingston Cellars	E&J Gallo Winery	11,230	11,150
4.	The Wine Cellars of Ernest & Julio Gallo	E&J Gallo Winery	9,300	9,500
5.	Almaden	Canandaigua Wine Co.	7,385	7,165
6.	Inglenook	Canandaigua Wine Co.	7,250	6,960
7.	Sutter Home	Sutter Home Winery	5,285	6,255
8.	Woodbridge	Robert Mondavi Winery	4,350	4,685
9.	Glen Ellen	Heublein Wines Group	3,350	3,475
10.	Vendange	Sebastiani Vineyards	2,465	3,200
	Total Top 10		75,310	79,990

Source: Adapted from IMPACT DATABANK.

over market research; this mind-set can be detrimental to a business. For example, the Greyhound Bus Company first pursued the African American market by placing advertising on African American radio stations. However, instead of creating a new commercial, Greyhound used its popular Country & Western music ad, which later was considered to have failed in that market.

OPPORTUNITY ANALYSIS   The eighth function of marketing is *opportunity analysis*, which involves assessing the costs, benefits, and risks associated with marketing decisions. Three steps are required to perform a *cost/benefit analysis*: (1) compute the total costs associated with a decision, (2) estimate the total benefits from the decision, and (3) compare the total costs with the total benefits. As expected benefits exceed total costs, an opportunity becomes more attractive. Sometimes the variables included in a cost/benefit analysis cannot be quantified or even measured, but usually reasonable estimates can be made to allow the analysis to be performed. One key factor to be considered is risk. Cost/benefit analyses should also be performed when a company is evaluating alternative ways to be socially responsible.

SOCIAL RESPONSIBILITY   The final function of marketing, according to Evans and Bergman, is to determine how best to meet the firm's social responsibility obligations. *Social responsibility* can include offering products and services that are safe and reasonably priced. Demands by special-interest groups on business organizations greatly increased during the 1980s. Arguments still rage today, though, about how socially responsible firms should be. A clear social policy can represent a major strength for organizations, whereas a poor social policy can be a weakness.

Some strategists view social responsibility as a focus that detracts from, or is counter to, their profit-minded pursuits. Although there may be some clearly distinct economic versus social concerns, there is a rather broad area in which economic and social concerns are consistent with one another. Many corporate activities are profitable, and at the same time are socially responsible. When a firm engages in social activities, it must do so in a way that receives economic advantages.

In perhaps the largest philanthropic gift ever by one individual, Ted Turner in 1997 donated $1 billion, one-third of his entire net worth, to United Nations charities. Turner, who owns 10 percent of Time Warner Inc., said, "I'm putting every rich person in the world on notice that they're going to be hearing from me about giving money. If you want to lead, you got to blow the horn and get out in front of the parade." Turner clearly believes firms should be highly socially responsible.

FINANCE/ACCOUNTING

Financial condition is often considered the single best measure of a firm's competitive position and overall attractiveness to investors. Determining an organization's financial strengths and weaknesses is essential to formulating strategies effectively. A firm's liquidity, leverage, working capital, profitability, asset utilization, cash flow, and equity can eliminate some strategies as being feasible alternatives. Financial factors often alter existing strategies and change implementation plans.

FINANCE/ACCOUNTING FUNCTIONS According to James Van Horne, the *functions of finance/accounting* comprise three decisions: the investment decision, the financing decision, and the dividend decision.[18] Financial ratio analysis is the most widely used method for determining an organization's strengths and weaknesses in the investment, financing, and dividend areas. Because the functional areas of business are so closely related, financial ratios can signal strengths or weaknesses in management, marketing, production, research and development, and computer information systems activities.

The *investment decision*, also called *capital budgeting*, is the allocation and reallocation of capital and resources to projects, products, assets, and divisions of an organization. Once strategies are formulated, capital budgeting decisions are required to implement strategies successfully. The *financing decision* concerns determining the best capital structure for the firm and includes examining various methods by which the firm can raise capital (for example, by issuing stock, increasing debt, selling assets, or using a combination of these approaches). The financing decision must consider both short-term and long-term needs for working capital. Two key financial ratios that indicate whether a firm's financing decisions have been effective are the debt-to-equity ratio and the debt-to-total-assets ratio.

Dividend decisions concern issues such as the percentage of earnings paid to stockholders, the stability of dividends paid over time, and the repurchase or issuance of stock. Dividend decisions determine the amount of funds that are retained in a firm compared to the amount paid out to stockholders. Three financial ratios that are helpful in evaluating a firm's dividend decisions are the earnings-per-share ratio, the dividends-per-share ratio, and the price-earnings ratio. The benefits of paying dividends to investors must be balanced against the benefits of retaining funds internally, and there is no set formula on how to balance this trade-off. For the reasons listed here, dividends are sometimes paid out even when funds could be better reinvested in the business or when the firm has to obtain outside sources of capital:

1. Paying cash dividends is customary. Failure to do so could be thought of as a stigma. A dividend change is considered a signal about the future.

2. Dividends represent a sales point for investment bankers. Some institutional investors can buy only dividend-paying stocks.

3. Shareholders often demand dividends, even in companies with great opportunities for reinvesting all available funds.

4. A myth exists that paying dividends will result in a higher stock price.

BASIC TYPES OF FINANCIAL RATIOS   Financial ratios are computed from an organization's income statement and balance sheet. Computing financial ratios is like taking a picture because the results reflect a situation at just one point in time. Comparing ratios over time and to industry averages is more likely to result in meaningful statistics that can be used to identify and evaluate strengths and weaknesses. Trend analysis, illustrated in Figure 5–3, is a useful technique that incorporates both the time and industry average dimensions of financial ratios. Note that the dotted lines reveal projected ratios. Some Web sites such as Wall Street Research Net at www.wsrn.com calculate financial ratios and provide data with charts. Four major sources of industry-average financial ratios follow:

1. Dun & Bradstreet's *Industry Norms and Key Business Ratios*—Fourteen different ratios are calculated in an industry-average format for 800 different types of businesses. The ratios are presented by Standard Industrial Classification (SIC) number and are grouped by annual sales into three size categories.

2. Robert Morris Associates' *Annual Statement Studies*—Sixteen different ratios are calculated in an industry-average format. Industries are referenced by SIC

FIGURE 5–3
A Financial Ratio Trend Analysis

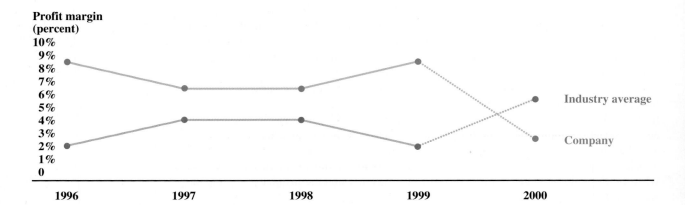

numbers published by the Bureau of the Census. The ratios are presented in four size categories by annual sales for all firms in the industry.

3. *Almanac of Business & Industrial Financial Ratios*—Twenty-two financial ratios and percentages are provided in an industry-average format for all major industries. The ratios and percentages are given for 12 different company-size categories for all firms in a given industry.

4. Federal Trade Commission Reports—The FTC publishes quarterly financial data, including ratios on manufacturing companies. FTC reports include analyses by industry group and asset size.

Table 5–4 provides a summary of key financial ratios showing how each ratio is calculated and what each ratio measures. However, all the ratios are not significant for all industries and companies. For example, accounts receivable turnover and average collection period are not very meaningful to a company that does primarily a cash receipts business. Key financial ratios can be classified into the following five types:

1. *Liquidity ratios* measure a firm's ability to meet maturing short-term obligations.
   Current ratio
   Quick (or acid-test) ratio

2. *Leverage ratios* measure the extent to which a firm has been financed by debt.
   Debt-to-total-assets ratio
   Debt-to-equity ratio
   Long-term debt-to-equity ratio
   Times-interest-earned (or coverage) ratio

3. *Activity ratios* measure how effectively a firm is using its resources.
   Inventory-turnover
   Fixed assets turnover
   Total assets turnover
   Accounts receivable turnover
   Average collection period

4. *Profitability ratios* measure management's overall effectiveness as shown by the returns generated on sales and investment.
   Gross profit margin
   Operating profit margin
   Net profit margin
   Return on total assets (ROA)
   Return on stockholders' equity (ROE)
   Earnings per share
   Price-earnings ratio

5. *Growth ratios* measure the firm's ability to maintain its economic position in the growth of the economy and industry.
   Sales
   Net income
   Earnings per share
   Dividends per share

Financial ratio analysis is not without some limitations. First of all, financial ratios are based on accounting data, and firms differ in their treatment of such items as depreciation, inventory valuation, research and development expenditures, pension plan costs, mergers, and taxes. Also, seasonal factors can influence comparative ratios. Therefore, conformity to industry composite ratios does not establish with certainty that a firm is performing normally or that it is well managed. Likewise, departures from industry averages

TABLE 5–4
A Summary of Key Financial Ratios

RATIO	HOW CALCULATED	WHAT IT MEASURES
LIQUIDITY RATIOS		
Current Ratio	$$\frac{\text{Current assets}}{\text{Current liabilities}}$$	The extent to which a firm can meet its short-term obligations
Quick Ratio	$$\frac{\text{Current assets minus inventory}}{\text{Current liabilities}}$$	The extent to which a firm can meet its short-term obligations without relying upon the sale of its inventories
LEVERAGE RATIOS		
Debt-to-Total-Assets Ratio	$$\frac{\text{Total debt}}{\text{Total assets}}$$	The percentage of total funds that are provided by creditors
Debt-to-Equity Ratio	$$\frac{\text{Total debt}}{\text{Total stockholders' equity}}$$	The percentage of total funds provided by creditors versus by owners
Long-Term Debt-to-Equity Ratio	$$\frac{\text{Long-term debt}}{\text{Total stockholders' equity}}$$	The balance between debt and equity in a firm's long-term capital structure
Times-Interest-Earned Ratio	$$\frac{\text{Profits before interest and taxes}}{\text{Total interest charges}}$$	The extent to which earnings can decline without the firm becoming unable to meet its annual interest costs
ACTIVITY RATIOS		
Inventory Turnover	$$\frac{\text{Sales}}{\text{Inventory of finished goods}}$$	Whether a firm holds excessive stocks of inventories and whether a firm is selling its inventories slowly compared to the industry average
Fixed Assets Turnover	$$\frac{\text{Sales}}{\text{Fixed assets}}$$	Sales productivity and plant and equipment utilization
Total Assets Turnover	$$\frac{\text{Sales}}{\text{Total assets}}$$	Whether a firm is generating a sufficient volume of business for the size of its asset investment
Accounts Receivable Turnover	$$\frac{\text{Annual credit sales}}{\text{Accounts receivable}}$$	The average length of time it takes a firm to collect credit sales (in percentage terms)
Average Collection Period	$$\frac{\text{Accounts receivable}}{\text{Total credit sales/365 days}}$$	The average length of time it takes a firm to collect on credit sales (in days)
PROFITABILITY RATIOS		
Gross Profit Margin	$$\frac{\text{Sales minus cost of goods sold}}{\text{Sales}}$$	The total margin available to cover operating expenses and yield a profit
Operating Profit Margin	$$\frac{\text{Earnings before interest and taxes (EBIT)}}{\text{Sales}}$$	Profitability without concern for taxes and interest
Net Profit Margin	$$\frac{\text{Net income}}{\text{Sales}}$$	After-tax profits per dollar of sales
Return on Total Assets (ROA)	$$\frac{\text{Net income}}{\text{Total assets}}$$	After-tax profits per dollar of assets; this ratio is also called return on investment (ROI)
Return on Stockholders' Equity (ROE)	$$\frac{\text{Net income}}{\text{Total stockholders' equity}}$$	After-tax profits per dollar of stockholders' investment in the firm
Earning Per Share (EPS)	$$\frac{\text{Net income}}{\text{Number of shares of common stock outstanding}}$$	Earnings available to the owners of common stock
Price-earning Ratio	$$\frac{\text{Market price per share}}{\text{Earnings per share}}$$	Attractiveness of firm on equity markets.
GROWTH RATIOS		
Sales	Annual percentage growth in total sales	Firm's growth rate in sales
Income	Annual percentage growth in profits	Firm's growth rate in profits
Earnings Per Share	Annual percentage growth in EPS	Firm's growth rate in EPS
Dividends Per Share	Annual percentage growth in dividends per share	Firm's growth rate in dividends per share

158

do not always indicate that a firm is doing especially well or badly. For example, a high inventory turnover ratio could indicate efficient inventory management and a strong working capital position, but it also could indicate a serious inventory shortage and a weak working capital position.

It is important to recognize that a firm's financial condition depends not only on the functions of finance, but also on many other factors that include (1) management, marketing, production/operations, research and development, and computer information systems decisions; (2) actions by competitors, suppliers, distributors, creditors, customers, and shareholders; and (3) economic, social, cultural, demographic, environmental, political, governmental, legal, and technological trends. Even natural environment liabilities can affect financial ratios, as indicated in the Natural Environment Perspective. So financial ratio analysis, like all other analytical tools, should be used wisely.

PRODUCTION/OPERATIONS

The *production/operations functions* of a business consists of all those activities that transform inputs into goods and services. Production/operations management deals with inputs, transformations, and outputs that vary across industries and markets. A manufacturing operation transforms or converts inputs such as raw materials, labor, capital, machines, and facilities into finished goods and services. As indicated in Table 5–5, Roger Schroeder suggested that production/operations management comprises five functions or decision areas: process, capacity, inventory, workforce, and quality.

Production/operations activities often represent the largest part of an organization's human and capital assets. In most industries, the major costs of producing a product or service are incurred within operations, so production/operations can have great value as a competitive weapon in a company's overall strategy. Strengths and weaknesses in the five functions of production can mean the success or failure of an enterprise.

Many production/operations managers are finding that cross-training of employees can help their firms respond to changing markets faster. Cross-training of workers can

NATURAL ENVIRONMENT
Environmental Liability on the Balance Sheet

Environmental liability may be the largest recognized or unrecognized liability on a company's balance sheet. More American firms are finding themselves liable for cleanup costs and damages stemming from waste disposal practices of the past, in some cases going back 100 years. Environmental liabilities associated with air and water pollution, habitat destruction, deforestation, and medical problems can be immense. For this reason, many financial institutions now inquire about environmental liabilities as part of their commercial lending proce-

dures. Firms such as American Insurance Company specialize in providing environmental liability insurance to companies.

Environmental Protection Agency (EPA) regulations take up more than 11,000 pages; they vary with location and size of firm and are added to daily. The complexity of these regulations can translate into liabilities for the environmentally reactive firm. Proactive firms, on the other hand, are adding a "green executive" and department to oversee management of environmental policies and practices of the firm. The responsi-

bility of green executives includes thinking through environmental regulations, marketing needs, public attitudes, consumer demands, and potential problems. Ideally, green executives should promote development of a corporate culture in which all managers and employees become "green," or environmentally sensitive. Such a culture would represent an internal strength to the firm.

TABLE 5–5
The Basic Functions of Production Management

FUNCTION	DESCRIPTION
1. Process	Process decisions concern the design of the physical production system. Specific decisions include choice of technology, facility layout, process flow analysis, facility location, line balancing, process control, and transportation analysis.
2. Capacity	Capacity decisions concern determination of optimal output levels for the organization—not too much and not too little. Specific decisions include forecasting, facilities planning, aggregate planning, scheduling, capacity planning, and queuing analysis.
3. Inventory	Inventory decisions involve managing the level of raw materials, work in process, and finished goods. Specific decisions include what to order, when to order, how much to order, and materials handling.
4. Workforce	Workforce decisions are concerned with managing the skilled, unskilled, clerical, and managerial employees. Specific decisions include job design, work measurement, job enrichment, work standards, and motivation techniques.
5. Quality	Quality decisions are aimed at ensuring that high-quality goods and services are produced. Specific decisions include quality control, sampling, testing, quality assurance, and cost control.

Source: Adapted from R. Schroeder, *Operations Management* (New York: McGraw-Hill Book Co., 1981): 12.

increase efficiency, quality, productivity, and job satisfaction. For example, at General Motors's Detroit Gear & Axle plant, costs related to product defects were reduced 400 percent in 2 years as a result of cross-training workers. A shortage of qualified labor in America is another reason cross-training is becoming a common management practice.

There is much reason for concern that many organizations have not taken sufficient account of the capabilities and limitations of the production/operations function in formulating strategies. Scholars contend that this neglect has had unfavorable consequences on corporate performance in America. As shown in Table 5–6, James Dilworth outlined several types of strategic decisions that a company might make with production/operations implications of those decisions. Production capabilities and policies can also greatly affect strategies:

> Given today's decision-making environment with shortages, inflation, technological booms, and government intervention, a company's production/operations capabilities and policies may not be able to fulfill the demands dictated by strategies. In fact, they may dictate corporate strategies. It is hard to imagine that an organization can formulate strategies today without first considering the constraints and limitations imposed by its existing production/operations structure.[19]

RESEARCH AND DEVELOPMENT

The fifth major area of internal operations that should be examined for specific strengths and weaknesses is research and development (R&D). Many firms today conduct no R&D, and yet many other companies depend on successful R&D activities for survival. Firms pursuing a product development strategy especially need to have a strong R&D orientation.

R&D expenditures overall for U.S. companies increased 5.6 percent in 1997. Microsoft increased its R&D expenditures 300 percent in 1997. IBM received more than 2,000 patents in 1997, up from 1,867 in 1996 and marking the fifth year in a row of leading all U.S. firms in number of patents received. Total R&D expenditures for all U.S. firms exceeded $200 billion for the first time in 1997.

TABLE 5–6
Impact of Strategy Elements on Production Management

POSSIBLE ELEMENTS OF STRATEGY	CONCOMITANT CONDITIONS THAT MAY AFFECT THE OPERATIONS FUNCTION AND ADVANTAGES AND DISADVANTAGES
1. Compete as low-cost provider of goods or services	Discourages competition Broadens market Requires longer production runs and fewer product changes Requires special-purpose equipment and facilities
2. Compete as high-quality provider	Often possible to obtain more profit per unit, and perhaps more total profit from a smaller volume of sales Requires more quality-assurance effort and higher operating cost Requires more precise equipment, which is more expensive Requires highly skilled workers, necessitating higher wages and greater training efforts
3. Stress customer service	Requires broader development of servicepeople and service parts and equipment Requires rapid response to customer needs or changes in customer tastes, rapid and accurate information system, careful coordination Requires a higher inventory investment
4. Provide rapid and frequent introduction of new products	Requires versatile equipment and people Has higher research and development costs Has high retraining costs and high tooling and changeover in manufacturing Provides lower volumes for each product and fewer opportunities for improvements due to the learning curve
5. Strive for absolute growth	Requires accepting some projects or products with lower marginal value, which reduces ROI Diverts talents to areas of weakness instead of concentrating on strengths
6. Seek vertical integration	Enables company to control more of the process May not have economies of scale at some stages of process May require high capital investment as well as technology and skills beyond those currently available within the organization
7. Maintain reserve capacity for flexibility	Provides ability to meet peak demands and quickly implement some contingency plans if forecasts are too low Requires capital investment in idle capacity Provides capability to grow during the lead time normally required for expansion
8. Consolidate processing (Centralize)	Can result in economies of scale Can locate near one major customer or supplier Vulnerability: one strike, fire, or flood can halt the entire operation
9. Disperse processing of service (Decentralize)	Can be near several market territories Requires more complex coordination network: perhaps expensive data transmission and duplication of some personnel and equipment at each location If each location produces one product in the line, then other products still must be transported to be available at all locations If each location specializes in a type of component for all products, the company is vulnerable to strike, fire, flood, etc. If each location provides total product line, then economies of scale may not be realized
10. Stress the use of mechanization, automation, robots	Requires high capital investment Reduces flexibility May affect labor relations Makes maintenance more crucial
11. Stress stability of employment	Serves the security needs of employees and may develop employee loyalty Helps to attract and retain highly skilled employees May require revisions of make-or-buy decisions, use of idle time, inventory, and subcontractors as demand fluctuates

Source: *Production and Operations Management: Manufacturing and Nonmanufacturing*, Second Edition, by J. Dilworth. Copyright © 1983 by Random House, Inc. Reprinted by permission of Random House, Inc.

Organizations invest in R&D because they believe that such investment will lead to superior product or services and give them competitive advantages. Research and development expenditures are directed at developing new products before competitors do, improving product quality, or improving manufacturing processes to reduce costs.[20]

One article on planning emphasized that effective management of the R&D function requires a strategic and operational partnership between R&D and the other vital business functions. A spirit of partnership and mutual trust between general and R&D managers is evident in the best-managed firms today. Managers in these firms jointly explore; assess; and decide the what, when, why, and how much of R&D. Priorities, costs, benefits, risks, and rewards associated with R&D activities are discussed openly and shared. The overall mission of R&D thus has become broad-based, including supporting existing businesses, helping launch new businesses, developing new products, improving product quality, improving manufacturing efficiency, and deepening or broadening the company's technological capabilities.[21]

The best-managed firms today seek to organize R&D activities in a way that breaks the isolation of R&D from the rest of the company and promotes a spirit of partnership between R&D managers and other managers in the firm. R&D decisions and plans must be integrated and coordinated across departments and divisions by sharing experiences and information. The strategic-management process facilitates this new cross-functional approach to managing the R&D function.

INTERNAL AND EXTERNAL R&D Cost distributions among R&D activities vary by company and industry, but total R&D costs generally do not exceed manufacturing and marketing start-up costs. Four approaches to determining R&D budget allocations commonly are used: (1) financing as many project proposals as possible, (2) using a percentage-of-sales method, (3) budgeting about the same amount that competitors spend for R&D, or (4) deciding how many successful new products are needed and working backward to estimate the required R&D investment.

R&D in organizations can take two basic forms: (1) internal R&D, in which an organization operates its own R&D department, and/or (2) contract R&D, in which a firm hires independent researchers or independent agencies to develop specific products. Many companies use both approaches to develop new products. A widely used approach for obtaining outside R&D assistance is to pursue a joint venture with another firm. R&D strengths (capabilities) and weaknesses (limitations) play a major role in strategy formulation and strategy implementation.

Most firms have no choice but to continually develop new and improved products because of changing consumer needs and tastes, new technologies, shortened product life cycles, and increased domestic and foreign competition. A shortage of ideas for new products, increased global competition, increased market segmentation, strong special-interest groups, and increased government regulation are several factors making the successful development of new products more and more difficult, costly, and risky. In the pharmaceutical industry, for example, only one out of every 10,000 drugs created in the laboratory ends up on pharmacists' shelves. Scarpello, Boulton, and Hofer emphasized that different strategies require different R&D capabilities:

> The focus of R&D efforts can vary greatly depending on a firm's competitive strategy. Some corporations attempt to be market leaders and innovators of new products, while others are satisfied to be market followers and developers of currently available products. The basic skills required to support these strategies will vary, depending on whether R&D becomes the driving force behind competitive strategy. In cases where new product introduction is the driving force for strategy, R&D activities must be extensive. The R&D unit must then be able to advance scientific and technological knowledge, exploit that knowledge, and manage the risks associated with ideas, products, services, and production requirements.[22]

COMPUTER INFORMATION SYSTEMS

Information ties all business functions together and provides the basis for all managerial decisions. It is the cornerstone of all organizations. Information represents a major source of competitive advantage or disadvantage. Assessing a firm's internal strengths and weaknesses in information systems is a critical dimension of performing an internal audit. The company motto of Mitsui, a large Japanese trading company, is "Information is the lifeblood of the company." A satellite network connects Mitsui's 200 worldwide offices.

A computer information system's purpose is to improve the performance of an enterprise by improving the quality of managerial decisions. An effective information system thus collects, codes, stores, synthesizes, and presents information in such a manner that it answers important operating and strategic questions. The heart of an information system is a database containing the kinds of records and data important to managers.

A *computer information system* receives raw material from both the external and internal evaluation of an organization. It gathers data about marketing, finance, production, and personnel matters internally, and social, cultural, demographic, environmental, economic, political, government, legal, technological, and competitive factors externally. Data is integrated in ways needed to support managerial decision making.

There is a logical flow of material in a computer information system, whereby data is input to the system and transformed into output. Outputs include computer printouts, written reports, tables, charts, graphs, checks, purchase orders, invoices, inventory records, payroll accounts, and a variety of other documents. Payoffs from alternative strategies can be calculated and estimated. *Data* becomes *information* only when it is evaluated, filtered, condensed, analyzed, and organized for a specific purpose, problem, individual, or time.

An effective computer information system utilizes computer hardware, software, models for analysis, and a database. Some people equate information systems with the advent of the computer, but historians have traced recordkeeping and noncomputer data processing to Babylonian merchants living in 3500 B.C. Benefits of an effective information system include an improved understanding of business functions, improved communications, more informed decision making, analysis of problems, and improved control.

Because organizations are becoming more complex, decentralized, and globally dispersed, the function of information systems is growing in importance. Spurring this advance is the falling cost and increasing power of computers. There are costs and benefits associated with obtaining and evaluating information, just as with equipment and land. Like equipment, information can become obsolete and may need to be purged from the system. An effective information system is like a library, collecting, categorizing, and filing data for use by managers throughout the organization. Information systems are a major strategic resource, monitoring environment changes, identifying competitive threats, and assisting in the implementation, evaluation, and control of strategy.

We are truly in an information age. Firms whose information-system skills are weak are at a competitive disadvantage. On the other hand, strengths in information systems allow firms to establish distinctive competencies in other areas. Low-cost manufacturing and good customer service, for example, can depend on a good information system.

Watson and Rainer found that executive information systems provide managerial support in six key areas: electronic mail, access to external news, access to external databases, word processing, spreadsheets, and automated filing.[23] A good executive information system provides graphic, tabular, and textual information. Graphic capabilities are needed so current conditions and trends can be examined quickly; tables provide greater detail and enable variance analyses; textual information adds insight and interpretation to data.

STRATEGIC PLANNING SOFTWARE The computer revolution today is being compared in magnitude to the industrial revolution. Computers are now common at the desks of almost every professional and administrative employee of industry, government, and academia. The proliferation of computers has aided strategic management because software products can be designed to enhance participation and to provide integration, uniformity, analysis, and economy. Strategic planning software can allow firms to tap the knowledge base of everyone in the firm. There are a number of commercially available software products designed to train and assist managers in strategic planning, including *Business Advantage, Business Simulator, SUCCESS, ANS-PLAN-A, Strategy!, CheckMATE, EXCEL, STRATPAC, SIMPLAN, REVEAL, COSMOS,* and *BASICS P-C.*[24]

Some strategic decision support systems, however, are too sophisticated, expensive, or restrictive to be used easily by managers in a firm. This is unfortunate because the strategic-management process must be a people process to be successful. People make the difference! Strategic planning software thus should be simple and unsophisticated. Simplicity allows wide participation among managers in a firm and participation is essential for effective strategy implementation.

One strategic planning software product that parallels this text and offers managers and executives a simple yet effective approach for developing organizational strategies is *CheckMATE.* This IBM-compatible, personal computer software performs planning analyses and generates strategies a firm could pursue. *CheckMATE,* a Windows-based program, incorporates the most modern strategic planning techniques. No previous experience with computers or knowledge of strategic planning is required of the user. *CheckMATE* thus promotes communication, understanding, creativity, and forward thinking among users.

CheckMATE is not a spreadsheet program or database; it is an expert system that carries a firm through strategy formulation and implementation. A major strength of the new *CheckMATE* strategic planning software is its simplicity and participative approach. The user is asked approptiate questions, responses are recorded, information is assimilated, and results are printed. Individuals can work through the software independently and then meet to develop joint recommendations for the firm.

The *CheckMATE* software utilizes the most modern strategic planning analytical matrices to generate alternative strategies firms could pursue. Specific analytical procedures included in the *CheckMATE* program are Strategic Position and Action Evaluation (SPACE) analysis, Threats-Opportunities-Weaknesses-Strengths (TOWS) analysis, Internal-External (IE) analysis, and Grand Strategy Matrix analysis. These widely used strategic planning analyses are described in Chapter 6.

Twenty-three customized industry applications of *CheckMATE* are available in a new Windows format. An individual license costs $195. More information about *CheckMATE* can be obtained at www.checkmateplan.com or 843-669-6960 (phone).

INTERNAL AUDIT CHECKLISTS

The checklists of questions provided in this section can be helpful in determining specific strengths and weaknesses in the functional area of business. An answer of *no* to any question could indicate a potential weakness, although the strategic significance and implications of negative answers, of course, will vary by organization, industry, and severity of the weakness. Positive or *yes* answers to the checklist questions suggest potential areas of strength. The questions provided in Table 5–7 are not all-inclusive, but they can facilitate internal audit efforts.

TABLE 5–7
Internal Audit Checklist of Questions

MANAGEMENT

1. Does the firm use strategic-management concepts?
2. Are company objectives and goals measurable and well communicated?
3. Do managers at all hierarchical levels plan effectively?
4. Do managers delegate authority well?
5. Is the organization's structure appropriate?
6. Are job descriptions and job specifications clear?
7. Is employee morale high?
8. Are employee turnover and absenteeism low?
9. Are organizational reward and control mechanisms effective?

MARKETING

1. Are markets segmented effectively?
2. Is the organization positioned well among competitors?
3. Has the firm's market share been increasing?
4. Are present channels of distribution reliable and cost-effective?
5. Does the firm have an effective sales organization?
6. Does the firm conduct market research?
7. Are product quality and customer service good?
8. Are the firm's products and services priced appropriately?
9. Does the firm have an effective promotion, advertising, and publicity strategy?
10. Are marketing planning and budgeting effective?
11. Do the firm's marketing managers have adequate experience and training?

FINANCE

1. Where is the firm financially strong and weak as indicated by financial ratio analyses?
2. Can the firm raise needed short-term capital?
3. Can the firm raise needed long-term capital through debt and/or equity?
4. Does the firm have sufficient working capital?
5. Are capital budgeting procedures effective?
6. Are dividend payout policies reasonable?
7. Does the firm have good relations with its investors and stockholders?
8. Are the firm's financial managers experienced and well trained?

PRODUCTION

1. Are suppliers of raw materials, parts, and subassemblies reliable and reasonable?
2. Are facilities, equipment, machinery, and offices in good condition?
3. Are inventory-control policies and procedures effective?
4. Are quality-control policies and procedures effective?
5. Are facilities, resources, and markets strategically located?
6. Does the firm have technological competencies?

RESEARCH AND DEVELOPMENT

1. Does the firm have R&D facilities? Are they adequate?
2. If outside R&D firms are used, are they cost-effective?
3. Are the organization's R&D personnel well qualified?
4. Are R&D resources allocated effectively?
5. Are management information and computer systems adequate?
6. Is communication between R&D and other organizational units effective?
7. Are present products technologically competitive?

COMPUTER INFORMATION SYSTEMS

1. Do all managers in the firm use the information system to make decisions?
2. Is there a chief information officer or director of information systems position in the firm?
3. Are data in the information system updated regularly?
4. Do managers from all functional areas of the firm contribute input to the information system?
5. Are there effective passwords for entry into the firm's information system?
6. Are strategists of the firm familiar with the information systems of rival firms?
7. Is the information system user-friendly?
8. Do all users of the information system understand the competitive advantages that information can provide firms?
9. Are computer training workshops provided for users of the information system?
10. Is the firm's information system continually being improved in content and user-friendliness?

THE INTERNAL FACTOR EVALUATION (IFE) MATRIX

A summary step in conducting an internal strategic-management audit is to construct an *Internal Factor Evaluation (IFE) Matrix*. This strategy-formulation tool summarizes and evaluates the major strengths and weaknesses in the functional areas of a business, and it also provides a basis for identifying and evaluating relationships among those areas. Intuitive judgments are required in developing an IFE Matrix, so the appearance of a scientific approach should not be interpreted to mean this is an all-powerful technique. A thorough understanding of the factors included is more important than the actual numbers. Similar to the EFE Matrix and Competitive Profile Matrix described in Chapter 4, an IFE Matrix can be developed in five steps:

1. List critical success factors as identified in the internal-audit process. Use a total of from 10 to 20 internal factors, including both strengths and weaknesses. List strengths first and then weaknesses. Be as specific as possible, using percentages, ratios, and comparative numbers.

2. Assign a weight that ranges from 0.0 (not important) to 1.0 (all-important) to each factor. The weight assigned to a given factor indicates the relative importance of the factor to being successful in the firm's industry. Regardless of whether a key factor is an internal strength or weakness, factors considered to have the greatest effect on organizational performance should be assigned the highest weights. The sum of all weights must equal 1.0.

3. Assign a 1-to-4 rating to each factor to indicate whether that factor represents a major weakness (rating = 1), a minor weakness (rating = 2), a minor strength (rating = 3), or a major strength (rating = 4). Ratings are thus company-based, whereas the weights in Step 2 are industry-based.

4. Multiply each factor's weight by its rating to determine a weighted score for each variable.

5. Sum the weighted scores for each variable to determine the total weighted score for the organization.

Regardless of how many factors are included in an IFE Matrix, the total weighted score can range from a low of 1.0 to a high of 4.0, with the average score being 2.5. Total weighted scores well below 2.5 characterize organizations that are weak internally, whereas scores significantly above 2.5 indicate a strong internal position. Like the EFE Matrix, an IFE Matrix should include from 10 to 20 key factors. The number of factors has no effect upon the range of total weighted scores because the weights always sum to 1.0.

When a key internal factor is both a strength and a weakness, the factor should be included twice in the IFE Matrix, and a weight and rating should be assigned to each statement. For example, the Playboy logo both helps and hurts Playboy Enterprises; the logo attracts customers to the *Playboy* magazine, but it keeps the Playboy cable channel out of many markets.

TABLE 5–8
A Sample Internal Factor Evaluation Matrix for Circus Circus Enterprises

KEY INTERNAL FACTORS	WEIGHT	RATING	WEIGHTED SCORE
INTERNAL STRENGTHS			
1. Largest casino company in the United States	.05	4	.20
2. Room occupancy rates over 95% in Las Vegas	.10	4	.40
3. Increasing free cash flows	.05	3	.15
4. Owns 1 mile on Las Vegas Strip	.15	4	.60
5. Strong management team	.05	3	.15
6. Buffets at most facilities	.05	3	.15
7. Minimal comps provided	.05	3	.15
8. Long-range planning	.05	4	.20
9. Reputation as family-friendly	.05	3	.15
10. Financial ratios	.05	3	.15
INTERNAL WEAKNESSES			
1. Most properties are located in Las Vegas	.05	1	.05
2. Little diversification	.05	2	.10
3. Family reputation, not high rollers	.05	2	.10
4. Laughlin properties	.10	1	.10
5. Recent loss of joint ventures	.10	1	.10
TOTAL	1.00		2.75

An example of an IFE Matrix for Circus Circus Enterprises is provided in Table 5–8. Note that the firm's major strengths are its size, occupancy rates, property, and long-range planning as indicated by the rating of 4. The major weaknesses are locations and recent joint venture. The total weighted score of 2.75 indicates that the firm is above average in its overall internal strength.

In multidivisional firms, each autonomous division or strategic business unit should construct an IFE Matrix. Divisional matrices then can be integrated to develop an overall corporate IFE Matrix.

CONCLUSION

Management, marketing, finance/accounting, production/operations, research and development, and computer information systems represent the core operations of most businesses. A strategic-management audit of a firm's internal operations is vital to organizational health. Many companies still prefer to be judged solely on their bottom-line performance. However, an increasing number of successful organizations are using the internal audit to gain competitive advantages over rival firms.

Systematic methodologies for performing strength-weakness assessments are not well developed in the strategic-management literature, but it is clear that strategists must identify and evaluate internal strengths and weaknesses in order to formulate and choose among alternative strategies effectively. The EFE Matrix, Competitive Profile Matrix, IFE Matrix, and a clear statement of mission provide the basic information needed to formulate competitive strategies successfully. The process of performing an internal audit represents an opportunity for managers and employees throughout the organization to participate in determining the future of the firm. Involvement in the process can energize and mobilize managers and employees.

We invite you to visit the DAVID page on the Prentice Hall Web site at
www.prenhall.com/davidsm
for this chapter's World Wide Web exercises.

TAKE IT TO THE NET

KEY TERMS AND CONCEPTS

ISSUES FOR REVIEW AND DISCUSSION

1. Explain why prioritizing the relative importance of strengths and weaknesses to include in an IFE Matrix is an important strategic-management activity.

2. How can delegation of authority contribute to effective strategic management?

3. Diagram a formal organizational chart that reflects the following positions: a president, two executive officers, four middle managers, and eighteen lower-level managers. Now, diagram three overlapping and hypothetical informal group structures. How can this information be helpful to a strategist in formulating and implementing strategy?

4. How could a strategist's attitude toward social responsibility affect a firm's strategy? What is your attitude toward social responsibility?

5. Which of the three basic functions of finance/accounting do you feel is most important in a small electronics manufacturing concern? Justify your position.

6. Do you think aggregate R&D expenditures for American firms will increase or decrease next year? Why?

7. Explain how you would motivate managers and employees to implement a major new strategy.

8. Why do you think production/operations managers often are not directly involved in strategy-formulation activities? Why can this be a major organizational weakness?

9. Give two examples of staffing strengths and two examples of staffing weaknesses of an organization with which you are familiar.

10. Would you ever pay out dividends when your firm's annual net profit is negative? Why? What effect could this have on a firm's strategies?

11. If a firm has zero debt in its capital structure, is that always an organizational strength? Why or why not?

12. Describe the production/operations system in a police department.

13. After conducting an internal audit, a firm discovers a total of 100 strengths and 100 weaknesses. What procedures then could be used to determine the most important of these? Why is it important to reduce the total number of key factors?

14. Select one of the suggested readings at the end of this chapter. Look up that article and give a 5-minute oral report to the class summarizing the article and your views on the topic.

15. Why do you believe cultural products affect all the functions of business?

16. Do you think cultural products affect strategy formulation, implementation, or evaluation the most? Why?

17. Identify cultural products at your college or university. Do these products, viewed collectively or separately, represent a strength or weakness for the organization?

18. Describe the computer information system at your college or university.

19. Explain the difference between data and information in terms of each being useful to strategists.

20. What are the most important characteristics of an effective computer information system?

NOTES

1. Robert Grant, "The Resource-Based Theory of Competitive Advantage: Implications for Strategy Formulation," *California Management Review* (Spring 1991): 116.

2. Reprinted by permission of the publisher from "Integrating Strength-Weakness Analysis into Strategic Planning," by William King, *Journal of Business Research II*, no. 4: p. 481. Copyright 1983 by Elsevier Science Publishing Co., Inc.

3. Igor Ansoff, "Strategic Management of Technology," *Journal of Business Strategy* 7, no. 3 (Winter 1987): 38.

4. Claude George, Jr., *The History of Management Thought*, 2nd ed. (Englewood Cliffs, N.J.: Prentice-Hall, 1972): 174.

5. Edgar Schein, *Organizational Culture and Leadership* (San Francisco: Jossey-Bass, 1985): 9.

6. John Lorsch, "Managing Culture: The Invisible Barrier to Strategic Change," *California Management Review* 28, no. 2 (1986): 95–109.

7. Y. Allarie and M. Firsirotu, "How to Implement Radical Strategies in Large Organizations," *Sloan Management Review* (Spring 1985): 19.

8. Adam Smith, *Wealth of Nations* (New York: Modern Library, 1937): 3–4.

9. Richard Daft, *Management*, 3rd ed. (Orlando, Fla.: Dryden Press, 1993): 512.

10. Shelley Kirkpatrick and Edwin Locke, "Leadership: Do Traits Matter?" *Academy of Management Executive* 5, no. 2 (May 1991): 48.

11. Peter Drucker, *Management Tasks, Responsibilities, and Practice* (New York: Harper & Row, 1973): 463.

12. Brian Dumaine, "What the Leaders of Tomorrow See," *Fortune* (July 3, 1989): 51.

13. J. M. Bryson and P. Bromiley, "Critical Factors Affecting the Planning and Implementation of Major Products," *Strategic Management Journal* 14, no. 5 (July 1993): 319.

14. Robert Waterman, Jr., "The Renewal Factor," *Business Week* (September 14, 1987): 104.

15. J. Evans and B. Bergman, *Marketing* (New York: Macmillan, 1982): 17.

16. John Wilke and Bob Ortega, "Anheuser's Sales Practices Under Probe," *The Wall Street Journal* (October 3, 1997): A2.

17. Quoted in Robert Waterman, Jr., "The Renewal Factor," *Business Week* (September 14, 1987): 108.

18. J. Van Horne, *Financial Management and Policy* (Englewood Cliffs, N.J.: Prentice-Hall, 1974): 10.

19. W. Boulton and B. Saladin, "Let's Make Production-Operations Management Top Priority for Strategic Planning in the 1980s," *Managerial Planning* 32, no. 1 (July–August 1983): 19.

20. Vida Scarpello, William Boulton, and Charles Hofer, "Reintegrating R&D into Business Strategy," *Journal of Business Strategy* 6, no. 4 (Spring 1986): 50.

21. Philip Rouseel, Kamal Saad, and Tamara Erickson, "The Evolution of Third Generation R&D," *Planning Review* 19, no. 2 (March–April 1991): 18–26.

22. Scarpello, Boulton, and Hofer, 50, 51.

23. Hugh Watson and Kelly Rainer, Jr., "A Manager's Guide to Executive Support Systems," *Business Horizons* (March–April 1991): 49.

24. Robert Mockler, "A Catalog of Commercially Available Software for Strategic Planning," *Planning Review* 19, no. 3 (May/June 1991): 28. Also, John Sterling, "Strategic Management Software Review," *Planning Review* (January–February 1992): 29–33.

CURRENT READINGS

Bamberger, Peter and Avi Fiegenbaum. "The Role of Strategic Reference Points in Explaining the Nature and Consequences of Human Resource Strategy." *Academy of Management Review* 21, no. 4 (October 1996): 926–958.

Brynjolfsson, Erik, Amy Austin Renshaw, and Marshall Van Alstyne. "The Matrix of Change." *Sloan Management Review* 38, no. 2 (Winter 1997):37–54.

Christensen, C. M. and J. L. Bower. "Customer Power, Strategic Investment, and the Failure of Leading Firms." *Strategic Management Journal* 17, no. 3 (March 1996): 197–218.

Cohen, Susan G. and Diane E. Bailey. "What Makes Teams Work: Group Effectiveness Research from the Shop Floor to the Executive Suite." *Journal of Management* 23, no. 3 (1997): 239–290.

Deadrick, Diana L., R. Bruce McAfee, and Myron Glassman. "Customers for Life: Does It Fit Your Culture?" *Business Horizons* 40, no. 4 (July–August 1997): 11–16.

Denison, Daniel R. "What IS the Difference Between Organizational Culture and Organizational Climate? A Native's Point of View on a Decade of Paradigm Wars." *Academy of Management Review* 21, no. 3 (July 1996): 619–654.

Doka, Kenneth J. "Dealing with Diversity: The Coming Challenge to American Business." *Business Horizons* 39, no. 3 (May–June 1996): 67–71.

Geletkanycz, M.A. "The Salience of 'Culture's Consequences': The Effects of Cultural Values on Top Executive Commitment to the Status Quo." *Strategic Management Journal* 18, no. 8 (September 1997): 615–634.

Grundy, Tony. "Human Resource Management—A Strategic Approach." *Long Range Planning* 30, no. 4 (August 1997): 507–517.

Heracleous, Loizos and Brian Langham. "Strategic Change and Organizational Culture at Hay Management Consultants." *Long Range Planning* 29, no. 4 (August 1996): 485–494.

Joachimsthaler, Erich and David A. Baker. "Building Brands Without Mass Media." *Harvard Business Review* (January–February 1997): 39–52.

Marino, Kenneth E. "Developing Consensus on Firm Competencies and Capabilities." *Academy of Management Executive* 10, no. 3 (August 1996): 40–51.

Meenaghan, Tony. "Ambush Marketing—A Threat to Corporate Sponsorship." *Sloan Management Review* 38, no. 1 (Fall 1996): 103–113.

Nemetz, Patricia L. and Sandra L. Christensen. "The Challenge of Cultural Diversity: Harnessing a Diversity of Views to Understand Multiculturalism." *Academy of Management Journal*, 21, no. 2 (April 1996): 434–462.

Ryan, Chuck and Walter E. Riggs. "Redefining the Product Life Cycle: The Five-Element Product Wave." *Business Horizons* 39, no. 5 (September–October 1996): 33–40.

Rindfleisch, Aric. "Marketing as Warfare: Reassessing a Dominant Metaphor." *Business Horizons* 39, no. 5 (September–October 1996): 3–10.

Stimpert, J. L. and I. M. Duhaime. "In the Eyes of the Beholder: Conceptualizations of Relatedness Held by the Managers of Large Diversified Firms." *Strategic Management Journal* 18, no. 2 (February 1997): 111–126.

Stuart, T. E. and J. M. Podolny. "Local Search and the Evolution of Technological Capabilities." *Strategic Management Journal* 17, Special Issue (Summer 1996): 21–38.

Waddock, S. A. and S. B. Graves. "The Corporate Social Performance—Financial Performance Link." *Strategic Management Journal* 18, no. 4 (April 1997): 303–320.

EXPERIENTIAL EXERCISES

Experiential Exercise 5A

PERFORMING A FINANCIAL RATIO ANALYSIS FOR HERSHEY FOODS

PURPOSE

Financial ratio analysis is one of the best techniques for identifying and evaluating internal strengths and weaknesses. Potential investors and current shareholders look closely at firms' financial ratios, making detailed comparisons to industry averages and to previous periods of time. Financial ratio analyses provide vital input information for developing an IFE Matrix.

INSTRUCTIONS

Step 1 On a separate sheet of paper, number from 1 to 20. Referring to Hershey's income statement and balance sheet (pp. 34–35), calculate 20 financial ratios for 1997 for the company. Use Table 5–4 as a reference.

Step 2 Go to your college library and find industry average financial ratios for the confectionery industry. Record the industry average values in a second column on your paper.

Step 3 In a third column, indicate whether you consider each ratio to be a strength, a weakness, or a neutral factor for Hershey.

Experiential Exercise 5B

CONSTRUCTING AN IFE MATRIX FOR HERSHEY FOODS

PURPOSE

This exercise will give you experience developing an IFE Matrix. Identifying and prioritizing factors to include in an IFE Matrix fosters communication among functional and divisional managers. Preparing an IFE Matrix allows human resource, marketing, production/operations, finance/accounting, R&D, and computer information systems managers to vocalize their concerns and thoughts regarding the business condition of the firm. This results in an improved collective understanding of the business.

INSTRUCTIONS

Step 1 Join with two other individuals to form a three-person team. Develop a team IFE Matrix for Hershey Foods.

Step 2 Compare your team's IFE Matrix to other teams' IFE Matrices. Discuss any major differences.

Step 3 What strategies do you think would allow Hershey to capitalize on its major strengths? What strategies would allow Hershey to improve upon its major weaknesses?

CONSTRUCTING AN IFE MATRIX FOR MY UNIVERSITY

PURPOSE

This exercise gives you the opportunity to evaluate your university's major strengths and weaknesses. As will become clearer in the next chapter, an organization's strategies are largely based upon striving to take advantage of strengths and improving upon weaknesses.

INSTRUCTIONS

Step 1 Join with two other individuals to form a three-person team. Develop a team IFE Matrix for your university. You may use the strength/weaknesses determined in Experiential Exercise 1D.

Step 2 Go to the board and diagram your team's IFE Matrix.

Step 3 Compare your team's IFE Matrix to other teams' IFE Matrices. Discuss any major differences.

Step 4 What strategies do you think would allow your university to capitalize on its major strengths? What strategies would allow your university to improve upon its major weaknesses?

Strategy Analysis and Choice

CHAPTER OBJECTIVES

After studying this chapter, you should be able to do the following:

1. Describe a three-stage framework for choosing among alternative strategies.

2. Explain how to develop a TOWS Matrix, SPACE Matrix, BCG Matrix, IE Matrix, and QSPM.

3. Identify important behavioral, political, ethical, and social responsibility considerations in strategy analysis and choice.

4. Discuss the role of intuition in strategic analysis and choice.

5. Discuss the role of organizational culture in strategic analysis and choice.

6. Discuss the role of a board of directors in choosing among alternative strategies.

NOTABLE
QUOTES

*S*trategic management is not a box of tricks or a bundle of techniques. It is analytical thinking and commitment of resources to action. But quantification alone is not planning. Some of the most important issues in strategic management cannot be quantified at all.—PETER DRUCKER

*O*bjectives are not commands; they are commitments. They do not determine the future; they are the means to mobilize resources and energies of an organization for the making of the future.—PETER DRUCKER

*L*ife is full of lousy options.—GENERAL P. X. KELLEY

*W*hen a crisis forces choosing among alternatives, most people will choose the worse possible one.—RUDIN'S LAW

*S*trategy isn't something you can nail together in slap-dash fashion by sitting around a conference table.—TERRY HALLER

*P*lanning is often doomed before it ever starts, either because too much is expected of it or because not enough is put into it.—T. J. CARTWRIGHT

*T*o acquire or not to acquire, that is the question.—ROBERT J. TERRY

*C*orporate boards need to work to stay away from the traps that force every member to go along with the majority. Devil's advocates represent one easy-to-implement solution.—CHARLES SCHWENK

*W*hether it's broke or not, fix it—make it better. Not just products, but the whole company if necessary.—BILL SAPORITO

*S*trategic analysis and choice largely involves making subjective decisions based on objective information. This chapter introduces important concepts that can help strategists generate feasible alternatives, evaluate those alternatives, and choose a specific course of action. Behavioral aspects of strategy formulation are described, including politics, culture, ethics, and social responsibility considerations. Modern tools for formulating strategies are described, and the appropriate role of a board of directors is discussed.

THE NATURE OF STRATEGY ANALYSIS AND CHOICE

As indicated by Figure 6.1, this chapter focuses on establishing long-term objectives, generating alternative strategies, and selecting strategies to pursue. Strategy analysis and choice seeks to determine alternative courses of action that could best enable the firm to achieve its mission and objectives. The firm's present strategies, objectives, and mission, coupled with the external and internal audit information, provide a basis for generating and evaluating feasible alternative strategies.

Unless a desperate situation faces the firm, alternative strategies will likely represent incremental steps to move the firm from its present position to a desired future position. For example, AT&T has a strategy to acquire other firms in the communication industry, perhaps even GTE Corporation, to combat increased competition from the recent Worldcom/MCI merger. Alternative strategies do not come out of the wild blue yonder; they are derived from the firm's mission, objectives, external audit, and internal audit; they are consistent with, or build upon, past strategies that have worked well!

THE PROCESS OF GENERATING AND SELECTING STRATEGIES

Strategists never consider all feasible alternatives that could benefit the firm, because there are an infinite number of possible actions and an infinite number of ways to implement those actions. Therefore, a manageable set of the most attractive alternative strategies must be developed. The advantages, disadvantages, trade-offs, costs, and benefits of these strategies should be determined. This section discusses the process that many firms use to determine an appropriate set of alternative strategies.

Identifying and evaluating alternative strategies should involve many of the managers and employees who earlier assembled the organizational mission statement, performed the external audit, and conducted the internal audit. Representatives from each department and division of the firm should be included in this process, as was the case in previous strategy-formulation activities. Recall that involvement provides the best opportunity for managers and employees to gain an understanding of what the firm is doing and why, and to become committed to helping the firm accomplish its objectives.

All participants in the strategy analysis and choice activity should have the firm's external and internal audit information by their sides. This information, coupled with the firm's mission statement, will help participants crystallize in their own minds particular strategies that they believe could benefit the firm most. Creativity should be encouraged in this thought process.

Alternative strategies proposed by participants should be considered and discussed in a meeting or series of meetings. Proposed strategies should be listed in writing. When all feasible strategies identified by participants are given and understood, the strategies should be ranked in order of attractiveness by all participants, with 1 = *should not be implemented*, 2 = *possibly should be implemented*, 3 = *probably should be implemented*, and 4 = *definitely should be implemented*. This process will result in a prioritized list of best strategies that reflects the collective wisdom of the group.

FIGURE 6–1

A Comprehensive Strategic-Management Model

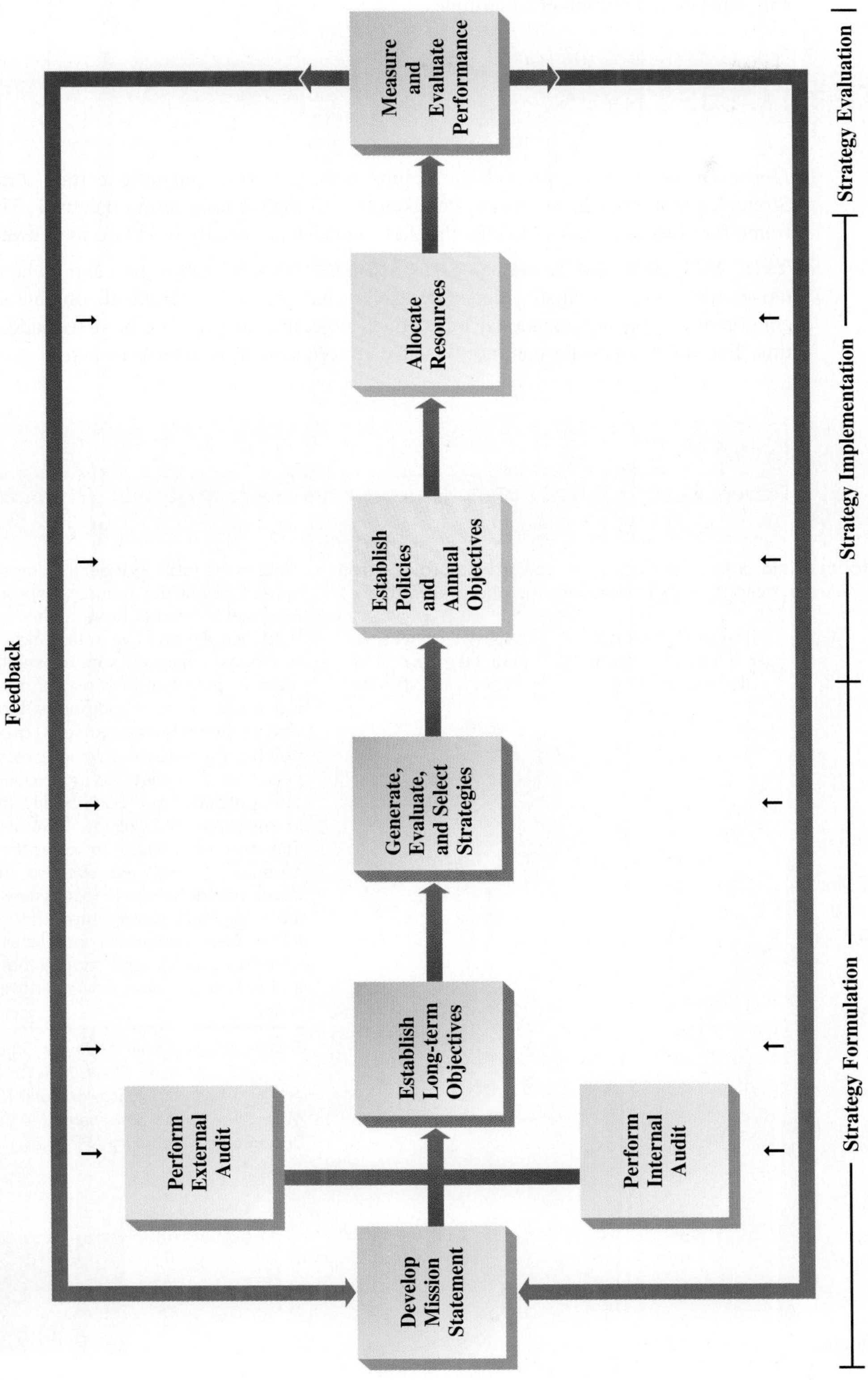

As indicated in the Natural Environment Perspective, the success of some strategies can depend on environmental attitudes.

LONG-TERM OBJECTIVES

Long-term objectives represent the results expected from pursuing certain strategies. Strategies represent the actions to be taken to accomplish long-term objectives. The time frame for objectives and strategies should be consistent, usually from two to five years.

THE NATURE OF LONG-TERM OBJECTIVES

Objectives should be quantitative, measurable, realistic, understandable, challenging, hierarchical, obtainable, and congruent among organizational units. Each objective should also be associated with a time line. Objectives are commonly stated in terms such as growth in assets, growth in

NATURAL ENVIRONMENT

Formulating Strategies Based on Environmental Attitudes

Americans can be grouped into categories based on their attitudes, actions, and concern toward natural environment deterioration and preservation.

CHARACTERISTICS	HIGH CONCERN FOR THE NATURAL ENVIRONMENT	LOW CONCERN FOR THE NATURAL ENVIRONMENT
Sex		
Male	34%	55%
Female	66	45
Education		
Less than High School	11	30
High School Graduate	39	39
Some College	22	20
College Graduate Or More	28	11
Occupation		
Executive/Professional	25	11
White Collar	18	15
Blue Collar	19	36
Marital Status		
Married	69	59
Not Married	30	41
Political/Social Ideology		
Conservative	43	36
Middle of the Road	26	41
Liberal	28	16
Region		
Northeast	31	17
Midwest	27	22
South	18	48
West	24	13
Median Income (in thousands)	$32.1	$21.2

Note in the table that persons most concerned about the natural environment tend to be female, have higher household income, and live in the Midwest or Northeast. These persons especially engage in activities such as not purchasing products from companies that are environmentally irresponsible, avoiding purchasing aerosol products, recycling paper and bottles, using biodegradable products, and contributing money to environmental groups. This information can be helpful to companies in formulating strategies such as market development (where to locate new facilities), product development (manufacturing new equipment or developing green products), and market penetration (whom to focus advertising efforts upon).

Source: Adapted from the Roper Organization, 205 East 42nd Street, New York, NY 10017. Also from Joe Schwartz and Thomas Miller, "The Earth's Best Friends," American Demographics (February 1991): 28.

sales, profitability, market share, degree and nature of diversification, degree and nature of vertical integration, earnings per share, and social responsibility. Clearly established objectives offer many benefits. They provide direction, allow synergy, aid in evaluation, establish priorities, reduce uncertainty, minimize conflicts, stimulate exertion, and aid in both the allocation of resources and the design of jobs.

Long-term objectives are needed at the corporate, divisional, and functional levels in an organization. They are an important measure of managerial performance. Many practitioners and academicians attribute a significant part of U.S. industry's competitive decline to the short-term, rather than long-term, strategy orientation of managers in the United States. Arthur D. Little argues that bonuses or merit pay for managers today must be based to a greater extent on long-term objectives and strategies. A general framework for relating objectives to performance evaluation is provided in Table 6–1. A particular organization could tailor these guidelines to meet its own needs, but incentives should be attached to both long-term and annual objectives.

Clearly stated and communicated objectives are vital to success for many reasons. First, objectives help stakeholders understand their role in an organization's future. They also provide a basis for consistent decision making by managers whose values and attitudes differ. By reaching a consensus on objectives during strategy-formulation activities, an organization can minimize potential conflicts later during implementation. Objectives set forth organizational priorities and stimulate exertion and accomplishment. They serve as standards by which individuals, groups, departments, divisions, and entire organizations can be evaluated. Objectives provide the basis for designing jobs and organizing activities to be performed in an organization. They also provide direction and allow for organizational synergy.

Without long-term objectives, an organization would drift aimlessly toward some unknown end! It is hard to imagine an organization or individual being successful without clear objectives. Success only rarely occurs by accident; rather, it is the result of hard work directed toward achieving certain objectives.

NOT MANAGING BY OBJECTIVES An unknown educator once said, "If you think education is expensive, try ignorance." The idea behind this saying also applies to establishing objectives. Strategists should avoid the following alternative ways to "not managing by objectives."

◆ Managing by Extrapolation—adheres to the principle "If it ain't broke, don't fix it." The idea is to keep on doing about the same things in the same ways because things are going well.

◆ Managing by Crisis—based on the belief that the true measure of a really good strategist is the ability to solve problems. Because there are plenty of crises and problems to go around for every person and every organization, strategists ought to bring their time and creative energy to bear on solving the most pressing problems of the day. Managing by crisis is actually a form of reacting rather than acting and of letting events dictate the whats and whens of management decisions.

ORGANIZATIONAL LEVEL	BASIS FOR ANNUAL BONUS OR MERIT PAY
Corporate	75% based on long-term objectives
	25% based on annual objectives
Division	50% based on long-term objectives
	50% based on annual objectives
Function	25% based on long-term objectives
	75% based on annual objectives

TABLE 6–1
Varying Performance Measures by Organizational Level

◆ Managing by Subjectives—built on the idea that there is no general plan for which way to go and what to do; just do the best you can to accomplish what you think should be done. In short, "Do your own thing, the best way you know how" (sometimes referred to as *the mystery approach to decision making* because subordinates are left to figure out what is happening and why).

◆ Managing by Hope—based on the fact that the future is laden with great uncertainty, and that if we try and do not succeed, then we hope our second (or third) attempt will succeed. Decisions are predicted on the hope that they will work and that good times are just around the corner, especially if luck and good fortune are on our side.[1]

A COMPREHENSIVE STRATEGY-FORMULATION FRAMEWORK

Important strategy-formulation techniques can be integrated into a three-stage decision-making framework, as shown in Figure 6–2. The tools presented in this framework are applicable to all sizes and types of organizations and can help strategists identify, evaluate, and select strategies.

Stage 1 of the formulation framework consists of the EFE Matrix, the IFE Matrix, and the Competitive Profile Matrix. Called the *Input Stage*, Stage 1 summarizes the basic input information needed to formulate strategies. Stage 2, called the *Matching Stage*, focuses upon generating feasible alternative strategies by aligning key external and internal factors. Stage 2 techniques include the Threats-Opportunities-Weaknesses-Strengths (TOWS) Matrix, the Strategic Position and Action Evaluation (SPACE) Matrix, the Boston Consulting Group (BCG) Matrix, the Internal-External (IE) Matrix, and the Grand Strategy Matrix. Stage 3, called the *Decision Stage*, involves a single technique, the Quantitative Strategic Planning Matrix (QSPM). A QSPM uses input information from Stage 1 to objectively evaluate feasible alternative strategies identified in Stage 2. A QSPM reveals the relative attractiveness of alternative strategies and thus provides an objective basis for selecting specific strategies.

FIGURE 6–2
The Strategy-Formulation Analytical Framework

STAGE 1: THE INPUT STAGE		
External Factor Evaluation (EFE) Matrix	Competitive Profile Matrix	Internal Factor Evaluation (IFE) Matrix

STAGE 2: THE MATCHING STAGE				
Threats-Opportunities-Weaknesses-Strengths (TOWS) Matrix	Strategic Position and Action Evaluation (SPACE) Matrix	Boston Consulting Group (BCG) Matrix	Internal-External (IE) Matrix	Grand Strategy Matrix

STAGE 3: THE DECISION STAGE
Quantitative Strategic Planning Matrix (QSPM)

All nine techniques included in the *strategy-formulation framework* require integration of intuition and analysis. Autonomous divisions in an organization commonly use strategy-formulation techniques to develop strategies and objectives. Divisional analyses provide a basis for identifying, evaluating, and selecting among alternative corporate-level strategies.

Strategists themselves, not analytic tools, are always responsible and accountable for strategic decisions. Lenz emphasized that the shift from a words-oriented to a numbers-oriented planning process can give rise to a false sense of certainty; it can reduce dialogue, discussion, and argument as a means to explore understandings, test assumptions and foster organizational learning.[2] Strategists therefore must be wary of this possibility and use analytical tools to facilitate, rather than diminish, communication. Without objective information and analysis, personal biases, politics, emotions, personalities, and *halo error* (the tendency to put too much weight on a single factor) unfortunately may play a dominant role in the strategy-formulation process.

THE INPUT STAGE

Procedures for developing an EFE Matrix, an IFE Matrix, and a Competitive Profile Matrix were presented in the previous two chapters. The information derived from these three matrices provides basic input information for the matching and decision stage matrices described later in this chapter.

The input tools require strategists to quantify subjectivity during early stages of the strategy-formulation process. Making small decisions in the input matrices regarding the relative importance of external and internal factors allows strategists to generate and evaluate alternative strategies more effectively. Good intuitive judgment is always needed in determining appropriate weights and ratings.

THE MATCHING STAGE

Strategy is sometimes defined as the match an organization makes between its internal resources and skills and the opportunities and risks created by its external factors.[3] The matching stage of the strategy-formulation framework consists of five techniques that can be used in any sequence: the TOWS Matrix, the SPACE Matrix, the BCG Matrix, the IE Matrix, and the Grand Strategy Matrix. These tools rely upon information derived from the input stage to match external opportunities and threats with internal strengths and weaknesses. *Matching* external and internal critical success factors is the key to effectively generating feasible alternative strategies! For example, a firm with excess working capital (an internal strength) could take advantage of the cablevision industry's 20 percent annual growth rate (an external opportunity) by acquiring a firm in the cablevision industry. This example portrays simple one-to-one matching. In most situations, external and internal relationships are more complex, and the matching requires multiple alignments for each strategy generated. The basic concept of matching is illustrated in Table 6–2.

Any organization, whether military, product-oriented, service-oriented, governmental, or even athletic, must develop and execute good strategies to win. A good offense without a good defense, or vice versa, usually leads to defeat. Developing strategies that use strengths to capitalize on opportunities could be considered an offense, whereas strategies designed to improve upon weaknesses while avoiding threats could be termed defensive. Every organization has some external opportunities and threats and internal strengths and

TABLE 6–2
Matching Key External and Internal Factors to Formulate Alternative Strategies

KEY INTERNAL FACTOR		KEY EXTERNAL FACTOR		RESULTANT STRATEGY
Excess working capacity (an internal strength)	+	20% annual growth in the cablevision industry (an external opportunity)	=	Acquire Visioncable, Inc.
Insufficient capacity (an internal weakness)	+	Exit of two major foreign competitors from the industry (an external opportunity)	=	Pursue horizontal integration by buying competitors' facilities
Strong R & D expertise (an internal strength)	+	Decreasing numbers of young adults (an external threat)	=	Develop new products for older adults
Poor employee morale (an internal weakness)	+	Strong union activity (an external threat)	=	Develop a new employee benefits package

weaknesses that can be aligned to formulate feasible alternative strategies. As indicated in the Information Technology Perspective, falling prices for wireless communication is an opportunity facing business firms.

THE THREATS-OPPORTUNITIES-WEAKNESSES-STRENGTHS (TOWS) MATRIX
The *Threats-Opportunities-Weaknesses-Strengths (TOWS) Matrix* is an important matching tool that helps managers develop four types of strategies: SO Strategies, WO Strategies, ST Strategies, and WT Strategies.[4] Matching key external and internal factors is the most difficult part of developing a TOWS Matrix and requires good judgment, and there is no one best set of matches. Note in Table 6–2 that the first, second, third, and fourth strategies are SO, WO, ST, and WT Strategies, respectively.

SO Strategies use a firm's internal strengths to take advantage of external opportunities. All managers would like their organizations to be in a position where internal strengths can be used to take advantage of external trends and events. Organizations generally will pursue WO, ST, or WT Strategies in order to get into a situation where they can apply SO Strategies. When a firm has major weaknesses, it will strive to overcome them and make them strengths. When an organization faces major threats, it will seek to avoid them in order to concentrate on opportunities. As indicated in the Information Technology Perspective,

INFORMATION TECHNOLOGY

Are You or Your Firm Wireless?

Wireless communication is becoming more the norm than the exception for many individuals and businesses. The number of wireless users in the United States is expected to increase from 48.9 million in 1997 to over 100 million in 2001, as the average price per minute of use falls from 15 cents to 8 cents. Today, the following wireless services are widely used:

- Digital satellite television
- Satellite location tracking
- Cellular phones
- Digital smart phones that combine cellu-

lar phone, two-way-radio, paging, and Internet

- Hand-held wireless computers
- Fixed-wireless local telephone service
- Wireless computer modems
- Wireless local-area computer networks
- Wireless cable television
- Infrared wireless devices and sensors

Soon, the following additional wireless communication services will be available:

- Satellite data broadcasting

- Satellite cellular-phone service
- Satellite high-speed Internet service
- Satellite sensing
- Digital television with Internet
- Wideband digital networks
- Wireless home security

Source: Adapted from Bill Hill, "The Communications Battleground," The Wall Street Journal (September 11, 1997): R4.

immense opportunities are available to many firms today from wireless communication advances in technology.

WO Strategies aim at improving internal weaknesses by taking advantage of external opportunities. Sometimes key external opportunities exist, but a firm has internal weaknesses that prevent it from exploiting those opportunities. For example, there may be a high demand for electronic devices to control the amount and timing of fuel injection in automobile engines (opportunity), but a certain auto parts manufacturer may lack the technology required for producing these devices (weakness). One possible WO Strategy would be to acquire this technology by forming a joint venture with a firm having competency in this area. An alternative WO Strategy would be to hire and train people with the required technical capabilities.

ST Strategies use a firm's strengths to avoid or reduce the impact of external threats. This does not mean that a strong organization should always meet threats in the external environment head-on. A recent example of ST Strategy occurred when Texas Instruments used an excellent legal department (a strength) to collect nearly $700 million in damages and royalties from nine Japanese and Korean firms that infringed on patents for semiconductor memory chips (threat). Rival firms that copy ideas, innovations, and patented products are a major threat in many industries. This is a major problem for U.S. firms selling products in China.

WT Strategies are defensive tactics directed at reducing internal weaknesses and avoiding environmental threats. An organization faced with numerous external threats and internal weaknesses may indeed be in a precarious position. In fact, such a firm may have to fight for its survival, merge, retrench, declare bankruptcy, or choose liquidation.

A schematic representation of the TOWS Matrix is provided in Figure 6–3. Note that a TOWS Matrix is composed of nine cells. As shown, there are four key factor cells, four

GLOBAL PERSPECTIVE
Is Africa Open for Business?

Still mired in poverty, corruption, dictatorships, and ethnic violence, Africa receives less than 5 percent of the world's net private capital flows. However, some African nations have established democratic governments, stamped out inflation, and are beginning to attract business. *The Wall Street Journal* suggests that the five best African areas to launch new investments are South Africa, Ghana, Uganda, Botswana, and the Ivory Coast. Comments on the latter four areas are given below:

GHANA

With $1.3 billion in foreign private investment in 1996, Ghana has become a peaceful, democratic, financial mecca in Africa. The country's gross domestic product grew 5.2 percent in 1996 and another 5 percent in 1997. Ghana offers low tariffs, low taxes, and low wages. The only real negative about Ghana is that inflation is about 35 percent annually.

UGANDA

Now a peaceful country, Uganda is a model of prudence, reform, and openness. Uganda's gross domestic product growth in 1997 reached 7 percent and is projected to do the same in fiscal 1998. Foreign private investment in Uganda grew from $3 million in 1992 to $148 million in 1996.

BOTSWANA

About the size of France and located near South Africa, Botswana is a peaceful nation of 1.3 million people. Rich in diamonds and having an excellent infrastructure, Botswana recently attracted large Hyundai Motor and AB Volvo plants. Botswana offers firms low wages, political stability, low taxes, and a convenient close export market in South Africa. Foreign private investment in Botswana reached $68 million in 1996.

IVORY COAST

The port city of Abidjan will host the eight-country West African stock exchange set to open in 1998. Many foreign companies now are investing in the Ivory Coast's cocoa, oil, telecommunications, power, and other sectors. Foreign private investment in the Ivory Coast was negative $192 million in 1996, but analysts expect positive flows in 1997 and thereafter.

Source: Adapted from Michael Phillips, "Into Africa," The Wall Street Journal (September 18, 1997): R6.

strategy cells, and one cell that is always left blank (the upper left cell). The four strategy cells, labeled *SO, WO, ST,* and *WT*, are developed after completing four key factor cells, labeled *S, W, O,* and *T*. There are eight steps involved in constructing a TOWS Matrix:

1. List the firm's key external opportunities.
2. List the firm's key external threats.
3. List the firm's key internal strengths.
4. List the firm's key internal weaknesses.
5. Match internal strengths with external opportunities and record the resultant SO Strategies in the appropriate cell.
6. Match internal weaknesses with external opportunities and record the resultant WO Strategies.
7. Match internal strengths with external threats and record the resultant ST Strategies.

FIGURE 6–3
The TOWS Matrix

	STRENGTHS—S 1. 2. 3. 4. 5. 6. 7. 8. 9. 10. List strengths	**WEAKNESSES—W** 1. 2. 3. 4. 5. 6. 7. 8. 9. 10. List weaknesses
Always leave blank		
OPPORTUNITIES—O 1. 2. 3. 4. 5. 6. 7. 8. 9. 10. List opportunities	**SO STRATEGIES** 1. 2. 3. 4. 5. 6. 7. 8. 9. 10. Use strengths to take advantage of opportunities	**WO STRATEGIES** 1. 2. 3. 4. 5. 6. 7. 8. 9. 10. Overcome weaknesses by taking advantage of opportunities
THREATS—T 1. 2. 3. 4. 5. 6. 7. 8. 9. 10. List threats	**ST STRATEGIES** 1. 2. 3. 4. 5. 6. 7. 8. 9. 10. Use strengths to avoid threats	**WT STRATEGIES** 1. 2. 3. 4. 5. 6. 7. 8. 9. 10. Minimize weaknesses and avoid threats

8. Match internal weaknesses with external threats and record the resultant WT Strategies.

The purpose of each Stage 2 matching tool is to generate feasible alternative strategies, not to select or determine which strategies are best! Not all of the strategies developed in the TOWS Matrix, therefore, will be selected for implementation. A sample TOWS Matrix for Cineplex Odeon, the large cinema company, is provided in Figure 6–4.

The strategy-formulation guidelines provided in Chapter 2 can enhance the process of matching key external and internal factors. For example, when an organization has both the

FIGURE 6–4
Cineplex Odeon TOWS Matrix

	STRENGTHS—S 1. Located in large population centers 2. Positive cash flow 3 years running 3. Double the industry concession sales rate 4. Many cost-cutting measures in place 5. Upgraded audio in many places 6. Profitable in Canada	WEAKNESSES—W 1. Poor labor relations 2. Current ratio of 0.25 3. Flat operating cost through falling revenue 4. Triple the G&A expenses of Carmike 5. Significant losses in the United States 6. Management concentrating on market share 7. Restrictive covenants set by lenders
OPPORTUNITIES—O 1. Approached by most major chains for potential merger 2. Opening economies in Eastern Europe 3. Rebounding attendance (up 6.4%) 4. Videotape industry worth estimated $18 billion vs. $6.4 billion for movie theaters 5. Foreign per capita income growth outpacing the United States	SO STRATEGIES 1. Open theaters in Eastern Europe (S1, O2, O5)	WO STRATEGIES 1. Pursue merger with American Cinemas (O1, O2, W3, W4, W5, W6)
THREATS—T 1. 80% of all households own VCRs 2. Aging population 3. Dependence on successful movies 4. Switch from bid to allocation for licenses 5. Seasonality for movie releases 6. Increased competition in exhibition	ST STRATEGIES 1. Open 50 video rental stores in 10 markets (S1, S6, T1, T3, T5, O4) 2. Construct 20 multidimensional entertainment complexes (S1, T3, T5, T6)	WT STRATEGIES 1. Reduce corporate overhead (W3, W4, T3, T5, T6) 2. Divest U.S. operations (T6, W2, W3, W4, W5, W6)

capital and human resources needed to distribute its own products (internal strength) and distributors are unreliable, costly, or incapable of meeting the firm's needs (external threat), then forward integration can be an attractive ST Strategy. When a firm has excess production capacity (internal weakness) and its basic industry is experiencing declining annual sales and profits (external threat), then concentric diversification can be an effective WT Strategy. It is important to use specific, rather than general, strategy terms when developing a TOWS Matrix. In addition, it is important to include the "S1,O2"-type notation after each strategy in the TOWS Matrix. This notation reveals the rationale for each alternative strategy.

THE STRATEGIC POSITION AND ACTION EVALUATION (SPACE)

MATRIX   *The Strategic Position and Action Evaluation (SPACE) Matrix*, another important Stage 2 *matching* tool, is illustrated in Figure 6–5. Its four-quadrant framework indicates whether aggressive, conservative, defensive, or competitive strategies are most appropriate for a given organization. The axes of the SPACE Matrix represent two internal dimensions (*financial strength* [FS] and *competitive advantage* [CA]) and two external dimensions (*environmental stability* [ES] and *industry strength* [IS]). These four factors are the most important determinants of an organization's overall strategic position.[5]

Depending upon the type of organization, numerous variables could make up each of the dimensions represented on the axes of the SPACE Matrix. Factors earlier included in the firm's EFE and IFE matrices should be considered in developing a SPACE Matrix. Other variables commonly included are given in Table 6–3. For example, return on investment, leverage, liquidity, working capital, and cash flow commonly are considered determining factors of an organization's financial strength. Like the TOWS Matrix, the SPACE Matrix should be tailored to the particular organization being studied and based on factual information as much as possible.

FIGURE 6–5
The SPACE Matrix

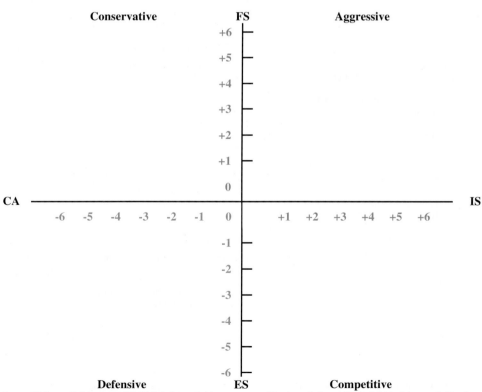

Source: H. Rowe, R. Mason, and K. Dickel, *Strategic Management and Business Policy: A Methodological Approach* (Reading, Massachusetts: Addison-Wesley Publishing Co. Inc., © 1982):155. Reprinted with permission of the publisher.

INTERNAL STRATEGIC POSITION	EXTERNAL STRATEGIC POSITION
FINANCIAL STRENGTH (FS)	**ENVIRONMENTAL STABILITY (ES)**
Return on investment	Technological changes
Leverage	Rate of inflation
Liquidity	Demand variability
Working capital	Price range of competing products
Cash flow	Barriers to entry into market
Ease of exit from market	Competitive pressure
Risk involved in business	Price elasticity of demand
COMPETITIVE ADVANTAGE (CA)	**INDUSTRY STRENGTH (IS)**
Market share	Growth potential
Product quality	Profit potential
Product life cycle	Financial stability
Customer loyalty	Technological know-how
Competition's capacity utilization	Resource utilization
Technological know-how	Capital intensity
Control over suppliers and distributors	Ease of entry into market
	Productivity, capacity utilization

TABLE 6–3
Example Factors That Make Up the SPACE Matrix Axes

Source: H. Rowe, R. Mason, and K. Dickel, *Strategic Management and Business Policy: A Methodological Approach* (Reading, Massachusetts: Addison-Wesley Publishing Co. Inc., © 1982): 155–156. Reprinted with permission of the publisher.

The steps required to develop a SPACE Matrix are as follows:

1. Select a set of variables to define financial strength (FS), competitive advantage (CA), environmental stability (ES), and industry strength (IS).

2. Assign a numerical value ranging from +1 (worst) to +6 (best) to each of the variables that make up the FS and IS dimensions. Assign a numerical value ranging from −1 (best) to −6 (worst) to each of the variables that make up the ES and CA dimensions.

3. Compute an average score for FS, CA, IS, and ES by summing the values given to the variables of each dimension and dividing by the number of variables included in the respective dimension.

4. Plot the average scores for FS, IS, ES, and CA on the appropriate axis in the SPACE Matrix.

5. Add the two scores on the *x*-axis and plot the resultant point on *X*. Add the two scores on the *y*-axis and plot the resultant point on *Y*. Plot the intersection of the new *xy* point.

6. Draw a *directional vector* from the origin of the SPACE Matrix through the new intersection point. This vector reveals the type of strategies recommended for the organization: aggressive, competitive, defensive, or conservative.

Some examples of strategy profiles that can emerge from a SPACE analysis are shown in Figure 6–6. The directional vector associated with each profile suggests the type of strategies to pursue: aggressive, conservative, defensive, or competitive. When a firm's directional vector is located in the *aggressive quadrant* (upper right quadrant) of the SPACE Matrix, an organization is in an excellent position to use its internal strengths to (1) take advantage of external opportunities, (2) overcome internal weaknesses, and (3) avoid external threats. Therefore, market penetration, market development, product development, backward integration, forward integration, horizontal integration, conglomerate diversification, concentric diversification, horizontal diversification, or a combination strategy all can be feasible, depending on the specific circumstances that face the firm.

FIGURE 6–6
Example Strategy Profiles

Aggressive Profiles

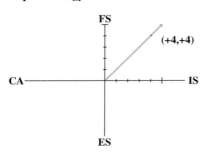

A financially strong firm that has achieved major competitive advantages in a growing and stable industry

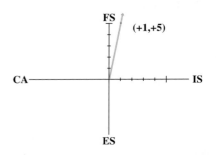

A firm whose financial strength is a dominating factor in the industry

Conservative Profiles

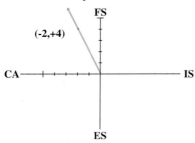

A firm that has achieved financial strength in a stable industry that is not growing; the firm has no major competitive advantages

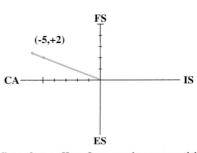

A firm that suffers from major competitive disadvantages in an industry that is technologically stable but declining in sales

Competitive Profiles

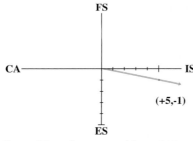

A firm with major competitive advantages in a high-growth industry

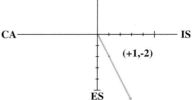

An organization that is competing fairly well in an unstable industry

Defensive Profiles

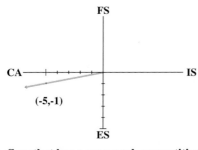

A firm that has a very weak competitive position in a negative growth, stable industry

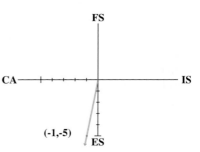

A financially troubled firm in a very unstable industry

Source: H. Rowe, R. Mason, and K. Dickel, *Strategic Management and Business Policy: A Methodological Approach* (Reading, Massachusetts: Addison-Wesley Publishing Co. Inc. © 1982): 155. Reprinted with permission of the publisher.

The directional vector may appear in the *conservative quadrant* (upper left quadrant) of the SPACE Matrix, which implies staying close to the firm's basic competencies and not taking excessive risks. Conservative strategies most often include market penetration, market development, product development, and concentric diversification. The directional vector may be located in the lower left or *defensive quadrant* of the SPACE Matrix, which suggests that the firm should focus on rectifying internal weaknesses and avoiding external threats. Defensive strategies include retrenchment, divestiture, liquidation, and concentric diversification. Finally, the directional vector may be located in the lower right or *competitive quadrant* of the SPACE Matrix, indicating competitive strategies. Competitive strategies include backward, forward, and horizonal integration; market penetration; market development; product development; and joint venture.

SPACE Matrix analysis for a bank is provided in Table 6–4. Note that competitive strategies are recommended.

THE BOSTON CONSULTING GROUP (BCG) MATRIX Autonomous divisions (or profit centers) of an organization make up what is called a *business portfolio*. When a firm's divisions compete in different industries, a separate strategy often must be

TABLE 6–4
A SPACE Matrix for a Bank

FINANCIAL STRENGTH	RATINGS
The bank's primary capital ratio is 7.23 percent, which is 1.23 percentage points over the generally required ratio of 6 percent.	1.0
The bank's return on assets is negative 0.77, compared to a bank industry average ratio of positive 0.70.	1.0
The bank's net income was $183 million, down 9 percent from a year earlier.	3.0
The bank's revenues increased 7 percent to $3.46 billion.	4.0
	9.0

INDUSTRY STRENGTH	
Deregulation provides geographic and product freedom.	4.0
Deregulation increases competition in the banking industry.	2.0
Pennsylvania's interstate banking law allows the bank to acquire other banks in New Jersey, Ohio, Kentucky, the District of Columbia, and West Virginia.	4.0
	10.0

ENVIRONMENTAL STABILITY	
Less-developed countries are experiencing high inflation and political instability.	−4.0
Headquartered in Pittsburgh, the bank historically has been heavily dependent on the steel, oil, and gas industries. These industries are depressed.	−5.0
Banking deregulation has created instability throughout the industry.	−4.0
	−13.0

COMPETITIVE ADVANTAGE	
The bank provides data processing services for more than 450 institutions in 38 states.	−2.0
Superregional banks, international banks, and nonbanks are becoming increasingly competitive.	−5.0
The bank has a large customer base.	−2.0
	−9.0

CONCLUSION

ES Average is $-13.0 \div 3 = -4.33$ IS Average is $+10.0 \div 3 = 3.33$
CA Average is $-9.0 \div 3 = -3.00$ FS Average is $+9.0 \div 4 = 2.25$
Directional Vector Coordinates: *x*-axis: $-3.00 + (+3.33) = +0.33$
                                          y-axis: $-4.33 + (+2.25) = -2.08$
The bank should pursue Competitive Strategies.

developed for each business. The *Boston Consulting Group (BCG) Matrix* and the *Internal-External (IE) Matrix* are designed specifically to enhance a multidivisional firm's efforts to formulate strategies.

The BCG Matrix graphically portrays differences among divisions in terms of relative market share position and industry growth rate. The BCG Matrix allows a multidivisional organization to manage its portfolio of businesses by examining the relative market share position and the industry growth rate of each division relative to all other divisions in the organization. *Relative market share position* is defined as the ratio of a division's own market share in a particular industry to the market share held by the largest rival firm in that industry. For example, in Table 6–5, the relative market share of Miller Lite in 1996 would be 8.5/19.5 = .44.

Relative market share position is given on the *x*-axis of the BCG Matrix. The midpoint on the *x*-axis usually is set at .50, corresponding to a division that has half the market share of the leading firm in the industry. The *y*-axis represents the industry growth rate in sales, measured in percentage terms. The growth rate percentages on the *y*-axis could range from −20 to +20 percent, with 0.0 being the midpoint. These numerical ranges on the *x*- and *y*-axes often are used, but other numerical values could be established as deemed appropriate for particular organizations.

An example of a BCG Matrix appears in Figure 6–7. Each circle represents a separate division. The size of the circle corresponds to the proportion of corporate revenue generated by that business unit, and the pie slice indicates the proportion of corporate profits generated by that division. Divisions located in Quadrant I of the BCG Matrix are called Question Marks, those located in Quadrant II are called Stars, those located in Quadrant III are called Cash Cows, and those divisions located in Quadrant IV are called Dogs.

TABLE 6–5
Top 10 Beer Brands—1996
(Ranked by unit sales)

		SALES (MIL. BARRELS)			MARKET SHARE (%)		
BRAND	**BREWER**	**1990**	**1995**	**1996**	**1990**	**1995**	**1996**
1. Budweiser	Anheuser-Busch Inc.	47.9	37.2	36.5	24.8	20.0	19.5
2. Bud Light	Anheuser-Busch Inc.	11.8	17.9	20.2	6.1	9.6	10.8
3. Miller Lite	Miller Brewing Co.	19.9	15.8	15.9	10.3	8.5	8.5
4. Coors Light	Adolph Coors	11.6	12.9	13.3	6.0	7.0	7.1
5. Busch	Anheuser-Busch Inc.	9.4	8.1	7.9	4.9	4.4	4.2
6. Natural Light	Anheuser-Busch Inc.	3.0	7.1	6.8	1.6	3.8	3.6
7. Miller Genuine Draft	Miller Brewing Co.	5.8	5.8	5.6	3.0	3.1	3.0
8. Miller High Life	Miller Brewing Co.	6.0	4.4	4.4	3.1	2.4	2.4
9. Busch Light Draft	Anheuser-Busch Inc.	1.9	4.2	4.4	1.0	2.3	2.4
10. Milwaukee's Best	Miller Brewing Co.	6.6	4.7	4.3	3.4	2.5	2.3
Total Top 10		123.9	118.1	119.3	64.2	63.6	63.8
All others		69.2	67.5	67.8	35.8	36.4	36.2
Total		193.1	185.6	187.1	100.0	100.0	100.0

Source: IMPACT DATABANK.

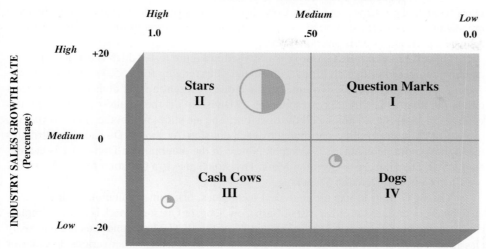

RELATIVE MARKET SHARE POSITION

FIGURE 6–7
The BCG Matrix

Source: Adapted from Boston Consulting Group, *Perspectives on Experience* (Boston, MA.: The Boston Consulting Group, 1974).

◆ Question Marks—Divisions in Quadrant I have a low relative market share position, yet compete in a high-growth industry. Generally these firms' cash needs
are high and their cash generation is low. These businesses are called *Question
Marks* because the organization must decide whether to strengthen them by pursuing an intensive strategy (market penetration, market development, or product
development) or to sell them.

◆ Stars—Quadrant II businesses (often called *Stars*) represent the organization's
best long-run opportunities for growth and profitability. Divisions with a high relative market share and a high industry growth rate should receive substantial investment to maintain or strengthen their dominant positions. Forward, backward, and
horizontal integration; market penetration; market development; product development; and joint ventures are appropriate strategies for these divisions to consider.

◆ Cash Cows—Divisions positioned in Quadrant III have a high relative market
share position but compete in a low-growth industry. Called *Cash Cows* because
they generate cash in excess of their needs, they often are milked. Many of
today's Cash Cows were yesterday's Stars. Cash Cow divisions should be managed to maintain their strong position for as long as possible. Product development or concentric diversification may be attractive strategies for strong Cash
Cows. However, as a Cash Cow division becomes weak, retrenchment or divestiture can become more appropriate.

◆ Dogs—Quadrant IV divisions of the organization have a low relative market share
position and compete in a slow- or no-market-growth industry; they are *Dogs* in
the firm's portfolio. Because of their weak internal and external position, these
businesses often are liquidated, divested, or trimmed down through retrenchment.
When a division first becomes a Dog, retrenchment can be the best strategy to pursue because many Dogs have bounced back, after strenuous asset and cost reduction, to become viable, profitable divisions.

The major benefit of the BCG Matrix is that it draws attention to the cash flow, investment characteristics, and needs of an organization's various divisions. The divisions of
many firms evolve over time: Dogs become Question Marks, Question Marks become Stars,
Stars become Cash Cows, and Cash Cows become Dogs in an ongoing counterclockwise

motion. Less frequently, Stars become Question Marks, Question Marks become Dogs, Dogs become Cash Cows, and Cash Cows become Stars (in a clockwise motion). In some organizations no cyclical motion is apparent. Over time, organizations should strive to achieve a portfolio of divisions that are Stars.

One example of a BCG Matrix is provided in Figure 6–8, which illustrates an organization composed of five divisions with annual sales ranging from $5,000 to $60,000. Division I has the greatest sales volume, so the circle representing that division is the largest one in the matrix. The circle corresponding to Division 5 is the smallest because its sales volume ($5,000) is least among all the divisions. The pie slices within the circles reveal the percent of corporate profits contributed by each division. As shown, Division 1 contributes the highest profit percentage, 39 percent. Notice in the diagram that Division 1 is considered a Star, Division 2 is a Question Mark, Division 3 also is a Question Mark, Division 4 is a Cash Cow, and Division 5 is a Dog.

The BCG Matrix, like all analytical techniques, has some limitations. For example, viewing every business as either a Star, Cash Cow, Dog, or Question Mark is an oversimplification; many businesses fall right in the middle of the BCG Matrix and thus are not easily classified. Furthermore, the BCG Matrix does not reflect whether or not various divisions or their industries are growing over time; that is, the matrix has no temporal qualities, but rather is a snapshot of an organization at a given point in time. Finally, other variables besides relative market share position and industry growth rate in sales, such as size of the market and competitive advantages, are important in making strategic decisions about various divisions.

THE INTERNAL-EXTERNAL (IE) MATRIX   The *Internal-External (IE) Matrix* positions an organization's various divisions in a nine-cell display illustrated in Figure 6–9. The IE Matrix is similar to the BCG Matrix in that both tools involve plotting organization divisions in a schematic diagram; this is why they are both called portfolio matrices. Also, the

FIGURE 6–8
An Example BCG Matrix

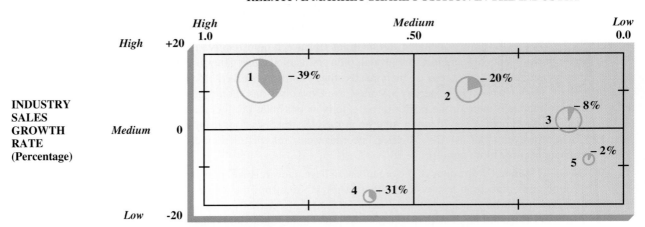

Division	Revenues	Percent Revenues	Profits	Percent Profits	Percent Market Share	Percent Growth Rate
1	$60,000	37	$10,000	39	80	+15
2	40,000	24	5,000	20	40	+10
3	40,000	24	2,000	8	10	1
4	20,000	12	8,000	31	60	-20
5	5,000	3	500	2	5	-10
Total	$165,000	100	$25,500	100		

FIGURE 6–9
The Internal-External (IE) Matrix

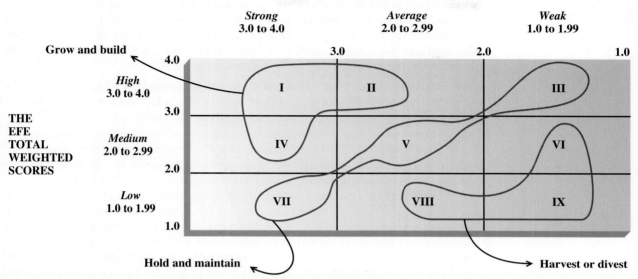

Note: The IE Matrix was developed from the General Electric (GE) Business Screen Matrix. For a description of the GE Matrix, see Michael Allen, "Diagramming GE's Planning for What's WATT" in *Corporate Planning: Techniques and Applications*, eds. R. Allio and M. Pennington (New York: AMACOM, 1979).

size of each circle represents the percentage sales contribution of each division, and pie slices reveal the percentage profit contribution of each division in both the BCG and IE Matrix.

But there are some important differences between the BCG Matrix and IE Matrix. First, the axes are different. Also, the IE Matrix requires more information about the divisions than the BCG Matrix. Further, the strategic implications of each matrix are different. For these reasons, strategists in multidivisional firms often develop both the BCG Matrix and the IE Matrix in formulating alternative strategies. A common practice is to develop a BCG Matrix and an IE Matrix for the present and then develop projected matrices to reflect expectations of the future. This before-and-after analysis forecasts the expected effect of strategic decisions on an organization's portfolio of divisions.

The IE Matrix is based on two key dimensions: the IFE total weighted scores on the *x*-axis and the EFE total weighted scores on the *y*-axis. Recall that each division of an organization should construct an IFE Matrix and an EFE Matrix for its part of the organization. The total weighted scores derived from the divisions allow construction of the corporate-level IE Matrix. On the *x*-axis of the IE Matrix, an IFE total weighted score of 1.0 to 1.99 represents a weak internal position; a score of 2.0 to 2.99 is considered average; and a score of 3.0 to 4.0 is strong. Similarly, on the *y*-axis, an EFE total weighted score of 1.0 to 1.99 is considered low; a score of 2.0 to 2.99 is medium; and a score of 3.0 to 4.0 is high.

The IE Matrix can be divided into three major regions that have different strategy implications. First, the prescription for divisions that fall into cells I, II, or IV can be described as *grow and build*. Intensive (market penetration, market development, and product development) or integrative (backward integration, forward integration, and horizontal integration) strategies can be most appropriate for these divisions. Second, divisions that fall into cells III, V, or VII can be managed best with *hold and maintain* strategies; market penetration and product development are two commonly employed strategies for these types of divisions. Third, a common prescription for divisions that fall into cells VI, VIII, or IX is *harvest or divest*. Successful organizations are able to achieve a portfolio of businesses positioned in or around cell I in the IE Matrix.

An example of a completed IE Matrix is given in Figure 6–10, which depicts an organization composed of four divisions. As indicated by the positioning of the circles, *grow and build* strategies are appropriate for Division 1, Division 2, and Division 3. Division 4 is a candidate for *harvest or divest*. Division 2 contributes the greatest percentage of company sales and thus is represented by the largest circle. Division 1 contributes the greatest proportion of total profits; it has the largest-percentage pie slice.

THE GRAND STRATEGY MATRIX   In addition to the TOWS Matrix, SPACE Matrix, BCG Matrix, and IE Matrix, the *Grand Strategy Matrix* has become a popular tool for formulating alternative strategies. All organizations can be positioned in one of the Grand Strategy Matrix's four strategy quadrants. A firm's divisions likewise could be positioned. As illustrated in Figure 6–11, the Grand Strategy Matrix is based on two evaluative dimensions: competitive position and market growth. Appropriate strategies for an organization to consider are listed in sequential order of attractiveness in each quadrant of the matrix.

Firms located in Quadrant I of the Grand Strategy Matrix are in an excellent strategic position. For these firms, continued concentration on current markets (market penetration and market development) and products (product development) are appropriate strategies. It is unwise for a Quadrant I firm to shift notably from its established competitive advantages. When a Quadrant I organization has excessive resources, then backward, forward, or horizontal integration may be effective strategies. When a Quadrant I firm is too heavily committed to a single product, then concentric diversification may reduce the risks associated with a narrow product line. Quadrant I firms can afford to take advantage of external opportunities in many areas: they can take risks aggressively when necessary.

FIGURE 6–10
An Example IE Matrix

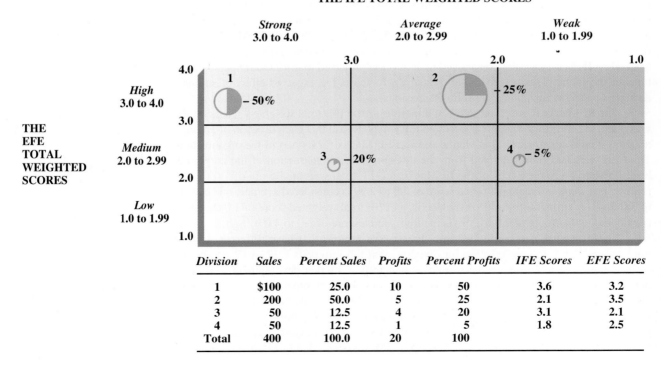

THE IFE TOTAL WEIGHTED SCORES

Division	Sales	Percent Sales	Profits	Percent Profits	IFE Scores	EFE Scores
1	$100	25.0	10	50	3.6	3.2
2	200	50.0	5	25	2.1	3.5
3	50	12.5	4	20	3.1	2.1
4	50	12.5	1	5	1.8	2.5
Total	400	100.0	20	100		

FIGURE 6–11
The Grand Strategy Matrix

RAPID MARKET GROWTH

Quadrant II

1. Market development
2. Market penetration
3. Product development
4. Horizontal integration
5. Divestiture
6. Liquidation

Quadrant I

1. Market development
2. Market penetration
3. Product development
4. Forward integration
5. Backward integration
6. Horizontal integration
7. Concentric diversification

WEAK
COMPETITIVE
POSITION

STRONG
COMPETITIVE
POSITION

Quadrant III

1. Retrenchment
2. Concentric diversification
3. Horizontal diversification
4. Conglomerate diversification
5. Divestiture
6. Liquidation

Quadrant IV

1. Concentric diversification
2. Horizontal diversification
3. Conglomerate diversification
4. Joint ventures

SLOW MARKET GROWTH

Source: Adapted from Roland Christensen, Norman Berg, and Malcolm Salter, *Policy Formulation and Administration* (Homewood, Ill.: Richard D. Irwin, 1976): 16–18.

Firms positioned in Quadrant II need to evaluate their present approach to the marketplace seriously. Although their industry is growing, they are unable to compete effectively, and they need to determine why the firm's current approach is ineffectual and how the company can best change to improve its competitiveness. Because Quadrant II firms are in a rapid-market-growth industry, an intensive strategy (as opposed to integrative or diversification) is usually the first option that should be considered. However, if the firm is lacking a distinctive competence or competitive advantage, then horizontal integration is often a desirable alternative. As a last result, divestiture or liquidation should be considered. Divestiture can provide funds needed to acquire other businesses or buy back shares of stock.

Quadrant III organizations compete in slow-growth industries and have weak competitive positions. These firms must make some drastic changes quickly to avoid further demise and possible liquidation. Extensive cost and asset reduction (retrenchment) should be pursued first. An alternative strategy is to shift resources away from the current business into different areas. If all else fails, the final options for Quadrant III businesses are divestiture or liquidation.

Finally, Quadrant IV businesses have a strong competitive position but are in a slow-growth industry. These firms have the strength to launch diversified programs into more promising growth areas. Quadrant IV firms have characteristically high cash flow levels and limited internal growth needs and often can pursue concentric, horizontal, or conglomerate diversification successfully. Quadrant IV firms also may pursue joint ventures.

THE DECISION STAGE

Analysis and intuition provide a basis for making strategy-formulation decisions. The matching techniques just discussed reveal feasible alternative strategies. Many of these strategies will likely have been proposed by managers and employees participating in the strategy analysis and choice activity. Any additional strategies resulting from the matching analyses could be discussed and added to the list of feasible alternative options. As indicated earlier in this chapter, participants could rate these strategies on a 1 to 4 scale so that a prioritized list of the best strategies could be achieved.

THE QUANTITATIVE STRATEGIC PLANNING MATRIX (QSPM) Other than ranking strategies to achieve the prioritized list, there is only one analytical technique in the literature designed to determine the relative attractiveness of feasible alternative actions. This technique is the *Quantitative Strategic Planning Matrix (QSPM)*, which comprises Stage 3 of the strategy-formulation analytical framework.[6] This technique objectively indicates which alternative strategies are best. The QSPM uses input from Stage 1 analyses and matching results from Stage 2 analyses to decide objectively among alternative strategies. That is, the EFE Matrix, IFE Matrix, and Competitive Profile Matrix that make up Stage 1, coupled with the TOWS Matrix, SPACE Analysis, BCG Matrix, IE Matrix, and Grand Strategy Matrix that make up Stage 2, provide the needed information for setting up the QSPM (Stage 3). The QSPM is a tool that allows strategists to evaluate alternative strategies objectively, based on previously identified external and internal critical success factors. Like other strategy-formulation analytical tools, the QSPM requires good intuitive judgment.

The basic format of the QSPM is illustrated in Table 6–6. Note that the left column of a QSPM consists of key external and internal factors (from Stage 1), and the top row consists of feasible alternative strategies (from Stage 2). Specifically, the left column of a QSPM consists of information obtained directly from the EFE Matrix and IFE Matrix. In a column adjacent to the critical success factors, the respective weights received by each factor in the EFE Matrix and the IFE Matrix are recorded.

TABLE 6–6
The Quantitative Strategic Planning Matrix—QSPM

		STRATEGIC ALTERNATIVES		
KEY FACTORS	**WEIGHT**	**STRATEGY 1**	**STRATEGY 2**	**STRATEGY 3**
KEY EXTERNAL FACTORS				
Economy				
Political/Legal/Governmental				
Social/Cultural/Demographic/Environmental				
Technological				
Competitive				
KEY INTERNAL FACTORS				
Management				
Marketing				
Finance/Accounting				
Production/Operations				
Research and Development				
Computer Information Systems				

The top row of a QSPM consists of alternative strategies derived from the TOWS Matrix, SPACE Matrix, BCG Matrix, IE Matrix, and Grand Strategy Matrix. These matching tools usually generate similar feasible alternatives. However, not every strategy suggested by the matching techniques has to be evaluated in a QSPM. Strategists should use good intuitive judgment in selecting strategies to include in a QSPM.

Conceptually, the QSPM determines the relative attractiveness of various strategies based on the extent to which key external and internal critical success factors are capitalized upon or improved. The relative attractiveness of each strategy within a set of alternatives is computed by determining the cumulative impact of each external and internal critical success factor. Any number of sets of alternative strategies can be included in the QSPM, and any number of strategies can make up a given set, but only strategies within a given set are evaluated relative to each other. For example, one set of strategies may include concentric, horizontal, and conglomerate diversification, whereas another set may include issuing stock and selling a division to raise needed capital. These two sets of strategies are totally different, and the QSPM evaluates strategies only within sets. Note in Table 6–6 that three strategies are included and they make up just one set.

A QSPM for a food company is provided in Table 6–7. This example illustrates all the components of the QSPM: Key Factors, Strategic Alternatives, Weights, Attractiveness Scores, Total Attractiveness Scores, and the Sum Total Attractiveness Score. The three new terms just introduced—(1) Attractiveness Scores, (2) Total Attractiveness Scores, and (3) the Sum Total Attractiveness Score—are defined and explained below as the six steps required to develop a QSPM are discussed.

Step 1 **List the firm's key external opportunities/threats and internal strengths/weaknesses in the left column of the QSPM.** This information should be taken directly from the EFE Matrix and IFE Matrix. A minimum of 10 external critical success factors and 10 internal critical success factors should be included in the QSPM.

Step 2 **Assign weights to each external and internal critical success factor.** These weights are identical to those in the EFE Matrix and the IFE Matrix. The weights are presented in a straight column just to the right of the external and internal critical success factors.

Step 3 **Examine the Stage 2 (matching) matrices and identify alternative strategies that the organization should consider implementing.** Record these strategies in the top row of the QSPM. Group the strategies into mutually exclusive sets if possible.

Step 4 **Determine the Attractiveness Scores (AS),** defined as numerical values that indicate the relative attractiveness of each strategy in a given set of alternatives. *Attractiveness Scores* are determined by examining each external or internal critical success factor, one at a time, and asking the question, "Does this factor affect the choice of strategies being made?" If the answer to this question is *yes*, then the strategies should be compared relative to that key factor. Specifically, Attractiveness Scores should be assigned to each strategy to indicate the relative attractiveness of one strategy over others, considering the particular factor. The range for Attractiveness Scores is 1 = *not attractive*, 2 = *somewhat attractive*, 3 = *reasonably attractive*, and 4 = *highly attractive*. If the answer to the above question is *no*, indicating that the respective critical success factor has no effect upon the specific choice being made, then do not assign Attractiveness Scores to the strategies in that set.

Step 5 **Compute the Total Attractiveness Scores.** *Total Attractiveness Scores* are defined as the product of multiplying the weights (Step 2) by the Attractiveness Scores (Step 4) in each row. The Total Attractiveness Scores indicate the relative attractiveness

TABLE 6–7
A QSPM for Campbell Soup Company

CRITICAL SUCCESS FACTORS	WEIGHT	JOINT VENTURE IN EUROPE AS	TAS	JOINT VENTURE IN ASIA AS	TAS
OPPORTUNITIES					
1. One European currency—Euro	.10	4	.40	2	.20
2. Rising health consciousness in selecting foods	.15	4	.60	3	.45
3. Free market economies arising in Asia	.10	2	.20	4	.40
4. Demand for soups increasing 10 percent annually	.15	3	.45	4	.60
5. NAFTA	.05	–	–	–	–
THREATS					
1. Food revenues increasing only 1 percent annually	.10	3	.30	4	.40
2. ConAgra's Banquet TV Dinners lead market with 27.4 percent share	.05	–	–	–	–
3. Unstable economies in Asia	.10	4	.40	1	.10
4. Tin cans are not biodegradable	.05	–	–	–	–
5. Low value of the dollar	.15	4	.60	2	.30
	1.0				
STRENGTHS					
1. Profits rose 30 percent	.10	4	.40	2	.20
2. New North American division	.10	–	–	–	–
3. New health-conscious soups are successful	.10	4	.40	2	.20
4. Swanson TV dinners' market share has increased to 25.1 percent	.05	4	.20	3	.15
5. One-fifth of all managers' bonuses is based on overall corporate performance	.05	–	–	–	–
6. Capacity utilization increased from 60 percent to 80 percent	.15	3	.45	4	.60
WEAKNESSES					
1. Pepperidge Farm sales have declined 7 percent	.05	–	–	–	–
2. Restructuring cost $302 million	.05	–	–	–	–
3. The company's European operation is losing money	.15	2	.30	4	.60
4. The company is slow in globalizing	.15	4	.60	3	.45
5. Pretax profit margin of 8.4 percent is only one-half industry average	.05	–	–	–	–
SUM TOTAL ATTRACTIVENESS SCORE	1.0		5.30		4.65

AS = Attractiveness Score; TAS = Total Attractiveness Score
Attractiveness Score: 1 = not acceptable; 2 = possibly acceptable; 3 = probably acceptable; 4 = most acceptable.

of each alternative strategy, considering only the impact of the adjacent external or internal critical success factor. The higher the Total Attractiveness Score, the more attractive the strategic alternative (considering only the adjacent critical success factor).

Step 6 **Compute the Sum Total Attractiveness Score.** Add Total Attractiveness Scores in each strategy column of the QSPM. The *Sum Total Attractiveness Scores* reveal which strategy is most attractive in each set of alternatives. Higher scores indicate more attractive strategies, considering all the relevant external and internal factors that could affect the strategic decisions. The magnitude of the difference between the Sum Total Attractiveness Scores in a given set of strategic alternatives indicates the relative desirability of one strategy over another.

In Table 6–7, two alternative strategies—establishing a joint venture in Europe and establishing a joint venture in Asia—are being considered by Campbell Soup.

Note that NAFTA has no impact on the choice being made between the two strategies, so a dash (–) appears several times across that row. Several other factors also have no effect on the choice being made, so dashes are recorded in those rows as well. If a particular factor affects one strategy but not the other, it affects the choice being made, so attractiveness scores should be recorded. The sum total attractiveness score of 5.30 in Table 6.7 indicates that the joint venture in Europe is a more attractive strategy when compared to the joint venture in Asia.

You should have a rationale for each AS score assigned. In Table 6–7, the rationale for the AS scores in the first row is that the unification of Western Europe creates more stable business conditions in Europe than in Asia. The AS score of 4 for the joint venture in Europe and 2 for the joint venture in Asia indicates that the European venture is most acceptable and the Asian venture is possibly acceptable, considering only the first critical success factor. AS scores, therefore, are not mere guesses; they should be rational, defensible, and reasonable. Avoid giving each strategy the same AS score.

POSITIVE FEATURES AND LIMITATIONS OF THE QSPM   A positive feature of the QSPM is that sets of strategies can be examined sequentially or simultaneously. For example, corporate-level strategies could be evaluated first, followed by division-level strategies, and then function-level strategies. There is no limit to the number of strategies that can be evaluated or the number of sets of strategies that can be examined at once using the QSPM.

Another positive feature of the QSPM is that it requires strategists to integrate pertinent external and internal factors into the decision process. Developing a QSPM makes it less likely that key factors will be overlooked or weighted inappropriately. A QSPM draws attention to important relationships that affect strategy decisions. Although developing a QSPM requires a number of subjective decisions, making small decisions along the way enhances the probability that the final strategic decisions will be best for the organization. A QSPM can be adapted for use by small and large for-profit and nonprofit organizations and can be applied to virtually any type of organization. A QSPM especially can enhance strategic choice in multinational firms because many key factors and strategies can be considered at once. It also has been applied successfully by a number of small businesses.[7]

The QSPM is not without some limitations. First, it always requires intuitive judgments and educated assumptions. The ratings and attractiveness scores require judgmental decisions, even though they should be based on objective information. Discussion among strategists, managers, and employees throughout the strategy-formulation process, including development of a QSPM, is constructive and improves strategic decisions. Constructive discussion during strategy analysis and choice may arise because of genuine differences of interpretation of information and varying opinions. Another limitation of the QSPM is that it can be only as good as the prerequisite information and matching analyses upon which it is based.

CULTURAL ASPECTS OF STRATEGY CHOICE

All organizations have a culture. *Culture* includes the set of shared values, beliefs, attitudes, customs, norms, personalities, heroes, and heroines that describe a firm. Culture is the unique way an organization does business. It is the human dimension that creates solidarity and meaning, and inspires commitment and productivity in an organization when strategy changes are made. All human beings have a basic need to make sense of their world, to feel in control, and to make meaning. When events threaten meaning, individuals react defensively. Managers and employees even may sabotage new strategies in an effort to recapture the status quo.

It is beneficial to view strategic management from a cultural perspective because success often rests upon the degree of support that strategies receive from a firm's culture.

If a firm's strategies are supported by cultural products such as values, beliefs, rites, rituals, ceremonies, stories, symbols, language, heroes, and heroines then managers often can implement changes swiftly and easily. However, if a supportive culture does not exist and is not cultivated, then strategy changes may be ineffective or even counterproductive. A firm's culture can become antagonistic to new strategies, and the result of that antagonism may be confusion and disarray.

Strategies that require fewer cultural changes may be more attractive because extensive changes can take considerable time and effort. Whenever two firms merge, culture-strategy linkages become especially important to evaluate and consider. For example, Boeing actively is integrating the culture of McDonnell Douglas with its own, and Westinghouse is trying to integrate its culture with CBS, Inc.

When two or three companies from different countries form a joint venture, such as the recent venture among Honeywell, NEC Corporation of Japan, and Compagnie des Machines Bull of France, merging corporate cultures can be a problem. Jerome Meyer, a Honeywell executive, is president and CEO of the new organization, the first multinational computer company. "We've not had an alliance of these dimensions before, with its geographic diversity and cultural conflict," said Michael Geran, an analyst with E. F. Hutton. "The skill to run it will be a tremendous challenge." He predicted that Meyer would become primarily "a referee."

Culture provides an explanation for the difficulties a firm encounters when it attempts to shift its strategic direction, as the following statement explains:

> Not only has the "right" corporate culture become the essence and foundation of corporate excellence, but success or failure of needed corporate reforms hinges on management's sagacity and ability to change the firm's driving culture in time and in tune with required changes in strategies.[8]

THE POLITICS OF STRATEGY CHOICE

All organizations are political. Unless managed, political maneuvering consumes valuable time, subverts organizational objectives, diverts human energy, and results in the loss of some valuable employees. Sometimes political biases and personal preferences get unduly embedded in strategy choice decisions. Internal politics affect the choice of strategies in all organizations. The hierarchy of command in an organization, combined with the career aspirations of different people and the need to allocate scarce resources, guarantees the formation of coalitions of individuals who strive to take care of themselves first and the organization second, third, or fourth. Coalitions of individuals often form around key strategy issues that face an enterprise. A major responsibility of strategists is to guide the development of coalitions, to nurture an overall team concept, and to gain the support of key individuals and groups of individuals.

In the absence of objective analyses, strategy decisions too often are based on the politics of the moment. With development of improved strategy-formation tools, political factors become less important in making strategic decisions. In the absence of objectivity, political factors sometimes dictate strategies, and this is unfortunate. Managing political relationships is an integral part of building enthusiasm and esprit de corps in an organization. Don Beeman and Tom Sharkey offer the following guidelines for minimizing the negative aspects of organizational politics:

1. Make clear the bases and processes for performance evaluation.
2. Differentiate rewards among high and low performers.

3. Make sure rewards are as immediately and directly related to performance as possible.

4. Minimize resource competition among managers.

5. Replace resource competition among managers.

6. Where highly cohesive political empires exist, break them apart by removing or splitting the most dysfunctional subgroups.

7. Be keenly sensitive to managers whose mode of operation is personalization of political patronage. Approach these persons with a directive to "stop political maneuvering." If it continues, remove them from the position and preferably the company.[9]

A classic study of strategic management in nine large corporations examined the political tactics of successful and unsuccessful strategists.[10] Successful strategists were found to let weakly supported ideas and proposals die through inaction and to establish additional hurdles or tests for strongly supported ideas considered unacceptable but not openly opposed. Successful strategists kept a low political profile on unacceptable proposals and strived to let most negative decisions come from subordinates or a group consensus, thereby reserving their personal vetoes for big issues and crucial moments. Successful strategists did a lot of chatting and informal questioning to stay abreast of how things were progressing and to know when to intervene. They led strategy but did not dictate it. They gave few orders, announced few decisions, depended heavily on informal questioning, and sought to probe and clarify until a consensus emerged.

Successful strategists generously and visibly rewarded key thrusts that succeeded. They assigned responsibility for major new thrusts to *champions*, the individuals most strongly identified with the idea or product and whose futures were linked to its success. They stayed alert to the symbolic impact of their own actions and statements so as not to send false signals that could stimulate movements in unwanted directions.

Successful strategists ensured that all major power bases within an organization were represented in, or had access to, top management. They interjected new faces and new views into considerations of major changes. (This is important because new employees and managers generally have more enthusiasm and drive than employees who have been with the firm a long time. New employees do not see the world the same old way nor act as screens against changes.) Successful strategists minimized their own political exposure on highly controversial issues and in circumstances where major opposition from key power centers was likely. In combination, these findings provide a basis for managing political relationships in an organization.

Because strategies must be effective in the marketplace and capable of gaining internal commitment, the following tactics used by politicians for centuries can aid strategists:

◆ *Equifinality*: It is often possible to achieve similar results using different means or paths. Strategists should recognize that achieving a successful outcome is more important than imposing the method of achieving it. It may be possible to generate new alternatives that give equal results but with far greater potential for gaining commitment.

◆ *Satisfying*: Achieving satisfactory results with an acceptable strategy is far better than failing to achieve optimal results with an unpopular strategy.

◆ *Generalization*: Shifting focus from specific issues to more general ones may increase strategists' options for gaining organizational commitment.

◆ *Focus on Higher-Order Issues*: By raising an issue to a higher level, many short-term interests can be postponed in favor of long-term interests. For instance, by focusing on issues of survival, the auto and steel industries were able to persuade unions to make concessions on wage increases.

◆ *Provide Political Access on Important Issues*: Strategy and policy decisions with significant negative consequences for middle managers will motivate intervention behavior from them. If middle managers do not have an opportunity to take a position on such decisions in appropriate political forums, they are capable of successfully resisting the decisions after they are made. Providing such political access provides strategists with information that otherwise might not be available and that could be useful in managing intervention behavior.[11]

THE ROLE OF A BOARD OF DIRECTORS

The widespread lack of involvement by *boards of directors* in the strategic-management process is changing in America. Historically, boards of directors mostly have been insiders who would not second-guess top executives on strategic issues. It generally has been understood that strategists are responsible and accountable for implementing strategy, so they, not board members, should formulate strategy. Consequently, chief executive officers usually avoided discussions of overall strategy with directors because the results of those discussions often restricted their freedom of action. The judgments of board members seldom were used on acquisitions, divestitures, large capital investments, and other strategic matters. Often, the board would meet only annually to fulfill its minimum legal requirements; in many organizations, boards served merely a traditional legitimizing role.

Today, boards of directors are composed mostly of outsiders who are becoming more involved in organizations' strategic management. The trend in America is toward smaller boards, now averaging 12 members rather than 18 as they did a few years ago. Smaller boards can discuss issues more easily; individuals in small groups take responsibility more personally. The percentage of minority individuals serving on the boards of directors of *Fortune* 1,000 companies doubled between 1992 and 1997. Although 85 percent of the 7,041 directors of Fortune 1,000 boards are white males, the percentage continues to fall. African American membership on these boards now is nearly 3 percent while women make up nearly 9 percent. Most shareholders realize that women and minorities strengthen a board and a company by bringing in new perspectives and preventing "CEO clones."

Just as directors are beginning to place more emphasis on staying informed about an organization's health and operations, they also are taking a more active role in ensuring that publicly issued documents are accurate representations of a firm's status. It is becoming widely recognized that a board of directors has legal responsibilities to stockholders and society for all company activities, for corporate performance, and for ensuring that a firm has an effective strategy. Failure to accept responsibility for auditing or evaluating a firm's strategy is considered a serious breach of a director's duties. Stockholders, government agencies, and customers are filing legal suits against directors for fraud, omissions, inaccurate disclosures, lack of due diligence, and culpable ignorance about a firm's operations with increasing frequency. Liability insurance for directors has become exceptionally expensive and has caused numerous directors to resign.

Boards of directors in corporate America today seriously are evaluating strategic plans, evaluating the top management team, and assuming responsibility for management succession. TIAA-CREF, the nation's largest pension fund, now regularly evaluates governance practices at more than 1,500 companies in which it owns a stake. *Business Week's* first annual board of director's evaluation[12] posited that good boards of directors actively perform the following responsibilities:

- ◆ Evaluate the CEO annually.
- ◆ Link the CEO's pay to specific goals.
- ◆ Evaluate long-range strategy.
- ◆ Evaluate board members' performance through a governance committee.
- ◆ Compensate board members only in company stock.
- ◆ Require each director to own a large amount of company stock.
- ◆ Ensure no more than two board members are insiders (work for the company).
- ◆ Require directors to retire at age 70.
- ◆ Place the entire board up for election every year.
- ◆ Limit the number of other boards a member can serve on.
- ◆ Ban directors who draw consulting fees or other monies from the company.
- ◆ Ban interlocking directorships.

Business Week's top 10 boards for 1996 were those of the following:

1. Campbell Soup
2. General Electric
3. IBM
4. Compaq Computer
5. Colgate Palmolive
6. Chrysler
7. Johnson & Johnson
8. Merck
9. Hercules
10. Exxon

Business Week's 10 lowest-rated boards of directors for 1996 were those of the following:

1. Archer Daniels Midland
2. Champion International
3. H. J. Heinz
4. Rollins Environmental
5. Nationsbank
6. AT&T
7. Kmart
8. Unisys
9. Ethyl
10. Fleming Companies

Two rulings particulary affected the role of boards of directors in the strategy-formulation process. First, the Supreme Court of Delaware ruled that the directors of the Trans Union Corporation violated the interests of shareholders when they hastily accepted a takeover bid from the Marmon Group; that ruling eroded the so-called business judgment rule, which protects directors from liability as long as their decisions represent a good-faith effort to serve the best interests of the corporation. One clear signal from the Trans Union case is that haste can be costly for board members.

In another landmark ruling that illustrates how boards of directors increasingly are being held responsible for the overall performance of organizations, the Federal Deposit Insurance Corporation forced Continental Illinois to accept the resignations of 10 of the troubled bank's outside directors. The impact of increasing legal pressures on board members is that directors are demanding greater and more regular access to financial performance information.

Some boardroom reforms that are lessening the likelihood of lawsuits today include increasing the percentage of outsiders on the board, separating the positions of CEO and chairperson, requiring directors to hold substantial amounts of stock in the firm, and decreasing the board size. Outsiders now outnumber insiders at 90 percent of all American firms' boards, and the average number of outsiders is three times that of insiders.

A direct response of increased pressure on directors to stay informed and execute their responsibilities is that audit committees are becoming commonplace. A board of directors should conduct an annual strategy audit in much the same fashion that it reviews the annual financial audit. In performing such an audit, a board could work jointly with operating management and/or seek outside counsel.

The trend among corporations toward decreased diversification, increased takeover activity, increased legal pressures, multidivisional structures, and multinational operations augments the problem of keeping directors informed. Boards should play a role beyond that of performing a strategic audit. They should provide greater input and advice in the strategy-formulation process to ensure that strategists are providing for the long-term needs of the firm. This is being done through the formation of three particular board committees: nominating committees to propose candidates for the board and senior officers of the firm; compensation committees to evaluate the performance of top executives and determine the terms and conditions of their employment; and public policy committees to give board-level attention to company policies and performance on subjects of concern such as business ethics, consumer affairs, and political activities.

Nearly 41 percent of all firms that have a board of directors have developed a mission statement for the board.[13] A board of directors' mission statement outlines the purpose and intent of the board and defines to whom, or for what, the board is held accountable. A board mission statement also indicates company expectations about the quality of preparation for and the process for conducting board meetings. Overall, the mission of boards of directors must be expanded. Companies should assign managers to join directors on board committees, rather than limit the board's contact with only a few top managers. Directors must assume a more activist stance in management development, rather than just react to management initiatives.

Powerful boards of directors are associated with high organizational performance. Powerful boards participate in corporate decisions more fully, share their experiences with the CEO regarding certain strategies, and are actively involved in industry analysis. Firms can develop more powerful boards by regularly reviewing board committee activities, evaluating board meetings, and involving the board more extensively in strategic issues. More companies are paying board members partly or totally in stock, which gives outside directors more reason to identify with the shareholders they represent rather than with the CEO they oversee.

CONCLUSION

The essence of strategy formulation is an assessment of whether an organization is doing the right things and how it can be more effective in what it does. Every organization should be wary of becoming a prisoner of its own strategy, because even the best strategies become obsolete sooner or later. Regular reappraisal of strategy helps management avoid complacency. Objectives and strategies should be consciously developed and coordinated and should not merely evolve out of day-to-day operating decisions.

An organization with no sense of direction and no coherent strategy precipitates its own demise. When an organization does not know where it wants to go, it usually ends up some place it does not want to be! Every organization needs to consciously establish and communicate clear objectives and strategies.

Modern strategy-formulation tools and concepts are described in this chapter and integrated into a practical three-stage framework. Tools such as the TOWS Matrix, SPACE Matrix, BCG Matrix, IE Matrix, and QSPM can enhance significantly the quality of strategic decisions, but they should never be used to dictate the choice of strategies. Behavioral, cultural, and political aspects of strategy generation and selection are always important to consider and manage. Due to increased legal pressure from outside groups, boards of directors are assuming a more active role in strategy analysis and choice. This is a positive trend for organizations.

We invite you to visit the DAVID page on the Prentice Hall Web site at
www.prenhall.com/
for this chapter's World Wide Web exercise.

TAKE IT TO THE NET

KEY TERMS AND CONCEPTS

Aggressive Quadrant	(p. 185)	Dogs	(p. 189)	SO Strategies	(p. 180)
Attractiveness Scores (AS)	(p. 195)	Environmental Stability (ES)	(p. 184)	ST Strategies	(p. 181)
Boards of Directors	(p. 200)	Financial Strength (FS)	(p. 184)	Stars	(p. 189)
Boston Consulting Group (BCG) Matrix	(p. 188)	Grand Strategy Matrix	(p. 192)	Strategic Position and Action Evaluation (SPACE) Matrix	(p. 184)
		Halo Error	(p. 179)		
Business Portfolio	(p. 187)	Industry Strength (IS)	(p. 184)	Strategy-Formulation Framework	(p. 179)
Cash Cows	(p. 189)	Input Stage	(p. 178)		
Champions	(p. 199)	Internal-External (IE) Matrix	(p. 190)	Sum Total Attractiveness Scores	(p. 196)
Competitive Advantage (CA)	(p. 184)	Long-Term Objectives	(p. 176)	Threats-Opportunities-Weaknesses-Strengths (TOWS) Matrix	(p. 180)
Competitive Quadrant	(p. 187)	Matching	(p. 179)		
Conservative Quadrant	(p. 187)	Matching Stage	(p. 178)	Total Attractiveness Scores (TAS)	(p. 195)
Culture	(p. 197)	Quantitative Strategic Planning Matrix (QSPM)	(p. 194)		
Decision Stage	(p. 178)			WO Strategies	(p. 181)
Defensive Quadrant	(p. 187)	Question Marks	(p. 189)	WT Strategies	(p. 181)
Directional Vector	(p. 185)	Relative Market Share Position	(p. 188)		

ISSUES FOR REVIEW AND DISCUSSION

1. How would application of the strategy-formulation framework differ from a small to a large organization?

2. What types of strategies would you recommend for an organization that achieves total weighted scores of 3.6 on the IFE and 1.2 on the EFE Matrix?

3. Given the following information, develop a SPACE Matrix for the XYZ Corporation: FS = +2; ES = −6; CA = −2; IS = +4.

4. Given the information in the table below, develop a BCG Matrix and an IE Matrix:

Divisions	1	2	3
Profits	$10	$15	$25
Sales	$100	$50	$100
Relative Market Share	0.2	0.5	0.8
Industry Growth Rate	+.20	+.10	−.10
IFE Total Weighted Scores	1.6	3.1	2.2
EFE Total Weighted Scores	2.5	1.8	3.3

5. Explain the steps involved in developing a QSPM.

6. How would you develop a set of objectives for your school of business?

7. What do you think is the appropriate role of a board of directors in strategic management? Why?

8. Discuss the limitations of various strategy-formulation analytical techniques.

9. Explain why cultural factors should be an important consideration in analyzing and choosing among alternative strategies.

10. How are the TOWS Matrix, SPACE Matrix, BCG Matrix, IE Matrix, and Grand Strategy Matrix similar? How are they different?

11. How would profit and nonprofit organizations differ in their applications of the strategy-formulation framework?

12. Select an article from the suggested readings at the end of this chapter and prepare a report on that article for your class.

NOTES

1. Steven C. Brandt, *Strategic Planning in Emerging Companies* (Reading, Massachusetts: Addison-Wesley, 1981). Reprinted with permission of the publisher.

2. R. T. Lenz, "Managing the Evolution of the Strategic Planning Process," *Business Horizons* 30, no. 1 (January–February 1987): 37.

3. Robert Grant, "The Resource-Based Theory of Competitive Advantage: Implications for Strategy Formulation," *California Management Review* (Spring 1991): 114.

4. Heinz Weihrich, "The TOWS Matrix: A Tool for Situational Analysis," *Long Range Planning* 15, no. 2 (April 1982): 61.

5. H. Rowe, R. Mason, and K. Dickel, *Strategic Management and Business Policy: A Methodological Approach* (Reading, Massachusetts: Addison-Wesley Publishing Co. Inc., 1982): 155–156. Reprinted with permission of the publisher.

6. Fred David, "The Strategic Planning Matrix—A Quantitative Approach," *Long Range Planning* 19, no. 5 (October 1986): 102. Andre Gib and Robert Margulies, "Making Competitive Intelligence Relevant to the User," *Planning Review* 19, no. 3 (May/June 1991): 21.

7. Fred David, "Computer-Assisted Strategic Planning in Small Businesses," *Journal of Systems Management* 36, no. 7 (July 1985): 24–34.

8. Y. Allarie and M. Firsirotu, "How to Implement Radical Strategies in Large Organizations," *Sloan Management Review* 26, no. 3 (Spring 1985): 19. Another excellent article is P. Shrivastava, "Integrating Strategy Formulation with Organizational Culture," *Journal of Business Strategy* 5, no. 3 (Winter 1985): 103–111.

9. Don Beeman and Thomas Sharkey, "The Use and Abuse of Corporate Politics," *Business Horizons* 30, no. 2 (March–April 1987): 30.

10. James Brian Quinn, *Strategies for Change: Logical Incrementalism* (Homewood, Ill.: Richard D. Irwin, 1980): 128–145. These political tactics are listed in A. Thompson and A. Strickland, *Strategic Management: Concepts and Cases* (Plano, Texas: Business Publications, 1984): 261.

11. William Guth and Ian MacMillan, "Strategy Implementation Versus Middle Management Self-Interest," *Strategic Management Journal* 7, no. 4 (July–August 1986): 321.

12. "Best and Worst Corporate Boards of Directors," *Business Week* (November 25, 1996): 82–98.

13. Ada Demb, Danielle Chouet, Tom Lossius, and Fred Neubauer, "Defining the Role of the Board," *Long Range Planning* 22, no. 1 (February 1989): 61–68.

CURRENT READINGS

Barker, V. L. III and I. M. Duhaime. "Strategic Change in the Turnaround Process: Theory and Empirical Evidence." *Strategic Management Journal* 18, no. 1 (January 1997): 13–38.

Chakravarthy, Bala. "A New Strategy Framework for Coping with Turbulence." *Sloan Management Review* 38, no. 2 (Winter 1997): 69–82.

Daily, Catherine M. and Charles Schwenk. "Chief Executive Officers, Top Management Teams, and Boards of Directors: Congruent or Countervailing Forces?" *Journal of Management* 22, no. 2 (1996): 185–208.

Dodllinger, M. J., P. A. Golden, and T. Saxton. "The Effect of Reputation on the Decision to Joint Venture." *Strategic Management Journal* 18, no. 2 (February 1997): 127–140.

Ferris, Gerald R., Dwight D. Frink, Dharm P. S. Bhawuk, Jing Zhou, and David C. Gilmore. "Reactions of Diverse Groups to Politics in the Workplace." *Journal of Management* 22, no. 1 (1996): 23–44.

Fischer, Frank, reviewed by. *Resistance and Power in Organizations*, edited by John Jermier, David Knights, and Walter Nord. *Academy of Management Review* 22, no. 2 (April 1997): 564–567.

Gould, Des. "Developing Directors Through Personal Coaching." *Long Range Planning* 30, no. 1 (February 1997): 29–37.

Higgins, James M. "Innovate or Evaporate: Creative Techniques for Strategists." *Long Range Planning* 29, no. 3 (June 1996): 370–380.

Hill, Terry and Roy Westbrook. "SWOT Analysis: It's Time for a Product Recall." *Long Range Planning* 30, no. 1 (February 1997): 46–52.

Iansiti, Marco and Jonathan West. "Technology Integration: Turning Great Research into Great Products." *Harvard Business Review* (May–June 1997): 69–82.

Johnson, Jonathan L., Catherine M. Daily, and Alan E. Ellstrand. "Boards of Directors: A Review and Research Agenda." *Journal of Management* 22, no. 3 (1996): 409–438.

O'Neal, Don and Howard Thomas. "Developing the Strategic Board." *Long Range Planning* 29, no. 3 (June 1996): 314–327.

Pennington, Ashly and Timothy Morris. "Power and Control in Professional Partnerships." *Long Range Planning* 29, no. 6 (December 1996): 842–849.

Seward, J. K. and J. P. Walsh. "The Governance and Control of Voluntary Corporate Spin-Offs." *Strategic Management Journal* 17, no. 1 (January 1996): 25–40.

Slevin, Dennis P. and Jeffrey G. Covin. "Strategy Formation Patterns, Performance, and the Significance of Context." *Journal of Management* 23, no. 2 (1997): 189–199.

Sundaramurthy, C. "Corporate Governance Within the Context of Anti-Takeover Provisions." *Strategic Management Journal* 17, no. 5 (May 1996): 377–394.

Sundaramurthy, C., J. M. Mahoney, and J. T. Mahoney. "Board Structure, Anti-Takeover Provisions, and Stockholder Wealth." *Strategic Management Journal* 18, no. 3 (March 1997): 231–246.

Sundaramurthy, Chamu, Paula Rechner, and Weiren Wang. "Governance Antecedents of Board Entrenchment: The Case of Classified Board Provisions." *Journal of Management* 22, no. 5 (1996): 783–793.

Zajac, Edward J. and James D. Westphal. "Who Shall Succeed? How CEO/Board Preferences and Power Affect the Choice of New CEOs." *Academy of Management Journal* 39, no. 1 (February 1996): 64–90.

EXPERIENTIAL EXERCISES

Experiential Exercise 6A

DEVELOPING A TOWS MATRIX FOR HERSHEY FOODS

PURPOSE

The most widely used strategy-formulation technique among American firms is the TOWS Matrix. This exercise requires development of a TOWS Matrix for Hershey. Matching key external and internal factors in a TOWS Matrix requires good intuitive and conceptual skills. You will improve with practice in developing a TOWS Matrix.

INSTRUCTIONS

Recall from Experiential Exercise 1A that you already may have determined Hershey's external opportunities/threats and internal strengths/weaknesses. This information could be used in completing this exercise. Follow the steps outlined below:

Step 1 On a separate sheet of paper, construct a large nine-cell diagram that will represent your TOWS Matrix. Label the cells appropriately.

Step 2 Record Hershey's opportunities/threats and strengths/weaknesses appropriately in your diagram.

Step 3 Match external and internal factors to generate feasible alternative strategies for Hershey. Record SO, WO, ST, and WT Strategies in appropriate cells of the TOWS Matrix. Use the proper notation to indicate the rationale for the strategies. You do not necessarily have to have strategies in all four strategy cells.

Step 4 Compare your TOWS Matrix to another student's TOWS Matrix. Discuss any major differences.

Experiential Exercise 6B

DEVELOPING A SPACE MATRIX FOR HERSHEY FOODS

PURPOSE

Should Hershey pursue aggressive, conservative, competitive, or defensive strategies? Develop a SPACE Matrix for Hershey to answer this question. Elaborate on the strategic implications of your directional vector. Be specific in terms of strategies that could benefit Hershey.

INSTRUCTIONS

Step 1 Join with two other persons in class and develop a joint SPACE Matrix for Hershey.

Step 2 Diagram your SPACE Matrix on the board. Compare your matrix with other teams' matrices.

Step 3 Discuss the implications of your SPACE Matrix.

DEVELOPING A BCG MATRIX FOR HERSHEY FOODS

PURPOSE

Portfolio matrices are widely used by multidivisional organizations to help identify and select strategies to pursue. A BCG analysis identifies particular divisions that should receive fewer resources than others. It may identify some divisions to be divested. This exercise can give you practice developing a BCG Matrix.

INSTRUCTIONS

Step 1 Place the following five column headings at the top of a separate sheet of paper: Divisions, Revenues, Profits, Relative Market Share Position, Industry Growth Rate.

Step 2 Complete a BCG Matrix for Hershey.

Step 3 Compare your BCG Matrix to other students' matrices. Discuss any major differences.

DEVELOPING A QSPM FOR HERSHEY FOODS

PURPOSE

This exercise can give you practice developing a Quantitative Strategic Planning Matrix to determine the relative attractiveness of various strategic alternatives.

INSTRUCTIONS

Step 1 Join with two other students in class to develop a joint QSPM for Hershey.

Step 2 Go to the blackboard and record your strategies and their Sum Total Attractiveness Scores. Compare your team's strategies and sum total attractiveness scores to those of other teams.

Step 3 Discuss any major differences.

FORMULATING INDIVIDUAL STRATEGIES

PURPOSE

Individuals and organizations are alike in many ways. Each has competitors and each should plan for the future. Every individual and organization faces some external opportunities and threats and has some internal strengths and weaknesses. Both individuals and organizations establish objectives and allocate resources. These and other similarities make it possible for individuals to use many strategic-management concepts and tools. This exercise is designed to demonstrate how the TOWS Matrix can be used by individuals to plan their futures. As one nears completion of a college degree and begins interviewing for jobs, planning can be particularly important.

INSTRUCTIONS

On a separate sheet of paper, construct a TOWS Matrix. Include what you consider to be your major external opportunities, your major external threats, your major strengths, and your major weaknesses. An internal weakness may be a low grade point average. An external opportunity may be that your university offers a graduate program that interests you. Match key external and internal factors by recording in the appropriate cell of the matrix alternative strategies or actions that would allow you to capitalize upon your strengths, overcome your weaknesses, take advantage of your external opportunities, and minimize the impact of external threats. Be sure to use the appropriate matching notation in the strategy cells of the matrix. Because every individual (and organization) is unique, there is no one right answer to this exercise.

Experiential Exercise 6F

THE MACH TEST

PURPOSE

The purpose of this exercise is to enhance your understanding and awareness of the impact that behavioral and political factors can have on strategy analysis and choice.

INSTRUCTIONS

Step 1 On a separate sheet of paper, number from 1 to 10. For each of the 10 statements given below, record a *1, 2, 3, 4,* or *5* to indicate your attitude, where

1 = I disagree a lot.
2 = I disagree a little.
3 = My attitude is neutral.
4 = I agree a little.
5 = I agree a lot.

1. The best way to handle people is to tell them what they want to hear.
2. When you ask someone to do something for you, it is best to give the real reason for wanting it, rather than a reason that might carry more weight.
3. Anyone who completely trusts anyone else is asking for trouble.
4. It is hard to get ahead without cutting corners here and there.
5. It is safest to assume that all people have a vicious streak, and it will come out when they are given a chance.
6. One should take action only when it is morally right.
7. Most people are basically good and kind.
8. There is no excuse for lying to someone else.
9. Most people forget more easily the death of their father than the loss of their property.
10. Generally speaking, people won't work hard unless they're forced to do so.

Step 2 Add up the numbers you recorded beside statements 1, 3, 4, 5, 9, and 10. This sum is Subtotal One. For the other four statements, reverse the numbers you recorded, so a *5* becomes a *1, 4* becomes *2, 2* becomes *4, 1* becomes *5,* and *3* remains *3.* Then add those four numbers to get Subtotal Two. Finally, add Subtotal One and Subtotal Two to get your Final Score.

YOUR FINAL SCORE

Your Final Score is your Machiavellian Score. Machiavellian principles are defined in a dictionary as "manipulative, dishonest, deceiving, and favoring political expediency over morality." These tactics are not desirable, are not ethical, and are not recommended in the strategic-management process! You may, however, encounter some highly Machiavellian individuals in your career, so beware. It is important for strategists not to manipulate others in the pursuit of organizational objectives. Individuals today recognize and resent manipulative tactics more than ever before. J.R. Ewing (on a television show in the 1980s, *Dallas*) was a good example of someone who was a high Mach (score over 30). The National Opinion Research Center used this short quiz in a random sample of American adults and found the national average Final Score to be 25.[1] The higher your score, the more Machiavellian (manipulative) you tend to be. The following scale is descriptive of individual scores on this test:

- ◆ Below 16: Never uses manipulation as a tool.
- ◆ 16 to 20: Rarely uses manipulation as a tool.
- ◆ 21 to 25: Sometimes uses manipulation as a tool.
- ◆ 26 to 30: Often uses manipulation as a tool.
- ◆ Over 30: Always uses manipulation as a tool.

TEST DEVELOPMENT

The Mach (Machiavellian) test was developed by Dr. Richard Christie, whose research suggests the following tendencies:

1. Men generally are more Machiavellian than women.
2. There is no significant difference between high Machs and low Machs on measures of intelligence or ability.
3. Although high Machs are detached from others, they are detached in a pathological sense.
4. Machiavellian Scores are not statistically related to authoritarian values.
5. High Machs tend to be in professions that emphasize the control and manipulation of individuals; for example, law, psychiatry, and behavioral science.
6. Machiavellianism is not significantly related to major demographic characteristics such as educational level or marital status.
7. High Machs tend to come from a city or have urban backgrounds.
8. Older adults tend to have lower Mach scores than younger adults.[2]

A classic book on power relationships, *The Prince*, was written by Niccolo Machiavelli. Several excerpts from *The Prince* are given below:

Men must either be cajoled or crushed, for they will revenge themselves for slight wrongs, while for grave ones they cannot. The injury therefore that you do to a man should be such that you need not fear his revenge.

We must bear in mind . . . that there is nothing more difficult and dangerous, or more doubtful of success, than an attempt to introduce a new order of things in any state. The innovator has for enemies all those who derived advantages from the old order of things, while those who expect to be benefitted by the new institution will be but lukewarm defenders.

A wise prince, therefore, will steadily pursue such a course that the citizens of his state will always and under all circumstances feel the need for his authority, and will therefore always prove faithful to him.

A prince should seem to be merciful, faithful, humane, religious, and upright, and should even be so in reality; but he should have his mind so trained that, when occasion requires it, he may know how to change to the opposite.[3]

NOTES

1. Richard Christie and Florence Geis, *Studies in Machiavellianism* (Orlando, Florida: Academic Press, 1970). Material in this exercise adapted with permission of the authors and the Academic Press.
2. Ibid., 82–83.
3. Niccolo Machiavelli, *The Prince* (New York: The Washington Press, 1963).

Experiential Exercise 6G

DEVELOPING A BCG MATRIX FOR MY UNIVERSITY

PURPOSE

A BCG Matrix is useful to develop for many nonprofit organizations, including colleges and universities. Of course, there are no profits for each division or department and in some cases no revenues. However, you can be creative in performing a BCG Matrix. For example, the pie slice in the circles can represent the number of majors receiving jobs upon graduation, or the number of faculty teaching in that area, or some other variable that you believe is important to consider. The size of the circles can represent the number of students majoring in particular departments or areas.

INSTRUCTIONS

Step 1 On a separate sheet of paper, develop a BCG Matrix for your university. Include all academic schools, departments, or colleges.

Step 2 Diagram your BCG Matrix on the blackboard.

Step 3 Discuss differences among the BCG Matrices on the board.

Experiential Exercise 6H

THE ROLE OF BOARDS OF DIRECTORS

PURPOSE

This exercise will give you a better understanding of the role of boards of directors in formulating, implementing, and evaluating strategies.

INSTRUCTIONS

Identify a person in your community who serves on a board of directors. Make an appointment to interview that person and seek answers to the questions given below. Summarize your findings in a five-minute oral report to the class.

On what board are you a member?
How often does the board meet?
How long have you served on the board?
What role does the board play in this company?
How has the role of the board changed in recent years?

What changes would you like to see in the role of the board?
To what extent do you prepare for the board meeting?
To what extent are you involved in strategic management of the firm?

Experiential Exercise 6I

LOCATING COMPANIES IN A GRAND STRATEGY MATRIX

PURPOSE

The Grand Strategy Matrix is a popular tool for formulating alternative strategies. All organizations can be positioned in one of the Grand Strategy Matrix's four strategy quadrants. The divisions of a firm likewise could be positioned. The Grand Strategy Matrix is based on two evaluative dimensions: competitive position and market growth. Appropriate strategies for an organization to consider are listed in sequential order of attractiveness in each quadrant of the matrix. This exercise gives you experience using a Grand Strategy Matrix.

INSTRUCTIONS

Using the year-end 1997 financial information given below, prepare a Grand Strategy Matrix on a separate sheet of paper. Write the respective company names in the appropriate quadrant of the matrix. Based on this analysis, what strategies are recommended for each company?

COMPANY	COMPANY SALES/PROFIT GROWTH (%)	INDUSTRY	INDUSTRY SALES/PROFITS GROWTH (%)
Eaton	+9/+33	Automotive Parts	+11/+27
General Signal	−5/−2	Automotive Parts	+11/+27
Pennzoil	+7/+35	Oil, Gas, & Coal	0/+13
Chevron	−7/+25	Oil, Gas, & Coal	0/+13
Microsoft	+39/+57	Computer Software	+19/+39
Novell	−27/Neg	Computer Software	+19/+39
Boise Cascade	+8/Neg	Forest Products	0/Neg
Bowater	−14/Neg	Forest Products	0/Neg

PART 3

STRATEGY IMPLEMENTATION

CHAPTER 7

Implementing Strategies: Management Issues

CHAPTER OBJECTIVES

After studying this chapter, you should be able to do the following:

1. Explain why strategy implementation is more difficult than strategy formulation.

2. Discuss the importance of annual objectives and policies in achieving organizational commitment for strategies to be implemented.

3. Explain why organizational structure is so important in strategy implementation.

4. Compare and contrast restructuring and reengineering.

5. Describe the relationships between production/operations and strategy implementation.

6. Explain how a firm can effectively link performance and pay to strategies.

7. Discuss employee stock ownership plans (ESOPs) as a strategic-management concept.

8. Describe how to modify an organizational culture to support new strategies.

NOTABLE QUOTES

You want your people to run the business as if it were their own.—WILLIAM FULMER

The ideal organizational structure is a place where ideas filter up as well as down, where the merit of ideas carries more weight than their source, and where participation and shared objectives are valued more than executive orders.—EDSON SPENCER

A management truism says structure follows strategy. However, this truism is often ignored. Too many organizations attempt to carry out a new strategy with an old structure.—DALE MCCONKEY

Poor Ike; when he was a general, he gave an order and it was carried out. Now, he's going to sit in that office and give an order and not a damn thing is going to happen.—HARRY TRUMAN

Changing your pay plan is a big risk, but not changing it could be a bigger one.—NANCY PERRY

In Japan, workers receive an average 25 percent of total pay in the form of a flexible bonus. In America, the average is still only 1 percent.—NANCY PERRY

Of course, objectives are not a railroad timetable. They can be compared to a compass bearing by which a ship navigates. A compass bearing is firm, but in actual navigation, a ship may veer off its course for many miles. Without a compass bearing, a ship would neither find its port nor be able to estimate the time required to get there.—PETER DRUCKER

The best game plan in the world never blocked or tackled anybody.—VINCE LOMBARDI

In most organizations, the top performers are paid too little and the worst performers too much.
—CASS BETTINGER

The strategic-management process does not end when the firm decides what strategy or strategies to pursue. There must be a translation of strategic thought into strategic action. This translation is much easier if managers and employees of the firm understand the business, feel a part of the company, and through involvement in strategy-formulation activities have become committed to helping the organization succeed. Without understanding and commitment, strategy-implementation efforts face major problems.

Implementing strategy affects an organization from top to bottom; it impacts all the functional and divisional areas of a business. It is beyond the purpose and scope of this text to examine all the business administration concepts and tools important in strategy implementation. This chapter focuses on management issues most central to implementing strategies in the year 2000, and Chapter 8 focuses on marketing, finance/accounting, R&D, and computer information systems issues.

THE NATURE OF STRATEGY IMPLEMENTATION

The strategy-implementation stage of strategic management stands out in Figure 7–1. Successful strategy formulation does not guarantee successful strategy implementation. It is always more difficult to do something (strategy implementation) than to say you are going to do it (strategy formulation)! Although inextricably linked, strategy implementation is fundamentally different from strategy formulation. Strategy formulation and implementation can be contrasted in the following ways:

- ◆ Strategy formulation is positioning forces before the action.
- ◆ Strategy implementation is managing forces during the action.
- ◆ Strategy formulation focuses on effectiveness.
- ◆ Strategy implementation focuses on efficiency.
- ◆ Strategy formulation is primarily an intellectual process.
- ◆ Strategy implementation is primarily an operational process.
- ◆ Strategy formulation requires good intuitive and analytical skills.
- ◆ Strategy implementation requires special motivation and leadership skills.
- ◆ Strategy formulation requires coordination among a few individuals.
- ◆ Strategy implementation requires coordination among many persons.

Strategy-formulation concepts and tools do not differ greatly for small, large, for-profit, or nonprofit organizations. However, strategy implementation varies substantially among different types and sizes of organizations. Implementing strategies requires such actions as altering sales territories, adding new departments, closing facilities, hiring new employees, changing an organization's pricing strategy, developing financial budgets, developing new employee benefits, establishing cost-control procedures, changing advertising strategies, building new facilities, training new employees, transferring managers among divisions, and building a better computer information system. These types of activities obviously differ greatly between manufacturing, service, and governmental organizations.

MANAGEMENT PERSPECTIVES   In all but the smallest organizations, the transition from strategy formulation to strategy implementation requires a shift in responsibility from strategists to divisional and functional managers. Implementation problems can arise because of this shift in responsibility, especially if strategy-formulation decisions come as a surprise to middle- and lower-level managers. Managers and employees are motivated more by perceived self-interests than by organizational interests,

FIGURE 7–1

A Comprehensive Strategic-Management Model

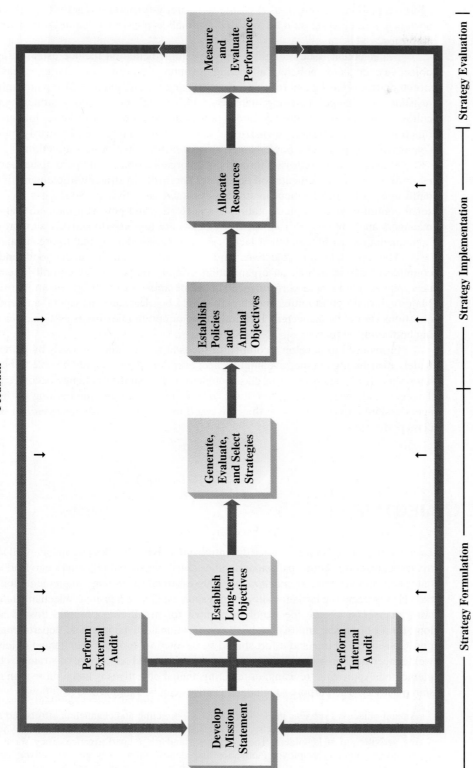

unless the two coincide. Therefore, it is essential that divisional and functional managers be involved as much as possible in strategy-formulation activities. Of equal importance, strategists should be involved as much as possible in strategy-implementation activities.

Management issues central to strategy implementation include establishing annual objectives, devising policies, allocating resources, altering an existing organizational structure, restructuring and reengineering, revising reward and incentive plans, minimizing resistance to change, matching managers with strategy, developing a strategy-supportive culture, adapting production/operations processes, developing an effective human resource function and, if necessary, downsizing. Management changes are necessarily more extensive when strategies to be implemented move a firm in a major new direction.

Managers and employees throughout an organization should participate early and directly in strategy-implementation decisions. Their role in strategy implementation should build upon prior involvement in strategy-formulation activities. Strategists' genuine personal commitment to implementation is a necessary and powerful motivational force for managers and employees. Too often, strategists are too busy to actively support strategy-implementation efforts, and their lack of interest can be detrimental to organizational success. The rationale for objectives and strategies should be understood and clearly communicated throughout an organization. Major competitors' accomplishments, products, plans, actions, and performance should be apparent to all organizational members. Major external opportunities and threats should be clear, and managers' and employees' questions should be answered. Top-down flow of communication is essential for developing bottom-up support.

Firms need to develop a competitor focus at all hierarchical levels by gathering and widely distributing competitive intelligence; every employee should be able to benchmark her or his efforts against best-in-class competitors so that the challenge becomes personal. This is a challenge for strategists of the firm. Firms should provide training for both managers and employees to ensure they have and maintain the skills necessary to be world-class performers.

ANNUAL OBJECTIVES

Establishing annual objectives is a decentralized activity that directly involves all managers in an organization. Active participation in establishing annual objectives can lead to acceptance and commitment. *Annual objectives* are essential for strategy implementation because they (1) represent the basis for allocating resources; (2) are a primary mechanism for evaluating managers; (3) are the major instrument for monitoring progress toward achieving long-term objectives; and (4) establish organizational, divisional, and departmental priorities. Considerable time and effort should be devoted to ensuring that annual objectives are well conceived, consistent with long-term objectives, and supportive of strategies to be implemented. Approving, revising, or rejecting annual objectives is much more than a rubber-stamp activity. The purpose of annual objectives can be summarized as follows:

> Annual objectives serve as guidelines for action, directing and channeling efforts and activities of organization members. They provide a source of legitimacy in an enterprise by justifying activities to stakeholders. They serve as standards of performance. They serve as an important source of employee motivation and identification. They give incentives for managers and employees to perform. They provide a basis for organizational design.[1]

INFORMATION TECHNOLOGY

How Extensively Is the Internet Used in Asia?

When it comes to using the Internet, Asia is light-years behind the United States and far behind Europe. "Even in Japan, the Internet is still in the experimental stage," says Mitsuru Shinozaki, Internet specialist at Keidanren. The following regional problems severely restrict use of the Internet for commercial or personal use throughout Asia:

1. Poor telecommunications infrastructure. Most countries, including China and India, have less than one telephone line per 100 people, compared to nearly 60 per 100 people in the United States.

2. A myriad of complex written and spoken languages. Asian languages mostly use non-Roman characters, and the Internet cannot handle them without special software.

3. There are dozens of highly diverse national boundaries, standards, and cultures.

4. There are relatively few desktop computers, and most of these are not regularly used for commerce. There are relatively few computer-literate businesspeople.

5. Most Asian cultures shun any type of electronic form of payment.

6. There are exceptionally high telecommunications and Internet connection charges.

Since creation of the Japanese version of Windows 95, personal computer shipments grew from 5.3 million in 1996 to 18.6 million in 1998. Use of the Internet tripled during this time in Japan, even though most customers and other businesses still will not use the Internet. The few Japanese companies that today have Web sites, such as Nippon Telephone & Telegraph; Fujitsu Ltd.; and Mitsubishi Motors Corp., direct customers off-line to complete purchases.

In Malaysia, Singapore, and Thailand, progress is rapidly being made to develop the infrastructure to support the Internet. China and India are working hard in this regard too, but these countries are still Third World in every aspect of the Internet, especially when compared to the United States.

Source: Adapted from Jack Gee, "Parlez-Vous Internet," Industry Week (April 21, 1997): 78–82.

Clearly stated and communicated objectives are critical to success in all types and sizes of firms. Annual objectives, stated in terms of profitability, growth, and market share by business segment, geographic area, customer groups, and product are common in organizations. Figure 7–2 illustrates how the Stamus Company could establish annual objectives based on long-term objectives. Table 7–1 reveals associated revenue figures that correspond to the objectives outlined in Figure 7–2. Note that, according to plan, the Stamus Company will slightly exceed its long-term objective of doubling company revenues between 1998 and the year 2000.

Figure 7–2 also reflects how a hierarchy of annual objectives can be established based on an organization's structure. Objectives should be consistent across hierarchical levels and form a network of supportive aims. *Horizontal consistency of objectives* is as important as *vertical consistency*. For instance, it would not be effective for manufacturing to achieve more than its annual objective of units produced if marketing could not sell the additional units.

Annual objectives should be measurable, consistent, reasonable, challenging, clear, communicated throughout the organization, characterized by an appropriate time dimension, and accompanied by commensurate rewards and sanctions. Too often, objectives are stated in generalities, with little operational usefulness. Annual objectives such as "to improve communication" or "to improve performance" are not clear, specific, or measurable. Objectives should state quantity, quality, cost, and time and also be verifiable. Terms such as "maximize," "minimize," "as soon as possible," and "adequate" should be avoided.

	1998	1999	2000
Division I Revenues	1.0	1.400	1.960
Division II Revenues	0.5	0.700	0.980
Division III Revenues	0.5	0.750	1.125
Total Company Revenues	2.0	2.850	4.065

TABLE 7-1

The Stamus Company's Revenue Expectations (in millions of dollars)

FIGURE 7–2
The Stamus Company's Hierarchy of Aims

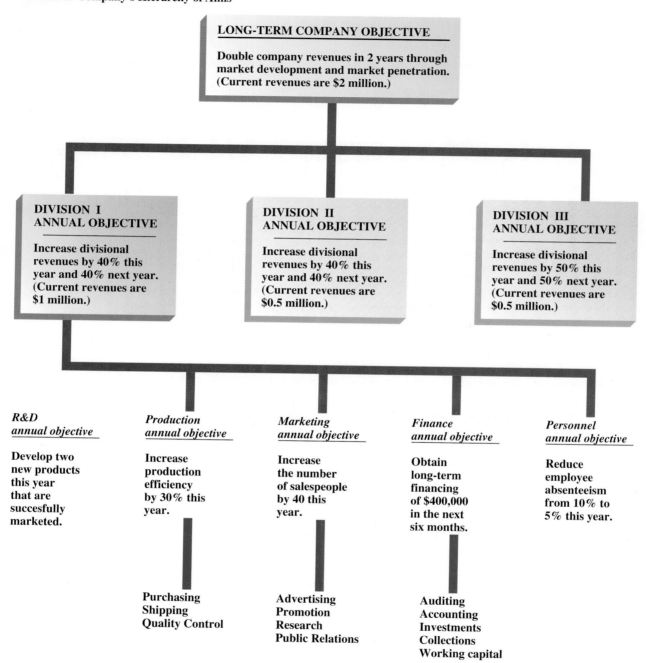

Annual objectives should be compatible with employees' and managers' values and should be supported by clearly stated policies. More of something is not always better! Improved quality or reduced cost may, for example, be more important than quantity. It is important to tie rewards and sanctions to annual objectives so that employees and managers understand that achieving objectives is critical to successful strategy implementation.

Clear annual objectives do not guarantee successful strategy implementation but they do increase the likelihood that personal and organizational aims can be accomplished. Overemphasis on achieving objectives can result in undesirable conduct, such as faking the numbers, distorting the records, and letting objectives become ends in themselves. Managers must be alert to these potential problems.

POLICIES

Changes in a firm's strategic direction do not occur automatically. On a day-to-day basis, policies are needed to make a strategy work. Policies facilitate solving recurring problems and guide the implementation of strategy. Broadly defined, *policy* refers to specific guidelines, methods, procedures, rules, forms, and administrative practices established to support and encourage work toward stated goals. Policies are instruments for strategy implementation. Policies set boundaries, constraints, and limits on the kinds of administrative actions that can be taken to reward and sanction behavior; they clarify what can and cannot be done in pursuit of an organization's objectives. For example, Carnival's new *Paradise* ship launched in the fall 1998 has a no-smoking policy anywhere, anytime aboard ship. It is the first cruise ship to comprehensively ban smoking. Another example of corporate policy relates to surfing the Web while at work. About 40 percent of companies today do not have a formal policy preventing employees from surfing the Internet, but software is being marketed now that allows firms to monitor how, when, where, and how long various employees use the Internet at work.

Policies let both employees and managers know what is expected of them, thereby increasing the likelihood that strategies will be implemented successfully. They provide a basis for management control, allow coordination across organizational units, and reduce the amount of time managers spend making decisions. Policies also clarify what work is to be done by whom. They promote delegation of decision making to appropriate managerial levels where various problems usually arise. Many organizations have a policy manual that serves to guide and direct behavior. About 80 percent of all corporations in the United States have instituted no-smoking policies. This is not true, however, in other countries. About 4.6 trillion cigarettes are smoked annually worldwide. Countries with the highest number of cigarettes smoked per capita are listed below (U.S. rate is 1,836):

South Korea	4,153
Japan	2,739
Hungary	2,689
Greece	2,648
Poland	2,534
Romania	2,172

Policies can apply to all divisions and departments (for example, "We are an equal opportunity employer"). Some policies apply to a single department ("Employees in this department must take at least one training and development course each year"). Whatever their scope and form, policies serve as a mechanism for implementing strategies and obtaining objectives. Policies should be stated in writing whenever possible. They represent the means for carrying out strategic decisions. Examples of policies that support a company strategy, a divisional objective, and a departmental objective are given in Table 7–2.

TABLE 7–2
A Hierarchy of Policies

Company Strategy: Acquire a chain of retail stores to meet our sales growth and profitability objectives.
Supporting policies:
1. "All stores will be open from 8 A.M. to 8 P.M. Monday through Saturday." (This policy could increase retail sales if stores currently are open only 40 hours a week.)
2. "All stores must submit a Monthly Control Data Report." (This policy could reduce expense-to-sales ratios.)
3. "All stores must support company advertising by contributing 5 percent of their total monthly revenues for this purpose." (This policy could allow the company to establish a national reputation.)
4. "All stores must adhere to the uniform pricing guidelines set forth in the Company Handbook." (This policy could help assure customers that the company offers a consistent product in terms of price and quality in all its stores.)

Divisional Objective: Increase the division's revenues from $10 million in 1998 to $15 million in 2000.
Supporting policies:
1. "Beginning in January 1999, this division's salespersons must file a weekly activity report that includes the number of calls made, the number of miles traveled, the number of units sold, the dollar volume sold, and the number of new accounts opened." (This policy could ensure that salespersons do not place too great an emphasis in certain areas.)
2. "Beginning in January 1999, this division will return to its employees 5 percent of its gross revenues in the form of a Christmas bonus." (This policy could increase employee productivity.)
3. "Beginning in January 1999, inventory levels carried in warehouses will be decreased by 30 percent in accordance with a Just-in-Time manufacturing approach." (This policy could reduce production expenses and thus free funds for increased marketing efforts.)

Production Department Objective: Increase production from 20,000 units in 1998 to 30,000 units in 2000.
Supporting policies:
1. "Beginning in January 1999, employees will have the option of working up to 20 hours of overtime per week." (This policy could minimize the need to hire additional employees.)
2. "Beginning in January 1999, perfect attendance awards in the amount of $100 will be given to all employees who do not miss a workday in a given year." (This policy could decrease absenteeism and increase productivity.)
3. "Beginning in January 1999, new equipment must be leased rather than purchased." (This policy could reduce tax liabilities and thus allow more funds to be invested in modernizing production processes.)

Some example issues that may require a management policy are as follows:

◆ To offer extensive or limited management development workshops and seminars
◆ To centralize or decentralize employee-training activities
◆ To recruit through employment agencies, college campuses, and/or newspapers
◆ To promote from within or hire from the outside
◆ To promote on the basis of merit or on the basis of seniority
◆ To tie executive compensation to long-term and/or annual objectives
◆ To offer numerous or few employee benefits
◆ To negotiate directly or indirectly with labor unions
◆ To delegate authority for large expenditures or to retain this authority centrally
◆ To allow much, some, or no overtime work
◆ To establish a high- or low-safety stock of inventory
◆ To use one or more suppliers
◆ To buy, lease, or rent new production equipment
◆ To stress quality control greatly or not
◆ To establish many or only a few production standards
◆ To operate one, two, or three shifts
◆ To discourage using insider information for personal gain
◆ To discourage sexual harassment

◆ To discourage smoking at work
◆ To discourage insider trading
◆ To discourage moonlighting

RESOURCE ALLOCATION

Resource allocation is a central management activity that allows for strategy execution. In organizations that do not use a strategic-management approach to decision making, resource allocation is often based on political or personal factors. Strategic management enables resources to be allocated according to priorities established by annual objectives. Nothing could be more detrimental to strategic management and to organizational success than for resources to be allocated in ways not consistent with priorities indicated by approved annual objectives.

All organizations have at least four types of resources that can be used to achieve desired objectives: financial resources, physical resources, human resources, and technological resources. Allocating resources to particular divisions and departments does not mean that strategies will be successfully implemented. A number of factors commonly prohibit effective resource allocation, including an overprotection of resources, too great an emphasis on short-run financial criteria, organizational politics, vague strategy targets, a reluctance to take risks, and a lack of sufficient knowledge.

Below the corporate level, there often exists an absence of systematic thinking about resources allocated and strategies of the firm. Yavitz and Newman explained why:

> Managers normally have many more tasks than they can do. Managers must allocate time and resources among these tasks. Pressure builds up. Expenses are too high. The CEO wants a good financial report for the third quarter. Strategy formulation and implementation activities often get deferred. Today's problems soak up available energies and resources. Scrambled accounts and budgets fail to reveal the shift in allocation away from strategic needs to currently squeaking wheels.[2]

The real value of any resource allocation program lies in the resulting accomplishment of an organization's objectives. Effective resource allocation does not guarantee successful strategy implementation because programs, personnel, controls, and commitment must breathe life into the resources provided. Strategic management itself is sometimes referred to as a "resource allocation process."

MANAGING CONFLICT

Interdependency of objectives and competition for limited resources often leads to conflict. *Conflict* can be defined as a disagreement between two or more parties on one or more issues. Establishing annual objectives can lead to conflict because individuals have different expectations and perceptions, schedules create pressure, personalities are incompatible, and misunderstandings between line and staff occur. For example, a collection manager's objective of reducing bad debts by 50 percent in a given year may conflict with a divisional objective to increase sales by 20 percent.

Establishing objectives can lead to conflict because managers and strategists must make trade-offs, such as whether to emphasize short-term profits or long-term growth, profit margin or market share, market penetration or market development, growth or stability, high risk or low risk, and social responsiveness or profit maximization. Conflict is unavoidable in organizations, so it is important that conflict be managed and resolved before dysfunctional consequences affect organizational performance. Conflict is not always bad. An absence of conflict can signal indifference and apathy. Conflict can serve to energize opposing groups into action and may help managers identify problems.

Various approaches for managing and resolving conflict can be classified into three categories: avoidance, defusion, and confrontation. *Avoidance* includes such actions as ignoring the problem in hopes that the conflict will resolve itself or physically separating the conflicting individuals (or groups). *Defusion* can include playing down differences between conflicting parties while accentuating similarities and common interests, compromising so that there is neither a clear winner nor loser, resorting to majority rule, appealing to a higher authority, or redesigning present positions. *Confrontation* is exemplified by exchanging members of conflicting parties so that each can gain an appreciation of the other's point of view, or holding a meeting at which conflicting parties present their views and work through their differences.

MATCHING STRUCTURE WITH STRATEGY

Changes in strategy often require changes in the way an organization is structured for two major reasons. First, structure largely dictates how objectives and policies will be established. For example, objectives and policies established under a geographic organizational structure are couched in geographic terms. Objectives and policies are stated largely in terms of products in an organization whose structure is based on product groups. The structural format for developing objectives and policies can significantly impact all other strategy-implementation activities.

The second major reason why changes in strategy often require changes in structure is that structure dictates how resources will be allocated. If an organization is structured based on customer groups, then resources will be allocated in that manner. Similarly, if an organization's structure is set up along functional business lines, then resources are allocated by functional areas. Unless new or revised strategies place emphasis in the same areas as old strategies, structural reorientation commonly becomes a part of strategy implementation.

Changes in strategy lead to changes in organizational structure. Structure should be designed to facilitate the strategic pursuit of a firm and, therefore, follows strategy. Without a strategy or reasons for being (mission), designing an effective structure is difficult. Chandler found a particular structure sequence to be often repeated as organizations grow and change strategy over time; this sequence is depicted in Figure 7–3.

There is no one optimal organizational design or structure for a given strategy or type of organization. What is appropriate for one organization may not be appropriate for a similar firm, although successful firms in a given industry do tend to organize themselves in a similar way. For example, consumer goods companies tend to emulate the divisional structure-by-product form of organization. Small firms tend to be functionally structured (centralized). Medium-size firms tend to be divisionally structured (decentralized). Large firms tend to use an SBU (strategic business unit) or matrix structure. As organizations grow, their structures generally change from simple to complex as a result of concatenation, or the linking together of several basic strategies.

Numerous external and internal forces affect an organization; no firm could change its structure in response to every one of these forces, because to do so would lead to chaos. However, when a firm changes its strategy, the existing organizational structure may become ineffective. Symptoms of an ineffective organizational structure include too many levels of management, too many meetings attended by too many people, too much

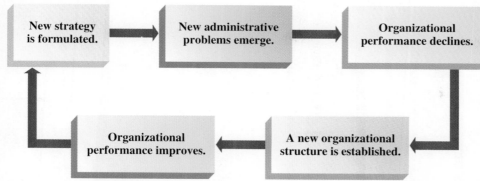

**FIGURE 7–3
Chandler's Strategy-
Structure Relationship**

Source: Adapted from Alfred Chandler, *Strategy and Structure* (Cambridge, Massachusetts: MIT Press, 1962).

attention being directed toward solving interdepartmental conflicts, too large a span of control, and too many unachieved objectives. Changes in structure can facilitate strategy-implementation efforts, but changes in structure should not be expected to make a bad strategy good, to make bad managers good, or to make bad products sell.

Structure undeniably can and does influence strategy. Strategies formulated must be workable, so if a certain new strategy required massive structural changes it would not be an attractive choice. In this way, structure can shape the choice of strategies. But a more important concern is determining what types of structural changes are needed to implement new strategies and how these changes can best be accomplished. We examine this issue by focusing on seven basic types of organizational structure: functional, divisional by geographic area, divisional by product, divisional by customer, divisional by process, strategic business unit (SBU), and matrix.

THE FUNCTIONAL STRUCTURE   The most widely used structure is the functional or centralized type because this structure is the simplest and least expensive of the seven alternatives. A *functional structure* groups tasks and activities by business function such as production/operations, marketing, finance/accounting, research and development, and computer information systems. A university may structure its activities by major functions that include academic affairs, student services, alumni relations, athletics, maintenance, and accounting. Besides being simple and inexpensive, a functional structure also promotes specialization of labor, encourages efficiency, minimizes the need for an elaborate control system, and allows rapid decision making. Some disadvantages of a functional structure are that it forces accountability to the top, minimizes career development opportunities, and is sometimes characterized by low employee morale, line/staff conflicts, poor delegation of authority, and inadequate planning for products and markets.

The 1980s and 1990s witnessed most large companies abandoning the functional structure in favor of decentralization and improved accountability. A company that still adheres to a functional design, however, is Food Lion, Inc., as shown in Figure 7–4.

THE DIVISIONAL STRUCTURE   The *divisional* or *decentralized structure* is the second most common type used by American businesses. As a small organization grows, it has more difficulty managing different products and services in different markets. Some form of divisional structure generally becomes necessary to motivate employees, control operations, and compete successfully in diverse locations. The divisional structure can be organized in one of four ways: by geographic area, by product or service, by customer, or by process. With a divisional structure, functional activities are performed both centrally and in each separate division.

FIGURE 7–4
Food Lion's Organizational Chart

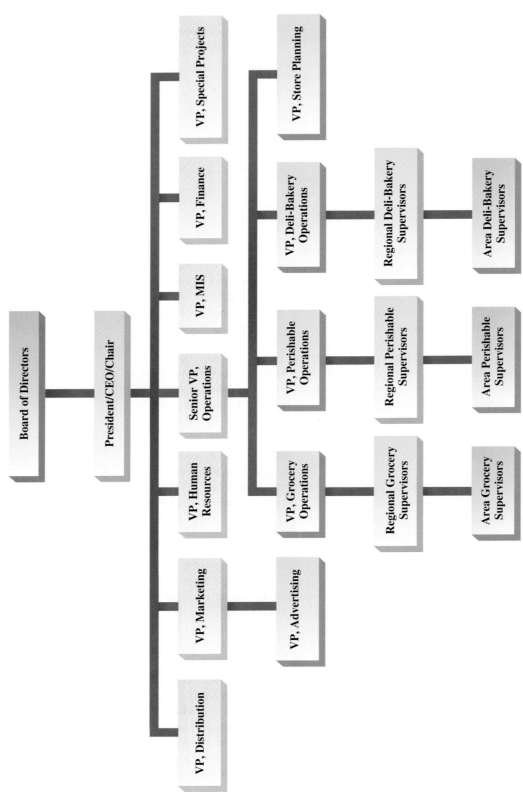

A divisional structure has some clear advantages. First and perhaps foremost, accountability is clear. That is, divisional managers can be held responsible for sales and profit levels. Because a divisional structure is based on extensive delegation of authority, managers and employees can easily see the results of their good or bad performances. As a result, employee morale is generally higher in a divisional structure than it is in a centralized structure. Other advantages of the divisional design are that it creates career development opportunities for managers, allows local control of local situations, leads to a competitive climate within an organization, and allows new businesses and products to be added easily. AT&T recently restructured by breaking large businesses into smaller, focused units, totaling 24 divisions and 19 subsidiaries.

The divisional design is not without some limitations, however. Perhaps the most important limitation is that a divisional structure is costly, for a number of reasons. First, each division requires functional specialists who must be paid. Second, there exists some duplication of staff services, facilities, and personnel; for instance, functional specialists are also needed centrally (at headquarters) to coordinate divisional activities. Third, managers must be well qualified because the divisional design forces delegation of authority; better-qualified individuals require higher salaries. A divisional structure can also be costly because it requires an elaborate, headquarters-driven control system. Finally, certain regions, products, or customers may sometimes receive special treatment, and it may be difficult to maintain consistent, companywide practices. Nonetheless, for most large organizations and many small firms, the advantages of a divisional structure more than offset the potential limitations.

A *divisional structure by geographic area* is appropriate for organizations whose strategies need to be tailored to fit the particular needs and characteristics of customers in different geographic areas. This type of structure can be most appropriate for organizations that have similar branch facilities located in widely dispersed areas. A divisional structure by geographic area allows local participation in decision making and improved coordination within a region. ABB (Asia Brown Bover, Ltd.) reorganized its management structure into three large geographic regions: Europe, the Americas, and Asia-Pacific. Percy Barnevik, ABB's chief executive officer, says the growing unification of Europe requires that the continent be treated as one market, and the opening up of markets under the North American Free Trade Agreement made establishment of one region for the Americas a logical step. Treating the Asia-Pacific region as one division ensures focused attention in the area of the world with the greatest growth potential.

The *divisional structure by product* is most effective for implementing strategies when specific products or services need special emphasis. Also, this type of structure is widely used when an organization offers only a few products or services, or when an organization's products or services differ substantially. The divisional structure allows strict control and attention to product lines, but it may also require a more skilled management force and reduced top management control. General Motors, DuPont, and Procter & Gamble use a divisional structure by product to implement strategies. Huffy, the largest bicycle company in the world, is another firm that is highly decentralized based on a divisional-by-product structure. Based in Ohio, Huffy's divisions are the Bicycle division, the Gerry Baby Products division, the Huffy Sports division, YLC Enterprises, and Washington Inventory Service. Harry Shaw, Huffy's chairman, believes decentralization is one of the keys to Huffy's success.

When a few major customers are of paramount importance and many different services are provided to these customers, then a *divisional structure by customer* can be the most effective way to implement strategies. This structure allows an organization to cater effectively to the requirements of clearly defined customer groups. For example, book publishing companies often organize their activities around customer groups such as colleges, secondary schools, and private commercial schools. Some airline companies have two major customer divisions: passengers and freight or cargo services. Merrill Lynch is organized into separate divisions that cater to different groups of customers, including wealthy individuals, institutional investors, and small corporations.

A *divisional structure by process* is similar to a functional structure, because activities are organized according to the way work is actually performed. However, a key difference between these two designs is that functional departments are not accountable for profits or revenues, whereas divisional process departments are evaluated on these criteria. An example of a divisional structure by process is a manufacturing business organized into six divisions: electrical work, glass cutting, welding, grinding, painting, and foundry work. In this case, all operations related to these specific processes would be grouped under the separate divisions. Each process (division) would be responsible for generating revenues and profits. The divisional structure by process can be particularly effective in achieving objectives when distinct production processes represent the thrust of competitiveness in an industry.

THE STRATEGIC BUSINESS UNIT (SBU) STRUCTURE As the number, size, and diversity of divisions in an organization increase, controlling and evaluating divisional operations become increasingly difficult for strategists. Increases in sales often are not accompanied by similar increases in profitability. The span of control becomes too large at top levels of the firm. For example, in a large conglomerate organization composed of 90 divisions, the chief executive officer could have difficulty even remembering the first names of divisional presidents. In multidivisional organizations an SBU structure can greatly facilitate strategy-implementation efforts.

The *SBU structure* groups similar divisions into strategic business units and delegates authority and responsibility for each unit to a senior executive who reports directly to the chief executive officer. This change in structure can facilitate strategy implementation by improving coordination between similar divisions and channeling accountability to distinct business units. In the 90-division conglomerate just mentioned, the 90 divisions could perhaps be regrouped into 10 SBUs according to certain common characteristics such as competing in the same industry, being located in the same area, or having the same customers.

Two disadvantages of an SBU structure are that it requires an additional layer of management, which increases salary expenses, and the role of the group vice-president is often ambiguous. However, these limitations often do not outweigh the advantages of improved coordination and accountability. Atlantic Richfield and Fairchild Industries are examples of firms that successfully use an SBU-type structure.

THE MATRIX STRUCTURE A *matrix structure* is the most complex of all designs because it depends upon both vertical and horizontal flows of authority and communication (hence the term *matrix*). In contrast, functional and divisional structures depend primarily on vertical flows of authority and communication. A matrix structure can result in higher overhead because it creates more management positions. Other characteristics of a matrix structure that contribute to overall complexity include dual lines of budget authority (a violation of the unity-of-command principle), dual sources of reward and punishment, shared authority, dual reporting channels, and a need for an extensive and effective communication system.

Despite its complexity, the matrix structure is widely used in many industries, including construction, health care, research, and defense. Some advantages of a matrix structure are that project objectives are clear, there are many channels of communication, workers can see visible results of their work, and shutting down a project can be accomplished relatively easily.

In order for a matrix structure to be effective, organizations need participative planning, training, clear mutual understanding of roles and responsibilities, excellent internal communication, and mutual trust and confidence. The matrix structure is being used more frequently by American businesses because firms are pursuing strategies that add new products, customer groups, and technology to their range of activities. Out of these changes are coming product managers, functional managers, and geographic-area managers, all of whom have important strategic responsibilities. When several variables, such as product, customer, technology, geography, functional area, and line of business, have roughly equal strategic priorities, a matrix organization can be an effective structural form.

RESTRUCTURING AND REENGINEERING

Restructuring and reengineering are becoming commonplace on the corporate landscape across the United States and Europe. *Restructuring*—also called *downsizing*, *rightsizing*, or *delayering*—involves reducing the size of the firm in terms of number of employees, number of divisions or units, and number of hierarchical levels in the firm's organizational structure. This reduction in size is intended to improve both efficiency and effectiveness. Restructuring is concerned primarily with shareholder well-being rather than employee well-being.

Unforgiving competition from leaner U.S. firms is forcing many European companies to downsize, laying off managers and employees. This was almost unheard of prior to the mid-1990s because European labor unions and laws required lengthy negotiations or huge severance checks before workers could be terminated. Unlike in the United States, labor union executives sit on most boards of directors of large European firms.

Job security in European companies is slowly moving toward a U.S. scenario in which firms lay off almost at will. From banks in Milan to factories in Mannhelm, European employers are starting to show people the door in an effort to streamline operations, increase efficiency, and compete against already slim and trim U.S. firms. Massive U.S.-style layoffs are still rare in Europe, but unemployment rates throughout the continent are rising quite rapidly. European firms still prefer to downsize by attrition and retirement rather than by blanket layoffs due to culture, laws, and unions. Electrolux, based in Switzerland, plans to cut 12,000 jobs and close 25 plants during 1998 and 1999.

In contrast, *reengineering* is concerned more with employee and customer well-being than shareholder well-being. Reengineering—also called process management, process innovation, or process redesign—involves reconfiguring or redesigning work, jobs, and processes for the purpose of improving cost, quality, service, and speed. Reengineering does not usually affect the organizational structure or chart, nor does it imply job loss or employee layoffs. Whereas restructuring is concerned with eliminating or establishing, shrinking or enlarging, and moving organizational departments and divisions, the focus of reengineering is changing the way work is actually carried out.

Reengineering is characterized by many tactical (short-term, business function–specific) decisions, whereas restructuring is characterized by strategic (long-term, affecting all business functions) decisions.

RESTRUCTURING Firms often employ restructuring when various ratios appear out of line with competitors as determined through benchmarking exercises. *Benchmarking* simply involves comparing a firm against the best firms in the industry on a wide variety of performance-related criteria. Some benchmarking ratios commonly used in rationalizing the need for restructuring are headcount-to-sales-volume, or corporate-staff-to-operating-employees, or span-of-control figures.

The primary benefit sought from restructuring is cost reduction. For some highly bureaucratic firms, restructuring can actually rescue the firm from global competition and demise. But the downside of restructuring can be reduced employee commitment, creativity, and innovation that accompanies the uncertainty and trauma associated with pending and actual employee layoffs.

Another downside of restructuring is that more people today do not aspire to become managers, and many present-day managers are trying to get off the management track.[3] Sentiment against joining management ranks is higher today than ever. About 80 percent of employees say they want nothing to do with management, a major shift from just a decade ago when 60 to 70 percent hoped to become managers. Managing others historically led to enhanced career mobility, financial rewards, and executive perks; but in today's global, more competitive, restructured arena, managerial jobs demand more hours and headaches with fewer financial rewards. Managers today manage more people spread over different locations, travel more, manage diverse functions, and are change agents even when they have nothing to do with the creation of the plan or even disagree with its approach. Employers today are looking for people who can do things, not for people who make other people do things. Restructuring in many firms has made a manager's job an invisible, thankless role. More workers today are self-managed, entrepreneurs, intrepreneurs, or team-managed. Managers today need to be counselors, motivators, financial advisors, and psychologists. They also run the risk of becoming technologically behind in their areas of expertise. "Dilbert" cartoons commonly portray managers as enemies or as morons.

An example of company restructuring is ITT Corporation, which is splitting itself into three companies—ITT Educational Services, World Directories, and ITT Destinations. ITT's restructuring includes taking on $2 billion in new debt and buying back 30 million shares of its own stock in order to deter Hilton Hotels from acquiring the company in a hostile takeover.

REENGINEERING The argument for a firm engaging in reengineering usually goes as follows: Many companies historically have been organized vertically by business function. This arrangement has led over time to managers' and employees' mind-sets being defined by their particular functions rather than by overall customer service, product quality, or corporate performance. The logic is that all firms tend to bureaucratize over time. As routines become entrenched, turf becomes delineated and defended, and politics takes precedence over performance. Walls that exist in the physical workplace can be reflections of "mental" walls.

In reengineering, a firm uses information technology to break down functional barriers and create a work system based on business processes, products, or outputs rather than on functions or inputs. Cornerstones of reengineering are decentralization, reciprocal interdependence, and information sharing. A firm that exemplifies complete information sharing is Springfield ReManufacturing Corporation, which provides to all employees a weekly income statement of the firm, as well as extensive information on other companies' performances.

There are numerous examples of firms that benefited in the 1990s from reengineering—including Union Carbide, which reduced its fixed costs by $400 million; Taco Bell, which raised its restaurant peak capacity from $400 per hour to $1,500 per hour; and AT&T which created a new business telephone system called PBX.

A benefit of reengineering is that it offers employees the opportunity to see more clearly how their particular jobs impact the final product or service being marketed by the firm. However, reengineering also can raise manager and employee anxiety which, unless calmed, can lead to corporate trauma.

LINKING PERFORMANCE AND PAY TO STRATEGIES

Most companies today are practicing some form of pay-for-performance for employees and managers other than top executives. The average employee performance bonus is 6.8

percent of pay for individual performance, 5.5 percent of pay for group productivity, and 6.4 percent of pay for companywide profitability.

Staff control of pay systems often prevents line managers from using financial compensation as a strategic tool. Flexibility regarding managerial and employee compensation is needed to allow short-term shifts in compensation that can stimulate efforts to achieve long-term objectives. NBC recently unveiled a new method for paying its affiliated stations. The compensation formula is 50 percent based on audience viewing of shows from 4 P.M. to 8 P.M. and 50 percent based on how many adults aged 25 to 54 watch NBC over the course of a day.

How can an organization's reward system be more closely linked to strategic performance? How can decisions on salary increases, promotions, merit pay, and bonuses be more closely aligned to support the long-term strategic objectives of the organization? There are no widely accepted answers to these questions, but a dual bonus system based on both annual objectives and long-term objectives is becoming common. The percentage of a manager's annual bonus attributable to short-term versus long-term results should vary by hierarchical level in the organization. A chief executive officer's annual bonus could, for example, be determined on a 75 percent short-term and 25 percent long-term basis. It is important that bonuses not be based solely on short-term results because such a system ignores long-term company strategies and objectives.

DuPont Canada has a 16 percent return-on-equity objective. If this objective is met, the company's 4,000 employees receive a "performance sharing cash award" equal to 4 percent of pay. If return-on-equity falls below 11 percent, employees get nothing. If return-on-equity exceeds 28 percent, workers receive a 10 percent bonus.

Profit sharing is another widely used form of incentive compensation. More than 30 percent of American companies have profit sharing plans, but critics emphasize that too many factors affect profits for this to be a good criterion. Taxes, pricing, or an acquisition would wipe out profits, for example. Also, firms try to minimize profits in a sense to reduce taxes.

Still another criterion widely used to link performance and pay to strategies is gain sharing. *Gain sharing* requires employees or departments to establish performance targets; if actual results exceed objectives, all members get bonuses. More than 26 percent of American companies use some form of gain sharing; about 75 percent of gain sharing plans have been adopted since 1980. Carrier, a subsidiary of United Technologies, has had excellent success with gain sharing in its six plants in Syracuse, New York; Firestone's tire plant in Wilson, North Carolina, has experienced similar success with gain sharing.

Criteria such as sales, profit, production efficiency, quality, and safety could also serve as bases for an effective *bonus system*. If an organization meets certain understood, agreed-upon profit objectives, every member of the enterprise should share in the harvest. A bonus system can be an effective tool for motivating individuals to support strategy-implementation efforts. BankAmerica, for example, recently overhauled its incentive system to link pay to sales of the bank's most profitable products and services. Branch managers receive a base salary plus a bonus based on the number of new customers and on sales of bank products. Every employee in each branch is also eligible for a bonus if the branch exceeds its goals. Thomas Peterson, a top BankAmerica executive, says, "We want to make people responsible for meeting their goals, so we pay incentives on sales, not on controlling costs or on being sure the parking lot is swept."

Five tests are often used to determine whether a performance-pay plan will benefit an organization:

1. *Does the plan capture attention?* Are people talking more about their activities and taking pride in early successes under the plan?

2. *Do employees understand the plan?* Can participants explain how it works and what they need to do to earn the incentive?

3. *Is the plan improving communications?* Do employees know more than they used to about the company's mission, plans, and objectives?

4. *Does the plan pay out when it should?* Are incentives being paid for desired results—and being withheld when objectives are not met?

5. *Is the company or unit performing better?* Are profits up? Has market share grown? Have gains resulted in part from the incentives?[4]

In addition to a dual bonus system, a combination of reward strategy incentives such as salary raises, stock options, fringe benefits, promotions, praise, recognition, criticism, fear, increased job autonomy, and awards can be used to encourage managers and employees to push hard for successful strategic implementation. The range of options for getting people, departments, and divisions to actively support strategy-implementation activities in a particular organization is almost limitless. Merck, for example, recently gave each of its 37,000 employees a 10-year option to buy 100 shares of Merck stock at a set price of $127. Steven Darien, Merck's vice-president of human resources, says, "We needed to find ways to get everyone in the workforce on board in terms of our goals and objectives. Company executives will begin meeting with all Merck workers to explore ways in which employees can contribute more."

Increasing criticism aimed at chief executive officers for their high pay has resulted in executive compensation being linked to performance of their firm more closely than ever before. CEO Deryck Maughan of Salomon saw an 87 percent drop in his pay when

GLOBAL PERSPECTIVE
How Much Are U.S. CEOs Paid versus the World?

The average CEO in the United States gets paid nearly double what the average CEO gets paid in Canada, Japan, and the United Kingdom and nearly a third more than the average CEO in Germany, Hong Kong, and France.

The difference, however, lies not in salary per se but rather in stock options and bonuses, which are rare abroad but commonplace here. Foreign countries, however, are beginning to approve stock options for their CEOs in

order to be competitive. Japan approved stock options in July 1997 and Germany in January 1998. Warrant bonds, similar to stock options, are being approved by foreign multinational firms.

TOP-PAID U.S. CEOS IN 1996 AND 1997

	1996			1997	
CEO	**COMPANY**	**TOTAL PAY (MILLIONS)**	**CEO**	**COMPANY**	**TOTAL PAY (MILLIONS)**
Millard Drexler	The Gap	$104.8	Sanford Wells	Travelers Group	$230.7
Lawrence Coss	Green Tree Financial	102.4	Roberto Goizueta	Coca-Cola	111.8
			Richard Scrushy	HealthSouth	106.7
Andrew Grove	Intel	97.9	Ray Irani	Occidental Petroleum	101.5
Sanford Wells	Travelers Group	91.6			
Theodore Waitt	Gateway 2000	81.3	Eugene Isenberg	Nabors Industries	84.5
Anthony O'Reilly	H. J. Heinz	64.6	Joseph Costello	Cadence Design Systems	66.8
Stephen Hibert	Conseco	51.4			
John Reed	Citicorp	46.2	Andrew Grove	Intel	52.2
Daniel Smith	Cascade Communications	35.6	Charles McCall	HBO & Company	51.4
			Philip Purcell	Morgan Stanley Dean Witter	50.8
Casey Cowell	U.S. Robotics	33.9			
			Robert Shapiro	Monsanto	49.3

Source: Adapted from "Executive Pay," *Business Week* (April 20, 1998):64.

his firm incurred a $963 million in pretax losses. CEO Charles Sanford of Bankers Trust saw a 57 percent drop in his pay as his firm's return-on-equity dropped nearly half to 13.5 percent. Although the linkage between CEO pay and corporate performance is getting closer, CEO pay in the United States still can be astronomical, as indicated in the Global Perspective. A close pay-performance linkage does not imply less pay. In fact, the opposite is true when the firm does well.

MANAGING RESISTANCE TO CHANGE

No organization or individual can escape change. But the thought of change raises anxieties because people fear economic loss, inconvenience, uncertainty, and a break in normal social patterns. Almost any change in structure, technology, people, or strategies has the potential to disrupt comfortable interaction patterns. For this reason, people resist change. The strategic-management process itself can impose major changes on individuals and processes. Reorienting an organization to get people to think and act strategically is not an easy task.

> The level of familiarity with strategic thinking in the U.S. is high, but acceptance is low. U.S. management has to undergo a cultural change, and it's difficult to force people to change their thinking; it's like ordering them to use personal computers. One obstacle is that top executives are often too busy fighting fires to devote time to developing managers who can think strategically. Yet, the best-run companies recognize the need to develop managers who can fashion and implement strategy.[5]

Resistance to change can be considered the single greatest threat to successful strategy implementation. Resistance in the form of sabotaging production machines, absenteeism, filing unfounded grievances, and an unwillingness to cooperate regularly occurs in organizations. People often resist strategy implementation because they do not understand what is happening or why changes are taking place. In that case, employees may simply need accurate information. Successful strategy implementation hinges upon managers' ability to develop an organizational climate conducive to change. Change must be viewed as an opportunity rather than as a threat by managers and employees.

Resistance to change can emerge at any stage or level of the strategy-implementation process. Although there are various approaches for implementing changes, three commonly used strategies are a force change strategy, an educative change strategy, and a rational or self-interest change strategy. A *force change strategy* involves giving orders and enforcing those orders; this strategy has the advantage of being fast, but it is plagued by low commitment and high resistance. The *educative change strategy* is one that presents information to convince people of the need for change; the disadvantage of an educative change strategy is that implementation becomes slow and difficult. However, this type of strategy evokes greater commitment and less resistance than does the force strategy. Finally, a *rational* or *self-interest change strategy* is one that attempts to convince individuals that the change is to their personal advantage. When this appeal is successful, strategy implementation can be relatively easy. However, implementation changes are seldom to everyone's advantage.

The rational change strategy is the most desirable, so this approach is examined a bit further. Managers can improve the likelihood of successfully implementing change by carefully designing change efforts. Jack Duncan described a rational or self-interest change strategy as consisting of four steps. First, employees are invited to participate in the process of change and the details of transition; participation allows everyone to give opinions, to feel a part of the change process, and to identify their own self-interests regarding the recommended change. Second, some motivation or incentive to change is required;

self-interest can be the most important motivator. Third, communication is needed so that people can understand the purpose for the changes. Giving and receiving feedback is the fourth step; everyone enjoys knowing how things are going and how much progress is being made.[6]

Igor Ansoff summarized the need for strategists to manage resistance to change as follows:

> Observation of the historical transitions from one orientation to another shows that, if left un-managed, the process becomes conflict-laden, prolonged, and costly in both human and financial terms. Management of resistance involves anticipating the focus of resistance and its intensity. Second, it involves eliminating unnecessary resistance caused by misperceptions and insecurities. Third, it involves mustering the power base necessary to assure support for the change. Fourth, it involves planning the process of change. Finally, it involves monitoring and controlling resistance during the process of change. . . .[7]

Due to diverse external and internal forces, change is a fact of life in organizations. The rate, speed, magnitude, and direction of changes vary over time by industry and organization. Strategists should strive to create a work environment in which change is recognized as necessary and beneficial so that individuals can adapt to change more easily. Adopting a strategic-management approach to decision making can itself require major changes in the philosophy and operations of a firm.

Strategists can take a number of positive actions to minimize managers' and employees' resistance to change. For example, individuals who will be affected by a change should be involved in the decision to make the change and in decisions about how to implement change. Strategists should anticipate changes and develop and offer training and development workshops so managers and employees can adapt to those changes. They also need to communicate the need for changes effectively. The strategic-management process can be described as a process of managing change. Robert Waterman describes how successful organizations involve individuals to facilitate change:

> Implementation starts with, not after, the decision. When Ford Motor Company embarked on the program to build the highly successful Taurus, management gave up the usual, sequential design process. Instead they showed the tentative design to the workforce and asked their help in devising a car that would be easy to build. Team Taurus came up with no less than 1,401 items suggested by Ford employees. What a contrast from the secrecy that characterized the industry before! When people are treated as the main engine rather than interchangeable parts, motivation, creativity, quality, and commitment to implementation go up.[8]

MANAGING THE NATURAL ENVIRONMENT

Monsanto, a large U.S. chemical company, is an excellent example of a firm that protects the natural environment. Monsanto's motto is "Zero Spills, Zero Releases, Zero Incidents, and Zero Excuses." As indicated in the Natural Environment Perspective, there needs to be more Monsanto-type companies in Asia, a continent that became more polluted in the 1990s.

The 1990s may well be remembered as the decade of the environment. Earth itself has become a stakeholder for all business firms. Consumer interest in businesses' preserving nature's ecological balance and fostering a clean, healthy environment is high and growing. Evidence of this growing interest is that circulation of the top three natural environmental magazines, *Audubon*, *Greenpeace*, and *Sierra*, is soaring. Advertising revenues from these three magazines increased nearly 25 percent annually in the 1990s, when the magazine industry in general experienced slow or no growth in advertising revenues. This consumer interest is spurring companies to reconcile environmental and economic considerations.

The ecological challenge facing all organizations requires managers to formulate strategies that preserve and conserve natural resources and control pollution. Special natural environmental issues include ozone depletion, global warming, depletion of rain forests, destruction of animal habitats, protecting endangered species, developing biodegradable products and packages, waste management, clean air, clean water, erosion, destruction of natural resources, and pollution control. Firms increasingly are developing green product lines that are biodegradable and/or are made from recycled products. Green products sell well.

The Environmental Protection Agency recently reported that U.S. citizens and organizations spend more than about $200 billion annually on pollution abatement. Environmental concerns touch all aspects of a business's operations, including workplace risk exposures, packaging, waste reduction, energy use, alternative fuels, environmental cost accounting, and recycling practices. As indicated in the Natural Environment Perspective, preserving the natural environment makes good business sense.

Managing as if the earth matters requires an understanding of how international trade, competitiveness, and global resources are connected. Managing environmental affairs can no longer be simply a technical function performed by specialists in a firm; more emphasis must be placed on developing an environmental perspective among all employees and managers of the firm. Many companies are moving environmental affairs from the staff side of the organization to the line side, to make the corporate environmental group report directly to the chief operating officer.

Societies have been plagued by environmental disasters to such an extent recently that firms failing to recognize the importance of environmental issues and challenges could suffer severe consequences. Managing environmental affairs can no longer be an incidental or secondary function of company operations. Product design, manufacturing, and ultimate disposal should not merely reflect environmental considerations, but be driven by

NATURAL ENVIRONMENT

Does Asia Smell Bad?

"Since I left Taiwan 10 years ago to study in the United States, the quality of life, the air, and the water is 10 times worse. It's not worth it to have our economy grow so rapidly and have our environment ruined," says Jeff Chiang. In Kaohsiung, Taiwan, you can light the groundwater with a match at times. This is true in many Asian cities. Many large bodies of water in Asia are nearly biologically dead, including the Black Sea, the Caspian Sea, and Lake Baikal, the largest body of fresh water in the world.

Every uptick in economic expansion that has brought prosperity to Asia has come with a surge in smoke, hazardous waste, and garbage. The unrelenting push for growth has led numerous Asian countries to destroy their green landscapes, so celebrated in paintings, and their sacred rivers, so adored in poetry.

Most steel towns of China have sulfurous black skies. China is home to four of the world's 10 dirtiest cities, including Shenyang. Children going to school in Bangkok lose 10 IQ points to lead exposure. Leaded gasoline became illegal in Thailand only in 1997. The soil around Korean petrochemical plants is contaminated.

Asians are coming to realize that preserving the natural environment is much more than just a quality-of-life issue; it is an economic one. Pollution inhibits economic development. Improving the natural environment is an important theme for many political candidates in Asia in 1998.

Asian countries purchased over $7 billion in air pollution equipment in 1997. U.S. companies lag behind the world in exporting pollution control equipment, exporting just 6 percent of their output in environmental protection products, compared to 20 percent for both German and Japanese firms. Global opportunities for U.S. environmental firms are tremendous.

Source: Adapted from Susan Moffat, "Asia Stinks," Fortune (December 9, 1996): 121–132.

them. Firms that manage environmental affairs will enhance relations with consumers, regulators, vendors, and other industry players—substantially improving their prospects of success.

Firms should formulate and implement strategies from an environmental perspective. Environmental strategies could include developing or acquiring green businesses, divesting or altering environment-damaging businesses, striving to become a low-cost producer through waste minimization and energy conservation, and pursuing a differentiation strategy through green product features. In addition to creating strategies, firms could include an environmental representative on the board of directors, conduct regular environmental audits, implement bonuses for favorable environmental results, become involved in environmental issues and programs, incorporate environmental values in mission statements, establish environmentally oriented objectives, acquire environmental skills, and provide environmental training programs for company employees and managers.

CREATING A STRATEGY-SUPPORTIVE CULTURE

Strategists should strive to preserve, emphasize, and build upon aspects of an existing *culture* that support proposed new strategies. Aspects of an existing culture that are antagonistic to a proposed strategy should be identified and changed. Substantial research indicates that new strategies are often market-driven and dictated by competitive forces. For this reason, changing a firm's culture to fit a new strategy is usually more effective than changing a strategy to fit an existing culture. Numerous techniques are available to alter an organization's culture, including recruitment, training, transfer, promotion, restructure of an organization's design, role modeling, and positive reinforcement.

Jack Duncan described *triangulation* as an effective, multi-method technique for studying and altering a firm's culture.[9] Triangulation includes the combined use of obtrusive observation, self-administered questionnaires, and personal interviews to determine the nature of a firm's culture. The process of triangulation reveals needed changes in a firm's culture that could benefit strategy.

Schein indicated that the following elements are most useful in linking culture to strategy:

1. Formal statements of organizational philosophy, charters, creeds, materials used for recruitment and selection, and socialization
2. Designing of physical spaces, facades, buildings
3. Deliberate role modeling, teaching, and coaching by leaders
4. Explicit reward and status system, promotion criteria
5. Stories, legends, myths, and parables about key people and events
6. What leaders pay attention to, measure, and control
7. Leader reactions to critical incidents and organizational crises
8. How the organization is designed and structured
9. Organizational systems and procedures
10. Criteria used for recruitment, selection, promotion, leveling off, retirement, and "excommunication" of people.[10]

In the personal and religious side of life, the impact of loss and change is easy to see.[11] Memories of loss and change often haunt individuals and organizations for years. Ibsen wrote, "Rob the average man of his life illusion and you rob him of his happiness at the same stroke."[12] When attachments to a culture are severed in an organization's attempt to change direction, employees and managers often experience deep feelings of grief. This phenomenon commonly occurs when external conditions dictate the need for a new strategy. Managers and employees often struggle to find meaning in a situation that changed many years before. Some people find comfort in memories; others find solace in the present. Weak linkages between strategic management and organizational culture can jeopardize performance and success. Deal and Kennedy emphasized that making strategic changes in an organization always threatens a culture:

> . . . people form strong attachments to heroes, legends, the rituals of daily life, the hoopla of extravaganza and ceremonies, and all the symbols of the workplace. Change strips relationships and leaves employees confused, insecure, and often angry. Unless something can be done to provide support for transitions from old to new, the force of a culture can neutralize and emasculate strategy changes.[13]

The old corporate culture at AT&T consisted of lifetime careers, intense loyalty to the company, up-from-the-ranks management succession, dedication to the service ethos, and management by consensus. As AT&T moved from a regulated monopoly to a highly competitive environment in the 1980s, the company made numerous changes to create a culture that supported the new strategy; it redesigned its organizational structure, articulated its value system explicitly, provided management training to modify behavior in support of new values, revised recruiting aims and practices, and modified old symbols. AT&T abandoned its familiar logo, a bell with a circle, and adopted a new logo, a globe encircled by electronic communications, that symbolizes its new strategies to compete with Sprint and MCI.

PRODUCTION/OPERATIONS CONCERNS WHEN IMPLEMENTING STRATEGIES

Production/operations capabilities, limitations, and policies can significantly enhance or inhibit attainment of objectives. Production processes typically constitute more than 70 percent of a firm's total assets. A major part of the strategy-implementation process takes place at the production site. Production-related decisions on plant size, plant location, product design, choice of equipment, kind of tooling, size of inventory, inventory control, quality control, cost control, use of standards, job specialization, employee training, equipment and resource utilization, shipping and packaging, and technological innovation can have a dramatic impact on the success or failure of strategy-implementation efforts.

> There was a time when people were "factors of production," managed little differently from machines or capital. No more. The best people will not tolerate it. And if that way of managing ever generated productivity, it has the reverse effect today. While capital and machines either are or can be managed toward sameness, people are individuals. They must be managed that way. When companies encourage individual expression, it is difficult for them not to be successful (renew). The only true source of success in a company is the individual.[14]

Examples of adjustments in production systems that could be required to implement various strategies are provided in Table 7–3 for both for-profit and nonprofit organizations. For instance, note that when a bank formulates and selects a strategy to add 10 new branches, a production-related implementation concern is site location. As indicated in the Natural Environment Perspective, pollution control someday may become an important concern in production decisions for companies with operations in Asia.

TABLE 7–3
Production Management and Strategy Implementation

TYPE OF ORGANIZATION	STRATEGY BEING IMPLEMENTED	PRODUCTION SYSTEM ADJUSTMENTS
Hospital	Adding a cancer center (Product Development)	Purchase specialized equipment and add specialized people.
Bank	Adding 10 new branches (Market Development)	Perform site location analysis.
Beer brewery	Purchasing a barley farm operation (Backward Integration)	Revise the inventory control system.
Steel manufacturer	Acquiring a fast-food chain (Conglomerate Diversification)	Improve the quality control system.
Computer company	Purchasing a retail distribution chain (Forward Integration)	Alter the shipping, packaging, and transportation systems.

Just in Time (JIT) production approaches have withstood the test of time. JIT significantly reduces the costs of implementing strategies. With JIT, parts and materials are delivered to a production site just as they are needed, rather than being stockpiled as a hedge against later deliveries. Harley-Davidson reports that at one plant alone, JIT freed $22 million previously tied up in inventory and greatly reduced reorder lead time. *Industry Week* made the following observation about JIT:

> Most of the nation's 1,000 largest industrial companies are experimenting with, or preparing to implement, "Just in Time" manufacturing schemes. Suppliers who can't, or won't, play by the new rules are finding themselves on the sidelines. "Just in Case" just isn't good enough any more.[15]

Factors that should be studied before locating production facilities include the availability of major resources, the prevailing wage rates in the area, transportation costs related to shipping and receiving, the location of major markets, political risks in the area or country, and the availability of trainable employees.

For high-technology companies, production costs may not be as important as production flexibility because major product changes can be needed often. Industries such as biogenetics and plastics rely on production systems that must be flexible enough to allow frequent changes and rapid introduction of new products. An article in *Harvard Business Review* explained why some organizations get into trouble:

> They too slowly realize that a change in product strategy alters the tasks of a production system. These tasks, which can be stated in terms of requirements for cost, product flexibility, volume flexibility, product performance, and product consistency, determine which manufacturing policies are appropriate. As strategies shift over time, so must production policies covering the location and scale of manufacturing facilities, the choice of manufacturing process, the degree of vertical integration of each manufacturing facility, the use of R&D units, the control of the production system, and the licensing of technology.[16]

A common management practice, cross-training of employees, can facilitate strategy implementation and can yield many benefits. Employees gain a better understanding of the whole business and can contribute better ideas in planning sessions. Production/operations managers need to realize, however, that cross-training employees can create problems related to the following issues:

1. It can thrust managers into roles that emphasize counseling and coaching over directing and enforcing.
2. It can necessitate substantial investments in training and incentives.
3. It can be very time-consuming.
4. Skilled workers may resent unskilled workers who learn their jobs.
5. Older employees may not want to learn new skills.

HUMAN RESOURCE CONCERNS WHEN IMPLEMENTING STRATEGIES

The job of human resource manager is changing rapidly as companies downsize and reorganize in the 1990s. Strategic responsibilities of the human resource manager include assessing the staffing needs and costs for alternative strategies proposed during strategy formulation and developing a staffing plan for effectively implementing strategies. This plan must consider how best to manage spiraling health care insurance costs. Employers' health coverage expenses consume an average 26 percent of firms' net profits, even though most companies now require employees to pay part of their health insurance premiums. The plan must also include how to motivate employees and managers during a time when layoffs are common and workloads are high.

The human resource department must develop performance incentives that clearly link performance and pay to strategies. The process of empowering managers and employees through involvement in strategic-management activities yields the greatest benefits when all organizational members understand clearly how they will benefit personally if the firm does well. Linking company and personal benefits is a major new strategic responsibility of human resource managers. Other new responsibilities for human resource managers may include establishing and administering an *employee stock ownership plan* (*ESOP*), instituting an effective child care policy, and providing leadership for managers and employees to balance work and family.

A well-designed strategic-management system can fail if insufficient attention is given to the human resource dimension. Human resource problems that arise when businesses implement strategies can usually be traced to one of three causes: (1) disruption of social and political structures, (2) failure to match individuals' aptitudes with implementation tasks, and (3) inadequate top management support for implementation activities.[17]

Strategy implementation poses a threat to many managers and employees in an organization. New power and status relationships are anticipated and realized. New formal and informal groups' values, beliefs, and priorities may be largely unknown. Managers and employees may become engaged in resistance behavior as their roles, prerogatives, and power in the firm change. Disruption of social and political structures that accompany strategy execution must be anticipated and considered during strategy formulation and managed during strategy implementation.

A concern in matching managers with strategy is that jobs have specific and relatively static responsibilities, although people are dynamic in their personal development. Commonly used methods that match managers with strategies to be implemented include transferring managers, developing leadership workshops, offering career development activities, promotions, job enlargement, and job enrichment.

A number of other guidelines can help ensure that human relationships facilitate rather than disrupt strategy-implementation efforts. Specifically, managers should do a lot of chatting and informal questioning to stay abreast of how things are progressing and to know when to intervene. Managers can build support for strategy-implementation efforts by giving few orders, announcing few decisions, depending heavily on informal questioning, and seeking to probe and clarify until a consensus emerges. Key thrusts that succeed should be rewarded generously and visibly. A sense of humor is important, too. According to Adia Personnel Services, 72 percent of personnel executives nationwide say that humor is appropriate in discussions with colleagues; 63 percent say humor is appropriate in job interviews; 58 percent say humor is appropriate in performance reviews; and 53 percent say humor is appropriate in tense meetings.

It is suprising that so often during strategy formulation, individual values, skills, and abilities needed for successful strategy implementation are not considered. It is rare that a firm selecting new strategies or significantly altering existing strategies possesses the right line and staff personnel in the right positions for successful strategy implementation. The need to match individual aptitudes with strategy-implementation tasks should be considered in strategy choice.

Inadequate support from strategists for implementation activities often undermines organizational success. Chief executive officers, small business owners, and government agency heads must be personally committed to strategy implementation and express this commitment in highly visible ways. Strategists' formal statements about the importance of strategic management must be consistent with actual support and rewards given for activities completed and objectives reached. Otherwise, stress created by inconsistency can cause uncertainty among managers and employees at all levels.

Perhaps the best method for preventing and overcoming human resource problems in strategic management is to actively involve as many managers and employees as possible in the process. Although time-consuming, this approach builds understanding, trust, commitment, and ownership and reduces resentment and hostility. The true potential of strategy formulation and implementation resides in people.

EMPLOYEE STOCK OWNERSHIP PLANS (ESOPs)

An ESOP is a tax-qualified, defined-contribution, employee-benefit plan whereby employees purchase stock of the company through borrowed money or cash contributions. ESOPs empower employees to work as owners; this is a primary reason why the number of ESOPs grew dramatically throughout the 1980s and 1990s to more than 10,000 plans covering more than 15 million employees. ESOPs now control more than $80 billion in corporate stock in the United States.

Besides reducing worker alienation and stimulating productivity, ESOPs allow firms other benefits, such as substantial tax savings. Principal, interest, and dividend payments on ESOP-funded debt are tax-deductible. Banks lend money to ESOPs at interest rates below prime. This money can be repaid in pretax dollars, lowering the debt service as much as 30 percent in some cases.

If an ESOP owns more than 50 percent of the firm, those who lend money to the ESOP are taxed on only 50 percent of the income received on the loans. ESOPs are not for every firm, however, because the initial legal, accounting, actuarial, and appraisal fees to set up an ESOP are about $50,000 for a small or mid-sized firm, with annual administration expenses of about $15,000. Analysts say ESOPs also do not work well in firms that have fluctuating payrolls and profits. Human resource managers in many firms conduct preliminary research to determine the desirability of an ESOP, and then facilitate its establishment and administration if benefits outweigh the costs.

To establish an ESOP, a firm sets up a trust fund and purchases shares of its stock, which are allocated to individual employee accounts. All full-time employees over age 21 usually participate in the plan. Allocations of stock to the trust are made on the basis of relative pay, seniority, or some other formula. When an ESOP borrows money to purchase stock, the debt is guaranteed by the company and thus appears on the firm's balance sheet. On average, ESOP employees get $1,300 worth of stock per year, but cannot take physical possession of the shares until they quit, retire, or die. The median level of employee ownership in ESOP plans is 30 to 40 percent, although the range is from about 10 to 100 percent.

Research confirms that ESOPs can have a dramatic positive effect on employee motivation and corporate performance, especially if ownership is coupled with expanded employee participation and involvement in decision making. Market surveys indicate that customers prefer to do business with firms that are employee-owned.

Many companies are following the lead of Polaroid, which established an ESOP as a tactic for preventing a hostile takeover. Polaroid's CEO MacAllister Booth says, "Twenty years from now we'll find that employees have a sizable stake in every major American corporation." (It is interesting to note here that Polaroid is chartered in the state of Delaware, which requires corporate suitors to acquire 85 percent of a target company's shares to complete a merger; over 50 percent of all American corporations are incorporated in Delaware for this reason.) Wyatt Cafeterias, a Southwestern U.S. operator of 120 cafeterias, also adopted the ESOP concept to prevent a hostile takeover. Employee productivity at Wyatt greatly increased since the ESOP began, as illustrated in the following quote:

> The key employee in our entire organization is the person serving the customer on the cafeteria line. In the past, because of high employee turnover and entry-level wages for many line jobs, these employees received far less attention and recognition than managers. We now tell the tea cart server, "You own the place. Don't wait for the manager to tell you how to do your job better or how to provide better service. You take care of it." Sure, we're looking for productivity increases, but since we began pushing decisions down to the level of people who deal directly with customers, we've discovered an awesome side effect—suddenly the work crews have this "happy to be here" attitude that the customers really love.[18]

Companies such as Avis, Procter & Gamble, BellSouth, ITT, Xerox, Delta, Austin Industries, Health Trust, The Parsons Corporation, Dyncorp, and Charter Medical have established ESOPs to assist strategists in divesting divisions, going private, and consummating leveraged buyouts. ESOPs can be found today in all kinds of firms, from small retailers to large manufacturers. Employees can own any amount from 1 percent to 100 percent of the company. Nearly all ESOPs are established in healthy firms, not failing firms.

BALANCING WORK LIFE AND HOME LIFE Work/family strategies have become so popular among companies in the 1990s that the strategies now represent a competitive advantage for those firms that offer such benefits as elder care assistance, flexible scheduling, job sharing, adoption benefits, an on-site summer camp, employee help lines, pet care, and even lawn service referrals. New corporate titles such as Work/Life Coordinator and Director of Diversity are becoming common. *Business Week* and the Center on Work and Family at Boston University have for the first time begun rating companies on their family-friendly strategies. The 10 U.S. companies that received the highest ratings for providing work-family benefits are given below in rank order:[19]

	1996	1997
1.	DuPont	MBNA America Bank
2.	Eddie Bauer	Motorola
3.	Eli Lilly	Barnett Banks
4.	First Tennessee Bank	Hewlett-Packard
5.	Hewlett-Packard	Unum Life Insurance
6.	Marriott International	Lincoln National
7.	MBNA America Bank	Merrill Lynch
8.	Merrill Lynch	DuPont
9.	Motorola	TRW
10.	Unum Life Insurance	Cigna

Human resource managers need to foster more effective balancing of professional and private lives because nearly 60 million people in the United States are now part of two-career families. A corporate objective to become more lean and mean must today include consideration for the fact that a good home life contributes immensely to a good work life.

> You can count on baby boomers to force the issue of family versus work onto the corporate agenda. Fully 73 percent of all women age 25 to 34 now work for pay, as do half of all women with babies under a year old. For them and their husbands, child care, flexible hours, and job sharing are pressing concerns.[20]

The work/family issue is no longer just a women's problem. Some specific measures that firms are taking to address this issue are providing spouse relocation assistance as an employee benefit, providing company resources for family recreational and educational use, establishing employee country clubs such as those at IBM and Bethlehem Steel, and creating family/work interaction opportunities. A recent study by Joseph Pleck of Wheaton College found that in companies that do not offer paternity leave for fathers as a benefit, most men take short informal paternity leaves anyway by combining vacation time and sick days.

Some organizations have developed family days, when family members are invited into the workplace, taken on plant or office tours, dined by management, and given a chance to see exactly what other family members do each day. Family days are inexpensive and increase the employee's pride in working for the organization. Flexible working hours during the week are another human resource response to the need for individuals to balance work life and home life. The work/family topic is being made part of the agenda at meetings and thus is becoming discussable in many organizations.

Research indicates that employees who are dissatisfied with child care arrangements are most likely to be absent or unproductive.[21] Lack of adequate child care in a community can be a deterrent in recruiting and retaining good managers and employees. Some benefits of on-site child care facilities are improved employee relations, reduced absenteeism and turnover, increased productivity, enhanced recruitment, and improved community relations.

A recent survey of women managers revealed that one-third would leave their present employer for another employer offering child care assistance. The Conference Board recently reported that more than 500 firms in the United States had created on-site or near-site child care centers for their employees, including Merck, Campbell Soup, Hoffman–La Roche, Stride-Rite, Johnson Wax, CIGNA, Champion International, Walt Disney World, and Playboy Resorts.

Other common child care service arrangements include employer-sponsored day care, child care information, and referral services. IBM, Steelcase, Honeywell, Citibank, 3M, and Southland have established contracts with third-party child care information and referral services.

The nation's largest employer-sponsored day care center is operated by Intermedics, a Texas-based medical instruments firm. Employee turnover declined 23 percent the first year Intermedics instituted the center. Due to the high cost of child care, numerous firms are forming partnerships to build and manage child care facilities. The largest collaboration so far is the new $2 million, 194-child day care center in Charlotte, financed and operated by IBM, American Express, Allstate, Duke Power, and University Research Park. The teacher-child ratio at this center is 50 percent lower than required by North Carolina law. Other large partnership child care centers have recently been built in Minneapolis, Rochester, Dallas–Fort Worth, and New York City. In Virginia, 22 companies recently pooled $100,000 to establish a parent-run child care cooperative. Other companies that effectively address child care concerns of managers and employees include Clorox and Nyloncraft. Even small businesses are beginning to offer child care benefits for employees.

Some small firms that now offer an on-site day care center for employees' children include Bowles Corporation in North Ferrisburg, Vermont; Byrne Electrical Specialists in Rockford, Michigan; Chalet Dental Clinic in Yakima, Washington; and Stackpole Ltd. in Brownsville, Tennessee.

CORPORATE FITNESS PROGRAMS   At least 10,000 U.S. employers now offer programs to improve or maintain their employees' health, such as programs to stop smoking, reduce cholesterol, promote regular exercise, and control high blood pressure. Another 1,000 American firms offer on-site, fully equipped fitness centers to promote good employee health. Perhaps the leader in this area is Johnson & Johnson, which provides an 11,000-square-foot fitness center, aerobics and other exercise classes, seminars on AIDS and alcohol abuse, and an indoor track. J & J's program is called Live for Life.

CONCLUSION

Successful strategy formulation does not at all guarantee successful strategy implementation. Although inextricably interdependent, strategy formulation and strategy implementation are characteristically different. In a single word, strategy implementation means *change*. It is widely agreed that "the real work begins after strategies are formulated." Successful strategy implementation requires support, discipline, motivation, and hard work from all managers and employees. It is sometimes frightening to think that a single individual can sabotage strategy-implementation efforts irreparably.

Formulating the right strategies is not enough, because managers and employees must be motivated to implement those strategies. Management issues considered central to strategy implementation include matching organizational structure with strategy, linking performance and pay to strategies, creating an organizational climate conducive to change, managing political relationships, creating a strategy-supportive culture, adapting production/operations processes, and managing human resources. Establishing annual objectives, devising policies, and allocating resources are central strategy-implementation activities common to all organizations. Depending on the size and type of organization, other management issues could be equally important to successful strategy implementation.

We invite you to visit the DAVID page on the Prentice Hall Web site at
www.prenhall.com/davidsm
for this chapter's World Wide Web exercises.

TAKE
IT TO
THE NET

KEY TERMS AND CONCEPTS

ISSUES FOR REVIEW AND DISCUSSION

1. Allocating resources can be a political and an ad hoc activity in firms that do not use strategic management. Why is this true? Does adopting strategic management ensure easy resource allocation? Why?

2. Compare strategy formulation with strategy implementation in terms of each being an art or a science.

3. Describe the relationship between annual objectives and policies.

4. Identify a long-term objective and two supporting annual objectives for a familiar organization.

5. Identify and discuss three policies that apply to your present business policy class.

6. Explain the following statement: Horizontal consistency of goals is as important as vertical consistency.

7. Describe several reasons why conflict may occur during objective-setting activities.

8. In your opinion, what approaches to conflict resolution would be best for resolving a disagreement between a personnel manager and a sales manager over the firing of a particular salesperson? Why?

9. Describe the organizational culture of your college or university.

10. Explain why organizational structure is so important in strategy implementation.

11. In your opinion, how many separate divisions could an organization reasonably have without using an SBU-type organizational structure? Why?

12. Would you recommend a divisional structure by geographic area, product, customer, or process for a medium-sized bank in your local area? Why?

13. What are the advantages and disadvantages of decentralizing the wage and salary function of an organization? How could this be accomplished?

14. Consider a college organization with which you are familiar. How did management issues affect strategy implementation in that organization?

15. As production manager of a local newspaper, what problems would you anticipate in implementing a strategy to increase the average number of pages in the paper by 40 percent?

16. Read an article from the suggested readings at the end of this chapter and give a summary report to the class revealing your thoughts on the topic.

17. Do you believe expenditures for child care or fitness facilities are warranted from a cost/benefit perspective? Why or why not?

18. Explain why successful strategy implementation often hinges on whether the strategy-formulation process empowers managers and employees.

NOTES

1. A. G. Bedeian and W. F. Glueck, *Management*, 3rd. ed. (Chicago: The Dryden Press, 1983): 212.

2. Boris Yavits and William Newman, *Strategy in Action: The Execution, Politics, and Payoff of Business Planning* (New York: The Free Press, 1982): 195.

3. "Want to Be a Manager? Many People Say No, Calling Job Miserable," *The Wall Street Journal* (April 4, 1997): 1. Also, Stephanie Armour, "Management Loses Its Allure," *USA Today* (October 10, 1997): 1B.

4. Yavits and Newman, 58.

5. Perry Pascarella, "The Toughest Turnaround of All," *Industry Week* (April 2, 1984): 33. Reprinted with permission from *Industry Week*, April 2, 1984. Copyright Renton Publishing Inc., Cleveland, Ohio.

6. Jack Duncan, *Management* (New York: Random House, 1983): 381–390.

7. H. Igor Ansoff, "Strategic Management of Technology," *Journal of Business Strategy* 7, no. 3 (Winter 1987): 38.

8. Robert Waterman, Jr., "How the Best Get Better," *Business Week* (September 14, 1987): 104.

9. Jack Duncan, "Organizational Culture: Getting a Fix on an Elusive Concept," *Academy of Management Executive*, no. 3 (August 1989): 229.

10. E. H. Schein, "The Role of the Founder in Creating Organizational Culture," *Organizational Dynamics* (Summer 1983): 13–28.

11. T. Deal and A. Kennedy, "Culture: A New Look Through Old Lenses," *Journal of Applied Behavioral Science* 19, no. 4 (1983): 498–504.

12. H. Ibsen, "The Wild Duck," in O. G. Brochett and L. Brochett (eds.), *Plays for the Theater* (New York: Holt, Rinehart & Winston, 1967). Also, R. Pascale, "The Paradox of 'Corporate Culture': Reconciling Ourselves to Socialization," *California Management Review* 28, 2 (1985): 26, 37–40.

13. T. Deal and A. Kennedy, *Corporate Cultures: The Rites and Rituals of Corporate Life* (Reading, Massachusetts: Addison-Wesley, 1982).

14. Robert Waterman, Jr., "The Renewal Factor," *Business Week* (September 14, 1987): 100.

15. "Just in Time: Putting the Squeeze on Suppliers," *Industry Week* (July 9, 1984): 59.

16. Robert Stobaugh and Piero Telesio, "Match Manufacturing Policies and Product Strategy," *Harvard Business Review* 61, no. 2 (March–April 1983): 113.

17. R. T. Lenz and Marjorie Lyles, "Managing Human Resource Problems in Strategy Planning Systems," *Journal of Business Strategy* 60, no. 4 (Spring 1986): 58.

18. J. Warren Henry, "ESOPs with Productivity Payoffs," *Journal of Business Strategy* (July–August 1989): 33.

19. "Balancing Work and Family," *Business Week* (September 16, 1996): 74–80. Also, Keith Hammonds, "Work and Family," *Business Week* (September 15, 1997): 96–99.

20. Ronald Henkoff, "Is Greed Dead?" *Fortune* (August 14, 1989): 49.

21. Richard Levine, "Childcare: Inching up the Corporate Agenda," *Management Review* 78, no. 1 (January 1989): 43.

CURRENT READINGS

Amason, Allen C. "Distinguishing the Effects of Functional and Dysfunctional Conflict on Strategic Decision Making: Resolving a Paradox for Top Management Teams." *Academy of Management Journal* 39, no. 1 (February 1996): 123–148.

Bruton, Garry D., J. Kay Keels, and Christopher L. Shook. "Downsizing the Firm: Answering the Strategic Questions." *Academy of Management Executive* 10, no. 2 (May 1996): 38–45.

Brynjolfsson, Erik, Amy Austin, and Renshaw and Marshall Van Alstyne. "The Matrix of Change." *Sloan Management Review* 38, no. 2 (Winter 1997): 37–54.

Dutton, J. E., S. J. Ashford, R. M. O'Neill, E. Hayes, and E. E. Wierba. "Reading the Wind: How Middle Managers Assess the Context for Selling Issues to Top Managers." *Strategic Management Journal* 18, no. 5 (May 1997): 407–417.

Eisenhardt, Kathleen M., Jean L. Kahwajy, and L. J. Bourgeois III. "Conflict and Strategic Choice: How Top Management Teams Disagree." *California Management Review* 39, no. 2 (Winter 1997): 42–62.

Ettorre, Barbara. "The Empowerment Gap: Hype vs. Reality." *Management Review* (July–August 1997): 10–14.

Gomez-Mejia, Luis and Robert M. Wiserman. "Reframing Executive Compensation: An Assessment and Outlook." *Journal of Management* 23, no. 3 (1997): 291–374.

Gould, R. Morgan. "Getting from Strategy to Action: Processes for Continuous Change." *Long Range Planning* 29, no. 3 (June 1996): 278–289.

Hatfield, D. E., J. P. Liebeskind, and T. C. Opler. "The Effects of Corporate Restructuring on Aggregate Industry Specialization." *Strategic Management Journal* 17, no. 1 (January 1996): 55–72.

Heifetz, Ronald A. and Donald L. Laurie. "The Work of Leadership." *Harvard Business Review* (January–February 1997): 124–134.

Huselid, Mark A., Susan E. Jackson, and Randall S. Schuler. "Technical and Strategic Human Resource Management Effectiveness as Determinants of Firm Peformance." *Academy of Management Journal* 40, no. 1 (February 1997). 171–188.

Imberman, Woodruff. "Gainsharing: A Lemon or Lemonade?" *Business Horizons* 39, no. 1 (January–February 1996): 36–40.

Kubasek, Nancy. "Following Canada's Lead: Preventing Prosecution for Environmental Crimes." *Business Horizons* 39, no. 5 (September–October 1996): 64–70.

London, Manuel. "Redeployment and Continuous Learning in the 21st Century: Hard Lessons and Positive Examples from the Downsizing Era." *Academy of Management Executive* 10, no. 4 (November 1996): 67–79.

Mabert, Vincent A. and Roger W. Schmenner. "Assessing the Roller Coaster of Downsizing." *Business Horizons* 40, no. 4 (July–August 1997): 45–53.

Magnan, M. L. and S. St-Onge. "Bank Performance and Executive Compensation: A Managerial Discretion Perspective." *Strategic Management Journal* 18, no. 7 (August 1997): 573–582.

Majchrzak, Ann and Qianwei Wang. "Breaking the Functional Mind-Set in Process Organizations." *Harvard Business Review* (September–October 1996): 92–101.

Malone, Thomas W. "Is Empowerment Just a Fad? Control, Decision Making, and IT." *Sloan Management Review* 38, no. 2 (Winter 1997): 23–36.

Markides, Constantinos C. and Peter J. Williamson. "Corporate Diversification and Organizational Structure: A Resource-Based View." *Academy of Management Journal* 39, no. 2 (April 1996): 340–367.

Maxwell, John W. "What To Do When Win-Win Won't Work: Environmental Strategies for Costly Regulation." *Business Horizons* 39, no. 5 (September–October 1996): 60–63.

McMaster, Mike. "Foresight: Exploring the Structure of the Future." *Long Range Planning* 29, no. 2 (April 1996): 149–155.

Montemayor, Edilberto F. "Congruence Between Pay Policy and Competitive Strategy in High-Performing Firms." *Journal of Management* 22, no. 6 (1996): 889–912.

Reichers, Arnon E., John P. Wanous, and James T. Austin. "Understanding and Managing Cynicism About Organizational Change." *Academy of Management Executive* 11, no. 1 (February 1997): 48–59.

Roth, Kendall and Sharon O'Donnell. "Foreign Subsidiary Compensation Strategy: An Agency Theory Perspective" *Academy of Management Journal* 39, no. 3 (June 1996): 678–703.

Shi, J. Stephen and Jane M. Kane. "Green Issues." *Business Horizons* 39, no. 1 (January–February 1996): 65–70.

Smith, K. G., C. M. Grimm, G. Young, and S. Wally. "Strategic Groups and Rivalrous Firm Behavior: Towards a Reconciliation." *Strategic Management Journal* 18, no. 2 (February 1997): 149–158.

Sparrowe, Raymond T. and Robert C. Liden. "Process and Structure in Leader-Member Exchange." *Academy of Management Review* 22, no. 2 (April 1997): 522–552.

Strebel, Paul. "Why Do Employees Resist Change?" *Harvard Business Review* (May–June 1996): 86–94.

Taylor, Sully, Schon Beechler, and Nancy Napier. "Toward an Integrative Model of Strategic International Human Resource Management." *Academy of Management Review* 21, no. 4 (October 1996): 959–985.

Ward, Peter T., Deborah J. Bickford, and G. Keong Leong. "Configurations of Manufacturing Strategy, Business Strategy, Environment and Structure." *Journal of Management* 22, no. 4 (1996): 597–607.

EXPERIENTIAL EXERCISES

REVISING HERSHEY'S ORGANIZATIONAL CHART

PURPOSE

Developing and altering organizational charts is an important skill for strategists to possess. This exercise can improve your skill in altering an organization's hierarchical structure in response to new strategies being formulated.

INSTRUCTIONS

Step 1 Turn back to Hershey's organizational chart given in the Cohesion Case (p. 33).

Step 2 On a separate sheet of paper, diagram an organizational chart that you believe would best suit Hershey's needs if the company decided to form a divisional structure by product.

Step 3 Provide as much detail in your chart as possible, including the names of individuals and the titles of positions.

MATCHING MANAGERS WITH STRATEGY

PURPOSE

For many years, strategists believed that good managers could adapt to handle any situation. Consequently, strategists rarely replaced or transferred managers as the need arose to implement new strategies. Today, this situation is changing. Research supports the notion that certain management characteristics are needed for certain strategic situations.[1] Chase Manhattan Bank, Heublein, Texas Instruments, Corning Glass, and General Electric are examples of companies that match managers to strategic requirements.

This exercise can improve your awareness and understanding of particular managerial characteristics that have been found to be most desirable for implementing certain types of strategies. Having the right managers in the right jobs can determine the success or failure of strategy-implementation efforts. This exercise is based on a framework that has proved to be useful in "matching managers to strategy."[2]

INSTRUCTIONS

Your task is to match specific managerial characteristics with particular generic strategies. Four broad types of strategies are examined:

1. Retrenchment/Turnaround
2. Intensive (market penetration, market development, and product development)
3. Liquidation/Divestiture
4. Integration (backward, forward, and horizontal)

Five managerial characteristics have been found to be associated with each of these strategies. On a separate sheet of paper, list the four types of strategies. Beside each strategy, record the appropriate letter of the five managerial characteristics that you believe are most needed to successfully implement those strategies. Each of the managerial characteristics in the following list should be used only once in completing this exercise.

A. Is technically knowledgeable—"knows the business"
B. Is "callous"—tough-minded, determined, willing to be the bad guy
C. Is "take charge"–oriented—strong leader
D. Is a good negotiator
E. Wants to be respected, not necessarily liked
F. Has good analytical ability
G. Is low glory-seeking—willing to do dirty jobs; does not want glamour
H. Has excellent staffing skills
I. Handles pressure well
J. Is a risk taker
K. Has good relationship-building skills
L. Has good organizational and team-building skills
M. Is oriented to getting out the most efficiency, not growth
N. Anticipates problems—"problem finder"
O. Has strong analytical and diagnostic skills, especially financial
P. Is an excellent business strategist
Q. Has good communication skills
R. Has personal magnetism
S. Is highly analytical—focuses on costs/benefits, does not easily accept current ways of doing things
T. Has good interpersonal influence

NOTES

1. Marc Gerstein and Heather Reisman, "Strategic Selection: Matching Executives to Business Conditions," *Sloan Management Review* 24, no. 2 (Winter 1983): 33–47.
2. Ibid., 37.

Experiential Exercise 7C

DO ORGANIZATIONS REALLY ESTABLISH OBJECTIVES?

PURPOSE

Objectives provide direction, allow synergy, aid in evaluation, establish priorities, reduce uncertainty, minimize conflicts, stimulate exertion, and aid in both the allocation of resources and the design of jobs. This exercise will enhance your understanding of how organizations use or misuse objectives.

INSTRUCTIONS

Step 1 Join with one other person in class to form a two-person team.

Step 2 Contact by telephone the owner or manager of an organization in your city or town. Request a 30-minute personal interview or meeting with that person for the purpose of discussing "business objectives." During your meeting, seek answers to the following questions:

1. Do you believe it is important for a business to establish and clearly communicate long-term and annual objectives? Why or why not?
2. Does your organization establish objectives? If yes, what type and how many? How are the objectives communicated to individuals? Are your firm's objectives in written form or simply communicated orally?
3. To what extent are managers and employees involved in the process of establishing objectives?
4. How often are your business objectives revised and by what process?

Step 3 Take good notes during the interview. Let one person be the note taker and one person do most of the talking. Have your notes typed up and ready to turn in to your professor.

Step 4 Prepare a five-minute oral presentation for the class, reporting the results of your interview. Turn in your typed report.

Experiential Exercise 7D

UNDERSTANDING MY UNIVERSITY'S CULTURE

PURPOSE

It is something of an art to uncover the basic values and beliefs that are buried deeply in an organization's rich collection of stories, language, heroes, heroines, and rituals, yet culture can be the most important factor in implementing strategies.

INSTRUCTIONS

Step 1 On a separate sheet of paper, list the following terms: hero/heroine, belief, metaphor, language, value, symbol, story, legend, saga, folktale, myth, ceremonial, rite, and ritual.

Step 2 For your college or university, give examples of each term. If necessary, speak with faculty, staff, alumni, administration, or fellow students of the institution to identify examples of each term. Refer back to p. 236 for definitions of the terms if needed.

Step 3 Report your findings to the class. Tell the class how you feel regarding cultural products being consciously used to help implement strategies.

CHAPTER 8

Implementing Strategies: Marketing, Finance/ Accounting, R&D, and CIS Issues

CHAPTER OUTLINE

◆ **THE NATURE OF STRATEGY IMPLEMENTATION**

◆ **MARKETING ISSUES**

◆ **FINANCE/ACCOUNTING ISSUES**

◆ **RESEARCH AND DEVELOPMENT (R&D) ISSUES**

◆ **COMPUTER INFORMATION SYSTEMS (CIS) ISSUES**

■ EXPERIENTIAL EXERCISE 8A
Developing a Product Positioning Map for Hershey Foods

■ EXPERIENTIAL EXERCISE 8B
Performing an EPS/EBIT Analysis for Hershey Foods

■ EXPERIENTIAL EXERCISE 8C
Preparing Pro Forma Financial Statements for Hershey Foods

■ EXPERIENTIAL EXERCISE 8D
Determining the Cash Value of Hershey Foods

■ EXPERIENTIAL EXERCISE 8E
Developing a Product Positioning Map for My University

■ EXPERIENTIAL EXERCISE 8F
Do Banks Require Pro Forma Statements?

CHAPTER OBJECTIVES

After studying this chapter, you should be able to do the following:

1. Explain market segmentation and product positioning as strategy-implementation tools.

2. Discuss procedures for determining the worth of a business.

3. Explain why pro forma financial analysis is a central strategy-implementation tool.

4. Explain how to evaluate the attractiveness of debt versus stock as a source of capital to implement strategies.

5. Discuss the nature and role of research and development in strategy implementation.

6. Explain how computer information systems can determine the success of strategy-implementation efforts.

NOTABLE QUOTES

*T*he greatest strategy is doomed if it's implemented badly.——BERNARD REIMANN

*O*rganizations should approach all tasks with the idea that they can be accomplished in a superior fashion.——THOMAS WATSON, JR.

*T*here is no "perfect" strategic decision. One always has to pay a price. One always has to balance conflicting objectives, conflicting opinions, and conflicting priorities. The best strategic decision is only an approximation——and a risk.——PETER DRUCKER

*T*he real question isn't how well you're doing today against your own history, but how you're doing against your competitors.——DONALD KRESS

*E*ffective organizational responses are retarded not so much by failing to recognize what needs to be done, but by not doing what ought to be done.——JOHN KEANE

*A*s market windows open and close more quickly, it is important that R&D be tied more closely to corporate strategy.——WILLIAM SPENSER

*M*ost of the time, strategists should not be formulating strategy at all; they should be getting on with implementing strategies they already have.——HENRY MINTZBERG

*T*he best plan is only a plan, that is, good intentions. Unless commitment is made, there are only promises and hopes, but no plan.——PETER DRUCKER

Strategies have no chance of being implemented successfully in organizations that do not market goods and services well, in firms that cannot raise needed working capital, in firms that produce technologically inferior products, or in firms that have a weak information system. This chapter examines marketing, finance/accounting, R&D, and computer information systems (CIS) issues that are central to effective strategy implementation. Special topics include market segmentation, market positioning, evaluating the worth of a business, determining to what extent debt and/or stock should be used as a source of capital, developing pro forma financial statements, contracting R&D outside the firm, and creating an information support system. Manager and employee involvement and participation are essential for success in marketing, finance/accounting, R&D, and CIS activities.

THE NATURE OF STRATEGY IMPLEMENTATION

The quarterback can call the best play possible in the huddle, but that does not mean the play will go for a touchdown. The team may even lose yardage unless the play is executed (implemented) well. Less than 10 percent of strategies formulated are successfully implemented! There are many reasons for this low success rate, including failing to segment markets appropriately, paying too much for a new acquisition, falling behind competitors in R&D, and not recognizing the benefit of computers in managing information.

Strategy implementation directly affects the lives of plant managers, division managers, department managers, sales managers, product managers, project managers, personnel managers, staff managers, supervisors, and all employees. In some situations, individuals may not have participated in the strategy-formulation process at all and may not appreciate, understand, or even accept the work and thought that went into strategy formulation. There may even be foot dragging or resistance on their part. Managers and employees who do not understand the business and are not committed to the business may attempt to sabotage strategy-implementation efforts in hopes that the organization will return to its old ways. The strategy-implementation stage of the strategic-management process is emphasized in Figure 8–1.

MARKETING ISSUES

Countless marketing variables affect the success or failure of strategy implementation, and the scope of this text does not allow addressing all those issues. However, two variables are of central importance to strategy implementation: *market segmentation* and *product positioning*. Market segmentation and product positioning rank as marketing's most important contributions to strategic management. Some examples of marketing decisions that may require policies are as follows:

1. To use exclusive dealerships or multiple channels of distribution
2. To use heavy, light, or no TV advertising
3. To limit (or not) the share of business done with a single customer
4. To be a price leader or a price follower
5. To offer a complete or limited warranty
6. To reward salespeople based on straight salary, straight commission, or a combination salary/commission

FIGURE 8–1
A Comprehensive Strategic-Management Model

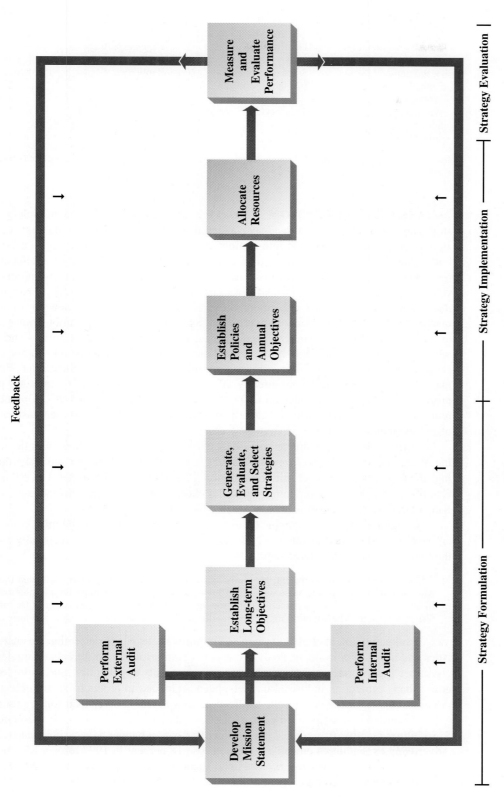

TABLE 8–1
**The Marketing Mix
Component Factors**

PRODUCT	PLACE	PROMOTION	PRICE
Quality	Distribution channels	Advertising	Level
Features and options	Distribution coverage	Personal selling	Discounts and
Style	Outlet location	Sales promotion	allowances
Brand name	Sales territories	Publicity	Payment terms
Packaging	Inventory levels and		
Product line	locations		
Warranty	Transportation carriers		
Service level			
Other services			

Source: E. Jerome McCarthy, *Basic Marketing: A Managerial Approach*, 9th ed. (Homewood, Illinois: Richard D. Irwin, Inc., 1987): 37–44.

MARKET SEGMENTATION Market segmentation is widely used in implementing strategies, especially for small and specialized firms. Market segmentation can be defined as the subdividing of a market into distinct subsets of customers according to needs and buying habits. Market segmentation is an important variable in strategy implementation for at least three major reasons. First, strategies such as market development, product development, market penetration, and diversification require increased sales through new markets and products. To implement these strategies successfully, new or improved market-segmentation approaches are required. Second, market segmentation allows a firm to operate with limited resources because mass production, mass distribution, and mass advertising are not required. Market segmentation can enable a small firm to compete successfully with a large firm by maximizing per-unit profits and per-segment sales. Finally, market segmentation decisions directly affect *marketing mix variables*: product, place, promotion, and price, as indicated in Table 8–1. For example, SnackWells, a pioneer in reduced-fat snacks, has shifted its advertising emphasis from low-fat to great taste as part of its new market segmentation strategy.

Perhaps the most dramatic late-1990s market segmentation strategy was the targeting of regional tastes. Firms from McDonald's to General Motors are increasingly modifying their products to meet different regional preferences within the United States. Campbell's has a spicier version of its nacho cheese soup for the Southwest, and Burger King offers breakfast burritos in New Mexico but not in South Carolina.

Geographic and demographic bases for segmenting markets are the most commonly employed, as illustrated in Table 8–2. Beer producers, for example, have generally divided the light beer market into three segments:

> The light beer market can be meaningfully separated into three motivation segments: those who are calorie-conscious, those who prefer less alcohol, and those who prefer a lighter taste. In fact, it is possible for one person to consume light beer on three separate occasions for three different reasons. The situation may therefore dictate the segment the consumer falls into.[1]

Evaluating potential market segments requires strategists to determine the characteristics and needs of consumers, analyze consumer similarities and differences, and develop consumer group profiles. Segmenting consumer markets is generally much simpler and easier than segmenting industrial markets, because industrial products, such as electronic circuits and forklifts, have multiple applications and appeal to diverse customer groups.

Advertising strategy follows market segmentation. In 1997, U.S. firms spent over $186 billion on advertising, a 6.2 percent increase over a banner advertising year in 1996. Advertising expenditures on cable television rose 18 percent in 1997 to over $5.3 billion, in contrast to only a 2 percent increase in ad spending on network television. Airlines and cigarette makers, on average, spent 20 percent less in 1997 than in 1996, while computer,

VARIABLE	TYPICAL BREAKDOWNS
GEOGRAPHIC	
Region	Pacific, Mountain, West North Central, West South Central, East North Central, East South Central, South Atlantic, Middle Atlantic, New England
County Size	A, B, C, D
City Size	Under 5,000; 5,000–20,000; 20,000–50,000; 50,000–100,000; 100,000–250,000; 250,000–500,000; 500,000–1,000,000; 1,000,000–4,000,000; 4,000,000 or over
Density	Urban, suburban, rural
Climate	Northern, southern
DEMOGRAPHIC	
Age	Under 6, 6–11, 12–19, 20–34, 35–49, 50–64, 65+
Sex	Male, female
Family Size	1–2, 3–4, 5+
Family Life Cycle	Young, single; young, married, no children; young, married, youngest child under 6; young, married, youngest child 6 or over; older, married, with children; older, married, no children under 18; older, single; other
Income	Under $10,000; $10,001–$15,000; $15,001–$20,000; $20,001–$30,000; $30,001–$50,000; $50,001–$70,000; $70,001–$100,000; over $100,000
Occupation	Professional and technical; managers, officials, and proprietors; clerical, sales; craftsmen, foremen; operatives; farmers; retired; students; housewives; unemployed
Education	Grade school or less; some high school; high school graduate; some college; college graduate
Religion	Catholic, Protestant, Jewish, other
Race	White, Asian, Hispanic, African American
Nationality	American, British, French, German, Scandinavian, Italian, Latin American, Middle Eastern, Japanese
PSYCHOGRAPHIC	
Social Class	Lower lowers, upper lowers, lower middles, upper middles, lower uppers, upper uppers
Personality	Compulsive, gregarious, authoritarian, ambitious
BEHAVIORAL	
Use Occasion	Regular occasion, special occasion
Benefits Sought	Quality, service, economy
User Status	Nonuser, ex-user, potential user, first-time user, regular user
Usage Rate	Light user, medium user, heavy user
Loyalty Status	None, medium, strong, absolute
Readiness Stage	Unaware, aware, informed, interested, desirous, intending to buy
Attitude Toward Product	Enthusiastic, positive, indifferent, negative, hostile

TABLE 8–2
Alternative Bases for Market Segmentation

Source: Adapted from Philip Kotler, *Marketing Management: Analysis, Planning and Control*, © 1984: 256. Adapted by permission of Prentice-Hall, Inc., Englewood Cliffs, New Jersey.

liquor, and stock brokerage firms spent 20 percent more. Companies such as Pizza Hut and McDonald's have recently used advertisements that feature their own employees. (These ads have not worked well.) Pizza Hut has a 23 percent market share of the $21 billion restaurant pizza market, followed by Domino's with 11 percent and Little Caesars with 8.5 percent.

Market segmentation matrices and decision trees can facilitate implementing strategies effectively. An example of a matrix for segmenting the lawn fertilizer market is provided in Figure 8–2. Similar matrices could be developed for almost any market, product, or service. Market segmentation strategies in the high-tech arcade business in the United

FIGURE 8–2

Tools for Segmenting the Lawn Fertilizer Market

Heavy users	High income	Central city
		Suburban
		Rural
	Low income	Central city
		Suburban
		Rural
Light users	High income	Central city
		Suburban
		Rural
	Low income	Central city
		Suburban
		Rural
Nonusers	High income	Central city
		Suburban
		Rural
	Low income	Central city
		Suburban
		Rural

Source: Fred Winter, "Market Segmentation: A Tactical Approach," *Business Horizons* (January–February 1984): 60, 61.

States has resulted in dominance by three major firms: GameWorks, which relies on repeat business from local teens and young adults; Dave & Buster's, which attracts a slightly older crowd of local residents; and DisneyQuest, which focuses on families and tourists.

Segmentation is a key to matching supply and demand, which is one of the thorniest problems in customer service. Segmentation often reveals that large, random fluctuations in demand actually consist of several small, predictable, and manageable patterns. Matching supply and demand allows factories to produce desirable levels without extra shifts, overtime, and subcontracting. Matching supply and demand also minimizes the number and severity of stockouts. The demand for hotel rooms, for example, can be dependent on foreign tourists, businesspersons, and vacationers. Focusing on these three market segments separately, however, can allow hotel firms to predict overall supply and demand more effectively.

Banks now are segmenting markets to increase effectiveness. "You're dead in the water if you aren't segmenting the market," says Anne Moore, president of a bank consulting firm in Atlanta.

PRODUCT POSITIONING After segmenting markets so that the firm can target particular customer groups, the next step is to find out what customers want and expect. This takes analysis and research. A severe mistake is to assume the firm knows what customers want and expect. Countless research studies reveal large differences between how customers define service and rank the importance of different service activities and how producers view services. Many firms have become successful by filling the gap between what customers and producers see as good service. What the customer believes is good service is paramount, not what the producer believes service should be.

Identifying target customers upon whom to focus marketing efforts sets the stage for deciding how to meet the needs and wants of particular consumer groups. Product positioning is widely used for this purpose. Positioning entails developing schematic representations that reflect how your products or services compare to competitors' on dimensions most important to success in the industry. The following steps are required in product positioning:

1. Select key criteria that effectively differentiate products or services in the industry.

2. Diagram a two-dimensional product positioning map with specified criteria on each axis.

3. Plot major competitors' products or services in the resultant four-quadrant matrix.

4. Identify areas in the positioning map where the company's products or services could be most competitive in the given target market. Look for vacant areas (niches).

5. Develop a marketing plan to position the company's products or services appropriately.

Because just two criteria can be examined on a single product positioning map, multiple maps are often developed to assess various approaches to strategy implementation. Multidimensional scaling could be used to examine three or more criteria simultaneously, but this technique requires computer assistance and is beyond the scope of this text. Some examples of product positioning maps are illustrated in Figure 8–3.

Some rules of thumb for using product positioning as a strategy-implementation tool are the following:

1. Look for the hole or *vacant niche*. The best strategic opportunity might be an unserved segment.

2. Don't squat between segments. Any advantage from squatting (such as a larger target market) is offset by a failure to satisfy one segment. In decision-theory terms, the intent here is to avoid suboptimization by trying to serve more than one objective function.

3. Don't serve two segments with the same strategy. Usually, a strategy successful with one segment cannot be directly transferred to another segment.

4. Don't position yourself in the middle of the map. The middle usually means a strategy that is not clearly perceived to have any distinguishing characteristics. This rule can vary with the number of competitors. For example, when there are only two competitors, as in U.S. presidential elections, the middle becomes the preferred strategic position.[2]

An effective product positioning strategy meets two criteria: (1) it uniquely distinguishes a company from the competition, and (2) it leads customers to expect slightly less service than a company can deliver. Firms should not create expectations that exceed the service the firm can or will deliver. Network Equipment Technology is an example of a company that keeps customer expectations slightly below perceived performance. This is a constant challenge for marketers. Firms need to inform customers about what to expect and then exceed the promise. Underpromise and then overdeliver!

FINANCE/ACCOUNTING ISSUES

In this section, we examine several finance/accounting concepts considered to be central to strategy implementation: acquiring needed capital, developing pro forma financial statements, preparing financial budgets, and evaluating the worth of a business. Some examples of decisions that may require finance/accounting policies are:

1. To raise capital with short-term debt, long-term debt, preferred stock, or common stock.

2. To lease or buy fixed assets.

FIGURE 8–3
Examples of Product Positioning Maps

A. A PRODUCT POSITIONING MAP FOR BANKS

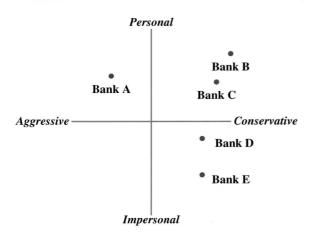

B. A PRODUCT POSITIONING MAP FOR PERSONAL COMPUTERS

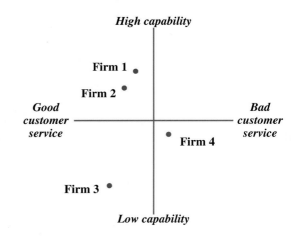

C. A PRODUCT POSITIONING MAP FOR MENSWEAR RETAIL STORES

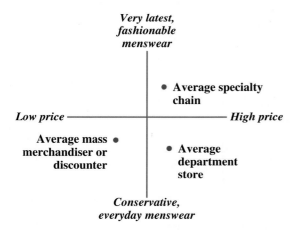

D. A PRODUCT POSITIONING MAP FOR THE RENTAL CAR MARKET

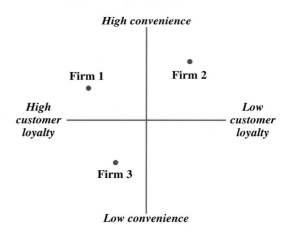

3. To determine an appropriate dividend payout ratio.
4. To use LIFO, FIFO, or a market-value accounting approach.
5. To extend the time of accounts receivable.
6. To establish a certain percentage discount on accounts within a specified period of time.
7. To determine the amount of cash that should be kept on hand.

ACQUIRING CAPITAL TO IMPLEMENT STRATEGIES Successful strategy implementation often requires additional capital. As indicated in the Global Perspective, countries and continents are like companies in that they actively strive to attract investment capital.

GLOBAL PERSPECTIVE
Which Areas of the World Attract the Most Foreign Capital (1996)?

As global competition for foreign investment dollars intensifies, China, Mexico, Indonesia, and Malaysia are winning while Russia, Hungary, Turkey, and Chile are losers. The following data (in billions of dollars) reveals regions and nations of the world that attracted the most capital investment dollars in 1996.

Source: Adapted from Urban Lehner, "Money Hungry," The Wall Street Journal (September 18, 1997): R4.

REGIONS			
East Asia/Pacific	$108.7	Indonesia	17.9
Latin America/Caribbean	74.3	Malaysia	16.0
Europe/Central Asia	31.2	Brazil	14.7
Sub-Saharan Africa	11.8	Thailand	13.3
South Asia	10.7	Argentina	11.3
Middle East/North Africa	6.9	India	8.0
		Turkey	4.7
NATIONS		Chile	4.6
China	$52.0	Russia	3.6
Mexico	28.1	Hungary	2.5

Besides net profit from operations and the sale of assets, two basic sources of capital for an organization are debt and equity. Determining an appropriate mix of debt and equity in a firm's capital structure can be vital to successful strategy implementation. An *Earnings Per Share/Earnings Before Interest and Taxes (EPS/EBIT) analysis* is the most widely used technique for determining whether debt, stock, or a combination of debt and stock is the best alternative for raising capital to implement strategies. This technique involves an examination of the impact that debt versus stock financing has on earnings per share under various assumptions as to EBIT.

Theoretically, an enterprise should have enough debt in its capital structure to boost its return on investment by applying debt to products and projects earning more than the cost of the debt. In low earning periods, too much debt in the capital structure of an organization can endanger stockholders' return and jeopardize company survival. Fixed debt obligations generally must be met, regardless of circumstances. This does not mean that stock issuances are always better than debt for raising capital. Some special concerns with stock issuances are dilution of ownership, effect on stock price, and the need to share future earnings with all new shareholders.

In the 1990s, interest rates were low, yet stock issuances remained very popular for the purpose of paying off corporate debt. Kmart is one firm that issued new stock worth over $1 billion to reduce its debt. Sony Corporation also raised nearly $3 billion by selling new shares of stock to reduce the company's debt. The lingerie maker Warnaco Group, which accounts for 30 percent of the women's bra market in the United States, recently sold 6 million shares to the public to reduce its debt.

Without going into detail on other institutional and legal issues related to the debt versus stock decision, EPS/EBIT may be best explained by working through an example. Let's say the Brown Company needs to raise $1 million to finance implementation of a market-development strategy. The company's common stock currently sells for $50 per share, and 100,000 shares are outstanding. The prime interest rate is 10 percent and the company's tax rate is 50 percent. The company's earnings before interest and taxes next year are expected to be $2 million if a recession occurs, $4 million if the economy stays as is, and $8 million if the economy significantly improves. EPS/EBIT analysis can be used to determine if all stock, all debt, or some combination of stock and debt is the best capital financing alternative. The EPS/EBIT analysis for this example is provided in Table 8–3.

As indicated by the EPS values of 9.5, 19.50, and 39.50 in Table 8–3, debt is the best financing alternative for the Brown Company if a recession, boom, or normal year is expected. An EPS/EBIT chart can be constructed to determine the break-even point, where one financing alternative becomes more attractive than another. Figure 8–4 indicates that issuing common stock is the least attractive financing alternative for the Brown Company.

EPS/EBIT analysis is a valuable tool for making capital financing decisions needed to implement strategies, but several considerations should be made whenever using this technique. First, profit levels may be higher for stock or debt alternatives when EPS levels are lower. For example, looking only at the earnings after taxes (EAT) values in Table 8–3, the common stock option is the best alternative, regardless of economic conditions. If the Brown Company's mission includes strict profit maximization, as opposed to the maximization of stockholders' wealth or some other criterion, then stock rather than debt is the best choice of financing.

Another consideration when using EPS/EBIT analysis is flexibility. As an organization's capital structure changes, so does its flexibility for considering future capital needs. Using all debt or all stock to raise capital in the present may impose fixed obligations, restrictive covenants, or other constraints that could severely reduce a firm's ability to raise additional capital in the future. Control is also a concern. When additional stock is issued to finance strategy implementation, ownership and control of the enterprise are diluted. This can be a serious concern in today's business environment of hostile takeovers, mergers, and acquisitions. Also, dilution of ownership can be an overriding concern in closely held corporations where stock issuances affect the decision-making power of majority stockholders. For example, the Smucker family owns 30 percent of the stock in Smucker's, a well-known jam and jelly company. When Smucker's acquired Dickson Family, Inc., the company used mostly debt rather than stock in order not to dilute the family ownership.

When using EPS/EBIT analysis, timing in relation to movements of stock prices, interest rates, and bond prices becomes important. In times of depressed stock prices, debt may prove to be the most suitable alternative from both a cost and a demand standpoint. However, when cost of capital (interest rates) is high, stock issuances become more attractive. In fact, even when interest rates are low, as in 1998, stock issuances can be very popular. The explosion of new mergers and acquisitions in the 1990s was fueled by equity at a time when stock prices were high. Using stock for acquisitions rather than debt enhances a

TABLE 8–3
EPS/EBIT Analysis for the Brown Company (in millions)

	COMMON STOCK FINANCING			DEBT FINANCING			COMBINATION FINANCING		
	RECESSION	NORMAL	BOOM	RECESSION	NORMAL	BOOM	RECESSION	NORMAL	BOOM
EBIT	$2.0	$ 4.0	$ 8.0	$2.0	$ 4.0	$ 8.0	$2.0	$ 4.0	$ 8.0
Interest[a]	0	0	0	.10	.10	.10	.05	.05	.05
EBT	2.0	4.0	8.0	1.9	3.9	7.9	1.95	3.95	7.95
Taxes	1.0	2.0	4.0	.95	1.95	3.95	.975	1.975	3.975
EAT	1.0	2.0	4.0	.95	1.95	3.95	.975	1.975	3.975
#Shares[b]	.12	.12	.12	.10	.10	.10	.11	.11	.11
EPS[c]	8.33	16.66	33.33	9.5	19.50	39.50	8.86	17.95	36.14

[a]The annual interest charge on $1 million at 10% is $100,000 and on $0.5 million is $50,000. This row is in $, not %.
[b]To raise all of the needed $1 million with stock, 20,000 new shares must be issued, raising the total to 120,000 shares outstanding. To raise one-half of the needed $1 million with stock, 10,000 new shares must be issued, raising the total to 110,000 shares outstanding.
[c]EPS = Earnings After Taxes (EAT) divided by shares (number of shares outstanding).

FIGURE 8–4
An EPS/EBIT Chart for the Brown Company

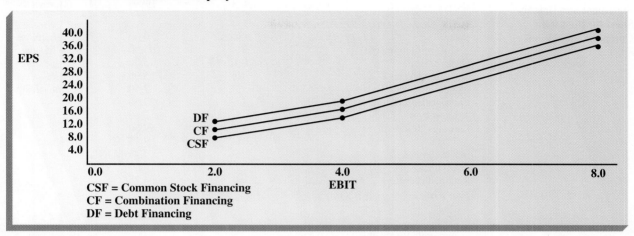

CSF = Common Stock Financing
CF = Combination Financing
DF = Debt Financing

firm's reported earnings because, unlike debt acquirers, stock acquirers do not have to deduct goodwill from their earnings for years to come.

PRO FORMA FINANCIAL STATEMENTS   *Pro forma (projected) financial statement analysis* is a central strategy-implementation technique because it allows an organization to examine the expected results of various actions and approaches. This type of analysis can be used to forecast the impact of various implementation decisions (for example, to increase promotion expenditures by 50 percent to support a market-development strategy, to increase salaries by 25 percent to support a market-penetration strategy, to increase research and development expenditures by 70 percent to support product development, or to sell $1 million of common stock to raise capital for diversification). Nearly all financial institutions require at least three years of projected financial statements whenever a business seeks capital. A pro forma income statement and balance sheet allow an organization to compute projected financial ratios under various strategy-implementation scenarios. When compared to prior years and to industry averages, financial ratios provide valuable insights into the feasibility of various strategy-implementation approaches.

A 1998 pro forma income statement and balance sheet for the Litten Company are provided in Table 8–4. The pro forma statements for Litten are based on five assumptions: (1) The company needs to raise $45 million to finance expansion into foreign markets; (2) $30 million of this total will be raised through increased debt and $15 million through common stock; (3) sales are expected to increase 50 percent; (4) three new facilities, costing a total of $30 million, will be constructed in foreign markets; and (5) land for the new facilities is already owned by the company. Note in Table 8–4 that Litten's strategies and their implementation are expected to result in a sales increase from $100 million to $150 million and in a net increase in income from $6 million to $9.75 million, in the forecasted year.

There are six steps in performing pro forma financial analysis:

1. Prepare the pro forma income statement before the balance sheet. Start by forecasting sales as accurately as possible.

2. Use the percentage-of-sales method to project cost of goods sold (CGS) and the expense items in the income statement. For example, if CGS is 70 percent of sales in the prior year (as it is in Table 8–4), then use that same percentage to calculate CGS in the future year—unless there is a reason to use a different

TABLE 8–4

A Pro Forma Income Statement and Balance Sheet for the Litten Company (in millions)

	PRIOR YEAR 1998	PROJECTED YEAR 1999	REMARKS
PRO FORMA INCOME STATEMENT			
Sales	100	150.00	50% increase
Cost of Goods Sold	70	105.00	70% of sales
Gross Margin	30	45.00	
Selling Expense	10	15.00	10% of sales
Administrative Expense	5	7.50	5% of sales
Earnings Before Interest and Taxes	15	22.50	
Interest	3	3.00	
Earnings Before Taxes	12	19.50	
Taxes	6	9.75	50% rate
Net Income	6	9.75	
Dividends	2	5.00	
Retained Earnings	4	4.75	
PRO FORMA BALANCE SHEET			
Assets			
Cash	5	7.75	Plug figure
Accounts Receivable	2	4.00	Incr. 100%
Inventory	20	45.00	
Total Current Assets	27	56.75	
Land	15	15.00	
Plant and Equipment	50	80.00	Add 3 new plants at $10 million each
Less Depreciation	10	20.00	
Net Plant and Equipment	40	60.00	
Total Fixed Assets	55	75.00	
Total Assets	82	131.75	
Liabilities			
Accounts Payable	10	10.00	
Notes Payable	10	10.00	
Total Current Liabilities	20	20.00	
Long-term Debt	40	70.00	Borrowed $30 million
Additional Paid-in Capital	20	35.00	Issued 100,000 shares at $150 each
Retained Earnings	2	6.75	2 + 4.75
Total Liabilities and Net Worth	82	131.75	

percentage. Items such as interest, dividends, and taxes must be treated independently and cannot be forecasted using the percentage-of-sales method.

3. Calculate the projected net income.

4. Subtract from the net income any dividends to be paid and add the remaining net income to Retained Earnings. Reflect the Retained Earnings total on both the income statement and balance sheet because this item is the key link between the two projected statements.

5. Project the balance sheet items, beginning with retained earnings and then forecasting stockholders' equity, long-term liabilities, current liabilities, total liabilities, total assets, fixed assets, and current assets (in that order). Use the cash account as the plug figure; that is, use the cash account to make the assets total the liabilities and net worth. Then, make appropriate adjustments. For example, if the cash needed to balance the statements is too small (or too large), make appropriate changes to borrow more (or less) money than planned.

6. List comments (remarks) on the projected statements. Any time a significant change is made in an item from a prior year to the projected year, an explanation (remark) should be provided. Remarks are essential because otherwise pro formas are meaningless.

FINANCIAL BUDGETS A *financial budget* is a document that details how funds will be obtained and spent for a specified period of time. Annual budgets are most common, although the period of time for a budget can range from one day to more than 10 years. Fundamentally, financial budgeting is a method for specifying what must be done to complete strategy implementation successfully. Financial budgeting should not be thought of as a tool for limiting expenditures but rather as a method for obtaining the most productive and profitable use of an organization's resources. Financial budgets can be viewed as the planned allocation of a firm's resources based on forecasts of the future.

There are almost as many different types of financial budgets as there are types of organizations. Some common types of budgets include cash budgets, operating budgets, sales budgets, profit budgets, factory budgets, capital budgets, expense budgets, divisional budgets, variable budgets, flexible budgets, and fixed budgets. When an organization is experiencing financial difficulties, budgets are especially important in guiding strategy implementation.

Perhaps the most common type of financial budget is the *cash budget*. The Financial Accounting Standards Board has mandated that every publicly held company in the United States must issue an annual cash-flow statement in addition to the usual financial reports. The statement includes all receipts and disbursements of cash in operations, investments, and financing. It supplements the Statement on Changes in Financial Position formerly included in the annual reports of all publicly held companies. A cash budget for the year 2000 for the Toddler Toy Company is provided in Table 8–5. Note that Toddler is not expecting to have surplus cash until November of 2000.

Financial budgets have some limitations. First, budgetary programs can become so detailed that they are cumbersome and overly expensive. Overbudgeting or underbudgeting can cause problems. Second, financial budgets can become a substitute for objectives.

TABLE 8–5
A Six-Month Cash Budget for the Toddler Toy Company in 2000

CASH BUDGET (IN THOUSANDS)	JULY	AUG	SEPT.	OCT.	NOV.	DEC.	JAN.
Receipts							
Collections	$12,000	$21,000	$31,000	$35,000	$22,000	$18,000	$11,000
Payments							
Purchases	14,000	21,000	28,000	14,000	14,000	7,000	
Wages and Salaries	1,500	2,000	2,500	1,500	1,500	1,000	
Rent	500	500	500	500	500	500	
Other Expenses	200	300	400	200	200	100	
Taxes	–	8,000	–	–	–	–	
Payment on Machine	–	–	10,000	–	–	–	
Total Payments	$16,200	$31,800	$41,400	$16,200	$16,200	$ 8,600	
Net Cash Gain (Loss) During Month	−4,200	−10,800	−10,400	18,800	5,800	9,400	
Cash at Start of Month If No							
Borrowing Is Done	6,000	1,800	−9,000	−19,400	−600	5,200	
Cumulative Cash (Cash at start plus							
gains or minus losses)	1,800	−9,000	−19,400	−600	5,200	14,600	
Less Desired Level of Cash	−5,000	−5,000	−5,000	−5,000	−5,000	−5,000	
Total Loans Outstanding to							
Maintain $5,000 Cash Balance	$3,200	$14,000	$24,400	$ 5,600	–	–	
Surplus Cash	–	–	–	–	$ 200	$ 9,600	

A budget is a tool and not an end in itself. Third, budgets can hide inefficiencies if based solely on precedent rather than periodic evaluation of circumstances and standards. Finally, budgets are sometimes used as instruments of tyranny that result in frustration, resentment, absenteeism, and high turnover. To minimize the effect of this last concern, managers should increase the participation of subordinates in preparing budgets.

EVALUATING THE WORTH OF A BUSINESS

Evaluating the worth of a business is central to strategy implementation because integrative, intensive, and diversification strategies are often implemented by acquiring other firms. Other strategies, such as retrenchment and divestiture, may result in the sale of a division of an organization or of the firm itself. Approximately 20,000 transactions occur each year in which businesses are bought or sold in the United States. In all these cases, it is necessary to establish the financial worth or cash value of a business to successfully implement strategies.

All the various methods for determining a business's worth can be grouped into three main approaches: what a firm owns, what a firm earns, or what a firm will bring in the market. But it is important to realize that valuation is not an exact science. The valuation of a firm's worth is based on financial facts, but common sense and intuitive judgment must enter into the process. It is difficult to assign a monetary value to factors—such as a loyal customer base, a history of growth, legal suits pending, dedicated employees, a favorable lease, a bad credit rating, or good patents—that may not be reflected in a firm's financial statements. Also, different valuation methods will yield different totals for a firm's worth, and no prescribed approach is best for a certain situation. Evaluating the worth of a business truly requires both qualitative and quantitative skills.

The first approach in evaluating the worth of a business is determining its net worth or stockholders' equity. Net worth represents the sum of common stock, additional paid-in capital, and retained earnings. After calculating net worth, add or subtract an appropriate amount for goodwill (such as high customer loyalty) and overvalued or undervalued assets. This total provides a reasonable estimate of a firm's monetary value. If a firm has goodwill, it will be listed on the balance sheet, perhaps as "intangibles."

The second approach to measuring the value of a firm grows out of the belief that the worth of any business should be based largely on the future benefits its owners may derive through net profits. A conservative rule of thumb is to establish a business's worth as five times the firm's current annual profit. A five-year average profit level could also be used. When using this approach, remember that firms normally suppress earnings in their financial statements to minimize taxes.

The third approach, letting the market determine a business's worth, involves three methods. First, base the firm's worth on the selling price of a similar company. A potential problem, however, is that sometimes comparable figures are not easy to locate, even though substantial information on firms that buy or sell to other firms is available in major libraries. The second approach is called the *price-earnings ratio method*. To use this method, divide the market price of the firm's common stock by the annual earnings per share and multiply this number by the firm's average net income for the past five years. The third approach can be called the *outstanding shares method*. To use this method, simply multiply the number of shares outstanding by the market price per share and add a premium. The premium is simply a per share dollar amount that a person or firm is willing to pay to control (acquire) the other company.

Business evaluations are becoming routine in many situations. Businesses have many strategy-implementation reasons for determining their worth in addition to preparing to be sold or to buy other companies. Employee plans, taxes, retirement, mergers, acquisitions, expansion plans, banking relationships, death of a principal, divorce, partnership agreements, and IRS audits are other reasons for a periodic valuation. It is just good business to have a reasonable understanding of what your firm is worth. This knowledge protects the interests of all parties involved.

DECIDING WHETHER TO GO PUBLIC Going public means selling off a percentage of your company to others in order to raise capital; consequently, it dilutes the owners' control of the firm. Going public is not recommended for companies with less than $10 million in sales because the initial costs can be too high for the firm to generate sufficient cash flow to make going public worthwhile. One dollar in four is the average total cost paid to lawyers, accountants, and underwriters when an initial stock issuance is under $1 million; one dollar in 20 will go to cover these costs for issuances over $20 million.

In addition to initial costs involved with a stock offering, there are costs and obligations associated with reporting and management in a publicly held firm. For firms with more than $10 million in sales, going public can provide major advantages: It can allow the firm to raise capital to develop new products, build plants, expand, grow, and market products and services more effectively.

Before going public, a firm must have quality management with a proven track record for achieving quality earnings and positive cash flow. The company also should enjoy growing demand for its products. Sales growth of about 5 or 6 percent a year is good for a private firm, but shareholders expect public companies to grow around 10 to 15 percent per year.

RESEARCH AND DEVELOPMENT (R&D) ISSUES

Research and development (R&D) personnel can play an integral part in strategy implementation. These individuals are generally charged with developing new products and improving old products in a way that will allow effective strategy implementation. R&D employees and managers perform tasks that include transferring complex technology, adjusting processes to local raw materials, adapting processes to local markets, and altering products to particular tastes and specifications. Strategies such as product development, market penetration, and concentric diversification require that new products be successfully developed and that old products be significantly improved. But the level of management support for R&D is often constrained by resource availability:

> If U.S. business is to maintain its position in the global business environment, then R&D support will have to become a major U.S. commitment. U.S. managers cannot continue to ignore it or take funds away from it for short-term profits and still have long-term strategic options. If one runs away from more aggressive product and process strategies, one should not be surprised by the fact that competitive advantages are lost to foreign competitors.[3]

Technological improvements that affect consumer and industrial products and services shorten product life cycles. Companies in virtually every industry are relying on the development of new products and services to fuel profitability and growth. Table 8–6 provides a breakdown of R&D expenditures in 1996 for the 10 American companies that spent the most on R&D. American companies in 1997 spent about $192 billion on R&D, a 4.3 percent increase from the $184 billion in 1996. Many companies are spending much more on R&D than the average. For example, Microsoft spent 300 percent more on R&D in 1997 than in 1996 in its effort to reinvent and enhance the personal computer experience. Daniel Ling of Microsoft says, "Transferring technology into development is always a challenge, always difficult, and always requires a lot of work."

Surveys suggest that the most successful organizations use an R&D strategy that ties external opportunities to internal strength and is linked with objectives. Well-formulated

TABLE 8–6

Ranking the Top 10 American Companies in R&D Spending in 1996

COMPANY	IN TOTAL DOLLARS (MILLIONS)	INCREASE (DECREASE) FROM PRIOR YEAR	R&D/ SALES
1. General Motors	$8,900	8.5%	5.6%
2. Ford Motor	6,821	3.0	4.6
3. IBM	3,934	16.2	5.2
4. Hewlett-Packard	2,718	18.1	7.1
5. Motorola	2,394	9.0	8.6
6. Lucent Technologies	2,056	(23.7)	13.0
7. TRW	1,981	5.3	20.1
8. Johnson & Johnson	1,905	16.6	8.8
9. Intel	1,808	39.5	8.7
10. Pfizer	1,684	16.8	14.9

R&D policies match market opportunities with internal capabilities and provide an initial screen to all ideas generated. R&D policies can enhance strategy-implementation efforts to:

1. Emphasize product or process improvements.
2. Stress basic or applied research.
3. Be leaders or followers in R&D.
4. Develop robotics or manual-type processes.
5. Spend a high, average, or low amount of money on R&D.
6. Perform R&D within the firm or to contract R&D to outside firms.
7. Use university researchers or private sector researchers.

There must be effective interactions between R&D departments and other functional departments in implementing different types of generic business strategies. Conflicts between marketing, finance/accounting, R&D, and information systems departments can be minimized with clear policies and objectives. Table 8–7 gives some examples of R&D activities that could be required for successful implementation of various strategies.

Many firms wrestle with the decision to acquire R&D expertise from external firms or to develop R&D expertise internally. The following guidelines can be used to help make this decision:

1. If the rate of technical progress is slow, the rate of market growth is moderate, and there are significant barriers to possible new entrants, then in-house R&D is the preferred solution. The reason is that R&D, if successful, will result in a temporary product or process monopoly that the company can exploit.
2. If technology is changing rapidly and the market is growing slowly, then a major effort in R&D may be very risky, because it may lead to development of an ultimately obsolete technology or one for which there is no market.
3. If technology is changing slowly but the market is growing fast, there generally is not enough time for in-house development. The prescribed approach is to obtain R&D expertise on an exclusive or nonexclusive basis from an outside firm.
4. If both technical progress and market growth are fast, R&D expertise should be obtained through acquisition of a well-established firm in the industry.[4]

There are at least three major R&D approaches for implementing strategies. The first strategy is to be the first firm to market new technological products. This is a glamorous and exciting strategy but also a dangerous one. Firms such as 3M, Polaroid, and General Electric have been successful with this approach, but many other pioneering firms have

TABLE 8–7
Research and Development Involvement in Selected Strategy-Implementation Situations

TYPE OF ORGANIZATION	STRATEGY BEING IMPLEMENTED	R&D ACTIVITY
Pharmaceutical company	Product development	Develop a procedure for testing the effects of a new drug on different subgroups.
Boat manufacturer	Concentric diversification	Develop a procedure to test the performance of various keel designs under various conditions.
Plastic container manufacturer	Market penetration	Develop a biodegradable container.
Electronics company	Market development	Develop a telecommunications system in a foreign country.

fallen, with rival firms seizing the initiative. Two firms also using this first R&D strategy are Global Ozone Solutions and American Thermalfo; these firms manufacture machines that extract ozone-depleting chlorofluorocarbons, or CFCs, from the air. As indicated in the Natural Environment Perspective, equipment like this is needed in Southeast Asia.

A second R&D approach is to be an innovative imitator of successful products, thus minimizing the risks and costs of start-up. This approach entails allowing a pioneer firm to develop the first version of the new product and to demonstrate that a market exists. Then, laggard firms develop a similar product. This strategy requires excellent R&D personnel and an excellent marketing department.

A third R&D strategy is to be a low-cost producer by mass-producing products similar to but less expensive than products recently introduced. Far Eastern countries used this approach effectively during the 1980s to crush the $8 billion U.S. consumer electronics industry. As a new product is accepted by customers, price becomes increasingly important in the buying decision. Also, mass marketing replaces personal selling as the dominant selling strategy. This R&D strategy requires substantial investment in plant and equipment, but fewer expenditures in R&D than the two approaches described earlier.

NATURAL ENVIRONMENT
Do Smoke and Smog Still Cover Southeast Asia?

During the latter months of 1997, smoke and smog from forest fires and industrial polluters covered most of Indonesia, Malaysia, and the Philippines. The real cause of this problem is politics. Indonesia, for example, is a country run like an empire, by soldiers and civil servants dispatched throughout its 13,000 islands from the main island of Java. Their job is to keep peace while providing basic services, but at the same time facilitating exploitation of Indonesia's enormous natural resources. Over recent years, the capital of Jakarta has funded huge expansion of plantation output of timber, palm oil, and rubber. Direct costs to burn these areas are far lower than

other methods of clearing land so widespread burning is common. Indonesia's environmental ministry says its budget is too small to police fire setting.

Lack of concern for polluting the natural environmental in Southeast Asia and resultant smoke and fog have caused numerous airplane crashes, ship collisions, and medical emergencies. Whole cities of people walk around with breathing masks. Passenger airliners have crashed. Pollution is a reason often given for the falling value of Southeast Asian currencies. As shown, during the second half of 1997, Asian currencies fell against the U.S. dollar:

Thailand (baht)	35%
Indonesia (rupiah)	23
Malaysia (ringgit)	17
Philippines (peso)	15
Japan (yen)	6
Singapore (dollar)	6

Source: Adapted from Peter Waldman, "Southeast Asian Smog Is Tied to Politics," The Wall Street Journal *(September 30, 1997): A10. Also, James Cox, "Asian Currencies and Stock Markets Continue Fall,"* USA Today *(September 2, 1997): 10A.*

R&D activities among American firms need to be more closely aligned to business objectives. There needs to be expanded communication between R&D managers and strategists. Corporations are experimenting with various methods to achieve this improved communication climate, including different roles and reporting arrangements for managers and new methods to reduce the time it takes research ideas to become reality.[5]

Perhaps the most current trend in R&D management has been lifting the veil of secrecy whereby firms, even major competitors, are joining forces to develop new products. Collaboration is on the rise due to new competitive pressures, rising research costs, increasing regulatory issues, and accelerated product development schedules. Companies not only are working more closely with each other on R&D, but they are also turning to consortia at universities for their R&D needs. More than 600 research consortia are now in operation in the United States. Lifting of R&D secrecy among many firms through collaboration has allowed marketing of new technologies and products even before they were available for sale.

COMPUTER INFORMATION SYSTEMS (CIS) ISSUES

Although no firm would use the same marketing or management approach for 20 years, many companies have 20-year-old *computer information systems* that threaten their very existence. Developing new user applications often takes a backseat to keeping an old system running. Countless firms still do not use the Internet. This unfortunate situation is happening at a time when the quantity and quality of information available to firms and their competitors is increasing exponentially.

Firms that gather, assimilate, and evaluate external and internal information most effectively are gaining competitive advantages over other firms. Recognizing the importance of having an effective computer information system will not be an option in the future; it will be a requirement. Information is the basis for understanding in a firm. Robert Kavner, president of AT&T Data Systems Group, says, "Modern corporations are organizing around information flow. With the growth of communications networks such as the Internet, the barriers of time and place have been breached. By mirroring people's work needs and habits, networked computing systems have made new modes of work possible."

It is estimated that the quantity of human knowledge is doubling every decade. In many industries, information is becoming the most important factor differentiating successful and unsuccessful firms. The process of strategic management is facilitated immensely in firms that have an effective information system. Many companies are establishing a new approach to information systems, one that blends the technical knowledge of the computer experts with the vision of senior management. Some guidelines that allow computer information systems to enhance strategy implementation are as follows:

1. Computer hardware and software should facilitate global information consistency.
2. All component parts should be accessible through a common order-processing system.
3. All divisions should be self-sufficient yet compatible in their information systems capabilities.
4. A basic purpose of information systems is to support cross-functional integration of the business functions.
5. Integration of voice and data communications is a goal of information systems.

INFORMATION TECHNOLOGY

How Harmful Are Hackers?

The Gap, Playboy Enterprises, Hitachi America, PeopleSoft, and Twentieth Century Fox average over 30 computer intrusion attempts daily. Thousands of companies today are plagued by computer hackers who include disgruntled employees, competitors, bored teens, sociopaths, thieves, spies, and hired agents. Computer vulnerability is a giant, expensive headache. Over 40 percent of U.S. corporations reported severe computer break-ins in 1996 and spent over $6 billion that year to safeguard their computers. These firms lost more than $10 billion due to computer hackers.

The FBI reports that 95 percent of computer break-ins go undetected and fewer than 15 percent are reported to law enforcement agencies. The FBI's senior expert on computer crime, Dennis Hughes, says "Hackers are driving us nuts. Everyone is getting hacked into. It's out of control." Hackers can download computer break-in programs free off the Internet, and hacker magazines provide easy, step-by-step tips. Hackers can read a computer screen from over a mile away, can intercept all passwords and e-mail messages, steal trade secrets and patents, and read all confidential messages such as bids on projects and new strategy initiatives.

To minimize the hacker threat, companies today must purchase expensive encryption software to scramble the traffic that flows through their computer networks; companies much teach all employees to be security-conscious; companies must construct several, not just one, complex computer firewalls to deter hackers. Hacker technology is getting exotic and developing faster than safeguards. Companies naive to the computer hacker threat are grossly negligent and vulnerable.

Even the U.S. federal government is becoming more worried about cyberterror. Research costs on cyberspace security related to the federal government are expected to reach $1 billion per year by 2004. Thomas Marsh, chair of President Clinton's Commission on Critical Infrastructure Protection, says, "Vulnerability is serious and increasing." Former senator Sam Nunn, also on the commission, says, "The only issue of equal or greater concern today is nuclear, chemical, or biological weapon proliferation."

Source: Adapted from Richard Behar, "Who's Reading Your E-Mail?" Fortune *(February 3, 1997): 57–70. Also, M.J. Zuckerman, "Clinton to Get Cyberterror Plan,"* USA Today *(October 9, 1997): 1A.*

6. Data and information obtained within the firm should be available to any department or person in the firm who can demonstrate a need for it, except for reasons of security or integrity of the database.

7. Information systems design should stress effectiveness in the business environment rather than efficiency in the technical environment.[6]

Information collection, retrieval, and storage can be used to create competitive advantages in ways such as cross-selling to customers, monitoring suppliers, keeping managers and employees informed, coordinating activities among divisions, and managing funds. Like inventory and human resources, information is becoming recognized as a valuable organizational asset that can be controlled and managed. Firms that implement strategies using the best information will reap competitive advantages in the 1990s. John Young, president and CEO of Hewlett-Packard, says, "There really isn't any right amount to spend on information systems. Many management teams spend too much time thinking about how to beat down the information system's cost, instead of thinking about how to get more value out of the information they could have available and how to link that to strategic goals of the company."

A good information system can allow a firm to reduce costs. For example, on-line orders from salespersons to production facilities can shorten materials ordering time and reduce inventory costs. Direct communications between suppliers, manufacturers, marketers, and customers can link elements of the value chain together as though they were one organization. Improved quality and service often result from an improved information system.

As indicated in the Information Technology Perspective, firms must increasingly be concerned about computer hackers and take specific measures to secure and safeguard corporate communications, files, orders, and business conducted over the Internet.

Dun & Bradstreet is an example of a company that has an excellent information system. Every D & B customer and client in the world has a separate nine-digit number. The database of information associated with each number has become so widely used that it is like a business social security number. D & B reaps great competitive advantages from its information system.

CONCLUSION

Successful strategy implementation depends upon cooperation among all functional and divisional managers in an organization. Marketing departments are commonly charged with implementing strategies that require significant increases in sales revenues in new areas and with new or improved products. Finance and accounting managers must devise effective strategy-implementation approaches at low cost and minimum risk to that firm. R&D managers have to transfer complex technologies or develop new technologies to successfully implement strategies. Information systems managers are being called upon more and more to provide leadership and training for all individuals in the firm. The nature and role of marketing, finance/accounting, R&D, and computer information systems activities, coupled with management activities described in Chapter 7, largely determine organizational success.

TAKE IT TO THE NET   We invite you to visit the DAVID page on the Prentice Hall Web site at **www.prenhall.com/davidsm** for this chapter's World Wide Web exercises.

KEY TERMS AND CONCEPTS

Cash Budget	(p. 263)	Marketing Mix Variables	(p. 254)	Product Positioning	(p. 252)
Computer Information Systems	(p. 268)	Outstanding Shares Method	(p. 264)	Research and Development	(p. 265)
EPS/EBIT Analysis	(p. 259)	Price-Earnings Ratio Method	(p. 264)	Vacant Niche	(p. 257)
Financial Budget	(p. 263)	Pro Forma Financial Statement	(p. 261)		
Market Segmentation	(p. 252)	Analysis			

ISSUES FOR REVIEW AND DISCUSSION

1. Suppose your company has just acquired a firm that produces battery-operated lawn mowers, and strategists want to implement a market-penetration strategy. How would you segment the market for this product? Justify your answer.

2. Explain how you would estimate the total worth of a business.

3. Diagram and label clearly a product positioning map that includes six fast-food restaurant chains.

4. Explain why EPS/EBIT analysis is a central strategy-implementation technique.

5. How would the R&D role in strategy implementation differ in small versus large organizations?

6. Discuss the limitations of EPS/EBIT analysis.

7. Explain how marketing, finance/accounting, R&D, and computer information systems managers' involvement in strategy formulation can enhance strategy implementation.

8. Consider the following statement: "Retained earnings on the balance sheet are not monies available to finance strategy implementation." It is true or false? Explain.

9. Explain why pro forma financial statement analysis is considered both a strategy-formulation and a strategy-implementation tool.

10. Describe some marketing, finance/accounting, R&D, and computer information systems activities that a small

restaurant chain might undertake to expand into a neighboring state.

11. Select one of the suggested readings at the end of this chapter, find that article in your college library, and summarize it in a five-minute oral report for the class.

12. Discuss the computer information systems at your college or university.

NOTES

1. Fred Winter, "Market Segmentation: A Tactical Approach," *Business Horizons* 27, no. 1 (January–February 1984): 59.

2. Ralph Biggadike, "The Contributions of Marketing to Strategic Management," *Academy of Management Review* 6, no. 4 (October 1981): 627.

3. Vida Scarpello, William Boulton, and Charles Hofer, "Reintegrating R&D into Business Strategy," *Journal of Business Strategy* 6, no. 4 (Spring 1986): 55.

4. Pier Abetti, "Technology: A Key Strategic Resource," *Management Review* 78, no. 2 (February 1989): 38.

5. William Spencer and Deborah Triant, "Strengthening the Link Between R&D and Corporate Strategy," *Journal of Business Strategy* 10, no. 1 (January/February 1989): 42.

6. Thomas Davenport, Michael Hammer, and Tauno Metsisto, "How Executives Can Shape Their Company's Information Systems," *Harvard Business Review* 67, no. 2 (March–April 1989): 131.

CURRENT READINGS

Argyres, N. "Capabilites, Technological Diversification and Divisionalization." *Strategic Management Journal* 17, no. 5 (May 1996): 395–410.

Berthon, Pierre, Leyland Pitt, and Richard T. Watson. "Marketing Communication and the World Wide Web." *Business Horizons* 39, no. 5 (September-October 1996): 24–32.

Datta, Y. "Market Segmentation: An Integrated Framework." *Long Range Planning* 29 no. 6 (December 1996): 797–811.

Hattan, Mary Louise and Kenneth J. Hatten. "Information Systems Strategy: Long Overdue—and Still Not Here." *Long Range Planning* 30, no. 2 (April 1997): 254–266.

Kochhar, R. "Explaining Firm Capital Structure: The Role of Agency Theory vs. Transaction Cost Economics." *Strategic Management Journal* 17, no. 9 (November 1996): 713–728.

Kuemmerle, Walter. "Building Effective R&D Capabilities Abroad." *Harvard Business Review* (March–April 1997): 61–72.

Lawler, John J. and Robin Elliot. "Artificial Intelligence in HRM: An Experimental Study of an Expert System." *Journal of Management* 22, no. 1 (1996): 85–112.

Mentzas, Gregory. "Implementing an IS Strategy—A Team Approach." *Long Range Planning* 30, no. 1 (February 1997): 84–95.

Sakakibara, M. "Heterogeneity of Firm Capabilities and Cooperative Research and Development: An Empirical Examiniation of Motives." *Strategic Management Journal* 18, Special Issue (Summer 1997): 143–164.

Segars, Albert H. and Varun Grover. "Designing Companywide Information Systems: Risk Factors and Coping Strategies." *Long Range Planning* 29, no. 3 (June 1996): 381–392.

Shanklin, William L. and David A. Griffith. "Crafting Strategies for Global Marketing in the New Millennium." *Business Horizons* 39, no. 5 (September–October 1996): 11–16.

Stone, Merlin, Neil Woodcock, and Muriel Wilson. "Managing the Change from Marketing Planning to Customer Relationship Management." *Long Range Planning* 29, no. 5 (October 1996): 675–683.

Tufano, Peter. "How Financial Engineering Can Advance Corporate Strategy." *Harvard Business Review* (January–February 1996): 136–146.

Venkatraman, N. "Beyond Outsourcing: Managing IT Resources as a Value Center." *Sloan Management Review* 38, no. 3 (Spring 1997): 51–64.

Wright, P. and S.P. Ferris. "Agency Conflict and Corporate Strategy: The Effect of Divestment on Corporate Value." *Strategic Management Journal* 18, no. 1 (January 1997): 77–87.

EXPERIENTIAL EXERCISES

Experiential Exercise 8A

DEVELOPING A PRODUCT POSITIONING MAP FOR HERSHEY FOODS

PURPOSE

Organizations continually monitor how their products and services are positioned relative to competitors. This information is especially useful for marketing managers, but is also used by other managers and strategists.

INSTRUCTIONS

Step 1 On a separate sheet of paper, develop a product positioning map for Hershey. Include Nestlé, Mars, and Hershey in your map.

Step 2 Go to the blackboard and diagram your product positioning map.

Step 3 Compare your product positioning map with those diagrammed by other students. Discuss any major differences.

Experiential Exercise 8B

PERFORMING AN EPS/EBIT ANALYSIS FOR HERSHEY FOODS

PURPOSE

An EPS/EBIT analysis is one of the most widely used techniques for determining the extent that debt and/or stock should be used to finance strategies to be implemented. This exercise can give you practice performing EPS/EBIT analysis.

INSTRUCTIONS

Let's say Hershey needs to raise $2 billion to introduce Hershey products in 20 new countries around the world in 1999. Determine whether Hershey should have used all debt, all stock, or a 50-50 combination of debt and stock to finance this market-development strategy. Assume a 44 percent tax rate and an 8 percent interest rate. Hershey's stock price is $50 per share. Hershey pays an annual dividend of $1.25 per share of common stock. The EBIT range for 1999 is between $300 and $500 million. A total of 90 million shares of common stock are outstanding. Develop an EPS/EBIT chart to reflect your analysis.

PREPARING PRO FORMA FINANCIAL STATEMENTS FOR HERSHEY FOODS

PURPOSE

This exercise is designed to give you experience preparing pro forma financial statements. Pro forma analysis is a central strategy-implementation technique because it allows managers to anticipate and evaluate the expected results of various strategy-implementation approaches.

INSTRUCTIONS

Step 1 Work with a classmate. Develop a 1998 pro forma income statement and balance sheet for Hershey. Assume that Hershey plans to raise $100 million in 1998 to introduce Hershey products in 20 new countries and plans to obtain 50 percent financing from a bank and 50 percent financing from a stock issuance. Make other assumptions as needed, and state them clearly in written form.

Step 2 Compute Hershey's current ratio, debt-to-equity ratio, and return-on-investment ratio for 1995, 1996, and 1997. How do your 1998 projected ratios compare to the 1996 and 1997 ratios? Why is it important to make this comparison?

Step 3 Bring your pro forma statements to class and discuss any problems or questions you encountered.

Step 4 Compare your pro forma statements to the statements of other students. What major differences exist between your analysis and the work of other students?

DETERMINING THE CASH VALUE OF HERSHEY FOODS

PURPOSE

It is simply good business practice to periodically determine the financial worth or cash value of your company. This exercise gives you practice determining the total worth of a company using several methods. Use 1997 as the sample year.

INSTRUCTIONS

Step 1 Calculate the financial worth of Hershey based on three methods: (1) the net worth or stockholders' equity, (2) the future value of Hershey's earnings, and (3) the price-earnings ratio.

Step 2 In a dollar amount, how much is Hershey worth?

Step 3 Compare your analyses and conclusions with those of other students.

Experiential Exercise 8E

DEVELOPING A PRODUCT POSITIONING MAP FOR MY UNIVERSITY

PURPOSE

The purpose of this exercise is to give you practice developing product positioning maps. Nonprofit organizations, such as universities, increasingly are using product positioning maps to determine effective ways to implement strategies.

INSTRUCTIONS

Step 1 Join with two other persons in class to form a group of three.

Step 2 Jointly prepare a product positioning map that includes your institution and four other colleges or universities in your state.

Step 3 Go to the blackboard and diagram your product positioning map.

Step 4 Discuss differences among the maps diagrammed on the board.

DO BANKS REQUIRE PRO FORMA STATEMENTS?

PURPOSE

The purpose of this exercise is to explore the practical importance and use of projected financial statements in the banking business.

INSTRUCTIONS

Contact two local bankers by phone and seek answers to the questions listed below. Record the answers you receive and report your findings to the class.

1. Does your bank require projected financial statements as part of a business loan application?

2. How does your bank use projected financial statements when they are part of a business loan application?

3. What special advice do you give potential business borrowers in preparing projected financial statements?

PART 4

STRATEGY
EVALUATION

CHAPTER 9

Strategy Review, Evaluation, and Control

CHAPTER OUTLINE

- ◆ THE NATURE OF STRATEGY EVALUATION
- ◆ A STRATEGY-EVALUATION FRAMEWORK
- ◆ PUBLISHED SOURCES OF STRATEGY-EVALUATION INFORMATION
- ◆ CHARACTERISTICS OF AN EFFECTIVE EVALUATION SYSTEM
- ◆ CONTINGENCY PLANNING
- ◆ AUDITING

- ◆ USING COMPUTERS TO EVALUATE STRATEGIES
- ◆ GUIDELINES FOR EFFECTIVE STRATEGIC MANAGEMENT

- ■ EXPERIENTIAL EXERCISE 9A
  Preparing a Strategy-Evaluation Report for Hershey Foods

- ■ EXPERIENTIAL EXERCISE 9B
  Evaluating My University's Strategies

- ■ EXPERIENTIAL EXERCISE 9C
  Who Prepares an Environmental Audit?

CHAPTER OBJECTIVES

After studying this chapter, you should be able to do the following:

1. Describe a practical framework for evaluating strategies.
2. Explain why strategy evaluation is complex, sensitive, and yet essential for organizational success.
3. Discuss the importance of contingency planning in strategy evaluation.
4. Discuss the role of auditing in strategy evaluation.
5. Explain how computers can aid in evaluating strategies.

NOTABLE QUOTES

Complicated controls do not work. They confuse. They misdirect attention from what is to be controlled to the mechanics and methodology of the control.—SEYMOUR TILLES

Strategic thinking lives through dialogue or dies through writer's cramp.—DAVID MOORE

Although Plan A may be selected as the most realistic . . . the other major alternatives should not be forgotten. They may well serve as contingency plans.—DALE MCCONKEY

Organizations are most vulnerable when they are at the peak of their success.—R. T. LENZ

As spans of control widen, computers will become even more necessary.—BRIAN DUMAINE

Strategy evaluation must make it as easy as possible for managers to revise their plans and reach quick agreement on the changes.—DALE MCCONKEY

While strategy is a word that is usually associated with the future, its link to the past is no less central. Life is lived forward but understood backward. Managers may live strategy in the future, but they understand it through the past.—HENRY MINTZBERG

Unless strategy evaluation is performed seriously and systematically, and unless strategists are willing to act on the results, energy will be used up defending yesterday. No one will have the time, resources, or will to work on exploiting today, let alone to work on making tomorrow.—PETER DRUCKER

I have a duty to the soldiers, their parents, and the country to remove immediately any commander who does not satisfy the highest performance demands. It is a mistake to put a person in a command that is not the right command. It is therefore my job to think through where that person belongs.
—GEORGE C. MARSHALL

The best-formulated and -implemented strategies become obsolete as a firm's external and internal environments change. It is essential, therefore, that strategists systematically review, evaluate, and control the execution of strategies. This chapter presents a framework that can guide managers' efforts to evaluate strategic-management activities, to make sure they are working, and to make timely changes. Computer information systems being used to evaluate strategies are discussed. Guidelines are presented for formulating, implementing, and evaluating strategies.

THE NATURE OF STRATEGY EVALUATION

The strategic-management process results in decisions that can have significant, long-lasting consequences. Erroneous strategic decisions can inflict severe penalties and can be exceedingly difficult, if not impossible, to reverse. Most strategists agree, therefore, that strategy evaluation is vital to an organization's well-being; timely evaluations can alert management to problems or potential problems before a situation becomes critical. Strategy evaluation includes three basic activities: (1) examining the underlying bases of a firm's strategy, (2) comparing expected results with actual results, and (3) taking corrective actions to ensure that performance conforms to plans. The strategy-evaluation stage of the strategic-management process is illustrated in Figure 9–1.

Adequate and timely feedback is the cornerstone of effective strategy evaluation. Strategy evaluation can be no better than the information on which it operates. Too much pressure from top managers may result in lower managers contriving numbers they think will be satisfactory.

Strategy evaluation can be a complex and sensitive undertaking. Too much emphasis on evaluating strategies may be expensive and counterproductive. No one likes to be evaluated too closely! The more managers attempt to evaluate the behavior of others, the less control they have. Yet, too little or no evaluation can create even worse problems. Strategy evaluation is essential to ensure that stated objectives are being achieved.

In many organizations, strategy evaluation is simply an appraisal of how well an organization has performed. Have the firm's assets increased? Has there been an increase in profitability? Have sales increased? Have productivity levels increased? Have profit margin, return on investment, and earnings-per-share ratios increased? Some firms argue that their strategy must have been correct if the answers to these types of questions are affirmative. Well, the strategy or strategies may have been correct, but this type of reasoning can be misleading, because strategy evaluation must have both a long-run and short-run focus. Strategies often do not affect short-term operating results until it is too late to make needed changes.

It is impossible to demonstrate conclusively that a particular strategy is optimal or even to guarantee that it will work. One can, however, evaluate it for critical flaws. Richard Rumelt offered four criteria that could be used to evaluate a strategy: consistency, consonance, feasibility, and advantage. Described in Table 9–1, *consonance* and *advantage* are mostly based on a firm's external assessment, whereas *consistency* and *feasibility* are largely based on an internal assessment.

Strategy evaluation is important because organizations face dynamic environments in which key external and internal factors often change quickly and dramatically. Success today is no guarantee for success tomorrow! An organization should never be lulled into complacency with success. Countless firms have thrived one year only to struggle for survival the following year. For example, Waste Management's profits dropped in 1997 to negative $1.27 billion. Other companies that experienced net profit losses in excess of

FIGURE 9–1
A Comprehensive Strategic-Management Model

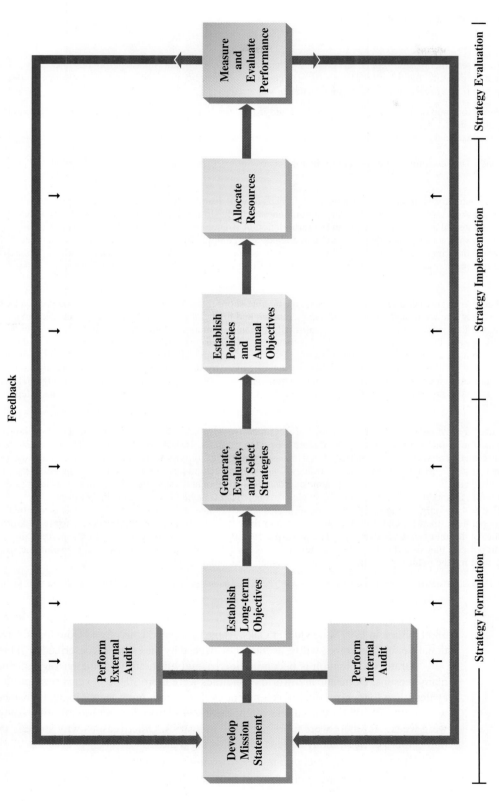

TABLE 9–1
Rumelt's Criteria for Evaluating Strategies

CONSISTENCY

A strategy should not present inconsistent goals and policies. Organizational conflict and interdepartmental bickering are often symptoms of a managerial disorder, but these problems may also be a sign of strategic inconsistency. There are three guidelines to help determine if organizational problems are due to inconsistencies in strategy:

• If managerial problems continue despite changes in personnel and if they tend to be issue-based rather than people-based, then strategies may be inconsistent.
• If success for one organizational department means, or is interpreted to mean, failure for another department, then strategies may be inconsistent.
• If policy problems and issues continue to be brought to the top for resolution, then strategies may be inconsistent.

CONSONANCE

Consonance refers to the need for strategists to examine *sets of trends* as well as individual trends in evaluating strategies. A strategy must represent an adaptive response to the external environment and to the critical changes occurring within it. One difficulty in matching a firm's key internal and external factors in the formulation of strategy is that most trends are the result of interactions among other trends. For example, the day care explosion came about as a combined result of many trends that included a rise in the average level of education, increased inflation, and an increase in women in the workforce. Although single economic or demographic trends might appear steady for many years, there are waves of change going on at the interaction level.

FEASIBILITY

A strategy must neither overtax available resources nor create unsolvable subproblems. The final broad test of strategy is its feasibility; that is, can the strategy be attempted within the physical, human, and financial resources of the enterprise? The financial resources of a business are the easiest to quantify and are normally the first limitation against which strategy is evaluated. It is sometimes forgotten, however, that innovative approaches to financing are often possible. Devices such as captive subsidiaries, sale-leaseback arrangements, and tying plant mortgages to long-term contracts have all been used effectively to help win key positions in suddenly expanding industries. A less quantifiable, but actually more rigid, limitation on strategic choice is that imposed by individual and organizational capabilities. In evaluating a strategy, it is important to examine whether an organization has demonstrated in the past that it possesses the abilities, competencies, skills, and talents needed to carry out a given strategy.

ADVANTAGE

A strategy must provide for the creation and/or maintenance of a competitive advantage in a selected area of activity. Competitive advantages normally are the result of superiority in one of three areas: 1) resources, 2) skills, or 3) position. The idea that the positioning of one's resources can enhance their combined effectiveness is familiar to military theorists, chess players, and diplomats. Position can also play a crucial role in an organization's strategy. Once gained, a good position is defensible—meaning that it is so costly to capture that rivals are deterred from full-scale attacks. Positional advantage tends to be self-sustaining as long as the key internal and environmental factors that underlie it remain stable. This is why entrenched firms can be almost impossible to unseat, even if their raw skill levels are only average. Although not all positional advantages are associated with size, it is true that larger organizations tend to operate in markets and use procedures that turn their size into advantage, while smaller firms seek product/market positions that exploit other types of advantage. The principal characteristics of good position is that it permits the firm to obtain advantage from policies that would not similarly benefit rivals without the same position. Therefore, in evaluating strategy, organizations should examine the nature of positional advantages associated with a given strategy.

Source: Adapted from Richard Rumelt, "The Evaluation of Business Strategy," in W. F. Glueck, ed., *Business Policy and Strategic Management* (New York: McGraw-Hill, 1980): 359–367.

$800 million in 1997 were Quaker Oaks, Apple Computer, Unisys, and Dow Jones. Organizational trouble can come swiftly, as further evidenced by the examples described in Table 9–2.

Strategy evaluation is becoming increasingly difficult with the passage of time, for many reasons. Domestic and world economies were more stable in years past, product life cycles were longer, product development cycles were longer, technological advancement was slower, change occurred less often, there were fewer competitors, foreign companies were weak, and there were more regulated industries. Other reasons why strategy evaluation is more difficult today include the following trends:

1. A dramatic increase in the environment's complexity
2. The increasing difficulty of predicting the future with accuracy

A few large Fortune 500 companies that experienced more than a 15 percent decline in revenues for 1997 are:		**TABLE 9–2** **Examples of** **Organizational Trouble**

Bradlees
Coastal
Mobil
LAM Research
WHX
Apple Computer

These large companies experienced more than a 50 percent decline in profits in 1997:

Whitman	Gateway 2000
Arco Chemical	Ceridian
Value City Department Stores	3Com
Sonoco Products	Bowater
Amerada Hess	Fort James
Occidental Petroleum	Willamette Industries
CVS	Enron
International Multifoods	United Stationers
Smart & Final	Cendant
Columbia/HCA Healthcare	Lucent Technologies
Trigon Healthcare	Frontier
Tupperware	SBC Communications
Alumax	Cilcorp
Engelhard	Florida Progress
Advanta	

3. The increasing number of variables
4. The rapid rate of obsolescence of even the best plans
5. The increase in the number of both domestic and world events affecting organizations
6. The decreasing time span for which planning can be done with any degree of certainty[1]

A fundamental problem facing managers today is how to effectively control employees in light of modern organizational demands for greater flexibility, innovation, creativity, and initiative from employees.[2] How can managers today ensure that empowered employees acting in an entrepreneurial manner do not put the well-being of the business at risk? Recall that Kidder, Peabody, & Company lost $350 million when one of their traders allegedly booked fictitious profits; Sears, Roebuck and Company took a $60 million charge against earnings after admitting that its automobile service businesses were performing unnecessary repairs. The costs to companies such as these in terms of damaged reputations, fines, missed opportunities, and diversion of management's attention are enormous.

When empowered employees are held accountable for and pressured to achieve specific goals and are given wide latitude in their actions to achieve them, there can be dysfunctional behavior. For example, Nordstrom, the upscale fashion retailer known for outstanding customer services, recently was subjected to lawsuits and fines when employees underreported hours worked in order to increase their sales per hour—the company's primary performance criterion. Nordstrom's customer service and earnings were enhanced until the misconduct was reported, at which time severe penalties were levied against the firm.

THE PROCESS OF EVALUATING STRATEGIES   Strategy evaluation is necessary for all sizes and kinds of organizations. Strategy evaluation should initiate managerial questioning of expectations and assumptions, should trigger a review of objectives and values, and should stimulate creativity in generating alternatives and formulating criteria of evaluation.[3] Regardless of the size of the organization, a certain amount of *management by wandering around* at all levels is essential to effective strategy evaluation. Strategy-evaluation activities should be performed on a continuing basis, rather than at the end of specified periods of time or just after problems occur. Waiting until the end of the year, for example, could result in a firm closing the barn door after the horses have already escaped.

Evaluating strategies on a continuous rather than a periodic basis allows benchmarks of progress to be established and more effectively monitored. Some strategies take years to implement; consequently, associated results may not become apparent for years. Successful strategists combine patience with a willingness to take corrective actions promptly when necessary. There always comes a time when corrective actions are needed in an organization! Centuries ago, a writer (perhaps Solomon) made the following observations about change:

> There is a time for everything,
> A time to be born and a time to die,
> A time to plant and a time to uproot,
> A time to kill and a time to heal,
> A time to tear down and a time to build,
> A time to weep and a time to laugh,
> A time to mourn and a time to dance,
> A time to scatter stones and a time to gather them,
> A time to embrace and a time to refrain,
> A time to search and a time to give up,
> A time to keep and a time to throw away,
> A time to tear and a time to mend,
> A time to be silent and a time to speak,
> A time to love and a time to hate,
> A time for war and a time for peace.[4]

In a study that examined the timing of strategy evaluation in many organizations, Lindsay and Rue hypothesized that strategy-evaluation activities would be conducted more frequently as environmental complexity and instability increased.[5] However, the researchers found a surprising inverse relationship between planning review frequency and organizational environment. Top managers in dynamic environments performed strategy-evaluation activities less frequently than those in stable environments. Lindsay and Rue concluded that forecasting is more difficult under complex and unstable environmental conditions, so strategists may see less need for frequent evaluation of their long-range plans. Evidence for this conclusion was stronger for large firms than for small ones.

Managers and employees of the firm should be continually aware of progress being made toward achieving the firm's objectives. As critical success factors change, organizational members should be involved in determining appropriate corrective actions. If assumptions and expectations deviate significantly from forecasts, then the firm should renew strategy-formulation activities, perhaps sooner than planned. In strategy evaluation, like strategy formulation and strategy implementation, people make the difference. Through involvement in the process of evaluating strategies, managers and employees become committed to keeping the firm moving steadily toward achieving objectives.

A STRATEGY-EVALUATION FRAMEWORK

Table 9–3 summarizes strategy-evaluation activities in terms of key questions that should be addressed, alternative answers to those questions, and appropriate actions for an organization to take. Notice that corrective actions are almost always needed except when (1) external and internal factors have not significantly changed and (2) the firm is progressing satisfactorily toward achieving stated objectives. Relationships among strategy-evaluation activities are illustrated in Figure 9–2.

REVIEWING BASES OF STRATEGY   As shown in Figure 9–2, *reviewing the underlying bases of an organization's strategy* could be approached by developing a revised EFE Matrix and IFE Matrix. A *revised IFE Matrix* should focus on changes in the organization's management, marketing, finance/accounting, production/operations, R&D, and computer information systems strengths and weaknesses. A *revised EFE Matrix* should indicate how effective a firm's strategies have been in response to key opportunities and threats. This analysis could also address such questions as the following:

1. How have competitors reacted to our strategies?
2. How have competitors' strategies changed?
3. Have major competitors' strengths and weaknesses changed?
4. Why are competitors making certain strategic changes?
5. Why are some competitors' strategies more successful than others?
6. How satisfied are our competitors with their present market positions and profitability?
7. How far can our major competitors be pushed before retaliating?
8. How could we more effectively cooperate with our competitors?

Numerous external and internal factors can prohibit firms from achieving long-term and annual objectives. Externally, actions by competitors, changes in demand, changes in technology, economic changes, demographic shifts, and governmental actions may prohibit objectives from being accomplished. Internally, ineffective strategies may have been chosen or implementation activities may have been poor. Objectives may have been too optimistic. Thus, failure to achieve objectives may not be the result of unsatisfactory work by managers and employees. All organizational members need to know this to encourage

TABLE 9–3
A Strategy-Evaluation Assessment Matrix

HAVE MAJOR CHANGES OCCURRED IN THE FIRM'S INTERNAL STRATEGIC POSITION?	HAVE MAJOR CHANGES OCCURRED IN THE FIRM'S EXTERNAL STRATEGIC POSITION?	HAS THE FIRM PROGRESSED SATISFACTORILY TOWARD ACHIEVING ITS STATED OBJECTIVES?	RESULT
No	No	No	Take corrective actions
Yes	Yes	Yes	Take corrective actions
Yes	Yes	No	Take corrective actions
Yes	No	Yes	Take corrective actions
Yes	No	No	Take corrective actions
No	Yes	Yes	Take corrective actions
No	Yes	No	Take corrective actions
No	No	Yes	Continue present strategic course

FIGURE 9–2
A Strategy-Evaluation Framework

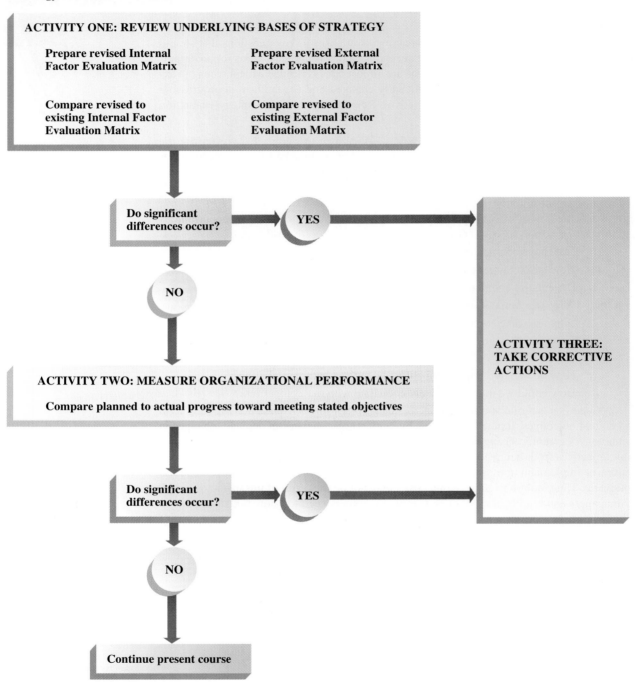

their support for strategy-evaluation activities. Organizations desperately need to know as soon as possible when their strategies are not effective. Sometimes managers and employees on the front line discover this well before strategists.

External opportunities and threats and internal strengths and weaknesses that represent the bases of current strategies should continually be monitored for change. It is not really a question of whether these factors will change, but rather when they will change and in what ways. Some key questions to address in evaluating strategies are given here.

1. Are our internal strengths still strengths?
2. Have we added other internal strengths? If so, what are they?
3. Are our internal weaknesses still weaknesses?
4. Do we now have other internal weaknesses? If so, what are they?
5. Are our external opportunities still opportunities?
6. Are there now other external opportunities? If so, what are they?
7. Are our external threats still threats?
8. Are there now other external threats? If so, what are they?
9. Are we vulnerable to a hostile takeover?

MEASURING ORGANIZATIONAL PERFORMANCE Another important strategy-evaluation activity is *measuring organizational performance*. This activity includes comparing expected results to actual results, investigating deviations from plans, evaluating individual performance, and examining progress being made toward meeting stated objectives. Both long-term and annual objectives are commonly used in this process. Criteria for evaluating strategies should be measurable and easily verifiable. Criteria that predict results may be more important than those that reveal what already has happened. For example, rather than simply being informed that sales last quarter were 20 percent under what was expected, strategists need to know that sales next quarter may be 20 percent below standard unless some action is taken to counter the trend. Really effective control requires accurate forecasting.

Failure to make satisfactory progress toward accomplishing long-term or annual objectives signals a need for corrective actions. Many factors, such as unreasonable policies, unexpected turns in the economy, unreliable suppliers or distributors, or ineffective strategies, can result in unsatisfactory progress toward meeting objectives. Problems can result from ineffectiveness (not doing the right things) or inefficiency (doing the right things poorly).

Determining which objectives are most important in the evaluation of strategies can be difficult. Strategy evaluation is based on both quantitative and qualitative criteria. Selecting the exact set of criteria for evaluating strategies depends on a particular organization's size, industry, strategies, and management philosophy. An organization pursuing a retrenchment strategy, for example, could have an entirely different set of evaluative criteria from an organization pursuing a market-development strategy. Quantitative criteria commonly used to evaluate strategies are financial ratios, which strategists use to make three critical comparisons: (1) comparing the firm's performance over different time periods, (2) comparing the firm's performance to competitors', and (3) comparing the firm's performance to industry averages. Some key financial ratios that are particularly useful as criteria for strategy evaluation are as follows:

1. Return on investment
2. Return on equity
3. Profit margin
4. Market share
5. Debt to equity
6. Earnings per share
7. Sales growth
8. Asset growth

But there are some potential problems associated with using quantitative criteria for evaluating strategies. First, most quantitative criteria are geared to annual objectives rather than long-term objectives. Also, different accounting methods can provide different results on many quantitative criteria. Third, intuitive judgments are almost always involved in deriving quantitative criteria. For these and other reasons, qualitative criteria are also important in evaluating strategies. Human factors such as high absenteeism and turnover rates, poor production quality and quantity rates, or low employee satisfaction can be underlying causes of declining performance. Marketing, finance/accounting, R&D, or computer information systems factors can also cause financial problems. Seymour Tilles identified six qualitative questions that are useful in evaluating strategies:

1. Is the strategy internally consistent?
2. Is the strategy consistent with the environment?
3. Is the strategy appropriate in view of available resources?
4. Does the strategy involve an acceptable degree of risk?
5. Does the strategy have an appropriate time framework?
6. Is the strategy workable?[6]

Some additional key questions that reveal the need for qualitative or intuitive judgments in strategy evaluation are as follows:

1. How good is the firm's balance of investments between high-risk and low-risk projects?
2. How good is the firm's balance of investments between long-term and short-term projects?
3. How good is the firm's balance of investments between slow-growing markets and fast-growing markets?
4. How good is the firm's balance of investments among different divisions?
5. To what extent are the firm's alternative strategies socially responsible?
6. What are the relationships among the firm's key internal and external strategic factors?
7. How are major competitors likely to respond to particular strategies?

TAKING CORRECTIVE ACTIONS   The final strategy-evaluation activity, *taking corrective actions*, requires making changes to reposition a firm competitively for the future. As indicated in the Global Perspective, expanding into Hong Kong is a popular action or strategy used by many firms. Other examples of changes that may be needed are altering an organization's structure, replacing one or more key individuals, selling a division, or revising a business mission. Other changes could include establishing or revising objectives, devising new policies, issuing stock to raise capital, adding additional salespersons, allocating resources differently, or developing new performance incentives. Taking corrective actions does not necessarily mean that existing strategies will be abandoned or even that new strategies must be formulated.

> The probabilities and possibilities for incorrect or inappropriate actions increase geometrically with an arithmetic increase in personnel. Any person directing an overall undertaking must check on the actions of the participants as well as the results, that they have achieved. If either the actions or results do not comply with preconceived or planned achievements, then corrective actions are needed.[7]

No organization can survive as an island; no organization can escape change. Taking corrective actions is necessary to keep an organization on track toward achieving stated objectives. In his thought-provoking books, *Future Shock* and *The Third Wave*, Alvin Toffler argued that business environments are becoming so dynamic and complex that they threaten people and organizations with *future shock*, which occurs when the nature, types, and speed of changes overpower an individual's or organization's ability and capacity to adapt. Strategy evaluation enhances an organization's ability to adapt successfully to changing circumstances. Brown and Agnew referred to this notion as *corporate agility*.[8]

GLOBAL PERSPECTIVE
Is Hong Kong the Winner?

Many Asian cities desire and even claim to have Asia's leading financial center, but Hong Kong is the clear winner. Hong Kong offers companies a free and open economy, the largest stock market in Asia except Tokyo, low tax rates, an advanced telecommunications system, an abundant supply of educated and experienced bi- and trilingual workers and professionals, a beautiful deepwater seaport, and close proximity to many other large Asian cities. Tokyo, despite its size and huge economy, remains comparably disadvantaged with English not being widely spoken, a long distance to other large Asian cities, and high operating costs. Other Asian cities such as Bangkok, Jakarta, Singapore, Shanghai, and Manila talk of financial leadership, but traffic jams, poor telephone service and infrastructure, and other problems make them no Hong Kong.

Evidence of Hong Kong's financial dominance is evidenced in the following list of new company equity issues in Asian cities and countries in 1996. This list reveals where new companies are locating in the Far East.

Source: Adapted from Sara Webb, "Still on Top," The Wall Street Journal (September 18, 1997): R18.

NATION OR CITY	NUMBER OF ISSUES	VALUE (IN MILLIONS)
Hong Kong	97	$ 8,312
Indonesia	69	6,159
Japan	20	4,869
Australia	16	4,592
Malaysia	136	4,039
Singapore	52	3,545
China	38	2,428
India	12	2,076
Taiwan	43	2,051
Philippines	33	1,893
South Korea	11	1,261
Thailand	41	1,050

As indicated in the Natural Environment Perspective, utilities across the United States increasingly are having to report where their power is derived so consumers can distinguish between polluters and nonpolluters.

Taking corrective actions raises employees' and managers' anxieties. Research suggests that participation in strategy-evaluation activities is one of the best ways to overcome individuals' resistance to change. According to Erez and Kanfer, individuals accept change best when they have a cognitive understanding of the changes, a sense of control over the situation, and an awareness that necessary actions are going to be taken to implement the changes.[9]

Strategy evaluation can lead to strategy-formulation changes, strategy-implementation changes, both formulation and implementation changes, or no changes at all. Strategists cannot escape having to revise strategies and implementation approaches sooner or later. Hussey and Langham offered the following insight on taking corrective actions:

> Resistance to change is often emotionally based and not easily overcome by rational argument. Resistance may be based on such feelings as loss of status, implied criticism of present competence, fear of failure in the new situation, annoyance at not being consulted, lack of understanding of the need for change, or insecurity in changing from well-known and fixed methods. It is necessary, therefore, to overcome such resistance by creating situations of participation and full explanation when changes are envisaged.[10]

Corrective actions should place an organization in a better position to capitalize upon internal strengths; to take advantage of key external opportunities; to avoid, reduce, or mitigate external threats; and to improve internal weaknesses. Corrective actions should have a proper time horizon and an appropriate amount of risk. They should be internally consistent and socially responsible. Perhaps most importantly, corrective actions strengthen an

NATURAL ENVIRONMENT
How Much Will You Pay for Green Electricity?

Since January 1, 1998, residential and industrial customers in California and parts of New England are able to choose their supplier of electricity just as everyone today may select their long-distance telephone carrier. More states are following suit as utility deregulation expands nationwide. The Environmental Protection Agency and others want to require all utilities in all states to disclose where their power is derived because 36 percent of all U.S. emissions of carbon dioxide, the dominant greenhouse gas, is produced by electric utilities. The Federal Trade Commission is considering a proposal to require all utilities to disclose on their bills a breakdown of their generation mix and a list of any resultant air pollutants.

Utilities are finding that environmentalism sells and that customers are, in fact, willing to pay more for power derived from noncoal sources. Branding the power generated as "green" will soon become the major meaningful differentiator in the whole energy sector, according to many analysts. California is finding that households and businesses are willing to pay, on average, $5.50 extra a month for electricity generated from a mix of geothermal and hydroelectric facilities rather than from coal-burning sources. A few New England utility companies now offering environmentally correct electricity include AllEnergy, Enova Energy, Northfield Mountain Energy, and Working Assets Green Power, Inc.

Source: Adapted from "For Sale: Environmentally Correct Electricity," The Wall Street Journal (July 23, 1997): B1, B5.

organization's competitive position in its basic industry. Continuous strategy evaluation keeps strategists close to the pulse of an organization and provides information needed for an effective strategic-management system. Carter Bayles described the benefits of strategy evaluation as follows:

> Evaluation activities may renew confidence in the current business strategy or point to the need for actions to correct some weaknesses, such as erosion of product superiority or technological edge. In many cases, the benefits of strategy evaluation are much more far-reaching, for the outcome of the process may be a fundamentally new strategy that will lead, even in a business that is already turning a respectable profit, to substantially increased earnings. It is this possibility that justifies strategy evaluation, for the payoff can be very large.[11]

PUBLISHED SOURCES OF STRATEGY-EVALUATION INFORMATION

A number of publications are helpful in evaluating a firm's strategies. For example, in its May and June issue each year, *Fortune* identifies and evaluates the Fortune 1,000 (the largest manufacturers) and the Fortune 50 (the largest retailers, transportation companies, utilities, banks, insurance companies, and diversified financial corporations in the United States). In these issues *Fortune* also ranks the best and worst performers on various factors such as return on investment, sales volume, and profitability.

Fortune annually evaluates organizations in 25 industries. Eight key attributes serve as evaluative criteria: quality of management; innovativeness; quality of products or services; long-term investment value; financial soundness; community and environmental responsibility; ability to attract, develop, and keep talented people; and use of corporate assets. *Fortune*'s 1997 evaluation in Table 9–4 reveals the firms considered best in their respective industries.[12]

Fortune and the Hay Group published the first-ever global list of the world's most admired companies in late 1997.[13] Some foreign companies that rank best in their industry over all U.S. competitors are the last three entries noted in Table 9–4.

COMPANY	INDUSTRY
J.P. Morgan	Money Center Banks
Golden West Financial	Savings Institutions
Merrill Lynch	Securities
Northwestern Mutual Life	Insurance: Life, Health
Berkshire Hathaway	Insurance: Property, Casualty
Norwest	Superregional Banks
American Express	Consumer Credit
Boeing	Aerospace
Southwest Airlines	Airlines
United Parcel Service	Mail, Package & Freight Delivery
Caterpillar	Industrial & Farm Equipment
Ryder System	Trucking
Toyota Motor Sales U.S.A.	Motor Vehicles & Parts
Norfolk Southern	Railroads
Nike	Apparel
Cardinal Health	Wholesalers
Herman Miller	Furniture
Nestlé USA	Food
Walgreen	Food & Drug Stores
Wal-Mart Stores	General Merchandise
Gillette	Soaps, Cosmetics
United Health Care	Health Care
Manpower	Temporary Help
Coca-Cola	Beverages
Fortune Brands	Tobacco
FPL Group	Electric & Gas Utilities
Burlington Resources	Mining, Crude Oil
Shell Oil	Petroleum Refining
Enron	Pipelines
USA Waste Services	Waste Management
Fluor	Engineering, Construction
Tyco International	Metal Products
Alcoa	Metals
Corning	Building Materials, Glass
Merck	Pharmaceuticals
Unifi	Textiles
Goodyear Tire & Rubber	Rubber & Plastic Products
DuPont	Chemicals
Kimberly-Clark	Forest & Paper Products
Omnicon Group	Advertising, Marketing
Tribune	Publishing, Printing
Walt Disney	Entertainment
Mirage Resorts	Hotels, Casinos, Resorts
Brunswick	Recreational Equipment
First Data	Computer & Data Services
Hewlett-Packard	Computers & Office Equipment
3M	Scientific & Photo Equipment
SBC Communications	Telecommunications
General Electric	Electronical Equipment
EMC	Computer Peripherals
Microsoft	Computer Software
Cicso Systems	Electrical Networks
Intel	Semiconductors
British Airways	Airlines
Toyota Motor	Motor Vehicles and Parts
Royal Dutch/Shell	Petroleum Refining

TABLE 9–4
***Fortune*'s 1997 Top Industry Performers**

Source: Edward Robinson, "America's Most Admired Companies," *Fortune* (March 3, 1997): 68–75.

Another excellent evaluation of corporations in America, "The Annual Report on American Industry," is published annually in the January issue of *Forbes*. It provides a detailed and comprehensive evaluation of hundreds of American companies in many different industries. *Business Week*, *Industry Week*, and *Dun's Business Month* also periodically publish detailed evaluations of American businesses and industries. Although published sources of strategy-evaluation information focus primarily on large, publicly held businesses, the comparative ratios and related information are widely used to evaluate small businesses and privately owned firms as well.

CHARACTERISTICS OF AN EFFECTIVE EVALUATION SYSTEM

Strategy evaluation must meet several basic requirements to be effective. First, strategy-evaluation activities must be economical; too much information can be just as bad as too little information; and too many controls can do more harm than good. Strategy-evaluation activities also should be meaningful; they should specifically relate to a firm's objectives. They should provide managers with useful information about tasks over which they have control and influence. Strategy-evaluation activities should provide timely information; on occasion and in some areas, managers may need information daily. For example, when a firm has diversified by acquiring another firm, evaluative information may be needed frequently. However, in an R&D department, daily or even weekly evaluative information could be dysfunctional. Approximate information that is timely is generally more desirable as a basis for strategy evaluation than accurate information that does not depict the present. Frequent measurement and rapid reporting may frustrate control rather than give better control. The time dimension of control must coincide with the time span of the event being measured.

Strategy evaluation should be designed to provide a true picture of what is happening. For example, in a severe economic downturn, productivity and profitability ratios may drop alarmingly, although employees and managers are actually working harder. Strategy evaluations should portray this type of situation fairly. Information derived from the strategy-evaluation process should facilitate action and should be directed to those individuals in the organization who need to take action based on it. Managers commonly ignore evaluative reports that are provided for informational purposes only; not all managers need to receive all reports. Controls need to be action-oriented rather than information-oriented.

The strategy-evaluation process should not dominate decisions; it should foster mutual understanding, trust, and common sense! No department should fail to cooperate with another in evaluating strategies. Strategy evaluations should be simple, not too cumbersome, and not too restrictive. Complex strategy-evaluation systems often confuse people and accomplish little. The test of an effective evaluation system is its usefulness, not its complexity.

Large organizations require a more elaborate and detailed strategy-evaluation system because it is more difficult to coordinate efforts among different divisions and functional areas. Managers in small companies often communicate with each other and their employees daily and do not need extensive evaluative reporting systems. Familiarity with local environments usually makes gathering and evaluating information much easier for small organizations than for large businesses. But the key to an effective strategy-evaluation system may be the ability to convince participants that failure to accomplish certain objectives within a prescribed time is not necessarily a reflection of their performance.

There is no one ideal strategy-evaluation system. The unique characteristics of an organization, including its size, management style, purpose, problems, and strengths, can determine a strategy-evaluation and control system's final design. Robert Waterman offered the following observation about successful organizations' strategy-evaluation and control systems:

> Successful companies treat facts as friends and controls as liberating. Morgan Guaranty and Wells Fargo not only survive but thrive in the troubled waters of bank deregulation, because their strategy evaluation and control systems are sound, their risk is contained, and they know themselves and the competitive situation so well. Successful companies have a voracious hunger for facts. They see information where others see only data. They love comparisons, rankings, anything that removes decision-making from the realm of mere opinion. Successful companies maintain tight, accurate financial controls. Their people don't regard controls as an imposition of autocracy, but as the benign checks and balances that allow them to be creative and free.[14]

CONTINGENCY PLANNING

A basic premise of good strategic management is that firms plan ways to deal with unfavorable and favorable events before they occur. Too many organizations prepare contingency plans just for unfavorable events; this is a mistake, because both minimizing threats and capitalizing on opportunities can improve a firm's competitive position.

Regardless of how carefully strategies are formulated, implemented, and evaluated, unforeseen events such as strikes, boycotts, natural disasters, arrival of foreign competitors, and government actions can make a strategy obsolete. To minimize the impact of potential threats, organizations should develop contingency plans as part of the strategy-evaluation process. *Contingency plans* can be defined as alternative plans that can be put into effect if certain key events do not occur as expected. Only high-priority areas require the insurance of contingency plans. Strategists cannot and should not try to cover all bases by planning for all possible contingencies. But in any case, contingency plans should be as simple as possible.

Some contingency plans commonly established by firms include the following:

1. If a major competitor withdraws from particular markets as intelligence reports indicate, what actions should our firm take?
2. If our sales objectives are not reached, what actions should our firm take to avoid profit losses?
3. If demand for our new product exceeds plans, what actions should our firm take to meet the higher demand?
4. If certain disasters occur—such as loss of computer capabilities; a hostile takeover attempt; loss of patent protection; or destruction of manufacturing facilities due to earthquakes, tornados, or hurricanes—what actions should our firm take?
5. If a new technological advancement makes our new product obsolete sooner than expected, what actions should our firm take?

Too many organizations discard alternative strategies not selected for implementation although the work devoted to analyzing these options would render valuable information. Alternative strategies not selected for implementation can serve as contingency plans in case the strategy or strategies selected do not work.

When strategy-evaluation activities reveal the need for a major change quickly, an appropriate contingency plan can be executed in a timely way. Contingency plans can promote a strategist's ability to respond quickly to key changes in the internal and external bases of an organization's current strategy. For example, if underlying assumptions about the economy turn out to be wrong and contingency plans are ready, then managers can make appropriate changes promptly.

In some cases, external or internal conditions present unexpected opportunities. When such opportunities occur, contingency plans could allow an organization to capitalize on them quickly. Linneman and Chandran reported that contingency planning gave users such as DuPont, Dow Chemical, Consolidated Foods, and Emerson Electric three major benefits: It permitted quick response to change, it prevented panic in crisis situations, and it made managers more adaptable by encouraging them to appreciate just how variable the future can be. They suggested that effective contingency planning involves a seven-step process as follows:

1. Identify both beneficial and unfavorable events that could possibly derail the strategy or strategies.

2. Specify trigger points. Calculate about when contingent events are likely to occur.

3. Assess the impact of each contingent event. Estimate the potential benefit or harm of each contingent event.

4. Develop contingency plans. Be sure that contingency plans are compatible with current strategy and are economically feasible.

5. Assess the counterimpact of each contingency plan. That is, estimate how much each contingency plan will capitalize on or cancel out its associated contingent event. Doing this will quantify the potential value of each contingency plan.

6. Determine early warning signals for key contingent events. Monitor the early warning signals.

7. For contingent events with reliable early warning signals, develop advance action plans to take advantage of the available lead time.[15]

AUDITING

A frequently used tool in strategy evaluation is the audit. *Auditing* is defined by the American Accounting Association (AAA) as "a systematic process of objectively obtaining and evaluating evidence regarding assertions about economic actions and events to ascertain

TABLE 9–5
Key Strategy-Evaluation Questions

1. Do you feel that the strategic-management system exists to provide service to you in your day-to-day work? How has it helped you in this respect?
2. Has the strategic-management system provided the service that you feel was promised at the start of its design and implementation? In which areas has it failed and exceeded, in your opinion?
3. Do you consider that the strategic-management system has been implemented with due regard to costs and benefits? Are there any areas in which you consider the costs to be excessive?
4. Do you feel comfortable using the system? Could more attention have been paid to matching the output of the system to your needs and, if so, in what areas?
5. Is the system flexible enough in your opinion? If not, where should changes be made?
6. Do you still keep a personal store of information in a notebook or elsewhere? If so, will you share that information with the system? Do you see any benefits in so doing?
7. Is the strategic-management system still evolving? Can you influence this evolution and, if not, why not?
8. Does the system provide timely, relevant, and accurate information? Are there any areas of deficiency?
9. Do you think that the strategic-management system makes too much use of complex procedures and models? Can you suggest areas in which less complicated techniques might be used to advantage?
10. Do you consider that there has been sufficient attention paid to the confidentiality and security of the information in the system? Can you suggest areas for improvement of these aspects of its operation?

Source: Adapted from K. J. Radford, *Information Systems for Strategic Decisions*. © 1978: 220–221. Adapted by permission of Prentice-Hall, Inc., Englewood Cliffs, New Jersey. Also, Lloyd Byars, *Strategic Management* (New York: Harper & Row, 1984): 237.

TABLE 9–6
The Planning Process Audit

1. To what extent do you feel top management has been committed to the pursuit of stated corporate strategy?
2. To what extent do you feel committed to the pursuit of stated corporate strategy?
3. Has top management's decision making been consistent with stated corporate strategy?
4. Has decision making been more or less centralized than anticipated?
5. Do you feel you have received sufficient resource support (financial and human) to pursue your stated plans?
6. Do everyday, operational plans seem to support the overall corporate strategy?
7. How would you rate the extent and quality of the coordination of plans among functional areas/departments/divisions?
8. How would you rate the extent and quality of the communication of plans to lower organizational levels?
9. Does the reward system (pay, promotions, etc.) seem to be tied to your planning efforts?
10. Do the written plans seem to adequately represent the actual goals toward which managers seem to be working?
11. How complex is the present planning process?
12. How formal is the present planning process?
13. Do you feel you have the right types and amounts of external information to fulfill your planning responsibilities?
14. Do you feel you have the right types and amounts of internal information to fulfill your planning responsibilities? If not, what other internal information do you feel you need?
15. Would any other training help you do a better job of planning? If yes, what other specific training would help?
16. What are the major problems of the current planning system?
17. How might the planning process be improved upon?

Source: C. Aaron Kelly, "Auditing the Planning Process," *Managerial Planning* 32, no. 4 (January–February 1984): 13. Used with permission.

the degree of correspondence between those assertions and established criteria, and communicating the results to interested users."[16] People who perform audits can be divided into three groups: independent auditors, government auditors, and internal auditors. Independent auditors basically are certified public accountants (CPAs) who provide their services to organizations for a fee; they examine the financial statements of an organization to determine whether they have been prepared according to generally accepted accounting principles (GAAP) and whether they fairly represent the activities of the firm. Independent auditors use a set of standards called generally accepted auditing standards (GAAS). Public accounting firms often have a consulting arm that provides strategy-evaluation services.

Two government agencies—the General Accounting Office (GAO) and the Internal Revenue Service (IRS)—employ government auditors responsible for making sure that organizations comply with federal laws, statutes, and policies. GAO and IRS auditors can audit any public or private organization. The third group of auditors are employees within an organization who are responsible for safeguarding company assets, for assessing the efficiency of company operations, and for ensuring that generally accepted business procedures are practiced. To evaluate the effectiveness of an organization's strategic-management system, internal auditors often seek answers to the questions posed in Table 9–5. C. Aaron Kelly developed the *Planning Process Audit* presented in Table 9–6.

THE ENVIRONMENTAL AUDIT For an increasing number of firms, overseeing environmental affairs is no longer a technical function performed by specialists; it rather has become an important strategic-management concern. Product design, manufacturing, transportation, customer use, packaging, product disposal, and corporate rewards and sanctions should reflect environmental considerations. Firms that effectively manage environmental affairs are benefiting from constructive relations with employees, consumers, suppliers, and distributors.

Shimell emphasized the need for organizations to conduct environmental audits of their operations and to develop a Corporate Environmental Policy (CEP).[17] Shimell contended that an environmental audit should be as rigorous as a financial audit and should include training workshops in which staff can help design and implement the policy. The CEP should be budgeted and requisite funds allocated to ensure that it is not a public relations facade. A Statement of Environmental Policy should be published periodically to inform shareholders and the public of environmental actions taken by the firm.

Instituting an environmental audit can include moving environmental affairs from the staff side of the organization to the line side. Some firms are also introducing environmental criteria and objectives in their performance appraisal instruments and systems. Conoco, for example, ties compensation of all its top managers to environmental action plans. Occidental Chemical includes environmental responsibilities in all its job descriptions for positions.

USING COMPUTERS TO EVALUATE STRATEGIES

When properly designed, installed, and operated, a computer network can efficiently acquire information promptly and accurately. Networks can allow diverse strategy-evaluation reports to be generated for—and responded to by—different levels and types of managers. For example, strategists will want reports concerned with whether the mission, objectives, and strategies of the enterprise are being achieved. Middle managers could require strategy-implementation information such as whether construction of a new facility is on schedule or a product's development is proceeding as expected. Lower-level managers could need evaluation reports that focus on operational concerns such as absenteeism and turnover rates, productivity rates, and the number and nature of grievances.

Business today has become so competitive that strategists are being forced to extend planning horizons and to make decisions under greater degrees of uncertainty. As a result, more information has to be obtained and assimilated to formulate, implement, and evaluate strategic decisions. In any competitive situation, the side with the best intelligence (information) usually wins; computers enable managers to evaluate vast amounts of information quickly and accurately. Use of the Internet, World Wide Web, e-mail, and search engines can make the difference today between a firm that is up-to-date or out-of-date in the currentness of information the firm uses to make strategic decisions. As indicated in the Information Technology Perspective, breaches in computer security must be a concern for businesses.

A limitation of computer-based systems to evaluate and monitor strategy execution is that personal values, attitudes, morals, preferences, politics, personalities, and emotions are not programmable. This limitation accents the need to view computers as tools, rather than as actual decision-making devices. Computers can significantly enhance the process of effectively integrating intuition and analysis in strategy evaluation. The General Accounting Office of the United States Government offered the following conclusions regarding the appropriate role of computers in strategy evaluation:

> The aim is to enhance and extend judgment. Computers should be looked upon not as a provider of solutions, but rather as a framework which permits science and judgment to be brought together and made explicit. It is the explicitness of this structure, the decision-maker's ability to probe, modify, and examine "What if?" alternatives, that is of value in extending judgment.[18]

INFORMATION TECHNOLOGY

How Widespread Are Computer Security Breaches?

Nearly 50 percent of American companies experienced security breaches in 1997, up from 37 percent in 1996. Prevalence of security breaches among U.S. firms can be categorized as follows:

Virus contamination	27%
Notebook thefts	24
Insider abuse of Internet access	13
Fraud	6.9
Unauthorized access by insider	6.7
Theft of proprietary information	5.8
Financial fraud	5.3
Sabotage	4.5
System penetration by outsiders	3.5
Wiretapping	1.4
Eavesdropping	1.1

Despite the computer security threat, U.S. businesses are rapidly increasing their commerce over the Internet. General Electric, for example, recently moved its 40,000 customers from electronic data interchange (EDI) transactions to the Internet. Boeing recently established its Boeing Part Page, a Web site that enables all its customers to order parts and get price quotations over the Internet.

In response to the computer security threat, an abundance of new technology and tools are now available to secure Web sites and lessen the threat of computer security breaches. The tools include firewalls, digital IDs, certifica-

tion, encryption, scrambling, and digital dollars. A growing number of companies are hiring a full-time computer security person. Computer security is a profession that is growing about 20 percent per year in the United States.

Source: Adapted from Laton McCartney, "A Safety Net," Industry Week (April 21, 1997): 74–81.

GUIDELINES FOR EFFECTIVE STRATEGIC MANAGEMENT

Failing to follow certain guidelines in conducting strategic management can foster criticisms of the process and create problems for the organization. An integral part of strategy evaluation must be to evaluate the quality of the strategic-management process. Issues such as "Is strategic management in our firm a people process or paper process?" should be addressed.

> Even the most technically perfect strategic plan will serve little purpose if it is not implemented. Many organizations tend to spend an inordinate amount of time, money, and effort on developing the strategic plan, treating the means and circumstances under which it will be implemented as afterthoughts! Change comes through implementation and evaluation, not through the plan. A technically imperfect plan that is implemented well will achieve more than the perfect plan that never gets off the paper on which it is typed.[19]

Strategic management must not become a self-perpetuating bureaucratic mechanism. Rather, it must be a self-reflective learning process that familiarizes managers and employees in the organization with key strategic issues and feasible alternatives for resolving those issues. Strategic management must not become ritualistic, stilted, orchestrated, or too formal, predictable, and rigid. Words supported by numbers, rather than numbers supported by words, should represent the medium for explaining strategic issues and organizational responses. A key role of strategists is to facilitate continuous organizational learning and change. Robert Waterman emphasized this, saying:

Successful companies know how to keep things moving. If they share a habit pattern, it's the habit of habit breaking. Sometimes they seem to like change for its own sake. IBM's chief executive John Akers says, "IBM never reorganizes except for a good business reason, but if they haven't reorganized in a while, that's a good business reason." Successful companies are deliberate bureaucracy-busters. They delight in smashing pettifogging encumbrances that Harry Quadracci calls "playing office."[20]

R. T. Lenz offered some important guidelines for effective strategic management:

Keep the strategic-management process as simple and nonroutine as possible. Eliminate jargon and arcane planning language. Remember, strategic management is a process for fostering learning and action, not merely a formal system for control. To avoid routinized behavior, vary assignments, team membership, meeting formats, and the planning calendar. The process should not be totally predictable, and settings must be changed to stimulate creativity. Emphasize word-oriented plans with numbers as back-up material. If managers cannot express their strategy in a paragraph or so, they either do not have one or do not understand it. Stimulate thinking and action that challenge the assumptions underlying current corporate strategy. Welcome bad news. If strategy is not working, managers desperately need to know it. Further, no pertinent information should be classified as inadmissable merely because it cannot be quantified. Build a corporate culture in which the role of strategic management and its essential purposes are understood. Do not permit "technicians" to co-opt the process. It is ultimately a process for learning and action. Speak of it in these terms. Attend to psychological, social, and political dimensions, as well as the information infrastructure and administrative procedures supporting it.[21]

An important guideline for effective strategic management is open-mindedness. A willingness and eagerness to consider new information, new viewpoints, new ideas, and new possibilities is essential; all organizational members must share a spirit of inquiry and learning. Strategists such as chief executive officers, presidents, owners of small businesses, and heads of government agencies must commit themselves to listen to and understand managers' positions well enough to be able to restate those positions to the managers' satisfaction. In addition, managers and employees throughout the firm should be able to describe the strategists' positions to the satisfaction of the strategists. This degree of discipline will promote understanding and learning.

No organization has unlimited resources. No firm can take on an unlimited amount of debt or issue an unlimited amount of stock to raise capital. Therefore, no organization can pursue all the strategies that potentially could benefit the firm. Strategic decisions thus always have to be made to eliminate some courses of action and to allocate organizational resources among others. Most organizations can afford to pursue only a few corporate-level strategies at any given time. It is a critical mistake for managers to pursue too many strategies at the same time, thereby spreading the firm's resources so thin that all strategies are jeopardized. Joseph Charyk, CEO of The Communication Satellite Corporation (Comsat), said, "We have to face the cold fact that Comsat may not be able to do all it wants. We must make hard choices on which ventures to keep and which to fold."

Strategic decisions require trade-offs such as long-range versus short-range considerations or maximizing profits versus increasing shareholders' wealth. There are ethics issues too. Strategy trade-offs require subjective judgments and preferences. In many cases, a lack of objectivity in formulating strategy results in a loss of competitive posture and profitability. Most organizations today recognize that strategic-management concepts and techniques can enhance the effectiveness of decisions. Subjective factors such as attitudes toward risk, concern for social responsibility, and organizational culture will always affect strategy-formulation decisions, but organizations need to be as objective as possible in considering qualitative factors.

CONCLUSION

This chapter presents a strategy-evaluation framework that can facilitate accomplishment of annual and long-term objectives. Effective strategy evaluation allows an organization to capitalize on internal strengths as they develop, to exploit external opportunities as they emerge, to recognize and defend against threats, and to mitigate internal weaknesses before they become detrimental.

Strategists in successful organizations take the time to formulate, implement, and then evaluate strategies deliberately and systematically. Good strategists move their organization forward with purpose and direction, continually evaluating and improving the firm's external and internal strategic position. Strategy evaluation allows an organization to shape its own future rather than allowing it to be constantly shaped by remote forces that have little or no vested interest in the well-being of the enterprise.

Although not a guarantee for success, strategic management allows organizations to make effective long-term decisions, to execute those decisions efficiently, and to take corrective actions as needed to ensure success. Computer networks and the Internet help to coordinate strategic-management activities and to ensure that decisions are based on good information. A key to effective strategy evaluation and to successful strategic management is an integration of intuition and analysis.

A potentially fatal problem is the tendency for analytical and intuitive issues to polarize. This polarization leads to strategy evaluation that is dominated by either analysis or intuition, or to strategy evaluation that is discontinuous, with a lack of coordination among analytical and intuitive issues.[22]

Strategists in successful organizations realize that strategic management is first and foremost a people process. It is an excellent vehicle for fostering organizational communication. People are what make the difference in organizations.

The real key to effective strategic management is to accept the premise that the planning process is more important than the written plan, that the manager is continuously planning and does not stop planning when the written plan is finished. The written plan is only a snapshot as of the moment it is approved. If the manager is not planning on a continuous basis—planning, measuring, and revising—the written plan can become obsolete the day it is finished. This obsolescence becomes more of a certainty as the increasingly rapid rate of change makes the business environment more uncertain.[23]

We invite you to visit the DAVID page on the Prentice Hall Web site at
www.prenhall.com/davidsm
for this chapter's World Wide Web exercises.

 **TAKE IT TO THE NET**

KEY TERMS AND CONCEPTS

Advantage (p. 280)
Auditing (p. 294)
Consistency (p. 280)
Consonance (p. 280)
Contingency Plans (p. 293)
Corporate Agility (p. 288)

Feasibility (p. 280)
Future Shock (p. 288)
Management by Wandering Around (p. 284)
Measuring Organizational Performance (p. 287)
Planning Process Audit (p. 295)

Reviewing the Underlying Bases of an Organization's Strategy (p. 285)
Revised EFE Matrix (p. 285)
Revised IFE Matrix (p. 285)
Taking Corrective Actions (p. 288)

ISSUES FOR REVIEW AND DISCUSSION

1. Why has strategy evaluation become so important in business today?

2. BellSouth Services is considering putting divisional EFE and IFE matrices on-line for continual updating. How would this affect strategy evaluation?

3. What types of quantitative and qualitative criteria do you think David Glass, CEO of Wal-Mart, uses to evaluate the company's strategy?

4. As owner of a local, independent supermarket, explain how you would evaluate the firm's strategy.

5. Under what conditions are corrective actions not required in the strategy-evaluation process?

6. Identify types of organizations that may need to evaluate strategy more frequently than others. Justify your choices.

7. As executive director of the state forestry commission, in what way and how frequently would you evaluate the organization's strategies?

8. Identify some key financial ratios that would be important in evaluating a bank's strategy.

9. As owner of a chain of hardware stores, describe how you would approach contingency planning.

10. Strategy evaluation allows an organization to take a proactive stance toward shaping its own future. Discuss the meaning of this statement.

11. Select an article listed in the suggested readings for this chapter. Give a five-minute oral report to the class summarizing the article and your thoughts on the particular topic.

12. Identify guidelines that you think are most important for using strategic management effectively in organizations. Justify your answer.

NOTES

1. Dale McConkey, "Planning in a Changing Environment," *Business Horizons* (September–October 1988): 64.

2. Robert Simons, "Control in an Age of Empowerment," *Harvard Business Review* (March–April 1995): 80.

3. Dale Zand, "Reviewing the Policy Process," *California Management Review* 21, no. 1 (Fall 1978): 37.

4. Eccles. 3: 1–8.

5. W. Lindsay and L. Rue, "Impact of the Organization Environment on the Long-Range Planning Process: A Contingency View," *Academy of Management Journal* 23, no. 3 (September 1980): 402.

6. Seymour Tilles, "How to Evaluate Corporate Strategy," *Harvard Business Review* 41 (July–August 1963): 111–21.

7. Claude George, Jr., *The History of Management Thought* (Englewood Cliffs, New Jersey: Prentice-Hall, 1968), 165–66.

8. John Brown and Neil Agnew, "Corporate Agility," *Business Horizons* 25, no. 2 (March–April 1982): 29.

9. M. Erez and F. Kanfer, "The Role of Goal Acceptance in Goal Setting and Task Performance," *Academy of Management Review* 8, no. 3 (July 1983): 457.

10. D. Hussey and M. Langham, *Corporate Planning: The Human Factor* (Oxford, England: Pergamon Press, 1979): 138.

11. Carter Bayles, "Strategic Control: The President's Paradox," *Business Horizons* 20, no. 4 (August 1977): 18.

12. Edward Robinson and Thomas Stewart, "America's Most Admired Companies," *Fortune* (March 2, 1998): 70–107.

13. Anne Fisher, "The World's Most Admired Companies," *Fortune* (October 27, 1997): 120.

14. Robert Waterman, Jr., "How the Best Get Better," *Business Week* (September 14, 1987): 105.

15. Robert Linneman and Rajan Chandran, "Contingency Planning: A Key to Swift Managerial Action in the Uncertain Tomorrow," *Managerial Planning* 29, no. 4 (January–February 1981): 23–27.

16. American Accounting Association, *Report of Committee on Basic Auditing Concepts* (1971): 15–74.

17. Pamela Shimell, "Corporate Environmental Policy in Practice," *Long Range Planning* 24, no. 3 (June 1991): 10.

18. GAO *Report* PAD—80–21, 17.

19. McConkey, 66.

20. Robert H. Waterman, Jr., *The Renewal Factor: How the Best Get and Keep the Competitive Edge* (New York: Bantam, 1987).

21. R. T. Lenz, "Managing the Evolution of the Strategic Planning Process," *Business Horizons* 30, no. 1 (January–February 1987): 39.

22. Michael McGinnis, "The Key to Strategic Planning: Integrating Analysis and Intuition," *Sloan Management Review* 26, no. 1 (Fall 1984): 49.

23. McConkey, 72.

CURRENT READINGS

Atkinson, Anthony A., John H. Waterhouse, and Robert B. Wells. "A Stakeholder Approach to Strategic Performance Measurement." *Sloan Management Review* 38, no. 3 (Spring 1997): 25–38.

Banker, R. D., H. H. Chang, and S. K. Majumdar. "A Framework for Analyzing Changes in Strategic Performance." *Strategic Management Journal* 17, no. 9 (November 1996): 693–712.

Hamilton, Robert D. III, Virginia A. Taylor, and Roger J. Kashlak. "Designing a Control System for a Multinational Subsidiary." *Long Range Planning* 29, no. 6 (December 1996): 857–868.

Hitt, Michael A., Robert E. Hoskisson, Richard A. Johnson, and Douglas D. Moesel. "The Market for Corporate Control and Firm Innovation." *Academy of Management Journal* 39, no. 5 (October 1996): 1084–1119.

Kroll, M., P. Wright, L. Toombs, and H. Leavell. "Forms of Control: A Critical Determinant of Acquisition Performance and CEO Rewards." *Strategic Management Journal* 18, no. 2 (February 1997): 85–96.

Lassar, W. M. and J. L. Kerr. "Strategy and Control in Supplier-Distributor Relationships: An Agency Perspective." *Strategic Management Journal* 17, no. 8 (October 1996): 613–632.

Leifer, Richard and Peter K. Mills. "An Information Processing Approach for Deciding upon Control Strategies and Reducing Control Loss in Emerging Organizations." *Journal of Management* 22, no. 1 (1996): 113–138.

Muralidharan, Raman. "Strategic Control for Fast-Moving Markets: Updating the Strategy and Monitoring Performance." *Long Range Planning* 30, no. 1 (February 1997): 64–73.

Noda, T. and J. L. Bower. "Strategy Making as Iterated Processes of Resource Allocation." *Strategic Management Journal* 17, Special Issue (Summer 1996): 159–192.

Slater, Stanley F., Eric M. Olson, and Venkateshwar K. Reddy. "Strategy-Based Performance Measurement." *Business Horizons* 40, no. 4 (July–August 1997): 37–44.

EXPERIENTIAL EXERCISES

Experiential Exercise 9A

PREPARING A STRATEGY-EVALUATION REPORT FOR HERSHEY FOODS

PURPOSE

This exercise can give you experience locating strategy-evaluation information in your college library. Published sources of information can significantly enhance the strategy-evaluation process. Performance information on competitors, for example, can help put into perspective a firm's own performance.

INSTRUCTIONS

Step 1 Use *F & S Index of Corporations and Industries, Business Periodicals Index,* and *The Wall Street Journal Index* in your college library to locate strategy-evaluation information on Hershey, Mars, and Nestlé. Read 5 to 10 articles written in the last 6 months that discuss these firms or the confectionery industry.

Step 2 Summarize your research findings by preparing a strategy-evaluation report for your instructor. Include in your report a summary of Hershey's strategies and performance in 1998 and a summary of your conclusions regarding the effectiveness of Hershey's strategies.

Step 3 Based on your analysis, do you feel Hershey is pursuing effective strategies? What recommendations would you offer Kenneth Wolfe, Hershey's chief executive officer?

Experiential Exercise 9B

EVALUATING MY UNIVERSITY'S STRATEGIES

PURPOSE

An important part of evaluating strategies is determining the nature and extent of changes in an organization's external opportunities/threats and internal strengths/weaknesses. Changes in these underlying critical success factors can indicate a need to change or modify the firm's strategies.

INSTRUCTIONS

As a class, discuss positive and negative changes in your university's external and internal factors during your college career. Begin by listing on the board new or emerging opportunities and threats. Then identify strengths and weaknesses that have changed significantly during your college career. In light of the external and internal changes identified, discuss whether your university's strategies need modifying. Are there any new strategies that you would recommend? Make a list to recommend to your department chair, dean, or chancellor.

WHO PREPARES AN ENVIRONMENTAL AUDIT?

PURPOSE

The purpose of this activity is to determine the nature and prevalence of environmental audits among companies in your state.

INSTRUCTIONS

Contact by phone at least five different plant managers or owners of large businesses in your area. Seek answers to the questions listed below. Present your findings in a written report to your instructor.

1. Does your company conduct an environmental audit? If yes, please describe the nature and scope of the audit.

2. Are environmental criteria included in the performance evaluation of managers? If yes, please specify the criteria.

3. Are environmental affairs more a technical function or a management function in your company?

4. Does your firm offer any environmental workshops for employees? If yes, please describe them.

PART 5

GLOBAL ISSUES IN STRATEGIC MANAGEMENT

CHAPTER 10

International Strategic Management

CHAPTER OUTLINE

CHAPTER OBJECTIVES

After studying this chapter, you should be able to do the following:

1. Describe the effects of a world economy and global competitors on strategic management.

2. Discuss the nature and strategic implications of diverse cultures around the world.

3. Discuss ramifications of the North American Free Trade Agreement (NAFTA).

4. Discuss changes in Japan as they affect strategy decisions.

5. Discuss changes in Mexico as they affect strategy decisions.

6. Discuss changes in Russia as they affect strategy decisions.

7. Discuss changes in Europe as they affect strategy decisions.

8. Discuss changes in China as they affect strategy decisions.

9. Provide guidelines for firms interested in initiating, continuing, or expanding international operations.

NOTABLE
QUOTES

*I*n the 1990s, globalization will mature from a buzzword to a pervasive reality. Companies will have to meet global standards for quality, design, pricing, and service.—BRIAN DUMAINE

*M*arket research is unfamiliar. The closest thing to a market survey that many East Europeans have experienced is a government interrogation.—JOHN QUELCH

*S*ad but true, U.S. businesspeople have the lowest foreign language proficiency of any major trading nation. U.S. business schools do not emphasize foreign languages, and students traditionally avoid them.—RONALD DULEK

*J*apan is not going to change. We love to work hard and Americans don't. . . . The result is that we'll continue to work hard and amass huge surpluses of money. We'll buy up your land and you'll live there and pay rent.—WATARU HIRAIZUMI

*T*he inclination of Japanese, Taiwanese, and Korean workers to sacrifice themselves for the good of the firm, in ways that we may find strange, surely bears some relation to their performance and rising competitiveness.—PHILIP WEST

*F*or Americans in the Southwest U.S., the major foreign country that affects business operations is clear. It's Mexico.—KEN THURSTON

*O*ne can master a few phrases of Chinese or Japanese, learn that Seoul is west of Tokyo, buy the proper gifts, learn to eat with chopsticks, and still be far from understanding what is really going on in the Far East.—PHILIP WEST

*A*mericans can be more successful if they recognize that foreign managers see them differently than they see themselves.—ARTHUR WHITEHILL

This chapter focuses on international strategic-management issues. Each day, U.S. businesses enter global markets and rival foreign firms enter U.S. markets. One-third of all college students in the United States who receive advanced degrees in science, math, and engineering are foreign citizens.

> Recently, I heard a story about former President George Bush being in a coma for three years and waking to find Dan Quayle standing at his bedside. Upon seeing the vice-president, the president began asking questions. "How long have I been asleep?" The president then inquires about the state of the U.S. economy. To his surprise, Quayle tells him that the budget and the trade deficits have been reduced to zero. Then, the president asks about inflation, which he figures must be at an all-time high. Again, to his surprise, Quayle says that inflation is not a problem. Having his doubts, the president asks for specifics. "How much," he asks "does a first-class stamp cost?" "Very reasonable," Quayle responds, "only 30 yen."[1]

THE NATURE OF GLOBAL COMPETITION

For centuries before Columbus discovered America and surely for centuries to come, businesses have searched and will continue to search for new opportunities beyond their national boundaries. There has never been a more internationalized and economically competitive society than today's. Some American industries, such as textiles, semiconductors, and consumer electronics, are in complete disarray as a result of the international challenge.

Organizations that conduct business operations across national borders are called *international firms* or *multinational corporations*. The term *parent company* refers to a firm investing in international operations, while *host country* is the country where that business is conducted. As illustrated in Figure 10–1, the strategic-management process is conceptually the same for multinational firms as for purely domestic firms; however, the process is more complex for international firms due to the presence of more variables and relationships. Social, cultural, demographic, environmental, political, governmental, legal, technological, and competitive opportunities and threats that face a multinational corporation are almost limitless, and the number and complexity of these factors increase dramatically with the number of products produced and the number of geographic areas served.

More time and effort are required to identify and evaluate external trends and events in multinational corporations. Geographical distance, cultural and national differences, and variations in business practices often make communication between domestic headquarters and overseas operations difficult. Strategy implementation can be more difficult because different cultures have different norms, values, and work ethics.

The fall of communism and advancements in telecommunications are drawing countries, cultures, and organizations worldwide closer together. Foreign revenue as a percent of total company revenues already exceeds 50 percent in hundreds of U.S. firms, including Exxon, Gillette, Dow Chemical, Citicorp, Colgate-Palmolive, and Texaco. Joint ventures and partnerships between domestic and foreign firms are becoming the rule rather than the exception!

World trade centers are proliferating in the United States and abroad because of growing interest in foreign trade. Trade centers were built in Cedar Rapids, Iowa; Santa Ana, California; Hartford, Connecticut; Pomona, California; Long Beach, California; St. Paul, Minnesota; Toledo, Ohio; and Wichita, Kansas. These new world trade centers offer many specialized services, such as assisting small businesses in exporting or importing, and housing foreign banks, export firms, and law offices.

Fully 95 percent of the world's population lives outside the United States, and this group is growing 70 percent faster than the American population! The lineup of competitors

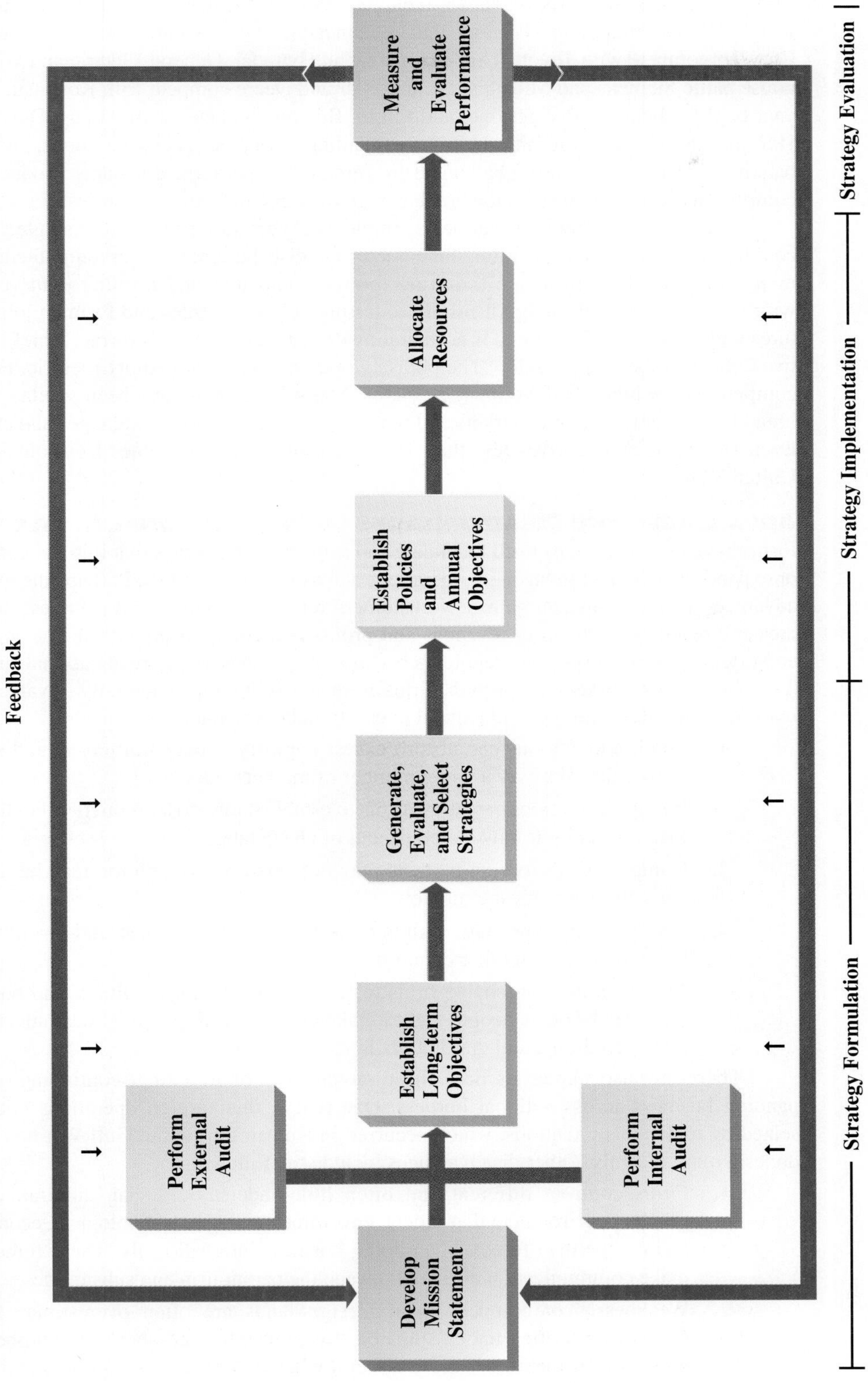

FIGURE 10–1
A Comprehensive Strategic-Management Model

in virtually all industries today is global. Six of the world's 10 largest public companies (in annual revenues) are based in Japan, including Mitsubishi, the largest corporation in the world. Global competition is more than a management fad. General Motors, Ford, and Chrysler compete with Toyota, Daimler Benz, and Hyundai. General Electric and Westinghouse battle Siemens and Mitsubishi. Caterpillar and Deere compete with Komatsu. Goodyear battles Michelin, Bridgestone, and Pirelli. Boeing competes with Airbus. Only a few U.S. industries, such as furniture, printing, retailing, consumer packaged goods, and retail banking, are not yet greatly challenged by foreign competitors. But many products and components in these industries too are now manufactured in foreign countries.

International operations can be as simple as exporting a product to a single foreign country, or as complex as operating manufacturing, distribution, and marketing facilities in many countries. U.S. firms are acquiring foreign companies and forming joint ventures with foreign firms, and foreign firms are acquiring U.S. companies and forming joint ventures with U.S. firms. This trend is accelerating dramatically. AT&T's former Chief Executive Officer, Robert Allen, said, "The phrase *global markets* is not empty rhetoric. Foreign competitors are here. And we must be there." Many U.S. firms have been spoiled by the breadth and plenty of home markets and remain ignorant of foreign languages and culture. Even Hershey Foods derives less than 10 percent of its total revenues from outside the United States.

ADVANTAGES AND DISADVANTAGES OF INTERNATIONAL OPERATIONS

Firms have numerous reasons to formulate and implement strategies that initiate, continue, or expand involvement in business operations across national borders. Perhaps the greatest advantage is that firms can gain new customers for their products and services, thus increasing revenues. Growth in revenues and profits is a common organizational objective and often an expectation of shareholders because it is a measure of organizational success.

In addition to seeking growth, firms have the following potentially advantageous reasons to initiate, continue, and expand international operations:

1. Foreign operations can absorb excess capacity, reduce unit costs, and spread economic risks over a wider number of markets.

2. Foreign operations can allow firms to establish low-cost production facilities in locations close to raw materials and/or cheap labor.

3. Competitors in foreign markets may not exist, or competition may be less intense than in domestic markets.

4. Foreign operations may result in reduced tariffs, lower taxes, and favorable political treatment in other countries.

5. Joint ventures can enable firms to learn the technology, culture, and business practices of other people and to make contacts with potential customers, suppliers, creditors, and distributors in foreign countries.

There are also numerous potential disadvantages of initiating, continuing, or expanding business across national borders. One risk is that foreign operations could be seized by nationalistic factions, which occurred in Kuwait during the Gulf War and in Indonesia more recently. Other disadvantages include the following:

1. Firms confront different and often little-understood social, cultural, demographic, environmental, political, governmental, legal, technological, economic, and competitive forces when doing business internationally. These forces can make communication difficult between the parent firm and subsidiaries.

2. Weaknesses of competitors in foreign lands are often overestimated, and strengths are often underestimated. Keeping informed about the number and nature of competitors is more difficult when doing business internationally.

3. Language, culture, and value systems differ among countries, and this can create barriers to communication and problems managing people.

4. Gaining an understanding of regional organizations such as the European Economic Community, the Latin American Free Trade Area, the International Bank for Reconstruction and Development, and the International Finance Corporation is difficult and often required in doing business internationally.

5. Dealing with two or more monetary systems can complicate international business operations.

CULTURES AROUND THE WORLD

To successfully compete in world markets, U.S. managers must obtain a better knowledge of historical, cultural, and religious forces that motivate and drive people in other countries. In Japan, for example, business relations operate within the context of *Wa*, which stresses group harmony and social cohesion. In China, business behavior revolves around *guanxi*, or personal relations. In Korea, activities involve concern for *inhwa*, or harmony based on respect of hierarchical relationships, including obedience to authority.[2]

In Europe, it is generally true that the farther north on the continent, the more participatory the management style. Most European workers are unionized and enjoy more frequent vacations and holidays than U.S. workers. A 90-minute lunch break plus 20-minute morning and afternoon breaks are common in European firms. Guaranteed permanent employment is commonly a part of employment contracts in Europe. In socialist countries such as France, Belgium, and the United Kingdom, the only ground for immediate dismissal from work is a criminal offense. A six-month trial period at the beginning of employment is usually part of the contract with a European firm. Many Europeans resent pay-for-performance, commission salaries, and objective measurement and reward systems. This is true especially of workers in southern Europe. Many Europeans also find the notion of team spirit difficult to grasp because the unionized environment has dichotomized worker-management relations throughout Europe.

A weakness that U.S. firms have in competing with Pacific Rim firms is a lack of understanding of Far Eastern cultures, including how Asians think and behave. Spoken Chinese, for example, has more in common with spoken English than with spoken Japanese or Korean. Managers around the world face the responsibility of having to exert authority while at the same time trying to be liked by subordinates. U.S. managers consistently put more weight on being friendly and liked, whereas Asian and European managers exercise authority often without this concern. Americans tend to use first names instantly in business dealings with foreigners, but foreigners find this presumptuous. In Japan, for example, first names are used only among family members and intimate friends; even long-time business associates and coworkers shy away from the use of first names. Other cultural differences or pitfalls that U.S. managers need to know are given in Table 10–1.

AMERICAN VERSUS FOREIGN CULTURES   U.S. managers have a low tolerance for silence, whereas Asian managers view extended periods of silence as important for organizing and evaluating one's thoughts. U.S. managers are much more action-oriented than their counterparts around the world; they rush to appointments, conferences, and meetings, and then feel the day has been productive. But for foreign managers, resting, listening, meditating, and thinking is considered productive. Sitting through a conference without talking is unproductive in the United States, but it is viewed as positive in Japan if one's silence helps preserve unity.

TABLE 10–1
Cultural Pitfalls That You Need To Know

Waving is a serious insult in Greece and Nigeria, particularly if the hand is near someone's face.
Making a "goodbye" wave in Europe can mean "no," but means "come here" in Peru.
In China, last names are written first.
A man named Carlos Lopez-Garcia should be addressed as Mr. Lopez in Latin America, but as Mr. Garcia in Brazil.
Breakfast meetings are considered uncivilized in most foreign countries.
Latin Americans average being 20 minutes late to business appointments.
Direct eye contact is impolite in Japan.
Don't cross your legs in Arab or many Asian countries—it's rude to show the sole of your shoe.
In Brazil, touching your thumb and first finger—an American "OK" sign—is the equivalent of raising your middle finger.
Nodding or tossing your head back in southern Italy, Malta, Greece, and Tunisia means "no." In India, this body motion means "yes."
Snapping your fingers is vulgar in France and Belgium.
Folding your arms across your chest is a sign of annoyance in Finland.
In China, leave some food on your plate to show that your host was so generous that you couldn't finish.
Do not eat with your left hand when dining with clients from Malaysia or India.
One form of communication works the same worldwide. It's the smile, so take that along wherever you go.

U.S. managers also put greater emphasis on short-term results than foreign managers. In marketing, for example, Japanese managers strive to achieve "everlasting customers," whereas many Americans strive to make a one-time sale. Marketing managers in Japan see making a sale as the beginning, not the end, of the selling process. This is an important distinction. Japanese managers often criticize U.S. managers for worrying more about shareholders, whom they do not know, than employees, whom they do know. Americans refer to "hourly employees," whereas Japanese refer to "lifetime employees." As indicated in the Global Perspective, even the varying pervasiveness of the Internet into homes and businesses of various countries may have an effect on the constantly evolving culture of different people.

Rose Knotts recently summarized some important cultural differences between U.S. and foreign managers:[3]

1. Americans place an exceptionally high priority on time, viewing time as an asset. Many foreigners place more worth on relationships. This difference results in foreign managers often viewing U.S. managers as "more interested in business than people."

2. Personal touching and distance norms differ around the world. Americans generally stand about 3 feet from each other in carrying on business conversations, but Arabs and Africans stand about one foot apart. Touching another person with the left hand in business dealings is taboo in some countries. American managers need to learn the personal space rules of foreign managers with whom they interact in business.

3. People in some cultures do not place the same significance on material wealth as American managers often do. Lists of the "largest corporations" and "highest-paid" executives abound in the United States. "More is better" and "bigger is better" in the United States, but not everywhere. This can be a consideration in trying to motivate individuals in other countries.

4. Family roles and relationships vary in different countries. For example, males are valued more than females in some cultures, and peer pressure, work situations, and business interactions reinforce this phenomenon.

GLOBAL PERSPECTIVE
Which Countries Have the Greatest Internet Access?

The following information reveals the extent of Internet access at home and at work among people in 22 different countries.

Source: Adapted from Bodil Jones, "Who's on the Net?" Management Review (September 1997): 6.

Country	Access at Home	Access at Work
United States	27%	25%
Sweden	10	21
Hong Kong	16	20
Australia	14	19
Finland	7	17
Canada	15	14
Netherlands	6	10
Switzerland	6	10
Mexico	2	9
Great Britain	6	8
Germany	5	6
Chile	3	6
Japan	3	6
Cyprus	3	4
Spain	3	4
Greece	2	4
Belgium	1	4
France	2	3
Italy	1	3
Peru	1	3
Turkey	0	3
Portugal	2	2

5. Language differs dramatically across countries, even countries where people speak the same language. Words and expressions commonly used in one country may be greedy or disrespectful in another.

6. Business and daily life in some societies is governed by religious factors. Prayer times, holidays, daily events, and dietary restrictions, for example, need to be respected by American managers not familiar with these practices in some countries.

7. Time spent with the family and quality of relationships are more important in some cultures than the personal achievement and accomplishments espoused by the traditional American manager. For example, where a person is in the hierarchy of a firm's organizational structure, how large the firm is, and where the firm is located are much more important factors to American managers than to many foreign managers.

8. Many cultures around the world value modesty, team spirit, collectivity, and patience much more than the competitiveness and individualism which are so important in America.

9. Punctuality is a valued personal trait when conducting business in America, but it is not revered in many of the world's societies. Eating habits also differ

dramatically across cultures. For example, belching is acceptable in many countries as evidence of satisfaction with the food that has been prepared. Chinese cultures consider it good manners to sample a portion of each food served.

10. To prevent social blunders when meeting with managers from other lands, one must learn and respect the rules of etiquette of others. Sitting on a toilet seat is viewed as unsanitary in most countries, but not the United States. Leaving food or drink after dining is considered impolite in some countries. Bowing instead of shaking hands is customary in many countries. Many cultures view Americans as unsanitary for locating toilet and bathing facilities in the same area, while Americans view people of some cultures as unsanitary for not taking a bath or shower every day.

11. Americans often do business with individuals they do not know, but this practice is not accepted in many other cultures. In Mexico and Japan, for example, an amicable relationship is often mandatory before conducting business.

In many countries, effective managers are those who are best at negotiating with government bureaucrats rather than those who inspire workers. Many U.S. managers are uncomfortable with nepotism and bribery, which are common in many countries. In almost every country except the United States, bribery is tax-deductible.

The United States has gained a reputation for defending women from sexual harassment and minorities from discrimination, but not all countries embrace the same values. For example, in the Czech Republic, it is considered a compliment when the boss openly flirts with his female secretary and invites her to dinner. U.S. managers in the Czech Republic who do not flirt seem cold and uncaring to some employees.

American managers in China have to be careful about how they arrange office furniture because Chinese workers believe in *feng shui*, the practice of harnessing natural forces. American managers in Japan have to be careful about *nemaswashio* whereby Japanese workers expect supervisors to alert them privately of changes rather than informing them in a meeting. Japanese managers have little appreciation for versatility, expecting all managers to be the same. In Japan, "If a nail sticks out, you hit it into the wall," says Brad Lashbrook, an international consultant for Wilson Learning.

Probably the biggest obstacle to the effectiveness of U.S. managers, or managers from any country working in another, is the fact that it is almost impossible to change the attitude of a foreign workforce. "The system drives you; you cannot fight the system or culture," says Bill Parker, president of Phillips Petroleum in Norway.

THE GLOBAL CHALLENGE

Foreign competitors are battering U.S. firms in many industries. In its simplest sense, the international challenge faced by U.S. business is twofold: (1) how to gain and maintain exports to other nations and (2) how to defend domestic markets against imported goods. Few companies can afford to ignore the presence of international competition. Firms that seem insulated and comfortable today may be vulnerable tomorrow; for example, foreign banks do not yet compete or operate in most of the United States.

America's economy is becoming much less American. A world economy and monetary system is emerging. Corporations in every corner of the globe are taking advantage of the opportunity to share in the benefits of worldwide economic development. Markets are shifting rapidly and in many cases converging in tastes, trends, and prices. Innovative transport systems are accelerating the transfer of technology, and shifts in the nature and location of production systems are reducing the response time to changing market conditions.

More and more countries around the world are welcoming foreign investment and capital. As a result, labor markets have steadily become more international. East Asian countries have become market leaders in labor-intensive industries, Brazil offers abundant natural resources and rapidly developing markets, and Germany offers skilled labor and technology. The drive to improve the efficiency of global business operations is leading to greater functional specialization. This is not limited to a search for the familiar low-cost labor in Latin America or Asia. Other considerations include the cost of energy, availability of resources, inflation rates, existing tax rates, and the nature of trade regulations. Yang Shangkun insists that China's door is still open to foreign capital and technology, despite the continued strength of the Communist Party.

The ability to identify and evaluate strategic opportunities and threats in an international environment is a prerequisite competency for strategists. The nuances of competing in international markets are seemingly infinite. Language, culture, politics, attitudes, and economies differ significantly across countries. The availability, depth, and reliability of economic and marketing information in different countries vary extensively, as do industrial structures, business practices, and the number and nature of regional organizations. Differences between domestic and multinational operations that affect strategic management are summarized in Table 10–2.

TABLE 10–2
Differences Between U.S. and Multinational Operations that Affect Strategic Management

FACTOR	U.S. OPERATIONS	INTERNATIONAL OPERATIONS
Language	English used almost universally	Local language must be used in many situations
Culture	Relatively homogeneous	Quite diverse, both between countries and within a country
Politics	Stable and relatively unimportant	Often volatile and of decisive importance
Economy	Relatively uniform	Wide variations among countries and between regions within countries
Government interference	Minimal and reasonably predictable	Extensive and subject to rapid change
Labor	Skilled labor available	Skilled labor often scarce, requiring training or redesign of production methods
Financing	Well-developed financial markets	Poorly developed financial markets / Capital flows subject to government control
Market research	Data easy to collect	Data difficult and expensive to collect
Advertising	Many media available; few restrictions	Media limited; many restrictions; low literacy rates rule out print media in some countries
Money	U.S. dollar used	Must change from one currency to another; changing exchange rates and government restrictions are problems
Transportation/ Communication	Among the best in the world	Often inadequate
Control	Always a problem; centralized control will work	A worse problem. Centralized control won't work. Must walk a tightrope between overcentralizing and losing control through too much decentralizing
Contracts	Once signed, are binding on both parties, even if one party makes a bad deal	Can be voided and renegotiated if one party becomes dissatisfied
Labor relations	Collective bargaining; can lay off workers easily	Often cannot lay off workers; may have mandatory worker participation in management; workers may seek change through political process rather than collective bargaining
Trade barriers	Nonexistent	Extensive and very important

Source: R. G. Murdick, R. C. Moor, R. H. Eckhouse, and T. W. Zimmerer, *Business Policy: A Framework for Analysis*, 4th ed. (Columbus, Ohio: Grid Publishing Company, 1984): 275.

THE IMPACT OF DIVERSE INDUSTRIAL POLICIES Some *industrial policies* include providing government subsidies, promoting exports, restructuring industries, nationalizing businesses, imposing regulations, changing tax laws, instituting pollution standards, and establishing import quotas. The vicissitudes of foreign affairs make identifying and selecting among alternative strategies more challenging for multinational corporations (MNCs) than for their domestic counterparts.

> Strategic management has proven to be a valuable tool in the successful firm's repertoire. Firms traveling on the path of international business face more risks than their domestic counterparts, but also may reap greater rewards. Properly done, strategic management offers these firms a map to guide them on their journey through the perilous paths of international business.[4]

Perhaps the greatest threat to domestic firms engaged in international operations is the national and international debt situation. When countries become excessively leveraged, they frequently turn to slashing imports and boosting exports to generate trade surpluses capable of servicing their debt. Faced with these policies, domestic firms producing for export markets can often no longer import essential inputs. When a debtor country is successful in boosting its exports, domestic firms often encounter a protectionist backlash in foreign countries.

Multinational business strategists can contribute to the solution of economic trade problems and improve their firms' competitive positions by maintaining and strengthening communication channels with domestic and foreign governments. Strategists are commonly on the front line of trade and financial crises around the world, so they often have direct knowledge of the gravity and interrelated nature of particular problems. Strategists should relay this knowledge and experience to political leaders. A steady stream of counsel and advice from international business strategists to policymakers and lawmakers is needed.

Strategists in multinational corporations need an understanding of foreign governments' industrial policies. Industrial policies differ from country to country as governments take different actions to develop their own economies. For example, cooperation between business and government in Japan is so good that some experts doubt whether a clear distinction exists there between government and business; some even use the term "Japan, Inc." when referring to the Japanese government and particularly the Ministry for International Trade and Industry (MITI).

Multinational corporations face unique and diverse risks such as expropriation of assets, currency losses through exchange rate fluctuations, unfavorable foreign court interpretations of contracts and agreements, social/political disturbances, import/export restrictions, tariffs, and trade barriers. Strategists in MNCs are often confronted with the need to be globally competitive and nationally responsive at the same time. With the rise in world commerce, government and regulatory bodies are more closely monitoring foreign business practices. The United States Foreign Corrupt Practices Act, for example, defines corrupt practices in many areas of business. A sensitive issue is that some MNCs sometimes violate legal and ethical standards of the home country, but not of the host country.

Before entering international markets, firms should scan relevant journals and patent reports, seek the advice of academic and research organizations, participate in international trade fairs, form partnerships, and conduct extensive research to broaden their contacts and diminish the risk of doing business in new markets. Firms can also reduce the risks of doing business internationally by obtaining insurance from the United States government's Overseas Private Investment Corporation (OPIC).

GLOBALIZATION Globalization is a process of worldwide integration of strategy formulation, implementation, and evaluation activities. Strategic decisions are made based on their impact upon global profitability of the firm, rather than on just domestic or other individual country considerations. A global strategy seeks to meet the needs of customers

FIGURE 10–2
The Typical Evolution of an MNC

Begin Export Operations	*Conduct Licensing Activities*	*Add Foreign Sales Representatives*	*Build Foreign Manufacturing Facilities*	*Establish a Foreign Division of the Firm*	*Establish Several Foreign Business Units*	*An MNC*

Source: Adapted from C. A. Bartlett, "How Multinational Organizations Evolve," *Journal of Business Strategy* (Summer 1982): 20–32. Also, D. Shanks, "Strategic Planning for Global Competition," *Journal of Business Strategy* (Winter 1985): 83.

worldwide with the highest value at the lowest cost. This may mean locating production in countries with the lowest labor costs or abundant natural resources, locating research and complex engineering centerswhere skilled scientists and engineers can be found, and locating marketing activities close to the markets to be served. A global strategy includes designing, producing, and marketing products with global needs in mind, instead of considering individual countries alone. A global strategy integrates actions against competitors into a worldwide plan.

Globalization of industries is occurring for many reasons, including a worldwide trend toward similar consumption patterns, the emergence of global buyers and sellers, and instant transmission of money and information across continents. The European Economic Community (EEC), religions, the Olympics, the World Bank, world trade centers, the Red Cross, the Internet, environmental conferences, telecommunications, and economic summits all contribute to global interdependencies and the emerging global marketplace.

David Shanks, manager of the Strategic Management Unit of Arthur D. Little, suggested that three major factors are driving many domestic firms into international operations: (1) the maturing economies of industrialized nations, (2) the emergence of new geographic markets and business arenas, and (3) the globalization of financial systems.[5] The typical evolution of a domestic firm into a multinational corporation is illustrated in Figure 10–2.

It is clear that different industries become global for different reasons. Convergence of income levels and standardization is what made designer clothing a universal product. The need to amortize massive R&D investments over many markets is a major reason why the aircraft manufacturing industry became global. Monitoring globalization in one's industry is an important strategic-management activity. Knowing how to use that information for one's competitive advantage is even more important. For example, firms may look around the world for the best technology and select one that has the most promise for the largest number of markets. When firms design a product, they design it to be marketable in as many countries as possible. When firms manufacture a product, they select the lowest cost source, which may be Japan for semiconductors, Sri Lanka for textiles, Malaysia for simple electronics, and Europe for precision machinery. MNCs design manufacturing systems to accommodate world markets. One of the riskiest strategies for a domestic firm is to remain solely a domestic firm in an industry that is rapidly becoming global.

MEXICO

POLITICS Mexico is a much better place for doing business in 1998 than in 1994 when Ernesto Zedillo, holding a Ph.D. from Yale, first was elected president. Zedillo and his government have made significant political, social, and economic progress in Mexico. He has basically reinvented Mexico's economic model with a focus on export-led growth, higher savings rates, and careful management of finances. Direct foreign investment into Mexico is forecasted to rise to $10.8 billion in the year 2000. Mexico's gross domestic product grew nearly 9 percent in 1997, the fastest annual growth rate in 20 years. Wages, inflation, and the value of the peso are under control.

Passage of the North American Free Trade Agreement (NAFTA) and the resultant lower tariffs have spurred trade between the United States and Mexico. NAFTA enabled Mexico to export its way out of the severe 1994 peso crisis. In January 1998, Mexico passed Japan as the second-largest market for U.S. products, trailing only Canada. Passage of NAFTA did not, as Ross Perot predicted, "create a giant sucking sound as U.S. jobs move south." U.S. unemployment rates remain low.

In the 1997 regional Mexican elections, a mayor of Mexico City was elected for the first time rather than being appointed by the president. The winner was Cuauhtemoc Cardenas, a leftist Democratic Revolutionary Party candidate who likely will challenge Zedillo for the presidency in the year 2000. Receiving only 21 percent of the mayoral vote, the old, autocratic Institutional Revolutionary Party (PRI) appears to be losing power after ruling Mexico from 1924 to 1994. PRI, which opposes privatization of industries, rigs elections, buys politicians, owns law enforcement officers, hires gangs of murderers, and supports drug traffickers, is losing power in Mexico.

President Zedillo, a member of the conservative middle-class National Action Party, is dedicated to fighting the drug trade, privatizing industry, reducing corruption, promoting democracy, and improving the natural environment. Zedillo is good for Mexico and offers hope. But his government has much work to be done before he runs for reelection in the year 2000. Nearly 80 percent of Mexico's wealth rests with 30 families. About 20 percent of the population lives on roughly a dollar per day income. About 60 percent of Mexican workers take home less than $140 per month. The minimum wage is still 80 cents per hour. Unemployment rates and interest rates are high. Banks are reluctant to make loans because consumer and business delinquency rates are high.

Shipment of illegal drugs to the United States via Mexico has climbed every year and now exceeds $120 billion per year. This level is more than twice the value of Mexico's legal exports. Over 20 percent of the Mexican population in rural areas is actually employed by drug traffickers, who have built schools and hospitals for their workers and invested in local banks. The U.S. Drug Enforcement Administration estimates that 75 percent of all drugs entering the United States from South America now come through Mexico, up from 25 percent in the 1980s. Pornography, prostitution, drug addiction, drug trafficking, illegal immigration, and pollution still are severe problems for business and society.

THE U.S.–MEXICAN BORDER   Stretching 2,100 miles from the Pacific Ocean to the Gulf of Mexico, this 180-mile wide strip of land is North America's fastest-growing region. With 11 million people and $150 billion in output, this region is an economy larger than Poland. For the 6.1 million residents on the U.S. side, the average hourly wage plus benefits is $7.71, but for the 5.1 million residents on the Mexican side, the average is $1.36. The First and Third Worlds meet along this border, which features shantytowns just down the street from luxury residential neighborhoods.

There are now over 1,500 *maquiladoras*, assembly plants on the Mexican side of the border. Many analysts contend that the *maquiladoras* are a vital key to continued U.S. global competitiveness. Mexico now ranks only behind China as global investors' favorite location for establishing business in the developing world. Amidst the swelter of economic activity, deep disparities and contrasts are likely to persist. But the two sides of the border are now so interdependent that they can only move forward together.

Tijuana, 15 minutes from San Diego, is the television-manufacturing capital of the world. Plants of Sony, Samsung, Matsushita, and others produce 14 million units annually.

Per capita income in San Diego is $25,000; in Tijuana, $3,200. Tijuana's *maquiladoras* employed 118,000 in 1996, up 28 percent from the prior year.

Cuidad Juarez, midway between the Pacific Ocean and the Gulf of Mexico and just 15 minutes from El Paso, has 235 factories employing 178,000, the largest concentration of *maquiladoras* anywhere along the border. General Motors alone has 17 auto parts plants. But explosive industrial growth and uncontrolled urban expansion have far surpassed municipal services such as sewers and street paving. Juarez and El Paso share the worst air pollution anywhere on the border.

Nuevo Laredo, 15 minutes from Laredo, Texas, is home to the largest rail and truck crossings of the Rio Grande River from Mexico into the United States. More than 4,000 loaded trucks cross the Rio Grande at Nuevo Laredo, which is home to Wal-Mart's largest distribution center.

CULTURE Mexico always has been and still is an authoritarian society in terms of schools, churches, businesses, and families. Employers seek workers who are agreeable, respectful, and obedient, rather than innovative, creative, and independent. Mexican workers tend to be activity-oriented rather than problem solvers. When visitors walk into a Mexican business, they are impressed by the cordial friendly atmosphere. This is almost always true because Mexicans desire harmony rather than conflict; desire for harmony is an overriding social fabric in worker-manager relations. There is a much lower tolerance for adversarial relations or friction at work in Mexico as compared to the United States.

Mexican employers are paternalistic, providing workers with more than a paycheck, but in return, they expect allegiance. Weekly food baskets, free meals, free bus service, and free day care are often a part of compensation. The ideal working conditions for a Mexican worker is the family model, with everyone working together, doing their share, according to their designated roles. Mexican workers do not expect or desire a work environment where self-expression and initiative are encouraged. Whereas U.S. business embodies individualism, achievement, competition, curiosity, pragmatism, informality, spontaneity, and doing more than expected on the job, Mexican businesses stress collectivism, continuity, cooperation, belongingness, formality, and doing exactly what you're told.

In Mexico, business associates only rarely entertain at their home, a place reserved exclusively for close friends and family. Business meetings and entertaining are nearly always done at a restaurant. Preserving one's honor, saving face, and looking important is also exceptionally important in Mexico. This is why Mexicans do not accept criticism and change easily; many find it humiliating to acknowledge having made a mistake. A meeting among employees and managers in a business located in Mexico is a forum for giving orders and directions rather than for discussing problems or participating in decision making. Mexican workers desire to be closely supervised, cared for, and corrected in a civil manner. Opinions expressed by employees are often regarded as back talk in Mexico. Mexican supervisors are viewed as weak if they explain the rationale for their orders to workers.

Mexicans do not feel compelled to follow rules that are not associated with a particular person in authority they know well or work for. Thus, signs to wear ear plugs or safety glasses, or attendance or seniority policies, and even one-way street signs are often ignored. Whereas Americans follow the rules, Mexicans often do not.

Life is slower in Mexico than in the United States. People do not wear watches. The first priority is often assigned to the last request, rather than the first. Telephone systems break down. Banks may suddenly not have pesos. Phone repair can take months. Electricity for an entire plant or town can be down for hours or even days. Business and government offices open and close at different hours. Buses and taxis may be hours off schedule.

Meeting times for appointments are not rigid. Tardiness is common everywhere. Doing business effectively in Mexico requires knowledge of the Mexican way of life, culture, beliefs, and customs.

As noted, Mexican minimum wage is 80 cents per hour. Easier access to Mexico's abundant, low-cost, high-quality labor has spurred U.S. firms to locate manufacturing facilities in Mexico. Jerry Perlman, former president and chairman of Zenith Electronics Corporation, said, "If we didn't have support operations in Mexico, our annual operating costs would be $350 million to $400 million higher, and we'd be out of business." Despite low wages in Mexico, Mexicans are acquiring a global reputation for quality work, as evidenced by Ford Motor Company's $1 billion Hermosillo plant, which recently tied the Daimler-Benz plant in Germany for the auto industry's first-place award for lowest production defects.

NEW BUSINESS OPPORTUNITIES Mexico's a good place for business for many reasons, including the fact that Mexicans are a hard-working people; 12-hour workdays are common. Also, the corporate income tax rate in Mexico is 35 percent, there are no taxes on dividends, local governments do not tax corporate income, there are no constraints on dividend and capital repatriation, and franchisers are allowed unlimited repatriation of royalties. Also, the fisheries, petrochemicals, and trucking industries have been deregulated, and more than 100 state businesses from airlines to petrochemicals have been privatized. By law, Mexican children must attend school for 10 years, and 88 percent of the citizenry is literate.

U.S. electronics and garment companies have established *maquiladoras* on the U.S.–Mexico border. AT&T, for example, moved its cordless-phone repair operation to Mexico from Singapore. DuPont Company and SCI Systems also are expanding their facilities in Guadalajara. Wal-Mart opened five warehouse clubs, called Club Aurrera, in a joint venture with Cifra, Mexico's largest retailer. Sears, Roebuck is spending $150 million to open new stores in Mexico. Southwestern Bell Corporation of St. Louis acquired Telefonos de Mexico, the state phone monopoly, and PepsiCo acquired Gamesa, the huge snack food firm. Unilever Group acquired part of Conasupo, the Mexican commodities company. Nissan plans a $1 billion expansion of its assembly plant in Aguascalientes. Compaq Computer, Lotus Development Corporation, and Microsoft have opened large subsidiaries in Mexico City.

RUSSIA

President Boris Yelsin has notified his country and the world that he will not seek reelection in the year 2000. Candidates are already jockeying to succeed him. Three frontrunners are former Prime Minister Viktor Chernomyrdin; First Deputy Prime Minister Boris Nemtsov; and Alexander Lebed, a former general. There could be political and economic turmoil in Russia leading up to this election.

Since the breakup of the Soviet Union in 1991, Russia and 11 other countries have made uneven progress toward economic reform, free markets, and openness to foreign investment and trade. Each of the countries is pursuing a political and economic reform agenda, although the pace of implementation varies significantly. The majority of these economies are now experiencing declining output, rising unemployment, difficult inflationary battles, and rapidly decaying infrastructures.

CORRUPTION In recent years, Russia privatized nearly 200,000 businesses that employed 70 percent of the nation's workforce. Privatizing simply meant giving the firm to its workers. Being untrained and unorganized, these workers most often, in turn, gave the firm to the top directors, who have largely become rich barons. Nearly 90 percent of Russian employees still live below the poverty level. "Imagine if Lee Iacocca had thought about nothing all day but how to steal from Chrysler," says Mikhail Harshan. "This is the situation in 99 percent of Russian businesses." Many Russians eat cabbage, bread, and potatoes at nearly every meal; most live in crowded apartments sharing bedrooms and bathrooms with other families.

The climate for business in Russia worsened from 1996 to 1998 due to further director stealing, the war in Chechnya, continued devaluation of the ruble, high unemployment, high inflation, skyrocketing taxes, and increased crime. Russian tax laws are among the world's most punitive and confusing, so firms keep business off the books to avoid paying out about 90 percent of profits to the government. Tax receipts by the Russian government are far lower than expected or needed to run the country.

It is almost impossible today to run a business in Russia legally. Racketeering, money laundering, financial scams, and organized criminal activity plague business. President Boris Yeltsin's greatest failure is the state's forced criminalization of the economy. More than 500 businesspeople are murdered annually, such as American businessman Paul Tatum, murdered in Moscow after disputes with the city over control of his Radisson Slavjanskaya Hotel. Over 40,000 Russian enterprises are connected in some way to organized crime. Ten of Russia's 25 largest banks are operated by organized crime bosses. There are daily reports of business disputes being settled fatally. A U.S. businessman disappeared in Moscow in mid-1997 while two Philip Morris employees and their families narrowly escaped with their lives.

Even President Yeltsin's executive branch of the government is now described as crooked, unpredictable, and capricious in dealing with businesses. But Yeltsin's capitalism and free economy is now so firmly entrenched in Russia that there is little fear of a return to the old communism.

The risk of business investments in Russia decreases from south to north and west to east. Thus, investments in Siberia and along the Pacific coast are more stable and much less corrupt than those near Moscow or the Russian areas bordering Europe. Because the ruble is virtually of no value in Russia, companies need to pay their workers with something besides money, such as apartments, health care, and medical and food products. Bartering is an excellent way to motivate Russian workers.

Russia's economic problems are evidenced in the fact that the number of domestic airline passengers plunged for the sixth straight year in 1996 to 26.9 million, from a peak of 90.7 million in 1990. U.S. companies investing in Russia today speak of getting a toehold there, not a foothold. It is just too risky.

A $1.5 billion agreement between the Russian government and Exxon over oil drilling was shockingly abandoned by Russia in late 1997 because Exxon was meticulous in following the letter of the law.

THE RUSSIAN CULTURE   In America, unsuccessful business entrepreneurs are viewed negatively as failures, whereas successful small business owners enjoy high esteem and respect. In Russia, however, there is substantial social pressure against becoming a successful entrepreneur. Being a winner in Russia makes you the object of envy and resentment, a member of the elite rather than of the masses. Personal ambition and success are often met with vindictiveness and derision. Initiative is met with indifference at best and punishment at worst. In the face of public ridicule and organized crime, however, thousands of Russians, particularly young persons, are opening all kinds of businesses. Public scorn and their own guilt from violating the values they were raised with do not deter many. Because Russian society scorns success, publicizing achievements, material possessions, awards, or privileges earned by Russian workers is not an effective motivation tool for those workers.

The Russian people are best known for their drive, boundless energy, tenacity, hard work, and perseverance in spite of immense obstacles. This is as true today as ever. The notion that the average Russian is stupid or lazy is nonsense; Russians on average are more educated than their American counterparts and bounce up more readily from failure.

In the United States, business ethics and personal ethics are essentially the same. Deception is deception and a lie is a lie whether in business or personal affairs in America. However, in Russia, business and personal ethics are separate. To deceive someone, bribe someone, or lie to someone to promote a business transaction is ethical in Russia, but to deceive a friend or trusted colleague is unethical. There are countless examples of foreign firms being cheated by Russian business partners. The implication of this fact for American businesses is to forge strong personal relationships with their Russian business partners whenever possible; spend time with the Russians eating, relaxing, and exercising; and in the absence of a personal relationship, be exceptionally cautious with agreements, partnerships, payments, and granting credit.

The Russian people have great faith, confidence, and respect for American products and services. Russians generally have low self-confidence. American ideas, technology, and production practices are viewed by Russians as a panacea that can save them from a gloomy existence. For example, their squeaky telephone system and lack of fax machines make them feel deprived. This mind-set presents great opportunity in Russia for American products of all kinds.

Russia has historically been an autocratic state. This cultural factor is evident in business; Russian managers generally exercise power without ever being challenged by subordinates. Delegation of authority and responsibility is difficult and often nonexistent in Russian businesses. The American participative management style is not well received in Russia.

A crackdown on religion is underway in Russia. In 1997, the government considered a law to recognize only Russian Orthodoxy, Judaism, Islam, and Buddhism as indigenous religions. All other faiths and churches, including all Christian demoninations, would have to apply each year for permission to practice in Russia. Permission simply may not be granted. President Yeltsin opposes the antireligion movement and new law, but is losing the battle to prevent religious persecution—especially directed at Christians—throughout the country. The lower house of Russia's parliament, the State Duma, is dominated by Communists who favor antireligion and resist further economic reforms.

TRADE   The major barriers to increased U.S. exports to Russia are a substantial value-added tax, high import duties, and onerous Russian excise levies. In addition, the government has imposed strict quality and safety standards on the majority of goods entering Russia. However, Russian standards authorities have permitted only a tightly circumscribed number of groups to perform this testing in the United States. The customs clearance process at Russian borders points is frequently cumbersome and unpredictable. Local transportation problems also complicate the process of getting goods to the Russian market.

The 10 best prospects for U.S. exports to Russia are telecommunications equipment, computers and computer peripherals, pollution control equipment, oil and gas field machinery, construction equipment, medical equipment, electric power systems equipment, automotive parts and services, building products, and food processing and packaging equipment. The increasing ability of local organizations to pay for substantive improvements in Russia's deteriorated infrastructure also will stimulate imports of more U.S. products.

In terms of population, Russia is larger than all the other former Soviet bloc countries combined and is the fifth-largest country in the world. Russia has more oil reserves than

Saudi Arabia, vast quantities of timber and gold, and first-rate scientists. Russia spans 11 time zones. Donald Kendall, former CEO of PepsiCo, said the Soviet disintegration "means chaos in the short term but immense business opportunities in the long term. If U.S. companies wait until all the problems are solved, somebody else will get the business."

SMALL BUSINESS　Many American entrepreneurs have gotten ideas for launching businesses in Russia by living in Russia and seeing for themselves how bad the services are. Stories abound about such woes as sheets coming back from the laundry with holes in them, shirts coming back from the dry cleaners missing buttons, scratchy copies of movie videos, and the widespread rudeness of shop employees. Even searching for a good meal is difficult. Lisa Dobbs, a trained French chef and wife of a foreign correspondent turned good food into a money-making enterprise. She called a Western news organization and offered to cook lunch and dinner every day for its Moscow employees. It accepted. Soon she formed Moscow Catering Co./ Kalitnikovski Produkti. Today, the catering firm has 18 employees and is swamped with orders. It recently began selling prepared food.

American entrepreneurs in Russia face numerous roadblocks. Just registering one's company with the Russian government can take 6 months. Most renovated commercial real estate in Moscow is too expensive for small firms, forcing them to settle in dingy, overcrowded office buildings.

But the opportunities for foreign entrepreneurs in Russia are huge. After-tax profits can be repatriated without restriction. Many entrepreneurs initially in business to meet the needs of foreigners are finding that demand from Russians drives growth.

Today, entrepreneurs in Russia are offering everything from catering services to video rentals to fitness centers. "There's a lot of money to be made," says Michael L. Oster, managing director of Oster & Co., a Moscow real estate and development firm. "Basically, there's still a need for just about everything." The potential for political unrest in Russia is troubling to businesspeople in that country, but the opportunities for entrepreneurs are limitless.

MONEY　Russia now recognizes individual rights, including equality, privacy, freedom of speech, conscience, and free choice of work. However, these newly won freedoms have contributed to skyrocketing prices and consumer discontent. A major problem facing Russia is economic disarray. The ruble is grossly overvalued at the official exchange rate of $1.79, but the black market rate is 3 cents. Companies doing business with Russian firms must hedge against the drop of the ruble's dollar value. Many companies will not do business with the former Soviets until the ruble is converted to a gold standard like all major currencies of the world because the two-tier exchange rate is unwieldy.

JOINT VENTURES　A joint venture strategy offers an excellent way to enter the Russian market. Joint ventures create a mechanism to generate hard currency, which is important due to problems valuing the ruble. Russia's joint venture law has been revised to allow foreigners to own up to 99 percent of the venture and to allow a foreigner to serve as chief executive officer.

The list of U.S. companies that have active joint ventures with Russia include Archer-Daniels-Midland, Chevron, Combustion Engineering, Dresser Industries, Hewlett-Packard, Honeywell, Johnson & Johnson, MCI, Marriott, McDonald's, Ogilvy & Mather, Radisson, RJR/Nabisco, and Young & Rubicam. In the aerospace industry, Russian firms are cooperating with Germany's Messerschmitt Company; in computers, with IBM; in manufacturing, with Combustion Engineering, Honeywell, and Siemens; in nuclear power, with Asea, Brown Boveri, and Siemens; and in telecommunications, with Nokia. PepsiCo, Inc., recently formed a joint venture with Moscow Metropolitan to sell PepsiCo food products in Moscow's subway stations.

Most analysts believe Russia will become a market that many U.S. firms will want to enter. Those firms that start mastering the complexities early and keep informed about the latest developments may likely gain the biggest rewards. Thousands of businesses in Russia have been given financial independence and broad management autonomy. Poor telecommunications equipment, however, often isolates foreign managers in Russia from the parent company. Russia's telephone system is comparable to the U.S. phone system of the 1930s.

GUIDELINES FOR STRATEGIC VENTURES The following guidelines are appropriate when considering a strategic venture into Russia. First, avoid regions with ethnic conflicts and violence. Also, make sure the potential partner has a proper charter that has been amended to permit joint venture participation. Be aware that businesspeople in these lands have little knowledge of marketing, contract law, corporate law, fax machines, voice mail, and other business practices that Westerners take for granted.

Business contracts with Russian firms should address natural environment issues because Westerners often get the blame for air and water pollution problems and habitat destruction. Work out a clear means of converting rubles to dollars before entering a proposed joint venture because neither Russian banks nor authorities can be counted on to facilitate foreign firms' getting dollar profits out of a business. Recognize that chronic shortages of raw materials hamper business in Russia, so make sure an adequate supply of competitively priced, good-quality raw materials is reliably available. Finally, make sure the business contract limits the circumstances in which expropriation would be legal. Specify a lump sum in dollars if expropriation should occur unexpectedly, and obtain expropriation insurance before signing the agreement.

A number of organizations in Russia assist foreign companies interested in initiating, continuing, or expanding business operations there. Some of these organizations are Amtorg, the Consultation Center of the Chamber of Commerce and Industry, Inpred, Interfact, and the U.S. Commercial Office (USCO). Inpred, for example, is a consulting firm in Russia that helps Western managers operate within regulations. Inpred also helps foreign firms locate partners in the republics and develop contracts, and contacts officials to set up meetings between Russian and foreign businesspersons. USCO annually sponsors about 25 trade fairs and exhibitions that introduce foreign companies and individuals to the new Russian markets, customers, buyers, and sellers.

CHINA

DEMOGRAPHICS As indicated in Table 10–3, China is almost exactly the same size as the United States, but differs in many other respects. The world's tallest building is the new 1,518-foot Shanghai World Financial Center in Shanghai, China, replacing the Petronas Towers in Juala Lumpur, Malaysia. Hong Kong was peacefully annexed, and long-time Communist dictator President Deng Xiaoping died and was replaced without incident. The Shanghai building and recent events symbolize the great economic progress China made from 1996 to 1998.

One of last remaining tenets of Marxism, the taboo against private ownership of large industrial enterprises, has been abandoned in China. President Jiang Zemin encourages all types of state- and locally owned companies to issue shares of stock to diversify their ownership. State-owned enterprises accounted for 62 percent of industrial production in 1986 but today account for only 35 percent. China today is powered by small private businesses, foreign-owned companies, joint ventures, agricultural collectives, and profitable village- and township-owned businesses.

	U.S.	CHINA	HONG KONG
Area (in thousands of sq. miles)	3,679	3,696	.415
Population (in millions)	265	1,200	6.3
Average urban population growth rate (1990–1994)	1.3%	4.1%	1.7%
Labor force (in millions, 1994)	131	715	3
Life expectancy	77	69	78
% of people with access to safe water	100	67	100
% of people with access to sanitation	95	24	85
% adult illiteracy	4	19	8
Infant mortality (per 1,000 live births)	8	30	5
Exports (in billions), 1996	$625	$151	$140
Imports (in billions), 1996	$795	$139	$153

TABLE 10–3
Comparing the United States, China, and Hong Kong

Source: Adapted from Marcus Brauchli and Joseph Kahn, "Hong Kong Yields China Both Victory and Challenge," *The Wall Street Journal* (July 1, 1997): 10.

POLITICS   Under the leadership of President Jiang Zemin, China is making rapid progress toward becoming a stable, economic trading partner in Asia. China is moving forward quickly with privatization, deregulation, reform through stock issuances to workers, stock listings, divestitures, mergers, bankruptcies, and sale of the country's 370,000 state-run enterprises. More than half of these enterprises are losing money, which undermines the health of state banks and overall reform. About half of the 113 million workers employed by these enterprises are not needed and do not work, yet still receive full benefits.

China still has more than 120 television manufacturers, 700 beer companies, and 30,000 rubber belt makers. But the state is encouraging merger and consolidation, which is transforming the economic landscape. There were 1,100 Chinese company mergers in 1997, up 33 percent from 1996. Jiang's plan is to create large, private, efficient, Chinese companies that can compete effectively and globally.

Jiang is also focusing on improving health care, pensions, education, unemployment, and poverty relief by strengthening the rule of law, promoting greater separation of government and business, and guaranteeing human rights. In 1998, China extended direct elections from villages to townships. Jiang has cut the number of specialized economic departments to ease bureaucratic meddling in business.

Jiang, however, is tightening control over the press and publishing and upholds the ruling role of the Communist Party. The Chinese government will retain control over only about 1,000 enterprises, including all those involved in infrastructure, telecommunications, certain raw materials, and the military. Labor protests in China climbed 50 percent to 3,000 in 1996 as unemployment rates climbed to 15 percent. Another 1,400 protests were reported in the first half of 1997. But what is different this time compared to 1989 when China smashed similar demonstrations in Tiananmen Square is that appeasement and conciliation, not violence, is used to end the protests. Beijing has evolved a policy of engaging protesters in dialogue and trying to mediate.

China still only takes in about 12 percent of gross domestic product in taxes, about one-third the level of most developed countries. This leaves the country strapped for cash in providing even the most basic social needs. For example, China spent only 3.8 percent of its GDP on health care, compared with about 10 percent in developed countries. Instead, state-controlled banks and companies had to take care of society's needs, which bankrupted more than half of these institutions. However, China is releasing state companies from the burden of providing health care, pensions, and housing by setting up national health and retirement systems.

Jiang Zemin's reform agenda consists of five key strategies:

1. **Restructure state enterprises.** Convert state enterprises into corporations owned by shareholders.

2. **Strengthen financial markets.** Expand capital markets by authorizing hundreds of new stock listings annually.

3. **Sell state assets.** Require all but 1,000 of China's 305,000 state enterprises to sell to shareholders or go bankrupt.

4. **Build social services.** Build low-cost housing, set up pension programs, and retrain workers to relieve burderns on state enterprises.

5. **Reduce Tariffs.** Reduce tariffs from 17 percent in 1997 to 15 percent in 2000 as part of a bid to join the World Trade Organization.[6]

OPPORTUNITIES U.S. firms increasingly are doing business in China as market reforms create a more businesslike arena daily. Foreign direct investment in China reached a massive $47 billion in 1996 and another $40 billion in 1997. This placed China second behind the United States, with annual $85 billion, as the most desirable country in the world for foreign investment.

China has set aside $3.6 billion annually to clear bad debts of state-run enterprises to help them plan to merge, divest, or declare bankruptcy. China's massive privatization program enables foreign firms to acquire state-run enterprises at bargain prices and thus gain a foothold in the Chinese market. Motorola, for example, had $3.4 billion in sales in 1996 from Hong Kong and China. Asia accounted for 21 percent of Intel's revenue in 1996, compared to 11 percent in 1995, primarily due to skyrocketing personal computer sales in China. IBM's sales within China are growing 50 percent annually, to more than $700 million in 1997.

In an effort to appease opponents of China entering the World Trade Organization (WTO), China in late 1997 reduced its average tariff rates by 26 percent, from 23 percent to 17 percent, on 4,800 items shipped in and out of the country. These cuts have accelerated national economic growth even more. If China is admitted soon, as expected, into the WTO, this should further accelerate economic development and trade. The major reason why the United States has historically not supported China's acceptance into WTO has been that country's human rights violations.

China Telecom, a state company, eclipsed AT&T as the world's largest provider of mobile phone services. China lays enough phone cable each year to rewire California. In late 1997, China added its 100 millionth phone line. China plans to spend $60 billion on telecommunications infrastructure through the year 2000, almost all through state-owned businesses. Telecommunications is a top priority in China.

China is modernizing its stock and bond markets so that companies can depend less on banks for financing.

Evidence of the success of China's market reforms is the government's attitude toward Hong Kong. As promised, China is operating Hong Kong as a separate democratic state with freedom of religion, press, and speech, and a fair legal system. Hong Kong is the centerpiece of China's efforts to reform, privatize, and expand imports and exports worldwide. The map in Figure 10–3 illustrates Hong Kong's strategic location for China. With its 6.3 million people, magnificent harbor, financial wealth, 500 banks from 43 countries, the world's eighth-largest stock market, and minimum taxation, Hong Kong serves as the gateway to fast-growing China. U.S. companies alone have 178 regional headquarters in Hong Kong and $10.5 billion in direct investment.

China's approach toward Taiwan has even changed from adversarial and confrontational to diplomatically appealing to Taiwanese to observe the Hong Kong experience and

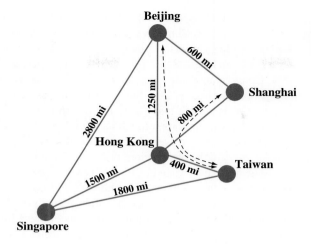

FIGURE 10–3
Hong Kong's Strategic Location

consider reuniting with mainland China. Taiwan's President Lee Teng-Hui says unification depends on assurances of democracy; China may soon grant these as needed.

There is a growing list of U.S. success stories in China. Holiday Inn has a 448-room hotel in Lhasa, Tibet. Boeing is selling 14 percent of its production to Chinese airlines. Ford and Chrysler are making money manufacturing automobiles or component parts. Playboy Enterprises operates nearly 200 sportswear boutiques in Chinese stores. Nike, Compaq Computer, Hughes, General Electric, and Weyerhaeuser are making money in their operations in China.

RISKS IN DOING BUSINESS Risks that still restrain firms from initiating business with China include the following:

◆ Poor infrastructure
◆ Disregard for the natural environment
◆ Absence of a legal system
◆ Rampant corruption
◆ Lack of freedom of press, speech, and religion
◆ Severe human rights violations
◆ Little respect for patents, copyrights, brands, and logos
◆ Counterfeiting, fraud, and pirating of products
◆ Little respect for legal contracts
◆ No generally accepted accounting principles

McDonald's, for instance, was recently evicted from its site in Beijing after operating its largest store in the world for only two of 20 years on its lease agreement. DuPont's herbicide Londax that kills weeds in rice fields was recently pirated and manufactured extensively in China. Scores of U.S. firms such as BellSouth have lost millions of dollars in China due to "illegal business actions." You can walk into any store in Beijing and buy a pirated copy of Microsoft's Windows 95 software.

At least 20 percent of credit loans in China are nonperforming; China's banking system is in shambles. Fully 75 percent of domestic credit goes to ailing state-run businesses that generate only 1 percent of industrial production. Managers of state-run enterprises are not very ethical either, often stealing money from the business.

Technological research is almost nonexistent in China. China's factories operate with ancient equipment, old-fashioned production methods, and little regard for the needs of the marketplace. Quality control is poor, and there basically are no books or records. Ninety percent of people in China live below the poverty level; 10 percent are very rich. Urban unemployment has grown to 15 percent, but may be even higher if idle farmers and furloughed workers are included. Retail prices grew only 3 percent in 1997, after hitting 24 percent in 1994. Concern about deflation or recession is real as China posts big trade surpluses and foreign reserves exceed $121 billion. A major reason for falling prices is increased competition, but this is putting many state-run enterprises out of business. Exports from China are rising rapidly but imports into China are falling. Private factories in China are now laying off workers faster than even the state-owned companies. State-owned enterprises have fired or drastically cut the pay of more than 10 million workers annually in recent years.

The minimum wage in China is 12 cents per hour but many firms pay even less. Chinese workers usually have no health care and no compensation for injury. Few factories have fire extinguishers. Bribes are often paid to officials to avoid fines and shutdowns. Labor unions are illegal and nonexistent in China. Child labor is commonplace. Political and religious oppression and imprisonment occur. Levi Strauss has pulled all its business operations out of China in protest to its human rights violations.

STRATEGY   *Business Week* offers the following formula for success in doing business with China:

> Pick partners wisely. Avoid forming ventures with inefficient state-owned enterprises. Search for entrepreneurial companies owned by local governments, or go it alone. Insist on management control.

> Focus on fundamentals. Capitalize on China rapidly becoming a market economy by executing the basics, such as marketing, distribution, and service.

> Guard know-how. Do not hand over state-of-the-art technology just to get an agreement. Aggressively fight theft of intellectual property because China wants to shed its bad reputation in this regard.

> Fly low. Begin with a series of small ventures rather than big, costly, high-profile projects that often get snarled in bureaucratic red tape and politics.[7]

JAPAN

Keizo Obuchi was elected in July 1998 as Japan's prime minister. Obuchi's program of deregulating Japanese industries and restoring consumer confidence in Japanese financial markets is aggressively underway. But much work is needed.

The Japanese economy is experiencing its most serious slowdown since the early 1970s. The Japanese yen fell 50 percent against the dollar from 1996 to 1998. The Nikkei stock index tumbled from its December 1989 peak of 38,915 to 18,000 in late 1997. Property values in Japan declined 60 percent between 1990 and 1997. These declines decimated individual interest in investing money in Japanese securities or property. Individuals in Japan hold $10 trillion in personal financial assets, but less than 3 percent of that is in mutual funds, compared to the U.S. individuals' average 14 percent of savings in mutual funds. Japanese individuals' investment in stocks has dropped to 10 percent of savings compared to 36 percent on average for Americans. Nearly all Japanese individual savings are now kept in post office or insurance accounts drawing less than 1 percent in annual interest.[8] Industries have huge amounts of excess capital.

The decline in asset values left Japanese banks with substantial nonperforming loans and precarious balance sheets. As a result, bank lending has been weak despite low interest rates. Residential housing construction has benefited from low interest rates and falling

NATURAL ENVIRONMENT

How Much Carbon Dioxide Is Your Firm Emitting?

Global warming isn't just a fear. It's a fact. Carbon dioxide is the major culprit and the most common air pollutant. Plants, of course, breathe in carbon dioxide, which is the reason why widespread cutting of trees and rain forests as well as clearing of land and harvesting kelp in the oceans are so detrimental to the natural environment. The following statistics reveal annual carbon-dioxide emissions for various countries worldwide. Note that the United States is guiltiest.

	TOTAL TONS (MILLIONS)	TONS PER CAPITA
United States	5,475	20.52
China	3,196	2.68
Russia	1,820	12.26
Japan	1,126	9.03
India	910	0.90
Germany	833	10.24
United Kingdom	539	9.29
Ukraine	437	8.48
Canada	433	14.83
Italy	411	7.19
South Korea	370	8.33
Mexico	359	3.93

Continents and countries' relative share of harmful CO_2 emissions is given below:

Eastern Europe and former Soviet Union	27%
United States	22%
Western Europe	17%
Other Asian countries	13%
China	11%
Latin America	4%
Africa	3%

Source: *Adapted from "Clear Skies Are Goal as Pollution Is Turning into a Commodity,"* The Wall Street Journal *(October 3, 1997): A4.*

land prices, but constraints on government-supported housing finance may temper this growth. Commercial construction has declined throughout the downturn, although public construction projects initiated as part of four government stimulus packages have compensated somewhat.

Private consumption has given a boost to slowly rising economic activity. Income tax rebates and low inflation have helped bolster consumer expenditures. Business's policy of keeping layoffs to a minimum during economic slowdowns has also helped consumption levels remain steady. The Japanese are the world's best consumers. With only 2 percent of the global population, the Japanese consume two-thirds of the world's branded products.[9]

Japan's labor markets are very weak. At 3.3 percent, unemployment is high by Japanese standards. Recruitment of new college graduates is depressed, and many firms have so much redundant employment that no hiring will occur until at least 2000.

TRADE TRENDS Japan is the world's third-largest merchandise exporter and importer (behind the United States and Germany). Machinery and equipment make up about 75 percent of Japan's exports.

The United States is by far Japan's single largest trading partner. The United States has about a 23 percent share of Japan's import market, and 30 percent of Japanese exports go to the United States. Japan has been the second-largest market for U.S. products for many years. About 70 percent of U.S. exports to Japan are manufactured goods. By comparison, about 84 percent of U.S. exports to the rest of the world are manufactured. In addition, a relatively large share of U.S. exports to Japan consists of intracompany shipments from Japanese subsidiaries in the United States to their parent firms in Japan.

TRADE CLIMATE   Japan's large trade surpluses with the United States and other industrial nations have resulted in almost continuous trade friction between Japan and these countries over the last two decades. Japan's trade surplus with the United States has bulged to more than $4 billion monthly. Consequently, the primary goal of U.S. trade policy with Japan has been to open the Japanese market to imports and foreign investment. Informal obstacles have largely prevented manufactured goods, especially high-technology products, from entering Japan's markets. These barriers include administrative guidance; opaque customs procedures, testing standards, and certification requirements; restrictive public procurement and industrial promotion policies; intellectual property regulations; and impenetrable local distribution channels.

Some deregulation has opened Japan's markets in recent years, but its trade structure remains substantially different from that of any other industrial country. Japanese exports are mainly manufactured goods, and its imports are raw materials, food, and industrial components. Most of Japan's imported goods come from its foreign subsidiaries. Deregulation and other market-opening measures that have resulted from U.S. policy initiatives may lead to some change to this trade pattern during the remainder of this century.

Although no larger in size than California, Japan supports a population five times that of California's. Japan is changing rapidly. Masakagu Yamazaki uses the term "flexible individualism" to summarize the changes occurring in Japanese society and business. Workaholic attitudes in Japan are being replaced by greater emphasis on leisure activities and consumption of leisure products and services. Rising incomes, an aging population, and more women in the workforce are increasing the demand for services in all sectors of the Japanese economy. Japanese people save much more of their income than Americans, averaging 17 percent versus 4 percent, but prices in Japan are among the highest in the world. An apple costs $2 and dinner for four can cost $600.

A comparison of educational levels of Japanese and American young people appears in Table 10–4. Teachers in Japan enjoy much more respect, status, job security, and higher pay than their counterparts in America. Japanese teachers visit their students' homes, are available after school to assist students, and supervise learning on vacation days. Education is compulsory for children ages 6 to 15 in Japan, and 95 percent of 5-year-olds and 70 percent of 4-year-olds go to kindergarten. The school year is 240 days, and many children spend Sunday and holidays being tutored or studying. Some of the forces behind the educational system in Japan are relative homogeneity in the population, an occupational system in which selection and promotion are based on educational credentials, a relatively equal distribution of educational opportunities across the population, steep competition for entry into prestigious universities, and devotion of families to enhancing the life chances of children. Many analysts contend that as we approach the year 2000 and beyond, countries around the world will be as competitive as their underlying education systems. U.S. firms could be at a disadvantage compared to Japanese firms if this holds true because the analysts are primarily referring to secondary education, literacy rates, and average education level of the populace.

Japanese women increasingly are pursuing careers outside the home, a practice that was taboo until the mid-1980s. However, women still hold only 1 percent of managerial positions in Japan despite their making up 40 percent of Japan's workforce. The 1986 Japanese law banning sex discrimination at work established no penalties for violations. Most Japanese men and women still believe that when a woman marries, taking care of her husband and children should be her priority. The Japanese government is encouraging companies to promote more women into managerial positions, but the managerial job in Japan typically requires late hours, afterwork drinking sessions with colleagues, and a pledge of allegiance to the company until retirement. Many Japanese women do not aspire to that lifestyle, so women on the career track in Japan still remain an oddity.

TABLE 10–4
The Educational Levels of Young Japanese and Young Americans Compared

	AMERICANS	JAPANESE
Literacy rate	80.0%	99.0%
High school completion rate	72.2%	90.0%
Length of school year	180 days	240 days
High school seniors spending less than 5 hours per week on homework	76.0%	35.0%
Financing of education:		
National	6.2%	47.3%
State	49.0%	28.1%
Local	44.8%	24.6%
Teacher salaries	Determined locally	By national law, teachers are paid 10% more than the top civil servant.

Sources: U.S. Department of Education and Japanese Ministry of Education.

Research and development has become a basic mission of the Japanese government and nearly all Japanese firms. It is a mission of the whole country. Japan plans to develop a futuristic space shuttle, a colony of space platforms, and an orbiting factory for manufacturing made-in-space products. Aerospace companies in the United States and worldwide consider the Japanese market to be a great opportunity and are developing strategies to capitalize on Japan's commitment to commercialize space.

Some U.S. companies have done especially well in Japanese markets, including Coca-Cola, Schick, Wella, Vicks, Scott, Del Monte, Kraft, Campbell, Unilever, Twinings, Kellogg, Borden, Ragu, and Oscar Mayer. These are all household names in Japan. Schick razor blades have 70 percent of the safety-blade market there, McDonald's has 30 percent of the fast-food hamburger market, Coca-Cola has 50 percent of the market for carbonated soft drinks, Pampers has 22 percent of the disposable-diaper market, and Kodak has 15 percent of the amateur color film market. IBM has 40 percent of the market for computers, and Caterpillar has 43 percent of the market for bulldozers.

JAPANESE MANAGEMENT STYLE   The Japanese place great importance upon group loyalty and consensus, a concept called *Wa*. Nearly all corporate activities in Japan encourage Wa among managers and employees. Wa requires that all members of a group agree and cooperate; this results in constant discussion and compromise. Japanese managers evaluate the potential attractiveness of alternative business decisions in terms of the long-term effect on the group's Wa. This is why silence, used for pondering alternatives, can be a plus in a formal Japanese meeting. Discussions potentially disruptive to Wa are generally conducted in very informal settings, such as at a bar, so as to minimize harm to the group's Wa. Entertaining is an important business activity in Japan because it strengthens Wa. Formal meetings are often conducted in informal settings. When confronted with disturbing questions or opinions, Japanese managers tend to remain silent, whereas Americans tend to respond directly, defending themselves through explanation and argument.

Most Japanese managers are reserved, quiet, distant, introspective, and other-oriented, whereas most U.S. managers are talkative, insensitive, impulsive, direct, and individual-oriented. Americans often perceive Japanese managers as wasting time and carrying on pointless conversations, whereas U.S. managers often use blunt criticism, ask prying questions, and make quick decisions. These kinds of cultural differences have disrupted many potentially productive Japanese-American business endeavors. Viewing the Japanese communication style as a prototype for all Asian and Oriental cultures is a related stereotype that must be avoided.

Americans have more freedom to control their own fate than do the Japanese. Life is much different in the United States than in Japan; the United States offers more upward mobility to its people. This is a great strength of the United States. Sherman explained:

> America is not like Japan and can never be. America's strength is the opposite: It opens its doors and brings the world's disorder in. It tolerates social change that would tear most other societies apart. This openness encourages Americans to adapt as individuals rather than as a group. Americans go west to California to get a new start; they move east to Manhattan to try to make the big time; they move to Vermont or to a farm to get close to the soil. They break away from their parents' religions or values or class; they rediscover their ethnicity. They go to night school; they change their names.[10]

GLOBAL EXPANSION   Japan is shifting from a strategy of exports to direct investment in the United States and Europe. Japan surpassed the United Kingdom in 1992 as the largest direct investor in the United States. The number of Americans working for Japanese subsidiaries in the United States now exceeds 500,000. The 10 largest Japanese employers in the United States in rank order are Matsushita Electric, Sony, Toyota, Honda, Hitachi, Toshiba, Nissan, NEC, Mitsubishi, and Fujitsu. However, over 50 percent of Japanese companies operating in the United States today face worker lawsuits on race, color, religion, age, sex, and equal employment.

The Japanese are expected to continue investing heavily in Great Britain because the British welcome the Japanese, although other European countries are divided in their attitudes toward Japan. More than 40 percent of all Japanese investment in Europe is in Britain. The Confederation of British Industry predicts that by the year 2000, an astonishing 16 percent of British factory workers will have Japanese bosses.

There are only three major industries—pharmaceuticals, chemicals, and telecommunications equipment—in which European companies are more competitive than Japanese companies. Five of the top 10 construction firms in the world are Japanese: Shimizu, Kajima, Jaisei, Takenaka, and Ohbayashi. Until European countries develop a more unified approach towards Japanese investment, England could be "exporting" Japanese products to Europe in great quantities.

During the 1990–1994 era, Japan's direct investment strategy focused largely on the United States and Europe. However, during the 1995–1999 era, Japan's focus shifted to Asia for several reasons: First, Japan wants to capitalize on Asian countries' growing markets and rapidly developing economies. Japan wants to lessen its dependence on the United States. Finally, Japan wants to be in a position to determine its own destiny in light of China's explosive growth and expansionist policies.

Asians now buy more Japanese exports than the United States, and Japanese firms are plowing these profits back into Asia. Shintaro Ishihara says, "Japan is a nation of Asian people with Asian blood. It seems natural that we recognize that we exist first for Asia." Japan's emphasis on new trade, investment, financial, and technological moves are in Asia.

To support their country's re-Asianization policy, the Japanese people are putting greater emphasis on learning the languages, foods, and cultural habits of their Asian neighbors from Manchuria to Indonesia. Japanese firms are building plants, forming alliances, and making business friends extensively in Korea, Vietnam, Thailand, Indonesia, Malaysia, Philippines, India, Taiwan, and China. Already the world's largest aid donor, Japan has targeted Asian countries as its primary recipient in order to bolster its Asian influence. Indonesia is Japan's largest aid recipient, followed by China, the Philippines, India, and Thailand. There is a growing acceptance of Japanese culture throughout Asia. Projections are for Japan's U.S. investment to decline to just over $30 billion.

LIFETIME EMPLOYMENT   The principle of lifetime employment is as strong as ever in Japan, despite Westerners' view that this policy will wilt under global competition.

Japanese law makes it illegal to fire employees, so firms cannot cut labor costs when demand falls. But this single disadvantage of a lifetime employment policy is counterbalanced by numerous advantages. For example, Japanese workers even view productivity-enhancing technologies and automation as positive because there is no downside risk of them losing their jobs. With the lifetime employment policy, Japanese firms undertake expensive training programs without fear that any workers will take their skills to rival firms. U.S. firms are only one-seventh as likely as Japanese firms to offer new employees formal training.

Another benefit of the lifetime employment is the long-term accountability built into the system; this enhances managerial decision making. Labor unions in Japan work for the business; a strike may last an hour at most. CEOs in Japan are salaried employees compensated at levels of 10 times that of lower-level managers; this compares to U.S. CEOs being paid on average 100 times the salary of lower-level managers. Stock options for CEOs are prohibited in Japan. Japanese workers are paid and promoted according to seniority rather than competence. This system promotes teamwork and eliminates a possible source of friction and jealousy among workers. Because older workers and managers are not going to be leapfrogged in promotion, they mentor and help younger, inexperienced workers and managers much more readily than in the United States. Workers in Japanese firms function as part of a clearly identified team, and assignments are given to the team rather than to individuals. Offenders of team norms risk being ostracized by the group. Lifetime employment in Japan has a bright and stable future. It is a policy that U.S. firms should consider implementing.

THE EUROPEAN UNION

Europe is one of the most open markets for U.S. companies, which are in a position to benefit from an integrated and borderless European Union (EU) and a new single currency. In order to capitalize fully, however, they must be allowed to participate in the coming wave of privatizations. In addition, U.S. exports are threatened by new product standards and rules on testing and certification, growing incompatibility in business regulations, and remaining barriers in such areas as telecommunications, heavy electrical equipment, and audiovisual services. Eliminating these obstacles is a primary trade objective of the U.S. government. U.S. companies also stand to benefit from increased marketing efforts in the EU, particularly in Germany and Italy. In 1995, U.S. firms had a 13.2 percent share of United Kingdom imports, but only a 6.5 percent in the rest of the EU. Each percentage point rise in the U.S. share of the EU market signifies a $13 billion increase in the value of U.S. exports.

Since World War II, Western European countries have had distinct national markets in which governments protected their own businesses and imposed stiff tariffs on outside firms. Jealousy, regulation, diverse economic conditions, and tensions among nations have characterized Europe for years. Viewed as separate entities, European countries have not represented a sufficiently large customer base to warrant many international companies establishing business operations in Europe. Consequently, Europe has been economically stagnant since World War II, especially compared with the United States and the Far East. For several years during the 1980s, the combined results of the largest 100 companies in Europe, excluding the oil companies, showed a profit level of zero percent. Unemployment in Europe still remains high and companies generally are not competitive in world markets.

There are also still wide differences in product tastes across European countries. For example, the French want top-loading washing machines, whereas the British want front-loading washers. The Portuguese eat only 4 pounds of beef per capita each year, whereas the French eat 13.2 pounds. Germans eat 3.8 pounds of poultry each year, whereas the Spanish eat 8.8 pounds. Electrical outlets in Britain are different from those in Holland.

With the exception of a few industries such as chemicals, most sectors of the European economy are marked by chronic overcapacity and high fixed costs, such as steel, detergents, pharmaceuticals, transportation, and banking. There is no reason why Europe's $2 billion turbine generator business should support 10 producers. Similar overcapacity problems plague other industries, such as locomotive manufacturing. European companies are moving quickly, however, to correct the overcapacity problems, and survivors will likely emerge as strong competitors in world markets. Differences among European countries are narrowing due to a massive increase in the flow of people and information across national borders, and European companies are moving rapidly to develop and market products that will be well received all over Europe. The Europlug, for example, has recently been developed and marketed in Europe as the electrical plug that "will work everywhere."

UNIFICATION AND THE EURO   Unification of Western Europe and the approaching adoption of a single currency are perhaps the single most important world events affecting business strategies in the 1990s. Fifteen countries speaking with one voice is more attractive to multinational corporations than 15 countries speaking with 15 voices. A proliferation of cross-border mergers, acquisitions, and alliances in Europe is creating a new generation of European firms large enough to take on U.S. and Japanese companies. In some industries, such as packaging and electric generating equipment, European firms have already replaced American firms as world leaders.

Unification of Western Europe and the planned adoption of the euro have reduced or eliminated trade barriers between European countries; people, goods, services, and capital now flow freely across national boundaries. European banks can operate in different countries without prohibitive barriers. Trucks pass freely between national borders instead of having to wait for hours at places such as the Mount Blanc tunnel between France and Italy, where custom agents used to check documents and cargo. The Eurotunnel under the English Channel is spurring business between England and Europe. The estimated annual savings to European companies from the unification is $75 billion to $90 billion.

Unification also brought common licensing of food and beverage products in Europe, common radio and television signals, common health and safety standards, elimination of duplication in distribution systems, and standardization of product lines. It has also prompted increased competitor analysis and alliances, decentralization of businesses, new marketing efforts, new strategies, more emphasis on service, improved telecommunications and information flow, and increased momentum for a single monetary system evolving in Europe.

Perhaps the most far-reaching feature of European unification is the planned establishment of a single financial market. The January 1, 1999, scheduled introduction of a single European currency, the euro, is expected to accelerate European downsizing.

Much stronger competitors in Europe have emerged from unification, and consumers throughout Europe are benefiting from lower prices and better choices. However, European companies still pay the world's highest wages and generally have trouble offering goods at globally competitive prices. The social welfare system in Europe is especially costly to firms. Most European workers and managers enjoy lifetime employment guarantees. There is a fear throughout Europe that rising unemployment, already at 10.5 percent, may bring back overregulation and protectionism, which would hurt firms' efforts to become more globally competitive.

European industries expected to represent the greatest threat to U.S. firms in the near future are publishing, communications equipment, pharmaceuticals, and civilian aerospace. Representing a lesser but still significant threat to U.S. firms will be European banks and producers of food, beverages, computers, electronics, and autos. U.S. industries that appear for the moment to be least affected by European unification are retailing, trucking, airlines, and insurance.

MERGERS AND ACQUISITIONS Because Brussels is headquarters of the European Union, significant business and economic activity has shifted there from other national capitals in Europe. A wave of mergers and acquisitions is sweeping Europe as companies try to consolidate strength in core markets. For example, Banco de Bilbao and Banco Vizcaya, Spain's third- and sixth-largest banks, recently combined to form the only Spanish bank to rank among the top 30 in Europe. Consolidations in the paper industry have resulted in strong competitors such as Stora Kopparbergs Bergslags and Svanska Cellusosa in Sweden and Finnpap and Kymmene in Finland. Nestlé in Switzerland has acquired a number of other food companies in both Europe and the United States. Two large accounting firms in England, Coopers & Lybrand and Deloitte & Touche Tohmatsu, recently merged, creating the largest accounting firm in Europe. Eurocom S.A., France's largest advertising agency, merged with Roux, Seguela, Cayzac & Goudard, creating by far the largest ad agency in Europe.

Some examples of European firms that have acquired U.S. firms are Pechiney of France, which acquired Triangle Industries; Grand Metropolitan of Britain, which acquired Pillsbury, Burger King, and Green Giant; Hoechst of Germany, which acquired Celanese; and Nestlé of Switzerland, which acquired Carnation.

Japanese firms are also making large acquisitions in Western Europe. For example, Fujitsu acquired Britain's last true computer maker, ICL. Mitsubishi Electric has a stated goal to increase its investment in Europe by as much as 30 percent a year. Olivetti in Italy depends on Canon and Sanyo for office equipment, and Fiat depends on Hitachi for construction gear. Nissan, Toyota, and Honda are all building manufacturing plants in Britain and expect to raise overall Japanese market share of automobiles in Britain from 12 percent to 17 percent by 1998.

After Great Britain, the European country receiving the next most extensive Japanese investment is Germany; Germany already imports 40 percent of all Japanese exports to Europe. Dusseldorf, Germany, has Europe's largest number of Japanese residents—over 7,000. Mitsubishi Electric and Toshiba are leading an array of Japanese firms planning investment of over $400 million annually in the Dusseldorf region alone.

GUIDELINES FOR SUCCESS AS A GLOBAL COMPETITOR

As indicated in the Information Technology Perspective, use of the Internet can be an effective and efficient way to enhance business globally. Another guideline for success as a global competitor is to make full use of STAT-USA on the World Wide Web. Updated monthly, this is the U.S. government's premier Internet publisher of business information.

Robert Allio offered seven guidelines for winning global battles for customer loyalty and market share:

1. Get to new global markets first. Trying to gain market share from well-entrenched competitors is exceptionally difficult.

2. Counterattack at home. Parent firms often finance expansion into host countries with profits generated at home. Competitor cash flow can be reduced by attacking them at home. An example is the 3M attack on Japanese markets for audiotape and videotape.

3. Invest in new technology. Successful firms in the 1990s are going to utilize the most efficient technology.

4. Consider alternative sourcing. Locate manufacturing facilities in low labor cost areas of the world. An example of this is Dominion Textile of Canada's building a denim manufacturing facility in Tunisia.

5. Install the right managerial system. Ensure that managers in foreign markets understand the nuances of culture and language in host countries.

6. Take early losses if necessary. Sacrifice short-term profits for long-term rewards. An example is Japanese firms' taking losses for 7 years in order to capture the European motorcycle market.

7. Join forces with competitors. Collaborate with competitors who have expertise in other parts of the value chain. Examples are Chrysler's deal with Mitsubishi and AT&T's linkup with Olivetti.[11]

Jeremy Main said there is no universal formula for going global, but any company serious about joining the race should do most or all of the following:

1. Make yourself at home in all three of the world's most important markets—North America, Europe, and Asia.

2. Develop new products for the whole world.

3. Replace profit centers based on countries or regions with ones based on product lines.

4. "Glocalize," as the Japanese call it: Make global decisions on strategic questions about products, capital, and research, but let local units decide tactical questions about packaging, marketing, and advertising.

5. Overcome parochial attitudes, such as the not-invented-here syndrome. Train people to think internationally, send them off on frequent trips, and give them the latest communications technology, such as teleconferencing.

6. Open the senior ranks to foreign employees.

7. Do whatever seems best wherever it seems best, even if people at home lose jobs or responsibilities.

8. In markets that you cannot penetrate on your own, find allies.[12]

INFORMATION TECHNOLOGY

Why Pay for Long-Distance Telephone Calls?

Computers enable persons to write each other by e-mail and even to have a voice conversation with another computer user. In late 1997, companies such as IDT unveiled Net2Phone Direct, which allows a person or business to dial an 800 or local access number, and have a voice conversation with another person by phone with the medium for transmission being the Internet rather than a phone company. The cost is 8 cents a minute within the United States, 18 cents to London, and 29 cents to Japan, all much cheaper than traditional long-distance calling. So whatever your corporate expense for long-distance phone calls may be, they probably are an inefficient use of company resources.

Large phone companies such as AT&T and MCI all but ignored developments in Internet telephony during the 1990s, but now are scrambling to reposition themselves. MCI, for example, has a calling plan that charges residential customers just 5 cents a minute for long-distance calls made on Sundays with no registration needed. Sprint now allows "registered" customers to make free long-distance calls on Monday nights (7–11 P.M.) during the National Football League season. AT&T still commands 50 percent to 60 percent of the consumer telephone market, followed by MCI with 15 percent to 20 percent and Sprint with about 10 percent, but smaller firms such as IDT and various Internet providers are gaining market share.

Source: Adapted from Kevin Maney, "Internet Long-Distance No Longer Needs a PC," USA Today (September 8, 1997): B1, B6.

David Garfield, former president of Ingersoll-Rand Company, offered three strategy suggestions to make domestic firms more competitive internationally:

1. The best defense is a good offense. Companies need to fight tooth and claw for exports and battle foreign competition on foreign ground wherever possible. This is preferable to competing intensely in domestic markets.

2. Investments that will improve competitive advantage should receive priority attention. Domestic firms should strive to reduce labor costs, lower overhead, compress production cycles, and improve the quality of products and services.

3. Domestic industries and firms need to help one another. They should give preference to American suppliers and distributors; they should encourage one another to take action to improve competitiveness in technology, quality, service, and cost.[13]

CONCLUSION

Success in business increasingly depends upon offering products and services that are competitive on a world basis, not just on a local basis. If the price and quality of a firm's products and services are not competitive with those available elsewhere in the world, the firm may soon face extinction. Global markets have become a reality in all but the most remote areas of the world. Certainly throughout the United States, even in small towns, firms feel the pressure of world competitors. Nearly half of all the automobiles sold in the United States, for example, are made in Japan and Germany.

Culture, industrial policies, joint venturing, and exporting are important in the strategic-management process of international firms. As world economies and consumption patterns become increasingly similar and interrelated, political and economic changes represent major opportunities for, and threats to, U.S. firms. To be successful in the late 1990s, businesses must offer products and services that exhibit a price/quality relationship competitive with similar products and services available worldwide.

We invite you to visit the DAVID page on the Prentice Hall Web site at
www.prenhall.com/davidsm
for this chapter's World Wide Web exercises.

TAKE IT TO THE NET

KEY TERMS AND CONCEPTS

European Economic Community	(p. 311)	Host Country	(p. 308)	Multinational Corporations	(p. 308)
European Union (EU)	(p. 333)	Industrial Policies	(p. 316)	Parent Company	(p. 308)
Global Markets	(p. 310)	International Firms	(p. 308)	Wa	(p. 331)

ISSUES FOR REVIEW AND DISCUSSION

1. Compare and contrast American culture with other cultures worldwide. How do differences in culture affect strategic management?

2. Explain why consumption patterns are becoming similar worldwide. What are the strategic implications of this trend?

3. What are the advantages and disadvantages of beginning export operations in a foreign country?

4. Why do you believe the airline industry is only slowly becoming global?

5. What recommendations do you have for firms wanting to do business with Russia?

6. What strategies are most commonly being pursued by Japanese firms? Why?

7. How does unification of Western Europe affect the strategies of U.S. firms?

8. What guidelines for success as a global competitor do you believe are most important?

9. Select one of the readings at the end of this chapter and prepare a 3-minute report to the class on this topic.

10. Do you believe *Guanxi*, *Inhwa*, or *Wa* would help facilitate strategic management in an organization? Why?

11. Compare and contrast the trade climate in Mexico, China, Japan, Russia, and the European Union.

12. Compare and contrast the political climate in Mexico, China, Japan, Russia, and the European Union.

13. Compare and contrast the culture in Mexico, China, Japan, Russia, and the European Union.

NOTES

1. Gephardt, Richard A. "U.S.–Japanese Trade Relations," *Vital Speeches of the Day* LV, no. 15 (May 15, 1989).

2. Jon Alston, "Wa, Guanxi, and Inhwa: Managerial Principles in Japan, China and Korea," *Business Horizons* 32, no. 2 (March–April 1989): 26.

3. Rose Knotts, "Cross-Cultural Management: Transformations and Adaptations," *Business Horizons* (January–February 1989): 29–33.

4. Ellen Fingerhut and Daryl Hatano, "Principles of Strategic Planning Applied to International Corporations," *Managerial Planning* 31, no. 5 (September–October 1983): 4–14. Also, Narendra Sethi, "Strategic Planning Systems for Multinational Companies," *Long Range Planning* 15, no. 3 (June 1982): 80–9.

5. David Shanks, "Strategic Planning for Global Competition," *Journal of Business Strategy* 5, no. 3 (Winter 1985): 80.

6. Mark Clifford, "Can China Reform Its Economy?" *Business Week* (September 29, 1997): 117–124.

7. "How You Can Win in China?" *Business Week* (May 26, 1997): 65.

8. Brian Fowler, "Japan Business Survey," *The Wall Street Journal* (September 29, 1997): B11.

9. Fowler., B12.

10. Stratford Sherman, "How to Beat the Japanese," *Fortune* (April 10, 1989): 145.

11. Robert Allio, "Formulating Global Strategy," *Planning Review* 17, no. 2 (March–April 1989): 27.

12. Jeremy Main, "How to Go Global—And Why," *Fortune* (August 28, 1989): 76.

13. David Garfield, "The International Challenge to U.S. Business," *Journal of Business Strategy* 5, no. 4 (Spring 1985): 28, 29.

CURRENT READINGS

Barkema, H. G., J. H. J. Bell, and J. M. Pennings. "Foreign Entry, Cultural Barriers, and Learning." *Strategic Management Journal* 17, no. 2 (February 1996): 151–161.

Barnes, John W., Matthew H. Crook, Taira Koybaeva, and Edwin R. Stafford. "Why Our Russian Alliances Fail." *Long Range Planning* 30, no. 4 (August 1997): 540–550.

Baron, David P. "Integrated Strategy, Trade Policy, and Global Competition." *California Management Review* 39, no. 2 (Winter 1997): 145–155.

Birkinshaw, J. "Entrepreneurship in Multinational Corporations: The Characteristics of Subsidiary Initiatives." *Strategic Management Journal* 18, no. 3 (March 1997): 207–230.

Chae, Myung-Su and John S. Hill. "The Hazards of Strategic Planning for Global Markets." *Long Range Planning* 29, no. 6 (December 1996): 880–891.

Filatotchev, Igor, Robert E. Hoskisson, Trevor Buck, and Mike Wright. "Corporate Restructuring in Russian Privatizations: Implications for U.S. Investors." *California Management Review* 38, no. 2 (Winter 1996): 87–105.

Foster, M. J. "South China: Are the Rewards Still Worth the Risks?" *Long Range Planning* 30, no. 4 (August 1997): 585–593.

Gouttefarde, Claire. "American Values in the French Workplace." *Business Horizons* 39, no. 2 (March–April 1996): 60–69.

Gowan, Mary, Santiago Ibarreche, and Charles Lackey. "Doing the Right Things in Mexico." *Academy of Management Executive* 10, no. 1 (February 1996): 74–81.

Greer, Charles R. and Gregory K. Stephens. "Employee Relations Issues for U.S. Companies in Mexico." *California Management Review* 38, no. 3 (Spring 1996): 121–145.

Hitt, M. A., M. T. Dacin, B. B. Tyler, and D. Park. "Understanding the Differences in Korean and U.S. Executives' Strategic Orientations." *Strategic Management Journal* 18, no. 2 (February 1997): 159–169.

Krug, J. A. and W. H. Hegarty. "Postacquisition Turnover Among U.S. Top Management Teams: An Analysis of the Effects of Foreign vs. Domestic Acquisitions of U.S. Targets." *Strategic Management Journal* 18, no. 8 (September 1997): 667–677.

Lomi, Alessandro and Erik R. Larsen. "Interacting Locally and Evolving Globally: A Computational Approach to the Dynamics of Organizational Population." *Academy of Management Journal* 39, no. 5 (October 1996): 1084–1119.

Lovelock, Christopher H. and George S. Yip. "Developing Global Strategies for Service Businesses." *California Management Review* 38, no. 2 (Winter 1996): 64–86.

Luo, Yadong. "Evaluating the Performance of Strategic Alliances in China." *Long Range Planning* 29, no. 4 (August 1996): 534–542.

Magretta, Joan. "Growth Through Global Sustainability: An Interview with Monsanto's CEO, Robert B. Shapiro." *Harvard Business Review* (January–February 1997): 78–90.

Northcott, Jim. "Mapping the Future for Countries." *Long Range Planning* 29, no. 2 (April 1996): 203–207.

Peng, Mike W. and Peggy Sue Heath. "The Growth of the Firm in Planned Economies in Transition: Institutions, Organizations, and Strategic Choice." *Academy of Management Review* 21, no. 2 (April 1996): 492–528.

Pincus, Laura B. and James A. Belohlav. "Legal Issues in Multinational Business Strategy: To Play the Game, You Have to Know the Rules." *Academy of Management Executive* 10, no. 3 (August 1996): 52–61.

Puffer, Sheila M., Daniel J. McCarthy, and Anatoly V. Zhuplev. "Meeting of the Mind-sets in a Changing Russia." *Business Horizons* 39, no. 6 (November–December 1996): 52–60.

Reuer, J. J. and K. D. Miller. "Agency Costs and the Performance Implications of International Joint Venture Internalization." *Strategic Management Journal* 18, no. 6 (June 1997): 425–438.

Sambharya, R. B. "Foreign Experience of Top Management Teams and International Diversification Strategies of U.S. Multinational Corporations." *Strategic Management Journal* 17, no. 9 (November 1996): 739–749.

Schuler, Randall S., Susan E. Jackson, Ellen Jackofsky, and John W. Slocum, Jr. "Managing Human Resources in Mexico: A Cultural Understanding." *Business Horizons* 39, no. 3 (May–June 1996): 55–61.

Serapio, Manuel G., Jr., and Wayne F. Cascio. "End-Games in International Alliances." *Academy of Management Executive* 10, no. 1 (February 1996): 62–73.

Smith, Esmond D., Jr., and Cuong Pham. "Doing Business in Vietnam: A Cultural Guide." *Business Horizons* 39, no. 3 (May–June 1996): 47–51.

Stewart, Rosemary. "German Management: A Challenge to Anglo-American Managerial Assumptions." *Business Horizons* 39, no. 3 (May–June 1996): 52–54.

Tallman, Stephen and Jiatao Li. "Effects of International Diversity and Product Diversity on the Performance of Multinational Firms." *Academy of Management Journal* 39, no. 1 (February 1996): 179–196.

Tezuka, Hiroyuki. "Success as the Source of Failure? Competition and Cooperation in the Japanese Economy." *Sloan Management Review* 38, no. 2 (Winter 1997): 83–93.

Vanhonacker, Wilfried. "Entering China: An Unconventional Approach." *Harvard Business Review* (March–April 1997): 130–141.

Very, P., M. Lubatkin, R. Calori and J. Veiga. "Relative Standing and the Performance of Recently Acquired European Firms." *Strategic Management Journal* 18, no. 8 (September 1997): 593–614.

Werther, William B., Jr. "Toward Global Convergence." *Business Horizons* 39, no. 1 (January–February 1996): 3–9.

Williamson, Peter J. "Asia's New Game." *Harvard Business Review* (September–October 1997): 55–65.

EXPERIENTIAL EXERCISES

Experiential Exercise 10A

DETERMINING THE COMPETITIVE ENVIRONMENT FOR HERSHEY'S PRODUCTS IN OTHER COUNTRIES

PURPOSE

Organizations are exploring potential markets in other countries. The purpose of this exercise is to assess the relative attractiveness of various foreign countries for distributing and possibly manufacturing Hershey products.

INSTRUCTIONS

Step 1 Select a European, Asian, African, South American, or Central American country of your choice.

Step 2 Go to your college library. Research your chosen country to identify social, cultural, demographic, geographic, political, legal, governmental, economic, technological, and competitive forces or trends that affect the candy and pasta market there. Decide whether you would recommend that Hershey begin or increase export operations or manufacturing operations in that country.

Step 3 Prepare a three-page typed report to Hershey's president of international operations, Patrice Le Maire. Give the results of your research and your specific recommendations to your professor.

Experiential Exercise 10B

DETERMINING MY UNIVERSITY'S RECRUITING EFFORTS IN FOREIGN COUNTRIES

PURPOSE

A competitive climate is emerging among colleges and universities around the world. Colleges and universities in Europe and Japan are increasingly recruiting American students to offset declining enrollments. Foreign students already make up more than one-third of the student body at many American universities. The purpose of this exercise is to identify particular colleges and universities in foreign countries that represent a competitive threat to American institutions of higher learning.

INSTRUCTIONS

Step 1 Select a foreign country. Conduct research to determine the number and nature of colleges and universities in that country. What are the major institutions in that country? What programs are those institutions recognized for offering? What percentage of undergraduate and graduate students attending those institutions are American? Do those institutions actively recruit American students?

Step 2 Prepare a report for the president or chancellor of your college or university that summarizes your research findings. Present your report to your professor.

LESSONS IN DOING BUSINESS GLOBALLY

PURPOSE

The purpose of this exercise is to discover some important lessons learned by local businesses who do business internationally.

INSTRUCTIONS

Contact several local business leaders by phone. Find at least three firms that engage in international or export operations. Ask the businessperson to give you several important lessons his or her firm has learned in doing business globally. Record the lessons on paper and report your findings to the class.

NAME INDEX

COMPANY INDEX